SPURGEON'S
✦SERMONS✦
ON PRAYER

SPURGEON'S ✦ SERMONS ✦ ON PRAYER

Charles H. Spurgeon

Spurgeon's Sermons on Prayer

Copyright © 2007 Hendrickson Publishers Marketing, LLC
P.O. Box 3473
Peabody, MA 01961-3473

ISBN: 978-1-59856-161-6

Printed in the United States of America

Second Printing — April 2013

Cover Art: Julius Schnorr von Carolsfeld (1794-1872). Depiction of David
as the Psalmist praying for deliverance from his enemies. From *Die Bibel
in Bildern*.
Image supplied courtesy of the Pitts Theology Library, Candler School
of Theology, Emory University. Used with Permission.

Table of Contents

Twelve Sermons on Prayer

Great Prayers of the Bible

Published on Thursday, December 30, 1909; delivered on
Thursday evening, August 7, 1873, at the Metropolitan Tabernacle,
Newington. No. 3178.

Now when all the people were baptized, it came to pass, that Jesus also
being baptized, and praying, the heaven was opened, and the Holy Ghost
descended in a bodily shape like a dove upon him, and a voice came from
heaven, which said, "Thou art my beloved Son; in thee I am well pleased."
—LUKE 3:21–22

And it came to pass in those days, that he went out into a mountain to pray,
and continued all night in prayer to God. And when it was day, he called
unto him his disciples: and of them he chose twelve, whom also he named
apostles.—LUKE 6:12–13

And it came to pass about an eight days after these sayings, he took Peter
and John and James, and went up into a mountain to pray. And as he
prayed, the fashion of his countenance was altered, and his raiment was
white and glistering.—LUKE 9:28–29

And when he had sent the multitudes away, he went up into a mountain
apart to pray: and when the evening was come, he was there alone. But
the ship was now in the midst of the sea, tossed with waves: for the wind
was contrary. And in the fourth watch of the night Jesus went unto them,
walking on the sea.—MATTHEW 14:23–25

Then they took away the stone from the place where the dead was laid. And
Jesus lifted up his eyes, and said, "Father, I thank thee that thou hast heard
me. And I knew that thou hearest me always: but because of the people
which stand by I said it, that they may believe that thou hast sent me."
—JOHN 11:41–42

And the Lord said, "Simon, Simon, behold, Satan hath desired to have you,
that he may sift you as wheat: but I have prayed for thee, that thy faith fail
not: and when thou art converted, strengthen thy brethren."
—LUKE 22:31–32

And when Jesus had cried with a loud voice, he said, "Father, into thy hands
I commend my spirit": and having said thus, he gave up the ghost.
—LUKE 23:46

The Prayers of Christ

*of heaven and earth, that thou hast hid these things from the wise and
prudent, and hast revealed them unto babes: even so, Father; for so it seemed
good in thy sight. All things are delivered to me of my Father: and no man
knoweth who the Son is, but the Father; and who the Father is, but the Son,
and he to whom the Son will reveal him."*—LUKE 10:21–22

Preface

⌒᷾ᵔᵔᷮ⌒

Charles Haddon Spurgeon, 1834–1892

Ask most people today who Charles Haddon Spurgeon was, and you might be surprised at the answers. Most know he was a preacher, others remember that he was Baptist, and others go so far as to remember that he lived in England during the nineteenth century. All of this is true. Yet Charles Haddon Spurgeon was so much more.

Born into a family of Congregationalists in 1834, Spurgeon's father and grandfather were both Independent preachers. This designation seems benign today, but in the mid-nineteenth century, it describes a family committed to a Nonconformist path— meaning they did not conform to the established Church of England. Spurgeon grew up in a rural village, a village virtually cut off from the Industrial Revolution rolling over most of England.

Spurgeon was born again at a Primitive Methodist meeting in 1850, at age sixteen. He soon became a Baptist (to the sorrow of his mother) and almost immediately began to preach. Considered a preaching prodigy — "a boy wonder of the fens" — Spurgeon attracted huge audiences and garnered a reputation that reached throughout the countryside and into London. As a result of his great success, Spurgeon was invited to preach at the New Park Street Chapel in London in 1854, when he was just nineteen. When he first preached at the church, they were unable to fill even two hundred seats. Within the year, Spurgeon filled the twelve-hundred-seat church to overflowing; he soon began preaching in larger and larger venues, outgrowing each, until finally in 1861, the Metropolitan Tabernacle was completed, which seated six thousand persons. This would be Spurgeon's home base for the rest of his career, until his death in 1892, at age fifty-seven.

Spurgeon married Susannah Thompson in 1856 and soon they had twin sons, Charles and Thomas, who would later follow him in his work. Spurgeon opened Pastors' College, a training school for preachers, that trained over nine hundred preachers during his lifetime. He also opened orphanages for underprivileged boys and girls, providing educations to each of the orphans. And with Susannah, he developed a program to publish and distribute Christian literature. He is said to have preached to over ten million people in his forty years of ministry. His sermons sold over twenty-five thousand copies each week, and were translated into twenty languages. He was utterly committed to spreading the Gospel, through preaching and through the written word.

During Spurgeon's lifetime, the Industrial Revolution transformed England from a rural, agricultural society, to an urban, industrial society, with all the attendant difficulties and horrors of a society in major transition. The people displaced by these sweeping changes, the factory workers, the shopkeepers, these became Spurgeon's congregation. From a small village himself and transplanted to a large and inhospitable city, he was a common man, and he understood innately the spiritual needs of the common people. He was a communicator who made the Gospel so relevant, who spoke so brilliantly to people's deepest needs, that listeners welcomed his message.

Keep in mind that Spurgeon preached in the days before microphones or speakers; in other words, he preached without benefit of amplifier systems. Once he preached to a crowd of over twenty-three thousand people without mechanical amplification of any sort. He himself was the electrifying presence on the platform: he did not stand and simply read a stilted sermon. Spurgeon used an outline, developing his themes extemporaneously, and speaking "in common language to common people." His sermons were filled with stories and poetry, drama and emotion. He was larger than life, always in motion, striding back and forth across the stage. He gestured broadly, acted out stories, used humor, and painted word pictures. For Spurgeon, preaching was about communicating the truth of God, and he would use any gift at his disposal to accomplish this.

Spurgeon's preaching was anchored in his spiritual life, a life rich in prayer and the study of Scripture. He was not tempted by fashion, be it theological, social, or political. Scripture was the cornerstone of Spurgeon's life and his preaching. He was an expositional preacher mostly, exploring a passage of Scripture for its meanings both within the text as well as in the lives of each member of his congregation. To Spurgeon, Scripture is alive and specifically relevant to people's lives, whatever their social status, economic situation, or time in which they live.

One has a sense that Spurgeon embraced God's revelation completely: God's revelation through Jesus Christ, through Scripture, and through his own prayer and study. For him, revelation was not a finished act: God still reveals Himself, if one made oneself available. Some recognize Spurgeon for the mystic he was, one who was willing and eager to explore the mysteries of God, able to live with those bits of truth that do not conform to a particular system of theology, perfectly comfortable with saying "This I know, and this I don't know—yet will I trust."

This collection of sermons is Spurgeon on the topic of prayer, his personal invitation into that interaction with the Holy One, the Creator of the Universe. These sermons are not a series: they were not created or intended to be sequential. Rather, they are stand-alone sermons, meant to explore specific aspects of prayer as found in the Bible.

Each of these sermons was preached at different times of Spurgeon's career, and each has distinct characteristics. They have not been homogenized or edited to sound as though they are all of a kind. Instead, they reflect the preacher himself, allowing the voice of this remarkable man to ring clearly as he guides the reader into a particular account, a particular event—to experience, with Spurgeon, God's particular revelation.

As you read, listen. These words meant to be heard, not merely read. Listen carefully and you will hear the cadences of this remarkable preaching, the echoes of God's timeless truth traveling across the years. And above all, enjoy Spurgeon's enthusiasm, his fire, his devotion, his zeal to recognize and respond to God's timeless invitation to engage the Creator himself.

Twelve Sermons

on Prayer

The Golden Key of Prayer

Delivered on Sunday morning, March 12, 1865, at the Metropolitan
Tabernacle, Newington. No. 619.

*"Call unto me, and I will answer thee, and shew thee great and mighty things,
which thou knowest not."* —Jeremiah 33:3

Some of the most learned works in the world smell of the midnight oil;
but the most spiritual and most comforting books and sayings of men usually
have a savor about them of prison-damp. I might quote many instances: John
Bunyan's *Pilgrim* may suffice instead of a hundred others; and this good text
of ours, all moldy and chill with the prison in which Jeremiah lay, has nevertheless a brightness and a beauty about it, which it might never have had if it
had not come as a cheering word to the prisoner of the Lord, shut up in the
court of the prison house. God's people have always in their worst condition
found out the best of their God. He is good at all times; but he seems to be
at his best when they are at their worst. "How could you bear your long
imprisonment so well?" said one to the Landgrave of Hesse, who had been
shut up for his attachment to the principles of the Reformation. He replied,
"The divine consolations of martyrs were with me." Doubtless there is a consolation more deep, more strong than any other, which God keeps for those
who, being his faithful witnesses, have to endure exceeding great tribulation
from the enmity of man. There is a glorious aurora for the frigid zone; and
stars glisten in northern skies with unusual splendor. Rutherford had a quaint
saying, that when he was cast into the cellars of affliction, he remembered that
the great king always kept his wine there, and he began to seek at once for the
wine bottles, and to drink of the "wines on the lees well refined." They who
dive in the sea of affliction bring up rare pearls. You know, my companions in
affliction, that it is so. You whose bones have been ready to come through the
skin through long lying upon the weary couch; you who have seen your
earthly goods carried away from you, and have been reduced well near to
penury; you who have gone to the grave yet seven times, till you have feared
that your last earthly friend would be borne away by unpitying Death; you
have proved that he is a faithful God, and that as your tribulations abound, so
your consolations also abound by Christ Jesus.

My prayer is, in taking this text this morning, that some other prisoners of the Lord may have its joyous promise spoken home to them; that you who are straitly shut up and cannot come forth by reason of present heaviness of spirit, may hear him say, as with a soft whisper in your ears, and in your hearts, "Call unto me, and I will answer thee, and shew thee great and mighty things, which thou knowest not."

The text naturally splits itself up into three distinct particles of truth. Upon these let us speak as we are enabled by God the Holy Spirit. First, prayer commanded—"Call unto me"; secondly, an answer promised—"And I will answer thee"; thirdly, faith encouraged—"And shew thee great and mighty things, which thou knowest not."

I. The first head is *prayer commanded.*

We are not merely counseled and recommended to pray, but bidden to pray. This is great condescension. A hospital is built: it is considered sufficient that free admission shall be given to the sick when they seek it; but no order in council is made that a man must enter its gates. A soup kitchen is well provided for in the depth of winter. Notice is promulgated that those who are poor may receive food on application; but no one thinks of passing an Act of Parliament, compelling the poor to come and wait at the door to take the charity. It is thought to be enough to proffer it without issuing any sort of mandate that men shall accept it. Yet so strange is the infatuation of man on the one hand, which makes him need a command to be merciful to his own soul, and so marvelous is the condescension of our gracious God on the other, that he issues a command of love without which not a man of Adam born would partake of the gospel feast, but would rather starve than come.

In the matter of prayer it is even so. God's own people need, or else they would not receive it, a command to pray. How is this? Because, dear friends, we are very subject to fits of worldliness, if indeed that be not our usual state. We do not forget to eat: we do not forget to take the shop shutters down: we do not forget to be diligent in business: we do not forget to go to our beds to rest: but we often do forget to wrestle with God in prayer and to spend, as we ought to spend, long periods in consecrated fellowship with our Father and our God. With too many professors the ledger is so bulky that you cannot move it, and the Bible, representing their devotion, is so small that you might almost put it in your waistcoat pocket. Hours for the world! Moments for Christ! The world has the best, and our closet the parings of our time. We give our strength and freshness to the ways of mammon, and our fatigue and languor to the ways of God. Hence it is that we need to be commanded to attend to that very act which it ought to be our greatest happiness, as it is our highest privilege to perform, i.e., to meet with our God. "Call unto me," says he, for he knows that we are apt to forget to call upon God. "What meanest thou, O sleeper? Arise, call upon thy God," is an exhortation which is needed by us as well as by Jonah in the storm.

He understands what heavy hearts we have sometimes, when under a sense of sin. Satan says to us, "Why should you pray? How can you hope to prevail? In vain, you say, I will arise and go to my Father, for you are not worthy to be one of his hired servants. How can you see the king's face after you have played the traitor against him? How will you dare to approach unto the altar when you have yourself defiled it, and when the sacrifice which you would bring there is a poor polluted one?" O brethren, it is well for us that we are commanded to pray, or else in times of heaviness we might give it up. If God command me, unfit as I may be, I will creep to the footstool of grace; and since he says, "Pray without ceasing," though my words fail me and my heart itself will wander, yet I will still stammer out the wishes of my hungering soul and say, "O God, at least teach me to pray and help me to prevail with you."

Are we not commanded to pray also because of our frequent unbelief? Unbelief whispers, "What profit is there if you should seek the Lord upon such and such a matter?" This is a case quite out of the list of those things wherein God has interposed, and, therefore (says the devil), if you were in any other position you might rest upon the mighty arm of God; but here your prayer will not avail you. Either it is too trivial a matter, or it is too connected with temporals, or else it is a matter in which you have sinned too much, or else it is too high, too hard, too complicated a piece of business, you have no right to take that before God! So suggests the foul fiend of hell. Therefore, there stands written as an everyday precept suitable to every case into which a Christian can be cast, "Call unto me—call unto me." Are you sick? Would you be healed? Cry unto me, for I am a Great Physician. Does providence trouble you? Are you fearful that you shall not provide things honest in the sight of man? Call unto me! Do your children vex you? Do you feel that which is sharper than an adder's tooth—a thankless child? Call unto me. Are your griefs little yet painful, like small points and pricks of thorns? Call unto me! Is your burden heavy as though it would make your back break beneath its load? Call unto me! "Cast thy burden upon the LORD, and he shall sustain thee: he shall never suffer the righteous to be moved."

In the valley—on the mountain—on the barren rock—in the briny sea, submerged, anon, beneath the billows, and lifted up by and by upon the crest of the waves—in the furnace when the coals are glowing—in the gates of death when the jaws of hell would shut themselves upon you—cease not, for the commandment evermore addresses you with, "Call unto me." Still prayer is mighty and must prevail with God to bring you your deliverance. These are some of the reasons why the privilege of supplication is also in holy Scripture spoken of as a duty: there are many more, but these will suffice this morning.

We must not leave our first part till we have made another remark. We ought to be very glad that God has given us this command in his Word that it may be sure and abiding. You may turn to fifty passages where the same precept is uttered. I do not often read in Scripture, "Thou shalt not kill"; "Thou shalt not covet." Twice the law is given, but I often read gospel precepts, for if the law be given twice, the gospel is given seventy times seven. For every precept which I cannot keep, by reason of my being weak through the flesh, I find a thousand precepts, which it is sweet and pleasant for me to keep, by reason of the power of the Holy Spirit which dwells in the children of God; and this command to pray is insisted upon again and again. It may be a seasonable exercise for some of you to find out how often in Scripture you are told to pray. You will be surprised to find how many times such words as these are given: "Call upon me in the day of trouble, and I will deliver thee"—"Ye people, pour out your heart before him"—"Seek ye the LORD while he may be found; call ye upon him while he is near"—"Ask, and it shall be given you; seek, and ye shall find; knock, and it shall be opened unto you"—"Watch and pray, lest ye enter into temptation"—"Pray without ceasing"—"Come boldly unto the throne of grace"—"Draw nigh to God and he will draw nigh to you." "Continue in prayer." I need not multiply where I could not possibly exhaust. I pick two or three out of this great bag of pearls. Come, Christian, you ought never to question whether you have a right to pray: you should never ask, "May I be permitted to come into his presence?" When you have so many commands (and God's commands are all promises, and all enablings), you may come boldly unto the throne of heavenly grace, by the new and living way through the rent veil.

But there are times when God not only commands his people to pray in the Bible, but he also commands them to pray directly by the motions of his Holy Spirit. You who know the inner life comprehend me at once. You feel on a sudden, possibly in the midst of business, the pressing thought that you must retire to pray. It may be, you do not at first take particular notice of the inclination, but it comes again, and again, and again—"Retire and pray!" I find that in the matter of prayer, I am myself very much like a water-wheel which runs well when there is plenty of water, but which turns with very little force when the brook is growing shallow; or, like the ship which flies over the waves, putting out all her canvas when the wind is favorable, but which has to tack about most laboriously when there is but little of the favoring breeze. Now, it strikes me that whenever our Lord gives you the special inclination to pray, that you should double your diligence. You ought always to pray and not to faint; yet when he gives you the special longing after prayer, and you feel a peculiar aptness and enjoyment in it, you have, over and above the command which is constantly binding, another command which should compel you to cheerful obedience. At such times I think we may stand in the position of David, to whom the Lord said, "When thou hearest a sound of a going in the tops of the mulberry trees, then shalt thou bestir thyself." That going in the tops of the mulberry trees may have been the footfalls of angels hastening to the help of David, and then David was to smite the Philistines, and when God's mercies are coming, their footfalls are our desires to pray; and our desires to pray should be at once an indication that the set time to favor Zion is come. Sow plentifully now, for you can sow in hope; plow joyously now, for your harvest is sure. Wrestle now, Jacob, for you are about to be made a prevailing prince, and your name shall be called Israel. Now is your time, spiritual merchant-men; the market is high, trade much; your profit shall be large. See to it that you use right well the golden hour, and reap your harvest while the sun shines. When we enjoy visitations from on high, we should be peculiarly constant in prayer; and if some other duty less pressing should be set aside for a season, it will not be amiss and we shall be no loser; for when God bids us specially pray by the monitions of his spirit, then should we bestir ourselves in prayer.

II. Let us now take the second head—*an answer promised.*

We ought not to tolerate for a minute the ghastly and grievous thought that God will not answer prayer. His nature, as manifested in Christ Jesus, demands it. He has revealed himself in the gospel as a God of love, full of grace and truth; and how can he refuse to help those of his creatures who humbly in his own appointed way seek his face and favor?

When the Athenian senate, upon one occasion, found it most convenient to meet together in the open air, as they were sitting in their deliberations, a sparrow, pursued by a hawk, flew in the direction of the senate. Being hard pressed by the bird of prey, it sought shelter in the bosom of one of the sena-tors. He, being a man of rough and vulgar mold, took the bird from his

bosom, dashed it on the ground and so killed it. Whereupon the whole senate
rose in uproar, and without one single dissenting voice, condemned him to
die, as being unworthy of a seat in the senate with them, or to be called an
Athenian, if he did not render succor to a creature that confided in him. Can
we suppose that the God of heaven, whose nature is love, could tear out of his
bosom the poor fluttering dove that flies from the eagle of justice into the
bosom of his mercy? Will he give the invitation to us to seek his face, and
when we as he knows, with so much trepidation of fear, yet summon courage
enough to fly into his bosom, will he then be unjust and ungracious enough
to forget to hear our cry and to answer us? Let us not think so hardly of the
God of heaven.

Let us recollect next, his past character as well as his nature. I mean the
character which he has won for himself by his past deeds of grace. Consider,
my brethren, that one stupendous display of bounty—if I were to mention a
thousand I could not give a better illustration of the character of God than
that one deed—"He that spared not his own Son, but freely delivered him up
for us all"—and it is not my inference only, but the inspired conclusion of an
apostle—"how shall he not with him also freely give us all things?" If the Lord
did not refuse to listen to my voice when I was a guilty sinner and an enemy,
how can he disregard my cry now that I am justified and saved! How is it that
he heard the voice of my misery when my heart knew it not, and would not
seek relief, if after all he will not hear me now that I am his child, his friend?
The streaming wounds of Jesus are the sure guarantees for answered prayer.
George Herbert represents in that quaint poem of his, "The Bag," the Savior
saying,

> If ye have anything to send or write,
> (I have no bag, but here is room):
> Unto my Father's hands and sight,
> (Believe me) it shall safely come.
> That I shall mind, what you impart,
> Look, you may put it very near my heart.
> Or if hereafter any of my friends
> Will use me in this kind, the door
> Shall still be open; what he sends
> I will present, and somewhat more,
> Not to his hurt.

Surely, George Herbert's thought was that the atonement was in itself a
guarantee that prayer must be heard, that the great gash made near the Savior's
heart, which let the light into the very depths of the heart of Deity, was a

proof that he who sits in heaven would hear the cry of his people. You misread Calvary, if you think that prayer is useless.

But, beloved, we have the Lord's own promise for it, and he is a God that cannot lie. "Call upon me in the day of trouble, and I will answer thee." Has he not said, "Whatsoever ye shall ask in prayer, believe that ye shall have it and ye shall have it." We cannot pray, indeed, unless we believe this doctrine; "for he that cometh to God must believe that he is, and that he is the rewarder of them, that diligently seek him"; and if we have any question at all about whether our prayer will be heard, we are comparable to him that wavers; "For he that wavereth is like a wave of the sea driven with the wind and tossed. For let not that man think that he shall receive any thing of the Lord."

Furthermore, it is not necessary, still it may strengthen the point, if we add that our own experience leads us to believe that God will answer prayer. I must not speak for you; but I may speak for myself. If there be anything I know, anything that I am quite assured of beyond all question, it is that praying breath is never spent in vain. If no other man here can say it, I dare to say it, and I know that I can prove it. My own conversion is the result of prayer, long, affectionate, earnest, importunate. Parents prayed for me; God heard their cries, and here I am to preach the gospel. Since then I have adventured upon some things that were far beyond my capacity as I thought; but I have never failed, because I have cast myself upon the Lord

You know as a church that I have not scrupled to indulge large ideas of what we might do for God; and we have accomplished all that we purposed. I have sought God's aid, and assistance, and help, in all my manifold undertakings, and though I cannot tell here the story of my private life in God's work, yet if it were written it would be a standing proof that there is a God that answers prayer. He has heard my prayers, not now and then, nor once nor twice, but so many times, that it has grown into a habit with me to spread my case before God with the absolute certainty that whatsoever I ask of God, he will give to me. It is not now a "perhaps" or a possibility. I know that my Lord answers me, and I dare not doubt, it were indeed folly if I did. As I am sure that a certain amount of leverage will lift a weight, so I know that a certain amount of prayer will get anything from God. As the rain cloud brings the shower, so prayer brings the blessing. As spring scatters flowers, so supplication ensures mercies. In all labor there is profit, but most of all in the work of intercession: I am sure of this, for I have reaped it.

As I put trust in the queen's money, and have never failed yet to buy what I want when I produce the cash, so put I trust in God's promises, and mean to do so till I find that he shall once tell me that they are base coin, and will not do to trade with in heaven's market. But why should I speak? O brothers and sisters, you all know in your own selves that God hears prayer; if you do not, then where is your Christianity? where is your religion? You will need to learn what are the first elements of the truth; for all saints, young or old, set it down as certain that he does hear prayer.

Still remember that prayer is always to be offered in submission to God's will; that when we say, God hears prayer, we do not intend by that, that he always gives us literally what we ask for. We do mean, however, this, that he gives us what is best for us; and that if he does not give us the mercy we ask for in silver, he bestows it upon us in gold. If he does not take away the thorn in the flesh, yet he says, "My grace is sufficient for thee," and that comes to the same in the end.

Lord Bolingbroke said to the Countess of Huntingdon, "I cannot understand, your ladyship, how you can make out earnest prayer to be consistent with submission to the divine will." "My lord," she said, "that is a matter of no difficulty. If I were a courtier of some generous king, and he gave me permission to ask any favor I pleased of him, I should be sure to put it thus, 'Will your majesty be graciously pleased to grant me such-and-such a favor; but at the same time though I very much desire it, if it would in any way detract from your majesty's honor, or if in your majesty's judgment it should seem better that I did not have this favor, I shall be quite as content to go without it as to receive it.' So you see I might earnestly offer a petition, and yet I might submissively leave it in the king's hands." So with God. We never offer up prayer without inserting that clause, either in spirit or in words, "Nevertheless, not as I will, but as thou wilt; not my will but thine be done." We can pray without an "if" only when we are quite sure that our will must be God's will, because God's will is fully our will.

A much slandered poet has well said, *Man, regard thy prayers as a
  purpose of love to thy soul,*
Esteem the providence that led to them as an index of God's good will;
So shalt thou pray aright, and thy words shall meet with acceptance.
Also, in pleading for others, be thankful for the fullness of thy prayer;
For if thou art ready to ask, the Lord is more ready to bestow.
The salt preserveth the sea, and the saints uphold the earth;
Their prayers are the thousand pillars that prop the canopy of nature.
Verily, an hour without prayer, from some terrestrial mind,
*Were a curse in the calendar of time, a spot of the blackness of
  darkness.*
Perchance the terrible day, when the world must rock into ruins,

Will be one unwhitened by prayer—shall He find faith on the earth?
For there is an economy of mercy, as of wisdom, and power, and means;
Neither is one blessing granted unbesought from the treasury of good:
And the charitable heart of the Being, to depend upon whom is
  happiness,
Never withholdeth a bounty, so long as his subject prayeth;
Yea, ask what thou wilt, to the second throne in heaven,
It is thine, for whom it was appointed; there is no limit unto prayer:
But and if thou cease to ask, tremble, thou self-suspended creature,
For thy strength is cut off as was Samson's: and the hour of thy doom is
  come.

III. I come to our third point, which I think is full of encouragement to all those who exercise the hallowed art of prayer: encouragement to faith, "[I will] shew thee great and mighty things,
which thou knowest not."

Let us just remark that this was originally spoken to a prophet in prison;
and, therefore, it applies in the first place to every teacher, and, indeed, as
every teacher must be a learner, it has a bearing upon every learner in divine
truth. The best way by which a prophet and teacher and learner can know the
reserved truths, the higher and more mysterious truths of God, is by waiting
upon God in prayer. I noticed very specially yesterday in reading the book of
the prophet Daniel, how Daniel found out Nebuchadnezzar's dream. The
soothsayers, the magicians, the astrologers of the Chaldees, brought out their
curious books and their strange-looking instruments, and began to mutter
their abracadabra and all sorts of mysterious incantations, but they all failed.
What did Daniel do? He set himself to prayer, and knowing that the prayer of
a united body of men has more prevalence than the prayer of one, we find
that Daniel called together his brethren, and bade them unite with him in
earnest prayer that God would be pleased of his infinite mercy to open up the
vision. "Then Daniel went to his house, and made the thing known to Hana-
niah, Mishael, and Azariah, his companions, that they would desire mercies of
the God of heaven concerning this secret; that Daniel and his fellows should
not perish with the rest of the wise men of Babylon." And in the case of John,
who was the Daniel of the New Testament, you remember he saw a book in
the right hand of him that sat on the throne—a book sealed with seven seals
which none was found worthy to open or to look thereon. What did John do?
The book was by and by opened by the Lion of the Tribe of Judah, who had

prevailed to open the book; but it is written first before the book was opened, "I wept much." Yes, and the tears of John which were his liquid prayers, were, as far as he was concerned, the sacred keys by which the folded book was opened.

Brethren in the ministry, you who are teachers in the Sunday school, and all of you who are learners in the college of Christ Jesus, I pray you remember that prayer is your best means of study: like Daniel you shall understand the dream, and the interpretation thereof, when you have sought unto God; and like John you shall see the seven seals of precious truth unloosed, after that you have wept much. "Yea, if thou criest after knowledge, and liftest up thy voice for understanding; if thou seekest her as silver, and searchest for her as for hid treasures; then shalt thou understand the fear of the LORD, and find the knowledge of God." Stones are not broken, except by an earnest use of the hammer; and the stonebreaker usually goes down on his knees. Use the hammer of diligence, and let the knee of prayer be exercised, too, and there is not a stony doctrine in Revelation which is useful for you to understand, which will not fly into shivers under the exercise of prayer and faith. *"Bene orasse est bene studuisse"* was a wise sentence of Luther, which has been so often quoted, that we hardly venture but to hint at it. "To have prayed well is to have studied well." You may force your way through anything with the leverage of prayers. Thoughts and reasoning may be like the steel wedges which may open a way into truth; but prayer is the lever, the prize which forces open the iron chest of sacred mystery, that we may get the treasure that is hidden therein for those who can force their way to reach it. The kingdom of heaven still suffers violence, and the violent take it by force. Take care that we work away with the mighty implement of prayer, and nothing can stand against you.

We must not, however, stop there. We have applied the text to only one case; it is applicable to a hundred. We single out another. The saint may expect to discover deeper experience and to know more of the higher spiritual life, by being much in prayer. There are different translations of my text. One version renders it, "I will show thee great and fortified things, which thou knowest not." Another reads it, "Great and reserved things, which thou knowest not." Now, all the developments of spiritual life are not alike easy of attainment. There are the common frames and feelings of repentance, and faith, and joy, and hope, which are enjoyed by the entire family: but there is an upper realm of rapture, of communion, and conscious union with Christ, which is far from being the common dwelling place of believers. All believers see Christ; but all believers do not put their fingers into the prints of the nails, nor thrust their hand into his side. We have not till the high privilege of John to lean upon Jesus' bosom, nor of Paul, to be caught up into the third heaven.

In the ark of salvation we find a lower, second, and third story; all are in the ark, but all are not in the same story. Most Christians, as to the river of experience, are only up to the ankles; some others have waded till the stream is up to the knees; a few find it breast-high; and but a few—oh! how few!— find it a river to swim in, the bottom of which they cannot touch. My brethren, there are heights in experimental knowledge of the things of God which the eagle's eye of acumen and philosophic thought has never seen; and there are secret paths which the lion's whelp of reason and judgment has not as yet learned to travel. God alone can bear us there; but the chariot in which he takes us up, and the fiery steeds with which that chariot is dragged, are prevailing prayers. Prevailing prayer is victorious over the God of mercy. "... by his strength he had power with God: yea, he had power over the angel, and prevailed: he wept, and made supplication unto him: he found him in Beth-el, and there he spake with us." Prevailing prayer takes the Christian to Carmel, and enables him to cover heaven with clouds of blessing, and earth with floods of mercy. Prevailing prayer bears the Christian aloft to Pisgah and shows him the inheritance reserved; yes, and it elevates him to Tabor and transfigures him, till in the likeness of his Lord, as he is, so are we also in this world. If you would reach to something higher than ordinary groveling experience, look to the Rock that is higher than you, and look with the eye of faith through the windows of importunate prayer. To grow in experience then, there must be much prayer.

You must have patience with me while I apply this text to two or three more cases. It is certainly true of the sufferer under trial: if he waits upon God in prayer much he shall receive greater deliverances than he has ever dreamed of—"great and mighty things, which thou knowest not." Here is Jeremiah's testimony:—"Thou drewest near in the day that I called upon thee: thou saidst, Fear not. O LORD, thou hast pleaded the causes of my soul; thou hast redeemed my life." And David's is the same:—"I called upon the LORD in distress: the LORD answered me, and set me in a large place. . . . I will praise thee: for thou hast heard me, and art become my salvation." And yet again:—"Then they cried unto the LORD in their trouble, and he delivered them out of their distresses. And he led them forth by the right way, that they might go to a city of habitation." "My husband is dead," said the poor woman, "and my creditor is come to take my two sons as bondsmen." She hoped that Elijah would possibly say, "What are your debts? I will pay them." Instead of that, he multiplies her oil till it is written, "Go thou and pay thy debts, and"—what was the "and"?—"live thou and thy children upon the rest." So often it will happen that God will not only help his people through the miry places of the way, so that they may just stand on the other side of the slough, but he will bring them safely far on the journey.

That was a remarkable miracle, when in the midst of the storm, Jesus Christ came walking upon the sea, the disciples received him into the ship, and not only was the sea calm, but it is recorded, "Immediately the ship was at the land whither they went." That was a mercy over and above what they asked. I sometimes hear you pray and make use of a quotation which is not in the Bible:—"He is able to do exceeding abundantly above what we can ask or even think." It is not so written in the Bible. I do not know what we can ask or what we can think. But it is said, "He is able to do exceeding abundantly above what we ask or even think." Let us then, dear friends, when we are in great trial say only, "Now I am in prison; like Jeremiah I will pray as he did, for I have God's command to do it; and I will look out as he did, expecting that he will show me reserved mercies, which I know nothing of at present." He will not merely bring his people through the battle, covering their heads in it, but he will bring them forth with banners waving, to divide the spoil with the mighty, and to claim their portion with the strong. Expect great things of a God who gives such great promises as these.

Again, here is encouragement for the worker. Most of you are doing something for Christ; I am happy to be able to say this, knowing that I do not flatter you. My dear friends, wait upon God much in prayer, and you have the promise that he will do greater things for you than you know of. We know not how much capacity for usefulness there may be in us. That ass's jawbone lying there upon the earth, what can it do? Nobody knows what it can do. It gets into Samson's hands, what can it not do? No one knows what it cannot do now that a Samson wields it. And you, friend, have often thought yourself to be as contemptible as that bone, and you have said, "What can I do?" Yes, but when Christ by his Spirit grips you, what can you not do? Truly you may adopt Paul's language and say, "I can do all things through Christ who strengtheneth me."

However, do not depend upon prayer without effort. In a certain school there was one girl who knew the Lord, a very gracious, simple-hearted, trustful child. As usual, grace developed itself in the child according to the child's position. Her lessons were always best said of any in the class. Another girl said to her, "How is it that your lessons are always so well said?" "I pray God to help me," she said, "to learn my lesson." "Well," thought the other, "then I will do the same." The next morning when she stood up in the class she knew nothing; and when she was in disgrace she complained to the other, "Why I prayed God to help me learn my lesson and I do not know anything of it. What is the use of prayer?" "But did you sit down and try to learn it?" "Oh, no," she said, "I never looked at the book." "Ah," then said the other, "I asked God to help me to learn my lesson; but I then sat down to it studiously, and I kept at it till I knew it well, and I learned it easily, because my earnest desire, which I had expressed to God, was, help me to be diligent in endeavoring to do my duty."

So is it with some who come up to prayer meetings and pray, and then they fold their arms and go away hoping that God's work will go on. Like the woman singing, "Fly abroad, thou mighty gospel," but not putting a penny in the plate; so that her friend touched her and said, "But how can it fly if you don't give it wings to fly with?" There are many who appear to be very mighty in prayer, wonderous in supplications; but then they require God to do what they can do themselves, and, therefore, God does nothing at all for them. "I shall leave my camel untied," said an Arab once to Mahomet, "and trust to providence." "Tie it up," said Mahomet, "and then trust to providence."

So you that say, "I shall pray and trust my Church, or my class, or my work to God's goodness," may rather hear the voice of experience and wisdom, which says, "Do your best; work as if all rested upon your toil; as if your own aim would bring your salvation"; "and when you have done all, cast yourself on him without whom it is in vain to rise up early and to sit up late, and to eat the bread of carefulness; and if he speed you, give him the praise."

I shall not detain you many minutes longer, but I want to notice that this promise ought to prove useful for the comforting of those who are intercessors for others. You who are calling upon God to save your children, to bless your neighbors, to remember your husbands or your wives in mercy, may take comfort from this, "I will shew thee great and mighty things, which thou knowest not."

A celebrated minister in the last century, one Mr. Bailey, was the child of a godly mother. This mother had almost ceased to pray for her husband, who was a man of a most ungodly stamp, and a bitter persecutor. The mother prayed for her boy, and while he was yet eleven or twelve years of age, eternal mercy met with him. So sweetly instructed was the child in the things of the kingdom of God, that the mother requested him—and for some time he always did so—to conduct family prayer in the house. Morning and evening this little one laid open the Bible; and though the father would not deign to stop for the family prayer, yet on one occasion he was rather curious to know "what sort of an out the boy would make of it," so he stopped on the other side of the door, and God blessed the prayer of his own child under thirteen years of age to his conversion. The mother might well have read my text with streaming eyes, and said, "Yes, Lord, you have shown me great and mighty things which I knew not: you have not only saved my boy, but through my boy you have brought my husband to the truth."

You cannot guess how greatly God will bless you. Only go and stand at his door, you cannot tell what is in reserve for you. If you do not beg at all, you will get nothing; but if you beg he may not only give you, as it were, the bones, and broken meat, but he may say to the servant at his table, "Take that dainty meat, and set that before the poor man." Ruth went to glean; she expected to get a few good ears: but Boaz said, "Let her glean even among the sheaves, and rebuke her not"; he said moreover to her, "At mealtime come thou hither, and eat of the bread, and dip thy morsel in the vinegar." No, she found a husband where she expected to find only a handful of barley. So in prayer for others, God may give us such mercies that we shall be astounded at them, since we expected but little. Hear what is said of Job, and learn its lesson, "And the LORD said, My servant Job shall pray for you: for him will I accept: lest I deal with you after your folly, in that ye have not spoken of me the thing which is right, like my servant Job. . . . And the LORD turned the captivity of Job, when he prayed for his friends: also the LORD gave Job twice as much as he had before."

Now, this word to close with. Some of you are seekers for your own conversion. God has quickened you to solemn prayer about your own souls. You are not content to go to hell, you want heaven; you want washing in the precious blood; you want eternal life. Dear friends, I pray you take this text—God himself speaks it to you—"Call unto me, and I will answer thee, and shew thee great and mighty things, which thou knowest not." At once take God at his word. Get home, go into your chamber and shut the door, and try him. Young man, I say, try the Lord. Young woman, prove him, see whether he be true or not. If God be true, you cannot seek mercy at his hands through Jesus Christ and get a negative reply. He must, for his own promise and character bind him to it, open mercy's gate to you who knock with all your heart. God help you, believing in Christ Jesus, to cry aloud unto God, and his answer of peace is already on the way to meet you. You shall hear him say, "Your sins which are many are all forgiven."

The Lord bless you for his love's sake. Amen.

The Raven's Cry

Delivered on Sunday evening, January 14, 1866, at the Metropolitan
Tabernacle, Newington. No. 672.

He giveth to the beast his food, and to the young ravens which cry.
—PSALM 147:9

I shall open this sermon with a quotation. I must give you in Caryl's own
words his note upon ravens. "Naturalists tell us, that when the raven hath fed
his young in the nest till they are well fledged and able to fly abroad, then he
thrusts them out of the nest, and will not let them abide there, but puts them
to get their own living. Now when these young ones are upon their first flight
from their nest, and are little acquainted with means how to help themselves
with food, then the Lord provides food for them. It is said by credible authorities, that the raven is marvelous strict and severe in this; for as soon as his
young ones are able to provide for themselves, he will not fetch any more food
for them; yea, some affirm, the old ones will not suffer them to stay in the
same country where they were bred; and if so, then they must needs wander.
We say proverbially, 'Need makes the old wife trot'; we may say, and 'the
young ones too.' It hath been, and possibly is, the practice of some parents
towards their children, who, as soon as they can shift for themselves, and are
fit in any competency to get their bread, they turn them out of doors, as the
raven doth his young ones out of the nest. Now, saith the Lord in the text,
when the young ones of the raven are at this pinch, that they are turned off,
and wander for lack of meat, who then provides for them? do not I, the Lord?
do not I, who provide for the old raven, provide for his young ones, both while
they abide in the nest and when they wander for lack of meat?"

Solomon sent the sluggard to the ant, and learned himself lessons from
conies, greyhounds, and spiders: let us be willing to be instructed by any of
God's creatures, and go to the ravens' nest tonight to learn as in a school.

To the pure nothing is unclean, and to the wise nothing is trivial. Let the
superstitious dread the raven as a bird of ill omen, and let the thoughtless see
nothing but a winged thing in glossy black. We are willing to see more, and
doubtless shall not be unrewarded if we be but teachable. Noah's raven

brought him back no olive branch, but ours may tonight; and it may even come to pass that ravens may bring us meat tonight, as of old they fed Elms by Cherith's brook.

Our blessed Lord once derived a very potent argument from ravens, an argument intended to comfort and cheer those of his servants who were oppressed with needless anxieties about their temporal circumstances. To such he said, "Consider the ravens: for they neither sow nor reap; which neither have storehouse nor barn; and God feedeth them: how much more are ye better than the fowls?"

Following the Master's logic, which you will all agree must have been sound, for he was never untruthful in his reasonings any more than in his statements, I shall argue tonight on this wise: Consider the ravens as they cry; with harsh, inarticulate, croaking notes they make known their wants, and your heavenly Father answers their prayer and sends them food; you, too, have begun to pray and to seek his favor; are you not much better than they? Does God care for ravens, and will he not care for you? Does he hearken to the cries of the unfledged ravens in their nests, when hungry they cry unto him and watch to be fed? Does he, I say, supply them in answer to their cries, and will he not answer you, poor trembling children of men who are seeking his face and favor through Christ Jesus? The whole business of this evening will be just simply to work that one thought out. I shall aim tonight, under the guidance of the Holy Spirit, to say something to those who have been praying for mercy, but as yet have not received it; who have gone on their knees, perhaps for months, with one exceeding great and bitter cry, but as yet know not the way of peace. Their sin still hangs like a millstone about their neck; they sit in the valley of the shadow of death; no light has dawned upon them, and they are wringing their hands and moaning, "Has God forgotten to be gracious? Has he shut his ear against the prayers of seeking souls? Will he be mindful of sinners' piteous cries no more? Shall penitents' tears drop upon the earth and no longer move his compassion?" Satan, too, is telling you, dear friends, who are now in this state of mind, that God will never hear you, that he will let you cry till you die, that you shall pant out your life in sighs and tears, and that at the end you shall be cast into the lake of fire. I long tonight to give you some comfort and encouragement. I want to urge you to cry yet more vehemently; to come to the cross and lay hold of it, and vow that you will never leave its shadow till you find the boon which your soul covets. I want to move you, if God the Holy Ghost shall help me, so that you will say within yourselves, like Queen Esther, "I will go in unto the King, and if I perish, I perish"; and may you add to that the vow of Jacob, "I will not let thee go, except thou bless me!"

Here, then, is the question in hand: *God hears the young ravens; will he not hear you?*

I. I argue that he will, first, when I remember that it is only a raven that cries, and that you, in some sense, are much better than a raven. The raven is but a poor, unclean bird, whose instant death would make no sort of grievous gap in creation. If thousands of ravens had their necks wrung tomorrow, I do not know that there would be any vehement grief and sorrow in the universe about them; it would simply be a number of poor birds dead, and that would be all. But you are an immortal soul. The raven is gone when life is over, there is no raven any longer; but when your present life is past, you have not ceased to be; you are but launched upon the sea of life; you have but begun to live for ever. You will see earth's hoary mountains crumble to nothingness before your immortal spirit shall expire; the moon shall have paled her feeble light, and the sun's more mighty fires shall have been quenched in perpetual darkness, and yet your spirit shall still be marching on in its everlasting course—an everlasting course of misery, unless God hear your cry.

> *Oh, that truth immense,*
> *This mortal, immortality shall wear!*
> *The pulse of mind shall never cease to play;*
> *By God awakened, it for ever throbs,*
> *Eternal as his own eternity!*
> *Above the angels, or below the fiends:*
> *To mount in glory, or in shame descend—*
> *Mankind are destined by resistless doom.*

Do you think, then, that God will hear the poor bird that is and is not, and is here a moment and is blotted out of existence, and will he not hear you, an immortal soul, whose duration is to be co-equal with his own? I think it surely must strike you that if he hears the dying raven, he will also hear an undying man.

The ancients said of Jupiter that he was not at leisure to mind little things, but Jehovah condescends to care for the least of his creatures, and even looks into birds' nests; will he not mercifully care for spirits who are heirs of a dread eternity?

Moreover, I never heard of ravens that they were made in the image of God; but I do find that, defiled, deformed, and debased as our race is, yet originally God said, "Let us make man in our own image." There is something about man which is not to be found in the lower creatures, the best and noblest of whom are immeasurably beneath the meanest child of Adam. A council was held as to the creation of man; and in his mind, and even in the adaptation of his body to assist the mind, there is a marvelous display of the wisdom of the Most High. Bring hither the most deformed, obscure, and wicked of the human race, and—though I dare not flatter human nature morally—yet there is a dignity about the fact of manhood which is not to be found in all the beasts of the field, be they which they may. Behemoth and Leviathan are put in subjection beneath the foot of man. The eagle cannot soar so high as his soul mounts, nor the lion feed on such royal meat as his spirit hungers after. And do you think that God will hear so low and so mean a creature as a raven and yet not hear you, when you are one of the race that was formed in his own image? Oh! think not so hardly and so foolishly of him whose ways are always equal! I will put this to yourselves. Does not nature itself teach that man is to be cared for above the fowls of the air? If you heard the cries of young ravens, you might feel compassion enough for those birds to give them food if you knew how to feed them; but I cannot believe that any of you would succor the birds, and yet would not fly upon the wings of compassion to the rescue of a perishing infant whose cries you might hear from the place where it was cast by cruel neglect. If, in the stillness of the night, you heard the plaintive cry of a man expiring in sickness, unpitied in the streets, would you not arise and help him? I am sure you would if you are one who would help a raven. If you have any compassion for a raven, much more would you have pity upon a man. I know, it is whispered, that there are some simpletons who care more for homeless dogs than for homeless men and women; and yet it is far more probable that those who feel for dogs are those who care most tenderly for men; at any rate, I should feel a strong presumption in their favor if I needed aid. And do you not think that God, the all-wise One, when he cares for these unfledged birds in the nest, will be sure also to care for you? Your heart says, "Yes"; then henceforth answer the unbelief of your heart by turning its own just reasoning against it.

But I hear you say, "Ah! but the raven is not sinful as I am; it may be an unclean bird, but it cannot be so unclean as I am morally; it may be black in hue, but I am black with sin; a raven cannot break the Sabbath, cannot swear, cannot commit adultery; a raven cannot be a drunkard; it cannot defile itself with vices such as those with which I am polluted." I know all that, friend, and it may seem to you to make your case more hopeless; but I do not think it does so really. Just think of it for a minute. What does this prove? Why, that you are a creature capable of sinning, and, consequently, that you are an intelligent spirit living in a sense in which a raven does not live. You are a creature moving in the spirit world; you belong to the world of souls, in which the raven has no portion. The raven cannot sin, because it has no spirit, no soul; but you are an intelligent agent, of which the better part is your soul. Now, as the soul is infinitely more precious than the body, and as the raven—I am speaking popularly now—is nothing but body, while you are evidently soul as well as body, or else you would not be capable of sinning, I see even in that black, discouraging thought some gleam of light. Does God care for flesh, and blood, and bones, and black feathers, and will he not care for your reason, your will, your judgment, your conscience, your immortal soul? Oh, if you will but think of it, you must see that it is not possible for a raven's cry to gain an audience of the ear of divine benevolence, and yet for your prayer to be despised and disregarded by the Most High.

> *The insect that with puny wing,*
> *Just shoots along one summer's ray;*
> *The flow'ret, which the breath of Spring*
> *Wakes into life for half a day;*
> *The smallest mote, the tenderest hair,*
> *All feel our heavenly Father's care.*

Surely, then, he will have respect unto the cry of the humble, and will not refuse their prayer. I can hardly leave this point without remarking that the mention of a raven should encourage a sinner. As an old author writes, "Among fowls he doth not mention the hawk or falcon, which are highly prized and fed by princes; nor the sweet singing nightingale, or such like musical pretty birds, which men keep choicely and much delight in; but he chooses that hateful and malicious bird the croaking raven, whom no man values but as she eats up the carrion which might annoy him." Behold then, and wonder at the providence and kindness of God, that he should provide food for the raven, a creature of so dismal a hue, and of so untunable a tone, a creature that is so odious to most men, and ominous to some. There is a great providence of God seen in providing for the ant, who gathers her meat in summer; but a greater in the raven, who, though he forgets, or is careless to provide for himself, yet God provides and lays up for him. One would think the Lord should say of ravens, Let them shift for themselves or perish; no, the Lord God does not despise any work of his hands; the raven has his being from God, and therefore the raven shall be provided for by him; not only the fair innocent dove, but the ugly raven has his meat from God. Which clearly shows that the want of excellence in you, you black, raven-like sinner, will not prevent your cry from being heard in heaven. Unworthiness the blood of Jesus shall remove, and defilement he shall utterly cleanse away. Only believe on Jesus, and you shall find peace.

II. Then, in the next place, there is a great deal of difference between your cry and the cry of a raven. When the young ravens cry, I suppose they scarcely know what they want. They have a natural instinct which makes them cry for food, but their cry does not in itself express their want. You would soon find out, I suppose, that they meant food; but they have no articulate speech; they do not utter so much as a single word; it is just a constant, croaking, craving cry, and that is all. But you do know what you want, and few as your words are, your heart knows its own bitterness and dire distress. Your sighs and groans have an obvious meaning; your understanding is at the right hand of your necessitous heart. You know that you want peace and pardon; you know that you need Jesus, his precious blood, his perfect righteousness. Now, if God hears such a strange, chattering, indistinct cry as that of a raven, do you not think that he will also hear the rational and expressive prayer of a poor, needy, guilty soul who is crying unto him, "God be merciful to me a sinner"? Surely your reason tells you that!

Moreover, the young ravens cannot use arguments, for they have no understanding. They cannot say as you can,

He knows what arguments I'd take
To wrestle with my God,
I'd plead for his own mercy's sake,
And for a Savior's blood.

They have one argument, namely, their dire necessity, which forces their cry from them, but beyond this they cannot go; and even this they cannot set forth in order, or describe in language. But you have a multitude of arguments ready at hand, and you have an understanding with which to set them in array and marshal them to besiege the throne of grace. Surely, if the mere plea of the unuttered want of the raven prevails with God, much more shall you prevail with the Most High if you can argue your case before him, and come unto him with arguments in your mouth. Come, you despairing one, and try my Lord! I do beseech you now let that doleful ditty ascend into the ears of mercy! Open that bursting heart and let it out in tears, if words are beyond your power.

A raven, however, I fear, has sometimes a great advantage over some sinners who seek God in prayer, namely in this: young ravens are more in earnest about their food than some are about their souls. This, however, is no discouragement to you, but rather a reason why you should be more earnest than you have hitherto been. When ravens want food, they do not cease crying till they have got it; there is no quieting a hungry young raven till his mouth is full, and there is no quieting a sinner when he is really in earnest till he gets his heart full of divine mercy. I would that some of you prayed more vehemently! "The kingdom of heaven suffereth violence, and the violent take it by force." An old Puritan said, "Prayer is a cannon set at the gate of heaven to burst open its gates": you must take the city by storm if you would have it. You will not ride to heaven on a feather bed; you must go on pilgrimage. There is no going to the land of glory while you are sound asleep; dreamy sluggards will have to wake up in hell. If God has made you to feel in your soul the need of salvation, cry like one who is awake and alive; be in earnest; cry aloud; spare not; and then I think you will find that my argument will be quite fair, that in all respects a reasonable, argumentative, intelligent prayer, is more likely to prevail with God than the mere screaming, chattering noise of the raven; and that if he hears such a cry as the raven's, it is much more certain that he will hear yours.

III. Remember, that the matter of your prayer is more congenial to the ear of God than the raven's cry for meat. All that the young ravens cry for is food; give them a little carrion and they have done. Your cry must be much more pleasing to God's ear, for you entreat for forgiveness through the blood of his dear Son. It is a nobler occupation for the Most High to be bestowing spiritual than natural gifts. The streams of grace flow from the upper springs. I know he is so condescending that he does not dishonor himself even when he drops food into the young raven's mouth; but still, there is more dignity about the work of giving peace, and pardon, and reconciliation to the sons of men. Eternal love appointed a way of mercy from before the foundation of the world, and infinite wisdom is engaged with boundless power to carry out the divine design; surely the Lord must take much pleasure in saving the sons of men. If God is pleased to supply the beast of the field, do you not think that he delights much more to supply his own child? I think you would find more congenial employment in teaching your own children than you would in merely foddering your ox, or scattering barley among the fowls at the barn door; because there would be in the first work something nobler, which would more fully call up all your powers and bring out your inward self. I am not left here to conjecture. It is written, "He delighteth in mercy." When God uses his power he cannot be sad, for he is a happy God; but if there be such a thing possible as the Infinite Deity's being more happy at one time than at another, it is when he is forgiving sinners through the precious blood of Jesus.

Ah! sinner, when you cry to God you give him an opportunity to do that which he loves most to do, for he delights to forgive, to press his Ephraim to his bosom, to say of his prodigal son, "He was lost, but is found; he was dead, but is alive again." This is more comfortable to the Father's heart than the feeding of the fatted calf, or tending the cattle of a thousand hills. Since then, dear friends, you are asking for something which it will honor God far more to give than the mere gift of food to ravens, I think there comes a very forcible blow of my argumentative hammer tonight to break your unbelief in pieces. May God the Holy Ghost, the true Comforter, work in you mightily! Surely the God who gives food to ravens will not deny peace and pardon to seeking sinners. Try him! Try him at this moment! No, stir not! Try him now.

IV. We must not pause on any one point when the whole subject is so prolific. There is another source of comfort for you, namely, that the ravens are nowhere commanded to cry. When they cry, their petition is unwarranted by any specific exhortation from the divine mouth, while you have a warrant derived from divine exhortations to approach the throne of God in prayer. If a rich man should open his house to those who were not invited, he would surely receive those who were invited. Ravens come without being bidden, yet they are not sent away empty; you come as a bidden and an invited guest; how shall you be denied? Do you think you are not bidden? Listen to this: "Whosoever calleth on the name of the Lord shall be saved." "Call upon me in the day of trouble, and I will deliver thee, and thou shalt glorify me." "Go ye into all the world, and preach the gospel to every creature; he that believeth and is baptized shall he saved; he that believeth not shall be damned." "Believe in the Lord Jesus Christ, and thou shalt be saved." "Repent and be baptized, every one of you, in the name of the Lord Jesus."

These are exhortations given without any limitation as to character. They freely invite you; no, they bid you come. Oh! after this can you think that God will spurn you? The window is open, the raven flies in, and the God mercy does not chase it out; the door is open, and the word of promise bids you come; think not that he will give you a denial, but believe rather that he will "receive you graciously and love you freely," and then you shall "render to him the calves of your lips." At any rate try him! Try him even now!

V. Again, there is yet another and a far mightier argument. The cry of a young raven is nothing but the natural cry of a creature, but your cry, if it be sincere, is the result of a work of grace in your heart. When the raven cries to heaven, it is nothing but the raven's own self that cries; but when you cry "God be merciful to me a sinner," it is God the Holy Spirit crying in you. It is the new life, which God has given you crying to the source from whence it came to have further communion and communication with its great Original. It needs God himself to set a man praying in sincerity and in truth. We can, if we think it right, teach our children to "say their prayers," but we cannot teach them to "pray." You may make a "prayerbook," but you cannot put a grain of "prayer" into a book, for it is too spiritual a matter to be encased between leaves. Some of you, perhaps, may "read prayers" in the family; I will not denounce the practice, but I will say this much of it: you may read those "prayers" for seventy years, and yet you may never once pray, for prayer is quite a different thing from mere words. True prayer is the trading of the heart with God, and the heart never comes into spiritual commerce with the ports of heaven until God the Holy Ghost puts wind into the sails and speeds the ship into its haven. "Ye must be born again." If there be any real prayer in your heart, though you may not know the secret, God the Holy Ghost is there.

Now if he hears cries that do not come from himself, how much more will he hear those that do! Perhaps you have been puzzling yourself to know whether your cry is a natural or a spiritual one. This may seem very important, and doubtless is so; but whether your cry be either the one or the other, still continue to seek the Lord. Possibly, you doubt whether natural cries are heard by God; let me assure you that they are. I remember saying something on this subject on one occasion in a certain Ultra-Calvinistic place of worship. At that time I was preaching to children, and was exhorting them to pray, and I happened to say that long before any actual conversion I had prayed for common mercies, and that God had heard my prayers. This did not suit my good brethren of the superfine school; and afterward they all came around me professedly to know what I meant, but really to cavil and carp according to their nature and wont. "They compassed me about like bees; yea, like bees they compassed me about!" After a while, as I expected, they fell to their usual amusement of calling names. They began to say what rank Arminianism this was; and another expression they were pleased to honor with the title of "Fullerism"; a title, by the way, so honorable that I could heartily have thanked them for appending it to what I had advanced. But to say that God should hear the prayer of natural men was something worse than Arminianism, if indeed anything could be worse to them. They quoted that counterfeit passage, "The prayer of the wicked is an abomination unto the Lord," which I speedily answered by asking them if they would find me that text in the Word of God; for I ventured to assert that the devil was the author of that saying, and that it was not in the Bible at all. "The sacrifice of the wicked is an abomination to the LORD" is in the Bible, but that is a very different thing from the "prayer of the wicked"; and moreover, there is a decided difference between the word wicked there intended and the natural man about whom we were controverting. I do not think that a man who begins to pray in any sense, can be considered as being altogether among "the wicked" intended by Solomon, and certainly he is not among those who turn away their ear from hearing the law, of whom it is written that their prayer is an abomination. "Well, but," they said, "how could it be that God could hear a natural prayer?" And while I paused for a moment, an old woman in a red cloak pushed her way into the little circle around me, and said to them in a very forcible way, like a mother in Israel as she was, "Why do you raise this question, forgetting what God himself has said! What is this you say, that God does not hear natural prayer? Why, does not he hear the young ravens when they cry unto him, and do you think they offer spiritual prayers?" Straightway the men of war took to their heels; no defeat was more thorough; and for once in their lives they must have felt that they might possibly err.

Surely, brethren, this may encourage and comfort you. I am not going to set you just now to the task of finding out whether your prayers are natural or spiritual, whether they come from God's Spirit or whether they do not, because that might, perhaps, nonplus you; if the prayer proceeds from your very heart, we know how it got there though you may not. God hears the ravens, and I do believe he will hear you, and I believe, moreover, though I do not now want to raise the question in your heart, that he hears your prayer, because—though you may not know it—there is a secret work of the Spirit of God going on within you which is teaching you to pray.

VI. But I have mightier arguments, and nearer the mark. When the young ravens cry they cry alone, but when you pray you have a mightier one than you praying with you. Hear that sinner crying, "God be merciful to me a sinner." Hark! Do you hear that other cry which goes up with his? No, you do not hear it, because your ears are dull and heavy, but God hears it. There is another voice, far louder, and sweeter than the first, and far more prevalent, mounting up at the same moment and pleading, "Father, forgive them through my precious blood." The echo to the sinner's whisper is as majestic as the thunder's peal. Never sinner prays truly without Christ praying at the same time. You cannot see nor hear him, but never does Jesus stir the depths of your soul by his Spirit without his soul's being stirred too. Oh, sinner! your prayer when it comes before God is a very different thing from what it is when it issues forth from you.

Sometimes poor people come to us with petitions, which they wish to send to some company or great personage. They bring the petition and ask us to have it presented for them. It is very badly spelled, very queerly written, and we can but just make out what they mean; but still there is enough to let us know what they want. First of all we make out a fair copy for them, and then, having stated their case, we put our own name at the bottom, and if we have any interest, of course they get what they desire through the power of the name signed at the foot of the petition. This is just what the Lord Jesus Christ does with our poor prayers. He makes a fair copy of them, stamps them with the seal of his own atoning blood, puts his own name at the foot, and thus they go up to God's throne. It is your prayer, but oh! it is his prayer too, and it is the fact of its being his prayer that makes it prevail. Now, this is a sledge-hammer argument: if the ravens prevail when they cry all alone, if their poor chattering brings them what they want of themselves, how much more shall the plaintive petitions of the poor, trembling sinner prevail who can say, "For Jesus' sake," and who can clinch all his own arguments with the blessed plea, "The Lord Jesus Christ deserves it; O Lord, give it to me for his sake."

I do trust that these seeking ones to whom I have been speaking, who have been crying so long and yet are afraid that they shall never be heard, may not have to wait much longer, but may soon have a gracious answer of peace; and if they shall not just yet get the desire of their hearts, I hope that they may be encouraged to persevere till the day of grace shall dawn. You have a promise which the ravens have not, and that might make another argument if time permitted us to dwell upon it. Trembler, having a promise to plead, never fear but that you shall speed at the throne of grace!

And now, let me say to the sinner in closing, *if you have cried unsuccessfully, still cry on.* "Go again seven times," yes, and seventy times seven. Remember that the mercy of God in Christ Jesus is your only hope; cling to it, then, as a drowning man clings to the only rope within reach. If you perish praying for mercy through the precious blood, you will be the first that ever perished so. Cry on; just cry on; but oh! believe too; for believing brings the morning star and the day dawn. When John Ryland's wife Betty lay dying, she was in great distress of mind, though she had been for many years a Christian. Her husband said to her in his quaint but wise way, "Well, Betty, what ails you?" "Oh, John, I am dying, and I have no hope, John!" "But, my dear, where are you going then?" "I am going to hell!" was the answer. "Well," said he, covering up his deep anguish with his usual humor, and meaning to strike a blow that would be sure to hit the nail on the head and put her doubts to speedy flight, "what do you intend doing when you get there, Betty?" The good woman could give no answer, and Mr. Ryland continued, "Do you think you will pray when you get there?" "Oh, John," said she, "I should pray anywhere; I cannot help praying!" "Well, then," said he, "they will say, 'Here is Betty Ryland praying here; turn her out; we won't have anybody praying here; turn her out!'" This strange way of putting it brought light to her soul, and she saw at once the absurdity of the very suspicion of a soul really seeking Christ, and yet being cast away for ever from his presence. Cry on, soul; cry on! While the child can cry, it lives; and while you can besiege the throne of mercy, there is hope for you: but hear as well as cry, and believe what you hear, for it is by believing that peace is obtained.

But stay a while, I have something else to say. Is it possible that you may have already obtained the very blessing you are crying after? "Oh," say you, "I would not ask for a thing which I had already got; if I knew I had it, I would leave off crying, and begin praising and blessing God." Now, I do not know whether all of you seekers are in so safe a state, but I am persuaded that there are some seeking souls who have received the mercy for which they are asking. The Lord instead of saying to them tonight, "Seek my face," is saying, "Why do you cry unto me? I have heard you in an acceptable hour, and in an acceptable time have I succored you; I have blotted out your sins like a cloud, and like a thick cloud your iniquities; I have saved you; you are mine; I have cleansed you from all your sins; go your way and rejoice." In such a case, believing praise is more suitable than agonizing prayer.

"Oh," you say, "but it is not likely that I have the mercy while I am still seeking for it." Well, I do not know. Mercy sometimes falls down in a fainting fit outside the gate; is it not possible for her to be taken inside while she is in the fainting fit, and for her to think all the while that she is still on the outside? She can hear the dog barking still; but ah, poor soul, when she comes to, she will find that she is inside the wicket and is safe. So some of you may happen to have fallen into a swoon of despondency just when you are coming to Christ. If so, may sovereign grace restore you, and perhaps I may be the means tonight of doing it.

What is it you are looking after? Some of you are expecting to see bright visions, but I hope you never may be gratified, for they are not worth a penny a thousand. All the visions in the world since the days of miracles, put together, are but mere dreams after all, and dreams are nothing but vanity. People eat too much supper and then dream; it is indigestion, or a morbid activity of brain, and that is all. If that is all the evidence you have of conversion, you will do well to doubt it: I pray you never to rest satisfied with it; it is wretched rubbish to build your eternal hopes upon. Perhaps you are looking for very strange feelings—not quite an electric shock, but something very singular and peculiar. Believe me, you need never feel the strange motions which you prize so highly. All those strange feelings which some people speak of in connection with conversion may or may not be of any good to them, but certain I am that they really have nothing to do with conversion so as to be at all necessary to it. I will put a question or two to you. Do you believe yourself to be a sinner? "Yes," say you. But supposing I put that word "sinner" away: do you mean that you believe you have broken God's law, that you are a good-for-nothing offender against God's government? Do you believe that you have in your heart, at any rate, broken all the commandments, and that you deserve punishment accordingly? "Yes," say you, "I not only believe that, but I feel it: it is a burden that I carry about with me daily." Now something more: do you believe that the Lord Jesus Christ can put all this sin of yours away? Yes, you do believe that. Then, can you trust him to save you? you want saving; you cannot save yourself; can you trust him to save you? "Yes," you say, "I already do that." Well, my dear friend, if you really trust Jesus, it is certain that you are saved, for you have the only evidence of salvation which is continual with any of us. There are other evidences, which follow afterward, such as holiness and the graces of the Spirit, but the only evidence that is continual with the best of men living is this,

Nothing in my hands I bring,
Simply to thy cross I cling.

Can you use Jack the huckster's verse,

"I'm a poor sinner and nothing at all,
But Jesus Christ is my all-in-all"?

I hope you will go a great deal farther in experience on some points than this by and by, but I do not want you to advance an inch farther as to the ground of your evidence and the reason for your hope. Just stop there, and if now you look away from everything that is within you or without you to Jesus Christ, and trust to his sufferings on Calvary and to his whole atoning work as the ground of your acceptance before God, you are saved. You do not want anything more; you have passed from death unto life. "He that believeth on him is not condemned." "He that believeth hath everlasting life." If I were to meet an angel presently in that aisle as I go out of my door into my vestry, and he should say, "Charles Spurgeon, I have come from heaven to tell you that you are pardoned," I should say to him, "I know that without your telling me anything of the kind; I know it on a great deal better authority than yours"; and if he asked me how I knew it, I should reply, "The Word of God is better to me than the word of an angel, and he has said it, 'He that believeth on him is not condemned'; I do believe on him, and therefore I am not condemned, and I know it without an angel to tell me so." Do not, you troubled ones, be looking after angels, and tokens, and evidences, and signs. If you rest on the finished work of Jesus, you have already the best evidence of your salvation in the world; you have God's word for it; what more is needed? Cannot you take God's word? You can take your father's word; you can take your mother's word; why cannot you take God's word? Oh! what base hearts we must have to suspect God himself! Perhaps you say you would not do such a thing. Oh! but you do doubt God, if you do not trust Christ; for "he that believeth not hath made God a liar." If you do not trust Christ, you do in effect say that God is a liar. You do not want to say that, do you?

Oh! believe the truthfulness of God! May the Spirit of God constrain you to believe the Father's mercy, the power of the Son's blood, the willingness of the Holy Ghost, to bring sinners to himself! Come, my dear hearers, join with me in the prayer that you may be led by grace to see in Jesus all that you need.

Prayer is a creature's strength, his very breath and being;
Prayer is the golden key that can open the wicket of Mercy;
Prayer is the magic sound that saith to Fate, So be it;
Prayer is the slender nerve that moveth the muscles of Omnipotence.
Wherefore, pray, O creature, for many and great are thy wants;
Thy mind, thy conscience, and thy being,
Thy rights commend thee unto prayer,
The cure of all cares, the grand panacea for all pains,
Doubt's destroyer, ruin's remedy, the antidote to all anxieties.

Order and Argument in Prayer

Delivered on Sunday morning, July 15, 1866, at the Metropolitan Tabernacle, Newington. No. 700.

"Oh that I knew where I might find him! that I might come even to his seat! I would order my cause before him, and fill my mouth with arguments."
—JOB 23:3–4

In Job's uttermost extremity he cried after the Lord. The longing desire of an afflicted child of God is once more to see his Father's face. His first prayer is not, "Oh that I might be healed of the disease which now festers in every part of my body!" nor even, "Oh that I might see my children restored from the jaws of the grave, and my property once more brought from the hand of the spoiler!" but the first and uppermost cry is, "Oh that I knew where I might find him—[who is my God]! that I might come even to his seat!" God's children run home when the storm comes on. It is the heaven-born instinct of a gracious soul to seek shelter from all ills beneath the wings of Jehovah. "He that hath made his refuge God," might serve as the title of a true believer. A hypocrite, when he feels that he has been afflicted by God, resents the infliction, and, like a slave, would run from the master who has scourged him; but not so the true heir of heaven. He kisses the hand which smote him, and seeks shelter from the rod in the bosom of that very God who frowned upon him.

You will observe that the desire to commune with God is intensified by the failure of all other sources of consolation. When Job first saw his friends at a distance, he may have entertained a hope that their kindly counsel and compassionate tenderness would blunt the edge of his grief; but they had not long spoken before he cried out in bitterness, "Miserable comforters are ye all." They put salt into his wounds, they heaped fuel upon the flame of his sorrow, they added the gall of their upbraidings to the wormwood of his griefs. In the sunshine of his smile they once had longed to sun themselves, and now they dare to cast shadows upon his reputation, most ungenerous and undeserved. Alas for a man when his wine cup mocks him with vinegar, and his pillow pricks him with thorns! The patriarch turned away from his sorry friends and looked up to the celestial throne, just as a traveler turns from his empty skin bottle and betakes himself with all speed to the well. He bids farewell to earth-born hopes, and cries, "Oh that I knew where I might find my God!"

My brethren, nothing teaches us so much the preciousness of the Creator as when we learn the emptiness of all besides. When you have been pierced through and through with the sentence, "Cursed is he that trusteth in man, and maketh flesh his arm," then will you suck unutterable sweetness from the divine assurance, "Blessed is he that trusteth in the LORD, and whose hope the LORD is." Turning away with bitter scorn from earth's hives, where you found no honey, but many sharp stings, you will rejoice in him whose faithful word is sweeter than honey or the honeycomb.

It is further observable that though a good man hastens to God in his trouble, and runs with all the more speed because of the unkindness of his fellowmen, yet sometimes the gracious soul is left without the comfortable presence of God. This is the worst of all griefs; the text is one of Job's deep groans, far deeper than any which came from him on account of the loss of his children and his property: "Oh that I knew where I might find him!" The worst of all losses is to lose the smile of my God. Job now had a foretaste of the bitterness of his Redeemer's cry, "My God, my God, why hast thou forsaken me?" God's presence is always with his people in one sense, so far as secretly sustaining them is concerned, but his manifest presence they do not always enjoy. Like the spouse in the song, they seek their beloved by night upon their bed, they seek him but they find him not; and though they wake and roam through the city they may not discover him, and the question may be sadly asked again and again, "Saw ye him whom my soul loveth?" You may be beloved of God, and yet have no consciousness of that love in your soul. You may be as dear to his heart as Jesus Christ himself, and yet for a small moment he may forsake you, and in a little wrath he may hide himself from you.

But, dear friends, at such times the desire of the believing soul gathers yet greater intensity from the fact of God's light being withheld. Instead of saying with proud lip, "Well, if he leaves me, I must do without him; if I cannot have his comfortable presence, I must fight on as best may be," the soul says, "No, it is my very life; I must have my God. I perish, I sink in deep mire where there is no standing, and nothing but the arm of God can deliver me." The gracious soul addresses itself with a double zeal to find out God, and sends up its groans, its entreaties, its sobs and sighs to heaven more frequently and fervently. "Oh that I knew where I might find him!" Distance or labor are as nothing; if the soul only knew where to go, she would soon overleap the distance. She makes no stipulation about mountains or rivers, but vows that if she knew where, she would come even to his seat. My soul in her hunger would break through stone walls, or scale the battlements of heaven to reach her God, and though there were seven hells between me and him, yet would I face the flame if I might reach him, nothing daunted if I had but the prospect of at last standing in his presence and feeling the delight of his love. That seems to me to be the state of mind in which Job pronounced the words before us.

But we cannot stop upon this point, for the object of this morning's discourse beckons us onward. It appears that Job's end, in desiring the presence of God, was that he might pray to him. He had prayed, but he wanted to pray as in God's presence. He desired to plead as before one whom he knew would hear and help him. He longed to state his own case before the seat of the impartial Judge, before the very face of the all-wise God; he would appeal from the lower courts, where his friends judged unrighteous judgment, to the Court of King's Bench—the High Court of heaven—there, says he, "I would order my cause before him, and fill my mouth with arguments."

In this latter verse Job teaches us how he meant to plead and intercede with God. He does, as it were, reveal the secrets of his closet, and unveils the art of prayer. We are here admitted into the guild of suppliants; we are shown the art and mystery of pleading; we have here taught to us the blessed handicraft and science of prayer, and if we can be bound apprentice to Job this morning, for the next hour, and can have a lesson from Job's Master, we may acquire no little skill in interceding with God.

There are two things here set forth as necessary in prayer—ordering of our cause, and filling our mouth with arguments. We shall speak of those two things, and then if we have rightly learned the lesson, a blessed result will follow.

I. First, *it is needful that our suit be ordered before God.*

There is a vulgar notion that prayer is a very easy thing, a kind of common business that may be done anyhow, without care or effort. Some think that you have only to reach a book down and get through a certain number of very excellent words, and you have prayed and may put the book up again; others suppose that to use a book is superstitious, and that you ought rather to repeat extemporaneous sentences, sentences which come to your mind with a rush, like a herd of swine or a pack of hounds, and that when you have uttered them with some little attention to what you have said, you have prayed. Now neither of these modes of prayer was adopted by ancient saints. They appear to have thought a great deal more seriously of prayer than many do nowadays.

It seems to have been a mighty business with them, a long-practiced exercise, in which some of them attained great eminence, and were thereby singularly blessed. They reaped great harvests in the field of prayer, and found the mercy seat to be a mine of untold treasures.

The ancient saints were wont, with Job, to order their cause before God; that is to say, as a petitioner coming into court does not come there without thought to state his case on the spur of the moment, but enters into the audience chamber with his suit well prepared, having moreover learned how he ought to behave himself in the presence of the great One to whom he is appealing. It is well to approach the seat of the King of kings as much as possible with premeditation and preparation, knowing what we are about, where we are standing, and what it is which we desire to obtain. In times of peril and distress we may fly to God just as we are, as the dove enters the cleft of the rock, even though her plumes are ruffled; but in ordinary times we should not come with an unprepared spirit, even as a child comes not to his father in the morning till he has washed his face. See yonder priest; he has a sacrifice to offer, but he does not rush into the court of the priests and hack at the bullock with the first poleax upon which he can lay his hand, but when he rises he washes his feet at the brazen laver, he puts on his garments, and adorns himself with his priestly vestments; then he comes to the altar with his victim properly divided according to the law, and is careful to do according to the command, even to such a simple matter as the placing of the fat, and the liver, and the kidneys, and he takes the blood in a bowl and pours it in an appropriate place at the foot of the altar, not throwing it just as may occur to him, and kindles the fire not with common flame, but with the sacred fire from off the altar. Now this ritual is all superseded, but the truth which it taught remains the same; our spiritual sacrifices should be offered with holy carefulness. God forbid that our prayer should be a mere leaping out of one's bed and kneeling down, and saying anything that comes first to hand; on the contrary, may we wait upon the Lord with holy fear and sacred awe. See how David prayed when God had blessed him—he went in before the Lord. Understand that; he did not stand outside at a distance, but he went in before the Lord and he sat down—for sitting is not a bad posture for prayer, let who will speak against it—and sitting down quietly and calmly before the Lord he then began to pray, but not until first he had thought over the divine goodness, and so attained to the spirit of prayer. Then by the assistance of the Holy Ghost did he open his mouth. Oh that we oftener sought the Lord in this style! Abraham may serve us as a pattern; he rose up early—here was his willingness; he went three days' journey—here was his zeal; he left his servants at the foot of the hill—here was his privacy; he carried the wood and the fire with him—here was his preparation; and lastly, he built the altar and laid the wood in order, and then took the knife—here was the devout carefulness of his worship. David puts it, "In the morning will I direct my prayer unto thee, and will look up"; which I have frequently explained to you to mean that he marshaled his thoughts like men of war, or that he aimed his prayers like arrows. He did not take the arrow and put it on the bowstring and shoot, and shoot, and shoot anywhere; but after he had taken out the chosen shaft, and fitted it to the string, he took deliberate aim. He looked—looked well—at the white of the target; kept his eye fixed on it, directing his prayer, and then drew his bow with all his strength and let the arrow fly; and then, when the shaft had left his hand, what does he say? "I will look up." He looked up to see where the arrow went, to see what effect it had; for he expected an answer to his prayers, and was not as many who scarcely think of their prayers after they have uttered them. David knew that he had an engagement before him which required all his mental powers; he marshaled up his faculties and went about the work in a work-manlike manner, as one who believed in it and meant to succeed. We should plow carefully and pray carefully. The better the work, the more attention it deserves. To be anxious in the shop and thoughtless in the closet is little less than blasphemy, for it is an insinuation that anything will do for God, but the world must have our best.

If any ask what order should be observed in prayer, I am not about to give you a scheme such as many have drawn out, in which adoration, confession, petition, intercession, and ascription are arranged in succession. I am not persuaded that any such order is of divine authority. It is to no mere mechanical order I have been referring, for our prayers will be equally acceptable, and possibly equally proper, in any form; for there are specimens of prayers, in all shapes, in the Old and New Testament. The true spiritual order of prayer seems to me to consist in something more than mere arrangement. It is most fitting for us first to feel that we are now doing something that is real; that we are about to address ourselves to God, whom we cannot see, but who is really present; whom we can neither touch nor hear, nor by our senses can apprehend, but who, nevertheless, is as truly with us as though we were speaking to a friend of flesh and blood like ourselves. Feeling the reality of God's presence, our mind will be led by divine grace into a humble state; we shall feel like Abraham, when he said, "I have taken upon myself to speak unto God, I that am but dust and ashes." Consequently, we shall not deliver ourselves of our prayer as boys repeating their lessons, as a mere matter of rote, much less shall we speak as if we were rabbis instructing our pupils, or as I have heard some do, with the coarseness of a highwayman stopping a person on the road and demanding his purse of him; but we shall be humble yet bold petitioners, humbly importuning mercy through the Savior's blood. We shall not have the reserve of a slave but the loving reverence of a child, yet not an impudent, impertinent child, but a teachable, obedient child, honoring his Father, and therefore asking earnestly, but with deferential submission, to his Father's will. When I feel that I am in the presence of God, and take my rightful position in that presence, the next thing I shall want to recognize will be that I have no right to what I am seeking, and cannot expect to obtain it except as a gift of grace, and I must recollect that God limits the channel through which he will give me mercy—he will give it to me through his dear Son. Let me put myself then under the patronage of the great Redeemer. Let me feel that now it is no longer I that speak but Christ that speaks with me, and that while I plead, I plead his wounds, his life, his death, his blood, himself. This is truly getting into order.

The next thing is to consider what I am to ask for. It is most proper in prayer, to aim at great distinctness of supplication. There is much reason to complain of some public prayers, that those who offer them do not really ask God for anything. I must acknowledge, I fear, to having so prayed myself, and certainly to having heard many prayers of the kind, in which I did not feel that anything was sought for from God—a great deal of very excellent doctrinal and experimental matter uttered, but little real petitioning, and that little in a nebulous kind of state, chaotic and unformed. But it seems to me that prayer should be distinct, the asking for something definitely and distinctly because the mind has realized its distinct need of such a thing, and therefore must plead for it. It is well not to beat around the bush in prayer, but to come directly to the point. I like that prayer of Abraham's, "Oh that Ishmael might live before thee!" There is the name and the person prayed for, and the blessing desired, all put in a few words—"Ishmael might live before thee!" Many persons would have used a roundabout expression of this kind, "Oh that our beloved offspring might be regarded with the favor which you bear to those who," etc. Say "Ishmael," if you mean "Ishmael"; put it in plain words before the Lord.

Some people cannot even pray for the minister without using such circular descriptives that you might think it were the parish beadle, or somebody whom it did not do to mention too particularly. Why not be distinct, and say what we mean as well as mean what we say? Ordering our cause would bring us to greater distinctness of mind. It is not necessary, my dear brethren, in the closet to ask for every supposable good thing; it is not necessary to rehearse the catalog of every want that you may have, have had, can have, or shall have. Ask for what you now need, and, as a rule, keep to present need; ask for your daily bread—what you want now—ask for that. Ask for it plainly, as before God, who does not regard your fine expressions, and to whom your eloquence and oratory will be less than nothing and vanity. You are before the Lord; let your words be few, but let your heart be fervent.

You have not quite completed the ordering when you have asked for what you want through Jesus Christ. There should be a looking around the blessing which you desire, to see whether it is assuredly a fitting thing to ask; for some prayers would never be offered if men did but think. A little reflection would show to us that some things which we desire were better let alone. We may, moreover, have a motive at the bottom of our desire which is not Christ-like, a selfish motive, which forgets God's glory and caters only for our own case and comfort. Now although we may ask for things which are for our profit, yet still we must never let our profit interfere in any way with the glory of God. There must be mingled with acceptable prayer the holy salt of submission to the divine will. I like Luther's saying, "Lord, I will have my will of thee at this time." "What!" say you, "Like such an expression as that?" I do, because of the next clause, which was, "I will have my will, for I know that my will is thy will." That is well spoken, Luther; but without the last words it would have been wicked presumption. When we are sure that what we ask for is for God's glory, then, if we have power in prayer, we may say, "I will not let thee go except thou bless me": we may come to close dealings with God, and like Jacob with the angel, we may even put it to the wrestle and seek to give the angel the fall sooner than be sent away without the benediction. But we must be quite clear, before we come to such terms as those, that what we are seeking is really for the Master's honor.

Put these three things together, the deep spirituality which recognizes prayer as being real conversation with the invisible God—much distinctness which is the reality of prayer, asking for what we know we want—and withal much fervency, believing the thing to be necessary, and therefore resolving to obtain it if it can be had by prayer, and above all these complete submission, leaving it still with the Master's will—commingle all these, and you have a clear idea of what it is to order your cause before the Lord.

Still prayer itself is an art which only the Holy Ghost can teach us. He is the giver of all prayer. Pray for prayer—pray till you can pray; pray to be helped to pray, and give not up praying because you cannot pray, for it is when you think you cannot pray that you are most praying; and sometimes when you have no sort of comfort in your supplications, it is then that your heart all broken and cast down is really wrestling and truly prevailing with the Most High.

II. The second part of prayer is *filling the mouth with arguments*— not filling the mouth with words, nor good phrases, nor pretty expressions, but filling the mouth with arguments are the knocks of the rapper by which the gate is opened.

Why are arguments to be used at all? is the first inquiry; the reply being, Certainly not because God is slow to give, not because we can change the divine purpose, not because God needs to be informed of any circumstance with regard to ourselves or of anything in connection with the mercy asked: the arguments to be used are for our own benefit, not for his. He requires for us to plead with him, and to bring forth our strong reasons, as Isaiah says, because this will show that we feel the value of the mercy. When a man searches for arguments for a thing, it is because he attaches importance to that which he is seeking. Again, our use of arguments teaches us the ground upon which we obtain the blessing. If a man should come with the argument of his own merit, he would never succeed; the successful argument is always founded upon grace, and hence the soul so pleading is made to understand intensely that it is by grace and by grace alone that a sinner obtains anything of the Lord. Besides, the use of arguments is intended to stir up our fervency. The man who uses one argument with God will get more force in using the next, and will use the next with still greater power, and the next with more force still. The best prayers I have ever heard in our prayer meetings have been those which have been fullest of argument. Sometimes my soul has been fairly melted down when I have listened to brethren who have come before God feeling the mercy to be really needed, and that they must have it, for they first pleaded with God to give it for this reason, and then for a second, and then for a third, and then for a fourth and a fifth, until they have awakened the fervency of the entire assembly.

My brethren, there is no need for prayer at all as far as God is concerned, but what a need there is for it on our own account! If we were not constrained to pray, I question whether we could even live as Christians. If God's mercies came to us unasked, they would not be half so useful as they now are, when they have to be sought for; for now we get a double blessing, a blessing in the obtaining, and a blessing in the seeking. The very act of prayer is a blessing. To pray is as it were to bathe one's self in a cool, purling stream, and so to escape from the heats of earth's summer sun. To pray is to mount on eagle's wings above the clouds and get into the clear heaven where God dwells. To pray is to enter the treasure house of God and to enrich one's self out of an inexhaustible storehouse. To pray is to grasp heaven in one's arms, to embrace the Deity within one's soul, and to feel one's body made a temple of the Holy Ghost. Apart from the answer, prayer is in itself a benediction. To pray, my brethren, is to cast off your burdens; it is to tear away your rags; it is to shake off your diseases; it is to be filled with spiritual vigor; it is to reach the highest point of Christian health. God give us to be much in the holy art of arguing with God in prayer.

The most interesting part of our subject remains; it is a very rapid summary and catalog of a few of the arguments which have been used with great success with God. I cannot give you a full list; that would require a treatise such as Master John Owen might produce. It is well in prayer to plead with Jehovah his attributes. Abraham did so when he laid hold upon God's justice. Sodom was to be pleaded for, and Abraham begins, "Peradventure there be fifty righteous within the city: wilt thou also destroy and not spare the place for the fifty righteous that are therein? That be far from thee to do after this manner, to slay the righteous with the wicked: and that the righteous should be as the wicked, that be far from thee: Shall not the Judge of all the earth do right?" Here the wrestling begins. It was a powerful argument by which the patriarch grasped the Lord's left hand, and arrested it just when the thunderbolt was about to fall. But there came a reply to it. It was intimated to him that this would not spare the city, and you notice how the good man, when sorely pressed, retreated by inches; and at last, when he could no longer lay hold upon justice, grasped God's right hand of mercy, and that gave him a wondrous hold when he asked that if there were but ten righteous there the city might be spared. So you and I may take hold at any time upon the justice, the mercy, the faithfulness, the wisdom, the long-suffering, the tenderness of God, and we shall find every attribute of the Most High to be, as it were, a great battering ram, with which we may open the gates of heaven.

Another mighty piece of ordinance in the battle of prayer is God's promise. When Jacob was on the other side of the brook Jabbok, and his brother Esau was coming with armed men, he pleaded with God not to suffer Esau to destroy the mother and the children, and as a master reason he pleaded, "And thou saidst, surely I will do thee good." Oh, the force of that plea! He was holding God to his word: "Thou saidst." The attribute is a splendid horn of the altar to lay hold upon; but the promise, which has in it the attribute and something more, is yet a mightier holdfast. "Thou saidst." Remember how David put it. After Nathan had spoken the promise, David

said at the close of his prayer, "Do as thou hast said." That is a legitimate argument with every honest man, and has he said, and shall he not do it? "Let God
be true, and every man a liar." Shall not he be true? Shall he not keep his word?
Shall not every word that comes out of his lips stand fast and be fulfilled?

Solomon, at the opening of the temple, used this same mighty plea. He
pleads with God to remember the word which he had spoken to his father,
David, and to bless that place. When a man gives a promissory note, his honor
is engaged. He signs his hand, and he must discharge it when the due time
comes, or else he loses credit. It shall never be said that God dishonors his bills.
The credit of the Most High never was impeached, and never shall be. He is
punctual to the moment; he never is before his time, but he never is behind it.
You shall search this Book through, and you shall compare it with the experience of God's people, and the two tally from the first to the last; and many a
hoary patriarch has said with Joshua in his old age, "Not one thing hath failed
of all the good things which the LORD your God spake concerning you; all are
come to pass." My brother, if you have a divine promise, you need not plead
it with an "if" in it; you may plead with a certainty. If for the mercy which you
are now asking, you have God's solemnly pledged word, there will scarce be
any room for the caution about submission to his will. You know his will: that
will is in the promise; plead it. Do not give him rest until he fulfill it. He meant
to fulfill it, or else he would not have given it.

God does not give his words merely to quiet our noise, and to keep us
hopeful for a while, with the intention of putting us off at last; but when he
speaks, he speaks because he means to act.

A third argument to be used is that employed by Moses, the great name
of God. How mightily did he argue with God on one occasion upon this
ground! "[What wilt thou do for thy great name? The Egyptians will say,]
because the LORD was not able to bring this people into the land which he
sware unto them, therefore he hath slain them in the wilderness." There are
some occasions when the name of God is very closely tied up with the history
of his people. Sometimes in reliance upon a divine promise, a believer will be
led to take a certain course of action. Now, if the Lord should not be as good
as his promise, not only is the believer deceived, but the wicked world looking
on would say, "Aha! aha! Where is your God?" Take the case of our respected
brother, Mr. Muller, of Bristol. These many years he has declared that God
hears prayer, and firm in that conviction, he has gone on to build house after
house for the maintenance of orphans. Now, I can very well conceive that, if
he were driven to a point of want of means for the maintenance of those
thousand or two thousand children, he might very well use the plea, "What

wilt thou do for thy great name?" And you, in some severe trouble, when you have fairly received the promise, may say, "Lord, you have said, 'In six troubles I will be with thee, and in seven I will not forsake thee.' I have told my friends and neighbors that I put my trust in you, and if you do not deliver me now, where is your name? Arise, O God, and do this thing, lest your honor be cast into the dust."

Coupled with this, we may employ the further argument of the hard things said by the revilers. It was well done of Hezekiah, when he took Rabshakeh's letter and spread it before the Lord. Will that help him? It is full of blasphemy, will that help him? "Where are the gods of Arphad and Sepharvaim? Where are the gods of the cities which I have overthrown? Let not Hezekiah deceive you, saying that Jehovah will deliver you." Does that have any effect? Oh! yes, it was a blessed thing that Rabshakeh wrote that letter, for it provoked the Lord to help his people. Sometimes the child of God can rejoice when he sees his enemies get thoroughly out of temper and take to reviling. "Now," he says, "they have reviled the Lord himself; not me alone have they assailed, but the Most High himself. Now it is no longer the poor insignificant Hezekiah with his little band of soldiers, but it is Jehovah, the King of angels, who has come to fight against Rabshakeh. Now what will you do, O boastful soldier of proud Sennacherib? Shall you not be utterly destroyed, since Jehovah himself has come into the fray? All the progress that is made by popery, all the wrong things said by speculative atheists and so on, should be by Christians used as an argument with God, why he should help the gospel. Lord, see how they reproach the gospel of Jesus! Pluck your right hand out of your bosom! O God, they defy you! Antichrist thrusts itself into the place where your Son once was honored, and from the very pulpits where the gospel was once preached popery is now declared. Arise, O God, wake up your zeal, let your sacred passions burn! Your ancient foe again prevails. Behold the harlot of Babylon once more upon her scarlet-colored beast rides forth in triumph! Come, Jehovah, come, Jehovah, and once again show what your bare arm can do!" This is a legitimate mode of pleading with God, for his great name's sake.

So also may we plead the sorrows of his people. This is frequently done. Jeremiah is the great master of this art. He says, "Her Nazarites were purer than snow, they were whiter than milk, they were more ruddy in body than rubies, their polishing was of sapphire: their visage is blacker than a coal." "The precious sons of Zion, comparable to fine gold, how are they esteemed as earthen pitchers, the work of the hands of the potter!" He talks of all their griefs and straitnesses in the siege. He calls upon the Lord to look upon his suffering Zion; and before long his plaintive cries are heard. Nothing so eloquent with the father as his child's cry; yes, there is one thing more mighty still, and that is a moan—when the child is so sick that it is past crying, and lies moaning with that kind of moan which indicates extreme suffering and intense weakness. Who can resist that moan? Ah! and when God's Israel shall be brought very low so that they can scarcely cry but only their moans are heard, then comes the Lord's time of deliverance, and he is sure to show that he loves his people. Dear friends, whenever you also are brought into the same condition you may plead your moanings, and when you see a church brought very low you may use her griefs as an argument why God should return and save the remnant of his people.

Brethren, it is good to plead with God the past. Ah, you experienced people of God, you know how to do this. Here is David's specimen of it: "Thou hast been my help; leave me not, neither forsake me." He pleads God's mercy to him from his youth up. He speaks of being cast upon his God from his very birth, and then he pleads, "Now also when I am old and greyheaded, O God, forsake me not." Moses also, speaking with God, says, "Thou didst bring this people up out of Egypt." As if he would say, "Do not leave your work unfinished; you have begun to build, complete it. You have fought the first battle; Lord, end the campaign! Go on till you get a complete victory." How often have we cried in our trouble, "Lord, you did deliver me in such and such a sharp trial, when it seemed as if no help were near; you have never forsaken me yet. I have set up my Ebenezer in your name. If you had intended to leave me, why have you showed me such things? Have you brought your servant to this place to put him to shame?" Brethren, we have to deal with an unchanging God, who will do in the future what he has done in the past, because he never turns from his purpose, and cannot be thwarted in his design; the past thus becomes a very mighty means of winning blessings from him.

We may even use our own unworthiness as an argument with God. "Out of the eater came forth meat, and out of the strong came forth sweetness." David in one place pleads thus: "O LORD, forgive my iniquity, though it is great." That is a very singular mode of reasoning; but being interpreted it means, "Lord, why should you go about doing little things? You are a great God, and here is a great sinner. Here is a fitness in me for the display of your grace. The greatness of my sin makes me a platform for the greatness of your mercy. Let the greatness of your love be seen in me." Moses seems to have the same on his mind when he asks God to show his great power in sparing his sinful people. The power with which God restrains himself is great indeed. O brothers and sisters, there is such a thing as creeping down at the foot of the throne, crouching low and crying, "O God, break me not—I am a bruised reed. Oh! tread not on my little life; it is now but as the smoking flax. Will you hunt me? Will you come out, as David said, 'after a dead dog, after a flea'? Will you pursue me as a leaf that is blown in the tempest? Will you watch me, as Job says, as though I were a vast sea, or a great whale? No, but because I am so little, and because the greatness of your mercy can be shown in one so insignificant and yet so vile, therefore, O God, have mercy upon me."

There was once an occasion when the very godhead of Jehovah made a triumphant plea for the prophet Elijah. On that august occasion, when he had bidden his adversaries see whether their god could answer them by fire, you can little guess the excitement there must have been that day in the prophet's mind. With what stern sarcasm did he say, "Cry aloud: for he is a god; either he is talking, or he is pursuing, or he is in a journey, or peradventure he sleepeth, and must be awaked." And as they cut themselves with knives, and leaped upon the altar, oh, the scorn with which that man of God must have looked down upon their impotent exertions, and their earnest but useless cries! But think of how his heart must have palpitated, if it had not been for the strength of his faith, when he repaired the altar of God that was broken down, and laid the wood in order, and killed the bullock. Hear him cry, "Pour water on it. You shall not suspect me of concealing fire; pour water on the victim." When they had done so, he bids them, "Do it a second time"; and they did it a second time; and then he says, "Do it a third time." And when it was all covered with water, soaked and saturated through, then he stands up and cries to God, "O God, let it be known that thou only art God." Here everything was put to the test. Jehovah's own existence was now put, as it were, at stake, before the eyes of men by this bold prophet. But how well the prophet was heard! Down came the fire and devoured not only the sacrifice, but even the wood, and the stones, and even the very water that was in the trenches, for Jehovah God had answered his servant's prayer. We sometimes may do the same, and say unto him, "Oh, by your Deity, by your existence, if indeed you be God, now show yourself for the help of your people!"

Lastly, the grand Christian argument is the sufferings, the death, the merit, the intercession of Christ Jesus. Brethren, I am afraid we do not understand what it is that we have at our command when we are allowed to plead with God for Christ's sake. I met with this thought the other day: it was somewhat new to me, but I believe it ought not to have been. When we ask God to hear us, pleading Christ's name, we usually mean, "O Lord, your dear Son deserves this of you; do this unto me because of what he merits." But if we knew it we might go in the city, "Sir, call at my office, and use my name, and say that they are to give you such a thing." I should go in and use your name, and I should obtain my request as a matter of right and a matter of necessity.

This is virtually what Jesus Christ says to us. "If you need anything of God, all that the Father has belongs to me; go and use my name." Suppose you should give a man your checkbook signed with your own name and left blank, to be filled up as he chose; that would be very nearly what Jesus has done in these words, "If you ask anything in my name, I will give it you." If I had a good name at the bottom of the check, I should be sure that I should get it cashed when I went to the banker with it; so when you have got Christ's name, to whom the very justice of God has become a debtor, and whose merits have claims with the Most High, when you have Christ's name there is no need to speak with fear and trembling and bated breath. Oh, waver not and let not faith stagger! When you plead the name of Christ you plead that which shakes the gates of hell, and which the hosts of heaven obey, and God himself feels the sacred power of that divine plea.

Brethren, you would do better if you sometimes thought more in your prayers of Christ's griefs and groans. Bring before the Lord his wounds, tell the Lord of his cries, make the groans of Jesus cry again from Gethsemane, and his blood speak again from that frozen Calvary. Speak out and tell the Lord that with such griefs, and cries, and groans to plead, you cannot take a denial: such arguments as these will speed you.

III. If the Holy Ghost shall teach us how to order our cause, and how to fill our mouth with arguments, the result shall be that *we shall have our mouth filled with praises.*

The man who has his mouth full of arguments in prayer shall soon have his mouth full of benedictions in answer to prayer. Dear friend, you have your mouth full this morning, have you? What of? Full of complaining? Pray the Lord to rinse your mouth out of that black stuff, for it will little avail you, and it will be bitter in your bowels one of these days. Oh, have your mouth full of prayer, full of it, full of arguments, so that there is room for nothing else. Then come with this blessed mouthful, and you shall soon go away with whatsoever you have asked of God. Only delight yourself in him, and he will give you the desire of your heart.

It is said—I know not how truly—that the explanation of the text, "Open thy mouth wide and I will fill it," may be found in a very singular Oriental custom. It is said that not many years ago—I remember the circumstance being reported—the King of Persia ordered the chief of his nobility, who had done something or other which greatly gratified him, to open his mouth, and when he had done so, he began to put into his mouth pearls, diamonds, rubies, and emeralds, till he had filled it as full as it could hold, and then he bade him go his way. This is said to have been occasionally done in Oriental courts toward great favorites. Now certainly whether that be an explanation of the text or not, it is an illustration of it. God says, "Open thy mouth with arguments," and then he will fill it with mercies priceless, gems unspeakably valuable. Would not a man open his mouth wide when he had to have it filled in such a style? Surely the most simpleminded among you would be wise enough for that. Oh! let us then open wide our mouth when we have to plead with God. Our needs are great, let our askings be great, and the supply shall be great too. You are not straitened in him; you are straitened in your own bowels. The Lord give you large mouths in prayer, great potency, not in the use of language, but in employing arguments.

What I have been speaking to the Christian is applicable in great measure to the unconverted man. God give you to see the force of it, and to fly in humble prayer to the Lord Jesus Christ and to find eternal life in him.

Pleading

Delivered on Lord's Day morning, October 29, 1871, at the Metropolitan Tabernacle, Newington. No. 1018.

But I am poor and needy: make haste unto me, O God: thou art my help and my deliverer; O LORD, make no tarrying.—PSALM 70:5

Young painters were anxious, in the olden times, to study under the great masters. They concluded that they should more easily attain to excellence if they entered the schools of eminent men. At this present time, men will pay large premiums that their sons may be apprenticed or articled to those who best understand their trades or professions; now, if any of us would learn the sacred art and mystery of prayer, it is well for us to study the productions of the greatest masters of that science. I am unable to point out one who understood it better than did the psalmist David. So well did he know how to praise, that his psalms have become the language of good men in all ages; and so well did he understand how to pray, that if we catch his spirit, and follow his mode of prayer, we shall have learned to plead with God after the most prevalent sort. Place before you, first of all, David's Son and David's Lord, that most mighty of all intercessors, and, next to him, you shall find David to be one of the most admirable models for your imitation.

We shall consider our text, then, as one of the productions of a great master in spiritual matters, and we will study it, praying all the while that God will help us to pray after the like fashion.

In our text we have the soul of a successful pleader under four aspects: we view, first, *the soul confessing*: "I am poor and needy." You have, next, *the soul pleading*, for he makes a plea out of his poor condition, and adds, "Make haste unto me, O God!" You see, thirdly, *a soul in its urgency*, for he cries, "Make haste," and he varies the expression but keeps the same idea: "Make no tarrying." And you have, in the fourth and last view, *a soul grasping God*, for the psalmist puts it thus: "Thou art my help and my deliverer"; thus with both hands he lays hold upon his God, so as not to let him go till a blessing is obtained.

I. To begin, then, see in this model of supplication, *a soul confessing*. The wrestler strips before he enters upon the contest, and confession does the like for the man who is about to plead with God. A racer on the plains of prayer cannot hope to win, unless, by confession, repentance, and faith, he lays aside every weight of sin.

Now, let it be ever remembered that confession is absolutely needful to the sinner when he first seeks a Savior. It is not possible for you, O seeker, to obtain peace for your troubled heart, till you shall have acknowledged your transgression and your iniquity before the Lord. You may do what you will, yes, even attempt to believe in Jesus, but you shall find that the faith of God's elect is not in you, unless you are willing to make a full confession of your transgression, and lay bare your heart before God. We do not usually think of giving charity to those who do not acknowledge that they need it: the physician does not send his medicine to those who are not sick. There is too much to be done in the world of necessary work for us to undertake works of supererogation; and, surely, to clothe those who are not naked, and to feed those that are not hungry, is to attempt superfluous work, which will bring us no credit. God will not do this: you must be empty before you can be filled by him, and you must confess your emptiness, too, or else assuredly he will not come to fill the full, nor to lift up those who are already high enough in their own esteem. The blind man in the Gospels had to feel his blindness, and to sit by the wayside begging; if he had entertained a doubt as to whether he were blind or not, the Lord would have passed him by. He opens the eyes of those who confess their blindness, but of others, he says, "Because ye say we see, therefore, your sin remaineth." He asks of those who are brought to him, "What wilt thou that I should do unto thee?" in order that their need may be publicly avowed. It must be so with all of us: we must offer the confession, or we cannot gain the benediction.

Let me speak especially to you who desire to find peace with God, and salvation through the precious blood: you will do well to make your confession before God very frank, very sincere, very explicit. Surely you have nothing to hide, for there is nothing that you can hide. He knows your guilt already, but he would have *you* know it, and, therefore, he bids you confess it. Go into the details of your sin in your secret acknowledgments before God: strip yourself of all excuses, make no apologies; say, "Against you, you only, have I sinned, and done this evil in your sight: that you might be justified when you speak, and be clear when you judge." Acknowledge the evil of sin; ask God to make you feel it; do not treat it as a trifle, for it is none. To redeem the sinner from the effect of sin, Christ himself must needs die, and unless you be delivered from it you must die eternally. Therefore, play not with sin; do not confess it as though it were some venial fault, which would not have been noticed unless God had been too severe; but labor to see sin as God sees it, as an offense against all that is good, a rebellion against all that is kind; see it to be treason, to be ingratitude, to be a mean and base thing.

Do not think that you can improve your condition before God by painting your case in brighter colors than it should be. Blacken it: if it were possible, blacken it, but it is not possible. When you feel your sin most you have not half felt it; when you confess it most fully you do not know a tithe of it; but oh, to the utmost of your ability make a clean breast of it, and say, "I have sinned against heaven, and before you." Acknowledge the sins of your youth and your manhood, the sins of your body and of your soul, the sins of omission and of commission, sins against the law and offenses against the gospel; acknowledge all, neither for a moment seek to deny one portion of the evil with which God's law, your own conscience, and his Holy Spirit justly charge you. And oh, soul, if you would get peace and approval with God in prayer, confess the ill desert of your sin. Submit yourself to whatever divine justice may sentence you to endure: confess that the deepest hell is your desert, and confess this not with your lips only, but with your soul. Let this be the doleful ditty of your inmost heart:

Should sudden vengeance seize my breath,
I must pronounce thee just in death;
And, if my soul were sent to hell,
Thy righteous law approves it well.

If you will condemn yourself, God will acquit you; if you will put the rope about your neck, and sentence yourself, then he who otherwise would have sentenced you will say, "I forgive you, through the merit of my Son."

But never expect that the King of heaven will pardon a traitor, if he will not confess and forsake his treason. Even the tenderest father expects that the child should humble himself when he has offended, and he will not withdraw his frown from him till with tears he has said, "Father, I have sinned." Dare you expect God to humble himself to you, and would it not be so if he did not constrain you to humble yourself to him? Would you have him connive at your faults and wink at your transgressions? He will have mercy, but he must be holy. He is ready to forgive, but not to tolerate sin; and, therefore, he cannot let you be forgiven if you hug your sins, or if you presume to say, "I have not sinned." Hasten, then, O seeker, hasten, I pray you, to the mercy seat with this upon your lips: "I am poor and needy, I am sinful, I am lost; have pity on me." With such an acknowledgment you begin your prayer well, and through Jesus you shalt prosper in it.

Beloved hearers, the same principle applies to the church of God. We are praying for a display of the Holy Spirit's power in this church, and, in order to successful pleading in this matter, it is necessary that we should unanimously make the confession of our text, "I am poor and needy." We must own that we are powerless in this business. Salvation is of the Lord, and we cannot save a single soul. The Spirit of God is treasured up in Christ, and we must seek him of the great head of the church. We cannot command the Spirit, and yet we can do nothing without him. The wind blows where it lists. We must deeply feel and honestly acknowledge this. Will you not heartily assent to it, my brethren and sisters, at this hour. May I not ask you unanimously to renew the confession this morning? We must also acknowledge that we are not worthy that the Holy Spirit should condescend to work with us and by us. There is no fitness in us for his purposes, except he shall give us that fitness. Our sins might well provoke him to leave us: he has striven with us, he has been tender toward us, but he might well go away and say, "I will no more shine upon that church, and no more bless that ministry." Let us feel our unworthiness; it will be a good preparation for earnest prayer; for, mark you, brethren, God will have his church before he blesses it know that the blessing is altogether from himself. "Not by might, nor by power, but by my spirit, saith the LORD of hosts."

The career of Gideon was a very remarkable one, and it commenced with two most instructive signs. I think our heavenly Father would have all of us learn the very same lesson which he taught to Gideon, and when we have mastered that lesson, he will use us for his own purposes. You remember Gideon laid a fleece upon the barn floor, and in the morning all around was dry and the fleece alone was wet. God alone had saturated the fleece so that he could wring it out, and its moisture was not due to its being placed in a favorable situation, for all around was dry. He would have us learn that, if the dew of his grace fills any one of us with its heavenly moisture, it is not because we lie upon the barn floor of a ministry which God usually blesses, or because we are in a church which the Lord graciously visits; but we must be made to see that the visitations of his Spirit are fruits of the Lord's sovereign grace, and gifts of his infinite love, and not of the will of man, neither by man. But then the miracle was reversed, for, as old Thomas Fuller says, "God's miracles will bear to be turned inside out and look as glorious one way as another."

The next night the fleece was dry and all around was wet. For skeptics might have said, "Yes, but a fleece would naturally attract moisture, and if there were any in the air, it would be likely to be absorbed by the wool." But, lo, on this occasion, the dew is not where it might be expected to be, even though it lies thickly all around. Damp is the stone and dry is the fleece. So God will have us know that he does not give us his grace because of any natural adaptation in us to receive it, and even where he has given a preparedness of heart to receive, he will have us understand that his grace and his Spirit are most free in action, and sovereign in operation: and that he is not bound to work after any rule of our making. If the fleece be wet, he bedews it, and that not because it is a fleece, but because he chooses to do so. He will have all the glory of all his grace from first to last. Come then, my brethren, and become disciples to this truth. Consider that from the great Father of lights every good and perfect gift must come. We are his workmanship; he must work all our works in us. Grace is not to be commanded by our position or condition: the wind blows where it lists, the Lord works and no man can hinder; but if he works not, the mightiest and the most zealous labor is but in vain.

It is very significant that before Christ fed the thousands, he made the disciples sum up all their provisions. It was well to let them see how low the commissariat had become, for then when the crowds were fed, they could not say the basket fed them, nor that the lad had done it. God will make us feel how little are our barley loaves, and how small our fishes, and compel us to inquire, "What are they among so many?" When the Savior bade his disciples cast the net on the right side of the ship, and they dragged such a mighty shoal to land, he did not work the miracle till they had confessed that they had toiled all the night and had taken nothing. They were thus taught that the success of their fishery was dependent upon the Lord, and that it was not their net, nor their way of dragging it, nor their skill and art in handling their vessels, but that altogether and entirely their success came from their Lord. We must get down to this, and the sooner we come to it the better.

Before the ancient Jews kept the Passover, observe what they did. The unleavened bread is to be brought in, and the paschal lamb to be eaten; but there shall be no unleavened bread, and no paschal lamb, till they have purged out the old leaven. If you have any old strength and self-confidence; if you have anything that is your own, and is, therefore, leavened, it must be swept right out; there must be a bare cupboard before there can come in the heavenly provision, upon which the spiritual Passover can be kept. I thank God when he cleans us out; I bless his name when he brings us to feel our soul-poverty as a church, for then the blessing will be sure to come.

One other illustration will show this, perhaps, more distinctly still. Behold Elijah with the priests of Baal at Carmel. The test appointed to decide Israel's choice was this—the God that answers by fire, let him be God. Baal's priests invoked the heavenly flame in vain. Elijah is confident that it will come upon his sacrifice, but he is also sternly resolved that the false priests and the fickle people shall not imagine that he himself had produced the fire. He determines to make it clear that there is no human contrivance, trickery, or maneuver about the matter. The flame should be seen to be of the Lord, and of the Lord alone. Remember the stern prophet's command, "Fill four barrels with water, and pour it on the burnt sacrifice, and on the wood. And he said, Do it the second time. And they did it the second time. And he said, Do it the third time. And they did it the third time. And the water ran round about the altar; and he filled the trench also with water." There could be no latent fires there. If there had been any combustibles or chemicals calculated to produce fire after the manner of the cheats of the time, they would all have been damped and spoiled. When no one could imagine that man could burn the sacrifice, then the prophet lifted up his eyes to heaven, and began to plead, and down came the fire of the Lord, which consumed the burnt sacrifice and the wood, and the altar stones and the dust, and even licked up the water that was in the trench. Then when all the people saw it they fell on their faces, and they said, "The LORD, he is the God; the LORD, he is the God."

The Lord in this church, if he means greatly to bless us, may send us the trial of pouring on the water once, and twice, and thrice; he may discourage us, grieve us, and try us, and bring us low, till all shall see that it is not of the preacher, it is not of the organization, it is not of man, but altogether of God, the Alpha and the Omega, who works all things according to the council of his will.

Thus I have shown you that for a successful season of prayer the best beginning is confession that we are poor and needy.

II. Secondly, after the soul has unburdened itself of all weights of merit and self-sufficiency, it proceeds to prayer, and we have before us *a soul pleading.*

"I am poor and needy: make haste unto me, O God: Thou art my help and my deliverer; O LORD, make no tarrying." The careful reader will perceive four pleas in this single verse. Upon this topic I would remark that it is the habit of faith, when she is praying, to use pleas. Mere prayer sayers, who do not pray at all, forget to argue with God; but those who would prevail bring forth their reasons and their strong arguments, and they debate the question with the Lord. They who play at wrestling catch here and there at random, but those who are really wrestling have a certain way of grasping the opponent—a certain mode of throwing, and the like; they work according to order and rule. Faith's art of wrestling is to plead with God, and say with holy boldness, "Let it be thus and thus, for these reasons." Hosea tells us of Jacob at Jabbok, "and there he spake with us"; from which I understand that Jacob instructed us by his example. Now, the two pleas which Jacob used were God's precept and God's promise. First, he said, "[Thou] saidst unto me, Return unto thy country and to thy kindred": as much as if he put it thus:—"Lord, I am in difficulty, but I have come here through obedience to you. You did tell me to do this; now, since you command me to come hither, into the very teeth of my brother Esau, who comes to meet me like a lion, Lord, you cannot be so unfaithful as to bring me into danger and then leave me in it." This was sound reasoning, and it prevailed with God. Then Jacob also urged a promise: "Thou saidst, I will surely do thee good."

Among men, it is a masterly way of reasoning when you can challenge your opponent with his own words: you may quote other authorities, and he may say, "I deny their force"; but, when you quote a man against himself, you foil him completely. When you bring a man's promise to his mind, he must either confess himself to be unfaithful and changeable, or, if he holds to being the same, and being true to his word, you have him, and you have won your will of him. Oh, brethren, let us learn thus to plead the precepts, the promises, and whatever else may serve our turn; but let us always have something to plead. Do not reckon you have prayed unless you have pleaded, for pleading is the very marrow of prayer. He who pleads well knows the secret of prevailing with God, especially if he pleads the blood of Jesus, for that unlocks the treasury of heaven. Many keys fit many locks, but the master key is the blood and the name of him that died but rose again, and ever lives in heaven to save unto the uttermost. Faith's pleas are plentiful, and this is well, for faith is placed in diverse positions, and needs them all.

She has many needs, and having a keen eye she perceives that there are pleas to be urged in every case. I will not, therefore, tell you all faith's pleas, but I will just mention some of them, enough to let you see how abundant they are. Faith will plead all the attributes of God. "You are just; therefore spare the soul for whom the Savior died. You are merciful; blot out my transgressions. You are good; reveal your bounty to your servant. You are immutable—you have done thus and thus to others of your servants; do thus unto me. You are faithful; can you break your promise, can you turn away from your covenant?" Rightly viewed, all the perfections of Deity become pleas for faith.

Faith will boldly plead all God's gracious relationships. She will say to him, "Are you not the Creator? Will you forsake the works of your own hands? Are you not the Redeemer? You have redeemed your servant; will you cast me away?" Faith usually delights to lay hold upon the fatherhood of God. This is generally one of her master points: when she brings this into the field she wins the day. "You are a Father, and would you chasten us as though you would kill? A Father, and will you not provide? A Father, and have you no sympathy and no bowels of compassion? A Father, and can you deny what your own child asks of you?" Whenever I am impressed with the divine majesty, and so, perhaps, a little dispirited in prayer, I find the short and sweet remedy is to remember that, although he is a great King, and infinitely glorious, I am his child, and no matter who the father is, the child may always be bold with his father. Yes, faith can plead any and all of the relationships in which God stands to his chosen.

Faith, too, can ply heaven with the divine promises. I need not enlarge here, for this I trust you all do so continually. When you can as it were bring home the Lord's word to himself, it is well. That is the conquering argument, "Do as you have said." "You have spoken it, and you have made your promise to be yes and amen in Christ Jesus to your own glory by us; will you not fulfill it? Will you run back from your own word? Will you fail to carry out your own declaration? That be far from you, Lord!" Brethren, we want to be more business-like and common sense with God in pleading promises. If you were to go to one of the banks in Lombard Street, and see a man go in and out and lay a piece of paper on the table, and take it up again and nothing more; if he did that several times a day, I think there would soon be orders issued to the porter to keep the man out, because he was merely wasting the clerk's time, and doing nothing to purpose. Those city men who come to the bank in earnest present their checks, they wait till they receive their gold and then they go, but not without having transacted real business. They do not put the paper down, speak about the excellent signature and discuss the correctness of the document, but they want their money for it, and they are not content without it. These are the people who are always welcome at the bank and not the triflers. Alas, a great many people play at praying, it is nothing better. I say they play at praying, they do not expect God to give them an answer, and thus they are mere triflers, who mock the Lord. He who prays in a business-like way, meaning what he says, honors the Lord. The Lord does not play at promising,

Jesus did not sport at confirming the Word by his blood, and we must not make a jest of prayer by going about it in a listless, unexpecting spirit.

The Holy Spirit is in earnest, and we must be in earnest also. We must go for a blessing, and not be satisfied till we have it; like the hunter, who is not satisfied because he has run so many miles, but is never content till he takes his prey.

Faith, moreover, pleads the performances of God; she looks back on the past and says, "Lord, you did deliver me on such and such an occasion; will you fail me now?" She, moreover, takes her life as a whole, and pleads thus:

After so much mercy past,

Will you let me sink at last?

"Have you brought me so far that I may be put to shame at the end?" She knows how to bring the ancient mercies of God and make them arguments for present favors. But your time would all be gone if I tried to exhibit even a thousandth part of faith's pleas.

Sometimes, however, faith's pleas are very singular. As in this text, it is by no means according to the proud rule of human nature to plead—"I am poor and needy: make haste unto me, O God." It is like another prayer of David: "Pardon mine iniquity, for it is great." It is not the manner of men to plead so; they say, "Lord, have mercy on me, for I am not so bad a sinner as some." But faith reads things in a truer light, and bases her pleas on truth. "Lord, because my sin is great, and you are a great God, let your great mercy be magnified in me."

You know the story of the Syrophoenician woman; that is a grand instance of the ingenuity of faith's reasoning. She came to Christ about her daughter, and he answered her not a word. What do you think her heart said? Why, she said in herself, "It is well, for he has not denied me: since he has not spoken at all, he has not refused me." With this for an encouragement, she began to plead again. Presently Christ spoke to her sharply, and then her brave heart said, "I have gained words from him at last; I shall have deeds from him by and by." That also cheered her; and then, when he called her a dog, "Ah," she reasoned, "but a dog is a part of the family; it has some connection with the master of the house. Though if does not eat meat from the table, it gets the crumbs under it, and so I have you now, great Master, dog as I am; the great mercy that I ask of you, great as it is to me, is only a crumb to you; grant it then, I beseech you." Could she fail to leave her request? Impossible! When faith has a will, she always finds a way, and she will win the day when all things forebode defeat.

Faith's pleas are singular, but, let me add, faith's pleas are always sound; for after all, it is a very telling plea to urge that we are poor and needy. Is not

that the main argument with mercy? Necessity is the very best plea with benevolence, either human or divine. Is not our need the best reason we can urge? If
we would have a physician come quickly to a sick man, "Sir," we say, "it is no
common case, he is on the point of death, come to him, come quickly!" If we
wanted our city firemen to rush to a fire, we should not say to them, "Make
haste, for it is only a small fire"; but, on the contrary, we urge that it is an old
house, full of combustible materials, and there are rumors of petroleum and
gunpowder on the premises; besides, it is near a timber yard, hosts of wooden
cottages are close by, and before long we shall have half the city in a blaze. We
put the case as badly as we can. Oh, for wisdom to be equally wise in pleading
with God, to find arguments everywhere, but especially to find them in our
necessities.

They said two centuries ago that the trade of beggary was the easiest one
to carry on, but it paid the worst. I am not sure about the last at this time, but
certainly the trade of begging with God is a hard one, and undoubtedly it pays
the best of anything in the world. It is very noteworthy that beggars with men
have usually plenty of pleas on hand. When a man is hardly driven and starv-
ing, he can usually find a reason why he should ask aid of every likely person.
Suppose it is a person to whom he is already under many obligations, then the
poor creature argues, "I may safety ask of him again, for he knows me, and
has been always very kind." If he never asked of the person before, then he
says, "I have never worried him before; he cannot say he has already done all
he can for me; I will make bold to begin with him." If it is one of his own kin,
then he will say, "Surely you will help me in my distress, for you are a relation";
and if it be a stranger, he says, "I have often found strangers kinder than my own
blood; help me, I entreat you." If he asks of the rich, he pleads that they will
never miss what they give; and if he begs of the poor, he urges that they know
what want means, and he is sure they will sympathize with him in his great
distress. Oh that we were half as much on the alert to fill our mouths with
arguments when we are before the Lord. How is it that we are not half awake,
and do not seem to have our spiritual senses aroused. May God grant that we
may learn the art of pleading with the eternal God, for in that shall rest our
prevalence with him, through the merit of Jesus Christ.

**III. I must be brief on the next point. It is *a soul urgent*: "Make haste
unto me, O God: . . .**

O LORD, make no tarrying." We may well be urgent with God, if as yet
we are not saved, for our need is urgent; we are in constant peril, and the peril

is of the most tremendous kind. O sinner, within an hour, within a minute, you may be where hope can never visit you; therefore, cry, "Make haste, O God, to deliver me: make haste to help me, O LORD!" Yours is not a case that can bear lingering: you have not time to procrastinate; therefore, be urgent, for your need is so. And, remember, if you really are under a sense of need, and the Spirit of God is at work with you, you will and must be urgent. An ordinary sinner may be content to wait, but a quickened sinner wants mercy now. A dead sinner will lie quiet, but a living sinner cannot rest till pardon is sealed home to his soul. If you are urgent this morning, I am glad of it, because your urgency, I trust, arises from the possession of spiritual life. When you cannot live longer without a Savior, the Savior will come to you, and you shall rejoice in him.

Brethren, members of this church, as I have said on another point, the same truth holds good with you. God will come to bless you, and come speedily, when your sense of need becomes deep and urgent. Oh, how great is this church's need! We shall grow cold, unholy, and worldly; there will be no conversions, there will be no additions to our numbers; there will be diminutions, there will be divisions, there will be mischief of all kinds; Satan will rejoice, and Christ will be dishonored, unless we obtain a larger measure of the Holy Spirit. Our need is urgent, and when we feel that need thoroughly, then we shall get the blessing which we want.

Does any melancholy spirit say, "We are in so bad a state that we cannot expect a large blessing"? I reply, perhaps if we were worse, we should obtain it all the sooner. I do not mean if we were really so, but if we felt we were worse, we should be nearer the blessing. When we mourn that we are in an ill state, then we cry the more vehemently to God, and the blessing comes. God never refused to go with Gideon because he had not enough valiant men with him, but he paused because the people were too many. He brought them down from thousands to hundreds, and he diminished the hundred before he gave them victory. When you feel that you must have God's presence, but that you do not deserve it, and when your consciousness of this lays you in the dust, then shall the blessing be vouchsafed.

For my part, brethren and sisters, I desire to feel a spirit of urgency within my soul as I plead with God for the dew of his grace to descend upon this church. I am not bashful in this matter, for I have a license to pray. Mendicancy is forbidden in the streets, but, before the Lord I am a licensed beggar. Jesus has said, "men ought always to pray, and not to faint." You land on the shores of a foreign country with the greatest confidence when you carry a passport with you, and God has issued passports to his children, by which they come boldly to his mercy seat; he has invited you, he has encouraged you, he has bidden you come to him, and he has promised that whatsoever ye ask in prayer, believing, ye shall receive. Come, then, come urgently, come importunately, come with this plea, "I am poor and needy; make no tarrying, O my God," and a blessing shall surely come; it will not tarry. God grant we may see it, and give him the glory of it.

IV. I am sorry to have been so brief where I had need to have enlarged, but I must close with the fourth point. Here is another part of the art and mystery of prayer—*the soul grasping God.*

She has pleaded, and she has been urgent, but now she comes to close quarters; she grasps the covenant angel with one hand, "You are my help," and with the other, "You are my deliverer." Oh, those blessed "my's," those potent "my's." The sweetness of the Bible lies in the possessive pronouns, and he who is taught to use them as the psalmist did, shall come off a conqueror with the eternal God.

Now, sinner, I pray God you may be helped to say this morning to the blessed Christ of God, "You are my help and my deliverer." Perhaps you mourn that you cannot get that length, but, poor soul, have you any other help? If you have, then you cannot hold two helpers with the same hand. "Oh, no," say you, "I have no help anywhere. I have no hope except in Christ." Well, then, poor soul, since your hand is empty, that empty hand was made on purpose to grasp your Lord with: lay hold on him! Say to him, this day, "Lord, I will hang on you as poor lame Jacob did; now I cannot help myself, I will cleave to you: I will not let you go except you bless me." "Ah, it would be too bold," says one. But the Lord loves holy boldness in poor sinners; he would have you be bolder than you think of being. It is an unhallowed bashfulness that dares not trust a crucified Savior. He died on purpose to save such as you are; let him have his way with you, and do trust him.

"Oh," says one, "but I am so unworthy." He came to seek and save the unworthy. He is not the Savior of the self-righteous: he is the sinners' Savior—"friend of sinners" is his name. Unworthy one, lay hold on him! "Oh," says one, "but I have no right." Well, but that is the very reason you should grasp him, for right is for the court of justice, not for the hall of mercy. I would advise you not to try your rights, for you have no right but to be condemned; but you need no rights when dealing with Jesus. Nothing makes a charitable person refuse his alms like a beggar's saying, "I have a right." "No," says the giver, "if you have rights, go and get them; I will give you nothing." Since you have no right, your need shall be your claim: it is all the claim you want. I think I hear one say, "It is too late for me to plead for grace." It cannot be: it is impossible. While you live and desire mercy, it is not too late to seek it. Notice the parable of the man who wanted three loaves. I will tell you what crossed my mind when I read it: the man went to his friend at midnight; it was late, was it not? Why, his friend might have said, and, indeed, did in effect say to him, that it was too late, but yet the pleader gained the bread after all. In the parable the time was late, it could not have been later; for if it had been a little later than midnight, it would have been early in the next morning, and so not late at all. It was midnight, and it could not be later; and so, if it is downright midnight with your soul, yet, be of good cheer; Jesus is an out-of-season Savior; many of his servants are "born out of due time."

Any season is the right season to call upon the name of Jesus; therefore, only do not let the devil tempt you with the thought that it can be too late. Go to Jesus now, go at once, and lay hold on the horns of the altar by a venturesome faith, and say, "Sacrifice for sinners, you are a sacrifice for me. Intercessor for the graceless, you are an intercessor for me. You who distribute gifts to the rebellious, distribute gifts to me, for a rebel I have been. When we were yet without strength, in due time Christ died for the ungodly. Such am I, good Master; let the power of your death be seen in me to have my soul."

Oh, you that are saved and, therefore, love Christ, I want you, dear brethren, as the saints of God, to practice this last part of my subject; and be sure to lay hold upon God in prayer. "Thou art my help and my deliverer." As a church we throw ourselves upon the strength of God, and we can do nothing without him; but we do not mean to be without him; we will hold him fast. "Thou art my help and my deliverer." There was a boy at Athens, according to the old story, who used to boast that he ruled all Athens, and when they asked him how, he said, "Why, I rule my mother, my mother rules my father, and my father rules the city." He who knows how to be master of prayer will rule the heart of Christ, and Christ can and will do all things for his people, for the Father has committed all things into his hands. You can be omnipotent if you know how to pray, omnipotent in all things which glorify God. What does the Word itself say? "Let him take hold of my strength." Prayer moves the arm that moves the world. Oh for grace to grasp Almighty love in this fashion.

We want more holdfast prayer; more tugging, and gripping, and wrestling prayer, that says, "I will not let you go." That picture of Jacob at Jabbok shall suffice for us to close with. The covenant angel is there, and Jacob wants a blessing from him: he seems to put him off, but no put-offs will do for Jacob. Then the angel endeavors to escape from him, and tugs and strives: so he may, but no efforts shall make Jacob relax his grasp. At last the angel falls from ordinary wrestling to wounding him in the very seat of his strength; and Jacob will let his thigh go, and all his limbs go, but he will not let the angel go. The poor man's strength shrivels under the withering touch, but in his weakness he is still strong: he throws his arms about the mysterious man, and holds him as in a death grip. Then the other says, "Let me go, for the day breaketh." Mark, he did not shake him off, he said only, "Let me go"; the angel will do nothing to force him to relax his hold; he leaves that to his voluntary will. The valiant Jacob cries, "[No, I am set on it, I am resolved to win an answer to my prayer.] I will not let thee go, except thou bless me." Now, when the church begins to pray, it may be at first, the Lord will make as though he would have gone further, and we may fear that no answer will be given. Hold on, dear brethren. Be steadfast, unmovable, notwithstanding all. By and by, it may be, there will come discouragements where we looked for a flowing success; we shall find brethren hindering; some will be slumbering, and others sinning; backsliders and impenitent souls will abound; but let us not be turned aside. Let us be all the more eager.

And if it should so happen that we ourselves become distressed and dispirited, and feel we never were so weak as we are now, never mind, brethren; still hold on, for when the sinew is shrunk, the victory is near. Grasp with a tighter clutch than ever. Be this our resolution, "I will not let thee go, except thou bless me." Remember, the longer the blessing is coming, the richer it will be when it arrives. That which is gained speedily by a single prayer is sometimes only a second-rate blessing; but that which is gained after many a desperate tug, and many an awful struggle, is a full-weighted and precious blessing. The children of importunity are always fair to look upon. The blessing which costs us the most prayer will be worth the most. Only let us be persevering in supplication, and we shall gain a broad, far-reaching benediction for ourselves, the churches, and the world. I wish it were in my power to stir you all to fervent prayer; but I must leave it with the great author of all true supplication, namely, the Holy Spirit. May he work in us mightily, for Jesus' sake. Amen.

The Throne of Grace

Delivered on Lord's Day morning, November 19, 1871, at the Metropolitan Tabernacle, Newington. No. 1024.

The throne of grace. . . .—HEBREWS 4:16

These words are found embedded in that gracious verse, "Let us therefore come boldly unto the throne of grace, that we may obtain mercy, and find grace to help in time of need"; they are a gem in a golden setting. True prayer is an approach of the soul by the Spirit of God to the throne of God. It is not the utterance of words, it is not alone the feeling of desires, but it is the advance of the desires to God, the spiritual approach of our nature toward the Lord our God. True prayer is not a mere mental exercise, nor a vocal performance, but it is deeper far than that—it is spiritual commerce with the Creator of heaven and earth. God is a Spirit unseen of mortal eye, and only to be perceived by the inner man; our spirit within us, begotten by the Holy Ghost at our regeneration, discerns the Great Spirit, communes with him, prefers to him its requests, and receives from him answers of peace. It is a spiritual business from beginning to end; and its aim and object end not with man, but reach to God himself.

In order to such prayer, the work of the Holy Ghost himself is needed. If prayer were of the lips alone, we should need only breath in our nostrils to pray: if prayer were of the desires alone, many excellent desires are easily felt, even by natural men: but when it is the spiritual desire, and the spiritual fellowship of the human spirit with the Great Spirit, then the Holy Ghost himself must be present all through it, to help infirmity, and give life and power, or else true prayer will never be presented, but the thing offered to God will wear the name and have the form, but the inner life of prayer will be far from it.

Moreover, it is clear from the collection of our text, that the interposition of the Lord Jesus Christ is essential to acceptable prayer. As prayer will not be truly prayer without the Spirit of God, so it will not be prevailing prayer without the Son of God. He, the Great High Priest, must go within the veil for us; no, through his crucified person the veil must be entirely taken away; for, until then, we are shut out from the living God. The man who, despite the teaching of Scripture, tries to pray without a Savior, insults the Deity; and he who imagines that his own natural desires, coming up before God, unsprinkled with the precious blood, will be an acceptable sacrifice before God, makes a mistake; he has not brought an offering that God can accept, any more than if he had struck off a dog's neck, or offered a nuclear sacrifice. Wrought in us by the Spirit, presented for us by the Christ of God, prayer becomes power before the Most High, but not else.

In order, dear friends, that I may stir you up to prayer this morning, and that your souls may be led to come near to the Throne of Grace, I purpose to take these few words and handle them as God shall give me ability. You have begun to pray; God has begun to answer. This week has been a very memorable one in the history of this church. Larger numbers than ever before at one time have come forward to confess Christ—as plain an answer to the supplications of God's people, as though the hand of the Most High had been seen stretched out of heaven handing down to us the blessings for which we asked. Now, let us continue in prayer, yes, let us gather strength in intercession, and the more we succeed, the more earnest let us be to succeed yet more and more. Let us not be straitened in our own bowels, since we are not straitened in our God. This is a good day, and a time of glad tidings, and seeing that we have the King's ear, I am most anxious that we should speak to him for thousands of others; that they also, in answer to our pleadings, may be brought near to Christ.

In trying to speak of the text this morning, I shall take it thus: First, *here is a throne*; then, secondly, *here is grace*; then we will put the two together, and we shall see grace on a throne; and putting them together in another order, we shall see *sovereignty manifesting itself, and resplendent in grace.*

I. Our text speaks of *a throne*—"The Throne of Grace."

God is to be viewed in prayer as our Father; that is the aspect which is dearest to us; but still we are not to regard him as though he were such as we are; for our Savior has qualified the expression "Our Father," with the words "who art in heaven"; and close at the heels of that condescending name, in order to remind us that our Father is still infinitely greater than ourselves, he has bidden us say, "Hallowed be thy name; thy kingdom come"; so that our Father is still to be regarded as a King, and in prayer we come, not only to our Father's feet, but we come also to the throne of the Great Monarch of the universe. The mercy seat is a throne, and we must not forget this.

If prayer should always be regarded by us as an entrance into the courts of the royalty of heaven; if we are to behave ourselves as courtiers should in the presence of an illustrious majesty, then we are not at a loss to know the right spirit in which to pray. If in prayer we come to a throne, it is clear that our spirit should, in the first place, be one of *lowly reverence*. It is expected that the subject in approaching to the king should pay him homage and honor. The pride that will not own the king, the treason which rebels against the sovereign will should, if it be wise, avoid any near approach to the throne. Let pride bite the curb at a distance, let treason lurk in corners, for only lowly reverence may come before the king himself when he sits clothed in his robes of majesty. In our case, the king before whom we come is the highest of all monarchs, the King of kings, the Lord of lords. Emperors are but the shadows of his imperial power. They call themselves kings by right divine, but what divine right have they? Common sense laughs their pretensions to scorn. The Lord alone has divine right, and to him only does the kingdom belong. He is the blessed and only potentate. They are but nominal kings, to be set up and put down at the will of men, or the decree of providence, but he is Lord alone, the Prince of the kings of the earth.

He sits on no precarious throne,
Nor borrows leave to be.

My heart, be sure that you prostrate yourself in such a presence. If he be so great, place your mouth in the dust before him, for he is the most powerful of all kings; his throne has sway in all worlds; heaven obeys him cheerfully, hell trembles at his frown, and earth is constrained to yield him homage willingly or unwillingly. His power can make or can destroy. To create or to crush, either is easy enough to him. My soul be sure that when you draw near to the Omnipotent, who is as a consuming fire, you put your shoes from off your feet, and worship him with lowliest humility.

Besides, he is the most holy of all kings. His throne is a great white throne, unspotted, and clear as crystal. The heavens are not pure in his sight, "and his angels he charged with folly." And you, a sinful creature, with what lowliness should you draw near to him. Familiarity there may be, but let it not be unhallowed. Boldness there should be, but let it not be impertinent. Still you are on earth and he in heaven; still you are a worm of the dust, a creature crushed before the moth, and he the Everlasting: before the mountains were brought forth he was God, and if all created things should pass away again, yet still were he the same. My brethren, I am afraid we do not bow as we should before the Eternal Majesty; but, henceforth, let us ask the Spirit of God to put us in a right frame, that every one of our prayers may be a reverential approach to the Infinite Majesty above.

A throne, and, therefore, in the second place, to be approached with *devout joyfulness*. If I find myself favored by divine grace to stand among those favored ones who frequent his courts, shall I not feel glad? I might have been in his prison, but I am before his throne: I might have been driven from his presence for ever, but I am permitted to come near to him, even into his royal palace, into his secret chamber of gracious audience; shall I not then be thankful? Shall not my thankfulness ascend into joy, and shall I not feel that I am honored, that I am made the recipient of great favors when I am permitted to pray? Wherefore is your countenance sad, O suppliant, when you stand before the throne of grace? If you were before the throne of justice to be condemned for your iniquities, your hands might well be on your loins; but now you are favored to come before the King in his silken robes of love, let your face shine with sacred delight. If your sorrows be heavy, tell them to him, for he can assuage them; if your sins be multiplied, confess them, for he can forgive them. O ye courtiers in the halls of such a monarch, be exceeding glad, and mingle praises with your prayers.

It is a throne, and therefore, in the third place, whenever it is approached, it should be with *complete submission*. We do not pray to God to instruct him as to what he ought to do, neither for a moment must we presume to dictate the line of the divine procedure. We are permitted to say unto God, "Thus and thus would we have it," but we must evermore add, "But, seeing that we are ignorant and may be mistaken—seeing that we are still in the flesh, and, therefore, may be actuated by carnal motives—not as we will, but as you will." Who shall dictate to the throne? No loyal child of God will for a moment imagine that he is to occupy the place of the King, but he bows before him who has a right to be Lord of all; and though he utters his desire earnestly, vehemently, importunately, and pleads and pleads again, yet it is evermore with this needful reservation: "Your will be done, my Lord; and, if I ask anything that is not in accordance therewith, my inmost will is that you would be good enough to deny your servant; I will take it as a true answer if you refuse me, if I ask that which seems not good in your sight." If we constantly remembered this, I think we should be less inclined to push certain suits before the throne, for we should feel, "I am here in seeking my own ease, my own comfort, my own advantage, and, peradventure, I may be asking for that which would dishonor God; therefore will I speak with the deepest submission to the divine decrees."

But, brethren, in the fourth place, if it be a throne, it ought to be approached with enlarged expectations. Well does our hymn put it:

Thou art coming to a king:
Large petitions with thee bring.

We do not come, as it were, in prayer, only to God's almonry where he dispenses his favors to the poor, nor do we come to the back door of the house of mercy to receive the broken scraps, though that were more than we deserve; to eat the crumbs that fall from the Master's table is more than we could claim; but, when we pray, we are standing in the palace, on the glittering floor of the great King's own reception room, and thus we are placed upon a vantage ground. In prayer we stand where angels bow with veiled faces; there, even there, the cherubim and seraphim adore, before that selfsame throne to which our prayers ascend. And shall we come there with stunted requests, and narrow and contracted faith? No, it becomes not a King to be giving away pence and groats; he distributes pieces of broad gold; he scatters not as poor men must, scraps of bread and broken meat, but he makes a feast of fat things, of fat things full of marrow, of wines on the lees well refined.

When Alexander's soldier was told to ask what he would, he did not ask stintedly after the nature of his own merits, but he made such a heavy demand, that the royal treasurer refused to pay it, and put the case to Alexander, and Alexander in right kingly sort replied, "He knows how great Alexander is, and he has asked as from a king; let him have what he requests." Take heed of imagining that God's thoughts are as your thoughts, and his ways as your ways. Do not bring before God stinted petitions and narrow desires, and say, "Lord, do according to these," but, remember, as high as the heavens are above the earth, so high are his ways above your ways, and his thoughts above your thoughts, and ask, therefore, after a God-like sort, ask for great things, for you are before a great throne. Oh, that we always felt this when we came before the throne of grace, for then he would do for us exceeding abundantly above what we ask or even think.

And, beloved, I may add, in the fifth place, that the right spirit in which to approach the throne of grace, is that of *unstaggering confidence.* Who shall doubt the King? Who dares impugn the Imperial Word? It was well said that if integrity were banished from the hearts of all mankind besides, it ought still to dwell in the hearts of kings. Shame on a king if he can lie. The veriest beggar in the streets is dishonored by a broken promise, but what shall we say of a king if his word cannot be depended upon? Oh, shame upon us, if we are unbelieving before the throne of the King of heaven and earth. With our God before us in all his glory, sitting on the throne of grace, will our hearts dare to say we mistrust him? Shall we imagine either that he cannot, or will not, keep his promise? Banished be such blasphemous thoughts, and if they must come,

let them come upon us when we are somewhere in the outskirts of his dominions, if such a place there be, but not in prayer, when we are in his immediate
presence, and behold him in all the glory of his throne of grace. There, surely,
is the place for the child to trust its Father, for the loyal subject to trust his
monarch; and, therefore, far from it be all wavering or suspicion. Unstaggering faith should be predominant before the mercy seat.

Only one other remark upon this point, and that is, that if prayer be a
coming before the throne of God, it ought always to be conducted with the
deepest sincerity, and in the spirit which makes everything real. If you are dis-
loyal enough to despise the King, at least, for your own sake, do not mock him
to his face, and when he is upon his throne. If anywhere you dare repeat holy
words without heart, let it not be in Jehovah's palace. If a person should ask
for audience with royalty, and then should say, "I scarcely know why I have
come. I do not know that I have anything very particular to ask; I have no very
urgent suit to press"; would he not be guilty both of folly and baseness? As for
our great King, when we venture into his presence, let us have an errand
there. As I said the other Sabbath, let us beware of playing at praying. It is
insolence toward God. If I am called upon to pray in public, I must not dare
to use words that are intended to please the ears of my fellow worshipers, but
I must realize that I am speaking to God himself, and that I have business to
transact with the great Lord. And, in my private prayer, if, when I rise from
my bed in the morning, I bow my knee and repeat certain words, or when I
retire to rest at night go through the same regular form, I rather sin than do
anything that is good, unless my very soul does speak unto the Most High. Do
you think that the King of heaven is delighted to hear you pronounce words
with a frivolous tongue and a thoughtless mind? You know him not. He is a
Spirit, and they that worship him must worship him in spirit and in truth.

If you have any empty forms to prate, go and pour them out into the ears
of fools like yourself, but not before the Lord of Hosts. If you have certain
words to utter, to which you attach a superstitious reverence, go and say them
in the bedizened courts of the harlot Rome, but not before the glorious Lord
of Zion. The spiritual God seeks spiritual worshipers, and such he will accept,
and only such; but the sacrifice of the wicked is an abomination unto the
Lord, and only a sincere prayer is his delight.

Beloved, the gathering up of all our remarks is just this—prayer is no trifle. It is an eminent and elevated act. It is a high and wondrous privilege. Under
the old Persian Empire, a few of the nobility were permitted at any time to
come in unto the king, and this was thought to be the highest privilege possessed by mortals. You and I, the people of God, have a permit, a passport to

come before the throne of heaven at any time we will, and we are encouraged to come there with great boldness; but still let us not forget that it is no mean thing to be a courtier in the courts of heaven and earth, to worship him who made us and sustains us in being. Truly, when we attempt to pray, we may hear the voice saying, out of the excellent glory, "Bow the knee." From all the spirits that behold the face of our Father who is in heaven, even now, I hear a voice which says, "O come, let us worship and bow down: let us kneel before the LORD our Maker. For he is our God; and we are the people of his pasture, and the sheep of his hand." "O worship the LORD in the beauty of holiness: fear before him, all the earth."

II. Lest the glow and brilliance of the word "throne" should be too much for mortal vision, our text now presents us with the soft, gentle radiance of that delightful word—*"grace."*

We are called to the throne of grace, not to the throne of law. Rocky Sinai once was the throne of law, when God came to Paran with ten thousand of his holy ones. Who desired to draw near to that throne? Even Israel might not. Bounds were set about the mount, and if but a beast touched the mount, it was stoned or thrust through with a dart. O ye self-righteous ones who hope that you can obey the law, and think that you can be saved by it, look to the flames that Moses saw, and shrink, and tremble, and despair. To that throne we do not come now, for through Jesus the case is changed. To a conscience purged by the precious blood, there is no anger upon the divine throne, though to our troubled minds,

> Once 'twas a seat of burning wrath,
> And shot devouring flame;
> Our God appeared consuming fire,
> And jealous was his name.

And, blessed be God, we are not this morning to speak of the throne of ultimate justice. Before that we shall all come, and as many of us as have believed will find it to be a throne of grace as well as of justice; for he who sits upon that throne shall pronounce no sentence of condemnation against the man who is justified by faith. But I have not to call you this morning to the place from whence the resurrection trumpet shall ring out so shrill and clear. Not yet do we see the angels with their vengeful swords come forth to smite the foes of God; not yet are the great doors of the pit opened to swallow up the enemies who would not have the Son of God to reign over them. We are still on praying ground and pleading terms with God, and the throne to which we are bidden to come, and of which we speak at this time, is the throne of grace. It is a throne set up on purpose for the dispensation of grace; a throne from which every utterance is an utterance of grace; the scepter that is stretched out from it is the silver scepter of grace; the decrees proclaimed from it are purposes of grace; the gifts that are scattered down its golden steps are gifts of grace; and he that sits upon the throne is grace itself. It is the throne of grace to which we approach when we pray; and let us for a moment or two think this over, by way of consolatory encouragement to those who are beginning to pray; indeed, to all of us who are praying men and women.

If in prayer I come before a throne of grace, then *the faults of my prayer will be overlooked*. In beginning to pray, dear friends, you feel as if you did not pray. The groanings of your spirit, when you rise from your knees are such that you think there is nothing in them. What a blotted, blurred, smeared prayer it is. Never mind; you are not come to the throne of justice, else when God perceived the fault in the prayer he would spurn it—your broken words, your gaspings, and stammerings are before a throne of grace. When any one of us has presented his best prayer before God, if he saw it as God sees it, there is no doubt he would make great lamentation over it; for there is enough sin in the best prayer that was ever prayed to secure its being cast away from God. But it is not a throne of justice, I say again, and here is the hope for our lame, limping supplications. Our condescending lying does not maintain a stately etiquette in his court like that which has been observed by princes among men, where a little mistake or a flaw would secure the petitioner's being dismissed with disgrace. Oh, no; the faulty cries of his children are not severely criticized by him. The Lord High Chamberlain of the palace above, our Lord Jesus Christ, takes care to alter and amend every prayer before he presents it, and he makes the prayer perfect with his perfection, and prevalent with his own merits. God looks upon the prayer, as presented through Christ, and forgives all its own inherent faultiness. How this ought to encourage any of us who feel ourselves to be feeble, wandering, and unskilful in prayer. If you cannot plead with God as sometimes you did in years gone by, if you feel as if somehow or other you had grown rusty in the work of supplication, never give over, but come still, yes, and come oftener; for it is not a throne of severe criticism, it is a throne of grace to which you come.

Then, further, inasmuch as it is a throne of grace, *the faults of the petitioner himself shall not prevent the success of his prayer*. Oh, what faults there are in us! To come before a throne how unfit we are—we, that are all defiled with sin within and without! Dare any of you think of praying were it not that God's throne is a throne of grace? If you could, I confess I could not. An absolute

God, infinitely holy and just, could not in consistency with his divine nature answer any prayer from such a sinner as I am, were it not that he has arranged a plan by which my prayer comes up no longer to a throne of absolute justice, but to a throne which is also the mercy seat, the propitiation, the place where God meets sinners, through Jesus Christ. Ah, I could not say to you, "Pray," not even to you saints, unless it were a throne of grace, much less could I talk of prayer to you sinners; but now I will say this to every sinner here, though he should think himself to be the worst sinner that ever lived, cry unto the Lord and seek him while he may be found. A throne of grace is a place fitted for you: go to your knees; by simple faith go to your Savior, for he, he it is who is the throne of grace. It is in him that God is able to dispense grace unto the most guilty of mankind. Blessed be God, neither the faults of the prayer nor yet of the suppliant shall shut out our petitions from the God who delights in broken and contrite hearts.

If it be a throne of grace, then *the desires of the pleader will be interpreted*. If I cannot find words in which to utter my desires, God in his grace will read my desires without the words. He takes the meaning of his saints, the meaning of their groans. A throne that was not gracious would not trouble itself to make out our petitions; but God, the infinitely gracious One, will dive into the soul of our desires, and he will read there what we cannot speak with the tongue. Have you never seen the parent, when his child is trying to say something to him, and he knows very well what it is the little one has got to say, help him over the words and utter the syllables for him; and if the little one has half forgotten what he would say, you have seen the father suggest the word: and so the ever-blessed Spirit, from the throne of grace, will help us and teach us words, no, write in our hearts the desires themselves. We have in Scripture instances where God puts words into sinners' mouths. "Take with you words," says he, "and . . . say unto him, . . . receive us graciously" and "love [us] freely." He will put the desires, and put the expression of those desires into your spirit by his grace; he will direct your desires to the things which you ought to seek for; he will teach you your wants, though as yet you know them not; he will suggest to you his promises that you may be able to plead them; he will, in fact, be Alpha and Omega to your prayer, just as he is to your salvation; for as salvation is from first to last of grace, so the sinner's approach to the throne of grace is of grace from first to last. What comfort is this. Will we not, my dear friends, with the greater boldness draw near to this throne, as we suck out the sweet meaning of this precious word, "the throne of grace"?

If it be a throne of grace, then *all the wants of those who come to it will be supplied*. The King from off such a throne will not say, "You must bring to me gifts, you must offer to me sacrifices." It is not a throne for receiving tribute; it is a throne for dispensing gifts. Come, then, you who are poor as poverty itself; come, you that have no merits and are destitute of virtues; come, you that are reduced to a beggarly bankruptcy by Adam's fall and by your own transgressions; this is not the throne of majesty which supports itself by the taxation of its subjects, but a throne which glorifies itself by streaming forth like a fountain with floods of good things. Come you, now, and receive the wine and milk which are freely given, yes, come buy wine and milk without money and without price. All the petitioner's wants shall be supplied, because it is a throne of grace.

And so, *all the petitioner's miseries shall be compassionated.* Suppose I come to the throne of grace with the burden of my sins; there is One on the throne who felt the burden of sin in ages long gone by, and has not forgotten its weight. Suppose I come loaded with sorrow; there is One there who knows all the sorrows to which humanity can be subjected. Am I depressed and distressed? Do I fear that God himself has forsaken me? There is One upon the throne who said, "My God, my God, why hast thou forsaken me?" It is a throne from which grace delights to look upon the miseries of mankind with tender eye, to consider them and to relieve them. Come, then; come, then; come, then, ye that are not only poor, but wretched, whose miseries make you long for death, and yet dread it. You captive ones, come in your chains; you slaves, come with the irons upon your souls; you who sit in darkness, come forth all blindfold as you are. The throne of grace will look on you if you cannot look on it, and will give to you, though you have nothing to give in return, and will deliver you, though you cannot raise a finger to deliver yourself.

"The throne of grace." The word grows as I turn it over in my mind, and to me it is a most delightful reflection that if I come to the throne of God in prayer, I may feel a thousand defects, but yet there is hope. I usually feel more dissatisfied with my prayers than with anything else I do. I do not believe that it is an easy thing to pray in public so as to conduct the devotions of a large congregation aright. We sometimes hear persons commended for preaching well, but if any shall be enabled to pray well, there will be an equal gift and a higher grace in it. But, brethren, suppose in our prayers there should be defects of knowledge: it is a throne of grace, and our Father knows that we have need of these things. Suppose there should be defects of faith: he sees our little faith and still does not reject it, small as it is. He does not in every case measure out his gifts by the degree of our faith, but by the sincerity and trueness of faith. And if there should be grave defects in our spirit even, and failures in the fervency or in the humility of the prayer, still, though these should not lie there and are much to be deplored, grace overlooks all this, forgives all this, and still its merciful hand is stretched out to enrich us according to our needs. Surely this ought to induce many to pray who have not prayed, and should make us who have been long accustomed to use the consecrated art of prayer, to draw near with greater boldness than ever to the throne of grace.

III. But, now regarding our text as a whole, it conveys to us the idea of *grace enthroned*.

It is a throne, and who sits on it? It is grace personified that is here installed in dignity. And, truly, today grace is on a throne. In the gospel of Jesus Christ, grace is the most predominant attribute of God. How comes it to be so exalted? We reply, well, grace has a throne by conquest. Grace came down to earth in the form of the Well-beloved, and it met with sin. Long and sharp was the struggle, and grace appeared to be trampled under foot of sin; but grace at last seized sin, threw it on its own shoulders, and, though all but crushed beneath the burden, grace carried sin up to the cross and nailed it there, slew it there, put it to death for ever, and triumphed gloriously. For this cause at this hour grace sits on a throne, because it has conquered human sin, has borne the penalty of human guilt, and overthrown all its enemies.

Grace, moreover, sits on the throne because it has established itself there *by right*. There is no injustice in the grace of God. God is as just when he forgives a believer as when he casts a sinner into hell. I believe in my own soul that there is as much and as pure a justice in the acceptance of a soul that believes in Christ as there will be in the rejection of those souls who die impenitent, and are banished from Jehovah's presence. The sacrifice of Christ has enabled God to be just, and yet the justifier of him that believes. He who knows the word "substitution," and can spell its meaning aright, will see that there is nothing due to punitive justice from any believer, seeing that Jesus Christ has paid all the believer's debts, and now God would be unjust if he did not save those for whom Christ vicariously suffered, for whom his righteousness was provided, and to whom it is imputed. Grace is on the throne by conquest, and sits there by right.

Grace is enthroned this day, brethren, because Christ has finished his work and gone into the heavens. It is enthroned *in power*. When we speak of its throne, we mean that it has unlimited might. Grace sits not on the footstool of God; grace stands not in the courts of God, but it sits on the throne; it is the reigning attribute; it is the king today. This is the dispensation of grace, the year of grace: grace reigns through righteousness unto eternal life. We live in the era of reigning grace, for seeing he ever lives to make intercession for the sons of men, Jesus is able also to save them to the uttermost that come unto God by him. Sinner, if you were to meet grace in the byway, like a traveler on his journey, I would bid you make its acquaintance and ask its influence; if you should meet grace as a merchant on the exchange, with treasure in his hand, I would bid you court its friendship; it will enrich you in the hour of poverty; if you should see grace as one of the peers of heaven, highly exalted, I would bid you seek to get its ear; but, oh, when grace sits on the throne, I beseech you close in with it at once. It can be no higher, it can be no greater, for it is written "God is love," which is an alias for grace. Oh, come and bow before it; come and adore the infinite mercy and grace of God. Doubt not, halt not, hesitate not. Grace is reigning; grace is God; God is love. Oh that you, seeing grace is thus enthroned, would come and receive it. I say, then, that grace is enthroned by conquest, by right, and by power, and, I will add, it is enthroned in glory, for God glorifies his grace. It is one of his objects now to make his grace illustrious. He delights to pardon penitents, and so to show his pardoning grace; he delights to look upon wanderers and restore them, to show his reclaiming grace; he delights to look upon the brokenhearted and comfort them, that he may show his consoling grace. There is grace to be had of various kinds, or rather the same grace acting in different ways, and God delights to make his grace glorious. There is a rainbow around about the throne like unto an emerald, the emerald of his compassion and his love. O happy souls that can believe this, and believing it can come at once and glorify grace by becoming instances of its power.

IV. Lastly, our text, if rightly read, has in it sovereignty resplendent in glory—*the glory of grace.*

The mercy seat is a throne; though grace is there, it is still a throne. Grace does not displace sovereignty. Now, the attribute of sovereignty is very high and terrible; its light is like unto a jasper stone, most precious, and like unto a sapphire stone, or, as Ezekiel calls it, "the terrible crystal." Thus says the King, the Lord of hosts, "I will have mercy on whom I will have mercy, and I will have compassion on whom I will have compassion." "O man, who art thou, that repliest against God? Shall the thing formed say to him that formed it, Why hast thou made me thus?" "Hath not the potter power over the clay, of the same lump to make one vessel unto honor, and another unto dishonor?" These are great and terrible words, and are not to be answered. He is a King, and he will do as he wills. None shall stay his hand, or say unto him, What do you? But, ah! lest any of you should be downcast by the thought of his sovereignty, I invite you to the text. It is a throne—there is sovereignty; but to every soul that knows how to pray, to every soul that by faith comes to Jesus, the true mercy seat, divine sovereignty wears no dark and terrible aspect, but is full of love. It is a throne of grace, from which I gather that the sovereignty of God to a believer, to a pleader, to one who comes to God in Christ, is always exercised in pure grace. To you, to you who come to God in prayer, the sovereignty always runs thus: "I will have mercy on that sinner; though he deserves it not, though in him there is no merit, yet because I can do as I will with my own, I will bless him, I will make him my child, I will accept him; he shall be mine in the day when I make up my jewels."

On the mercy seat, God never executed sovereignty otherwise than in a way of grace. He reigns, but in this case grace reigns through righteousness unto eternal life by Jesus Christ our Lord.

There are these two or three things to be thought of, and I have done. On the throne of grace, sovereignty has placed itself under bonds of love. I must speak with words choice and picked here, and I must hesitate and pause to get right sentences, lest I err while endeavoring to speak the truth in plainness. God will do as he wills; but, on the mercy seat, he is under bonds—bonds of his own making, for he has entered into covenant with Christ, and so into covenant with his chosen. Though God is and ever must be a sovereign, he never will break his covenant, nor alter the Word that is gone out of his mouth. He cannot be false to a covenant of his own making. When I come to God in Christ, to God on the mercy seat, I need not imagine that by any act of sovereignty God will set aside his covenant. That cannot be: it is impossible.

Moreover, on the throne of grace, God is again bound to us by his promises. The covenant contains in it many gracious promises, exceeding great and precious. "Ask, and it shall be given you; seek, and ye shall find; knock, and it shall be opened unto you." Until God had said that word or a word to that effect, it was at his own option to hear prayer or not, but it is not so now; for now, if it be true prayer offered through Jesus Christ, his truth binds him to hear it. A man may be perfectly free, but the moment he makes a promise, he is not free to break it; and the everlasting God wants not to break his promise. He delights to fulfill it. He has declared that all his promises are yes and amen in Christ Jesus; but, for our consolation when we survey God under the high and terrible aspect of a sovereign, we have this to reflect on, that he is under covenant bonds of promise to be faithful to the souls that seek him. His throne must be a throne of grace to his people.

And, once more, and sweetest thought of all, every covenant promise has been endorsed and sealed with blood, and far be it from the everlasting God to pour scorn upon the blood of his dear Son. When a king has given a charter to a city, he may before have been absolute, and there may have been nothing to check his prerogatives, but when the city has its charter, then it pleads its rights before the king. Even thus God has given to his people a charter of untold blessing, bestowing upon them the sure mercies of David. Very much of the validity of a charter depends upon the signature and the seal, and, my brethren, how sure is the charter of covenant grace. The signature is the handwriting of God himself, and the seal is the blood of the Only-begotten. The covenant is ratified with blood, the blood of his own dear Son. It is not possible that we can plead in vain with God when we plead the blood-sealed covenant, ordered in all things and sure. Heaven and earth shall pass away, but the power of the blood of Jesus with God can never fail. It speaks when we are silent, and it prevails when we are defeated. Better things than that of Abel does it ask for, and its cry is heard. Let us come boldly, for we bear the promise in our hearts. When we feel alarmed because of the sovereignty of God, let us cheerfully sing,

The gospel bears my spirit up,
A faithful and unchanging God
Lays the foundation for my hope
In oaths, and promises, and blood.

May God the Holy Spirit help us to use aright from this time forward "the throne of grace." Amen.

Prayer Certified of Success

—◆—

Delivered on Lord's Day morning, January 19, 1873, at the Metropolitan Tabernacle, Newington. No. 1091

> *"And I say unto you, Ask, and it shall be given you; seek, and ye shall find; knock, and it shall be opened unto you. For every one that asketh receiveth; and he that seeketh findeth; and to him that knocketh it shall be opened."*
> —LUKE 11:9–10

To seek aid in time of distress from a supernatural being is an instinct of human nature. We say not that human nature unrenewed ever offers truly spiritual prayer, or ever exercises saving faith in the living God; but still, like a child crying in the dark, with painful longing for help from somewhere or other, it scarce knows where, the soul in deep sorrow almost invariably cries to some supernatural being for succor. None have been more ready to pray in time of trouble than those who have ridiculed prayer in their prosperity; and probably no prayers have been more true to the feelings of the hour than those which atheists have offered under the pressure of the fear of death.

In one of his papers in the *Tattler*, Addison describes a man, who, on board ship, loudly boasted of his atheism. A brisk gale springing up, he fell upon his knees and confessed to the chaplain that he had been an atheist. The common seamen who had never heard the word before, thought it had been some strange fish, but were more surprised when they saw it was a man, and learned out of his own mouth "that he never believed till that day that there was a God." One of the old tars whispered to the boatswain, that it would be a good deed to heave him overboard, but this was a cruel suggestion, for the poor creature was already in misery enough—his atheism had evaporated, and he in mortal terror cried to God to have mercy upon him.

Similar incidents have occurred, not once nor twice. Indeed, so frequently does boastful skepticism come down with a run at the last that we always expect it to do so. Take away unnatural restraint from the mind, and it may be said of all men that, like the comrades of Jonah, they cry every man unto his God in their trouble. As birds to their nests, hinds to their coverts, so men in agony fly to a superior being for succor in the hour of need.

God has given to all the creatures he has made some peculiar form of strength—one has such swiftness of foot that at the baying of a hound it escapes from danger by outstripping the wind; another, with outspread wing, is lifted beyond the fowler; a third, with horns, pushes down its enemy; and a fourth, with tooth and claw, tears in pieces its adversary. To man he gave but little strength compared with the animals among which he was placed in Eden, and yet he was king over all, because the Lord was his strength. So long as he knew where to look for the source of his power, man remained the unresisted monarch of all around him. That image of God in which he shone resplendent sustained his sovereignty over the fowls of the air, and the beasts of the field, and the fish of the sea.

By instinct man turned to his God in Paradise; and now, though he is to a sad degree a discrowned monarch, there lingers in his memory shadows of what he was, and remembrances of where his strength must still be found. Therefore, no matter where you find a man, you meet one who in his distress will ask for supernatural help. I believe in the truthfulness of this instinct, and that man prays because there is something in prayer. As when the Creator gives his creature the power of thirst, it is because water exists to meet its thirst; and as when he creates hunger there is food to correspond to the appetite; so when he inclines men to pray it is because prayer has a corresponding blessing connected with it.

We find a powerful reason for expecting prayer to be effectual in the fact that it is an institution of God. In God's Word we are over and over again commanded to pray. God's institutions are not folly. Can I believe that the infinitely wise God has ordained for me an exercise which is ineffectual, and is no more than child's play? Does he bid me pray, and yet has prayer no more result than if I whistled to the wind, or sang to a grove of trees? If there be no answer to prayer, prayer is a monstrous absurdity and God is the author of it; which it is blasphemy to assert. No man who is not a fool will continue to pray when you have once proved to him that prayer has no effect with God, and never receives an answer. Prayer is a work for idiots and madmen, and not for sane persons, if it be, indeed, true, that its effects end with the man who prays!

I shall not this morning enter into any arguments upon the matter; rather, I am coming to my text, which to me, at least, and to you who are followers of Christ, is the end of all controversy. Our Savior knew right well that many difficulties would arise in connection with prayer which might tend to stagger his disciples, and therefore he has balanced every opposition by an overwhelming assurance. Read those words, *"I say unto you,"* I—your Teacher, your Master, your Lord, your Savior, your God: "I say unto you, Ask, and it shall be given you; seek, and ye shall find; knock, and it shall be opened unto you."

In the text our Lord meets all difficulties first by *giving us the weight of his own authority*, "I say unto you "; next by *presenting us with a promise*, "Ask, and it shall be given you," and so on; and then by *reminding us of an indisputable fact*, "every one that asketh receiveth." Here are three mortal wounds for a Christian's doubts as to prayer.

I. First, then, *our Savior gives to us the weight of his own authority,* "I say unto you."

The first mark of a follower of Christ is, that he believes his Lord. We do not follow the Lord at all if we raise any questions upon points whereupon he speaks positively. Though a doctrine should be surrounded with ten thousand difficulties, the ipse dixit of the Lord Jesus sweeps them all away, so far as true Christians are concerned. Our Master's declaration is all the argument we want; "I say unto you" is our logic. Reason! we see you at your best in Jesus, for he is made of God unto us wisdom. He cannot err, he cannot lie, and if he says, "I say unto you," there is an end of all debate.

But, brethren, there are certain reasons which should lead us the more confidently to rest in our Master's word upon this point. There is power in every word of the Lord Jesus, but there is special force in the utterance before us. It has been objected to prayer that it is not possible that it should be answered, because the laws of nature are unalterable, and they must and will go on whether men pray or not. Not a drop of water will change its position in a single wave, or a particle of infectious matter be turned from its course, though all the saints in the universe should plead against tempest and plague. Now, concerning that matter, we are in no hurry to make answer; our adversaries have more to prove than we have, and among the rest they have to prove a negative. To us it does not seem needful to prove that the laws of nature are disturbed. God can work miracles, and he may work them yet again as he has done in days of yore, but it is no part of the Christian faith that God must needs work miracles in order to answer the prayers of his servants. When a man in order to fulfill a promise has to disarrange all his affairs, and, so to speak, to stop all his machinery, it proves that he is but a man, and that his wisdom and power are limited; but he is God indeed who, without reversing the engine, or removing a single cog from a wheel, fulfills the desires of his people as they come up before him. The Lord is so omnipotent that he can work results tantamount to miracles without in the slightest degree suspending any one of his laws. He did, as it were, in the olden times, stop the machinery of the universe to answer prayer, but now, with equally godlike glory, he orders events so as to answer believing prayers, and yet suspends no natural law.

But this is far from being our only or our main comfort; that lies in the fact that we hear the voice of one who is competent to speak upon the matter, and he says, "I say unto you, Ask, and it shall be given you." Whether the laws of nature are reversible or irreversible, "Ask, and it shall be given you; seek, and ye shall find." Now, who is he that speaks thus? It is he that made all things, without whom was not anything made that was made. Cannot he speak to this point. O you eternal Word, you who were in the beginning with God, balancing the clouds and fastening the foundations of the earth, you know what the laws and the unalterable constitutions of nature may be, and if you say, "Ask, and it shall be given you," then assuredly it will be so, be the laws of nature what they may. Besides, our Lord is by us adored as the sustainer of all things; and, seeing that all the laws of nature are operative only through his power, and are sustained in their motion by his might, he must be cognizant of the motion of all the forces in the world; and if he says, "Ask, and it shall be given you," he does not speak in ignorance, but knows what he affirms. We may be assured that there are no forces which can prevent the fulfillment of the Lord's own word. From the Creator and the Sustainer, the word "I say unto you" settles all controversy for ever.

But another objection has been raised which is very ancient indeed, and has a great appearance of force. It is raised not so much by skeptics, as by those who hold a part of the truth; it is this—that prayer can certainly produce no result, because the decrees of God have settled everything, and those decrees are immutable. Now, we have no desire to deny the assertion that the decrees of God have settled all events. It is our full belief that God has foreknown and predestinated everything that happens in heaven above or in the earth beneath, and that the foreknown station of a reed by the river is as fixed as the station of a king, and "the chaff from the hand of the winnower is steered as the stars in their courses." Predestination embraces the great and the little, and reaches unto all things; the question is, wherefore pray? Might it not as logically be asked wherefore breathe, eat, move, or do anything? We have an answer which satisfies us, namely, that our prayers are in the predestination, and that God has as much ordained his people's prayers as anything else, and when we pray we are producing links in the chain of ordained facts. Destiny decrees that I should pray—I pray; destiny decrees that I shall be answered, and the answer comes to me.

Moreover, in other matters we never regulate our actions by the unknown decrees of God; as for instance, a man never questions whether he shall eat or drink, because it may or may not be decreed that he shall eat or drink; a man never inquires whether he shall work or not on the ground that it is decreed how much he shall do or how little, as it is inconsistent with common sense to make the secret decrees of God a guide to us in our general conduct, so we feel it would be in reference to prayer, and therefore still we pray.

But we have a better answer than all this. Our Lord Jesus Christ comes forward, and he says to us this morning, "My dear children, the decrees of God need not trouble you; there is nothing in them inconsistent with your prayers being heard. 'I say unto you, Ask, and it shall be given you.'" Now, who is he that says this? Why, it is he that has been with the Father from the beginning—"The same was in the beginning with God."—and he knows what the purposes of the Father are and what the heart of God is, for he has told us in another place, "the Father himself loveth you." Now since he knows the decrees of the Father, and the heart of the Father, he can tell us with the absolute certainty of an eyewitness that there is nothing in the eternal purposes in conflict with this truth, that he that asketh receiveth, and he that seeketh findeth. He has read the decrees from beginning to end: has he not taken the book, and loosed the seven seals thereof, and declared the ordinances of heaven? He tells you there is nothing there inconsistent with your bended knee and streaming eye, and with the Father's opening the windows of heaven to shower upon you the blessings which you seek. Moreover, he is himself God: the purposes of heaven are his own purposes, and he who ordained the purpose here gives the assurance that there is nothing in it to prevent the efficacy of prayer. "I say unto you." O you that believe in him, your doubts are scattered to the winds; you know that he hears prayer.

But sometimes there arises in our mind a third difficulty, which is associated with our own judgment of ourselves and our estimate of God. We feel that God is very great, and we tremble in the presence of his majesty. We feel that we are very little, and that, in addition, we are also vile; and it does seem a thing incredible that such guilty nothings should have power to move the arm which moves the world. I wonder not if that fear should often hamper us in prayer. But Jesus answers it so sweetly: he says, "I say unto you, Ask, and it shall be given you." And I ask again, who is it that says, "I say unto you"? Why, it is he who knows both the greatness of God and the weakness of man. He is God, and out of the excellent Majesty I think I hear him say, "I say unto you, Ask, and it shall be given you." But he is also man like ourselves, and he says, "Dread not your littleness, for I, bone of your bone and flesh of your flesh, assure you that God hears man's prayer."

The words come to us with the harmony of blended notes; the God, the man, both speak to us—"Dread not my majesty, your prayer is heard. Fear not your own weakness; I as a man have been heard of God."

And yet, again, if the dread of sin should haunt us, and our own sorrow should depress us, I would remind you that Jesus Christ, when he says, "I say unto you," gives us the authority, not only of his person, but of his experience. Jesus was wont to pray. Never any prayed as he did. Nights were spent in prayer by him, and whole days in earnest intercession; and he says to us, "I say unto you, Ask, and it shall be given you." I think I see him coming fresh from the heather of the hills, among which he had knelt all night to pray, and he says, "My disciples, Ask, and it shall be given you, for I have prayed, and it has been given unto me." I think I hear him say it, with his face all bloody red and his garments as if he had trodden the wine vat, as he rises from Gethsemane, with his soul exceeding sorrowful even unto death. He was heard in that he feared, and therefore he says to us, "I say unto you, knock, and it shall be opened unto you." Yes, and I think I hear him speak thus from the cross, with his face bright with the first beam of sunlight after he had borne our sins in his own body on the tree, and had suffered all our griefs to the last pang. He had cried, "My God, my God, why hast thou forsaken me?" and now, having received an answer, he cries in triumph, "It is finished," and, in so doing, bids us also "ask, and it shall be given [us]." Jesus has proved the power of prayer.

"Oh, but," says one, "he has not proved what it is to pray in trouble like mine." How grossly you assess the Savior's trouble was worse than yours. There are no depths so deep that he has not dived to the bottom of them. Christ has prayed out of the lowest dungeon and out of the most horrible pit. "Yes, but he has not cried under the burden of sin." How can you speak so thoughtlessly! Was ever such a burden of sin borne by any man as was laid on him? True, the sins were not his own, but they were sins, and sins with all their crushing weight in them too; yet was he heard, and he was helped unto the end. Christ gives you, in his own experience, the divinest proof that the asking shall be followed by the receiving, even when sin lies at the door. This much is certain, if you, who are believers, cannot believe in the efficacy of prayer on the very word of Christ, it has come to a strange pass; for, O beloved, you are leaning all your soul's weight on Jesus. If he be not true, then are you trusting to a false Savior. If he speak not verities, then you are deceived. If you can trust him with your soul, you must of necessity trust him with your prayers.

Remember, too, that if Jesus our Lord could speak so positively here, there is a yet greater reason for believing him now, for he has gone within the veil, he sits at the right hand of God, even the Father, and the voice does not come to us from the man of poverty, wearing a garment without seam, but from the enthroned priest with the golden girdle about his loins, for it is he who now says, from the right hand of God, "I say unto you, Ask, and it shall be given you." Do you not believe in his name? How then can a prayer that is sincerely offered in that name fall to the ground? When you present your petition in Jesus' name, a part of his authority clothes your prayers. If your prayer be rejected, Christ is dishonored: you cannot believe that. You have trusted him; then believe that prayer offered through him must and shall win the day.

We cannot talk longer on this point, but we trust the Holy Spirit will impress it upon all our hearts.

II. We will now remember that *our Lord presents us with a promise.*

Note that the promise is given to several varieties of prayer. "I say unto you, Ask, and it shall be given you; seek, and ye shall find; knock, and it shall be opened unto you." The text clearly asserts that all forms of true prayer shall be heard, provided they be presented through Jesus Christ, and are for promised blessings. Some are vocal prayers, men *ask*; never should we fail to offer up every day and continually the prayer which is uttered by the tongue, for the promise is that the asker shall be heard. But there are others who, not neglecting vocal prayer, are far more abundant in active prayer, for by humble and diligent use of the means they seek for the blessings which they need. Their heart speaks to God by its longings, strivings, emotions, and labors. Let them not cease seeking, for they shall surely find. There are others who, in their earnestness, combine the most eager forms, both acting and speaking, for knocking is a loud kind of asking, and a vehement form of seeking. If our prayer be vocal speech with God, or if it be the practical use of means ordained, which is real prayer, or if it should, best of all, be the continued use of both, or if it be expressed only by a tear or a sigh, or even if it remain quite unexpressed in a trembling desire, it shall be heard. All varieties of true prayer shall meet with responses from heaven. Now observe that these varieties of prayer are put on an ascending scale. It is said first that we ask: I suppose that refers to the prayer which is a mere statement of our wants, in which we tell the Lord that we want this and that, and ask him to grant it to us. But as we learn the art of prayer, we go on further to seek: which signifies that we marshal our arguments, and plead reasons for the granting of our desires, and we begin to wrestle with God for the mercies needed. And if the blessing come not, we then rise to the third degree, which is knocking: we become importunate, we are not content with asking and giving reasons, but we throw the whole earnestness of our being into our requests, and practice the text which says, "the kingdom of heaven suffereth violence, and the violent take it by force." So the prayers grow from asking—which is the statement, to seeking—which is the pleading, and to knocking—which is the importuning; to each of these stages of prayer there is a distinct promise. He that asks shall have, what did he ask for more? but he that seeks going further shall find, shall enjoy, shall grasp, shall know that he has obtained; and he who knocks shall go further still, for he shall understand, and to him shall the precious thing be opened—he shall not merely have the blessing and enjoy it, but he will comprehend it, shall understand "with all saints what is the breadth, and length, and depth, and height."

I want, however, you to notice this fact, which covers all—whatever form your prayer may assume, it shall succeed. If you only ask, you shall receive; if you seek, you shall find; if you knock, it shall be opened; but in each case according to your faith shall it be unto you. The clauses of the promise before us are not put as we say in law, jointly: he that asks and seeks and knocks shall receive, but they are put severally—he that asks shall have; he that seeks shall find; he that knocks shall have it opened. It is not when we combine the whole three that we get the blessing, though doubtless if we did combine them, we should get the combined reply; but if we exercise only one of these three forms of prayer, we shall still get that which our souls seek after.

These three methods of prayer exercise a variety of our graces. It is a gloss of the fathers upon this passage that faith asks, hope seeks, and love knocks, and the gloss is worth repeating. Faith asks because she believes God will give; hope, having asked, expects, and, therefore, seeks for the blessing; love comes nearer still, and will not take a denial from God, but desires to enter into his house, and to sup with him, and, therefore, knocks at his door till he opens. But, again, let us come back to the old point: it matters not which grace is exercised; a blessing comes to each one. If faith asks, it shall receive; if hope seeks, it shall find; and if love knocks, it shall be opened to her.

These three modes of prayer suit us in different stages of distress. There am I, a poor mendicant at mercy's door, I ask, and I shall receive: but I lose my way, so that I cannot find him of whom I once asked so successfully; well then I may seek with the certainty that I shall find: and if I am in the last stage of all, not merely poor and bewildered, but so defiled as to feel shut out from God, like a leper shut out of the camp, then I may knock, and the door will open to me.

Each of these different descriptions of prayer is exceedingly simple. If anybody said, "I cannot ask," our reply would be, you do not understand the word. Surely everybody can ask. A little child can ask. Long before an infant can speak, it can ask—it need not use words in order to ask for what it wants, and there is not one among us who is incapacitated from asking. Prayers need not be fine. I believe God abhors fine prayers. If a person asks charity of you in elegant sentences, he is not likely to get it. Finery in dress or language is out of place in boggles. I heard a man in the street one day begging aloud by means of a magnificent oration. He used grand language in very pompous style, and I dare say he thought he was sure of getting piles of coppers by his borrowed speech, but I, for one, gave him nothing, but felt more inclined to laugh at his bombast. Is is not likely that many great prayers are about as useless? Many prayer meetings' prayers are a great deal too fine. Keep your figures and metaphors and parabolical expressions for your fellow creatures; use them to those who want to be instructed; but do not parade them before God. When we pray, the simpler our prayers are, the better; the plainest, humblest language which expresses our meaning is the best.

The next word is *seek*, and surely there is no difficulty about seeking? In finding there might be, but in seeking there is none. When the woman in the parable lost her money, she lit a candle and sought for it. I do not suppose she had ever been to the university, or qualified as a lady physician, or that she could have sat on the School Board as a woman of superior sense—but she could seek. Anybody who desires to do so can seek, be they man, woman, or child; and for their encouragement the promise is not given to some particular philosophical form of seeking, but "he that seeketh findeth."

Then there is *knocking*: well, that is a thing of no great difficulty. We used to do it when we were boys, sometimes—too much for the neighbors' comfort; and at home, if the knocker was a little too high, we had ways and means of knocking at the door even then; a stone would do it, or the heel of a boot; anything would make a knocking: it was not beyond our capacity by any means. Therefore, it is put in this fashion by Christ himself, as much as to tell us, "You need have no scholarship, no training, no talent, and no wit for prayer; ask, seek, knock, that is all, and the promise is to every one of these ways of praying."

Will you believe the promise? It is Christ who gives it. No lie ever fell from his lips. O doubt him not. Pray on if you have prayed, and if you have never prayed before, God help you to begin today!

III. Our third point is that *Jesus testifies to the fact that prayer is heard.*

Having given a promise, he then adds, in effect—"You may be quite sure that this promise will be fulfilled, not only because I say it, but because it is and always has been so." When a man says the sun will rise tomorrow morning, we believe it because it always has risen. Our Lord tells us that, as a matter of indisputable fact, all along the ages true asking has been followed by receiving. Remember that he who stated this fact knew it. If you state a fact you may reply, "Yes, as far as your observation goes, it is true," but the observation of Christ was unbounded. There was never a true prayer offered unknown to him. Prayers acceptable with the Most High come up to him by the way of the wounds of Christ. Hence the Lord Jesus Christ can speak by personal knowledge, and his declaration is that prayer has succeeded: "Every one that asketh receiveth; and he that seeketh findeth."

Now here we must, of course, suppose the limitations which would be made by ordinary common sense, and which are made by Scripture. It is not every one that frivolously or wickedly asks or pretends to ask of God that gets what he asks for. It is not every silly, idle, unconsidered request of unregenerate hearts that God will answer. By no manner of means—common sense limits the statement so far. Besides, Scripture limits it again, "Ye have not, because ye ask not" or "because ye ask amiss"—there is an asking amiss which will never obtain. If we ask that we may consume the good things upon our lust, we shall not have them, or if we ask for that which would not be to our good, we shall be heard by receiving no such answer as we desired. But those things being remembered, the statement of our Lord has no other qualification— "every one that asketh receiveth."

Let it be remembered that frequently even when the ungodly and the wicked have asked of God, they have received. Full often in the time of their distress they have called upon God, and he has answered them. "Say you so?" says one. No, I say not so, but so says Scripture. Ahab's prayer was answered, and the Lord said, "Seest thou how Ahab humbleth himself before me? because he humbleth himself before me, I will not bring the evil in his days: but in his son's days will I bring the evil upon his house." So, also, the Lord heard the prayer of Jehoahaz, the son of Jehu, who did evil in the sight of the Lord. 2 Kings 13:1–4. The Israelites also, when for their sins they were given over to their foes, cried to God for deliverance, and they were answered, yet the Lord himself testified concerning them that they did but flatter with their mouth.

Does this stagger you? Does he not hear the young ravens when they cry? Do you think he will not hear man, that is formed in his own image? Do you doubt it? Remember Nineveh. The prayers offered at Nineveh, were they spiritual prayers? Did you ever hear of a church of God in Nineveh? I have not, neither do I believe the Ninevites were ever visited by converting grace; but they were by the preaching of Jonah convinced that they were in danger from the great Jehovah, and they proclaimed a fast, and humbled themselves, and God heard their prayer, and Nineveh for a while was preserved. Many a time in the hour of sickness, and in the time of woe, God has heard the prayers of the unthankful and the evil. Do you think God gives nothing except to the good? Have you dwelled at the foot of Sinai and learned to judge according to the law of merit? What were you when you did begin to pray? Were you good and righteous? Has not God commanded you to do good to the evil? Will he command you to do what he will not do himself? Has he not said that he "sendeth rain on the just and on the unjust," and is it not so? Is he not daily blessing those who curse him, and doing good to those who despitefully use him? This is one of the glories of God's grace; and when there is nothing else good in the man, yet if there be a cry lifted up from his heart, the Lord deigns full often to send relief from trouble. Now, if God has heard the prayers even of men who have not sought him in the highest manner, and has given them temporary deliverances in answer to their cries, will he not much more hear you when you are humbling yourself in his sight, and desiring to be reconciled to him. Surely there is an argument here.

But to come more fully to the point with regard to real and spiritual prayers, every one that asketh receiveth, without any limit whatever. There has never been an instance yet of a man's really seeking spiritual blessings of God without his receiving them. The publican stood afar off, and so broken was his heart that he dared not look up to heaven, yet God looked down on him. Manasseh lay in the low dungeon. He had been a cruel persecutor of the saints; there was nothing in him that could commend him to God; but God heard him out of the dungeon, and brought him forth to liberty of soul. Jonah had by his own sin brought himself into the whale's belly, and he was a petulant servant of God at the best, but out of the belly of hell he cried and God heard him. "Every one that asketh receiveth; and he that seeketh findeth; and to him that knocketh it shall be opened." *Every one.* If I wanted evidence, I should be able to find it in this Tabernacle. I would ask anyone here who has found Christ, to bear witness that God heard his prayer. I do not believe that among the damned in hell there is one who dare say, "I sought the Lord and he rejected me."

There shall not be found at the last day of account, one single soul that can say, "I knocked at mercy's door, but God refused to open it." There shall not stand before the great white throne, a single soul that can plead, "O Christ, I would have been saved by you, but you would not save me. I gave myself up into your hands, but you did reject me. I penitently asked for mercy of you, but I had it not." Every one that asketh receiveth. It has been so until this day—it will be so till Christ himself shall come. If you doubt it, try it, and if you have tried it, try it again. Are you in rags?—that matters not; *"every one that asketh receiveth."* Are you foul with sin?—that signifies not; *"every one* that seeketh findeth." Do you feel yourself as if you were shut out from God altogether?—that matters not, either; "knock, and it *shall* be opened unto you. For every one that asketh receiveth." Is there no election there? Yes, yes, doubtless there is, but that does not alter this truth which has no limit to it whatsoever—*"every one."* What a rich text it is! *"Every one* that asketh receiveth."

When our Lord spoke thus, he could have pointed to his own life as evidence; at any rate, we can refer to it now and show that no one asked of Christ who did not receive. The Syrophoenician woman was at first repulsed when the Lord called her a dog, but when she had the courage to say, "yet the dogs eat of the crumbs which fall from their masters' table," she soon discovered that every one that asketh receiveth. She, also, who came behind him in the press and touched the hem of his garment, she was no asker, but she was a seeker, and she found.

I think I hear, in answer to all this, the lamentable wail of one who says, "I have been crying to God a long while for salvation; I have asked, I have sought, and I have knocked, but it has not come yet." Well, dear friend, if I be asked which is true, God or you, I know which I shall stand by, and I would advise you to believe God before you believe yourself. God will hear prayer, but do you know there is one thing before prayer? What is it? Why, the gospel is not—he that prays shall be saved, that is not the gospel; I believe he will be saved, but that is not the gospel I am told to preach to you. "Go ye into all the world, and preach the gospel to every creature. He"—what?—"He that believeth and is baptized shall be saved." Now, you have been asking God to save you—do you expect him to save you without your believing and being baptized? Surely you have not had the impudence to ask God to make void his own word! Might he not say to you, "Do as I bid you, believe my Son: he that believes on him has everlasting life." Let me ask you: do you believe Jesus Christ? Will you trust him? "Oh, I trust him," says one, "I trust him wholly." Soul, do not ask for salvation any more—you have it already—you are saved. If you trust Jesus with all your soul, your sins are forgiven you, and you are saved; and the next time you approach the Lord, go with praise as well as with prayer, and sing and bless his name.

"But how am I to know that I am saved?" says one. God says, "He that believeth and is baptized shall be saved." Have you believed, have you been baptized? If so, you are saved. How know I that? On the best evidence in all the world: God says you are—do you want any evidence but that? "I want to feel this." Feel! Are your feelings better than God's witness? Will you make God a liar by asking more signs and tokens than his sure word of testimony? I have no evidence this day that I dare trust in concerning my salvation but this, that I rest on Christ alone with all my heart, and soul, and strength. "Other refuge have I none," and if you have that evidence, it is all the evidence that you need seek for this day. Other witnesses of grace in your heart shall come by and by, and cluster about you, and adorn the doctrine you do profess, but now your first business is to believe in Jesus.

"I have asked for faith," says one. Well, what do you mean by that? To believe in Jesus Christ is the gift of God, but it must be your own act as well. Do you think God will believe for you, or that the Holy Ghost believes instead of us? What has the Holy Spirit to believe? You must believe for yourself, or be lost. He cannot lie. Will you not believe in him? He deserves to be believed; trust in him, and you are saved, and your prayer is answered.

I think I hear another say, "I trust I am already saved; but I have been look-ing for the salvation of others in answer to my prayers"; dear friend, you will get it. "Every one that asketh receiveth; and he that seeketh findeth; and to him that knocketh it shall be opened." "But I have sought the conversion of such a one for years with many prayers." You shall have it, or you shall know one day why you have it not, and shall be made content not to have it. Pray on in hope. Many a one has had his prayer for others answered after he has been dead. I think I have reminded you before of the father who had prayed for many years for his sons and daughters, and yet they were not converted, but all became exceedingly worldly. His time came to die. He gathered his chil-dren about his bed, hoping to bear such a witness for Christ at the last that it might be blessed to their conversion; but unhappily for him, he was in deep distress of soul, he had doubts about his own interest in Christ. He was one of God's children who are put to bed in the dark; this being above all the worst fear of his mind, that he feared his dear children would see his distress and be prejudiced against religion. The good man was buried and his sons came to the funeral, and God heard the man's prayer that very day, for as they went away from the grave one of them said to the other, "Brother, our father died a most unhappy death." "He did, brother; I was very much astonished at it, for

I never knew a better man than our father." "Ah," said the first brother, "if a holy man such as our father found it a hard thing to die, it will be a dreadful thing for us who have no faith when our time comes." That same thought had struck them all, and drove them to the cross, and so the good man's prayer was heard in a mysterious manner. Heaven and earth shall pass away, but while God lives, prayer must be heard. While God remains true to his word, supplication is not in vain. The Lord give you grace to exercise it continually. Amen.

Ejaculatory Prayer

—❧—

Delivered on Lord's Day evening, September 9, 1877, at the Metropolitan Tabernacle, Newington. No. 1390.

So I prayed to the God of heaven.—NEHEMIAH 2:4

Nehemiah had made inquiry as to the state of the city of Jerusalem, and the tidings he heard caused him bitter grief. "Why should not my countenance be sad," he said, "when the city, the place of my fathers' sepulchres, lieth waste, and the gates thereof are consumed with fire?" He could not endure that it should be a mere ruinous heap—that city which was once beautiful for situation and the joy of the whole earth. Laying the matter to heart, he did not begin to speak to other people about what they would do, nor did he draw up a wonderful scheme about what might be done if so many thousand people joined in the enterprise; but it occurred to him that he would do something himself. This is just the way that practical men start a matter. The unpractical will plan, arrange, and speculate about what may be done, but the genuine, thorough-going lover of Zion puts this question to himself—"What can you do? Nehemiah, what can you do yourself? Come, it has to be done, and you are the man that is to do it—at least, to do your share. What can you do?"

Coming so far, he resolved to set apart a time for prayer. He never had it off his mind for nearly four months. Day and night, Jerusalem seemed written on his heart, as if the name were painted on his eyeballs. He could see only Jerusalem. When he slept, he dreamed about Jerusalem. When he woke, the first thought was, "Poor Jerusalem!" and before he fell asleep again, his evening prayer was for the ruined walls of Jerusalem. The man of one thing, you know, is a terrible man; and when one single passion has absorbed the whole of his manhood, something will be sure to come of it. Depend upon that. The desire of his heart will develop into some open demonstration, especially if he talks the matter over before God in prayer. Something did come of this. Before long, Nehemiah had an opportunity. Men of God, if you want to serve God and cannot find the propitious occasion, wait a while in prayer and your opportunity will break on your path like a sunbeam. There was never a true and valiant heart that failed to find a fitting sphere somewhere or other in his service. Every diligent laborer is needed in some part of his vineyard. You may have to linger, you may seem as if you stood in the market idle, because the Master would not engage you, but wait there in prayer, and with your heart boiling over with a warm purpose, and your chance will come. The hour will need its man, and if you are ready, you, as a man, shall not be without your hour.

God sent Nehemiah an opportunity. That opportunity came, 'tis true, in a way which he could not have expected. It came through his own sadness of heart. This matter preyed upon his mind till he began to look exceedingly unhappy. I cannot tell whether others remarked it, but the king whom he served, when he went into court with the royal goblet, noticed the distress on the cupbearer's countenance, and he said to him, "Why is thy countenance sad, seeing thou art not sick? this is nothing else but sorrow of heart." Nehemiah little knew that his prayer was making the occasion for him. The prayer was registering itself upon his face. His fasting was making its marks upon his visage; and, though he did not know it, he was, in that way, preparing the opportunity for himself when he went in before the king. But you see, when the opportunity did come, there was trouble with it, for he says, "I was very sore afraid." You want to serve God, young man: you want to be at work. Perhaps you do not know what that work involves. It is not all pleasure. You are longing for the battle, young soldier: you have not smelled powder yet, but when you have been in a battle, and have had a few cuts, or a bullet or two have pierced you, you may not feel quite so eager for the fray. Yet the courageous man sets those things aside, and is ready to serve his country or his sovereign, and so the courageous Christian puts all difficulty aside, and he is ready to serve his comrades and his God, cost what it may. What if I should be sore afraid? Yet so let it be, my God, if thus there shall be an opportunity to seek and to secure the welfare of Jerusalem for your servant, who longs to promote it with all his heart. Thus have we traced Nehemiah up to the particular point where our text concerns him. The king, Artaxerxes, having asked him why he was sad, he had an opportunity of telling him that the city of his fathers was a ruin. Thereupon the king asks him what he really wishes; by the manner of the question, he would seem to imply an assurance that he means to help him. And here we are somewhat surprised to find that, instead of promptly answering the king—the answer is not given immediately—an incident occurs, a fact is related. Though he was a man who had lately given himself up to prayer and fasting, this little parenthesis occurs—"So I prayed to the God of heaven." My preamble leads up to this parenthesis. Upon this prayer I propose to preach.

The fact that Nehemiah prayed challenges attention. He had been asked a question by his sovereign. The proper thing you would suppose was to answer

it. Not so. Before he answered, he prayed to the God of heaven. I do not suppose the king noticed the pause. Probably the interval was not long enough to
be noticed, but it was long enough for God to notice it—long enough for
Nehemiah to have sought and have obtained guidance from God as to how to
frame his answer to the king. Are you not surprised to find a man of God having time to pray to God between a question and an answer? Yet Nehemiah
found that time. We are the more astonished at his praying, because he was so
evidently perturbed in mind, for, according to the second verse, he was very
sore afraid. When you are fluttered and put out, you may forget to pray. Do
you not, some of you, account it a valid excuse for omitting your ordinary
devotion? At least, if anyone had said to you, "You did not pray when you were
about that business," you would have replied, "How could I? There was a
question that I was obliged to answer. I dared not hesitate. It was a king that
asked it. I was in a state of confusion. I really was so distressed and terrified
that I was not master of my own emotions. I hardly knew what I did. If I did
not pray, surely the omission may be overlooked. I was in a state of wild
alarm." Nehemiah, however, felt that if he was alarmed it was a reason for
praying, not for forgetting to pray. So habitually was he in communion with
God that as soon as he found himself in a dilemma he flew away to God, just
as the dove would fly to hide herself in the clefts of the rock.

His prayer was the more remarkable on this occasion, because he must
have felt very eager about his object. The king asks him what it is he wants,
and his whole heart is set upon building up Jerusalem. Are you not surprised
that he did not at once say, "O king, live forever. I long to build up Jerusalem's
walls. Give me all the help you can"? But no, eager as he was to pounce upon
the desired object, he withdraws his hand until it is said, "So I prayed to the
God of heaven." I confess I admire him. I desire also to imitate him. I would
that every Christian's heart might have just that holy caution that did not permit him to make such haste as to find ill-speed. "Prayer and provender hinder
no man's journey." Certainly, when the desire of our heart is close before us,
we are anxious to seize it; but we shall be all the surer of getting the bird we
spy in the bush to be a bird we grasp in the hand if we quietly pause, lift up
our heart, and pray unto the God of heaven.

It is all the more surprising that he should have deliberately prayed just
then, because he had been already praying for the past three or four months
concerning the selfsame matter. Some of us would have said, "That is the
thing I have been praying for; now all I have got to do is to take it and use it.
Why pray any more? After all my midnight tears and daily cries, after setting
myself apart by fasting to cry unto the God of heaven, after such an anxious

conference, surely at last the answer has come. What is to be done but to take the good that God provides me with and rejoice in it?" But no, you will always find that the man who has prayed much is the man who prays more. "For unto every one that hath shall be given, and he shall have abundance." If you do but know the sweet art of prayer, you are the man that will be often engaged in it. If you are familiar with the mercy seat, you will constantly visit it.

For who that knows the power of prayer
But wishes to be often there?

Although Nehemiah had been praying all this while, he nevertheless must offer another petition. "So I prayed to the God of heaven."

One thing more is worth recollecting, namely, that he was in a king's palace, and in the palace of a heathen king too; and he was in the very act of handing up to the king the goblet of wine. He was fulfilling his part in the state festival, I doubt not, among the glare of lamps and the glitter of gold and silver, in the midst of princes and peers of the realm. Or even if it were a private festival with the king and queen only, yet still men generally feel so impressed on such occasions with the responsibility of their high position that they are apt to forget prayer. But this devout Israelite, at such a time and in such a place, when he stands at the king's foot to hold up to him the golden goblet, refrains from answering the king's question until first he has prayed to the God of heaven.

There is the fact, and I think it seems to prompt further inquiry. So we pass on to observe—the manner of this prayer.

Well, very briefly, it was what we call ejaculatory prayer—prayer which, as it were, hurls a dart and then it is done. It was not the prayer which stands knocking at mercy's door—knock, knock, knock; but it was the concentration of many knocks into one. It was begun and completed, as it were, with one stroke. This ejaculatory prayer I desire to commend to you as among the very best forms of prayer.

Notice, how very short it must have been. It was introduced—slipped in—sandwiched in—between the king's question and Nehemiah's answer; and, as I have already said, I do not suppose it took up any time at all that was appreciable—scarcely a second. Most likely the king never observed any kind of pause or hesitation, for Nehemiah was in such a state of alarm at the question that I am persuaded he did not allow any demur or vacillation to appear, but the prayer must have been offered like an electric flash, very rapidly indeed. In certain states of strong excitement, it is wonderful how much the mind gets through in a short time. You may, perhaps, have dreamed, and your dream occupied, to your idea, an hour or two at the very least, yet it is probably—no,

I think certain—that all dreaming is done at the moment you wake. You never dreamed at all when you were asleep: it was just in that instant when you woke that the whole of it went through your mind. As drowning men when rescued and recovered have been heard to say, that while they were sinking they say the whole panorama of their lives passes before them in a few seconds, so the mind must be capable of accomplishing much in a brief space of time. Thus the prayer was presented like the winking of an eye; it was done intuitively; yet done it was, and it proved to be a prayer that prevailed with God.

We know, also, that it must have been a silent prayer; and not merely silent as to sounds but silent as to any outward signs—perfectly secret. Artaxerxes never knew that Nehemiah prayed, though he stood probably within a yard of him. He did not even move his lips as Hannah did, nor did he deem it right even to close his eyes, but the prayer was strictly within himself offered unto God. In the innermost shrine of the temple—in the holy of holies of his own secret soul—there did he pray. Short and silent was the prayer. It was a prayer on the spot. He did not go to his chamber as Daniel did, and open the window. Daniel was right, but this was a different occasion. Nehemiah could not have been permitted to retire from the palace just then. He did not even turn his face to the wall or seek a corner of the apartment. No, but there and then, with the cup in his hand, he prayed unto the God of heaven, and then answered the question of the king. I have no doubt from the very wording of the text that it was a very intense and direct prayer. He says, "So I prayed to the God of heaven." That was Nehemiah's favorite name of God—the God of heaven. He knew whom he was praying to. He did not draw a bow at a venture and shoot his prayers anyhow, but he prayed to the God of heaven—a right straight prayer to God for the thing he wanted; and his prayer sped, though it occupied less, perhaps, than a second of time.

It was a prayer of a remarkable kind. I know it was so, because Nehemiah never forgot that he did pray it. I have prayed hundreds of times, and thousands of times, and not recollected any minute particular afterward either as to the occasion that prompted or the emotions that excited me; but there are one or two prayers in my life that I never can forget. I have not jotted them down in a diary, but I remember when I prayed, because the time was so special and the prayer was so intense, and the answer to it was so remarkable. Now, Nehemiah's prayer was never, never erased from his memory; and when these words of history were written down, he wrote that down. "So I prayed to the God of heaven"—a little bit of a prayer pushed in edgewise between a question and an answer—a mere fragment of devotion, as it seemed, and yet so important that it is put down in a historical document as a part of the history of the restitution and rebuilding of the city of Jerusalem, and a link in the circumstances which led up to that event of the most important character. Nehemiah felt it to be so, and therefore he makes the record—"So I prayed to the God of heaven."

Now, beloved friends, I come, in the third place, to recommend to you this excellent style of praying.

I shall speak to the children of God mainly, to you that have faith in God. I beg you often, no, I would ask you always to use this method of ejaculatory prayer. And I would to God, also, that some here who have never prayed before would offer an ejaculation to the God of heaven before they leave this house—that a short but fervent petition, something like that of the publican in the temple, might go up from you—"God be merciful to me a sinner."

To deal with this matter practically, then, it is the duty and privilege of every Christian to have set times of prayer. I cannot understand a man's keeping up the vitality of godliness unless he regularly retires for prayer, morning and evening at the very least. Daniel prayed three times a day, and David says, "Seven times a day do I praise thee." It is good for your hearts, good for your memory, good for your moral consistency that you should hedge about certain portions of time and say, "These belong to God. I shall do business with God at such and such a time, and try to be as punctual to my hours with him as I should be if I made an engagement to meet a friend." When Sir Thomas Abney was Lord Mayor of London, the banquet somewhat troubled him, for Sir Thomas always had prayer with his family at a certain time. The difficulty was how to quit the banquet to keep up family devotion; but so important did he consider it that he vacated the chair, saying to a person near that he had a special engagement with a dear friend which he must keep. And he did keep it, and he returned again to his place, none of the company being the wiser, but he himself being all the better for observing his wonted habit of worship.

But now, having urged the importance of such habitual piety, I want to impress on you the value of another sort of prayer, namely, the short, brief, quick, frequent ejaculations of which Nehemiah gives us a specimen. And I recommend this, because it hinders no engagement and occupies no time. You may be measuring off your calicoes, or weighing your groceries, or you may be casting up an account, and between the items you may say, "Lord, help me." You may breathe a prayer to heaven and say, "Lord, keep me." It will take no time. It is one great advantage to persons who are hard pressed in business that such prayers as those will not, in the slightest degree, incapacitate them from attending to the business they may have in hand. It requires you to go to no particular place. You can stand where you are, ride in a cab, walk along the streets, be the bottom sawyer in a saw pit, or the top one either, and yet pray just as well such prayers as these. No altar, no church, no so-called sacred place is needed; but wherever you are, just a little prayer as that will reach the ear of God, and win a blessing.

Such a prayer as that can be offered anywhere, under any circumstances. I do not know in what condition a man could be in which he might not offer some such prayer as that. On the land, or on the sea, in sickness or in health, amid losses or gains, great reverses or good returns, still might he breathe his soul in short, quick sentences to God. The advantage of such a way of pray-ing is that you can pray often and pray always. If you must prolong your prayer for a quarter of an hour, you might possibly be unable to spare the time, but if it only wants the quarter of a minute, why, then, it may come again and again and again and again—a hundred times a day. The habit of prayer is blessed, but the spirit of prayer is better; and the spirit of prayer it is which is the mother of these ejaculations; and, therefore, do I like them, because she is a plentiful mother. Many times in a day may we speak with the Lord our God.

Such prayer may be suggested by all sorts of surroundings. I recollect a poor man once paying me a compliment which I highly valued at the time. He was lying in a hospital, and when I called to see him, he said, "I heard you for some years, and now whatever I look at seems to remind me of something or other that you said, and it comes back to me as fresh as when I first heard it." Well, now, he that knows how to pray ejaculatory prayers will find everything about him helping him to the sacred habit. Is it a beautiful landscape? Say, "Blessed be God who has strewn these treasures of form and color through the world, to cheer the sight and gladden the heart." Are you in doleful dark-ness, and is it a foggy day? Say, "Lighten my darkness, O Lord." Are you in the midst of company? You will be reminded to pray, "Lord, keep the door of my lips." Are you quite alone? Then can you say, "Let me not be alone, but be with me, Father." The putting on of your clothes, the sitting at the breakfast table, the getting into the conveyance, the walking the streets, the opening of your ledger, the putting up of your shutters—everything may suggest such prayer as that which I am trying to describe if you be but in the right frame of mind for offering it.

These prayers are commendable, because they are truly spiritual. Wordy prayers may also be windy prayers. There is much of praying by book that has nothing whatever to recommend it. Pray with your heart, not with your hands. Or, if you would lift hands in prayer, let them be your own hands, not another man's. The prayers that come leaping out of the soul—the gust of strong emotion, fervent desire, lively faith—these are the truly spiritual; and no prayers but spiritual prayers will God accept.

This kind of prayer is free from any suspicion that it is prompted by the corrupt motive of being offered to please men. They cannot say that the secret ejaculations of our soul are presented with any view to our own praise, for no man knows that we are praying at all; therefore do I commend such prayers to you, and hope that you may abound therein. There have been hypocrites that have prayed by the hour. I doubt not there are hypocrites as regular at their devotions as the angels are before the throne of God, and yet is there no life, no spirit, no acceptance in their pretentious homage; but he that ejaculates—whose heart talks with God—he is no hypocrite. There is a reality, and force, and life about it.

Short, ejaculatory prayers are of great use to us. Oftentimes they check us. Bad-tempered people, if you were always to pray just a little before you let angry expressions fly from your lips, why, many times you would not say those naughty words at all. They advised a good woman to take a glass of water and hold some of it in her mouth five minutes before she scolded her husband. I dare say it was not a bad recipe, but if, instead of practicing that little eccentricity, she would just breathe a short prayer to God, it would certainly be more effectual, and far more scriptural. I can recommend it as a valuable prescription for the hasty and the peevish; for all who are quick to take offense and slow to forgive insult or injury. When in business you are about to close in with an offer about the propriety of which you have a little doubt, or a positive scruple, such a prayer as "Guide me, good Lord" would often keep you back from doing what you will afterward regret.

The habit of offering these brief prayers would also check your confidence in yourself. It would show your dependence upon God. It would keep you from getting worldly. It would be like sweet perfume burnt in the chamber of your soul to keep away the fever of the world from your heart.

Besides, they actually bring us blessing from heaven. Ejaculatory prayers, as in the case of Eliezer, the servant of Abraham; as in the case of Jacob when he said, even in dying, "I have waited for thy salvation, O God"; prayers such as Moses offered when we do not read that he prayed at all, and yet God said to him, "Wherefore criest thou unto me?"; ejaculation such as David frequently presented, these were all successful with the Most High. Therefore abound in them, for God loves to encourage and to answer them.

I might thus keep on recommending ejaculatory prayer, but I will say one more thing in its favor. I believe it is very suitable to some persons of a peculiar temperament who could not pray for a long time to save their lives. Their minds are rapid and quick. Well, time is not an element in the business. God does not hear us because of the length of our prayer, but because of the sincerity of it. Prayer is not to be measured by the yard, nor weighed by the pound. It is the might and force of it—the truth and reality of it—the energy and the intensity of it. You that are either of so little a mind or of so quick a mind that you cannot use many words, or continue long to think of one thing, it should be to your comfort that ejaculatory prayers are acceptable. And it may be, dear friend, that you are in a condition of body in which you cannot pray any other way. A headache such as some people are frequently affected with the major part of their lives—a state of body which the physician can explain to you—might prevent the mind from concentrating itself long upon one subject. Then it is refreshing to be able again and again and again—fifty or a hundred times a day—to address one's self to God in short, quick sentences, the soul's being all on fire. This is a blessed style of praying.

Now, I conclude by mentioning a few of the times when I think we ought to resort to this practice of ejaculatory prayer. Mr. Rowland Hill was a remarkable man for the depth of his piety, but when I asked at Wotton-under-Edge for his study, though I rather pressed the question, I did not obtain a satisfactory reply. At length the good minister said, "The fact is, we never found any. Mr. Hill used to study in the garden, in the parlor, in the bedroom, in the streets, in the woods, anywhere." "But where did he retire for prayer?" They said they supposed it was in his chamber, but that he was always praying—that it did not matter where he was, the good old man was always praying. It seemed as if his whole life, though he spent it in the midst of his fellowmen doing good, were passed in perpetual prayer. You know the story of his being in Walworth at Mr. George Clayton's chapel, and of his being seen in the aisles after everybody was gone, while he was waiting for his coachman. There was the old man toddling up and down the aisles, and as someone listened, he heard him singing to himself,

And when I shall die, receive me, I'll cry,
For Jesus has loved me, I cannot tell why;
But this thing I find, we two are so joined,
He won't be in heaven and leave me behind.

And with such rhymes and ditties, and choice words, he would occupy every moment of his life. He has been known to stand in the Blackfriars' road, with his hands under his coattails, looking in a shop window, and if you listened you might soon perceive that he was breathing out his soul before God.

He had got into a constant state of prayer. I believe it is the best condition in which a man can be—praying always, praying without ceasing, always drawing near to God with these ejaculations.

But if I must give you a selection of suitable times, I should mention such as these. Whenever you have a great joy, cry, "Lord, make this a real blessing to me." Do not exclaim with others, "Am I not a lucky fellow?" but say, "Lord, give me more grace, and more gratitude, now that you do multiply your favors." When you have got any arduous undertaking on hand or a heavy piece of business, do not touch it till you have breathed your soul out in a short prayer. When you have a difficulty before you, and you are seriously perplexed, when business has got into a tangle or a confusion which you cannot unravel or arrange, breathe a prayer. It need not occupy a minute, but it is wonderful how many snarls come loose after just a word of prayer.

Are the children particularly troublesome to you, good woman? Do you seem as if your patience were almost worn out with the worry and harass? Now for an ejaculatory prayer. You will manage them all the better, and you will bear with their naughty tempers all the more quietly. At any rate, your own mind will be the less ruffled. Do you think that there is a temptation before you? Do you begin to suspect that somebody is plotting against you? Now for a prayer: "Lead me in a plain path because of my enemies." Are you at work at the bench, or in a shop, or a warehouse, where lewd conversation and shameful blasphemies assail your ears? Now for a short prayer. Have you noticed some sin that grieves you? Let it move you to prayer. These things ought to remind you to pray. I believe the devil would not let people swear so much if Christian people always prayed every time they heard an oath. He would then see it did not pay. Their blasphemies might somewhat be hushed if they provoked us to supplication.

Do you feel your own heart going off the lines? Does sin begin to fascinate you? Now for a prayer—a warm, earnest, passionate cry: "Lord, hold me up." Did you see something with your eye, and did that eye infect your heart? Do you feel as if your feet were almost gone, and your steps had well near slipped? Now for a prayer: "Hold me, Lord, by my right hand." Has something quite unlooked-for happened? Has a friend treated you badly? Then, like David, say, "O LORD, . . . turn the counsel of Ahithophel into foolishness." Breathe a prayer now. Are you anxious to do some good? Be sure to have prayer over it. Do you mean to speak to that young man about his soul? Pray first, brother. Do you mean to address yourself to the members of your class and write them a letter this week about their spiritual welfare? Pray over every line, brother. It is always good to have praying going on while you are talking about Christ. I always find I can preach the better if I can pray while I am preaching.

And the mind is very remarkable in its activities. It can be praying while it is studying: it can be looking up to God while it is talking to man; and there can be one hand held up to receive supplies from God while the other hand is dealing out the same supplies which he is pleased to give. Pray as long as you live. Pray when you are in great pain; the sharper the pang, then the more urgent and importunate should your cry to God be. And when the shadow of death gathers around you, and strange feelings flush or chill you, and plainly tell that you near the journey's end, then pray. Oh! that is a time for ejaculation. Short and pithy prayers like this: "Hide not your face from me, O Lord"; or this, "Be not far from me, O God"; will doubtless suit you. "Lord Jesus, receive my spirit" were the thrilling words of Stephen in his extremity; and "Father, into thy hands I commend my spirit" were the words that your Master himself uttered just before he bowed his head and gave up the ghost. You may well take up the same strain and imitate him.

These thoughts and counsels are so exclusively addressed to the saints and faithful brethren in Christ that you will be prone to ask, "Is not there anything to be said to the unconverted?" Well, whatever has been spoken in their hearing may be used by them for their own benefit. But let me address myself to you, as pointedly as I can. Though you are not saved, yet you must not say, "I cannot pray." Why, if prayer is thus simple, what excuse can you have for neglecting it? It wants no measurable space of time. Such prayers as these God will hear, and you have, all of you, the ability and opportunity to think and to express them, if you have only that elementary faith in God which believes "that he is, and that he is a rewarder of them that diligently seek him." Cornelius had, I suppose, got about as far as this, when he was admonished by the angel to send for Peter, who preached to him peace by Jesus Christ to the conversion of his soul. Is there such a strange being in the Tabernacle tonight as a man or woman that never prays? How shall I expostulate with you? May I steal a passage from a living poet who, though he has contributed nothing to our hymn books, hums a note so suited to my purpose, and so pleasant to my ear that I like to quote it:

> More things are wrought by prayer
> Than this world dreams of. Wherefore let thy voice
> Rise like a fountain, flowing night and day:
> For what are men better than sheep or goats,
> That nourish a blind life within the brain,

If, knowing God, they lift not hands of prayer,
Both for themselves and those who call them friend?
For so the whole round world is every way
Bound by gold chains about the feet of God.

I do not suspect there is a creature here who never prays, because people generally pray to somebody or other. The man that never prays to God such prayers as he ought, prays to God such prayers as he ought not. It is an awful thing when a man asks God to damn him: and yet there are persons that do that. Suppose he were to hear you; he is a prayer-hearing God. If I address one profane swearer here, I would like to put this matter clearly to him. Were the Almighty to hear you. If your eyes were blinded and your tongue were struck dumb while you were uttering a wild imprecation, how would you bear the sudden judgment on your impious speech? If some of those prayers of yours were answered for yourself, and some that you have offered in your passion for your wife and for your child, were fulfilled to their hurt and your distraction, what an awful thing it would be. Well, God does answer prayer, and one of these days he may answer your prayers, to your shame and everlasting confusion. Would not it be well now, before you leave your seat, to pray, "Lord, have mercy upon me; Lord, save me; Lord, change my heart; Lord, give me to believe in Christ; Lord, give me now an interest in the precious blood of Jesus; Lord, save me now"? Will not each one of you breathe such a prayer as that? May the Holy Spirit lead you so to do, and if you once begin to pray aright, I am not afraid that you will ever leave off, for there is a something that holds the soul fast in real prayer. Sham prayers—what is the good of them? But real heart pleading—the soul talkng with God—when it once begins will never cease. You will have to pray till you exchange prayer for praise, and go from the mercy seat below to the throne of God above.

May God bless you all; all of you, I say; all who are my kindred in Christ and all for whose salvation I yearn. God bless you all and every one, for our dear Redeemer's sake. Amen.

Ask and Have

Delivered on Lord's Day morning, October 1, 1882, at the Metropolitan Tabernacle, Newington. No. 1682.

Ye lust, and have not: ye kill, and desire to have, and cannot obtain: ye fight and war, yet ye have not, because ye ask not. Ye ask, and receive not, because ye ask amiss, that ye may consume it upon your lusts.—JAMES 4:2–3

May these striking words be made profitable to us by the teaching of the Holy Spirit.

Man is a creature abounding in wants, and ever restless, and hence his heart is full of desires. I can hardly imagine a man existing who has not many desires of some kind or another. Man is comparable to the sea anemone with its multitude of tentacles which are always hunting in the water for food; or like certain plants which send out tendrils, seeking after the means of climbing. The poet says, "Man never is, but always to be, blest." He steers for which he thinks to be his port, but as yet he is tossed about on the waves. One of these days he hopes to find his heart's delight, and so he continues to desire with more or less expectancy.

This fact appertains both to the worst of men and the best of men. In bad men, desires corrupt into lusts: they long after that which is selfish, sensual, and consequently evil. The current of their desires sets strongly in a wrong direction. These lustings, in many cases, become extremely intense: they make the man their slave; they domineer over his judgment; they stir him up to violence: he fights and wars, perhaps he literally kills: in God's sight, who counts anger murder, he does kill full often. Such is the strength of his desires that they are commonly called passions; and when these passions are fully excited, then the man himself struggles vehemently, so that the kingdom of the devil suffers violence, and the violent take it by force.

Meanwhile, in gracious men, there are desires also. To rob the saints of their desires would be to injure them greatly, for by these they rise out of their lower selves. The desires of the gracious are after the best things: things pure and peaceable, laudable and elevating. They desire God's glory, and hence their desires spring from higher motives than those which inflame the unrenewed mind. Such desires in Christian men are frequently very fervent and forcible; they ought always to be so; and those desires begotten of the Spirit of God stir the renewed nature, exciting and stimulating it, and making the man to groan and to be in anguish and in travail until he can attain that which God has taught him to long for. The lusting of the wicked and the holy desiring of the righteous have their own ways of seeking gratification. The lusting of the wicked develops itself in contention; it kills, and desires to have; it fights and it wars; while on the other hand, the desire of the righteous when rightly guided betakes itself to a far better course for achieving its purpose, for it expresses itself in prayer fervent and importunate. The godly man when full of desire asks and receives at the hand of God.

At this time I shall by God's help try to set forth from our text, first, the poverty of lusting—"Ye lust, and have not." Secondly, I shall sadly show the poverty of many professing Christians in spiritual things, especially in their church capacity; they also long for, and have not. Thirdly, we shall speak in closing, upon the wealth wherewith holy desires will be rewarded if we will but use the right means. If we ask, we shall receive.

I. First, consider *the poverty of lusting*—"Ye lust, and have not."

Carnal lustings, however strong they may be, do not in many cases obtain that which they seek after: as says the text, "Ye . . . desire to have, and cannot obtain." The man longs to be happy, but he is not; he pines to be great, but he grows meaner every day; he aspires after this and after that which he thinks will content him, but he is still unsatisfied: he is like the troubled sea which cannot rest. One way or another, his life is disappointment; he labors as in the very fire, but the result is vanity and vexation of spirit. How can it be otherwise? If we sow the wind, must we not reap the whirlwind, and nothing else? Or, if peradventure the strong lustings of an active, talented, persevering man do give him what he seeks after, yet how soon he loses it. He has it so that he has it not. The pursuit is toilsome, but the possession is a dream. He sits down to eat, and lo! the feast is snatched away, the cup vanishes when it is at his lip. He wins to lose; he builds, and his sandy foundation slips from under his tower, and it lies in ruins. He that conquered kingdoms, died discontented on a lone rock in mid ocean; and he who revived his empire, fell never to rise again. As Jonah's gourd withered in a night, so have empires fallen on a sudden, and their lords have died in exile. So that what men obtain by warring and fighting is an estate with a short lease; the obtaining is so temporary that it still stands true, "[they] lust, and have not."

Or if such men have gifts and power enough to retain that which they

have won, yet in another sense they have it not while they have it, for the pleasure which they looked for in it is not there. They pluck the apple, and it turns
out to be one of those Dead Sea apples which crumble to ashes in the hand.
The man is rich, but God takes away from him the power to enjoy his wealth.
By his lustings and his warrings, the licentious man at last obtains the object
of his cravings, and after a moment's gratification, he loathes that which he so
passionately lusted for. He longs for the tempting pleasure, seizes it, and
crushes it by the eager grasp. See the boy hunting the butterfly, which flits
from flower to flower, while he pursues it ardently. At last it is within reach,
and with his cap he knocks it down; but when he picks up the poor remains,
he finds the painted fly spoiled by the act which won it. Thus may it be said of
multitudes of the sons of men—"Ye lust, and have not."

Their poverty is set forth in a threefold manner: "Ye kill, and desire to
have, and cannot obtain," "Ye have not, because ye ask not," and "Ye ask, and
receive not, because ye ask amiss."

If the lusters fail, it is not because they did not set to work to gain their
ends; for according to their nature they used the most practical means within
their reach, and used them eagerly too. According to the mind of the flesh, the
only way to obtain a thing is to fight for it, and James sets this down as the reason of all fighting. "Whence come wars and fightings among you? come they
not hence, even of your lusts that war in your members?" This is the form of
effort of which we read, "Ye fight and war, yet ye have not." To this mode of
operation men cling from age to age. If a man is to get along in this world,
they tell me he must contend with his neighbors, and push them from their
vantage ground; he must not be particular how they are to thrive, but he must
mind the main chance on his own account, and take care to rise, no matter
how many he may tread upon. He cannot expect to get on if he loves his
neighbor as himself. It is a fair fight, and every man must look to himself. Do
you think I am satirical? I may be, but I have heard this sort of talk from men
who meant it. So they take to fighting, and that fighting is often victorious, for
according to the text, "ye kill"—that is to say, they so fight that they overthrow
their adversary, and there is an end of him.

They are men of great strength, young lions that can go forth and rend
the prey, and yet it is said of them that they "lack and suffer hunger," while
they that wait upon the Lord shall not want any good thing. These lusters are
unrestrained in their efforts to gain their point; they stick at nothing, they kill,
and desire to have. Moreover, they fight with great perseverance, for the text
says, "Ye fight and war." Now, war is a continuation of the act of fighting,

prolonging it from campaign to campaign, and conducting it by the rules of military art till the victory is won.

Multitudes of men are living for themselves, competing here and warring there, fighting for their own hand with the utmost perseverance. They have little choice as to how they will do it. Conscience is not allowed to interfere in their transactions, but the old advice rings in their ears, "Get money; get money honestly if you can, but by any means get money." No matter though body and soul he ruined, and others be deluged with misery, fight on, for there is no discharge in this war. If you are to win, you must fight; and everything is fair in war. So they muster their forces, they struggle with their fellows, they make the battle of life hotter and hotter, they banish love, and brand tenderness as folly, and yet with all their schemes they obtain not the end of life in any true sense. Well says James, "Ye kill, and desire to have, and cannot obtain: ye fight and war, yet ye have not."

When men who are greatly set upon their selfish purposes do not succeed, they may possibly hear that the reason of their non-success is "because ye ask not." Is, then, success to be achieved by asking? So the text seems to hint, and so the righteous find it. Why does not this man of intense desires take to asking? The reason is, first, because it is unnatural to the natural man to pray; as well expect him to fly. He despises the idea of supplication. "Pray?" says he. "No, I want to be at work. I cannot waste time on devotions; prayers are not practical; I want to fight my way. While you are praying, I shall have beaten my opponent. I go to my countinghouse, and leave you to your Bibles and your prayers." He has no mind for asking of God. He declares that none but canting hypocrites care to pray, thus confessing that if he were to pray he would he a canting hypocrite. As for him, his praying is of quite another sort, and woe to those who come into his clutches; they will find that with him business is business, and pretty sharp business too. He will never stoop to pray; he is too proud. God-reliance he does not understand; self-reliance is his word. Self is his god, and to his god he looks for success. He is so proud that he reckons himself to be his own providence; his own right hand and his active arm shall get to him the victory. When he is very liberal in his views, he admits that though he does not pray, yet there may be some good in it, for it quiets people's minds, and makes them more comfortable: but as to any answer's ever coming to prayer, he scouts the idea, and talks both philosophically and theologically about the absurdity of supposing that God alters his course of conduct out of respect to the prayers of men and women. "Ridiculous," says he, "utterly ridiculous"; and, therefore, in his own great wisdom he returns to his fighting and his warring, for by such means he hopes to attain his end. Yet he obtains not. The whole history of mankind shows the failure of evil lustings to obtain their object.

For a while the carnal man goes on fighting and warring; but by and by he changes his mind, for he is ill, or frightened. His purpose is the same, but if it cannot be achieved one way, he will try another. If he must ask, well, he will ask; he will become religious, and do good to himself in that way. He finds that some religious people prosper in the world, and that even sincere Christians are by no means fools in business, and, therefore, he will try their plan. And now he comes under the third censure of our text—"Ye ask, and receive not." What is the reason why the man who is the slave of his lusts obtains not his desire, even when he takes to asking? The reason is because his asking is a mere matter of form; his heart is not in his worship. He buys a book containing what are called forms of prayer, and he repeats these, for repeating is easier than praying, and demands no thought.

I have no objection to your using a form of prayer if you pray with it; but I know a great many who do not pray with it, but only repeat the form. Imagine what would come to our families if instead of our children speaking to us frankly when they have any need, they were always to think it requisite to go into the library and hunt up a form of prayer, and read it to us. Surely there would be an end to all home-feeling and love; life would move in fetters. Our household would become a kind of boarding school, or barracks, and all would be parade and formality, instead of happy eyes looking up with loving trust into fond eyes that delight to respond. Many spiritual men use a form, but carnal men are pretty sure to do so, for they end in the form.

This man's prayer is asking amiss, because it is entirely for himself. He wants to prosper that he may enjoy himself; he wants to be great simply that he may be admired: his prayer begins and ends with self. Look at the indecency of such a prayer even if it be sincere. When a man so prays, he asks God to be his servant, and gratify his desires; no, worse than that, he wants God to join him in the service of his lusts. He will gratify his lusts, and God shall come and help him to do it. Such prayer is blasphemous, but a large quantity of it is offered, and it must be one of the most God-provoking things that heaven ever beholds. No, if a man will live to himself and his lusts, let him do so, and the farther he gets off from God, the more consistent he will he. Let him not mouth the Lord's Prayer as though God were his father, or drag in Christ's sacred name to sanctify his greed, or invoke the Spirit's blessed power in connection with his personal aggrandizement, or his selfish ambition. If he does so, he will be no better off than he was at the beginning: he will ask, and have not. His asking will miss because he asks amiss, that he may consume it upon his lusts.

If your desires are the longings of fallen nature, if your desires begin and end with your own self, and if the chief end for which you live is not to glorify God, but to glorify yourself, then you may fight, but you shall not have; you may rise up early and sit up late, but nothing worth gaining shall come of it. Remember how the Lord has spoken in the thirty-seventh Psalm: "Cease from anger, and forsake wrath: fret not thyself in any wise to do evil. . . . For yet a little while, and the wicked shall not be: yea, thou shalt diligently consider his place, and it shall not be. But the meek shall inherit the earth; and shall delight themselves in the abundance of peace."

So much upon the poverty of lusting.

II. Secondly, I have now before me a serious business, and that is, to show *how Christian churches may suffer spiritual poverty*, so that they, too, "desire to have, and cannot obtain."

Of course the Christian seeks higher things than the worldling, else were he not worthy of that name at all. At least professedly his object is to obtain the true riches, and to glorify God in spirit and in truth. Yes, but look, dear brethren, all churches do not get what they desire. We have to complain, not here and there, but in many places, of churches that are nearly asleep, and are gradually declining. Of course they find excuses. The population is dwindling, or another place of worship is attracting the people. There is always an excuse handy when a man wants one; but still there stands the fact—public worship is almost deserted in some places, the ministry has no rallying power about it, and those who put in an appearance are discontented or indifferent. In such churches there are no conversions. If they had half a dozen added to them in a year, they would want to sing the "Hallelujah Chorus"; but as to bringing thousands to Christ, they secretly fear that this would be an undesirable thing, for it might involve excitement, and they are so proper that they dread anything of that sort. To do nothing, and let men be damned, is in their judgment proper and respectable, but to be alive and energetic is a perilous state of affairs, for it might lead to fanaticism and indecorum. They are specially afraid of anything like "sensationalism." That ugly-looking word they set before us, very much as the Chinese try to frighten their enemies by painting horrible faces on their shields. Never mind that terrible word; it will hurt no one. These churches "have not," for no truth is made prevalent through their zeal, no sin is smitten, no holiness promoted, nothing is done by which God is glorified. And what is the reason of it?

First, even among professed Christians, there may be the pursuit of desirable things in a wrong method. "Ye fight and war, yet ye have not." Have not churches thought to prosper by competing with other churches? At such and such a place of worship they have a very clever man: we must get a clever man too; in fact, he must be a little cleverer than our neighbor's hero. That is the thing—a clever man! Ah me, that we should live in an age in which we talk about clever men in preaching the gospel of Jesus Christ! Alas, that this holy service should be thought to depend upon human cleverness!

Churches have competed with each other in architecture, in music, in apparel, and in social status. The leaders fancy that to succeed they must have something more handsome, artistic, or expensive than their neighbors: hence they build Gothic edifices in which the minister's voice gets up among the timbers, and is never properly heard, or else they purchase an organ with every stop except the full one. The opinion would seem to be widely spread that there is a deal of grace in an organ. To pray to God with a windmill like the Tartars would be very absurd; but to praise God with wind passing through a set of pipes is eminently proper. I never have seen the distinction, and do not see it now. Organ or no organ is not now the question, but I speak of instances in which these machines are set up as a matter of rivalry. Is it not the design of many to succeed by a finer building, better music, and a cleverer ministry than others? Is it not as much a matter of competition as a shop front and a dressed window are with drapers? Is this the way by which the Kingdom of God is to grow up among us? In some cases there is a measure of bitterness in the rivalry. It is not pleasant to little minds to see other churches prospering more than their own. They may be more earnest than we are, and be doing God's work better, but we are too apt to turn a jealous eye toward them, and we would rather they did not get on quite so well. "Do ye think that the scripture saith in vain, The spirit that dwelleth in us lusteth to envy"? If we could see a disturbance among them, so that they would break up and be ecclesiastically killed, we would not rejoice. Of course not; but neither should we suffer any deadly sorrow. In some churches an evil spirit lingers. I bring no railing accusation, and, therefore, say no more than this: God will never bless such means and such a spirit; those who give way to them will desire to have, but never obtain.

Meanwhile, what is the reason why they do not have a blessing? The text says, "because ye ask not"; I am afraid there are churches which do not ask.

Prayer in all forms is too much neglected. Private prayer is allowed to decay. I shall put it to the conscience of every man how far secret prayer is attended to; and how much of fellowship with God there is in secret among the members of our churches. Certainly its healthy existence is vital to church prosperity. Of family prayer it is more easy to judge, for we can see it. 1 fear that in these days many have quite given up family prayer. I pray you do not imitate them.

I wish you were all of the same mind as the Scotch laborer who obtained a situation in the house of a wealthy farmer who was known to pay well, and all his friends envied him that he had gone to live in such a service. In a short time he returned to his native village, and when they asked him why he had left his situation, he replied that he "could not live in a house which had no roof to it." A house without prayer is a house without a roof. We cannot expect blessings on your churches if we have none on your families.

As to the congregational prayer, the gathering together in what we call our prayer meetings, is there not a falling off? In many cases, the prayer meeting is despised, and looked down upon as a sort of second-rate gathering. There are members of churches who are never present, and it does not prick their consciences that they stay away. Some congregations mix up the prayer meeting with a lecture, so as to hold only one service in the week. I read the other day an excuse for all this: it is said that people are better at home, attending to family concerns. This is idle talk, for who among us wishes people to neglect their domestic concerns? It will be found that those attend to their own concerns best who are diligent to get everything in order, so that they may go out to assemblies for worship. Negligence of the house of God is often an index of negligence of their own houses. They are not bringing their children to Christ, I am persuaded, or they would bring them up to the services. Anyhow, the prayers of the church measure its prosperity. If we restrain prayer, we restrain the blessing. Our true success as churches can be had only by asking it of the Lord. Are we not prepared to reform and amend in this matter? Oh, for Zion's travailing hour to come, when an agony of prayer shall move the whole body of the faithful.

But some reply, "There are prayer meetings, and we do ask for the blessing, and yet it comes not." Is not the explanation to be found in the other part of the text, "Ye , , , receive not, because ye ask amiss"? When prayer meetings become a mere form, when brethren stand up and waste the time with their long orations, instead of speaking to God in earnest and burning words, when there is no expectation of a blessing, when the prayer is cold and chill, then nothing will come of it. He who prays without fervency does not pray at all.

We cannot commune with God, who is a consuming fire, if there is no fire in our prayers. Many prayers fail of their errand because there is no faith in them. Prayers which are filled with doubt, are requests for refusal. Imagine that you wrote to a friend and said, "Dear friend, I am in great trouble, and I therefore tell you, and ask for your help, because it seems right to do so. But though I thus write, I have no belief that you will send me any help; indeed, I should be mightily surprised if you did, and should speak of it as a great wonder."

Will you get the help, think you? I should say your friend would be sensible enough to observe the little confidence which you have in him; and he would reply that, as you did not expect anything, he would not astonish you. Your opinion of his generosity is so low that he does not feel called upon to put himself out of the way on your account. When prayers are of that kind, you cannot wonder if we "receive not, because we ask amiss." Moreover, if our praying, however earnest and believing it may be, is a mere asking that our church may prosper because we want to glory in its prosperity, if we want to see our own denomination largely increased, and its respectability improved, that we may share the honors thereof, then our desires are nothing but lustings after all. Can it be that the children of God manifest the same emulations, jealousies, and ambitions as men of the world? Shall religious work be a matter of rivalry and contest? Ah, then, the prayers which seek success will have no acceptance at the mercy seat. God will not hear us, but bid us begone, for he cares not for the petitions of which self is the object. "Ye have not, because ye ask not" or "because ye ask amiss."

III. Thirdly, I have a much more pleasing work to do, and that is to hint at *the wealth which awaits the use of the right means*, namely, of asking rightly of God.

I invite your most solemn attention to this matter, for it is vitally important. And my first observation is this, how very small after all is this demand which God makes of us. Ask! Why, it is the least thing he can possibly expect of us, and it is no more than we ordinarily require of those who need help from us. We expect a poor man to ask; and if he does not, we lay the blame of his lack upon himself. If God will give for the asking, and we remain poor, who is to blame? Is not the blame most grievous? Does it not look as if we were out of order with God, so that we will not even condescend to ask a favor of him? Surely there must be in our hearts a lurking enmity to him, or else instead of its being an unwelcome necessity, it would be regarded as a great delight.

However, brethren, whether we like it or not, remember, asking is the rule of the kingdom. "Ask, and ye shall receive." It is a rule that never will be altered in anybody's case. Our Lord Jesus Christ is the elder brother of the family, but God has not relaxed the rule for him. Remember this text: Jehovah says to his own Son, "Ask of me and I shall give thee the heathen for thine inheritance, and the uttermost parts of the earth for thy possession." If the royal and divine Son of God cannot be exempted from the rule of asking that he may have, you and I cannot expect the rule to be relaxed in our favor. Why should it be? What reason can be pleaded why we should be exempted from prayer? What argument can there be why we should be deprived of the privilege and delivered from the necessity of supplication? I can see none: can you? God will bless Elijah and send rain on Israel, but Elijah must pray for it. If the chosen nation is to prosper, Samuel must plead for it. If the Jews are to be delivered, Daniel must intercede. God will bless Paul, and the nations shall be converted through him, but Paul must pray. Pray he did without ceasing; his Epistles show that he expected nothing except by asking for it. If you may have everything by asking, and nothing without asking, I beg you to see how absolutely vital prayer is, and I beseech you to abound in it.

Moreover, it is clear to even the most shallow thinker that there are some things necessary for the church of God which we cannot get otherwise than by prayer. You can get that clever man I spoke about—the less, perhaps, you pray about him, the better; and that new church, and the new organ, and the choir, you can also get without prayer; but you cannot get the heavenly anointing: the gift of God is not to be purchased with money. Some of the members of a church in a primitive village in America thought that they would raise a congregation by hanging up a very handsome chandelier in the meetinghouse. People talked about this chandelier, and some went to see it, but the light of it soon grew dim. You can buy all sorts of ecclesiastical furniture, you can purchase any kind of paint, brass, muslin, blue, scarlet, and fine linen, together with flutes, harps, sackbuts [trombones], psalteries, and all kinds of music—you can get these without prayer; in fact, it would be an impertinence to pray about such rubbish; but you cannot get the Holy Ghost without prayer. "The wind bloweth where it listeth." He will not be brought near by any process or method at our command apart from asking. There are no mechanical means which will make up for his absence. If the Holy Spirit be not there, what is the use of that clever man of yours? Will anybody be converted? Will any soul be comforted? Will any children of God be renewed in spiritual life without the Holy Spirit? Neither can you get communion with God without prayer. He that will not pray cannot have communion with God.

Yet more, there is no real, spiritual communion of the church with its own members when prayer is suspended. Prayer must be in action, or else those blessings which are vitally essential to the success of the church can never come to it. Prayer is the great door of spiritual blessing, and if you close it, you shut out the favor.

Beloved brethren, do you not think that this asking which God requires is a very great privilege? Suppose there were an edict published that you must not pray: that would be a hardship indeed. If prayer rather interrupted than increased the stream of blessing, it would be a sad calamity. Did you ever see a dumb man under a strong excitement, or suffering great pain, and therefore anxious to speak? It is a terrible sight to see: the face is distorted, the body is fearfully agitated; the mute writhes and labors in dire distress. Every limb is contorted with a desire to help the tongue, but it cannot break its bonds. Hollow sounds come from the breast, and stutterings of ineffectual speech awaken attention, though they cannot reach so far as expression. The poor creature is in pain unspeakable. Suppose we were in our spiritual nature full of strong desires, and yet dumb as to the tongue of prayer, I think it would be one of the direst afflictions that could possibly befall us; we should be terribly maimed and dismembered, and our agony would be overwhelming. Blessed be his name, the Lord ordains a way of utterance, and bids our heart speak out to him.

Beloved, we must pray: it seems to me that it ought to be the first thing we ever think of doing when in need. If men were right with God, and loved him truly, they would pray as naturally as they breathe. I hope some of us are right with God, and do not need to be driven to prayer, for it has become an instinct of our nature. I was told by a friend yesterday the story of a little German boy, a story which his pastor loved to tell. The dear little child believed his God, and delighted in prayer. His schoolmaster had urged the scholars to be at school in time, and this child always tried to be so; but his father and mother were dilatory people, and one morning, through their fault alone, he just left the door as the clock struck the hour for the school to open. A friend standing near heard the little one cry, "Dear God, do grant I may be in time for school." It struck the listener that for once prayer could not be heard, for the child had quite a little walk before him, and the hour was already come. He was curious to see the result. Now it so happened this morning that the master, in trying to open the schoolhouse door, turned the key the wrong way, and could not stir the bolt, and they had to send for a smith to open the door. Hence a delay, and just as the door opened our little friend entered with the rest, all in good time. God has many ways of granting right desires. It was most natural that instead of crying and whining, a child that really loved God should speak to him about his trouble. Should it not be natural to you and to me spontaneously and at once to tell the Lord our sorrows and ask for help? Should not this be the first resort?

Alas, according to Scripture and observation, and I grieve to add, according to experience, prayer is often the last thing. Look at the sick man in the one hundred and seventh Psalm. Friends bring him various foods, but his soul abhors all manner of meat: the physicians do what they can to heal him, but he grows worse and worse, and draws near to the gates of death: "Then they cry unto the LORD in their trouble." That was put last which should have been first. "Send for the doctor. Prepare him nourishment. Wrap him in flannels!" All very well, but when will you pray to God? God will be called upon when the case grows desperate. Look at the mariners described in the same psalm. The bark [sailing ship] is well near wrecked. "They mount up to the heaven, they go down again to the depths: their soul is melted because of trouble." Still they do all they can to ride out the storm; but when "They reel to and fro, and stagger like a drunken man, and are at their wit's end[:] Then they cry unto the LORD in their trouble." Oh yes; God is sought unto when we are driven into a corner and ready to perish. And what a mercy it is that he hears such laggard prayers, and delivers the suppliants out of their troubles. But ought it to be so with you and with me, and with churches of Christ? Ought not the first impulse of a declining church to be, "Let us pray day and night until the Lord appears for us; let us meet together with one accord in one place, and never separate until the blessing descends upon us"?

Do you know, brothers, what great things are to be had for the asking? Have you ever thought of it? Does it not stimulate you to pray fervently? All heaven lies before the grasp of the asking man; all the promises of God are rich and inexhaustible, and their fulfillment is to be had by prayer. Jesus says, "All things are delivered unto me of my Father," and Paul says, "All things are your's; . . . and ye are Christ's." Who would not pray when all things are thus handed over to us? Yes, and promises that were first made to special individuals, are all made to us if we know how to plead them in prayer. Israel went through the Red Sea ages ago, and yet we read in the sixty-sixth Psalm, "There did we rejoice in him." Only Jacob was present at Peniel, and yet Hosea says, "here he spake with us."

Paul wants to give us a great promise for times of need, and he quotes from the Old Testament, "For he hath said, I will never leave thee, nor forsake thee." Where did Paul get that? That is the assurance which the Lord gave to Joshua: "I will not fail thee, nor forsake thee." Surely the promise was for Joshua only. No; it is for us. "No . . . scripture is of private interpretation"; all

Scripture is ours. See how God appears unto Solomon at night, and he says, "Ask what I shall give thee." Solomon asks for wisdom. "Oh, that is Solomon," say you. Listen, "If any of you lack wisdom, let him ask of God." God gave Solomon wealth, and fame into the bargain. Is not that peculiar to Solomon? No, for it is said of the true wisdom, "Length of days is in her right hand; and in her left hand riches and honor"; and is not this much like our Savior's word, "Seek ye first the kingdom of God, and his righteousness; and all these things shall be added unto you." Thus you see the Lord's promises have many fulfillments, and they are waiting now to pour their treasures into the lap of prayer. Does not this lift prayer up to a high level, when God is willing to repeat the biographies of his saints in us; when he is waiting to be gracious, and to load us with his benefits?

I will mention another truth which ought to make us pray, and that is, that if we ask, God will give to us much more than we ask. Abraham asked of God that Ishmael might live before him. He thought, "Surely this is the promised seed: I cannot expect that Sarah will bear a child in her old age. God has promised me a seed, and surely it must be this child of Hagar. Oh that Ishmael might live before thee." God granted him that, but he gave him Isaac as well, and all the blessings of the covenant. There is Jacob, he kneels down to pray, and asks the Lord to give him bread to eat and raiment to put on. But what did his God give him? When he came back to Bethel he had two bands, thousands of sheep and camels, and much wealth. God had heard him and done exceeding abundantly above what he asked. It is said of David, "[The king] asked life of thee, and thou gavest it him, even length of days," yea, gave him not only length of days himself, but a throne for his sons throughout all generations, till David went in and sat before the Lord, overpowered with the Lord's goodness.

"Well," say you, "but is that true of New Testament prayers?" Yes, it is so with the New Testament pleaders, whether saints or sinners. They brought a man to Christ sick of the palsy, and asked him to heal him, and he said, "Son, thy sins be forgiven thee." He had not asked that, had he? No, but God gives greater things than we ask for. Hear that poor, dying thief's humble prayer, "Lord, remember me when thou comest into thy kingdom." Jesus replies, "Today shalt thou be with me in paradise." He had not dreamed of such an honor. Even the story of the Prodigal teaches us this. He resolved to say, "I . . . am no more worthy to be called thy son; make me as one of thy hired servants." What is the answer? "This my son was dead, and is alive again." "Bring forth the best robe, and put it on him; and put a ring on his hand, and shoes on his feet." Once get into the position of an asker, and you shall have what you never asked for, and never thought to receive. The text is often misquoted: "[God] is able to do exceeding abundantly above all that we ask or think." We could ask, if we were but more sensible and had more faith, for the very greatest things, but God is willing to give us infinitely more than we do ask.

At this moment I believe that God's church might have inconceivable blessings if she were but ready now to pray. Did you ever notice that wonderful picture in the eighth chapter of the Revelation? It is worthy of careful notice. I shall not attempt to explain it in its connection, but merely point to the picture as it hangs on the wall by itself. Read on—"When he had opened the seventh seal, there was silence in heaven about the space of half an hour." Silence in heaven: there were no anthems, no hallelujahs, not an angel stirred a wing. Silence in heaven! Can you imagine it? And look! You see seven angels standing before God, and to them are given seven trumpets. There they wait, trumpet in hand, but there is no sound. Not a single note of cheer or warning during an interval which was sufficiently long to provoke lively emotion, but short enough to prevent impatience. Silence unbroken, profound, awful reigned in heaven. Action is suspended in heaven, the center of all activity. "And another angel came and stood at the altar, having a golden censer." There he stands, but no offering is presented: everything has come to a standstill. What can possibly set it in motion? "And there was given unto him much incense, that he should offer it with the prayers of all saints upon the golden altar which was before the throne." Prayer is presented together with the merit of the Lord Jesus.

Now, see what will happen. "And the smoke of the incense, which came with the prayers of the saints, ascended up before God out of the angel's hand." That is the key of the whole matter. Now you will see: the angel begins to work: he takes the censer, fills it with the altar fire, and flings it down upon the earth, "and there were voices, and thunderings, and lightnings, and an earthquake." "And the seven angels which had the seven trumpets prepared themselves to sound." Everything is moving now. As soon as the prayers of the saints were mixed with the incense of Christ's eternal merit, and begun to smoke up from the altar, then prayer became effectual. Down fell the living coals among the sons of men, while the angels of the divine providence, who stood still before, sound their thunderblasts, and the will of the Lord is done. Such is the scene in heaven in a certain measure even to this day. Bring hither the incense. Bring hither the prayers of the saints! Set them on fire with Christ's merits, and on the golden altar let them smoke before the Most High: then shall we see the Lord at work, and his will shall be done on earth as it is in heaven. God send his blessing with these words, for Christ's sake. Amen.

Robinson Crusoe's Text

~⚬~

Intended for reading on Lord's Day, December 27, 1885; delivered on August 30, 1885, at the Metropolitan Tabernacle, Newington. No. 1876.

Call upon me in the day of trouble: I will deliver thee, and thou shalt glorify me.—PSALM 50:15

One book charmed us all in the days of our youth. Is there a boy alive who has not read it? *"Robinson Crusoe"* was a wealth of wonders to me: I could have read it over a score times, and never have wearied. I am not ashamed to confess that I can read it even now with ever fresh delight. Robinson and his man Friday, though mere inventions of fiction, are wonderfully real to the most of us. But why am I running on in this way on a Sabbath evening? Is not this talk altogether out of order? I hope not. A passage in that book comes vividly before my recollection tonight as I read my text; and in it I find something more than an excuse. Robinson Crusoe has been wrecked. He is left in the desert island all alone. His case is a very pitiable one. He goes to his bed, and he is smitten with fever. This fever lasts upon him long, and he has no one to wait upon him—none even to bring him a drink of cold water. He is ready to perish. He had been accustomed to sin, and had all the vices of a sailor; but his hard case brought him to think. He opens a Bible which he finds in his chest, and he lights upon this passage, *"Call upon me in the day of trouble: I will deliver thee, and thou shalt glorify me."* That night he prayed for the first time in his life, and ever after there was in him a hope in God, which marked the birth of the heavenly life.

Defoe, who composed the story, was, as you know, a Presbyterian minister; and though not overdone with spirituality, he knew enough of religion to be able to describe very vividly the experience of a man who is in despair, and who finds peace by casting himself upon his God. As a novelist, he had a keen eye for the probable, and he could think of no passage more likely to impress a poor broken spirit than this. Instinctively he perceived the mine of comfort which lies within these words.

Now I have everybody's attention, and this is one reason why I thus commenced my discourse. But I have a further purpose; for although Robinson

Crusoe is not here, nor his man Friday either, yet there may be somebody here very like him, a person who has suffered shipwreck in life, and who has now become a drifting, solitary creature. He remembers better days, but by his sins he has become a castaway, whom no man seeks after. He is here tonight, washed up on shore without a friend, suffering in body, broken in estate, and crushed in spirit. In the midst of a city full of people, he has not a friend, nor one who would wish to own that he has ever known him. He has come to the bare bone of existence now. Nothing lies before him but poverty, misery, and death.

Thus says the Lord unto you, my friend, this night, *"Call upon me in the day of trouble: I will deliver thee, and thou shalt glorify me."* You have come here half hoping that there might be a word from God to your soul; "half hoping," I said; for you are as much under the influence of dread as of hope. You are filled with despair. To you it seems that God has forgotten to be gracious, and that he has in anger shut up the bowels of his compassion. The lying fiend has persuaded you that there is no hope, on purpose that he may bind you with the fetters of despair, and hold you as a captive to work in the mill of ungodliness as you live. You write bitter things against yourself, but they are as false as they are bitter. The Lord's mercies fail not. His mercy endures for ever; and thus in mercy does he speak to you, poor troubled spirit, even to you—*"Call upon me in the day of trouble: I will deliver thee, and thou shalt glorify me."* I have the feeling upon me that I shall at this time speak home, God helping me, to some poor burdened spirit. In such a congregation as this, it is not everybody that can receive a blessing by the word that is spoken, but certain minds are prepared for it of the Lord. He prepares the seed to be sown, and the ground to receive it. He gives a sense of need, and this is the best preparation for the promise. Of what use is comfort to those who are not in distress? The word tonight will be of no avail, and have but little interest in it, to those who have no distress of heart. But, however badly I may speak, those hearts will dance for joy which need the cheering assurance of a gracious God, and are enabled to receive it as it shines forth in this golden text. *"Call upon me in the day of trouble: I will deliver thee, and thou shalt glorify me."* It is a text which I would have written in stars across the sky, or sounded forth with trumpet at noon from the top of every tower, or printed on every sheet of paper which passes through the post. It should be known and read of all mankind.

Four things suggest themselves to me. May the Holy Ghost bless what I am able to say upon them!

I. The first observation is not so much in my text alone as in the text and the context. *Realism is preferred to ritualism.*

If you will carefully read the rest of the Psalm, you will see that the Lord is speaking of the rites and ceremonies of Israel, and he is showing that he has little care about formalities of worship when the heart is absent from them. I think we must read the whole passage: "I will not reprove thee for thy sacrifices or thy burnt offerings, to have been continually before me. I will take no bullock out of thy house, nor he goats out of thy folds. For every beast of the forest is mine, and the cattle upon a thousand hills. I know all the fowls of the mountains: and the wild beasts of the field are mine. If I were hungry, I would not tell thee: for the world is mine, and the fullness thereof. Will I eat the flesh of bulls, or drink the blood of goats? Offer unto God thanksgiving; and pay thy vows unto the Most High: and call upon me in the day of trouble: I will deliver thee, and thou shalt glorify me." Thus praise and prayer are accepted in preference to every form of offering which it was possible for the Jew to present before the Lord. Why is this?

First of all I would answer, real prayer is far better than mere ritual, because *there is meaning in it,* and when grace is absent, there is no meaning in ritual; it is as senseless as an idiot's game.

Did you ever stand in some Romish cathedral and see the daily service, especially if it happened to be upon a high day? What with the boys in white, and the men in violet, or pink, or red, or black, there were performers enough to stock a decent village. What with those who carried candlesticks, and those who carried crosses, and those who carried pots and pans, and cushions and books, and those who rang bells, and those who made a smoke, and those who sprinkled water, and those who bobbed their heads, and those who bowed their knees, the whole concern was very wonderful to look at, very amazing, very amusing, very childish. One wonders, when he sees it, whatever it is all about, and what kind of people those must be who are really made better by it. One marvels also what an idea pious Romanists must have of God if they imagine that he is pleased with such performances. Do you not wonder how the good Lord endures it? What must his glorious mind think of it all?

Albeit that the incense is sweet, and the flowers are pretty, and the ornaments are fine, and everything is according to ancient rubric; what is there in it? To what purpose that procession? To what end that decorated priest?—that gorgeous altar? Do these things mean anything? Are they not a senseless show?

The glorious God cares nothing for pomp and show; but when you call upon him in the day of trouble, and ask him to deliver you, there is meaning in your groan of anguish. This is no empty form; there is heart in it, is there not? There is meaning in the appeal of sorrow, and therefore God prefers the prayer of a broken heart to the finest service that ever was performed by priests and choirs.

There is meaning in the soul's bitter cry, and there is no meaning in the pompous ceremony. In the poor man's prayer there are mind, heart, and soul; and hence it is real unto the Lord. Here is a living soul seeking contact with the living God in reality and in truth. Here is a breaking heart crying out to the compassionate Spirit. Ah! you may bid the organ peal forth its sweetest and its loudest notes, but what is the meaning of mere wind passing through pipes? A child cries, and there is meaning in *that*. A man standing up in yonder corner groans out, "O God, my heart will break!" There is more force in his moan than in a thousand of the biggest trumpets, drums, cymbals, tambourines, or any other instruments of music wherewith men seek to please God nowadays. What madness to think that God cares for musical sounds, or ordered marchings, or variegated garments! In a tear, or a sob, or a cry, there is meaning, but in mere sound there is no sense, and God cares not for the meaningless. He cares for that which has thought and feeling in it.

Why does God prefer realism to ritualism? It is for this reason also that *there is something spiritual in the cry of a troubled heart*; and "God is a Spirit: and they that worship him must worship him in spirit and in truth." Suppose I were to repeat tonight the finest creed for accuracy that was ever composed by learned and orthodox men; yet, if I had no faith in it, and you had none, what were the use of the repetition of the words? There is nothing spiritual in mere orthodox statement if we have no real belief therein: we might as well repeat the alphabet, and call it devotion. And if we were to burst forth tonight in the grandest hallelujah that ever pealed from mortal lips, and we did not mean it, there would be nothing spiritual in it, and it would be nothing to God. But when a poor soul gets away into its chamber, and bows its knee, and cries, "God be merciful to me! God save me! God help me in this day of trouble!" there is spiritual life in such a cry, and, therefore, God approves it and answers it! Spiritual worship is that what he wants, and he will have it, or he will have nothing. "They that worship him must worship him in spirit and in truth." He has abolished the ceremonial law, destroyed the one altar at Jerusalem, burned the Temple, abolished the Aaronic priesthood, and ended for ever all ritualistic performance; for he seeks only true worshipers, who worship him in spirit and in truth.

Further, the Lord loves the cry of the broken heart because *it distinctly recognizes himself as this living God,* in very deed sought after in prayer. From much of outward devotion, God is absent. But how we mock God when we do not discern him as present, and do not come near unto his very self! When the heart, the mind, the soul, breaks through itself to get to its God, then it is that God is glorified, but not by any bodily exercises in which he is forgotten. Oh, how real God is to a man who is perishing, and feels that only God can save him! He believes that God is, or else he would not make so piteous a prayer to him. He said his prayers before, and little cared whether God heard or not; but he prays now, and God's hearing is his chief anxiety.

Besides, dear friends, God takes great delight in our crying to him in the day of trouble because *there is sincerity in it.* I am afraid that in the hour of our mirth and the day of our prosperity, many of our prayers and our thanksgivings are hypocrisy. Too many of us are like boys' tops, that cease to spin except they are whipped. Certainly we pray with a deep intensity when we get into great trouble. A man is very poor: he is out of a situation; he has worn his shoes out in trying to find work; he does not know where the next meal is coming from for his children; and if he prays now, it is likely to be very sincere prayer, for he is in real earnest on account of real trouble. I have sometimes wished for some very gentlemanly Christian people, who seem to treat religion as if it were all kid gloves, that they could have just a little time of the "roughing" of it, and really come into actual difficulties. A life of ease breeds hosts of falsehoods and presences, which would soon vanish in the presence of matter-of-fact trials.

Many a man has been converted to God in the bush of Australia by hunger, and weariness, and loneliness, who, when he was a wealthy man, surrounded by flatterers, never thought of God at all. Many a man on board ship on yon Atlantic has learned to pray in the cold chill of an iceberg, or in the horrors of the trough of the wave out of which the vessel could not rise. When the mast has gone by the board, and every timber has been strained, and the ship has seemed doomed, then have hearts begun to pray in sincerity; and God loves sincerity. When we mean it; when the soul melts in prayer; when it is, "I must have it, or be lost"; when it is no sham, no vain performance, but a real, heartbreaking, agonizing cry, then God accepts it. Hence he says, "Call upon me in the day of trouble." Such a cry is the kind of worship that he cares for, because there is sincerity in it, and this is acceptable with the God of truth.

Again, in the cry of the troubled one *there is humility.* We may go through a highly brilliant performance of religion, after the rites of some gaudy church; or we may go through our own rites, which are as simple as they can be; and we may be all the while saying to ourselves, "This is very nicely done." The preacher may be thinking, "Am I not preaching well?" The brother at the prayer meeting may feel within himself, "How delightfully fluent I am!" Whenever there is that spirit in us, God cannot accept our worship. Worship is not acceptable if it be devoid of humility. Now, when in the day of trouble a man goes to God, and says, "Lord, help me! I cannot help myself, but do you interpose for me," there is humility in that confession and cry, and hence the Lord takes delight in them.

You, poor woman over here, deserted by your husband, and ready to wish that you could die, I exhort you to call upon God in the day of trouble, for I know that you will pray a humble prayer. You, poor trembler over yonder; you have done very wrong, and are likely to be found out and disgraced for it, but I charge you to cry to God in prayer, for I am sure there will be no pride about your petition. You will be broken in spirit, and humble before God, and "a broken and a contrite heart, O God, thou wilt not despise."

Once more, the Lord loves such pleadings because *there is a measure of faith in them*. When the man in trouble cries, "Lord deliver me!" he is looking away from himself. You see, he is driven out of himself because of the famine that is in the land. He cannot find hope or help on earth, and therefore he looks toward heaven. Perhaps he has been to friends, and they have failed him, and, therefore, in sheer despair, he seeks his truest Friend. At last he comes to God; and though he cannot say that he believes in God's goodness as he ought, yet he has some dim and shadowy faith in it, or else he would not be coming to God in this his time of extremity. God loves to discover even the shadow of faith in his unbelieving creature. When faith does as it were, only cross over the field of the camera, so that across the photograph there is a dim trace of its having been there, God can spy it out, and he can and will accept prayer for the sake of that little faith. Oh, dear heart, where are you? Are you torn with anguish? Are you sore distressed? Are you lonely? Are you cast away? Then cry to God. None else can help you; now are you shut up to him. Blessed shutting up! Cry to him, for he can help you; and I tell you, in that cry of yours there will be a pure and true worship, such as God desires, far more than the slaughter of ten thousand bullocks, or the pouring out of rivers of oil. It is true, assuredly, from Scripture, that the groan of a burdened spirit is among the sweetest sounds that are ever heard by the ear of the Most High. Plaintive cries are anthems with him, to whom all mere arrangements of sound must be as child's play.

See then, poor, weeping, and distracted ones, that it is not ritualism; it is not the performance of pompous ceremonies, it is not bowing and scraping, it is not using sacred words; but it is crying to God in the hour of your trouble, which is the most acceptable sacrifice your spirit can bring before the throne of God.

II. Come we now to our second observation. May God impress it upon us all! In our text we have *adversity turned to advantage.* "Call upon me in the day of trouble: I will deliver thee."

We say it with all reverence, but God himself cannot deliver a man who is not in trouble, and therefore it is some advantage to be in distress, because God can then deliver you. Even Jesus Christ, the Healer of men, cannot heal a man who is not sick; so that it turns to our advantage to be sick, in order that Christ may heal us. Thus, my hearer, your adversity may prove your advantage by offering occasion and opportunity for the display of divine grace. It is great wisdom to learn the art of making honey out of gall, and the text teaches us how to do that; it shows how trouble can become gain. When you are in adversity, then call upon God, and you shall experience a deliverance which will be a richer and sweeter experience for your soul than if you had never known trouble. Here is the art and science of making gains out of losses, and advantages out of adversities.

Now let me suppose that there is some person here in trouble. Perhaps another deserted Robinson Crusoe is among us. I am not idly supposing that a tried individual is here; he is so. Well now, when you pray—and oh! I wish you would pray now—do you not see what a plea you have? You have first a plea from *the time*: "Call upon me in the day of trouble." You can plead, "Lord, this is a day of trouble! I am in great affliction, and my case is urgent at this hour." Then state what your trouble is—that sick wife, that dying child, that sinking business, that failing health, that situation which you have lost—that poverty which stares you in the face. Say unto the Lord of mercy, "My Lord, if ever a man was in a day of trouble, I am that man; and, therefore, I take leave and license to pray to you now, because you have said, 'Call upon me in the day of trouble.' This is the hour which you have appointed for appealing to you: this dark, this stormy day. If ever there was a man that had a right given him to pray by your own word, I am that man, for I am in trouble, and, therefore, I will make use of the very time as a plea with you. Do, I beseech you, hear your servant's cry in this midnight hour."

Next, you cannot only make use of the time as a plea; but you may *urge the trouble itself.* You may argue thus, "You have said, 'Call upon me in the day of trouble.' O Lord, you see how great my trouble is. It is a very heavy one. I cannot bear it, or get rid of it. It follows me to my bed; it will not let me sleep. When I rise up it is still with me; I cannot shake it off. Lord, my trouble is an unusual one: few are afflicted as I am; therefore give me extraordinary succor! Lord, my trouble is a crushing one; if you do not help me, I shall soon be broken up by it!" That is good reasoning and prevalent pleading.

Further, turn your adversity to advantage by pleading this command. You can go to the Lord now, at this precise instant, and say, "Lord, do hear me, for you have commanded me to pray! I, though I am evil, would not tell a man to ask a thing of me, if I intended to deny him; I would not urge him to ask help, if I meant to refuse it." Do you not know, brethren, that we often impute to the good Lord conduct which we should be ashamed of in ourselves? This must not be. If you said to a poor man, "You are in very sad circumstances; write to me tomorrow, and I will see to your affairs for you"; and if he did write to you, you would not treat his letter with contempt. You would be bound to consider his case. When you told him to write, you meant that you would help him if you could. And when God tells you to call upon him, he does not mock you: he means that he will deal kindly with you. You are not urged to pray in the hour of trouble, that you may experience all the deeper disappointment. God knows that you have trouble enough without the new one of unanswered prayer. The Lord will not unnecessarily add even a quarter of an ounce to your burden; and if he bids you call upon him, you may call upon him without fear of failure. I do not know who you are. You may be Robinson Crusoe, for all I know, but you may call on the Lord, for he bids you call; and, if you do call upon him, you can put this argument into your prayer:

Lord, thou hast bid me seek thy face,
And shall I seek in vain?
And shall the ear of sovereign grace
Be deaf when I complain?

So plead the time, and plead the trouble, and plead the command; and then plead with God *his own character*. Speak with him reverently, but believingly, in this fashion, "Lord, it is you yourself to whom I appeal. You have said, 'Call upon me.' If my neighbor had bidden me do so, I might have feared that perhaps he would not hear me, but would change his mind; but you are too great and good to change. Lord, by your truth and by your faithfulness, by your immutability and by your love, I, a poor sinner, heartbroken and crushed, call upon you in the day of trouble! Oh, help me, and help me soon; or else I die!" Surely you that are in trouble have many and mighty pleas. You are on firm ground with the angel of the covenant, and may bravely seize the blessing. I do not feel tonight as if the text encouraged me one half so much as it must encourage others of you, for I am not in trouble just now, and you are. I thank God I am full of joy and rest; but I am half-inclined to see if I cannot patch up a little bit of trouble for myself: surely if I were in trouble, and sitting in those pews, I would open my mouth, and drink in this text, and pray like David, or Elias, or Daniel, in the power of this promise, "Call upon me in the day of trouble: I will deliver thee, and thou shalt glorify me."

O you troubled ones, leap up at the sound of this word! Believe it. Let it go down into your souls. "The LORD looseth the prisoners." He has come to loose you. I can see my Master arrayed in his silken garments: his countenance is joyous as heaven, his face is bright as morning without clouds, and in his hand he bears a silver key. "Where do you go, my Master, with that silver key of yours?" "I go," says he, "to open the door to the captive, and to loosen every one that is bound." Blessed Master, fulfill your errand; but pass not these prisoners of hope! We will not hinder you for a moment; but do not forget these mourners! Go up these galleries, and down these aisles, and set free the prisoners of Giant Despair, and make their hearts to sing for joy because they have called upon you in the day of trouble, and you have delivered them, and they shall glorify you!

III. My third head is clearly in the text. Here we have *free grace laid under bonds*.

Nothing in heaven or earth can be freer than grace, but here is grace putting itself under bonds of promise and covenant. Listen. "Call upon me in the day of trouble: *I will deliver thee*." If a person has once said to you, "I will," you hold him; he has placed himself at the command of his own declaration. If he is a true man, and has plainly said, "I will," you have him in your hand. He is not free after giving a promise as he was before it; he has set himself a certain way, and he must keep to it. Is it not so? I say so with the deepest reverence toward my Lord and Master: he has bound himself in the text with cords that he cannot break. He must now hear and help those who call upon him in the day of trouble. He has solemnly promised, and he will fully perform.

Notice that this text is *unconditional as to the persons*. It contains the gist of that other promise—"Whosoever shall call upon the name of the Lord shall be saved." The people who are specially addressed in the text had mocked God; they had presented their sacrifices without a true heart; but yet the Lord said to each of them, "Call upon me in the day of trouble: I will deliver thee." Hence I gather that he excludes none from the promise. You atheist, you blasphemer, you unchaste and impure one, if you call upon the Lord now, in this the day of your trouble, he will deliver you! Come and try him. "If there be a God," say you? But there is a God, say I; come, put him to the test, and see. He says, "Call upon me in the day of trouble: I will deliver thee." Will you not prove him now? Come hither, you bondaged ones, and see if he does not free you! Come to Christ, all you that labor, and are heavy laden, and he will give you rest! In temporals and in spirituals, but specially in spiritual things, call upon him in the day of trouble, and he will deliver you. He is bound by this great unrestricted word of his, about which he has put neither ditch nor hedge; whosoever will call upon him in the day of trouble, shall be delivered.

Moreover, notice that this "I will" *includes all needful power which may be required for deliverance.* "Call upon me in the day of trouble: I will deliver thee." "But how can this be?" cries one. Ah! that I cannot tell you, and I do not feel bound to tell you: it rests with the Lord to find suitable ways and means. God says, "I will." Let him do it in his own way. If he says, "I will," depend upon it; he will keep his word. If it be needful to shake heaven and earth, he will do it; for he cannot lack power, and he certainly does not lack honesty; and an honest man will keep his word at all costs, and so will a faithful God. Hear him say, "I will deliver thee," and ask no more questions. I do not suppose that Daniel knew how God would deliver him out of the den of lions. I do not suppose that Joseph knew how he would be delivered out of the prison when his mistress had slandered his character so shamefully. I do not suppose that these ancient believers dreamed of the way of the Lord's deliverance; but they left themselves in God's hands. They rested upon God, and he delivered them in the best possible manner. He will do the like for you; only call upon him, and then stand still, and see the salvation of God.

Notice, *the text does not say exactly when.* "I will deliver thee" is plain enough; but whether it shall be tomorrow, or next week, or next year, is not so clear. You are in a great hurry; but the Lord is not. Your trial may not yet have wrought all the good to you that it was sent to do, and, therefore, it must last longer. When the gold is cast into the fining pot, it might cry to the goldsmith, "Let me out." "No," says he, "you have not yet lost your dross. You must tarry in the fire till I have purified you." God may, therefore, subject us to many trials; and yet if he says, "I will deliver thee," depend upon it; he will keep his word. The Lord's promise is like a good bill from a substantial firm. A bill may be dated for three months ahead; but anybody will discount it if it bears a trusted name. When you get God's "I will," you may always cash it by faith; and no discount need be taken from it, for it is current money of the merchant even when it is only "I will." God's promise for the future is good, bona fide stuff for the present, if you have but faith to use it. "Call upon me in the day of trouble: I will deliver thee," is tantamount to deliverance already received. It means, "If I do not deliver you now, I will deliver you at a time that is better than now, when, if you were as wise as I am, you would prefer to be delivered rather than now."

But promptitude is implied, for else deliverance would not be wrought. "Ah!" says one, "I am in such a trouble that if I do not get deliverance soon I shall die." Rest assured that you shall not die. You shall be delivered, and therefore you shall be delivered before you quite die of despair. He will deliver you in the best possible time. The Lord is always punctual. You never were kept waiting by him. You have kept him waiting long enough; but he is prompt to the instant. He never keeps his servants waiting one single tick of the clock beyond his own appointed, fitting, wise, and proper moment. "I will deliver thee" implies that his delays will not be too protracted, lest the spirit of man should fail because of hope deferred. The Lord rides on the wings of the wind when he comes to the rescue of those who seek him. Wherefore, be of good courage!

Oh, this is a blessed text! and yet what can I do with it? I cannot carry it home to those of you who want it most. Spirit of the living God, come, and apply these rich consolations to those hearts which are bleeding and ready to die!

Do notice this text once again. Let me repeat it, putting the emphasis in a different way: "Call upon me in the day of trouble: *I* will deliver *thee*." Pick up the threads of those two words. "I will deliver thee"; men would not; angels could not; but I will. God himself will set about the rescue of the man that calls upon him. It is yours to call: and it is God's to answer. Poor trembler, you begin to try to answer your own prayers! Why did you pray to God, then? When you have prayed, leave it to God to fulfill his own promise. He says, "[Do thou] call upon me . . .: I will deliver thee."

Now take up that other word: "I will deliver *thee*." I know what you are thinking, Mr. John. You murmur, "God will deliver everybody, I believe, but *not me*." But the text says, "I will deliver *thee*." It is the man that calls that shall get the answer. Mary, where are you? If you call upon God, he will answer *you*. He will give *you* the blessing even to your own heart and spirit, in your own personal experience. "Call upon me," says he, "in the day of trouble: I will deliver *thee*." Oh, for grace to take that personal pronoun home to one's soul, and to make sure of it as though you could see it with your own eyes!

The apostle tells us, "Through faith we understand that the worlds were framed by the Word of God." Assuredly I know that the worlds were made by

God. I am sure of it; and yet I did not see him making them. I did not see him when the light came because he said, "Let there be light." I did not see him divide the light from the darkness, and the waters that are beneath the firmament from the waters that are above the firmament, but I am quite sure that he did all this. All the evolution gentlemen in the world cannot shake my conviction that creation was wrought by God, though I was not there to see him make even a bird, or a flower. Why should I not have just the same kind of faith tonight about God's answer to my prayer if I am in trouble? If I cannot see how he will deliver me, why should I wish to see? He created the world well enough without my knowing how he was to do it, and he will deliver me without my having a finger in it. It is no business of mine to see how he works. My business is to trust in my God, and glorify him by believing that what he has promised he is able to perform.

IV. Thus we have had three sweet things to remember; and we close with a fourth, which is this: here are *God and the praying man taking shares*.

That is an odd word to close with, but I want you to notice it. Here are the shares. First, here is your share: "Call upon me in the day of trouble." Secondly, here is God's share: "I will deliver thee." Again, you take a share—for you shall be delivered. And then again it is the Lord's turn—"Thou shalt glorify me." Here is a compact, a covenant that God enters into with you who pray to him, and whom he helps. He says, "You shall have the deliverance, but I must have the glory. You shall pray; I will bless, and then you shall honor my holy name." Here is a delightful partnership: we obtain that which we so greatly need, and all that God gets is the glory which is due unto his name. Poor troubled heart! I am sure you do not demur to these terms. "Sinners," says the Lord, "I will give you pardon, but you must give me the honor of it." Our only answer is, "Yes, Lord, that we will, for ever and ever."

Who is a pardoning God like thee?
Or who has grace so rich and free?

"Come, souls," says he, "I will justify you, but I must have the glory of it." And our answer is, "Where is boasting, then? It is excluded. By the law of works? No, but by the law of faith." God must have the glory if we are justified by Christ.

"Come," says he, "I will put you into my family, but my grace must have the glory of it"; and we say, "Yes, that it shall, good Lord! Behold, what manner of love the Father has bestowed upon us that we should be called the sons of God."

"Now," says he, "I will sanctify you, and make you holy, but I must have the glory of it": and our answer is, "Yes, we will sing for ever—'We have washed our robes, and made them white in the blood of the Lamb. Therefore will we serve him day and night in his temple, giving him all praise.'"

"I will take you home to heaven," says God: "I will deliver you from sin and death and hell; but I must have the glory of it." "Truly," say we, "You shall be magnified. For ever and for ever we will sing, 'Blessing, and honor, and glory, and power, be unto him that sitteth upon the throne, and unto the Lamb for ever and ever.'"

Stop, you thief, there! What are you at? Running away with a portion of God's glory? What a villain he must be! Here is a man that was lately a drunkard, and God has loved him and made him sober, and he is wonderfully proud because he is sober. What folly! Have done, sir! Have done! Give God the glory of your deliverance from the degrading vice, or else you are still degraded by ingratitude. Here is another man. He used to swear once; but he has been praying now; he even delivered a sermon the other night, or at least an open-air address. He has been as proud about this as any peacock. O bird of pride, when you look at your fine feathers, remember your black feet, and your hideous voice! O reclaimed sinner, remember your former character, and be ashamed! Give God the glory if you have ceased to be profane. Give God the glory for every part of your salvation.

Alas! even some divines will give man a little of the glory. He has a free will, has he not? Oh, that Dagon of free will! How men will worship it! The man did something toward his salvation, by virtue of which he ought to receive some measure of honor! Do you really think so? Then say as you think. But we will have it from this pulpit, and we will declare it to the whole world, that when a man reaches heaven there shall not a particle of the glory be due to himself; he shall in no wise ascribe honor to his own feeble efforts; but unto God alone shall be the glory. "Give unto the LORD, O ye mighty, give unto the LORD glory and strength. Give unto the LORD the glory due unto his name."

"Call upon me in the day of trouble: I will deliver thee"—that is your part. But, "Thou shalt glorify me"—that is God's part. He must have all the honor from first to last.

Go out henceforth, you saved ones, and tell out what the Lord has done for you. An aged woman once said that if the Lord Jesus Christ really did save her, he should never hear the last of it. Join with her in that resolve. Truly my soul vows that my delivering Lord shall never hear the last of my salvation.

I'll praise him in life, and praise him in death,
And praise him as long as he lendeth me breath;
And say when the death-dew lies cold on my brow,
If ever I loved thee, my Jesus, 'tis now.

Come, poor soul, you that came in here tonight in the deepest of trouble; God means to glorify himself by you! The day shall yet come when you shall comfort other mourners by the rehearsal of your happy experience. The day may yet come when you that were a castaway shall preach the gospel to castaways. The day shall yet come, poor fallen woman, when you shall lead other sinners to the Savior's feet, where now you stand weeping! You abandoned of the devil, whom even Satan is tired of, whom the world rejects because you are worn out and stale—the day shall yet come when, renewed in heart, and washed in the blood of the Lamb, you shall shine like a star in the firmament, to the praise of the glory of his grace who has made you to be accepted in the Beloved! O desponding sinner, come to Jesus! Do call upon him, I entreat you! Be persuaded to call upon your God and Father. If you can do no more than groan, groan unto God. Drop a tear, heave a sigh, and let your heart say to the Lord, "O God, deliver me, for Christ's sake! Save me from my sin and the consequences of it." As surely as you thus pray, he will hear you, and say, "Your sins be forgiven you. Go in peace." So may it be. Amen.

A Free Grace Promise

❧

Intended for reading on Lord's Day, May 5, 1888, at the Metropolitan Tabernacle, Newington; delivered on Thursday evening, October 11, 1888. No. 2082.

And it shall come to pass, that whosoever shall call on the name of the LORD shall be delivered.—JOEL 2:32

Vengeance was in full career. The armies of divine justice had been called forth for war: "They shall run like mighty men; they shall climb the wall like men of war." They had invaded and devastated the land, and turned the land from being like the garden of Eden into a desolate wilderness. All faces gathered blackness: the people were "much pained." The sun itself was dim, the moon was dark, and the stars withdrew themselves: the earth quaked, and the heavens trembled. At such a dreadful time, when we might least have expected it, between the peals of thunder and the flashes of lightning, was heard this gentle word, "It shall come to pass, that whosoever shall call on the name of the LORD shall be delivered."

Let us carefully read the passage: "And I will shew wonders in the heavens and in the earth, blood, and fire, and pillars of smoke. The sun shall be turned into darkness, and the moon into blood, before the great and the terrible day of the LORD come. And it shall come to pass, that whosoever shall call on the name of the LORD shall be delivered." In the worst times that can ever happen, there is still salvation for men. When day turns to night, and life becomes death, and the staff of life is broken, and the hope of man has fled, there still remains in God, in the person of his dear Son, deliverance to all those who will call upon the name of the Lord. We do not know what is to happen: reading the roll of the future, we prophesy dark things; but still this light shall always shine between the rifts of the cloud rack: "Whosoever shall call on the name of the LORD shall be delivered."

This passage was selected by the apostle at Pentecost to be set in its place as a sort of morning star of gospel times. When the Spirit was poured out upon the servants and the handmaids, and sons and daughters began to prophesy, it was clear that the wondrous time had come, which had been foretold so long before. Then Peter, as he preached his memorable sermon, told the people, "Whosoever shall call on the name of the Lord shall be saved"; thus giving a fuller and yet more evangelical meaning to the word "delivered." Whosoever shall call on the name of the Lord shall be "delivered" from sin, death, and hell—shall, in fact, be so delivered as to be, in divine language, "saved"—saved from the guilt, the penalty, the power of sin, saved from the wrath to come. These gospel times are still the happy days in which "whosoever shall call on the name of the Lord shall be saved." In the Year of Grace we have reached a day and an hour in which "whosoever shall call on the name of the Lord shall be saved." To you at this moment is this salvation sent. The dispensation of immediate acceptance proclaimed at Pentecost has never ceased: its fullness of blessing has grown rather than diminished. The sacred promise stands in all its certainty, fullness, and freeness: it has lost none of all its breadth and length: "Whosoever shall call on the name of the Lord shall be saved."

I have nothing to do tonight but to tell you over again the old, old story of infinite mercy come to meet infinite sin—of free grace come to lead free will into a better line of things—of God himself appearing to undo man's ruin wrought by man, and to lift him up by a great deliverance. May the Holy Spirit graciously aid me while I shall talk to you very simply thus.

I. First, *there is something always wanted.*

That something is deliverance, or "salvation." It is always wanted. It is the requisite of man, wherever man is found. As long as there are men on the face of the earth, there will always be a need of salvation. I could wish that some of you had the instructive schooling which I received last Tuesday, when I was sitting to see inquirers. I had a very happy time in seeing a very large number of persons who had joyfully put their trust in Christ; but among them were some who could not trust—poor hearts, conscious of sin, though they did not think they were. These seemed bound hand and foot, shut up in the prison of despair, and darkened in heart. I tell you, I felt dismayed, as they baffled me: I felt a fool as they refused to be comforted. I could do nothing for them so far as argument and persuasion were concerned. I could pray with them: I could also set them praying, and they did pray: but they were cases in which, unless the arm of God were revealed, I was as powerless with them as when a man stands weeping over the body of his dead wife, and would restore her to life even at the cost of his own life, and yet he could produce neither hearing nor motion. Dear friends, while we mingle only with those who are saved, we forget how much need there is still of a divine salvation. If we could go through

London, into its dens and slums, we should think very differently of human need from what we do when we simply come from our own quiet domestic circle, and step into our pew and hear a sermon. The world is still sick and dying. The world is still corrupting and rotting. The world is a ship in which the water is rising fast, and the vessel is going down into the deep of destruction. God's salvation is wanted as much today as when the spirit preached it in Noah's day to the spirits in prison. God must step in, and bring deliverance, or there remains no hope.

Some want deliverance from present trouble. If you are in this need tonight through very sore distress, I invite you to take my text as your guide, and believe that "whosoever shall call on the name of the Lord shall be [delivered]." Depend upon it; in any form of distress—physical, mental, or whatever it may be—prayer is wonderfully available. "Call upon me," says God, "in the day of trouble: I will deliver thee, and thou shalt glorify me."

If you are so down at the heel that your foot is on the bare pavement; if you have come to this place in bodily sickness, and feel as if you should die on the seat in which you sit; if there be no physician to help you, and no friend to stretch out a generous hand, call upon God, I beseech you. You have come to the end of men; you are now at the beginning of God. See whether your Maker will forget you. See whether the great, generous heart of God does not still beat tenderly toward the sorrowful and the afflicted. If I saw you lying wounded on a battlefield, bleeding to death, I would say, "Call upon God." If I knew that you had not a house to go to, but must walk these streets all night, I would say, "Whosoever shall call on the name of the Lord shall be [delivered]." I will take the text in the broadest sense, and bid you, no, command you, to test your good and gracious God in the day of your calamity.

This is true whenever you come into a position of deep personal distress, even though it should not be of a physical kind. When you do not know how to act, but are bewildered and at your wits' end, when wave of trouble has followed wave of trouble till you are like the sailor in the storm who reels to and fro, and staggers like a drunken man; if now you cannot help yourself, because your spirit sinks and your mind fails, call upon God, call upon God, call upon God! Lost child in the wood, with the night fog thickening about you, ready to lie down and die, call upon your Father! Call upon God, you distracted one; for, "Whosoever shall call on the name of the Lord shall be [delivered]."

In the last great day when all secrets are known, it will seem ridiculous that ever persons took to writing tales and romances; for the real stories of what God has done for those who cry to him are infinitely more surprising. If men and women could but tell in simple, natural language how God has come to their rescue in the hour of imminent distress, they would set the harps of heaven a-ringing with new melodies, and the hearts of saints on earth a-glowing with new love to God for his wonderful kindness to the children of men. Oh, that men would praise the Lord for his goodness! Oh, that we could abundantly utter the memory of his great goodness to ourselves in the night of our weeping!

The text holds good concerning deliverance from future troubles. What is to happen in the amazing future we do not know. Some try to startle and alarm you with prophecies of what will soon happen; concerning whom I would warn you to be well upon your guard. Take small heed of what they say. Whatever is to happen according to the Word of God—if the sun shall be turned into darkness and the moon into blood—if God shall show great wonders in the heavens, and the earth, blood and fire, and pillars of smoke, yet remember that though you will then assuredly want deliverance, deliverance will still be near at hand. The text seems put in a startling connection in order to advise us that when the worst and most terrible convulsions shall occur, "Whosoever shall call on the name of the Lord shall be saved." The star Wormwood may fall, but we shall be saved if we call upon the name of the Lord. Plagues may be poured out, trumpets may sound, and judgments may follow one another as quickly as the plagues of Egypt, but, "Whosoever shall call on the name of the Lord shall be saved." When the need of deliverance shall apparently increase, the abundance of salvation shall increase with it. Fear not the direst of all wars, the bitterest of all famines, the deadliest of all plagues; for still, if we call upon the Lord, he is pledged to deliver us. This word of promise meets the most terrible of possibilities with a sure salvation.

Yes, and when you come to die, when to you the sun has turned into darkness, and the moon into blood, this text ensures deliverance in the last dread hour. Call upon the name of the Lord, and you shall be saved. Amid the pains of death, and the gloom of departure, you shall enjoy a glorious visitation, which shall turn darkness into light, and sorrow into joy. When you wake up amid the realities of the eternal future there will be nothing for you to dread in resurrection, or in judgment, or in the yawning mouth of hell. If you have called upon the name of the Lord, you shall still be delivered. Though the unpardoned are thrust down to the depth of woe, and the righteous scarcely are saved, yet you who have called upon the name of the Lord must be delivered. Stands the promise firm, whatever may be hidden in the great roll of the future; God cannot deny himself; he will deliver those who call upon his name.

What is wanted, then, is salvation; and I do think, beloved brethren, that you and I who preach the Word, and long to save souls, must very often go over this grand old truth about salvation to the guilty, deliverance to all who call upon the name of the Lord. Sometimes we talk to friends about the higher life, about attaining to very high degrees of sanctity; and all this is very proper and very good; but still the great fundamental truth is, "Whosoever shall call on the name of the Lord shall be saved." We urge our friends to be sound in doctrine, and to know what they do know, and to understand the revealed will of God; and very proper is this also; but still, first and foremost, this is the elementary, all-important truth—"Whosoever shall call on the name of the Lord shall be saved." To this old foundation truth we come back for comfort.

I sometimes rejoice in God, and joy in the God of my salvation, and spread my wings and mount up into communion with the heavenlies; but still there are other seasons when I hide my head in darkness, and then I am very glad of such a broad, gracious promise as this, "Whosoever shall call on the name of the Lord shall be saved." I find that my sweetest, happiest, safest state, is just as a poor, guilty, helpless sinner, to call upon the name of the Lord, and take mercy at his hands as one who deserves nothing but his wrath, while I dare hang the weight of my soul on such a sure promise as this, "Whosoever shall call on the name of the Lord shall be saved." Get where you may, however high your experience; be what you may, however great your usefulness; you will always want to come back to the same ground upon which the poorest and weakest of hearts must stand, and claim to be saved by almighty grace, through simply calling upon the name of the Lord.

Thus have I said enough upon what is always wanted—this deliverance, this salvation.

II. Now, secondly, let us attentively observe *the way in which this deliverance is to be had*. Help us, blessed Spirit, in this our meditation. It is to be had, according to the text, by calling upon the name of the Lord.

Is not the most obvious sense of this language, prayer? Are we not brought to the Lord by a prayer which trusts in God—by a prayer which asks God to give the deliverance that is needed, and expects to have it from the Lord, as a gift of grace? It amounts to much the same thing as that other word, "Believe and live"; for how shall they call on him of whom they have not heard? And if they have heard, yet vain is their calling if they have not believed as well as heard. But to "call on the name of the Lord" is briefly to pray a believing prayer; to cry to God for his help, and to leave yourself in his hands. This is very simple, is it not? There is no cumbersome machinery here, nothing complex and mysterious. No priestly help is wanted, except the help of that great High Priest, who intercedes for us within the veil. A poor, broken heart pours its distress into the ear of God, and calls upon him to fulfill his promise of help in the time of need—that is all. Thank God, nothing more is mentioned in our text. The promise is—"Whosoever shall call on the name of the Lord shall be saved."

What a suitable way of salvation it is to those who feel that they can do nothing! Ah, dear hearts! if we had to preach to them a very difficult and elaborate salvation, they would perish. They have not the mind, some of them, to follow our directions if they were at all intricate; and they have not enough hope to venture upon anything that looks at all difficult. But if it be true that "Whosoever shall call on the name of the Lord shall be saved," this method is simple and available, and they catch at it. He can pray to God who can do nothing else. Thank God, he need not want to do anything else; for if he can call for help, he gets deliverance, and, in that deliverance, he gets all that he will ever want between this place and heaven. He has called upon the name of the Lord, and all that is deficient in him will be supplied for time and for eternity. He will be delivered, not only now, but throughout all the future of his life, until he sees the face of God in glory everlasting.

The text, however, contains within it a measure of specific instruction: the prayer must be to the true God. "Whosoever shall call on the name of [Jehovah] shall be delivered." There is something distinctive here; for one would call on Baal, another would call on Ashtaroth, and a fourth on Moloch; but these would not be saved. The promise is special: "Whosoever shall call on the name of [Jehovah] shall be saved." You know that triune name, "Father, Son, and Holy Ghost"—call upon it. You know how the name of Jehovah is set forth most conspicuously in the person of the Lord Jesus—call upon him. Call upon the true God. Call upon no idol; call on no Virgin Mary, no saint, dead or living. Call on no image. Call on no impression of your mind! Call upon the living God—call upon him who reveals himself in the Bible—call upon him who manifests himself in the person of his dear Son; for whosoever shall call upon this God shall be saved. You may call upon the idols, but these will not hear you: "Eyes have they, but they see not; They have ears, but they hear not." You may not call upon men, for they are all sinners like yourselves. Priests cannot help their most zealous admirers; but, "Whosoever shall call on the name of [Jehovah] shall be saved." Mind, then, it is not the mere repetition of a prayer as a sort of charm, or a piece of religious witchcraft, but you must make a direct address to God, an appeal to the Most High to help you in your time of need. In presenting true prayer to the true God, you shall be delivered.

Moreover, the prayer should be intelligently presented. We read, "Whosoever shall call on the name of the Lord." Now, by the word "name" we understand the person, the character of the Lord. The more, then, you know about the Lord, and the better you know his name, the more intelligently will you call upon that name. If you know his power, you will call upon that power to help you. If you know his mercy, you will call upon him in his grace to save you. If you know his wisdom, you feel that he knows your difficulties, and can help you through them. If you understand his immutability, you will call upon him, as the same God who has saved other sinners, to come and save you. It will be well, therefore, for you to study the Scriptures much, and to pray the Lord to manifest himself to you that you may know him; since, in proportion to your acquaintance with him, will you with greater confidence be able to call upon his name. But, little as you may know, call on him according to the little you do know. Cast yourself upon him, whether your trouble tonight be external or internal; but especially if it be internal, if it be the trouble of sin, if it be the burden of guilt, if it be a load of horror and fear because of wrath to come, call upon the name of the Lord, for you shall be delivered. There stands his promise. It is not, "He may be delivered," but he "shall be." Note well the everlasting "shall" of God—irrevocable, unalterable, unquestionable, irresistible. His promise stands eternally the same. Has he said, and shall he not do it? "Whosoever shall call on the name of the Lord shall be saved."

This way of salvation, by calling upon the name of the Lord, glorifies God. He asks nothing of you but that you ask everything of him. You are the beggar, and he is the benefactor. You are in the trouble, and he is the Deliverer. All you have to do is to trust him, and beg of him. This is easy enough. This puts the matter into the hands of the Lord, and takes it out of your hands. Do you not like the plan? Put it in practice immediately! It will prove itself gloriously effectual.

Dear friends, I speak to some whom I know to be now present, who are under severe trial. You dare not look up. You seem to be given up; at any rate, you have given yourself up; and yet, I pray you, call upon the name of the Lord. You cannot perish praying; no one has ever done so. If you could perish praying, you would be a new wonder in the universe. A praying soul in hell is an utter impossibility. A man calling on God and rejected of God!—the supposition is not to be endured. "Whosoever shall call on the name of the Lord shall be saved." God himself must lie, he must quit his nature, forfeit his claim to mercy, destroy his character of love, if he were to let a poor sinner call upon his name, and yet refuse to hear him. There will come a day, but that is not now—there will come a day in the next state when he will say, "I called, but ye refused"; but it is not so now. While there is life, there is hope. "Today if ye will hear his voice, harden not your hearts," but call upon God at once; for this warrant of grace runs through all the regions of mortality, "Whosoever shall call on the name of the Lord shall be saved."

I recollect a time when, if I had heard a sermon on this subject, putting it plainly to me, I should have leaped into comfort and light in a single moment. Is it not such a time with you? I thought, I must do something, I must be something, I must in some way prepare myself for the mercy of God. I did not know that a calling upon God, a trusting myself in his hand, an invocation of his sacred name, would bring me to Christ, the Savior. But so it stands, and happy, indeed, was I when I found it out. Heaven is given away. Salvation may be had for the asking. I hope that many a captive heart here will at once leap to loose his chains, and cry, "It is even so. If God has said it, it must be true. There it is in his own Word. I have called upon him, and I must be delivered."

III. Now I come to notice, in the third place, *the people to whom this promise and this deliverance will be given.* "Whosoever shall call on the name of the LORD shall be delivered."

According to the connection, the people had been greatly afflicted—afflicted beyond all precedent, afflicted to the very brink of despair; but the Lord said, "Whosoever shall call on the name of the Lord shall be saved." Go down to the hospital. You may select, if you please, the hospital which deals with the effects of vice. In that house of misery you may stand at each bed and say, "Whosoever shall call on the name of the Lord shall be saved." You may then hasten to the jail. You may stop at every door of every cell, yes, even at the grating of the condemned cell, if there lie men and women there given up to death, and you may with safety say to each one, "Whosoever shall call on the name of the LORD shall be delivered."

I know what the Pharisees will say—"If you preach this, men will go on in sin." It has always been so, that the great mercy of God has been turned by some into a reason for continuing in sin; but God (and this is the wonder of it) has never restricted his mercy because of that. It must have been a terrible provocation of Almighty grace when men have perverted his mercy into an excuse for sin, but the Lord has never even taken the edges off from his mercy because men have misused it: he has still made it stand out bright and clear: "Whosoever shall call on the name of the Lord shall be saved." Still he cries, "Turn . . . and live." "Let the wicked forsake his way, and the unrighteous man his thoughts: and let him return unto the LORD, and he will have mercy upon him; and to our God, for he will abundantly pardon." Undimmed is that brave sun that shines on the foulest dunghills of vice. Trust Christ, and live. Call upon the name of the Lord, and you shall be pardoned; yes, you shall be rescued from the bondage of your sin, and be made a new creature, a child of God, a member of the family of his grace. The most afflicted, and the most afflicted by sin, are met with by this gracious promise, "Whosoever shall call on the name of the Lord shall be saved."

Yes, but there were some, according to Joel, who had the Spirit of God poured out upon them. What about them? Were they saved by that? Oh no! Those who had the Spirit of God so that they dreamed dreams and saw visions, yet had to come to the palace of mercy by this same gate of believing prayer—"Whosoever shall call on the name of the Lord shall be saved." Ah, poor souls! you say, to yourselves, "if we were deacons of churches, if we were pastors, oh, then we should be saved!" You do not know anything about it: church officers are no more saved by their office than you are by being without office. We owe nothing to our official position in this matter of salvation: in fact, we may owe our damnation to our official standing unless we look well to our ways. We have no preference over you plain folks. I do assure you, I am quite happy to take your hand, whoever you may be, and come to Christ on the same footing as yourself.

Nothing in my hand I bring,
Simply to thy cross I cling.

Often, when I have been cheering up a poor sinner, and urging him to believe in Christ, I have thought, "Well, if he will not drink this cup of comfort, I will even drink it up myself." I assure you, I need it as much as those to whom I carry it. I have been as big a sinner as any of you, and, therefore, I take the promise to myself. The divine cordial shall not be lost: I will accept it. I came to Jesus as I was, weary, and worn, and faint, and sick, and full of sin, and I trusted him on my own account, and found peace—peace on the same ground as my text sets before all of you. If I drink of this consolation, you may drink it too. The miracle of this cup is that fifty may drink, and yet it is just as full as ever. There is no restriction in the word "whosoever." You maidens that have the Spirit of God upon you, and you old men that dream, it is neither the Spirit of God nor the dreaming that will save you; but your calling on the sacred name. It is, "Whosoever shall call on the name of the Lord shall be saved."

Also, there were some upon whom the Spirit of God did not fall. They did not speak with tongues, nor prophesy the future, nor work miracles; but though they did none of these marvels, yet it stood true to them—"Whosoever shall call on the name of the Lord shall be saved." What though no supernatural gift was bestowed, though they saw no vision and could not speak with tongues, they called upon the name of the Lord, and they were saved. There is the same way of salvation for the little as well as for the great, for the poorest and most obscure as well as for those that are strong in faith, and lead the hosts of God to the battle.

But some were terribly afraid. I should think that a good many must have been sadly alarmed when there were in the earth blood and fire and pillars of smoke, the sun turned into darkness and the moon into blood: but, afraid as they were, if they called upon the name of the Lord, they were delivered. Now, Mrs. Much-afraid, what do you say to that? Mr. Ready-to-halt, did I hear your crutches sounding in the aisle just now, or was it an umbrella? Never mind, if you call upon the name of the Lord, you shall be saved. You that are so feeble in mind, so weak, so wounded that you hardly dare to trust, still it is written for your sakes also, "Whosoever shall call on the name of the Lord shall be saved."

"Ah!" says another, "but I am worse than that. I have no good feelings. I would give all that I have to own a broken heart. I wish I could even feel despair, but I am hard as a stone." I have been told that sorrowful story many times, and it almost always happens that those who most mourn their want of feeling are those who feel most acutely. Their hearts are like hell-hardened steel, so they say; but it is not true. But if it were true, "Whosoever shall call on the name of the Lord shall be saved." Do you think that the Lord wants you to give yourself a new heart first, and that then he will save you? My dear soul, you are saved when you have a new heart, and you do not want him to save you then, since you are saved. "Oh, but I must get good feelings!" Must you? Where are you going for them? Are you to rake the dunghill of your depraved nature to find good feelings there? Come without any good feeling. Come just as you are. Come, you that are like a frozen iceberg, that have nothing about you whatever, but that which chills and repels; come and call upon the name of the Lord, and you shall be saved. "Wonders of grace to God belong." It is not a small gospel that he has sent us to preach to small sinners, but ours is a great gospel for great sinners. "Whosoever shall call on the name of the Lord shall be saved."

"Ah, well!" says one, "I cannot think it is meant for me, for I am nobody." Nobody, are you there? I have a great love for nobodies. I am worried with somebodies, and the worst somebody in the world is my own somebody. How I wish I could always turn my own somebody out, and keep company with none but nobodies! Then I should make Jesus everybody. Nobody, where are you? You are the very person that I am sent to look after. If there is nothing of you, there shall be all the more of Christ. If you are not only empty, but cracked and broken; if you are done for, destroyed, ruined, utterly crushed and broken, to you is this word of salvation sent: "Whosoever shall call on the name of the Lord shall be saved."

I have set the gate wide open. If it were the wrong track, all the sheep would go through; but as it is the right road, I may set the gate open as long as I will, but yet the sheep will shun it, unless you, Great Shepherd, shall go around the field tonight, and lead them in. Take up in your own arms some sheep that you have purchased long ago with your dear heart's blood—take him upon your gracious shoulders, rejoicing as you do it, and place him within the field where the good pasture grows.

IV. I want you to dwell for a minute upon *the blessing itself.*

"Whosoever shall call on the name of the LORD shall be delivered." I need not say much about it because I have already expounded it. It is a very good rule, when a man makes you a promise, to understand it in the narrowest sense. It is fair to him that you should do so. Let him interpret it liberally, if he pleases; but he is actually bound to give you no more than the bare terms of his promise will imply. Now, it is a rule which all God's people may well practice, always to understand God's promises in the largest possible sense. If the words will bear a bigger construction than at the first sight they naturally suggest to you, you may put the larger construction upon them. "[He] is able to do exceeding abundantly above all that we ask or think." God never draws a line in his promise, that he may go barely up to it; but it is with the great God as it was with his dear Son, who, though he was sent to the lost sheep of the house of Israel, yet spent the greater part of his time in Galilee, which was called "Galilee of the Gentiles"; and went to the very verge of Canaan to find out a Canaanitish woman, that he might give her a blessing. You may put the biggest and most liberal sense, then, on such a text as this, for Peter did so. The New Testament is wont to give a broader sense to Old Testament words; and it does so most rightly, for God loves us to treat his words with the breadth of faith.

Come, then, if you are the subject of the judgments of God; if you believe that God's hand has visited you on account of sin, call upon him, and he will deliver you both from the judgment, and from the guilt that brought the judgment—from the sin, and from that which follows the sin. He will help you to escape. Try him now, I pray you.

And if your case should be different: if you are a child of God and you are in trouble, and that trouble eats into your spirit, and causes you daily wear of spirit and tear of heart—call upon the Lord. He can take away from you the fret and the trouble too. "Whosoever shall call on the name of the LORD shall be delivered." You may have to bear the trouble, but it shall be so transformed as to be rather a blessing than an evil, and you shall fall in love with your cross, since the nature of it has been changed.

If sin be the great cause of your present trouble, and that sin has brought you into bondage to evil habits; if you have been a drunkard and do not know how to learn sobriety; if you have been unchaste and have become entangled in vicious connections; call upon God, and he can break you away from the sin, and set you free from all its entanglements. He can cut you loose tonight with the great sword of his grace, and make you a free man. I tell you that, though you should be like a poor sheep between the jaws of a lion, ready to be devoured immediately by the monster, God can come and pluck you out from between the lion's jaws. The prey shall be taken from the mighty, and the lawful captive shall be delivered. Only call upon the name of the Lord! Call upon the name of the Lord, and you shall be delivered.

Yes, and I repeat what I said just now. If you have come under the power of disease, if you are near to die, if already death has written his name legibly upon your body, and you are afraid of death and hell; yet call upon the name of the Lord, and you shall be delivered at this last moment. Even now, when the pit gapes wide for you, and like Korah, Dathan, and Abiram, you are ready to go down alive into it, call upon the name of the Lord and you shall be delivered. If I were telling you what I had made up, or hammered out of my own brain, I could not expect you to believe me; but, as this Book is inspired, and as Joel spoke in the name of God, and as the apostles spoke in the name of Jehovah, this is the very truth of the God that made the heavens and the earth. "Whosoever shall call on the name of the LORD shall be delivered."

V. In conclusion, I must remind you of one mournful thought. Let me warn you *of the sadly common neglect of this blessing.*

You would think that everybody would call upon the name of the Lord; but read the text, "For in mount Zion and in Jerusalem shall be deliverance, as the LORD hath said." It shall be there as the Lord has said. Will they not have it then? Notice! "And in the remnant whom the LORD shall call." It seems to shrivel me up altogether, that word "remnant." What! Will they not come? Are they madmen? Will they not come? No, only a remnant; and even that remnant will not call upon the name of the Lord until first God calls them by his grace. This is almost as great a wonder as the love which so graciously invites them. Could even devils behave worse? If they were invited to call upon God, and be saved, would they refuse?

Unhappy business! The way is plain, but "few there be that find it." After all the preaching, and all the invitation, and the illimitable breadth of the promise, yet all that are saved are contained "in the remnant whom the LORD shall call." Is not our text a generous invitation; the setting open of the door, yes, the lifting of the door from off its hinges, that it never might be shut? And yet, "wide is the gate, and broad is the way, that leadeth to destruction, and many there be which go in thereat." There they come, streams of them, hurrying impatiently, rushing down to death and hell—yes, eagerly panting, hurrying, dashing against one another to descend to that awful gulf from which there is no return! No missionaries are wanted, no ministers are needed to plead with men to go to hell. No books of persuasion are wanted to urge them to rush onward to eternal ruin.

They hurry to be lost: they are eager to be destroyed. As when the wild bisons of the prairie hasten onward in their madness, until they come to a great gulf, and then rush down headlong, a cataract of life leaping to death, so is it with the sons of men! They choose their own delusions, and covet their own damnations, and that without end. This is all that sovereign mercy rescues after all—a remnant, and that remnant only because the arm of the Lord is revealed, and a miraculous power exerted upon their wills. This is the misery of it, that the guilty are not willing to be parted from their sins. They will not seek that which alone is their life, their joy, their salvation. They prefer hell to heaven, sin to holiness.

Never spoke the Master a word which observation more clearly proves than when he said, "Ye will not come to me, that ye might have life." You will attend your chapels, but you will not call on the Lord. Jesus cries, "Search the Scriptures; for in them ye think ye have eternal life; and they are they which testify of me. And ye will not come to me, that ye might have life." You will do anything rather than come to Jesus. You stop short of calling upon him. O my dear hearers, do not let it be so with you! Many of you are saved; I beseech you, intercede for those who are not saved. Oh, that the unconverted among you may be moved to pray. Before you leave this place, breathe an earnest prayer to God, saying, "God be merciful to me a sinner. Lord, I need to be saved. Save me. I call upon your name." Join with me in prayer at this moment, I entreat you. Join with me while I put words into your mouths, and speak them on your behalf—"Lord, I am guilty. I deserve your wrath. Lord, I cannot save myself. Lord, I would have a new heart and a right spirit, but what can I do? Lord, I can do nothing; come and work in me to will and to do of your good pleasure.

> *Thou alone hast power, I know,*
> *To save a wretch like me;*
> *To whom, or whither should I go*
> *If I should turn from thee?*

But I now do from my very soul call upon your name. Trembling, yet believing, I cast myself wholly upon you, O Lord. I trust the blood and righteousness of your dear Son; I trust your mercy, and your love, and your power, as they are revealed in him. I dare to lay hold upon this word of yours, that whosoever shall call on the name of the Lord shall be saved. Lord, save me tonight, for Jesus' sake. Amen."

Pleading, Not Contradiction

Delivered on Lord's Day morning, February 9, 1890, at the Metropolitan Tabernacle, Newington. No. 2129.

She said, "Truth, Lord: yet. . . ."—MATTHEW 15:27

Did you notice, in the reading of this narrative of the Syrophoenician woman, the two facts mentioned in the twenty-first and twenty-second verses? "Then Jesus went thence, and departed into the coasts of Tyre and Sidon. And, behold, a woman of Canaan came out of the same coasts." See, Jesus goes toward the coast of Sidon on the land side, and the woman of Canaan comes from the seashore to meet him; and so they come to the same town. May we find that case repeated this morning in this Tabernacle! May our Lord Jesus come into this congregation with power to cast out the devil; and may some one—no, may many—have come to this place on purpose to seek grace at his hands! Blessed shall be this day's meeting! See how the grace of God arranges things. Jesus and the seeker have a common attraction. He comes, and she comes. It would have been of no use, her coming from the seacoast of Tyre and Sidon, if the Lord Jesus had not also come down to the Israelite border of Phoenicia to meet her. His coming makes her coming a success. What a happy circumstance when Christ meets the sinner, and the sinner meets his Lord!

Our Lord Jesus, as the Good Shepherd, came that way, drawn by the instincts of his heart: he was seeking after lost ones, and he seemed to feel that there was one to be found on the borders of Tyre and Sidon, and, therefore, he must go that way to find that one. It does not appear that he preached, or did anything special upon the road; he left the ninety and nine by the sea of Galilee to seek that one lost sheep by the Mediterranean shore. When he had dealt with her, he went back again to his old haunts in Galilee.

Our Lord was drawn toward this woman, but she, also, was driven toward him. What made her seek him? Strange to say, a devil had a hand in it; but not so as to give the devil any of the praise. The truth was, that a gracious God used the devil himself to drive this woman to Jesus: for her daughter was "grievously vexed with a devil," and she could not bear to stay at home and see her child in such misery. Oh, how often does a great sorrow drive men and women to Christ, even as a fierce wind compels the mariner to hasten to the harbor! I have known a domestic affliction, a daughter sore vexed, influence the heart of a mother to seek the Savior; and, doubtless, many a father, broken in spirit by the likelihood of losing a darling child, has turned his face toward the Lord Jesus in his distress. Ah, my Lord! you have many ways of bringing your wandering sheep back; and among the rest you do even send the black dog of sorrow and of sickness after them. This dog comes into the house, and his howlings are so dreadful that the poor lost sheep flies to the Shepherd for shelter. God make it so this morning with any of you who have a great trouble at home! May your boy's sickness work your health! Yes, may your girl's death be the means of the father's spiritual life! Oh, that your soul and Jesus may meet this day! Your Savior drawn by love, and your poor heart driven by anguish—may you thus be brought to a gracious meeting place!

Now, you would suppose that as the two were seeking each other, the happy meeting and the gracious blessing would be very easily brought about; but we have an old proverb, that "the course of true love never does run smooth"; and for certain, the course of true faith is seldom without trials. Here was genuine love in the heart of Christ toward this woman, and genuine faith in her heart toward Christ; but difficulties sprang up which we should never have looked for. It is for the good of us all that they occurred, but we could not have anticipated them. Perhaps there were more difficulties in the way of this woman than of anybody else that ever came to Jesus in the days of his flesh. I never saw the Savior before in such a mood as when he spoke to this woman of great faith. Did you ever read of his speaking such rough words? Did such a hard sentence, at any other time, ever fall from his lips as, "It is not meet to take the children's bread, and to cast it to dogs"? Ah! he knew her well, and he knew that she could stand the trial, and would be greatly benefited by it, and that he would be glorified by her faith throughout all future ages: therefore with good reason he put her through the athletic exercises which train a vigorous faith. Doubtless, for our sakes, he drew her through a test to which he would never have exposed her had she been a weakling unable to sustain it. She was trained and developed by his rebuffs. While his wisdom tried her, his grace sustained her.

Now, see how he began. The Savior was come to the town, wherever it was; but he was not there in public; on the contrary, he sought seclusion. Mark tells us, in his seventh chapter, at the twenty-fourth verse, "From thence he arose, and went into the borders of Tyre and Sidon, and entered into an house, and would have no man know it: but he could not be hid. For a certain woman, whose young daughter had an unclean spirit, heard of him, and came and fell at his feet."

Why is he hiding from her? He does not usually avoid the quest of the seeking soul. "Where is he?" she asks of his disciples. They give her no information; they had their Master's orders to let him remain in hiding. He sought quiet, and needed it, and so they discreetly held their tongues. Yet she found him out, and fell at his feet. Half a hint was dropped; she took up the trail, and followed it until she discovered the house, and sought the Lord in his abode. Here was the beginning of her trial: the Savior was in hiding. "But he could not be hid" from her eager search; she was all ear and eye for him, and nothing can be hid from an anxious mother, eager to bless her child. Disturbed by her, the Blessed One comes into the street, and his disciples surround him. She determines to be heard over their heads, and, therefore, she begins to cry aloud, "Have mercy on me, O Lord, thou son of David." As he walks along, she still cries out with mighty cries and pleadings, till the streets ring with her voice, and he who "would have no man know it" is proclaimer in the market place. Peter does not like it; he prefers quiet worship. John feels a great deal disturbed by the noise: he lost a sentence just now, a very precious sentence, which the Lord was uttering. The woman's noise was very distracting to everybody, and so the disciples came to Jesus, and they said, "Send her away, send her away; do something for her, or tell her to be gone; for she cries after us, we have no peace for her clamor; we cannot hear you speak because of her piteous cries."

Meanwhile, she, perceiving them speaking to Jesus, comes nearer, breaks into the inner circle, falls down before him, worships him, and utters this plaintive prayer—"Lord, help me." There is more power in worship than in noise; she has taken a step in advance. Our Lord has not yet answered her a single word. He has heard what she said, no doubt; but he has not answered a word to her as yet. All that he has done is to say to his disciples, "I am not sent but unto the lost sheep of the house of Israel." That has not prevented her nearer approach, or stopped her prayer; for now she pleads, "Lord, help me." At length the Blessed One does speak to her. Greatly to our surprise, it is a chill rebuff. What a cold word it is! How cutting! I dare not say, how cruel! yet it seemed so. "It is not meet to take the children's bread, and to cast it to dogs."

Now, what will the woman do? She is near the Savior; she has an audience with him, such as it is; she is on her knees before him, and he appears to repulse her! How will she act now? Here is the point about which I am going to speak. She will not be repulsed, she perseveres, she advances nearer, she actually turns the rebuff into a plea. She has come for a blessing, and a blessing she believes that she shall have, and she means to plead for it till she wins it. So she deals with the Savior after a very heroic manner, and in the wisest possible style; from which I want every seeker to learn a lesson at this time, that he, like her, may win with Christ, and hear the Master say to him this morning, "Great is thy faith: be it unto thee even as thou wilt."

Three pieces of advice I gather from this woman's example. First, *agree with the Lord whatever he says.* Say, "Truth, Lord; truth, Lord." Say "Yes" to all his words. Secondly, plead with the Lord—"Truth, Lord: yet," "yet." Think of another truth, and mention it to him as a plea. Say, "Lord, I must maintain my hold; I must plead with you yet." And thirdly, *in any case have faith in the Lord, whatever he says.* However he tries you, still believe in him with unstaggering faith, and know of a surety that he deserves your utmost confidence in his love and power.

I. My first advice to every heart here seeking the Savior is this, *agree with the Lord.*

In the Revised Version we read that she said, "Yea, Lord," or, "Yes, Lord." Whatever Jesus said, she did not contradict him in the least. I like the old translation, "Truth, Lord," for it is very expressive. She did not say, "It is hard, or unkind"; but "It is true. It is true that it is not meet to take the children's bread, and to cast it to dogs. It is true that compared with Israel I am a dog: for me to gain this blessing would be like a dog's feeding on the children's bread. Truth, Lord; truth, Lord." Now, dear friend, if you are dealing with the Lord for life and death, never contradict his word. You will never come unto perfect peace if you are in a contradicting humor; for that is a proud and unacceptable condition of mind. He that reads his Bible to find fault with it will soon discover that the Bible finds fault with him. It may be said of the Book of God as of its Author: "If you walk contrary to me, I will walk contrary to you." Of this Book I may truly say, "With the froward thou wilt shew thyself froward."

Remember, dear friends, that *if the Lord remind you of your unworthiness and your unfitness, he tells you only what is true,* and it will be your wisdom to say, "Truth, Lord." Scripture describes you as having a depraved nature: say, "Truth, Lord." It describes you as going astray like a lost sheep, and the charge is true. It describes you as having a deceitful heart, and just such a heart you have. Therefore say, "Truth, Lord." It represents you as "without strength," and "without hope." Let your answer be, "Truth, Lord." The Bible never gives unrenewed human nature a good word, nor does it deserve it. It exposes our corruptions, and lays bare our falseness, pride, and unbelief. Cavil not at the faithfulness of the Word. Take the lowest place, and own yourself a sinner, lost, ruined, and undone. If the Scripture should seem to degrade you, do not take umbrage thereat, but feel that it deals honestly with you. Never let proud nature contradict the Lord, for this is to increase your sin.

This woman took the very lowest possible place. She not only admitted that she was like one of the little dogs, but she put herself under the table, and under the children's table, rather than under the master's table. She said, "The dogs eat of the crumbs which fall from their masters' table." Most of you have supposed that she referred to the crumbs that fell from the table of the master of the house himself. If you will kindly look at the passage, you will see that it is not so. "Their masters'" refers to several masters: the word is plural, and refers to the children who were the little masters of the little dogs. Thus she humbled herself to be not only as a dog to the Lord, but as a dog to the house of Israel—to the Jews. This was going very far indeed, for a Tyrian woman, of proud Sidonian blood, to admit that the house of Israel were to her as masters, that these disciples who had said just now, "Send her away," stood in the same relation to her as the children of the family stand in toward the little dogs under the table. Great faith is always sister to great humility. It does not matter how low Christ puts her, she sits *there*. "Truth, Lord." I earnestly recommend every hearer of mine to consent unto the Lord's verdict, and never to raise an argument against The Sinner's Friend. When your heart is heavy, when you have a sense of being the greatest of sinners, I pray you remember that you are a greater sinner than you think yourself to be. Though conscience has rated you very low, you may go lower still, and yet be in your right place; for, truth to tell, you are as bad as bad can be; you are worse than your darkest thoughts have ever painted you; you are a wretch most undeserving, and hell-deserving; and apart from sovereign grace, your case is hopeless. If you were now in hell, you would have no cause to complain against the justice of God, for you deserve to be there. I would to God that every hearer here who has not yet found mercy would consent to the severest declarations of God's Word; for they are all true, and true to him. Oh, that you would say, "Yes, Lord: I have not a syllable to say in self-defense"!

And, next, if it should appear to your humbled heart to be a very strange thing for you to think of being saved, do not fight against that belief. If a sense of divine justice should suggest to you—"What! You saved? Then you will be the greatest wonder on earth! What! You saved! Surely God will have gone beyond all former mercy in pardoning such a one as you are. In that case, he would have taken the children's bread and cast it to a dog. You are so unworthy, and so insignificant and useless, that even if you are saved, you will be good for nothing in holy service." How can you expect the blessing? Do not attempt to argue to the contrary. Seek not to magnify yourself; but cry: "Lord, I agree with your valuation of me. I freely admit that if I be forgiven, if I am made a child of God, and if I enter heaven, I shall be the greatest marvel of immeasurable love and boundless grace that ever yet lived in earth or heaven."

We should be the more ready to give our assent and consent to every syllable of the divine Word, since *Jesus knows better than we know ourselves.* The Word of God knows more about us than we can ever discover about ourselves. We are partial to ourselves, and hence we are half blind. Our judgment always fails to hold the balance evenly when our own case is in the weighing. What man is there who is not on good terms with himself? Your faults, of course, are always excusable; and if you do a little good, why, it deserves to be talked of, and to be estimated at the rate of diamonds of the first water. Each one of us is a very superior person; so our proud heart tells us. Our Lord Jesus does not flatter us; he lets us see our case as it is: his searching eye perceives the naked truth of things, and as "the faithful and true witness" he deals with us after the rule of uprightness. O seeking soul, Jesus loves you too well to flatter you. Therefore, I pray you, have such confidence in him that, however much he, by his Word and Spirit, may rebuke, reprove, and even condemn you, you may without hesitation reply, "Truth, Lord! Truth, Lord!"

Nothing can be gained by caviling with the Savior. A beggar stands at your door and asks for charity: he goes the wrong way to work if he begins a discussion with you, and contradicts your statements. If beggars must not be choosers, certainly they must not be controversialists. If a mendicant will dispute, let him dispute; but let him give up begging. If he cavils as to how he shall receive your gift, or how or what you shall give him, he is likely to be sent about his business. A critical sinner disputing with his Savior is a fool in capitals. As for me, my mind is made up that I will quarrel with anybody sooner than with my Savior; and especially I will contend with myself, and pick a desperate quarrel with my own pride, rather than have a shade of difference with my Lord. To contend with one's Benefactor is folly indeed! For the justly condemned to quibble with the Lawgiver in whom is vested the prerogative of pardon would be folly. Instead of that, with heart and soul I cry, "Lord, whatever I find in your Word, whatever I read in holy Scripture, which is the revelation of your mind, I do believe it, I will believe it, I must believe it; and I, therefore, say, 'Truth, Lord!' It is all true, though it condemn me for ever."

Now, mark this: if you find your heart agreeing with what Jesus says, even when he answers you roughly, you may depend upon it, *this is a work of grace;*

for human nature is very upstart, and stands very much upon its silly dignity, and, therefore, it contradicts the Lord, when he deals truthfully with it, and humbles it. Human nature, if you want to see it in its true condition, is that naked thing over yonder, which so proudly aims at covering itself with a dress of its own devising. See, it sews fig leaves together to make itself an apron! What a destitute object! With its withered leaves about it, it seems worse than naked! Yet this wretched human nature proudly rebels against salvation by Christ. It will not hear of imputed righteousness: its own righteousness is dearer far. Woe be to the crown of pride which rivals the Lord Christ! If, my hearer, you are of another mind, and are willing to own yourself a sinner, lost, ruined, and condemned, it is well with you. If you are of this mind, that whatever humbling truth the Spirit of God may teach you in the Word, or teach by the conviction of your conscience, you will at once agree therewith, and confess, "It is even so"; then the Spirit of God has brought you to this humble and truthful and obedient condition, and things are going hopefully with you.

The Lord Jesus has not come to save you proud and arrogant ones, who sit on your thrones and look down contemptuously on others. Sit there as long as you can, until your thrones and yourselves dissolve into perdition: there is no hope for you. But you who lie upon the dunghill, you who feel as worthless as the broken potsherds around you, you who mourn that you cannot rise from that dunghill without divine help—you are the men whom he will lift from your mean estate and set you among princes, even the princes of his people. See the spokes of yonder wheel! They that are highest shall be lowest; they that are lowest shall be raised on high. This is how the Lord turns things upside down, "He hath put down the mighty from their seats, and exalted them of low degree. He hath filled the hungry with good things; and the rich he hath sent empty away." If you find it in your heart to say, "Truth, Lord," to all that the Holy Spirit teaches, then surely that same Spirit is at work upon your soul, leading you to look to Jesus, and causing you to give your heart's consent to the way of salvation through the merit of the Redeemer's blood.

II. And now my second point is this: although you must not cavil with Christ, you may *plead with him*. "Truth, Lord," she says; but she adds, "yet."

Here, then, is my first lesson: *set one truth over against another*. Do not contradict a frowning truth, but bring up a smiling one to meet it. Remember how the Jews were saved out of the hands of their enemies in the days of

Haman and Mordecai. The king issued a decree that, on a certain day, the people might rise up against the Jews, and slay them, and take their possessions as a spoil. Now, according to the laws of the Medes and Persians, this could not be altered: the decree must stand. What then? How was it to be got over? Why, by meeting that ordinance by another. Another decree is issued, that although the people might rise against the Jews, yet the Jews might defend themselves; and if anybody dared to hurt them, they might slay them, and take their property to be a prey. One decree thus counteracted another.

How often we may use the holy art of looking from one doctrine to another! If a truth looks black upon me, I shall not be wise to be always dwelling upon it; but it will be my wisdom to examine the whole range of truth, and see if there be not some other doctrine which will give me hope. David practiced this when he said of himself, "So foolish was I, and ignorant: I was as a beast before thee." And then he most confidently added, "Nevertheless I am continually with thee: thou hast holden me by my right hand." He does not contradict himself; and yet the second utterance removes all the bitterness which the first sentence left upon the palate. The two sentences together set forth the supreme grace of God, who enabled a poor beast-like being to commune with himself. I beg you to learn this holy art of setting one truth side by side with another, that thus you may have a fair view of the whole situation, and may not despair.

For instance, I meet with men who say, "O sir, sin is an awful thing; it condemns me. I feel I can never answer the Lord for my iniquities, nor stand in his holy presence." This is assuredly true; but remember another truth: "The LORD hath laid on him the iniquity of us all"; "He hath made him to be sin for us, who knew no sin"; "There is therefore now no condemnation to them which are in Christ Jesus." Set the truth of the sin-bearing of our Lord over against the guilt and curse of sin due to yourself apart from your great Substitute.

"The Lord has an elect people," cries one, "and this discourages me." Why should it? Do not contradict that truth; believe it as you read it in God's Word: but hear how Jesus puts it: "I thank thee, O Father, Lord of heaven and earth, because thou hast hid these things from the wise and prudent, and hast revealed them unto babes." To you who are weak, simple, and trustful as babes, the doctrine is full of comfort. If the Lord will save a number that no man can number, why should he not save me? It is true it is written, "All that the Father giveth me shall come to me"; but it is also written, "And him that cometh to me I will in no wise cast out." Let the second half of the saying be accepted as well as the first half.

Some are stumbled by the sovereignty of God. He will have mercy on whom he will have mercy. He may justly ask, "Shall I not do as I will with my own?" Beloved, do not dispute the rights of the eternal God. It is the Lord: let him do as seems to him good. Do not quarrel with the King; but come humbly to him, and plead thus: "O Lord, you alone have the right to pardon; but then your Word declares that if we confess our sins, you are faithful and just to forgive us our sins; and you have said, that whosoever believes in the Lord Jesus Christ shall be saved." This pleading will prevail. Kick not at truth, lest you dash your naked foot against iron pricks. Yet, dwell not on one truth till it distracts you, but look at others till they cheer you. Submit to all truth, but plead on your own behalf that which seems to you to look favorably upon you. When you read, "Ye must be born again," do not be angry. It is true that to be born again is a work beyond your power: it is the work of the Holy Spirit; and this need of a work beyond your reach may well distress you. But that third chapter of John, which says, "Ye must be born again," also says, "God so loved the world, that he gave his only begotten Son, that whosoever believeth in him should not perish, but have everlasting life." Thus, it is clear that he that believes in Jesus is born again.

I pray thee, have an eye to all the land of truth, and when you seem to be persecuted in one city of truth, flee to another; for there is a refuge city even for you. Besides, there is a bright side to every truth, if you have but the wit to spy it out. The same key which locks will also unlock: very much depends on the turn of the key, and still more on the turn of your thought.

This brings me to a second remark: *draw comfort even from a hard truth.* Take this advice in preference to that which I have already given. The Authorized translation here is very good, but I must confess that it is not quite so true to the woman's meaning as the Revised Version. She did not say, "Truth, Lord: *yet*," as if she were raising an objection, as I have already put it to you; but she said, "Truth, Lord, *for*." I have gone with the old translation, because it expresses the way in which our mind too generally looks at things. We fancy that we set one truth over against another, whereas all truths are agreed, and cannot be in conflict. Out of the very truth which looks darkest we may gain consolation. She said, "Truth, Lord; *for* the dogs eat of the crumbs which fall from their masters' table." She did not draw comfort from another truth which seemed to neutralize the first; but, as the bee sucks honey from the nettle, so did she gather encouragement from the severe word of the Lord—"It is not meet to take the children's bread, and to cast it to dogs." She said, "That is true, Lord, for even the dogs eat the crumbs that fall from their masters' table." She had not to turn what Christ said upside down; she took it as it stood, and spied out comfort in it. Earnestly would I urge you to learn the art of deriving comfort from every statement of God's Word; not necessarily bringing up a second doctrine, but believing that even the present truth which bears a threatening aspect is yet your friend.

Do I hear you say, "How can I have hope? for salvation is of the Lord"? Why, that is the very reason why you should be filled with hope, and seek salvation of the Lord alone. If it were of yourself, you might despair; but as it is of the Lord, you may have hope.

Do you groan out, "Alas! I can do nothing"? What of that? The Lord can do everything. Since salvation is of the Lord alone, ask him to be its Alpha and Omega to you. Do you groan, "I know I must repent; but I am so unfeeling that I cannot reach the right measure of tenderness"? This is true, and, therefore, the Lord Jesus is exalted on high to give repentance. You will no more repent in your own power than you will go to heaven in your own merit; but the Lord will grant you repentance unto life; for this, also, is a fruit of the Spirit.

Beloved, when I was under a sense of sin, I heard the doctrine of divine sovereignty: "He [will have] mercy on whom he will have mercy"; but that did not frighten me at all; for I felt more hopeful of grace through the sovereign will of God than by any other way. If pardon be not a matter of human deserving, but of divine prerogative, then there is hope for me. Why should not I be forgiven as well as others? If the Lord had only three elect ones, and these were chosen according to his own good pleasure, why should not I be one of them? I laid myself at his feet, and gave up every hope but that which flowed from his mercy. Knowing that he would save a number that no man could number, and that he would save every soul that believed in Jesus, I believed and was saved. It was well for me that salvation did not turn upon merit; for I had no merit whatever. If it remained with sovereign grace, then I, also, could go through that door; for the Lord might as well save me as any other sinner; and inasmuch as I read, "Him that cometh to me I will in no wise cast out," I even came, and he did not cast me out,

Rightly understood, every truth in God's Word leads to Jesus, and no single word drives the seeking sinner back. If you be a fine fellow, full of your own righteousness, every gospel truth looks black on you; but if you be a sinner deserving nothing of God but wrath—if in your heart you do confess that you deserve condemnation, you are the kind of man that Christ came to save, you are the sort of man that God chose from before the foundation of the world, and you may, without any hesitancy, come and put your trust in Jesus, who is the sinner's Savior. Believing in him, you shall receive immediate salvation.

I will not give you further instances and particulars; for time would fail me. I leave you just there with this advice: it is not yours to raise questions, but submissively to say, "Truth, Lord." Then it is your wisdom to set one truth over against another, till you have learned the better plan of finding light in the dark truth itself. God help you to fetch honey from the rock and oil out of the flinty rock, by a simple and unquestioning faith in the Lord Jesus Christ.

III. Thirdly, in any case, whatever Christ says or does not say, *have faith in him.* Look at this woman's faith and try to copy it. It grew in its apprehension of Jesus.

First, he is *the Lord of mercy*: she cried, "Have mercy on me." Have faith enough, dear hearer, to believe that you need mercy. Mercy is not for the meritorious: the claim of the meritorious is for justice, not for mercy. The guilty need and seek mercy; and only they. Believe that God delights in mercy, delights to give grace where it cannot be deserved, delights to forgive where there is no reason for forgiveness but his own goodness. Believe also that the Lord Jesus Christ whom we preach to you is the incarnation of mercy: his very existence is mercy to you, his every word means mercy; his life, his death, his intercession in heaven, all mean mercy, mercy, mercy, nothing but mercy. You need divine mercy, and Jesus is the embodiment of divine mercy—he is the Savior for you. Believe in him, and the mercy of God is yours.

This woman also called him *Son of David*, in which she recognized his manhood and his kingship toward man. Think of Jesus Christ as God over all, blessed for ever, he that made the heaven and the earth, and upholds all things by the word of his power. Know that he became man, veiling his godhead in this poor clay of ours: he hung as a babe upon a woman's breast, he sat as a weary man upon the curb of a well, he died with malefactors on the cross; and all this out of love to man. Can you not trust this Son of David? David was very popular because he went in and out among the people, and proved himself the people's king. Jesus is such. David gathered to him a company of men who were greatly attached to him, because when they came to him they were a broken-down crew; they were in debt, and discontented; all the outcasts from Saul's dominions came around David, and he became a captain to them.

My Lord Jesus Christ is one chosen out of the people, chosen by God on purpose to be a brother to us, a brother born for adversity, a brother who has come to associate with us, despite our meanness and misery. He is the friend of men and women who are ruined by their guilt and sin. "This man receiveth sinners, and eateth with them." Jesus is the willing leader of a people sinful and defiled, whom he raises to justification and holiness, and makes to dwell with himself in glory for ever. Oh, will you not trust such a Savior as this? My Lord did not come into the world to save superior people, who think themselves born saints. I say again, you may sit upon thrones till you and your thrones go down to perdition. But Jesus came to save the lost, the ruined, the guilty, the unworthy. Let such come clustering around him like the bees around the queen bee, for he is ordained on purpose to collect the Lord's chosen ones, as it is written, "Unto him shall the gathering of the people be."

This believing woman might have been cheered by another theme. Our Lord said to his disciples, "I am not sent but unto the lost sheep of the house of Israel." "Ah!" thinks she, "he is a shepherd for lost sheep. Whatever his flock may be, *he is a shepherd*, and he has bowels of compassion for poor lost sheep: surely he is one to whom I may look with confidence." Ah, dear hearer! my Lord Jesus Christ is a shepherd by office and by nature, and if you are a lost sheep this is good tidings for you. There is a holy instinct in him which makes him gather the lambs with his arms, and causes him to search out the lost ones, who were scattered in the cloudy and dark day. Trust him to seek you; yes, come to him now, and leave yourselves with him.

Further than that, this woman had a faith in Christ that he was like *a great householder*. She seems to say, "Those disciples are children who sit at table, and he feeds them on the bread of his love. He makes for them so great a feast, and he gives to them so much food, that if my daughter were healed, it would be a great and blessed thing to me, but to him it would be no more than if a crumb fell under the table, and a dog fed thereon." She does not ask to have a crumb thrown to her, but only to be allowed to pick up a crumb that has fallen from the table. She asks not even for a crumb which the Lord may drop; but for one which the children have let fall: they are generally great crumb-makers. I notice in the Greek, that as the word for "dogs" is "little dogs", so the word rendered "crumbs" is "little crumbs"—small, unconsidered morsels, which fall by accident. Think of this faith. To have the devil cast out of her daughter was the greatest thing she could imagine; and yet she had such a belief in the greatness of the Lord Christ, that she thought it would be no more to him to make her daughter well than for a great housekeeper to let a poor little dog eat a tiny crumb that had been dropped by a child. Is not that splendid faith?

And now, can you exercise such a faith? Can you believe it—you, a condemned, lost sinner—that if God save you it will be the greatest wonder that ever was; and yet that to Jesus, who made himself a sacrifice for sin, it will be no more than if this day your dog or your cat should eat a tiny morsel that one of your children had dropped from the table? Can you think Jesus to be so great, that what is heaven to you will be only a crumb to him? Can you believe that he can save you readily? As for me, I believe my Lord to be such a Savior that I can trust my soul wholly to him, and that without difficulty. And I will tell you something else: if I had all your souls in my body, I would trust them all to Jesus. Yes, and if I had a million sinful souls of my own, I would freely trust the Lord Christ with the whole of them, and I would say, "I am persuaded that he is able to keep that which I have committed to him against that day."

Do not suppose that I speak thus because I am conscious of any goodness of my own. Far from it: my trust is in no degree in myself, or anything I can do or be. If I were good, I could not trust in Jesus. Why should I? I should trust myself. But because I have nothing of my own, I am obliged to live by trust, and I am rejoiced that I may do so. My Lord gives me unlimited credit at the Bank of Faith. I am very deeply in debt to him, and I am resolved to be more indebted still. Sinner as I am, if I were a million times as sinful as I am, and then had a million souls, each one a million times more sinful than my own, I would still trust his atoning blood to cleanse me, and himself to save me. By your agony and bloody sweat, by your cross and passion, by your precious death and burial, by your glorious resurrection and ascension, by your intercession for the guilty at the right hand of God, O Christ, I feel that I can repose in you. May you come to this point, all of you; that Jesus is abundantly able to save.

You have been a thief, have you? The last person that was in our Lord's near company on earth was the dying thief. "Oh!" but you say, "I have been foul in life; I have defiled myself with all manner of evil." But those with whom he associates now were all of them once unclean; for they confess that they have washed their robes, and made them white in his blood. Their robes were once so foul that nothing but his heart's blood could have made them white. Jesus is a great Savior, greater than my tongue can tell. I fail to speak his worth, and I should still fail to do so, even if I could speak heaven in every word, and express infinity in every sentence. Not all the tongues of men or of angels can fully set forth the greatness of the grace of our Redeemer. Trust him! Are you afraid to trust him? Then make a dash for it. Venture to do so.

Venture on him, venture wholly;

Let no other trust intrude.

"Look unto me," says he, "and be ye saved, all the ends of the earth: for I am God, and there is none else." Look! Look now! Look to him alone; and as you look to him with the look of faith, he will look on you with loving acceptance, and say, "Great is thy faith: be it unto thee even as thou wilt." You shall be saved at this very hour; and though you came into this house of prayer grievously vexed with a devil, you shall go out at peace with God, and as restful as an angel. God grant you this boon, for Christ's sake. Amen.

David's Prayer in the Cave

⁓᪥⁓

Intended for reading on Lord's Day, November 13, 1892; delivered on Lord's Day evening, May 18, 1890, at the Metropolitan Tabernacle, Newington. No. 2282.

Maschil of David; A Prayer when he was in the cave. — Title of Psalm 142

"A Prayer when he was in the cave." David did pray when he was in the cave. If he had prayed half as much when he was in the palace as he did when he was in the cave, it would have been better for him. But, alas! when he was king, we find him rising from his bed in the evening, and looking from the roof of the house, and falling into temptation. If he had been looking up to heaven, if his heart bad been in communion with God, he might never have committed that great crime which has so deeply stained his whole character.

"A Prayer when he was in the cave." God will hear prayer on the land, and on the sea, and even under the sea. I remember a brother, when in prayer, making use of that last expression. Somebody who was at the prayer meeting was rather astonished at it, and asked, "How would God hear prayer under the sea?" On inquiry, we found out that the man who uttered those words was a diver, and often went down to the bottom of the sea after wrecks; and he said that he had held communion with God while he had been at work in the depths of the ocean. Our God is not the God of the hills only; but of the valleys also; he is God of both sea and land. He heard Jonah when the disobedient prophet was at the bottom of the mountains, and the earth with her bars seemed to be about him for ever. Wherever you work, you can pray. Wherever you lie sick, you can pray. There is no place to which you can be banished where God is not near, and there is no time of day or night when his throne is inaccessible.

"A Prayer when he was in the cave." The caves have heard the best prayers. Some birds sing best in cages. I have heard that some of God's people shine brightest in the dark. There is many an heir of heaven who never prays so well as when he is driven by necessity to pray. Some shall sing aloud upon their beds of sickness, whose voices were hardly heard when they were well; and some shall sing God's high praises in the fire, who did not praise him as they should before the trial came. In the furnace of affliction the saints are often seen at their best. If any of you tonight are in dark and gloomy positions, if your souls are bowed down within you, may this become a special time for peculiarly prevalent communion and intercession, and may the prayer of the cave be the very best of your prayers!

I shall, tonight, use David's prayer in the cave to represent the prayers of godly men in trouble; but, first, I will talk of it as a picture of the condition of a soul under a deep sense of sin. This psalm of the cave has a great likeness to the character of a man under a sense of sin. I shall then use it to represent the condition of a persecuted believer; and, thirdly, I shall speak of it as revealing the condition of a believer who is being prepared for greater honor and wider service than he has ever attained before.

I. First, let me try and use this psalm as a picture of *the condition of a soul under a deep sense of sin.*

A little while ago, you were out in the open field of the world, sinning with a high hand, plucking the flowers which grow in those poisoned vales, and enjoying their deadly perfume. You were as happy as your sinful heart could be; for you were giddy, and careless, and thoughtless; but it has pleased God to arrest you. You have been apprehended by Christ, and you have been put in prison, and now your feet are fast in the stocks. Tonight, you feel like one who has come out of the bright sunshine and balmy air into a dark, noisome cavern, where you can see but little, where there is no comfort, and where there appears to you to be no hope of escape.

Well, now, according to the psalm before us, which is meant for you as well as for David, your first business should be to appeal unto God. I know your doubts; I know your fears of God; I know how frightened you are at the very mention of his name; but I charge you, if you would come out of your present gloom, go to God at once. See, the psalm begins, "I cried unto the LORD with my voice; with my voice unto the LORD did I make my supplication." Get home, and cry to God with your voice; but if you have no place where you can use your voice, cry to God in silence; but do cry to him. Look God-ward; if you look any other way, all is darkness. Look God-ward; there, and there only, is hope.

"But I have sinned against God," say you. But God is ready to pardon; he has provided a great atonement, through which he can justly forgive the greatest offenses. Look God-ward, and begin to pray. I have known men, who have hardly believed in God, do this; but they have had some faint desire to do so, and they have cried; it has been a poor prayer, and yet God has heard it. I have known some cry to God in very despair. When they hardly believed that there could be any use in it, still it was that or nothing; and they knew that it could not hurt them to pray, and so they took to their knees, and they cried. It is wonderful what poor prayers God will hear, and answer, too; prayers that have no legs to run with, and no hands to grasp with, and very little heart; but still, God has heard them, and he has accepted them. Get to your knees, you who feel yourselves guilty; get to your knees, if your hearts are sighing on account of sin. If the dark gloom of your iniquities is gathering about you, cry to God; and he will hear you.

The next thing to do is, make a full confession. David says, "I poured out my complaint before him; I shewed before him my trouble." The human heart longs to express itself; an unuttered grief will lie and smolder in the soul, till its black smoke puts out the very eyes of the spirit. It is not a bad thing sometimes to speak to some Christian friend about the anguish of your heart. I would not encourage you to put that in the first place; far from it; but still it may be helpful to some. But, anyhow, make a full confession unto the Lord. Tell him how you have sinned; tell him how you have tried to save your-self, and broken down; tell him what a wretch you are, how changeable, how fickle, how proud, how wanton, how your ambition carries you away like an unbridled steed. Tell him all your faults, as far as you can remember them; do not attempt to hide anything from God; you cannot do so, for he knows all; therefore, hesitate not to tell him everything, the darkest secret, the sin you would not wish even to whisper to the evening's gale. Tell it all; tell it all. Confession to God is good for the soul. "Whoso confesseth and forsaketh [his sins] shall have mercy."

I do press upon any of you who are now in the gloomy cave, that you seek a secret and quiet place, and, alone with God, pour out your heart before him. David says, "I shewed before him my trouble." Do not think that the use of pious words can be of any avail; it is not merely words that you have to utter; you have to lay all your trouble before God. As a child tells its mother its griefs, tell the Lord all your griefs, your complaints, your miseries, your fears. Tell them all out, and great relief will come to your spirit. So, first, appeal to God. Secondly, make confession to him.

Thirdly, acknowledge to God that there is no hope for you but in his mercy. Put it as David did, "I looked on my right hand, and beheld, but there was no man that would know me." There is but one hope for you; acknowl-edge that. Perhaps you have been trying to be saved by your good works. They are altogether worthless when you heap them together. Possibly you expect to be saved by your religiousness. Half of it is hypocrisy; and how can a man hope to be saved by his hypocrisy? Do you hope to be saved by your feelings? What are your feelings? As changeable as the weather; a puff of wind will change all your fine feelings into murmuring and rebellion against God. O friend, you cannot keep the law of God! That is the only other way to heaven. The perfect keeping of God's commandments would save you if you had never committed a sin; but, having sinned, even that will not save you now, for future obedience will not wipe out past disobedience. Here, in Christ Jesus, whom God sets forth as a propitiation for sin, is the only hope for you; lay hold on it. In the cave of your doubts and fears, with the clinging damp of your despair about you, chilled and numbed by the dread of the wrath to come, yet venture to make God in Christ your sole confidence, and you shall yet have perfect peace.

Then, further, if you are still in the cave of doubt and sin, venture to plead with God to set you free. You cannot present a better prayer than this one of David in the cave, "Bring my soul out of prison, that I may praise thy name." You are in prison tonight, and you cannot get out of it by yourself. You may get a hold of those bars, and try to shake them to and fro, but they are fast in their sockets; they will not break in your hands. You may meditate, and think, and invent, and excogitate; but you cannot open that great iron gate; but there is a hand that can break gates of brass, and there is a power that can cut in sunder bars of iron. O man in the iron cage, there is a hand that can crumble up your cage, and set you free! You need not be a prisoner; you need not be shut up; you may walk at large through Jesus Christ the Savior. Only trust him, and believingly pray that prayer tonight, "Bring my soul out of prison, that I may praise thy name," and he will set you free. Ah, sinners do praise God's name when they get out of prison! I recollect how, when I was set free, I felt like singing all the time, and I could quite well use the language of Charles Wesley,

Oh, for a thousand tongues to sing
My great Redeemer's praise!

My old friend, Dr. Alexander Fletcher, seems to rise before me now, for I remember hearing him say to the children that, when men came out of prison, they did praise him who had set them free. He said that he was going down the Old Bailey one day, and he saw a boy standing on his head, turning Catherine wheels, dancing hornpipes, and jumping about in all manner of ways, and he said to him, "What are you at? You seem to be tremendously happy"; and the boy replied, "Ah, old gentleman, if you had been locked up six months, and had just got out, you would be happy too!" I have no doubt that is very true. When a soul gets out of a far worse prison than there ever was at Newgate, then he must praise "free grace and dying love" and "ring those charming bells" again, and again, and again, and make his whole life musical with the praise of the emancipating Christ.

Now, that is my advice to you who are in the cave through soul trouble. May God bless it to you! You need not notice anything else that I am going to say tonight. If you are under a sense of sin, heed well what I have been saying; and let other people have the rest of the sermon that belongs more especially to them.

II. I pass on to my second point. This psalm may well help to set forth *the condition of a persecuted believer.*

A persecuted believer! Are there any such nowadays? Ah, dear friends, there are many such! When a man becomes a Christian, he straightway becomes different from the rest of his fellows. When I lived in a street, I was standing one day at the window, meditating what my sermon should be, and I could not find a text, when, all of a sudden, I saw a flight of birds. There was a canary, which had escaped from its cage, and was flying over the slates of the opposite houses, and it was being chased by some twenty sparrows, and other rough birds. Then I thought of that text, "Mine heritage is unto me as a speckled bird, the birds round about are against her." Why, they seemed to say to one another, "Here is a yellow fellow; we have not seen the like of him in London; he has no business here; let us pull off his bright coat, let us kill him, or make him as dark and dull as ourselves." That is just what men of the world try to do with Christians. Here is a godly man who works in a factory, or a Christian girl who is occupied in book-folding, or some other work where there is a large number employed; such persons will have a sad tale to tell of how they have been hunted about, ridiculed, and scoffed at by ungodly companions. Now you are in the cave.

It may be that you are in the condition described here; you hardly know what to do. You are as David was when he wrote the third verse, "When my spirit was overwhelmed within me." The persecutors have so turned against you, and it is so new a thing to you as a young believer, that you are quite perplexed, and hard put to it to know what you should do. They are so severe, they are so ferocious, they are so incessant, and they find out your tender points, and they know how to touch you just on the raw places, that you really do not know what to do. You are like a lamb in the midst of wolves; you know not which way to turn. Well, then, say to the Lord, as David did, "When my spirit was overwhelmed within me, then thou knewest my path." God knows exactly where you are, and what you have to bear. Have confidence that, when you know not what to do, he can and will direct your way if you trust him.

In addition to that, it may be that you are greatly tempted. David said, "They privily laid a snare for me." It is often so with young men in a warehouse, or with a number of clerks in an establishment. They find that a young fellow has become a Christian, and they try to trip him up. If they can, they will get up some scheme by which they can make him appear to have been guilty, even if he has not. Ah, you will want much wisdom! I pray God that you may never yield to temptation; but may hold your ground by divine grace. Young Christian soldiers often have a very rough time of it in the barracks; but I hope that they will prove themselves true soldiers, and not yield an inch to those who would lead them astray.

It will be very painful if, in addition to that, your friends turn against you. David said, "There was no man that would know me." Is it so with you? Are your father and mother against you? Is your wife or your husband against you? Do your brothers and sisters call you "a canting hypocrite"? Do they call you a "Methodist," or a "Presbyterian," not themselves knowing the meaning of the words? Do they point the finger of scorn at you when you get home? And often, when you go from the Lord's table, where you have been so happy, do you have to hear an oath the first thing when you enter the door? I know that it is so with many of you. The Church of Christ in London is like Lot in Sodom. In this particular neighborhood, especially, it is hard for Christian people to live at all. You cannot walk down the streets anywhere without having your ears assailed with filthy language; and your children cannot be permitted to run these streets because of the abominable impurity that is on every hand around about us. Things are growing worse with us, instead of better; they who look for brighter times must be looking with their eyes shut. There is grave occasion for Christians to pray for young people who are converted in such a city as this, for their worst enemies are often those of their own household. "I should not mind so much," says one, "if I had a Christian friend to fly to. I spoke to one the other day, and he did not seem to interest himself in me at all."

I will tell you what hurts a young convert. Here is one just saved; he has really, lovingly, given his heart to Christ, and the principal or manager where he works is a Christian man. He finds himself ridiculed, and he ventures to say a word to this Christian man. He snuffs him out in a moment; he has no sympathy with him. Well, there is another old professing Christian working near at the same bench; and the young convert begins to tell him a little about his trouble, and he is very grumpy and cross. I have noticed some

Christian people who appear to be shut up in themselves, and they do not seem to notice the troubles of beginners in the divine life. Let it not be so among you. My dear brothers and sisters, cultivate great love to those who, having come into the army of Christ, are much beset by adversaries. They are in the cave. Do not disown them; they are trying to do their best; stand side by side with them. Say, "I, too, am a Christian. If you are honoring that young man with your ridicule, let me have my portion of it. If you are pouring contempt upon him, give me a share of it, for I also believe as he believes."

Will you do that? Some of you will, I am sure. Will you stand by the man of God who vindicates the Lord's revealed truth? Some of you will; but there are plenty of fellows who want to keep a whole skin on their body, and if they can sneak away out of any fight for the right, they are glad to get home and go to bed, and there slumber till the battle is over. God help us to have more of the lion in us, and not so much of the cur! God grant us grace to stand by those who are out and out for God, and for his Christ, that we may be remembered with them in the day of his appearing!

It may be that the worst point about you is that you feel very feeble. You say, "I should not mind the persecution if I felt strong; but I am so feeble." Well, now, always distinguish between feeling strong and being strong. The man who feels strong is weak; the man who feels weak is the man who is strong. Paul said, "When I am weak, then am I strong." David prays, "Deliver me from my persecutors; for they are stronger than I." Just hide yourself away in the strength of God; pray much; take God for your refuge and your portion; have faith in him; and you will be stronger than your adversaries. They may seem to pull you over; but you will soon be up again. They may set before you puzzles that you cannot solve; they may come up with their scientific knowledge; and you may be at a discount: but never mind that; the God who has led you into the cave will turn the tables for you one of these days. Only hold on, and hold out, even to the end.

I am rather glad that there should be some trouble in being a Christian, for it has become such a very general thing now to profess to be one. If I am right, it is going to be a very much less common thing than it is now for a man to say, "I am a Christian." There will come times when there will be sharp lines drawn. Some of us will help to draw them if we can, when men shall not wear the Christian garb, and bear the Christian name, and then act like worldlings, and love the amusements and the follies of worldlings. It is time that there was a division in the house of the Lord, and that the "ayes" went into one lobby, and the " noes" into the other lobby. We have too long been mixed together; and I for one say, may the day soon come when every

Christian will have to run the gauntlet! It will be a good thing for genuine believers. It will just blow some of the chaff away from the wheat. We shall have all the purer gold when the fire gets hot, and the crucible is put into it, for then the dross will be separated from the precious metal. Be of good courage, my brother; if you are now in the cave, the Lord will bring you out of it in his own good time!

III. Now, to close, I want to speak a little about *the condition of a believer who is being prepared for greater honor and wider service.*

Is it not a curious thing that, whenever God means to make a man great, he always breaks him in pieces first? There was a man whom the Lord meant to make into a prince. How did he do it? Why, he met him one night, and wrestled with him! You always hear about Jacob's wrestling. Well, I dare say he did; but it was not Jacob who was the principal wrestler: "There wrestled a man with him until the breaking of the day." God touched the hollow of Jacob's thigh, and put it out of joint, before he called him "Israel"; that is, "a prince of God." The wrestling was to take all his strength out of him; and when his strength was gone, then God called him a prince. Now, David was to be king over all Israel. What was the way to Jerusalem for David? What was the way to the throne? Well, it was around by the cave of Adullam. He must go there, and be an outlaw, and an outcast, for that was the way by which he would be made king.

Have none of you ever noticed, in your own lives, that whenever God is going to give you an enlargement, and bring you out to a larger sphere of service, or a higher platform of spiritual life, you always get thrown down? That is his usual way of working; he makes you hungry before he feeds you; he strips you before he robes you; he makes nothing of you before he makes something of you. This was the way with David. He is to be king in Jerusalem; but he must go to the throne by the way of the cave. Now, are any of you here going to heaven, or going to a more heavenly state of sanctification, or going to a greater sphere of usefulness? Do not wonder if you go by the way of the cave. Why is that?

It is, first, because, if God would make you greatly useful, he must teach you how to pray. The man who is a great preacher, and yet cannot pray, will come to a bad end. A woman who cannot pray, and yet is noted for the conducting of Bible classes, has already come to a bad end. If you can be great without prayer, your greatness will be your ruin. If God means to bless you greatly, he will make you pray greatly, as he does David, who says in this part of his preparation for coming to his throne, "I cried unto the LORD with my voice; with my voice unto the LORD did I make my supplication."

Next, the man whom God would greatly honor must always believe in God when he is at his wits' end. "When my spirit was overwhelmed within me, then thou knewest my path." Are you never at your wits' end? Then God has not sent you to do business in great waters; for, if he has, you will reel to and fro and be at your wits' end, in a great storm, before long. Oh, it is easy to trust when you can trust yourself; but when you cannot trust yourself, when you are dead beat, when your spirit sinks below zero in the chill of utter despair, then is the time to trust in God. If that is your case, you have the marks of a man who can lead God's people, and be a comforter of others.

Next, in order to greater usefulness, many a man of God must be taught to stand quite alone. "I looked on my right hand, and beheld, but there was no man that would know me." If you want men to help you, you may make a very decent follower; but if you want no man, and can stand alone, God being your Helper, you shall be helped to be a leader. Oh, it was a grand thing when Luther stepped out from the ranks of Rome. There were many good men around him, who said, "Be quiet, Martin. You will get burned if you do not hold your tongue. Let us keep where we are, in the Church of Rome, even if we have to swallow down great lumps of dirt. We can believe the gospel, and still remain where we are." But Luther knew that he must defy Antichrist, and declare the pure gospel of the blessed God; and he must stand alone for the truth, even if there were as many devils against him as there were tiles on the housetops at Worms. That is the kind of man whom God blesses. I would to God that many a young man here might have the courage to feel, in his particular position, "I can stand alone, if need be. I am glad to have my master and my fellow-workmen with me; but if nobody will go to heaven with me, I will say farewell to them, and go to heaven alone through the grace of God's dear Son."

Once more, the man whom God will bless must be the man who delights in God alone. David says, "I cried unto thee, O LORD: I said, Thou art my refuge and my portion in the land of the living." Oh, to have God as our refuge, and to make God our portion! "You will lose your situation; you will lose your income; you will lose the approbation of your fellowmen." "Ah!" says the believer, "but I shall not lose my portion, for God is my portion. He is situation, and income, and everything to me; and I will hold by him, come what may." If you have learned to "delight thyself also in the LORD; . . . he will give thee the desires of thine heart." Now you are come into such a state that God can use you, and make much of you; but until you do make much of God, he never will make much of you. God deliver us from having our portion in this life, for, if we have, we are not among his people at all!

He whom God would use must be taught sympathy with God's poor people. Hence we get these words of David, in the sixth verse, "I am brought very low." Mr. Greatheart, though he must be strong to kill Giant Grim, and any others of the giants that infest the pilgrim path, must be a man who has gone that road himself, if he is to be a leader of others. If the Lord means to bless you, my brother, and to make you very useful in his church, depend upon it he will try you. Half, perhaps nine-tenths, of the trials of God's ministers are not sent to them on their own account; but they are sent for the good of other people. Many a child of God, who goes very smoothly to heaven, does very little for others; but another of the Lord's children, who has all the ins and outs and changes of an experienced believer's life, has them only that he may be the better fitted to help others; to sit down and weep with them that weep, or to stand up and rejoice with them that rejoice.

So then you, dear brethren, who have got into the cave, and you, my sisters, who have deep spiritual exercises, I want to comfort you by showing you that this is God's way of making something of you. He is digging you out; you are like an old ditch, you cannot hold any more, and God is digging you out to make more room for more grace. That spade will cut sharply, and dig up sod after sod, and throw it on one side. The very thing you would like to keep shall be cast away, and you shall be hollowed out, and dug out, that the word of Elisha may be fulfilled, "Make this valley full of ditches. For thus saith the LORD, Ye shall not see wind, neither shall ye see rain; yet that valley shall be filled with water." You are to be tried, my friend, that God may be glorified in you.

Lastly, if God means to use you, you must get to be full of praise. Listen to what David says, "Bring my soul out of prison, that I may praise thy name: the righteous shall compass me about; for thou shalt deal bountifully with me." May God give to my brothers and sisters here, who are just about being tried for their good, and afflicted for their promotion, grace to begin to praise him! It is the singers that go before; they that can praise best shall be fit to lead others in the work. Do not set me to follow a gloomy leader. Oh no, dear sirs, we cannot work to the tune of "The Dead March in Saul"! Our soldiers would never have won Waterloo if that had been the music for the day of battle. No, no; give us a Jubilate: "Sing unto the Lord who hath triumphed gloriously; praise his great name again and again." Then draw the sword, and strike home. If you are of a cheerful spirit, glad in the Lord, and joyous after all your trials and afflictions, and if you do but rejoice the more because you have been brought so low, then God is making something of you, and he will yet use you to lead his people to greater works of grace.

I have just talked to three kinds of people tonight. May God grant each of you grace to take what belongs to you! But if you see any of the first sort before you go out of the building, any who are in the cave of gloom under a sense of sin, if you want to go to the communion, but feel that you ought to stop and comfort them, mind that you do the latter. Put yourself second. There is a wonderful work to be done in those lobbies, and in those pews, after a service. There are some dear brethren and sisters who are always doing it; they call themselves my "dogs"; for they go and pick up the birds that I have wounded. I wish that they might be able to pick up many tonight. Oh, that some of you might always be on the alert to watch a face, and see whether there is any emotion there! Just paddle your own canoe alongside that little ship, and see whether you cannot get into communication with the poor troubled one on board, and say a word to cheer a sad heart. Always be doing this; for if you are in prison yourself, the way out of it is to help another out. God turned the captivity of Job when he prayed for his friends. When we begin to look after others, and seek to help others, God will bless us. So may it be, for his name's sake! Amen.

Great Prayers

of the Bible

The Mediation of Moses

Intended for reading on Lord's Day, February 3, 1895; delivered on Thursday evening, February 17, 1887, at the Metropolitan Tabernacle, Newington. No. 2398

And the LORD repented of the evil which he thought to do unto his people.
—EXODUS 32:14

I suppose that I need not say that this verse speaks after the manner of men. I do not know after what other manner we can speak. To speak of God after the manner of God, is reserved for God himself; and mortal men could not comprehend such speech. In this sense, the Lord often speaks, not according to literal fact, but according to the appearance of things to us, in order that we may understand so far as the human can comprehend the divine. The Lord's purposes never really change. His eternal will must forever be the same; for he cannot alter, since he would either have to alter for the better or for the worse. He cannot change for the better, for he is infinitely good; it were blasphemous to suppose that he could change for the worse. He who sees all things at once, and perceives at one glance the beginning and the end of all things, has no need to repent. "God is not a man, that he should lie; neither the son of man, that he should repent"; but, in the course of his action, there appears to us to be sometimes a great change, and as we say of the sun that it rises and sets, though it does not actually do so, and we do not deceive when we speak after that fashion, so we say concerning God, in the language of the text, "The LORD repented of the evil which he thought to do unto his people." It appears to us to be so, and it is so in the act of God; yet this statement casts no doubt upon the great and glorious doctrine of the immutability of God.

Speaking after the manner of men, the mediation of Moses wrought this change in the mind of God. God in Moses seemed to overcome God out of Moses. God in the Mediator, the man Christ Jesus, appears to be stronger for mercy than God apart from the Mediator. This saying of our text is very wonderful, and it deserves our most earnest and careful consideration.

Just think, for a minute, of Moses up there in the serene solitude with God. He had left the tents of Israel down below, and he had passed within the mystic circle of fire where none may come but he who is specially invited; and there, alone with God, Moses had a glorious season of fellowship with the Most High. He lent his listening ear to the instructions of the Almighty concerning the priesthood, and the tabernacle, and the altar; and he was enjoying a profound peace of mind, when, on a sudden, he was startled. The whole tone of the speech of the Lord seemed changed, and he said to Moses, "Go, get thee down; for thy people, which thou broughtest out of the land of Egypt, have corrupted themselves." I can hardly imagine what thoughts passed through the great leader's mind. How Moses must have trembled in the presence of God! All the joy that he had experienced seemed suddenly to vanish, leaving behind, however, somewhat of the strength which always comes out of fellowship with God. This Moses now needed if ever he needed it in all his life; for this was the crucial period in the history of Moses, this was his severest trial, when, alone with God on the mountain's brow, he was called to come out of the happy serenity of his spirit, and to hear the voice of an angry God, saying, "Let me alone, that my wrath may wax hot against them, and that I may consume them."

The language of God was very stern; and well it might be after all that he had done for that people. When the song of Miriam had scarcely ceased, when you might almost hear the echoes of that jubilant note, "Sing ye to the LORD, for he hath triumphed gloriously; the horse and his rider hath he thrown into the sea"; you might quickly have heard a very different cry, "Up, make us gods"; and, in the presence of the calf that Aaron made, the same people blasphemously exclaimed, "These be thy gods, O Israel, which brought thee up out of the land of Egypt." Such a prostitution of their tongues to horrid blasphemies against Jehovah, such a turning aside from the truth to the grossest of falsehoods, might well provoke the anger of a righteously jealous God.

It is noteworthy that Moses did not lose himself in this moment of trial. We read at once, "And Moses besought the LORD his God." He was undoubtedly a man of prayer, but he must have been continually in the spirit of prayer, or else I could conceive of him, at that moment, falling on his face, and lying there in silent horror. I could imagine him flying down the mountain in a passionate haste to see what the people had done; but it is delightful to find that he did neither of these two things, but that he began to pray. Oh, friends, if we habitually pray, we shall know how to pray when praying times become more pressing than usual! The man who is to wrestle with the angel must have been familiar with angels beforehand. You cannot go into your chamber, and shut to the door, and begin a mighty intercessory prayer if you have never been to the mercy seat before. No, Moses is "the man of God." You remember that he left us a prayer, in the ninetieth Psalm, bearing this title, "A Prayer of Moses the man of God." There is no man of God if there is no prayer, for prayer makes the man into "the man of God." So, instinctively, though startled and saddened to the last degree, Moses is on his knees, beseeching the Lord his God.

I. This, then, is the scene I have to bring before you, and my first observation shall be, that *nothing can hinder a truly loving spirit from pleading for the objects of its love.*

There were many things that might have hindered Moses from making intercessory prayer; and the first was, the startling greatness of the people's sin. God himself put it to Moses in strong language. He said, "Thy . . . people have corrupted themselves: They have turned aside quickly out of the way which I commanded them: they have made them a molten calf, and have worshipped it, and have sacrificed thereunto, and said, These be thy gods, O Israel, which have brought thee up out of the land of Egypt." This terrible accusation from the mouth of God, spoken as God would speak it, must have impressed Moses greatly with the awful character of Israel's sin; for, farther on, we find Moses saying to God, "Oh, this people have sinned a great sin, and have made them gods of gold." It has happened to you, I suppose, as it has to me, that in the sight of a great sin one has almost hesitated to pray about it. The person sinned so wantonly, under circumstances so peculiarly grievous, transgressed so willfully and so altogether without excuse, that you felt thrust back from the mercy seat and from pleading for such a sinner; but it was not so with Moses. Idolatry is a horrible sin, yet Moses is not kept back from pleading for its forgiveness. It astounds him, his own wrath waxes hot against it; but still, there he is, pleading for the transgressors. What else can he do but pray? And he does that after the best possible fashion. Oh, let us never say, when we see great sin, "I am appalled by it; I cannot pray about it; I am sickened by it; I loathe it." Some time ago, we had revelations of the most infamous criminality in this great city, which we cannot even now quite forget; and I must confess that I sometimes felt as if I could not pray for some of the wretches who sinned so foully; but we must shake off that kind of feeling, and, even in the presence of the most atrocious iniquity, we must still say, "I will pray even for these Jerusalem sinners, that God may deliver them from the bondage of their sin."

A second thing that might have hindered Moses was, not only the sin, but the manifest obstinacy of those who had committed the sin. Moses had it upon the evidence of the heart-searching God that these people were exceedingly perverse. The Lord said, "I have seen this people, and, behold, it is a stiff-necked people." Poor Moses had to learn, in after years, how true that saying was, for though he poured out his very soul for them, and was tender toward them as a nurse with a child, yet they often vexed and wearied his spirit so that he cried to the Lord, "Have I conceived all this people? have I begotten them, that thou shouldest say unto me, Carry them in thy bosom, as a nursing father beareth the sucking child, unto the land which thou swarest unto their fathers?" He was crushed beneath the burden of Israel's perversity; yet, though God himself had told him that they were a stiff-necked people, Moses besought the Lord concerning these obstinate sinners.

Then, thirdly, the prayer of Moses might have been hindered by the greatness of God's wrath; yet he said, "LORD, why doth thy wrath wax hot against thy people?" Shall I pray for the man with whom God is angry? Shall I dare to be an intercessor with God who is righteously wrathful? Why, some of us scarcely pray to the merciful God in this gospel dispensation in which he is so full of goodness and long-suffering; there are some who profess to be God's people who make but very little intercession for the ungodly. I am afraid that, if they had seen God angry, they would have said, "It is of no use to pray for those idolaters. God is not unjustly angry. He knows what he does, and I must leave the matter there." But mighty love dares to cast itself upon its face before even an angry God; it dares to plead with him, and to ask him, "Why doth thy wrath wax hot?" although it knows the reason, and lays no blame upon the justice of God. Yes, love and faith together bring such a holy daring into the hearts of men of God that they can go into the presence of the King of kings, and cast themselves down before him, even when he is in his wrath, and say, "O God, spare your people; have mercy upon those with whom you are justly angry!"

Perhaps it is an even more remarkable thing that Moses was not hindered from praying to God though, to a large degree at the time, and much more afterward, he sympathized with God in his wrath. We have read how Moses' anger waxed hot when he saw the calf, and the dancing; do you not see the holy man dashing the precious tablets upon the earth, regarding them as too sacred for the unholy eyes of idolaters to gaze upon? He saves them, as it were, from the desecration of contact with such a guilty people by breaking them to shivers upon the ground. Can you not see how his eyes flash fire as he tears down their idol, burns it in the fire, grinds it to powder, strews it upon the water, and makes them drink it? He is determined that it shall go into their very bowels; they shall be made to know what kind of a thing it was that they called a god. He was exceedingly wroth [wrathful] with Aaron; and when he bade the sons of Levi draw the sword of vengeance, and slay the audacious rebels, his wrath was fiercely hot, and rightly so. Yet he prays for the guilty people. Oh, never let your indignation against sin prevent your prayers for sinners! If the tempest comes on, and your eyes flash lightnings, and your lips speak thunderbolts, yet let the silver drops of pitying tears fall down your cheek, and pray the Lord that the blessed shower may be acceptable to himself, especially when you plead for Jesus' sake. Nothing can stay the true lover of men's souls from pleading for them; no, not even our burning indignation against infamous iniquity. We see it, and our whole blood boils at the sight; yet we betake ourselves to our knees, and cry, "God be merciful to these great sinners, and pardon them, for Jesus' sake!"

A still greater hindrance to the prayer of Moses than those I have mentioned was, God's request for the pleading to cease. The Lord himself said to the intercessor, "Let me alone." Oh, friends, I fear that you and I would have thought that it was time to leave off praying when the Lord with whom we were pleading said, "Let me alone; let me alone." But I believe that Moses prayed the more earnestly because of that apparent rebuff. Under the cover of that expression, if you look closely into it, you will see that Moses' prayer was really prevailing with God. Even before he had uttered it, while it was only being formed in his soul, Jehovah felt the force of it; else he would not have said, "Let me alone."

And Moses appeared to gain courage from that which might have checked a less earnest suppliant; he seemed to say to himself, "Evidently God feels the force of my strong desires, and I will therefore wrestle with him until I prevail." It was a real rebuff, and was, doubtless, intended by the Lord to be the test of the patience, the perseverance, the confidence, the self-denying love of Moses. Jehovah says, "Let me alone, that my wrath may wax hot against them, and that I may consume them"; but Moses will not let him alone. O you who love the Lord, give him no rest until he saves men; and though he himself should seem to say to you, "Let me alone," do not let him alone, for he wishes you to be importunate with him, like that widow was with the unjust judge! The wicked man granted the poor woman's request because of her continual coming; and God is testing and trying you to see whether you really mean your prayers. He will keep you waiting a while, and even seem to repulse you, that you may, with an undaunted courage, say, "I will approach you; I will break through all obstacles to get to you. Even if it be not according to the law, I will go in unto the King of kings; and if I perish, I perish; but I will pray for sinners even if I perish in the act."

And, dear friends, there is one thing more that might have hindered the prayer of Moses. I want to bring this all out, that you may see how tender-hearted love will pray in spite of every difficulty. Moses prayed against his own personal interests, for Jehovah said to him, "Let me alone, . . . that I may consume them"; and then, looking with a glance of wondrous satisfaction upon his faithful servant, he said, "I will make of thee a great nation." What an opportunity for an ambitious man! Moses may become the founder of a great nation if he will. You know how men and women, in those old days, panted to be the progenitors of innumerable peoples, and looked upon it as the highest honor of mortal men that their seed should fill the earth. Here is the opportunity for Moses to become the father of a nation that God will bless. All the benedictions of Abraham, and Isaac, and Jacob, are to be met in Moses and his seed; but no, he will not have it so. He turns to God, and cries to him still to bless the sinful people. It seems as if he passed over the offer that God made, *sub silentio*, as we say; leaving it in utter silence, he cries, "Spare thy people, and bless thine heritage."

II. Now I introduce to you a second thought, which is, that *nothing can deprive a loving spirit of its arguments in prayer for others.*

It is one thing to be willing to besiege the throne of grace; but it is quite another thing to get the ammunition of prayer. Sometimes you cannot pray, for prayer means the pleading of arguments; and there are times when arguments fail you, when you cannot think of any reason why you should pray. Now there was no argument in these people, nothing that Moses could see in them that he could plead with God for them; so he turned his eyes another way; he looked to God, and pleaded what he saw in him.

His first argument was, that the Lord had made them his people. He said, "Lord, why doth thy wrath wax hot against thy people?" The Lord had said to Moses, "Get thee down; for thy people, . . . have corrupted themselves." "No," says Moses, "they are not my people; they are your people." It was a noble "retort courteous," as it were, upon the ever-blessed One. "In your wrath you call them my people; but you know that they are none of mine; they are yours, you did choose their fathers, and you did enter into covenant with them; and I remind you that they are your chosen ones, the objects of your love and mercy; and, therefore, O Lord, because they are yours, will you not bless them?" Oh, use that argument in your supplications! If you cannot say of a sinner that he is God's chosen, at least you can say that he is God's creature; therefore use that plea, "O God, suffer not your creature to perish!"

Next, Moses pleads that the Lord had done great things for them, for he says, "Why doth thy wrath wax hot against thy people, which thou hast brought forth out of the land of Egypt with great power, and with a mighty hand?" "I never brought Israel out of Egypt," says Moses, "how could I have done it? I did not divide the Red Sea; I did not smite Pharaoh; you have done it, O Lord; you alone have done it; and if you have done all this, will you not finish what you have begun?" This was grand pleading on the part of Moses, and I do not wonder that it prevailed. Now, if you see any sign of grace, any token of God's work in the heart, plead it with the Lord. Say, "You have done so much, O Lord; be pleased to do the rest, and let these people be saved with your everlasting salvation!"

Then Moses goes on to mention, in the next place, that the Lord's name would be compromised if Israel should be destroyed. He says, "Wherefore should the Egyptians speak, and say, For mischief did he bring them out, to slay them in the mountains, and to consume them from the face of the earth?" If God's people are not saved, if Christ does not see of the travail of his soul, the majesty of God and the honor of the Redeemer will be compromised. Shall Christ die to no purpose? Shall the gospel be preached in vain? Shall the Holy Spirit be poured out without avail? Let us plead thus with God, and we shall not be short of arguments that we may urge with him.

Moses goes on to mention that God was in covenant with these people. See how he puts it in the thirteenth verse: "Remember Abraham, Isaac, and Israel, thy servants, to whom thou swarest by thine own self, and saidst unto them, I will multiply your seed as the stars of heaven, and all this land that I have spoken of will I give unto your seed, and they shall inherit it for ever." There is no pleading with God like reminding him of his covenant. Get a hold of a promise of God, and you may pray with great boldness, for the Lord will not run back from his own word; but get a hold of the covenant, and you may plead with the greatest possible confidence. If I may compare a single promise to one great gun in the heavenly siege-train, then the covenant may be likened to a whole park of artillery; with that, you may besiege heaven, and come off a conqueror. Moses pleads thus with the Lord: "How can you destroy these people, even though you are angry with them, and they deserve your wrath? You have promised to Abraham, and Isaac, and Jacob, that their seed shall inherit the land; and if they be destroyed, how can they enter into Canaan, and possess it?" This is grand pleading; but what bravery it was when Moses dared to say to God, "Remember your covenant, and turn from your fierce anger, and repent of your thoughts of evil against your people"! O Lord, teach us also how to plead like this!

Nor was Moses without another argument, the most wonderful of all. If you read in the next chapter, at the sixteenth verse, you will notice how Moses says to God, in effect, "I cannot be parted from these people; with them I will live; with them I will die. If you blot their name out of your book, blot out my name also. 'If thy presence go not with me, carry us not up hence. For wherein shall it be known here that I and thy people have found grace in thy sight? is it not in that thou goest with us?'" See how he puts it: "I and thy people . . . thou goest with us." "No," says Moses, "I will not be favored alone; I will sink or swim with these people." And I do think that this is how the Lord Jesus Christ pleads for his Church when he is interceding with God. "My Father," says he, "I must have my people. My Church is my bride, and I, the Bridegroom, cannot lose my spouse. I will die for her; and if I live, she must live also; and if I rise to glory, she must be brought to glory with me." You see, it is, "I and thy people"; this is the glorious conjunction of Christ with us as it was of Moses with the children of Israel. And, brethren, we never prevail in prayer so much as when we seem to link ourselves with the people for whom we pray. You cannot stand up above them, as though you were their superior, and then pray for them with any success; you must get down by the side of the sinner, and say, "Let us plead with God." Sometimes, when you are preaching to people, or when you are praying for them, you must feel as if you could die for them, if they might be saved; and if they were lost, it would seem as if you, too, had lost everything. Rutherford said that he should have two heavens if but one soul from Anwoth met him at God's right hand; and, doubtless, we shall have the same, and we have sometimes felt as if we had a hell at the thought of any of our hearers' being cast into hell. When you can pray like that, when you put yourself side by side with the soul for which you are pleading, you will succeed. You will be like Elisha, when he stretched himself upon the Shunammite's son, and put his mouth upon the child's mouth, his eyes upon the child's eyes, his hands upon the child's hands, and seemed to identify himself with the dead child. Then was he made the means of quickening to the lad. God help us to plead thus in our prayers for sinners!

There is one other thing, which I think has hardly ever been noticed, and that is the way in which Moses finished his prayer by pleading the sovereign mercy of the Lord. When you are pleading with a man, it is sometimes a very wise thing to stop your own pleading, and let the man himself speak, and then out of his own mouth get your argument. When Moses pleaded with God for the people, he had at first only half an answer; and he turned around to the Lord, and said, "You have favored me, and promised to me great things; now I ask something more of you. 'I beseech thee, shew me thy glory.'" I do not think that was idle curiosity on the part of Moses, but that he meant to use it as the great master plea in prayer. When the Lord said to him, "I will make all my goodness pass before thee," I think I see the tears in the eyes of Moses, and I seem to hear him say, "He cannot smite the people, he cannot destroy them. He is going to make all his goodness pass before me, and I know what that is, infinite love, infinite mercy, mercy that endures for ever." And then, when the Lord said, "I will proclaim the name of the LORD before thee; and will be gracious to whom I will be gracious, and will shew mercy on whom I will shew mercy," how the heart of Moses must have leaped within him as he said, "There it is, that glorious truth of divine sovereignty; the Lord will show mercy on whom he will show mercy. Why, then, he can have mercy on these wicked wretches who have been making a god out of a calf, and bowing before it!" I do delight, sometimes, to fall back upon the sovereignty of God, and say, "Lord, here is a wicked wretch; I cannot see any reason why you should save him! I can see many reasons why you should damn him; but then you do as you will. Oh, magnify your sovereign grace by saving this great sinner! Let men see what a mighty King you are, and how royally you do handle the silver scepter of your pardoning mercy."

That is a grand argument, for it gives God all the glory; it puts him upon the throne; it acknowledges that he is an absolute Sovereign, who is not to be dictated to, or held in with bonds and cords. Shall he not do as he wills with his own? We need often to listen to the sublime truth that thunders out from the throne of God, "I will have mercy on whom I will have mercy, and I will have compassion on whom I will have compassion. So, then, it is not of him that wills, nor of him that runs, but of God that shows mercy." Out of this truth comes the best plea that ever trembles on a pleader's lips: "Great King, eternal, immortal, invisible, have mercy upon us! Divine Sovereign, exercise your gracious dispensing power, and let the guilty rebels live!"

III. Now, in the third place, let me say that *nothing can hinder a pleading spirit of success.* The text says, "The LORD repented of the evil which he thought to do unto his people."

If you and I know how to plead for sinners, there is no reason why we should not succeed, for, first, there is no reason in the character of God. Try, if you can, to get some idea of what God is; and though you tremble before his sovereignty, and adore his holiness, and magnify his justice, remember that he is still, first and foremost, love. "God is love," and that love shines in all the divine attributes. It is undiminished in its glory by any one of them. All the attributes of God are harmonious with each other, and love seems to be the very center of the circle. Let us never be afraid of pleading with God. He will never take it ill on our part that we pray for sinners, for it is so much after his own mind. "As I live, saith the Lord GOD, I have no pleasure in the death of the wicked; but that the wicked turn from his way, and live." The character of God is infinitely gracious; even in its sovereignty, it is grace that reigns; therefore, let us never be afraid of pleading with the Lord. We shall surely succeed, for there is nothing in God's character to hinder us.

And, next, there is nothing in God's thought to hinder the pleader's success. Look at the text: "The LORD repented of the evil which he thought to do unto his people." I will therefore never be hindered in my pleading by any idea of the divine purpose, whatever that purpose may be. There are some who have dreaded what they call "the horrible decrees of God." No divine decree is horrible to me; and it shall never hinder me in pleading with the Lord for the salvation of men. He is God; therefore let him do what seems him good; absolute authority is safe enough in his hands. But even if he had thought to do evil to his people, there is no reason why we should cease from praying; we may yet succeed, for so the text has it, "[Jehovah] repented of the evil which he thought to do unto his people."

I will go yet farther, and say that there is nothing even in God's act to hinder us from pleading with success. If God has begun to smite the sinner, as long as that sinner is in this world, I will still pray for him. Remember, how, when the fiery rain was falling upon Sodom and Gomorrah, and the vile cities of the plain were being covered with its bituminous sleet, Zoar was preserved in answer to the prayers of Lot. Look at David; he was a great sinner, and he had brought upon his people a terrible plague, and the destroying angel stood with his drawn sword stretched out over Jerusalem; but when David saw the angel, he said to the Lord, "Lo, I have sinned, and I have done wickedly: but these sheep, what have they done?" So the Lord was entreated for the land, and the plague was stayed from Israel. Why, if I saw you between the very jaws of hell, so long as they had not actually engulfed you, I would pray for you! God forbid that we should sin against any guilty ones by ceasing to pray for them, however desperate their case! My text seems to me to put this matter with astonishing force and power; the evil which God had thought to do was prevented by the intercession of his servant Moses.

IV. I had many more things to say to you, but I must leave them unsaid, and conclude by reminding you, in only a sentence or two, that *nothing in the mediation of Moses can match our greater intercessor, the Lord Jesus Christ.*

Remember, brethren, that he not only prayed, and willingly offered himself to die for us, but he actually died for us. His name was blotted from the book of the living; he died that we might live. He went not to God saying, "Peradventure, I may make atonement for the guilty"; but he made the atonement; and his pleading for sinners is perpetually prevalent. God is hearing Christ at this moment as he makes intercession for the transgressors, and he is giving him to see of the travail of his soul. This being the case, nothing ought to prevent any sinner from pleading for himself through Jesus Christ. If you think that God means to destroy you, yet go and pray to him, for "The LORD repented of the evil which he thought to do unto his people." Thus may he deal in mercy with you, for his dear Son's sake! Amen.

Achsah's Asking, a Pattern of Prayer

⊸ᘐᗢ⊷

Intended for reading on Lord's Day, June 11, 1893; delivered on Lord's Day evening, June 2, 1889, at the Metropolitan Tabernacle, Newington, No. 2312

> *And Caleb said, He that smiteth Kirjath-sepher, and taketh it, to him will I give Achsah my daughter to wife. And Othniel the son of Kenaz, Caleb's younger brother, took it: and he gave him Achsah his daughter to wife. And it came to pass, when she came to him, that she moved him to ask of her father a field: and she lighted from off her ass; and Caleb said unto her, What wilt thou? And she said unto him, Give me a blessing: for thou hast given me a south land; give me also springs of water. And Caleb gave her the upper springs and the nether springs.* —JUDGES 1:12–15

In domestic life we often meet with pictures of life in the house of God. I am sure that we are allowed to find them there, for our Savior said, "If ye then, being evil, know how to give good gifts unto your children: how much more shall your heavenly Father give the Holy Spirit to them that ask him?" God is a Father, and he likens himself to us as fathers; and we who are believers are God's children; and we are permitted to liken ourselves to our own children; and just as our children would deal with us, and we would deal with them, so may we deal with God, and expect God to deal with us. This little story of a daughter and her father is recorded twice in the Bible. You will find it in the fifteenth chapter of the book of Joshua, as well as in this first chapter of the book of Judges. It is not inserted twice without good reasons. I am going to use it tonight simply in this manner—the way in which this woman went to her father, and the way in which her father treated her, may teach us how to go to our Father who is in heaven, and what to expect if we go to him in that fashion.

I would hold up this good woman, Achsah, before you tonight as a kind of model, or parable. Our parable shall be Achsah, the daughter of Caleb; she shall be the picture of the true successful pleader with our Father in heaven.

I. And the first thing that I ask you to notice is, *her consideration of* *the matter* **before she went to her father. She was newly married, and she had an estate to go with her to her husband.**

She naturally wished that her husband should find in that estate all that was convenient and all that might be profitable, and looking it all over, she saw what was wanted. Before you pray, know what you are needing. That man, who blunders down on his knees, with nothing in his mind, will blunder up again, and get nothing for his pains. When this young woman goes to her father to ask for something, she knows what she is going to ask. She will not open her mouth till first her heart has been filled with knowledge as to what she requires. She saw that the land her father gave her would be of very little use to her husband and herself because it wanted water springs. So she therefore goes to her father with a very definite request, "Give me also springs of water."

My dear friends, do you always, before you pray, think of what you are going to ask? "Oh!" says somebody, "I utter some good words." Does God want your words? Think what you are going to ask before you begin to pray, and then pray like businessmen. This woman does not say to her father, "Father, listen to me," and then utter some pretty little oration about nothing; but she knows what she is going to ask for, and why she is going to ask it. She sees her need, and she prizes the boon she is about to request. Oh, take note, you who are much in prayer, that you rush not to the holy exercise "as the horse rusheth into the battle"; that you venture not out upon the sea of prayer without knowing within a little whereabouts will be your port! I do believe that God will make you think of many more things while you are in prayer; the Spirit will help your infirmities, and suggest to you other petitions; but before a word escapes your lips, I counsel you to do what Achsah did: know what you really need.

This good woman, before she went to her father with her petition, asked her husband's help. When she came to her husband, "she moved him to ask of her father a field." Now, Othniel was a very brave man, and very brave men are generally very bashful men. It is your cowardly man who is often forward and impertinent; but Othniel was so bashful that he did not like asking his uncle Caleb to give him anything more; it looked like grasping. He had received a wife from him, and he had received land from him, and he seemed to say, "No, my good wife, it is all very well for you to put me up to this, but I do not feel like asking for anything more for myself." Still, learn this lesson, good wives: prompt your husbands to pray with you. Brothers, ask your brothers to pray with you. Sisters, be not satisfied to approach the throne of grace alone; but ask your sister to pray with you. It is often a great help in prayer for two of you to agree touching the thing that concerns Christ's kingdom. A cordon of praying souls around the throne of grace will be sure to prevail. God help us to be anxious in prayer to get the help of others! A friend, some time ago, said to me, "My dear pastor, whenever I cannot pray for myself, and there are times when I feel shut up about myself, I always take to praying for you: 'God bless him, at any rate!' and I have not long been praying for you before I begin to feel able to pray for myself." I should like to come in for many of those odd bits of prayer. Whenever any of you get stuck in the mud, do pray for me. It will do you good, and I shall get a blessing. Remember how it is written of Job, "The LORD turned the captivity of Job, when he prayed for his friends." While he prayed for himself, he remained a captive; but when he prayed for those unfriendly friends of his, then the Lord smiled upon him, and loosed his captivity. So it is a good thing in prayer to imitate this woman, Achsah. Know what you want, and then ask others to join with you in prayer. Wife, especially ask your husband; husband, especially ask your wife. I think there is no sweeter praying on earth than the praying of a husband and a wife together when they plead for their children, and when they invoke a blessing upon each other, and upon the work of the Lord.

Next, Achsah bethought herself of this one thing, that she was going to present her request to her father. I suppose that she would not have gone to ask of anybody else; but she said to herself, "Come, Achsah, Caleb is your father. The boon I am going to ask is not of a stranger, who does not know me; but of a father, in whose care I have been ever since I was born." This thought ought to help us in prayer, and it will help us when we remember that we do not go to ask of an enemy, nor to plead with a stranger; but we say, "Our Father which art in heaven." Do you mean it? Do you really believe that God is your Father? Do you feel the spirit of sonship in your heart? If so, this ought to help you to pray with a believing tone. Your Father will give you whatever you need. If there was anything that I wanted, and I should ask it of him, I expect that my dear father, old and feeble as he is, would give it to me if it were within the range of his possibility; and surely, our great and glorious Father, with whom we have lived ever since we were newborn, has favored us so much that we ought to ask very boldly, and with a childlike familiarity, resting assured that our Father will never be vexed with us because we ask these things. Indeed, he knows what things we have need of before we ask him.

So this good woman, Achsah, feeling that it was her father of whom she was going to ask, and seeing that her husband hesitated to join her in her request, made the best of her way to go and pray alone. "Well, well, Othniel, I would have liked you to have gone with me; but as you will not, I am going alone." So she gets upon the ass, which was a familiar way for ladies to ride in that day, and she rides off to her father. The grand old man sees his daughter coming, and by the very look of her he knows that she is coming on business; there is a something about her eye that tells him she is coming with a request. This was not the first time that she had asked something of him. He knew her usual look when she was about to petition him; so he goes to meet her, and she alights from her ass, a token of great and deep respect, just as Rebecca, when she saw Isaac, alighted from the camel. She wished to show how deeply she reverenced that grand man, of whom it was an honor to be a child. Caleb survived Joshua a little while, and still in his old age went out to fight the Canaanites, and conquered Hebron, which the Lord had given him. Achsah pays reverence to her father; but yet she is very hearty in what she is going to say to him.

Now, dear friends, learn again from this good woman how to pray. She went humbly, yet eagerly. If others will not pray with you, go alone; and when you go, go very reverently. It is a shameful thing that there should ever be an irreverent prayer. You are on earth, and God is in heaven; multiply not your words as though you were talking to your equal. Do not speak to God as though you could order him about, and have your will of him, and he were to be a lackey to you. Bow low before the Most High; own yourself unworthy to approach him, speaking in the tone of one who is pleading for that which must be a gift of great charity. So shall you draw near to God aright; but while you are humble, have desire in your eyes, and expectation in your countenance. Pray as one who means to have what he asks. Say not, as one did, "I ask once for what I want; and if I do not get it, I never ask again." That is unchristian. Plead on if you know that what you are asking is right. Be like the importunate widow; come again, and again, and again. Be like the prophet's servant, "Go again seven times." You will at last prevail. This good woman had not to use importunity. The very look of her showed that she wanted something; and, therefore, her father said, "What wilt thou?"

I think that, at the outset of our meditation, we have learned something that ought to help us in prayer. If you put even this into practice, though no more was said, you might go away blessed thereby. God grant us to know our need, to be anxious to have the help of our fellow believers; but to remember that, as we go to our Father, even if nobody will go with us, we may go alone, through Jesus Christ our Lord, and plead our case with our Father in heaven!

II. Now, secondly, in this story of Achsah, kindly notice *her encouragment*. Here we have it: "She lighted from off her ass; and Caleb said unto her, What wilt thou?"

"Oh!" says one, "I could ask anything if my father said to me, 'What wilt thou?'" This is precisely what your great Father does say to you tonight, "What wilt thou?" With all the magnanimity of his great heart, God manifests himself to the praying man or pleading woman, and he says, "'What wilt thou?' What is your petition, and what is your request?"

What do I gather from that question, "What wilt thou"? Why, this. First, you should know what you want. Could some Christians here, if God were to say to each of them, "What wilt thou?" answer him? Do you not think that we get into such an indistinct, indiscriminate kind of a way of praying that we do not quite know what we do really want? If it is so with you, do not expect to be heard till you know what you want. Get a distinct, definite request realized by your mind as a pressing want; get it right before your mind's eye as a thing that you must have. That is a blessed preparation for prayer. Caleb said to his daughter, "What wilt thou?" and Christ says to you tonight, "Dear child of mine, what do you want of me? Blood-bought daughter, what do you want of me?" Will you not, some of you, begin to find a request or two if you have not one ready on the tip of your tongue? I hope that you have many petitions lying in the center of your hearts, and that they will not be long in leaping to your lips.

Next, as you ought to know what you want, you are to ask for it. God's way of giving is through our asking. I suppose that he does that in order that he may give twice over, for a prayer is itself a blessing as well as the answer to prayer. Perhaps it sometimes does us as much good to pray for a blessing as to get the blessing. At any rate, this is God's way, "Ask, and ye shall receive." He puts even his own Son, our blessed Savior, under this rule, for he says even to him, "Ask of me, and I shall give thee the heathen for thine inheritance, and the uttermost parts of the earth for thy possession." It is a rule, then, without exception, that you are to know what you want, and you are to ask for it. Will you do this, dear friend, while the Lord says to you, "What wilt thou?"

And when Caleb said, "What wilt thou?" did he not as good as say to Achsah, "You shall have what you ask for"? Come, now, tonight is a sweet, fair night for praying in; I do not know a night when it is not so; but tonight is a delightful night for prayer. You shall have what you ask. "All things, whatsoever ye shall ask in prayer, believing, ye shall receive." Desires written in your heart by the Holy Ghost will all of them be fulfilled. Come, then, bethink you of these three things: you must know what you want, you must ask for what you want, and you shall have what you want. Your Father says to you, as Caleb said to Achsah, "What wilt thou?"

And, once more, it shall be a pleasure to your Father to hear you ask. There stands Caleb, that good, brave, grand man, and he says to his daughter, "What wilt thou?" He likes to see her open that mouth that is so dear to him; he loves to listen to the music of her voice. The father delights to hear his child tell him what she wants; and it shall be no displeasure to your God to hear you pray tonight. It shall be a joy to him to have your petition spread before him. Many fathers would quite as soon that their children did not tell them all their wants; in fact, the fewer their wants, the better pleased will their parents be; but our Father in heaven feels a pleasure in giving to us all we need, for giving does not impoverish him, and withholding would not enrich him. He as much delights to give as the sun delights to shine. It is the very element of God to be scattering bounties. Come, then, and pray to him; you will thus please him more than you will please yourself. I wish that I could so speak tonight that every child of God here would say, "The preacher is talking to me. He means that I have to pray, and that God will hear me, and bless me." Yes, that is precisely what I do mean. Take my advice, and prove it yourself tonight; and see if it be not so, that God takes delight in your poor, feeble, broken prayer, and grants your humble petition.

Thus we have seen Achsah's consideration before prayer, and her encouragement to pray.

III. Now comes *her prayer* itself.

As soon as she found that she had an audience with her father of the kindliest sort, she said to him, "Give me a blessing." I like that petition; it is a good beginning, "Give me a blessing." I should like to put that prayer into every believing mouth here tonight, "Give me a blessing. Whatever you do not give me, give me a blessing. Whatever else you give me, do not fail to give me a blessing." A father's blessing is an inheritance to a loving child. "Give me a blessing." What is the blessing of God? If he shall say, "You are blessed," you may defy the devil to make you cursed. If the Lord calls you blessed, you are blessed. Though covered with boils, as Job was, you are blessed. Though near to death, like Lazarus, with the dogs licking his sores, you are blessed. If you should be dying, like Stephen, beneath the stones of murderous enemies, if God bless you, what more can you wish for? No, Lord, put me anywhere that you will, as long as I get your blessing. Deny me what you will, only give me your blessing. I am rich in poverty, if you do bless me. So Achsah said to her father, "Give me a blessing." I wish that prayer might be prayed by everybody here tonight. Printers here tonight, pray for once, if you have not prayed before, "Lord, give me a blessing." Soldiers, pray your gracious God to give you a blessing. Young men and maidens, old men and fathers, take this prayer of Achsah's upon your hearts tonight, "Give me a blessing." Why, if the Lord shall hear that prayer from everybody in this place, what a blessed company we shall be; and we shall go our way to be a blessing to this City of London beyond what we have ever been before!

Notice next, in Achsah's prayer, how she mingled gratitude with her petition: "Give me a blessing: for thou hast given me a south land." We like, when people ask anything of us, to hear them say, "You did help me, you know, sir, a month ago"; but if they seem to come to you, and quite forget that you ever helped them, and never thank you, never say a word about it, but come begging again and again, you say to yourself, "Why, I helped that fellow a month ago! He never says a word about that." "Have I not seen you before?" "No, sir, I do not know that you ever have." "Ah!" you say to yourself, "he will get no more out of me. He is not grateful for what he has had." I do believe that ingratitude seals up the springs of blessing. When we do not praise God for what we have received from him, it seems to me but just that he should say, "I am not going to cast my pearls before swine. I shall not give my precious things to those who set no value upon them." When you are praying, take to praising also; you will gather strength thereby. When a man has to take a long jump, you have seen him go back a good distance, and then run forward to get a spring. Go back in grateful praise to God for what he has done for you in days gone by, and then got a spring for your leap for a future blessing, or a present blessing. Mingle gratitude with all your prayers.

There was not only gratitude in this woman's prayer, but she used former gifts as a plea for more: "Thou hast given me a south land; give me also." Oh yes, that is grand argument with God: "You have given me; therefore, give me some more." You cannot always use this argument with men, for if you remind them that they have given you so much, they say, "Well, now, I think that somebody else must have a turn. Could you not go next door?" It is never so with God. There is no argument with him like this, "Lord, you have done this to me; you are always the same; your all-sufficiency is not abated; therefore, do again what you have done!" Make every gift that God gives you a plea for another gift; and when you have that other gift, make it a plea for another gift: he loves you to do this. Every blessing given contains the eggs of other blessings within it. You must take the blessing, and find the hidden eggs, and let them be hatched by your earnestness, and there shall be a whole brood of blessings springing out of a single blessing. See to that.

But this good woman used this plea in a particular way: she said, "Thou hast given me a south land; give me also springs of water." This was as much as to say, "Though you have given me the south land, and I thank you for it, it is no good to me unless I have water for it. It is a very hot bit of ground, this south land; it wants irrigating. My husband and I cannot get a living from it unless you give us springs of water." Do you see the way you are to pray? "Lord, you have given me so much, and it will all be good for nothing if you do not give me more. If you do not finish, it is a pity that you did ever begin; you have given me very many mercies, but if I do not have many more, all your generosity will be lost. You do not begin to build unless you mean to finish; and so I come to you to say, 'You have given me a south land, but it is dry; give me also springs of water to make it of real value to me.'" In this prayer of Achsah's there is a particularity and a speciality: "Give me also springs of water." She knew what she was praying for; and that is the way to pray. When you ask of God, ask distinctly: "Give me springs of water." You may say, "Give me my daily bread." You may cry, "Give me a sense of pardoned sin." You may distinctly ask for anything which God has promised to give; but mind that, like this woman, you are distinct and plain in what you ask of God: "Give me springs of water."

Now, it seems to me, tonight, as if I could pray that prayer, "Give me springs of water." "Lord, you have given me a south land, all this congregation, Sunday after Sunday, all this multitude of people; but, Lord, how can I preach to them if you do not give me springs of water? All my fresh springs are in you. What is the use of the hearers if there be not the power of the Holy Spirit going with the Word to bless them? Give me springs of water." Now, I can suppose a Sunday school teacher here tonight saying, "Lord, I thank you for my interesting class, and for the attention that the scholars pay to what I say to them; but, Lord, what is the good of my children to me unless you give me springs of water? Oh, that, out of myself, out of my very soul, might flow rivers of living water for my dear scholars, and that I might have the power of your Holy Spirit with all my teaching! Give me springs of water." I can imagine a Christian parent here saying, "Lord, I thank you for my wife and my children; I thank you that you have given me servants over whom I have influence; I thank you for all these; but what is the use of my being the head of a family unless you give me springs of grace that, like David, I may bless my household, and see my children grow up in your fear? Give me springs of water." The point of this petition is this, "O Lord, what you have given me is of little good to me unless you give me something more." O dear hearers, if God has given you money, pray that he will give you grace to use it aright; or else, if you hoard it up or spend it, it may, in either case, prove a curse to you! Pray, "Give me springs of water; give me grace to use my wealth aright." Some here have many talents. Riches in the brain are among the best of riches. Be thankful to God for your talents; but cry, "Lord, give me of your grace, that I may use my talents for your glory. Give me springs of water, or else my talents shall be a dry and thirsty land, yielding no fruit unto you. Give me springs of water." You see, the prayer is not merely for water; but for springs of water. "Give me a perpetual, eternal, ever-flowing fountain. Give me grace that shall never fail; but shall flow, and flow on, and flow for ever. Give me a constant supply: 'Give me springs of water.'"

This woman's prayer, then, I have thus tried to commend to you. Oh, that we might all have grace to copy her!

IV. Now, lastly, see *her success*. Upon this I will not detain you more than a minute or two. "Caleb gave her the upper springs and the nether springs."

Observe, her father gave her what she asked. She asked for springs, and he gave her springs. "If a son shall ask bread of any of you that is a father, will he give him a stone? or if he ask a fish, will he for a fish give him a serpent?" God gives us what we ask for when it is wise to do so. Sometimes we make mistakes, and ask for the wrong thing; and then he is kind enough to put the pen through the petition, and write another word into the prayer, and answer the amended prayer rather than the first foolish edition of it. Caleb gave Achsah what she asked.

Next, he gave her in large measure. She asked for springs of water, and he gave her the upper springs and the nether springs. The Lord "is able to do exceeding abundantly above all that we ask or think." Some use that passage in prayer, and misquote it, "above what we can ask or even think." That is not in the Bible, because you can ask or even think anything you like; but it is "above all that we ask or think." Our asking or our thinking falls short; but God's giving never does.

And her father gave her this without a word of upbraiding. He did not say, "Ah, you Achsah, you are always begging of me!" He did not say, "Now that I have given you to your husband, it is too bad of him to let you come and ask for more from me, when I have given you plenty already." There are some gruff old fathers who would speak like that to their daughters, and say, "No, no, no! Come, come, I cannot stand this; you have a good portion already, my girl, and I have others to think of as well as you." No, Caleb gave her the upper and the nether springs, and never said a word by way of blaming her; but I will be bound to say that he smiled on her, as he said, "Take the upper and the nether springs, and may you and your husband enjoy the whole! You have asked, after all, only what my heart delights to give you." Now, may the Lord grant unto us tonight to ask of him in wisdom, and may he not have to upbraid us, but give us all manner of blessings both of the upper and the nether springs, both of heaven and earth, both of eternity and time, and give them freely, and not say even a single word by way of upbraiding us!

I have done with this last point when I have asked a plain question or two. Why is it that, tonight, some of you dear friends have a very parched-up inheritance? The grass will not grow, and the corn will not grow; nothing good seems to grow. You have been plowing, and turning the plot up, and sowing, and weeding, and yet nothing comes of it. You are a believer, and you have an inheritance; but you are not very much given to song, not very cheery, not very happy; and you are sitting here tonight, and singing, to the tune Job,

Lord, what a wretched land is this,

That yields us no supply!

Well, why is that? There is no need for it. Your heavenly Father does not want you to be in that miserable condition. There is something to be had that would lift you out of that state, and change your tone altogether. May every child of God here go to his Father, just like Achsah went to Caleb! Pour out your heart before the Lord, with all the simple ease and naturalness of a trustful, loving child.

Do you say, "Oh, I could not do that"? Then I shall have to ask you this question: "Are we truly the children of God if we never feel toward him any of that holy boldness?" Do you not think that every child must feel a measure of that confidence toward his father? If there is a son in the world who says, "No, I-I-I really could not speak to my father," well, I shall not make any inquiries, but I know that there is something wrong up at his home, there is something not right either with the father or with the boy. Wherever there is a loving home, you never hear the son or daughter say, "You know, I-I-I could not ask my father." I hope that we have none of us got into that condition with regard to our earthly fathers; let none of us be in that condition with regard to our heavenly Father.

My soul, ask what thou wilt,
Thou canst not be too bold;
Since his own blood for thee he spilt
What else can he withhold?

Come, then, while in the pew tonight, before we gather at the communion table, and present your petition with a childlike confidence, and expect it to be heard, and expect tonight to have fellowship with the Father, and with his Son Jesus Christ.

And you, poor sinners, who cannot pray like children, what are you to do? Well, you remember how the Savior said to the Syrophoenician woman, "It is not meet to take the children's bread, and to cast it unto the dogs." But she answered, "Yes, Lord: yet the dogs under the table eat of the children's crumbs." You come in for the crumbs tonight; for if a man is satisfied to eat crumbs with the dogs, God will not be satisfied till he makes him eat bread with the children. If you will take the lowest place, God will give you a higher place before long. Come to Jesus, and trust in him henceforth and for ever. Amen.

The Prayer of Jabez

∼◈∼

Delivered at the Metropolitan Tabernacle, Newington. No. 994.

"Oh that thou wouldest bless me indeed!"—1 CHRONICLES 4:10

We know very little about Jabez, except that he was more honorable than his brethren, and that he was called Jabez because his mother bore him with sorrow. It will sometimes happen that where there is the most sorrow in the antecedents, there will be the most pleasure in the sequel. As the furious storm gives place to the clear sunshine, so the night of weeping precedes the morning of joy. Sorrow is the harbinger; gladness is the prince it ushers in. Cowper says,

The path of sorrow, and that path alone,
Leads to the place where sorrow is unknown.

To a great extent we find that we must sow in tears before we can reap in joy. Many of our works for Christ have cost us tears. Difficulties and disappointments have wrung our soul with anguish. Yet those projects that have cost us more than ordinary sorrow, have often turned out to be the most honorable of our undertakings. While our grief called the offspring of desire "Benoni," the son of my sorrow, our faith has been afterward able to give it a name of delight, "Benjamin," the son of my right hand. You may expect a blessing in serving God if you are enabled to persevere under many discouragements. The ship is often long coming home, because detained on the way by excess of cargo. Expect her freight to be the better when she reaches the port. More honorable than his brethren was the child whom his mother bore with sorrow. As for this Jabez, whose aim was so well pointed, his fame so far sounded, his name so lastingly embalmed—he was a man of prayer. The honor he enjoyed would not have been worth having if it had not been vigorously contested and equitably won. His devotion was the key to his promotion. Those are the best honors that come from God, the award of grace with the acknowledgment of service. When Jacob was surnamed Israel, he received his princedom after a memorable night of prayer. Surely it was far more honorable to him than if it had been bestowed upon him as a flattering distinction by some earthly emperor. The best honor is that which a man gains in communion with the Most High. Jabez, we are told, was more honorable than his brethren, and his prayer is forthwith recorded, as if to intimate that he was also more prayerful than his brethren. We are told of what petitions his prayer consisted. All through it was very significant and instructive. We have time to take only one clause of it—indeed, that one clause may be said to comprehend the rest: "Oh that thou wouldest bless me indeed!" I commend it as a prayer for yourselves, dear brethren and sisters; one which will be available at all seasons; a prayer to begin Christian life with, a prayer to end it with, a prayer which would never be unseasonable in your joys or in your sorrows.

Oh that thou, the God of Israel, the covenant God, would bless me indeed! The very pith of the prayer seems to lie in that word, "indeed." There are many varieties of blessing. Some are blessings only in name: they gratify our wishes for a moment, but permanently disappoint our expectations. They charm the eye, but pall on the taste. Others are mere temporary blessings: they perish with the using. Though for a while they regale the senses, they cannot satisfy the higher cravings of the soul. But, "Oh that thou wouldest bless me indeed!" I wot [know] whom God blesses shall be blessed. The thing good in itself is bestowed with the goodwill of the giver, and shall be productive of so much good fortune to the recipient that it may well be esteemed as a blessing "indeed," for there is nothing comparable to it. Let the grace of God prompt it, let the choice of God appoint it, let the bounty of God confer it, and then the endowment shall be something godlike indeed; something worthy of the lips that pronounce the benediction, and verily to be craved by every one who seeks honor that is substantial and enduring. "Oh that thou wouldest bless me indeed!" Think it over, and you will see that there is a depth of meaning in the expression.

We may set this in contrast with human blessings: "Oh that thou wouldest bless me indeed!" It is very delightful to be blessed by our parents, and those venerable friends whose benedictions come from their hearts, and are backed up by their prayers. Many a poor man has had no other legacy to leave his children except his blessing, but the blessing of an honest, holy, Christian father is a rich treasure to his son. One might well feel it were a thing to be deplored through life if he had lost a parent's blessing. We like to have it. The blessing of our spiritual parents is consolatory. Though we believe in no priest-craft, we like to live in the affections of those who were the means of bringing us to Christ, and from whose lips we were instructed in the things of God. And how very precious is the blessing of the poor! I do not wonder that Job treasured that up as a sweet thing. "When the ear heard me, then it blessed me." If you have relieved the widow and the fatherless, and their thanks are returned to you in benediction, it is no mean reward. But, dear friends, after all—all that parents, relatives, saints, and grateful persons can do in the way of blessing, falls very far short of what we desire to have. O Lord, we would have the blessings of our fellow creatures, the blessings that come from their hearts; but, "Oh that *thou* wouldest bless me indeed!" for you can bless with authority. Their blessings may be but words, but yours are effectual. They may often wish what they cannot do, and desire to give what they have not at their own disposal, but your will is omnipotent. You did create the world with but a word. Oh, that such omnipotence would now bespeak me your blessing! Other blessings may bring us some tiny cheer, but in your favor is life. Other blessings are mere tittles in comparison with your blessing; for your blessing is the title "to an inheritance incorruptible" and unfading, to "a kingdom which cannot be moved."

Well therefore might David pray in another place, "With thy blessing let the house of thy servant be blessed for ever." Perhaps in this place, Jabez may have put the blessing of God in contrast with the blessings of men. Men will bless you when you do well for yourself. They will praise the man who is successful in business. Nothing succeeds like success. Nothing has so much the approval of the general public as a man's prosperity. Alas! they do not weigh men's actions in the balances of the sanctuary, but in quite other scales. You will find those about you who will commend you if you are prosperous; or like Job's comforters, condemn you if you suffer adversity. Perhaps there may be some feature about their blessings that may please you, because you feel you deserve them. They commend you for your patriotism: you have been a patriot. They commend you for your generosity: you know you have been self-sacrificing. Well, but after all, what is there in the verdict of man? At a trial, the verdict of the policeman who stands in the court, or of the spectators who sit in the courthouse, amounts to just nothing. The man who is being tried feels that the only thing that is of importance at all will be the verdict of the jury, and the sentence of the judge. So it will little avail us whatever we may do, how others commend or censure. Their blessings are not of any great value. But, "Oh that thou wouldest bless me," that you would say, "Well done, good and faithful servant." Commend the feeble service that through your grace my heart has rendered. That will be to bless me indeed.

Men are sometimes blessed in a very fulsome sense by flattery. There are always those who, like the fox in the fable, hope to gain the cheese by praising the crow. They never saw such plumage, and no voice could be so sweet as yours. The whole of their mind is set, not on you, but on what they are to gain by you. The race of flatterers is never extinct, though the flattered usually flatter themselves it is so. They may conceive that men flatter others, but all is so palpable and transparent when heaped upon themselves, that they accept it with a great deal of self-complacency, as being perhaps a little exaggerated, but, after all, exceedingly near the truth. We are not very apt to take a large discount off the praises that others offer us; yet, were we wise, we should press to our bosom those who censure us; and we should always keep at arm's length those who praise us, for those who censure us to our face cannot possibly be making a market of us; but with regard to those who extol us, rising early, and using loud sentences of praise, we may suspect, and we shall very seldom be unjust in the suspicion, that there is some other motive in the praise which they render to us than that which appears on the surface.

Young man, are you placed in a position where God honors you? Beware of flatterers. Or have you come into a large estate? Have you abundance? There are always flies where there is honey. Beware of flattery. Young woman, are you fair to look upon? There will be those about you that will have their designs, perhaps their evil designs, in lauding your beauty. Beware of flatterers. Turn aside from all these who have honey on their tongue, because of the poison of asps that is under it. Bethink you of Solomon's caution, "meddle not with him that flattereth with his lips." Cry to God, "Deliver me from all this vain adulation, which nauseates my soul." So shall you pray to him the more fervently, "Oh that thou wouldest bless me indeed!" Let me have your benediction, which never says more than it means; which never gives less than it promises. If you take then the prayer of Jabez as being put in contrast with the benedictions which come from men, you see much force in it.

But we may put it in another light, and compare the blessing Jabez craved with those blessings that are temporal and transient. There are many bounties given to us mercifully by God for which we are bound to be very grateful; but we must not set too much store by them. We may accept them with gratitude, but we must not make them our idols. When we have them, we have great need to cry, "'Oh that thou wouldest bless me indeed,' and make these inferior blessings real blessings"; and if we have them not, we should with greater vehemence cry, "Oh, that we may be rich in faith, and if not blessed with these external favors, may we be blessed spiritually, and then we shall be blessed indeed."

Let us review some of these mercies, and just say a word or two about them.

One of the first cravings of men's hearts is wealth. So universal the desire to gain it, that we might almost say it is a natural instinct. How many have thought if they once possessed it they should be blessed indeed! But there are ten thousand proofs that happiness consists not in the abundance which a man possesses. So many instances are well known to you all, that I need not quote any to show that riches are not a blessing indeed. They are rather apparently than really so. Hence, it has been well said, that when we see how much a man has we envy him; but could we see how little he enjoys we should pity him. Some that have had the most easy circumstances have had the most uneasy minds. Those who have acquired all they could wish, had their wishes been at all sane, have been led by the possession of what they had to be discontented because they had not more.

> But the base miser starves amidst his store,
> Broods on his gold, and griping still at more,
> Sits sadly pining, and believes he's poor.

Nothing is more clear to any one who chooses to observe it, than that riches are not the chief good at whose advent sorrow flies, and in whose presence joy perennial springs. Full often wealth cozens the owner. Dainties are spread on his table, but his appetite fails; minstrels wait his bidding, but his ears are deaf to all the strains of music; holidays he may have as many as he pleases, but for him recreation has lost all its charms: or he is young, fortune has come to him by inheritance, and he makes pleasure his pursuit till sport becomes more irksome than work, and dissipation worse than drudgery. You know how riches make themselves wings; like the bird that roosted on the tree, they fly away. In sickness and despondency these ample means that once seemed to whisper, "Soul, . . . take thine ease," prove themselves to be poor comforters. In death they even tend to make the pang of separation more acute, because there is the more to leave, the more to lose. We may well say, if we have wealth, "My God, put me not off with these husks; let me never make a god of the silver and the gold, the goods and the chattels, the estates and investments, which in your providence you have given me. I beseech you, bless me indeed. As for these worldly possessions, they will be my bane unless I have your grace with them." And if you have not wealth, and perhaps the most of you will never have it, say, "My Father, you have denied me this outward and seeming good, enrich me with your love, give me the gold of your favor, bless me indeed; then allot to others whatever you will, you shall divide my portion, my soul shall wait your daily will; do you bless me indeed, and I shall be content."

Another transient blessing which our poor humanity fondly covets and eagerly pursues is fame. In this respect we would fain be more honorable than our brethren, and outstrip all our competitors. It seems natural to us all to wish to make a name, and gain some note in the circle we move in at any rate, and we wish to make that circle wider if we can. But here, as of riches, it is indisputable that the greatest fame does not bring with it any equal measure of gratification. Men, in seeking after notoriety or honor, have a degree of pleasure in the search which they do not always possess when they have gained their object. Some of the most famous men have also been the most wretched of the human race. If you have honor and fame, accept it; but let this prayer go up, "My God, bless me indeed, for what profit were it, if my name were in a thousand mouths, if you should spew it out of your mouth? What matter, though my name were written on marble, if it were not written in the Lamb's Book of Life? These blessings are only apparently blessings, windy blessings, blessings that mock me. Give me your blessing: then the honor which comes of you will make me blessed indeed." If you happen to have lived in obscurity, and have never entered the lists for honors among your fellowmen, be content to run well your own course and fulfill truly your own vocation. To lack fame is not the most grievous of ills; it is worse to have it like the snow, that whitens the ground in the morning, and disappears in the heat of the day. What matters it to a dead man that men are talking of him? Get the blessing indeed.

There is another temporal blessing which wise men desire, and legitimately may wish for rather than the other two—*the blessing of health.* Can we ever prize it sufficiently? To trifle with such a boon is the madness of folly. The highest eulogiums that can be passed on health would not be extravagant. He that has a healthy body is infinitely more blessed than he who is sickly, whatever his estates may be. Yet if I have health, my bones well set, and my muscles well strung, if I scarcely know an ache or pain, but can rise in the morning, and with elastic step go forth to labor, and cast myself upon my couch at night, and sleep the sleep of the happy, yet, oh, let me not glory in my strength! In a moment it may fail me. A few short weeks may reduce the strong man to a skeleton. Consumption may set in, the cheek may pale with the shadow of death. Let not the strong man glory in his strength. The Lord "delighteth not in the strength of the horse: he taketh not pleasure in the legs of a man." And let us not make our boast concerning these things. Say, you that are in good health, "My God, bless me indeed. Give me the healthy soul. Heal me of my spiritual diseases. Jehovah Rophi, come and purge out the leprosy that is in my heart by nature: make me healthy in the heavenly sense, that I may not be put aside among the unclean, but allowed to stand among the congregation of your saints. Bless my bodily health to me that I may use it rightly, spending the strength I have in your service and to your glory; otherwise, though blessed with health, I may not be blessed indeed."

Some of you, dear friends, do not possess the great treasure of health. Wearisome days and nights are appointed you. Your bones are become an almanac, in which you note the changes of the weather. There is much about you that is fitted to excite pity. But I pray that you may have the blessing indeed, and I know what that is. I can heartily sympathize with a sister that said to me the other day, "I had such nearness to God when I was sick, such full assurance, and such joy in the Lord, and I regret to say I have lost it now; that I could almost wish to be ill again, if thereby I might have a renewal of communion with God." I have oftentimes looked gratefully back to my sick chamber. I am certain that I never did grow in grace one-half so much anywhere as I have upon the bed of pain. It ought not to be so. Our joyous mercies ought to be great fertilizers to our spirit; but not unfrequently our griefs are more salutary than our joys. The pruning knife is best for some of us. Well, after all, whatever you have to suffer, of weakness, of debility, of pain, and anguish, may it be so attended with the divine presence, that this light affliction may work out for you a far more exceeding and eternal weight of glory, and so you may be blessed indeed.

I will dwell upon only one more temporal mercy, which is very precious— I mean *the blessing of home*. I do not think any one can ever prize it too highly, or speak too well of it. What a blessing it is to have the fireside, and the dear relationships that gather around the word "home"—wife, children, father, brother, sister! Why, there are no songs in any language that are more full of music than those dedicated to "Mother." We hear a great deal about the German "Fatherland"—we like the sound. But the word "father" is the whole of it. The "land" is nothing: the "father" is key to the music. There are many of us, I hope, blessed with a great many of these relationships. Do not let us be content to solace our souls with ties that must ere long be sundered. Let us ask that over and above them may come the blessing indeed. I thank you, my God, for my earthly father; but oh, be you my Father, then am I blessed indeed. I thank you, my God, for a mother's love; but comfort you my soul as one whom a mother comforts, then am I blessed indeed. I thank you, Savior, for the marriage bond; but be you the bridegroom of my soul. I thank you for the tie of brotherhood; but be you my brother born for adversity, bone of my bone, and flesh of my flesh.

The home you have given me, I prize, and thank you for it; but I would dwell in the house of the Lord for ever, and be a child that never wanders, wherever my feet may travel, from my Father's house with its many mansions. You can thus be blessed indeed. If not domiciled under the paternal care of the

Almighty, even the blessing of home, with all its sweet familiar comforts, does not reach to the benediction which Jabez desired for himself. But do I speak to any here that are separated from kith and kin? I know some of you have left behind you in the bivouac of life graves where parts of your heart are buried, and that which remains is bleeding with just so many wounds. Ah, well! the Lord bless you indeed! Widow, your maker is your husband. Fatherless one, he has said, "I will not leave you comfortless: I will come to you." Oh, to find all your relationships made up in him, then you will be blessed indeed! I have perhaps taken too long a time in mentioning these temporary blessings, so let me set the text in another light. I trust we have had human blessings and temporary blessings, to fill our hearts with gladness, but not to foul our hearts with worldliness, or to distract our attention from the things that belong to our everlasting welfare.

Let us proceed, thirdly, to speak of *imaginary blessings*. There are such in the world. From them may God deliver us. "Oh that thou wouldest bless me indeed!" Take the Pharisee. He stood in the Lord's house, and he thought he had the Lord's blessing, and it made him very bold, and he spoke with unctuous self-complacency, "God, I thank thee, that I am not as other men are," and so on. He had the blessing, and well indeed he supposed himself to have merited it. He had fasted twice in the week, paid tithes of all that he possessed, even to the odd farthing on the mint and the extra halfpenny on the cumin he had used. He felt he had done everything. His the blessing of a quiet or a quiescent conscience; good, easy man. He was a pattern to the parish. It was a pity everybody did not live as he did; if they had, they would not have wanted any police. Pilate might have dismissed his guards, and Herod his soldiers. He was just one of the most excellent persons that ever breathed. He adored the city of which he was a burgess! Yes; but he was not blessed indeed. This was all his own overweening conceit. He was a mere windbag, nothing more, and the blessing which he fancied had fallen upon him, had never come. The poor publican whom he thought accursed, went to his home justified rather than he. The blessing had not fallen on the man who thought he had it. Oh, let every one of us here feel the sting of this rebuke, and pray: "Great God, save us from imputing to ourselves a righteousness which we do not possess. Save us from wrapping ourselves up in our own rags, and fancying we have put on the wedding garments. Bless me indeed. Let me have the true righteousness. Let me have the true worthiness which you can accept, even that which is of faith in Jesus Christ."

Another form of this imaginary blessing is found in persons who would scorn to be thought self-righteous. Their delusion, however, is near akin. I hear them singing,

I do believe, I will believe,
That Jesus died for me;
And on his cross he shed his blood,
From sin to set me free.

You believe it, you say. Well, but how do you know? Upon what authority do you make so sure? Who told you? "Oh, I believe it." Yes, but we must mind what we believe. Have you any clear evidence of a special interest in the blood of Jesus? Can you give any spiritual reasons for believing that Christ has set you free from sin? I am afraid that some have got a hope that has not got any ground, like an anchor without any fluke—nothing to grasp, nothing to lay hold upon. They say they are saved, and they stick to it. They are, and think it wicked to doubt it; but yet they have no reason to warrant their confidence. When the sons of Kohath carried the ark, and touched it with their hands, they did rightly; but when Uzzah touched it, he died. There are those who are ready to be fully assured; there are others to whom it will be death to talk of it. There is a great difference between presumption and full assurance. Full assurance is reasonable: it is based on solid ground. Presumption takes for granted, and with brazen face pronounces that to be its own to which it has no right whatever. Beware, I pray you, of presuming that you are saved. If with your heart you do trust in Jesus, then are you saved; but if you merely say, "I trust in Jesus," it does not save you. If your heart be renewed, if you shall hate the things that you did once love, and love the things that you did once hate; if you have really repented; if there be a thorough change of mind in you; if you be born again, then have you reason to rejoice: but if there be no vital change, no inward godliness; if there be no love to God, no prayer, no work of the Holy Spirit, then your saying, "I am saved," is but your own assertion, and it may delude, but it will not deliver you. Our prayer ought to be, "'Oh that thou wouldest bless me indeed,' with real faith, with real salvation, with the trust in Jesus that is the essential of faith; not with the conceit that begets credulity. God preserve us from imaginary blessings!" I have met with persons who said, "I believe I am saved because I dreamed it." Or, "Because I had a text of Scripture that applied to my own case." "Such and such a good man said so and so in his sermon." Or, "Because I took to weeping and was excited, and felt as I never felt before." Ah! but nothing will stand the trial but this, "Do you abjure all confidence in everything but the finished work of Jesus, and do you come to Christ to be reconciled in him to God?" If you do not, your dreams, and visions, and fancies, are but dreams, and visions, and fancies, and will not serve your turn when most you need them. Pray the Lord to bless you indeed, for of that sterling verity in all your walk and talk there is a great scarcity.

Too much I am afraid, that even those who are saved—saved for time and eternity—need this caution, and have good cause to pray this prayer that they may learn to make a distinction between some things which they think to be spiritual blessings, and others which are blessings indeed. Let me show you what I mean. Is it certainly a blessing to get an answer to your prayer after your own mind? I always like to qualify my most earnest prayer with, "Not as I will, but as thou wilt." Not only ought I to do it, but I would like to do it, because otherwise I might ask for something which it would be dangerous for me to receive. God might give it me in anger, and I might find little sweetness in the grant, but much soreness in the grief it caused me. You remember how Israel of old asked for flesh, and God gave them quails; but while the meat was yet in their mouths the wrath of God came upon them. Ask for the meat, if you like, but always put in this: "Lord, if this is not a real blessing, do not give it me." "Bless me indeed."

I hardly like to repeat the old story of the good woman whose son was ill—a little child near death's door—and she begged the minister, a Puritan, to pray for its life. He did pray very earnestly, but he put in, "If it be thy will, save this child." The woman said, "I cannot bear that: I must have you pray that the child shall live. Do not put in any ifs or buts." "Woman," said the minister, "it may be you will live to rue the day that ever you wished to set your will up against God's will." Twenty years afterward, she was carried away in a fainting fit from under Tyburn gallows-tree, where that son was put to death as a felon. Although she had lived to see her child grow up to be a man, it would have been infinitely better for her had the child died, and infinitely wiser had she left it to God's will. Do not be quite so sure that what you think an answer to prayer is any proof of divine love. It may leave much room for you to seek unto the Lord, saying, "Oh that thou wouldest blessed me indeed!" So sometimes great exhilaration of spirit, liveliness of heart, even though it be religious joy, may not always be a blessing. We delight in it, and oh, sometimes when we have had gatherings for prayer here, the fire has burned, and our souls have glowed! We felt at the time how we could sing,

> *My willing soul would stay*
> *In such a frame as this,*
> *And sit and sing herself away*
> *To everlasting bliss.*

So far as that was a blessing we are thankful for it; but I should not like to set such seasons up, as if my enjoyments were the main token of God's favor; or as if they were the chief signs of his blessing. Perhaps it would be a greater blessing to me to be broken in spirit, and laid low before the Lord at the present time. When you ask for the highest joy, and pray to be on the mountain with Christ, remember it may be as much a blessing, yes, a blessing indeed, to be brought into the Valley of Humiliation, to be laid very low, and constrained to cry out in anguish, "Lord, save, or I perish!"

If today he deigns to bless us
With a sense of pardon'd sin,
He tomorrow may distress us,
Make us feel the plague within,
All to make us
Sick of self, and fond of him.

These variable experiences of ours may be blessings indeed to us, when, had we been always rejoicing, we might have been like Moab, settled on our lees, and not emptied from vessel to vessel. It fares ill with those who have no changes; they fear not God. Have we not, dear friends, sometimes envied those persons that are always calm and unruffled, and are never perturbed in mind? Well, there are Christians whose evenness of temper deserves to be emulated. And as for that calm repose, that unwavering assurance which comes from the Spirit of God, it is a very delightful attainment; but I am not sure that we ought to envy anybody's lot because it is more tranquil or less exposed to storm and tempest than our own. There is a danger of saying, "Peace, peace," where there is no peace, and there is a calmness which arises from callousness. Dupes there are who deceive their own souls. They have no doubts, they say, but it is because they have little heartsearching. They have no anxieties, because they have not much enterprise or many pursuits to stir them up. Or it may be they have no pains, because they have no life. Better go to heaven, halt and maimed, than go marching on in confidence down to hell. "Oh that thou wouldest bless me indeed!" My God, I will envy no one of his gifts or his graces, much less of his inward mood or his outward circumstances, if only you will "bless me indeed." I would not be comforted unless you comfort me, nor have any peace but Christ my peace, nor any rest but the rest which comes from the sweet savor of the sacrifice of Christ. Christ shall be all in all, and none shall be anything to me save himself. O that we might always feel that we are not to judge as to the manner of the blessing, but must leave it with God to give us what we would have, not the imaginary blessing, the superficial and apparent blessing, but the blessing indeed!

Equally, too, with regard to our work and service, I think our prayer should always be, "Oh that thou wouldest bless me indeed!" It is lamentable to see the work of some good men, though it is not ours to judge them, how very pretentious, but how very unreal it is. It is really shocking to think how some men pretend to build up a church in the course of two or three evenings. They will report, in the corner of the newspapers, that there were forty-three persons convinced of sin, and forty-six justified, and sometimes thirty-eight sanctified; I do not know what besides of wonderful statistics they give as to all that is accomplished. I have observed congregations that have been speedily gathered together, and great additions have been made to the church all of a sudden. And what has become of them? Where are those churches at the present moment? The dreariest deserts in Christendom are those places that were fertilized by the patent manures of certain revivalists. The whole church seemed to have spent its strength in one rush and effort after something, and it ended in nothing at all. They built their wooden house, and piled up the hay, and made a stubble spire that seemed to reach the heavens, and there fell one spark, and all went away in smoke; and he that came to labor next time—the successor of the great builder—had to get the ashes swept away before he could do any good. The prayer of every one that serves God should be, "Oh that thou wouldest bless me indeed!" Plod on, plod on. If I build only one piece of masonry in my life, and nothing more, if it be gold, silver, or precious stones, it is a good deal for a man to do; of such precious stuff as that, to build even one little corner which will not show, is a worthy service. It will not be much talked of, but it will last. There is the point: it will last. "Establish thou the work of our hands upon us; yea, the work of our hands establish thou it." If we are not builders in an established church, it is of little use to try at all. What God establishes will stand, but what men build without his establishment will certainly come to nothing. "Oh that thou wouldest bless me indeed!" Sunday school teacher, be this your prayer. Tract distributer, local preacher, whatever you may be, dear brother or sister, whatever your form of service, do ask the Lord that you may not be one of those plaster builders using sham compo that requires only a certain amount of frost and weather to make it crumble to pieces. Be it yours, if you cannot build a cathedral, to build at least one part of the marvelous temple that God is piling for eternity, which will outlast the stars.

I have one thing more to mention before I bring this sermon to a close. The blessings of God's grace are blessings indeed, which in right earnest we ought to seek after. By these marks shall you know them. Blessings indeed, are such blessings as come from the pierced hand; blessings that come from

Calvary's bloody tree, streaming from the Savior's wounded side—your pardon, your acceptance, your spiritual life: the bread that is meat indeed, the blood that is drink indeed—your oneness to Christ, and all that comes of it—these are blessings indeed. Any blessing that comes as the result of the Spirit's work in your soul is a blessing indeed; though it humble you, though it strip you, though it kill you, it is a blessing indeed. Though the harrow go over and over your soul, and the deep plow cut into your very heart; though you be maimed and wounded, and left for dead, yet if the Spirit of God do it, it is a blessing indeed. If he convinces you of sin, of righteousness, and of judgment, even though you have not hitherto been brought to Christ, it is a blessing indeed. Anything that he does, accept it; do not be dubious of it; but pray that he may continue his blessed operations in your soul. Whatsoever leads you to God is in like manner a blessing indeed. Riches may not do it. There may be a golden wall between you and God. Health will not do it: even the strength and marrow of your bones may keep you at a distance from your God. But anything that draws you nearer to him is a blessing indeed. What though it be a cross that raises you? yet if it raise you to God, it shall be a blessing indeed. Anything that reaches into eternity with a preparation for the world to come, anything that we can carry across the river—the holy joy that is to blossom in those fields beyond the swelling flood, the pure cloudless love of the brotherhood which is to be the atmosphere of truth for ever—anything of this kind that has the eternal broad arrow on it—the immutable mark—is a blessing indeed. And anything which helps me to glorify God is a blessing indeed. If I be sick, and that helps me to praise him, it is a blessing indeed. If I be poor, and I can serve him better in poverty than in wealth, it is a blessing indeed. If I be in contempt, I will rejoice in that day and leap for joy, if it be for Christ's sake—it is a blessing indeed. Yes, my faith shakes off the disguise, snatches the visor from the fair forehead of the blessing, and counts it all joy to all into diverse trials for the sake of Jesus and the recompense of reward that he has promised. Oh, that we may be blessed indeed!

Now, I send you away with these three words: "Search." See whether the blessings are blessings indeed, and be not satisfied unless you know that they are of God, tokens of his grace, and earnests of his saving purpose. "Weigh." That shall be the next word. Whatever you have, weigh it in the scale, and ascertain if it be a blessing indeed, conferring such grace upon you as causes you to abound in love, and to abound in every good word and work. And lastly, "Pray." So pray that this prayer may mingle with all your prayers, that whatsoever God grants or whatever he withholds you may be blessed indeed. Is it a joy time with you? Oh, that Christ may mellow your joy, and prevent the intoxication of earthly blessedness from leading you aside from close walking with him! In the night of sorrow, pray that he will bless you indeed, lest the wormwood also intoxicate you and make you drunk, lest your afflictions should make you think hardly of him. Pray for the blessing, which having, you are rich to all the intents of bliss, or which lacking, you are poor and destitute, though plenty fill your store. "If thy presence go not with me, carry us not up hence." But "Oh that thou wouldest bless me indeed!"

Letter from Mr. Spurgeon, read at the Tabernacle on Lord's Day, June 11: Beloved Friends,—Whom I have in constant and affectionate remembrance, I am obliged again to take up the note of mourning, for I have been all the week suffering, and the most of it confined to my bed. The severe weather has driven me back, and caused a repetition of all my pains. Nevertheless, the Lord's will be done. Let Him have his way with me, for he is Love. I have been wearying to preach again, but it may be my dumb Sabbaths are appointed for my chastisement, and their number is not yet fulfilled. We must work for God while we can, for not one of us knows how soon he may be unable to take a share in the service. At the same time, how unimportant we are! God's work goes on without us. We all need him, but he needs no one of us. Beloved, hitherto I have had much solace in hearing that the Lord's work among you goes on. I pray you make earnest intercession that this may continue. I hope weeknight services will not droop. If you stay away, let it be when I am there, but *not now*. May the Deacons and Elders find themselves at every meeting for worship surrounded by an untiring band of helpers. May abundance of grace rest on you all, especially on the sick, the poor, and the bereaved. Pray for me, I entreat you. Perhaps if *the church* met for prayer I should be speedily restored. I know thousands do pray, but should not the church do so as a church! I fear I must give up all hope of preaching on the 25th; but I trust the Lord will be merciful to me, and send me among you on the first Sabbath of July. Next Sunday there should be a collection for the Association, an object very dear to me. With deep Christian love, Your suffering Pastor,

C. H. Spurgeon.

The Two Guards,
Praying and Watching

Intended for reading on Lord's Day, May 1, 1892; delivered on Thursday evening, July 24, 1890, at the Metropolitan Tabernacle, Newington. No. 2254

Nevertheless we made our prayer unto our God, and set a watch against them day and night, because of them.—NEHEMIAH 4:9

Nehemiah, and the Jews with him, were rebuilding the walls of Jerusalem. Sanballat and others were angry with them, and tried to stop the work. They determined to pounce upon the people on a sudden, and slay them, and so to put an end to what they were doing. Our text tells us what Nehemiah and his companions did in this emergency: "Nevertheless we made our prayer unto our God, and set a watch against them day and night, because of them."

These people had not only to build the wall of Jerusalem, but to watch against their enemies at the same time. Their case is ours. We have to work for Christ. I hope that all of us who love him are trying to do what we can to build up his kingdom; but we need also to watch against deadly foes. If they can destroy us, of course they will also destroy our work. They will do both, if they can. The powers of evil are mad against the people of God. If they can in any way injure or annoy us, you may rest assured that they will do so. They will leave no stone unturned, if it can serve their purpose. No arrows will be left in the quivers of hell while there are godly men and women at whom they can be aimed. Satan and his allies aim at our hearts every poisoned dart they have.

Nehemiah had been warned of the attack that was to be made upon the city. The Jews who lived near these Samaritans had heard their talk of what they meant to do, and they came and told Nehemiah of the plotting of the adversaries. We also have been warned. As our Lord said to Peter, "Simon, Simon, behold, Satan hath desired to have you, that he may sift you as wheat," so has he, in his Word, told us that there is a great and terrible evil power which is seeking our destruction. If Satan can do it, he will not only sift us as wheat, but he will cast us into the fire that we may be destroyed. Brethren, we are not ignorant of his devices. You are not left in a fool's paradise, to dream of security from trial, and to fancy that you are past temptation.

It is well for these people, also, that, being in danger, and being aware of the malice of their enemies, they had a noble leader to incite them to the right course to be pursued. Nehemiah was well qualified for his work. He gave the Jews very shrewd, sensible, and yet spiritual advice, and this was a great help to them in their hour of need. Beloved, we have a better Leader than Nehemiah; we have our Lord Jesus Christ himself, and we have his Holy Spirit, who dwells in us, and shall abide with us. I beg you to listen to his wise and good advice. I think that he will give it to you through our explanation of the text. He will say to you what Nehemiah, in effect, said to these people, "Watch and pray." Although the adversaries of the Jews conspired together, and came to fight against Jerusalem, and to hinder the work of rebuilding the wall, Nehemiah says, "Nevertheless we made our prayer unto our God, and set a watch against them day and night, because of them."

In the text, I see two guards; first, prayer: "We made our prayer unto our God." The second guard is watchfulness: "[We] set a watch." When I have spoken on these two subjects, I shall take as my third topic, the two guards together. "We made our prayer . . ., and set a watch." We must have them both, if we would defeat the enemy.

First, then, dear friends, think of *the first guard*: "We made our prayer unto our God."

Speaking of this prayer, I would hold it up as a pattern for our prayers in a like condition. It was *a prayer that meant business*. Sometimes when we pray, I am afraid that we are not transacting business at the throne of grace; but Nehemiah was as practical in his prayer as he was in the setting of the watch. Some brethren get up in our prayer meetings, and say some very good things; but what they really ask for, I am sure I do not know. I have heard prayers of which I have said, when they were over, "Well, if God answers that prayer, I have not the least idea of what he will give us." It was a very beautiful prayer, and there was a great deal of explanation of doctrine and experience in it; but I do not think that God wants to have doctrine or experience explained to him. The fault about the prayer was, that there was not anything asked for in it. I like, when brethren are praying, that they should be as businesslike as a good carpenter at his work. It is of no use to have a hammer with an ivory handle, unless you aim it at the nail you mean to drive in up to the head; and if that is your object, an ordinary hammer will do as well as a fine one, perhaps better. Now, the prayers of Nehemiah and the Jews were petitions for divine protection. They knew what they wanted, and they asked for it definitely. Oh, for more definiteness in prayer! I am afraid that our prayers are often clouds, and we get mists for answers. Nehemiah's prayer meant business. I wish we could always pray in this way. When I pray, I like to go to God just as I go to a banker when I have a check to be cashed. I walk in, put the check down on the counter, the clerk gives me my money, I take it up, and go about my business. I do not know that I ever stopped in a bank five minutes to talk with the clerks; when I have received my change, I go away and attend to other matters. That is how I like to pray; but there is a way of praying that seems like lounging near the mercy seat, as though one had no particular reason for being found there. Let it not be so with you, brethren. Plead the promise, believe it, receive the blessing God is ready to give, and go about your business. The prayer of Nehemiah and his companions meant business.

In the next place, it was *a prayer that overcame difficulties*. The text begins with a long word, "nevertheless." If we pull it to pieces, we get three words, never the less; when certain things happen, we will pray never the less; on the contrary, we will cry to our God all the more. Sanballat sneered; but we prayed never the less, but all the more because of his sneers. Tobiah uttered a cutting jest; but we prayed never the less, but all the more because of his mocking taunt. If men make a jest of your religion, pray none the less. If they even become cruel and violent to you, pray none the less; never the less, not a word less, not a syllable less, not a desire less, and not any faith less. What are your difficulties, dear friend, in coming to the mercy seat? What hindrance lies in your way? Let nothing obstruct your approach to the throne of grace. Turn all stumbling-stones into stepping-stones; and come, with holy boldness, and say, notwithstanding all opposition, never the less "we made our prayer unto our God." Nehemiah's prayer meant business, and overcame difficulties.

Notice, next, that it was *a prayer that came before anything else*. It does not say that Nehemiah set a watch, and then prayed; but "nevertheless we made our prayer unto our God, and set a watch." Prayer must always be the forehorse of the team. Do whatever else is wise, but not until you have prayed. Send for the physician if you are sick; but first pray. Take the medicine if you have a belief that it will do you good; but first pray. Go and talk to the man who has slandered you, if you think you ought to do so; but first pray. "Well, I am going to do so and so," says one, "and I shall pray for a blessing on it afterward." Do not begin it until you have prayed. Begin, continue, and end everything with prayer; but especially begin with prayer. Some people would never begin what they are going to do if they prayed about it first, for they could not ask God's blessing upon it. Is there anybody here who is going out of this Tabernacle to a place where he should not go? Will he pray first? He knows that he cannot ask a blessing on it; and, therefore, he ought not to go there. Go nowhere where you cannot go after prayer. This would often be a good guide in your choice of where you should go. Nehemiah first prayed, and then set a watch.

Once more, it was *a prayer that was continued.* If I read the passage aright, "we made our prayer unto our God, and set a watch against them day and night," it means that, as long as they watched, they prayed. They did not pray their prayer, and then leave off, and go away, as naughty boys do when they give runaway knocks at a door. Having begun to pray, they continued praying. So long as there were any enemies about, the prayer and the watching were never parted. They continued still to cry to him who keeps Israel as long as they set the watchman of the night to warn them of the foe.

When shall we leave off praying, brothers and sisters? Well, they say that we shall do so when we get to heaven. I am not clear about that. I do not believe in the intercession of saints for us; but I remember that it is written in the book of Revelation, that the souls under the altar cried, "How long, O Lord?" Those souls were waiting for the resurrection, waiting for the coming of Christ, waiting for the triumph of his kingdom; and I cannot conceive of their waiting there without often crying, "O Lord, how long? Remember your Son, glorify his name, accomplish the number of your elect." But certainly, as long as we are here, we must pray. One lady professed that she had long been perfect, said that her mind was in such complete conformity with the mind of God, that she need not pray any longer. Poor creature! What did she know about the matter? She needed to begin at the first letter of the alphabet of salvation, and pray, "God be merciful to me a sinner!" When people imagine they need not to pray, the Lord have mercy upon them!

Long as they live let Christians pray,
For only while they pray they live.

The prayer which Nehemiah offered was, next, *a prayer that was homemade.* There may be some of you who like prayers made for you; and it may be that, if all the congregation are to join in the supplication, and every voice is to speak, the prayer must be prepared even as the hymn is; but ready-made prayers always seem to me very much like ready-made clothes; they are meant to fit everybody, and it is very seldom that they fit anybody. For real business at the mercy seat, give me a homemade prayer, a prayer that comes out of the deeps of my heart, not because I invented it, but because God the Holy Spirit put it there, and gave it such a living force that I could not help letting it come out. Though your words are broken, and your sentences are disconnected; if your desires are earnest, if they are like coals of juniper, burning with a vehement flame, God will not mind how they find expression. If you have no words, perhaps you will pray better without them. There are prayers that break the backs of words; they are too heavy for any human language to carry.

This prayer, then, whatever it may have been as to its words, was one the pleaders made: "We made our prayer unto our God."

It is very important to notice, that it was *a prayer that went to the home of prayer*: "We made our prayer unto our God." You have heard of the man who prayed at Boston, "the hub of the universe," and the report in the paper the next morning was, that "The Rev. Dr. So-and-so prayed the finest prayer that was ever addressed to a Boston audience." I am afraid that there are some prayers of that sort, that are prayed to the congregation. That is not the kind of prayer that God loves. Forget that there is anybody present, forget that a human ear is listening to your accents; and let it be said of your prayer, "Nevertheless we made our prayer unto our God."

It is a very commonplace remark to make, that prayer must go to God if it is to be of any avail; but it is very necessary to make it. When prayer does not go to God, what is the good of it? When you come out of your closet, and feel that you have only gone through a form, how much are you benefited? Make your prayers unto your God. Speak in his ear, knowing that he is there; and come away knowing that he has replied to you, that he has lifted up the light of his countenance upon you. That is the kind of prayer we need for our protection against our enemies both day and night.

Only once more upon this first point. I gather from the words before me that it was *a prayer saturated with faith*. We made our prayer unto—God? No, "unto our God." They had taken Jehovah to be their God, and they prayed to him as their God. They had a full assurance that, though he was the God of the whole earth, yet he was specially their God; and so they made their prayer unto the God who had given himself to them, and to whom they belonged by covenant relationship. "We made our prayer unto our God." Those two little words carry a vast weight of meaning. The door of prayer seems to turn on those two golden hinges—"our God." If you and I are to be delivered from the evil that is in the world, if we are to be kept building the church of God, we must have for our first guard, mighty, believing prayer, such as Nehemiah and his Jewish friends presented unto the Lord.

I have now to speak to you about *the second guard*: **"[We] set a watch against them day and night, because of them."**

This setting of the watch was *a work appointed*. "[We] set a watch." Nehemiah did not say, "Now, some of you fellows, go and watch," leaving the post of watchmen open to any who chose to take it; but they "set a watch." A certain number of men had to go on duty at a certain point, at a certain hour, and remain for a certain length of time, and be on guard against the adversary. "[We] set a watch." Brethren, if we are to watch over ourselves, and we must do so, we must do it with a definite purpose. We must not say, "I must try to be watchful." No, no; you must be watchful; and your watchfulness must be as distinct and definite an act as your prayer. "[We] set a watch." Some of you have seen the guards changed in the barracks; there is a special time for each company to mount guard. When you go to bed at night, pray the Lord to guard you during the darkness. In the morning, set a watch when you go to your business. Set a watch when you go to the dinner table; set a watch when you return home. Oh, how soon we may be betrayed into evil unless we set a watch!

It was *a work carefully done*; for Nehemiah says, "[We] set a watch against them day and night, because of them." Those three last words would be better rendered, "over against them"; that is, wherever there was an enemy, there he set a watch. They are likely to come up this way. Very well, set a watch there. Perhaps they may shift about, and come up this way. Very well, set a watch there. Possibly they may come climbing over the wall in front here. "Well, set a watch there." "[We] set a watch [over] against them." One brother has a very hot temper. Brother, set a watch there. Another is very morose at home, critical, picking holes in other people's coats. Brother, set a watch there. One friend has a tendency to pride, another to unbelief. Set a watch wherever the foe is likely to come. "We made our prayer unto our God, and set a watch [over] against them."

It was *a work continued*; Nehemiah says, "[We] set a watch against them day and night." What! Is there to be someone sitting up all night? Of course there is. If Sanballat had told them when he meant to attack them, they might have gone to sleep at other times; but as he did not give them that information, they had to set a watch "day and night." The devil will not give you notice when he is going to tempt you; he likes to take men by surprise; therefore, set a watch day and night.

It was *a work quickened by knowledge*. They knew that Sanballat would come if he could, so they set a watch. The more you know of the plague of your own heart, the more you will set a watch against it. The more you know of the temptations that are in the world through lust, the more you should set a watch. The older you are, the more you should watch. "Oh!" says an aged friend, "you should not say that; it is the young people who go wrong." Is it? In the Old Testament or in the New, have you an instance of a young believer who went astray? The Bible tells us of many old men who were tripped up by Satan when they were not watching; so you have need to set a watch even when your hair turns gray, for you will not be out of gunshot of the devil until you have passed through the gate of pearl into the golden streets of the New Jerusalem.

You and I, dear friends, have need to set a watch against the enemies of our holy faith. Some people ask me, "Why do you talk so much about the 'downgrade'? Let men believe what they like. Go on with your work for God, and pray to him to set them right." I believe in praying and setting a watch. We have to guard with jealous care "the faith which was once delivered unto the saints." When you find, as you do find now, professing Christians and professing Christian ministers denying every article of the faith, or putting another meaning upon all the words than they must have been understood to bear, and preaching lies in the name of the Most High, it is time that somebody set a watch against them. A night watchman's place is not an easy berth; but I am willing to take that post for my blessed Master's sake. Those professed servants of Christ who enter into an unholy alliance with men who deny the faith will have to answer for it at the last great day. As for us, brethren, when our Lord comes, let him find us watching as well as praying.

But, dear friends, to come home to ourselves, we must set a watch against our own personal adversaries. I hope that, in one sense, you have no personal enemies; that you owe nobody a grudge; but that you live in peace and love toward all mankind. But there are Christian people here, who will go to homes where everybody in the house is against them. Many a godly woman goes from the sanctuary to a drunken husband; many children, converted to God, see anything but what they like to see in their homes. What are they to do in such circumstances? Set a watch. Dear woman, how do you know but that you shall be the means of saving your unconverted husband? If so, you must set a watch; do not give him a bit of your mind; you will not convert him that way. And you, dear children, who have come to Christ, and joined the church, mind that you are dutiful and obedient, for otherwise you will destroy all hope of bringing your parents to the Savior. Set a watch. "Oh!" say you, "if I do a little wrong, they magnify it." I know they do; therefore, set a watch; be more careful. Set a watch over your temper, set a watch over your tongue, set a watch over your actions. Be patient, be gentle, be loving. May the Spirit of God work all this in you!

But there is another set of enemies much more dreadful than these adversaries that are without us, the foes within, the evil tendencies of our corrupt nature, against which we must always set a watch. Perhaps you say, "How can

I do this?" Well, first, know what they are. People who are beginning the Christian life should seek to know where their weak points are. I should not wonder, dear friend, if your weak point lies where you think that you are strong. Where you think, "Oh, I shall never go wrong there!"—that is the very place where you are likely to fall. Set a watch wherever any weakness has appeared; and if you have, in the past of your Christian life, grieved the Holy Spirit by anything wrong, set a double watch there. Where you have tripped once, you may trip again; for you are the same man. Set a watch, also, dear friend, whenever you feel quite secure. Whenever you feel certain that you cannot be tempted in a particular direction, that proves that you are already as proud as Lucifer. Set a watch, set a watch, set a watch. Avoid every occasion of sin. If any course of conduct would lead you into sin, do not go in that direction. I heard a man say, as an excuse for drinking, "You see, if ever I take a glass of beer, I seem to lose myself, and I must have two or three more." Well, then, if that is the case with you, do not take a glass of beer. "But," says one, "if I get into company, I forget myself." Then, do not go into company. Better go to heaven as a hermit, than go to hell with a multitude. Pluck out your right eye, and cut off your right hand, sooner than that these should cause you to fall into sin. Do not go where you are likely to be tempted. "Well," says one, "but my business calls me into the midst of temptation." I grant you that your business may compel you to go where there are ungodly men; for how could some live at all, if they had not to come into contact with the ungodly?—they would have to go out of the world. Well, then, if that is your case, put on the whole armor of God, and do not go without being prepared to fight the good fight of faith. Set a watch, set a watch, set a watch.

Watch against the beginnings of sin. Remember, Satan never begins where he leaves off; he begins with a little sin, and he goes on to a greater one. When he first tempts men, he does not aim at all he hopes to accomplish; but he tries to draw them aside by little and little, and he works up by degrees to the greater sin he wants them to commit. I do not believe that, at the present time, a Christian man can be too precise. We serve a very precise God: "the LORD thy God is a jealous God." Keep out of many things in which professing Christians now indulge themselves. The question is, whether they are Christians at all. If we must not judge them, at any rate, let us judge for ourselves, and settle it, once for all, that we dare not go where they go; indeed, we have no wish to do so.

Watch for what God has to say to you. In your reading of the Bible, if the Holy Spirit applies a text of Scripture to you with special force, regard it as a hint from your heavenly Father that there is a lesson in it for you. I am often surprised at the way in which the morning text will often instruct me through the whole day. Persons who come to hear the Word of God preached, often find that, within two or three days, there is a reason why the preacher delivered that particular sermon, and a reason why they were led to hear it.

Whenever you see a professing Christian going astray from the way of holiness, do not talk about it, and so increase the mischief. "It is an ill bird that fouls its own nest." Instead of speaking of another's fall, set a watch for yourself, and say, "That is where he slipped, and that is where I may stumble if the grace of God does not keep me." Remember our Savior's words to the three disciples with him in Gethsemane, "Watch and pray, that ye enter not into temptation."

I finish by putting *the two guards together*. "We made our prayer unto our God, and set a watch against them."

Dear friends, neither of these two guards is sufficient alone. *Prayer alone* will not avail. To pray and not to watch, is presumption. You pretend to trust in God, and yet you are throwing yourself into danger, as the devil would have had Christ do, when he tempted him to cast himself down from the pinnacle of the temple. If you pray to be kept, then be watchful.

Prayer without watchfulness is hypocrisy. A man prays to be kept from sin, and then goes into temptation; his prayer is evidently a mere piece of mockery, for he does not carry it out in his practice.

Sometimes, however, ignorance may lead to prayer without watching. There are other things which ought not to be omitted. Let me tell you a simple story. There was a little schoolgirl who did not often know her lessons, and there was another girl, who sat near her, who always said her lessons correctly. Her companion said to her, "Jane, how is it that you always know your lessons?" Jane replied, "I pray to God to help me, and so I know them." The next day, the other little girl stood up, but she did not know her lesson; and afterward she said to her friend, "I prayed to God about my lesson, but I did not know it any better than I did yesterday." Jane said, "But did you try to learn the lesson?" "No," she said; "I prayed about it, and I thought that was sufficient." Of course she did not know her lesson without learning it. In the same manner, you must watch as well as pray. There must be the daily guard put upon tongue, and thought, and hand; or else prayer will be in vain.

I have known some people run great risks, and yet say that they have prayed to the Lord to preserve them. I have heard, dozens of times, these words, "I made it a matter of prayer," and I have been ready to grow angry with the man who has uttered them. He has done a wrong thing, and he has excused himself because he says that he made it a matter of prayer. A young man married an ungodly young woman, and yet he said that he made it a matter of prayer! A Christian woman married an ungodly man, and when someone blamed her for disobeying the Word of God, she said that she made it a matter of prayer! If you had really sought divine guidance, you would not have dared to do what the Scriptures expressly forbid to a child of God. Prayer without watching is not sufficient to preserve us from evil.

On the other hand, dear friends, *watching without praying* is equally futile. To say, "I will keep myself right," and never pray to God to keep you, is self-confidence, which must lead to evil. If you try to watch, and do not pray, you will go to sleep, and there will be an end to your watching. It is only by praying and watching that you will be able to keep on your guard. Besides, watching grows wearisome without prayer, and we soon give it up, unless we have a sweet interlude of prayer to give us rest, and to help us to continue watching.

I will not keep you longer when I have said this: *put the two together*, watch and pray, or, as my text has it, pray and watch. One will help the other. Prayer will call out the watchman, prayer will incite him to keep his eyes open, prayer will be the food to sustain him during the night, prayer will be the fire to warn him. On the other hand, watching will help prayer, for watching proves prayer to be true. Watching excites prayer, for every enemy we see will move us to pray more earnestly. Moreover, watching is prayer. If there be true watching, the watching itself is prayer. The two blend the one into the other. Beloved friends, I send you away with my text ringing in your ears, "We made our prayer unto our God, and set a watch against them day and night."

But I have not been speaking to all who are here. Some of you do not pray, some of you cannot set a watch. The message for you is, "Ye must be born again." You cannot attempt Christian duties till first you have the Christian life; and the only way to get the Christian life is to have faith in the Lord Jesus Christ. Come to the fountain which he has filled with his precious blood; wash there, and be clean; and then, quickened by his Spirit, set a watch. I am looking to see some people brought to Christ at this service, for although I have been preaching to God's people, if they will watch for you, and pray for you, there will come a blessing to you through their watching and praying. The Lord grant that it may come to many of you! "Seek ye the LORD while he may be found, call ye upon him while he is near." May many seek and find the Lord tonight; and may many call upon him in truth! "Whosoever shall call upon the name of the Lord shall be saved." God grant that it may be so to everybody here, for Jesus' sake! Amen.

The Young Man's Prayer

Delivered on Sunday morning, June 7, 1863, at the Metropolitan Tabernacle, Newington. No. 513.

O satisfy us early with thy mercy; that we may rejoice and be glad all our days.—PSALM 90:14

Israel had suffered a long night of affliction. Dense was the darkness while they abode in Egypt, and cheerless was the glimmering twilight of that wilderness which was covered with their graves. Amid a thousand miracles of mercy, what must have been the sorrows of a camp in which every halt was marked with many burials, until the whole track was a long cemetery? I suppose that the mortality in the camp of Israel was never less than fifty each day—if not three times that number—so that they learned experimentally that verse of the psalm, "For we are consumed by thine anger, and by thy wrath are we troubled." Theirs was the weary march of men who wander about in search of tombs; they traveled toward a land which they could never reach, weary with a work the result of which only their children should receive. You may easily understand how these troubled ones longed for the time when the true day of Israel should dawn, when the black midnight of Egypt and the dark twilight of the wilderness should both give way to the rising sun of the settled rest in Canaan. Most fitly was the prayer offered by Moses—the representative man of all that host—"O satisfy us early with thy mercy"; hasten the time when we shall come to our promised rest; bring on speedily the season when we shall sit under our own vines and our own fig trees, "that we may rejoice and be glad all our days."

This prayer falls from the lips of yonder brother, whose rough pathway for many a mile has descended into the Valley of Deathshade. Loss after loss has he experienced, till as in Job's case, the messengers of evil have trodden upon one another's heels. His griefs are new every morning, and his trials fresh every evening. Friends forsake him and prove to be deceitful brooks; God breaks him with a tempest; he finds no pause in the ceaseless shower of his troubles. Nevertheless, his hope is not extinguished, and his constant faith lays hold upon the promise, that "weeping may endure for a night, but joy cometh in the morning." He understands that God will not always chide, neither does he keep his anger for ever; therefore he watches for deliverance even as they that watch for the morning, and his most appropriate cry is, "'O satisfy us early with thy mercy'; lift up the light of your countenance upon us, show your marvelous lovingkindness in this present hour of need. O my God, make haste to help me, be a very present help in time of trouble; fly to my relief lest I perish from the land; awake, for my rescue, that I may rejoice and be glad all my days."

See yonder sick bed! Tread lightly, lest perchance you disturb the brief slumbers of that daughter of affliction. She has tossed to and fro days and nights without number, counting her minutes by her pains, and numbering her hours with the paroxysms of her agony. From that couch of suffering where many diseases have conspired to torment the frail body of this child of woe, where the soul itself has grown weary of life, and longs for the wings of a dove, I think this prayer may well arise, "O satisfy us early with thy mercy." When will the eternal day break upon my long night? When will the shadows flee away? Sweet Sun of Glory! when will you rise with healing beneath your wings? I shall be satisfied when I wake up in your likeness, O Lord; hasten that joyful hour; give me a speedy deliverance from my bed of weakness, that I may rejoice and be glad throughout eternal days.

I think the prayer would be equally appropriate from many a distressed conscience where conviction of sin has rolled heavily over the soul, till the bones are sore vexed, and the spirit is overwhelmed. That poor heart indulges the hope that Jesus Christ will one day comfort it, and become its salvation: it has a humble hope that these woundings will not last for ever but shall all be healed by mercy's hand; that he who looses the bands of Orion will one day deliver the prisoner out of his captivity. Oh! conscience-stricken sinner, you may on your knees now cry out—"O satisfy me early with your mercy; keep me not always in this house of bondage; let me not plunge for ever in this slough of despondency; set my feet upon a rock; wash me from my iniquities; clothe me with garments of salvation, and put the new song into my mouth, that I may rejoice and be glad all my days."

Still it appears to me that without straining so much as one word even in the slightest degree, I may take my text this morning as the prayer of a young heart, expressing its desire for present salvation. To you, young men and maidens, shall I address myself, and may the good Spirit cause you in the days of your youth to remember your Creator, while the evil days come not, nor the years draw near, when you shall say, We have no pleasure in them. I hope the angel of the Lord has said unto me, "Run, speak to that young man," and that like the good housewife in the Proverbs, I shall have a portion also for the maidens!

I shall use the text in two ways; first, as the ground of my address to the young; and then, secondly, as a model for your address to God.

I. *We will make our text the groundwork of a solemn pleading with young men and women to give their hearts to Christ this day.*

The voice of wisdom reminds you in this our text, that you are not pure in God's sight, but *need his mercy*. Early as it is with you, you must come before God on the same footing as those who seek him at the eleventh hour. Here is nothing said about merit, nothing concerning the natural innocence of youth, and the beauty of the juvenile character. You are not thus flattered and deceived; but holy Scripture guides you aright, by dictating to you an evangelical prayer, such as God will deign to accept—"O satisfy us early *with thy mercy*." Young man, though as yet no outward crimes have stained your character, yet your salvation must be the work of reigning grace, and that for several reasons. *Your nature is at the present moment full of sin, and saturated with iniquity,* and hence you are the object of God's most righteous anger. How can he meet an heir of wrath on terms of justice? His holiness cannot endure you. What if you be made an heir of glory, will not this be grace and grace alone? If ever you are made meet to be a partaker with the saints in light, this must surely be love's own work. Inasmuch as your nature, altogether apart from your actions, deserves God's reprobation, it is mercy which spares you, and if the Lord be pleased to renew your heart, it will be to the praise of the glory of his grace. Be not proud, repel not this certain truth, that you are an alien, a stranger, an enemy, born in sin and shaped in iniquity, by nature an heir of wrath, even as others; yield to its force, and seek that mercy which is as really needed by you as by the hoary-headed villain who rots into his grace, festering with debauchery and lust.

> *True you are young, but there's a stone*
> *Within the youngest breast;*
> *Or half the crimes which you have done*
> *Would rob you of your rest.*

Besides, your conscience reminds you that your outward lives *have not been what they should be.* How soon did we begin to sin! While we were yet little children we went astray from the womb, speaking lies. How rebellious we were! How we chose our own will and way, and would by no means submit ourselves to our parents! How in our riper youth we thought it sport to scatter firebrands, and carry the hot coals of sin in our bosom. We played with the serpent, charmed with its azure scales, but forgetful of its poisoned fangs. Far be it from us to boast with the Pharisee—"God, I thank thee, that I am not as other men are"; but rather let the youngest pray with the publican—"God be merciful to me a sinner." A little child, but seven years of age, cried when under conviction of sin—"Can the Lord have mercy upon such a great sinner as I am, who have lived seven years without fearing and loving him?" Ah! my friends, if this babe could thus lament, what should be the repentance of those who are fifteen, or sixteen, or seventeen, or eighteen, or twenty, or who have passed the year of manhood? What shall you say, since you have lived so long, wasting your precious days—more priceless than pearls, neglecting those golden years, despising divine things, and continuing in rebellion against God? Lord, you know that young though we be, we have multitudes of sins to confess, and, therefore, it is mercy, mercy, mercy, which we crave at your hands. Remember, beloved young friends, that if you be saved in the morning of life, *you will be wonderful instances of preventing mercy.* It is great mercy which blots out sin, but who shall say that it is not equally great mercy which prevents it? To bring home yonder sheep which has long gone astray, with its wool all torn, its flesh bleeding, and its bones broken, manifests the tender care of the good Shepherd; but, oh! to reclaim the lamb at the commencement of its strayings, to put it into the fold, and to keep it there, and nurture it. What a million mercies are here compressed into one!

The young saint may sweetly sing—
I still had wander'd but for thee;
Lord, 'twas thine own all-powerful word,
Sin's fetters broke, and set me free,
Henceforth to own thee as my Lord.

To pluck the seared brand from out of the fire when it is black and scorched with the flame, there are depths of mercy here; but are there not heights of love, when the young wood is planted in the courts of the Lord and made to flourish as a cedar? However soon we are saved, the glory of perfection has departed from us, but how happy is he who tarries but a few years in a state of nature; as if the fall and the rising again walked hand in hand. No soul is without spot or wrinkle, but some stains are spots the young believer is happily delivered from. Habits of vice and continuance in crime he has not known. He never knew the drunkard's raging thirst; the black oath of the shearer never cancered his mouth. This younger son has not been long in the far country; he comes back before he has long fed the swine. He has been black in the sight of God, but in the eyes of men and in the open vision of onlookers, the young believer seems as if he had never gone astray. Here is great mercy, mercy for which heaven is to be praised for ever and ever. This, I think, I may call *distinguishing* grace, with an emphasis. All election distinguishes, and all grace is discriminating; but that grace which adopts the young child so early, is distinguishing in the highest degree. As Jenubath, the young son of Hadad, was brought up in the court of Pharaoh and weaned in the king's palace, so are some saints sanctified from the womb. Happy is it for any young man, an elect one out of the elect is he, if he be weaned upon the knees of piety and handled upon the lap of holiness; if he be lighted to his bed with the lamps of the sanctuary and lulled to his sleep with the name of Jesus! If I may breathe a prayer in public for my children, let them be clothed with a little ephod, like young Samuel, and nourished in the chambers of the temple, like the young prince Joash. O my dear young friends, it is mercy, mercy in a distinguishing and peculiar degree, to be saved early, because of your fallen nature, because of sin committed, and yet more because of sin prevented, and distinguishing favor bestowed.

But I have another reason for endeavoring to plead with the young this morning, hoping that the Spirit of God will plead with them. I remark that salvation, if it comes to you, must not only be mercy, *but it must be mercy through the cross.* I infer that from the text, because the text desires it to be a satisfying mercy, and there is no mercy which ever can satisfy a sinner, but mercy through the cross of Christ. Many preach a mercy apart from the cross. Many say that God is merciful, and, therefore, surely he will not condemn them; but in the pangs of death, and in the terrors of conscience, the uncovenanted mercy of God is no solace to the soul. Some proclaim a mercy which is dependent upon human effort, human goodness, or merit, but no soul ever yet did or could find any lasting satisfaction in this delusion. Mercy by mere ceremonies, mercy by outward ordinances, is but a mockery of human thirst. Like Tantalus, who is mocked by the receding waters, so is the ceremonialist who tries to drink where he finds all comfort flying from him. Young man, the cross of Christ has that in it which can give you solid, satisfying comfort, if you put your trust in it. It can satisfy *your judgment.* What is more logical than the great doctrine of substitution?—God so terribly just that he will by no means spare the guilty, and that justice wholly met by him who stood in the room, place, and stead of his people! Here is that which will satisfy your *conscience.* Your conscience knows that God must punish you; it is one of those truths which God stamped upon it when he first made you what you are; but when your soul sees Christ punished instead of you, it pillows its head right softly. There is no resting place for conscience but at the cross. Priests may preach what they will, and philosophers may imagine what they please, but there is in the conscience of man, in its unrestingness, an indication that the cross of Christ must have come from God, because that conscience never ceases from its disquiet till it hides in the wounds of the Crucified. Never again shall conscience alarm you with dreadful thoughts of the wrath to come, if you lay hold of that mercy which is revealed in Jesus Christ. Here, too, is satisfaction *for all your fears*. Do they pursue you today like a pack of hungry dogs in full pursuit of the stag? Fly to Christ and your fears have vanished! What has that man to fear for whom Jesus died? Need he alarm himself when Christ stands in his stead before the eternal throne and pleads there for him? Here, too, is satisfaction *for your hopes*. He that gets Christ gets all the future wrapped up in him.

There's pardon for transgressions past;
It matters not how black their cast.

There are also peace, and joy, and safety for all the years and for all the eternity to come in the same Christ Jesus who has put away your sin. Oh! I would young man, I would young woman, that you would put your trust in Jesus now, for in him there is an answer to this prayer—"O satisfy us early with thy mercy."

Furthermore, anxiously would I press this matter of a youthful faith upon you, *because you have a dissatisfaction even now*. Do I not speak the truth, when looking into the bright eyes of the gayest among you, I venture to say that you are not perfectly satisfied? You feel that something is lacking. My lad, your boyish games cannot quite satisfy you; there is a something in you more noble than toys and games can gratify. Young man, your pursuits of business furnish you with some considerable interest and amusement, but still there is an aching void—you know there is—and although pleasure promises to fill it, you have begun already to discover that you have a thirst which is not to be quenched with water, and a hunger which is not to be satisfied with bread. You know it is so. The other evening when you were quite alone, when you were quietly thinking matters over, you felt that this present world was not enough for you. The majesty of a mysterious longing which God had put in you lifted up itself and claimed to be heard! Did it not? The other day, after the party was over at which you had so enjoyed yourself, when it was all done, and everybody was gone and you were quite quiet, did you not feel that even if you had these things every day of your life, yet you could not be content? You want you know not what, but something you do want to fill your heart. We look back upon our younger days and think that they were far happier than our present state, and we sometimes fancy that we used to be satisfied then, but I believe that our thoughts imagine a great falsehood. I do from my soul confess that I never was satisfied till I came to Christ; when I was yet a child I had far more wretchedness than ever I have now; I will even add more weariness, more care, more heartache, than I know at this day. I may be singular in this confession, but I make it, and know it to be the truth. Since that dear hour when my soul cast itself on Jesus, I have found solid joy and peace, but before that all those supposed thrills of early youth, all the imagined ease and joy of boyhood, were but vanity and vexation of spirit to me. You do feel, if I know anything about you, that you are not quite satisfied now. Well, then, let me say to you again, that I would have you come to Jesus, for depend upon it, there is that in Him which can thoroughly satisfy you.

What can you want more to satisfy *your heart* than love to him? Our hearts all crave for an object upon which they may be set. We often surrender ourselves to an unworthy object which betrays us, or proves too narrow to accommodate our heart's desire. But if you love Jesus, you will love one who deserves your warmest affection, who will amply repay your fullest confidence, and will never betray it. You say that not only does your heart want something, but your *head.* My witness is that there is in the gospel of Christ the richest food for the brain. Before you know Christ, you read, you search, you study, and you put what you learn into a wild chaos of useless confusion; but after you have found Christ, everything else that you learn is put in its proper place. You get Christ as the central sun, and then every science and fact begins to revolve around about him just as the planets travel in their perpetual circle around the central orb. Without Christ we are ignorant, but with him we understand the most excellent of sciences, and all others shall fall into their proper place.

This is an age when, without a true faith in Christ, the young mind has a dreary pilgrimage before it. False guides are standing, arrayed in all sorts of garbs, ready to lead you first to doubt this book of Scripture, then to distrust the whole, then to mistrust God and Christ, and then to doubt your own existence, and to come into the dreary dreamland, where nothing is certain, but where everything is myth and fiction. Give your heart to Christ, young man, and he will furnish you with anchors and good anchor-hold to your mind, so that when stormy winds of skepticism sweep across the sea, and other barks [sailing ships] are wrecked, you shall outride the storm and shall evermore be safe. It is a strange thing that people should be so long before they are satisfied. Look at some of my hearers today. They mean to be satisfied with money, and when they were apprentices they thought they should be so satisfied when they earned journeymen's wages; but they came to be journeymen, and then they were not satisfied till they were foremen; and then they felt they never should be satisfied till they had a concern of their own. They got a concern of their own, and took a house in the city, but then they felt they could not be content till they had taken the adjoining premises; then they had more advertising and more work to do, and now they begin to feel that they never shall be quite easy till they have purchased a snug little villa in the country. Yes, there are some here who have the villa, and handsome grounds, and so on; but they will not be satisfied till they see all their children married; and when they have seen all their children married, they will not be at rest then; they think they will, but they will not. There is always a something yet beyond. "Man never is, but always to be blessed," as Young puts it.

There are Fortunate Isles for the mariner to reach, and failing these there is no haven for him even in the safest port. We know some, too, who instead of pursuing wealth, are looking after fame. They have been honored for that clever piece of writing, but they are emulous of more honor; they must write better still; and when they have achieved some degree of notoriety through a second attempt, they will feel that now they have a name to keep up, and they must have that name widened, and the circle of their influence must extend. The fact is, that neither wealth, nor honor, nor anything that is of mortal birth can ever fill the insatiable, immortal soul of man. The heart of man has an everlasting hunger given to it, and if you could put worlds into its mouth, it would still crave for more; it is so thirsty, that if all the rivers drained themselves into it, still, like the deep sea which is never full, the heart would yet cry out for more. Man is truly like the horse leech; ever he says, "Give! give! give!" and until the cross be given to the insatiable heart, till Jesus Christ, who is the fullness of him that fills all in all, be bestowed, the heart of man never can be full.

Where shall we find a satisfied man but in the Church of Christ? And in the Church of Christ I find him, not in the pulpit merely, where success and position might satisfy, but I find him in the pew humbly receiving the truth. I find him in the pew, not among the rich, where earthly comforts might tend to make him satisfied, but among the poor, where cold and nakedness might cause him to complain. I could point you today to the workman who earns every bit of bread he eats with more sweat of his brow than you would dream of, but he is content. I could point you to the poor work girl who scarce earns enough to hold body and soul together, and yet in this house of God her heart often leaps for joy, for she is wholly resigned. I could show you the bedridden woman whose bones come through the skin through long lying upon a bed which friendship would fain make soft, but which is all too hard for her weakness, and yet she is content, though a parish pittance be all that is given her to feed upon. I say we have no need to exaggerate, or strain, or use hyperboles; we do find in the Church of Christ those who have been and are satisfied with the mercy of God. Now, would it not be a fine thing to begin life with being satisfied? There are some who do not end it with this attainment; they hunt after satisfaction till they come to their dying beds, and then do not find it at last; but oh! to begin life with being satisfied! Not to say at some future date I will be satisfied, but to be content now; not when I have climbed to such and such a pinnacle I shall have enough, but to have enough now, to begin with satisfaction before you launch upon a world of troubles! You may do so, my brother; you may do so, my young sister, if now with a true heart you look to him who hangs upon yonder cross, and commit your soul into his keeping, praying this prayer—"O satisfy us *early* with thy mercy."

The reason which our text gives I must comment upon for a moment. Our text says—"O satisfy us early with thy mercy; *that we may rejoice and be glad all our days.*" We never rejoice in the true sense of the term; we never possess solid gladness, till we are satisfied with God's mercy. It is all a mockery and a pretense; the reality never comes to us till God's mercy visits our hearts; but after that what joy we know! Tell me that the Christian is miserable! O sir, you do not know what the Christian is. We need not appear before you with laughing faces, for our joy is deeper than yours, and needs not to tell itself out in immodest signs. The *poor* trader puts all his goods in the window, but the rich man has rich stores even in the dark cellar; his warehouses are full, and he makes no show. Still waters run deep, and we are sometimes still in our joy because of the depth of our delight. Say we are not happy! Sirs, we would not change one moment of our joy for a hundred years of yours! We hear your joy, and we understand that it is like the crackling of thorns under a pot, which crackle all the louder because they burn so furiously and will so soon be gone. But ours is a steady fire. We do mourn sometimes; we mourn oftener than we ought to do; we are free to confess this; but it is not our religion which makes us mourn; it is because we do not live up to it; for when we live up to it, and have the company of Jesus,

> We would not change our blest estate
> For all that earth calls good or great;
> And while our faith can keep her hold,
> We envy not the sinner's gold.

Our sickbeds are often as the doorstep of heaven; even when we are cast down, there is a sweet solace in our sorrow, and a profound joy about our apparent grief which we would not give away; God gave it to us and the world cannot destroy it. They who love Jesus Christ early, have the best hope of enjoying the happiest days as Christians. *They will have the most service*, and the service of God is perfect delight. Their youthful vigor will enable them to do more than those who enlist when they are old and decrepit. The joy of the

Lord is our strength; and on the other hand, to use our strength for God is a fountain of joy. Young man, if you give fifty years of service unto God, surely you shall rejoice all your days. The earlier we are converted, having the longer time to study in Christ's college, *the more profound shall be our knowledge of him.* We shall have more time for communion, more years for fellowship. We shall have more seasons to prove the power of prayer, and more opportunities to test the fidelity of God than we should if we came late. Those who come late are blessed by being helped to learn so much, but those that come in early shall surely outstrip them. Let me be young, like John, that I may have years of loving service, and like him may have much of intimate acquaintance with my Lord. Surely those who are converted early may reckon upon more joy, because *they never will have to contend with and to mourn over what later converts must know.* Your bones are not broken, you can run without weariness, you have not fallen as some have done, you can walk without fainting. Often the gray-headed man who is converted at sixty or seventy, finds the remembrance of his youthful sins clinging to him; when he would praise, an old lascivious song revives upon his memory; when he would mount up to heaven, he suddenly remembers some scene in a haunt of vice which he would be glad to forget. But you, saved by divine grace before you thus fall into the jaw of the lion, or under the paw of the bear, will certainly have cause for rejoicing all your life. If I may have heavenly music upon earth, let me begin it now, Lord. Put not away the viol and the harp for my fingers when they tremble with age; let me use them while yet I am young. Now, Lord, if there be a banquet, do not bring me in at the end of the feast, but let me begin to feast today. If I am to be married unto Jesus, let it not be when my hair is gray, but marry me to Jesus now. What better time for joy than today? Now shall my joys swell and grow like a river, which rolls on to a mightier breadth and depth as its course is prolonged! I shall rejoice and be glad in you all my days, good Lord, if you will now begin with me, in this the morning of my days.

I cannot put my thoughts together this morning as I could desire, but I still feel an earnest longing to shoot the arrow to its mark, and, therefore, one or two stray thoughts before I turn to the prayer itself, and these shall be very brief. My dear young friends, you who are of my own age, or younger still, I beseech you ask to be satisfied with God's mercy early, *for you may die early.* It has been our grief this week, to stand by the open grave of one who was, alas! too soon, as we thought, snatched away to heaven. You may never number the full ripe years of manhood. We say that our years are threescore and ten, but to you they may not even be a score; your sun may go down while it is yet noon. God often reaps his corn green; long before the autumn comes he cuts down his sheaves. "Because I will do this unto thee, prepare to meet thy God." Then, on the other hand, if you should live, *in whose service could you spend your days better than in the service of God?* What more happy employment, what more blessed position than to be found, like Samuel, a waiting servant upon God while yet you need a mother's care. *Remember how early temptations beset you.* Would you not wish to secure your early days? And how can you cleanse your ways, except by taking heed unto them according to God's Word? Do you not know, too, *that the Church wants you?* Your young blood shall keep her veins full of vigor, and make her sinews strong. *Should not the love of Jesus Christ win you?* If he died and shed his blood for men, does he not deserve their best service? Would you desire to give to God an offering of the end of your days? What would you have thought of the Jew who brought an old bullock—who, after having used an ox in his own fields till it was worn out, should then consecrate it to God? Let the lambs be offered; let the firstlings of the herd be brought; let God have the first sheaves of the harvest. Surely he deserves something better than to have the devil's leavings put upon his holy altar! "Oh! but," you say, "would he accept me if I came to him early?" Why, you have more promises than the old man has. It is written that God will be found of them that seek him, but it is specially written, "Those that seek me early shall find me." You have a peculiar promise given to you. If there were any who could be rejected, it could not by any possibility be the young. If there were one whom Jesus Christ could leave, it would not be you, for he gathers the lambs in his bosom. "Suffer the little children to come unto me, and forbid them not: for of such is the kingdom of God." May not that cheer you, however young you be? Jesus Christ loves to see young men and maidens join in his praise. We find that the best of saints in the Old and New Testament were those who came to Jesus young. Certain it is, that the pick and cream of the Church in modern times will be found among those who are early converts. Look at those who are Church officials and ministers, and in most cases—and the exception only proves the rule—in most cases the leaders in our Israel are those who, as young Hannibal was devoted by his parents to the great cause of his country, were devoted by their parents to the great cause of Zion and to the interests of Jerusalem. If you would be strong for God, eminent in his service, and joyful in his ways; if you would understand the heights and depths of the love of Christ which passes knowledge; if you would give yourselves before your bones are broken and before your spirit has become tinctured through and through with habits of iniquity, then offer this prayer—"O satisfy us early with thy mercy; that we may rejoice and be glad all our days."

II. And now very briefly we shall take the text as your address to God.

Every word here is significant. *"O."* This teaches us *that the prayer is to be earnest.* I will suppose that I have led some of you young people here now to breathe this prayer to God. Am I so unhappy as to suppose that none of you will do it? Are there not some who now say, "I will with my whole heart, God the Holy Spirit helping me, now in my pew offer this supplication to heaven." It begins with an "O." Dull prayers will never reach God's throne. What comes from our heart coldly can never get to God's heart. Dull, dead prayers, ask God to deny them. We must pray out of our very souls. The soul of our prayer must be the prayer of our soul. *"O satisfy us."* Young man, the Lord is willing to open the door to those who knock, but you must knock hard. He is fully prepared to give to those who ask, but you must ask earnestly. The kingdom of heaven suffers violence. It is not a gentle grasp which will avail; you must *wrestle* with the angel. Give no sleep to your eyes nor slumber to your eyelids till you have found the Savior. Remember, if you do but find him, it will well repay you though you shed drops of blood in the pursuit. If instead of tears you had given your heart's gore, and if instead of sighs you were to give the shrieks of a martyr, it would well recompense you if you did but find Jesus; therefore be earnest. If you find him not, remember you perish, and perish with a great destruction; the wrath of God abides on you, and hell must be your portion; therefore as one that pleads for his life, so plead for mercy. Throw your whole spirit into it, and let that spirit be heated to a glowing heat. Be not satisfied to stand at the foot of the throne, and say, "Let God save me if he will." No, but put it thus, "Lord, I cannot take a denial; O satisfy me; O save me." Such a prayer is sure to be accepted.

Again, *make it a generous prayer*, when you are at it. *"O satisfy us early!"* I am glad to see among our young sisters in the catechumen class, such a spirit of love for one another, so that when one is converted she is sure to look around for another; the scores in that class who have found the Lord are always searching out some stray young woman in the street, or some hopeful ones attending the congregation, whom they try to bring in, that Jesus may be glorified. The very first duty of a convert is to labor for the conversion of others, and surely it will not spoil your prayer, young man, if when you are praying for yourself, you will put it in the plural—"O satisfy *us*." Pray for your brothers and sisters. I am sure we are verily guilty in this thing. Those that sprang from the same loins as ourselves, would to God that they were all saved with the same salvation. You may, some of you, be happy enough to be members of a family in which all are converted. Oh, that we could all say the same! May the remembrance of this text provoke you and me to pray for unconverted brothers and sisters more than we have ever done. "O satisfy *us*"; if you have brought in the eldest, Lord, stay not till the youngest be converted; if my brother preaches the Word, if my sister rejoices in your fear, then let other sisters know and taste of your love. You young people in shops, in warehouses, in factories, pray this prayer, and do not exclude even those who have begun to blaspheme, but even in their early youth pray for them—"O satisfy *us* with thy mercy."

See to it, dear friends, in the next place, *that your prayer be thoroughly evangelical.* "O satisfy us early *with thy mercy.*" The prayer of the publican is the model for us all. No matter how amiable or how excellent we may be, we must all come together and say, "God be merciful to me a sinner." Do not come with any hereditary godliness; do not approach the Lord with the fact of your infant sprinkling; do not come before him to plead your mother's covenant. Come as a sinner, as a black, foul, filthy sinner, having nothing to rely on or to trust to but the merit of God in Christ Jesus; and let the prayer be just such as a thief might offer or a prostitute might present: "O satisfy us early with thy mercy."

Let the prayer be put up now *at once.* The text says, "O satisfy us *early.*" Why not today? Oh that it had been done years ago! But there was time enough, you thought. There is time enough, but there is none to spare. Acquaint yourself *now* with God, and be at peace. "Today is the accepted time; today is the day of salvation." I would to God we would not pray our prayers meaning to have them heard so late. Let it be—"O satisfy us *early.*" The man who truly repents always wants to have pardon on the spot; he feels as if he could not rise from his knees till God has been favorable to him, and mark you, when a man has really come to that point that he must be saved now or else he feels that it will be too late, then has come the solemn juncture when God will say—"Be it unto thee even as thou wilt."

I must leave this poor sermon of mine with the people of God to pray over it. Sometimes when most I long to plead with men's souls, I find the brain distracted although the heart is warm. God knows, could I plead with the young I would do it even unto tears. I do feel it such a solemn thing for our country. Happy shall she be if her sons and daughters give their young days to God! It will be such a blessed thing for London, if our young men in business and our young women in families become missionaries for Christ. But what a happy thing it will be for them! What joy shall they know! What transports shall they feel! What a blessing will they be to their households! What happy families they will be! Unconverted fathers shall be made to feel the power of godliness through their daughters, and mothers who despise religion shall not dare to neglect it any longer because they see it exemplified and illustrated in their sons. We want missionaries everywhere. This great city never can by any possibility become the Lord's except by individual action. We must have all Christians at work, and since we cannot get the old ones to work as we would; since preach as we may, they will settle on their lees, we long for new recruits, whose ardor shall rekindle the dying enthusiasm of the seniors. We want to see fresh minds come in all aglow with holy fervor to keep the fire still blazing on the altar. For Jesus Christ's sake I do implore you, you who number but few years, offer this supplication in your pew. Do it now. It is a brother's heart that begs the favor. It is for your own soul's sake, that you may be blessed on earth, and that you may have the joys of heaven. There is a prayer-hearing God. The mercy seat is still open. Christ still waits. May the Spirit of God compel you now to come before him in supplication. Now may he compel you to come in, with this as your cry—"O satisfy us early with thy mercy; that we may rejoice and be glad all our days."

The Student's Prayer

—◦◦◦—

Delivered in 1877 at the Metropolitan Tabernacle, Newington. No. 1344.

Make me to understand the way of thy precepts: so shall I talk of thy wondrous works.—PSALM 119:27

When we seek any good thing from God, we ought also to consider how we may use it for his glory. It is meet that desires for good things should flow from good motives. When the heart is not only gracious but grateful, it will turn to God with double purpose, desiring the mercy and desiring to use it to his praise. The grace of God, which brings salvation, does marvelously whet the appetite for good things; it does more; it provokes an intense anxiety to glorify God's name in the world, even before it has imparted the ability to do any good thing. Vehement passion and abject helplessness meeting together, and struggling in the breast, often lead to despondency, but they ought far rather to stimulate prayer.

Directly we are saved by grace, we are eager after supplies for our soul's wants. "As newborn babes, desire the sincere milk of the Word, that ye may grow thereby." This is the first stage of spiritual childhood; like the infant who cries for the bottle, and takes its little fill and feasts, all to itself, and all for itself. There follows on this another yearning, a desire for fellowship with the saints, although we feel too weak and too foolish to enter into such good company as we take the older disciples to be, or even to talk to them. But I will tell you what we can do. We may all venture to ask the Lord to instruct us and make us understand his ways so that our conversation may be welcome to his people: and so he will. "Wherefore comfort yourselves together, and edify one another, even as also ye do." This is the second stage of development. Then comes a third grade; and come it surely will, if you follow on to know the Lord. "Then will I teach transgressors thy ways; and sinners shall be converted unto thee." Speak not, my brother, on this wise—"You have told me, O my God, to covet earnestly the best gifts. I do covet them, Lord, you know, not to consume them upon my lusts, but to use them for your service. I gladly will accept your talents as a trust, not to trifle with them, not to vaunt them as the toys of my vanity, but by your grace as a wise and faithful steward to bring you all the profit and all the interest, for I am greedy to get gain out of all those endowments you do entrust to my care. "Make me to understand the way of thy precepts: so shall I talk of thy wondrous works."

I would have you further observe, on the threshold of our meditation, that there is not really any grave duty a man can be called on to discharge, no responsible office he may be elected to fill, nor even any plan or purpose he lays it on his heart to accomplish, which does not require diligent preparation on his own part to fit himself, to train his faculties, and to discipline his mind. What you call unskilled labor may possibly be utilized by efficient officers, but unskilful labor is a sheer waste of power. How much more imperative the demand that we should be endowed with the requisite faculties and qualified by suitable instruction if we have any work to do for God, or any office, however humble, in the service of the great King! Zeal without knowledge would only betray us into reckless presumption. When called to talk of God's wondrous works, we ought not to rush upon that exercise at once unfitted and unprepared, but we should wait upon the Lord, that the eyes of our understanding may be enlightened, that our stammering tongues may be unloosed, and that our lips may be attuned to tell the noble tale in grateful strains. We must first obtain for ourselves an understanding of the way of the Lord's precepts before we can make it plain to others. He who tries to teach, but has never been taught himself, will make a sorry mess of it. He who has no understanding, and yet wants to make others understand, must assuredly fail. Some there are who cannot teach and will not learn, and it is because they will not learn that they cannot teach. I believe aptness for being taught is at the bottom of aptness to teach. The psalmist had both. He says, "Make me to understand the way of thy precepts." There he would be taught. Then, says he, "shall I talk of thy wondrous works." There he would be teaching.

In pondering the text, it has appeared to me to set forth three things: first, the prayer of a student; secondly, the occupation of a scholar; and thirdly, the intimate relation there is between them.

I. I see in it *a student's prayer.*

I hope, my beloved brethren and sisters in Christ, that we are all students in the school of Christ—all disciples or scholars—and I trust we shall adopt the student's prayer as our own: "Make me to understand the way of thy precepts." You know that prayer is to study what fire is to the sacrifice; I beseech you, therefore, join heartily in the petition of the text.

The student's prayer deals with the main subject of the conversation which is to be that student's occupation, namely, the way of God's precepts.

You and I, brethren, have to teach those things which relate to the counsels and commandments of the Lord. It is not our province to guide men in politics or to tutor them in science. Those things are better taught by men of mark, whose time and attention are absorbed in those profound and laborious researches. As for us who are Christians, and servants of Christ, our business is to teach men the things of God. To that one topic we do well to keep, both for our own good and for the good of others. If we have many studies to engage us, our thoughts will soon be scattered; and if we multiply our pursuits, we shall be incapable of concentrating all our energies upon the grand topic which divine wisdom has selected for us—"the way of thy precepts."

In the way of God's legal precepts we have great need of sound understanding, that we may be competent to instruct others. It is well to be initiated in the law, to discern its wonderful comprehensiveness, spirituality, and severity; to know the way of the law—a way too hard to be trodden by any mortal man so as to win salvation thereby. It is well to survey the way of the Lord's precepts, to see how exceedingly broad and yet at the same time how remarkably narrow it is; for "thy commandment is exceeding broad," and yet, "strait is the gate, and narrow is the way, which leadeth unto life, and few there be that find it." It is well for us to know exactly what the law teaches, and what the law designs; why we were made subject to its prescript, and how we may be delivered from its penalties.

Great need, too, have we to understand the way of God's gospel precepts— what these precepts are: "repent," "believe," "be converted," and the like; to be able to see their relation, where they stand, not as means to an end, but as results of divine grace—commands but yet promises, the duty of man but yet the gift of God. Happy is that preacher and teacher who understands the way of the gospel precepts, and never lets them clash with the precepts of the law, so as to teach a mingle-mangle, half law and half gospel, but who knows the way of God's legal precepts, and sees them all ablaze with divine wrath on account of sin, and discerns the way of the gospel precepts, and sees them all bright and yet all crimson with the precious blood of him that opened up for us the way of acceptance.

The way of God's precepts! Does not that mean that we ought to be acquainted with the relative position which the precepts occupy, for it is very easy, brethren, unless God gives us understanding, to preach up one precept to the neglect of another. It is possible for a ministry and a teaching to be lopsided, and those who follow it may become rather the caricatures of Christianity than Christians harmoniously proportioned. O Lord, what foolish creatures we are! When you do exhort us one way, we run to such an extreme therein that we forget that you have given us any other counsel than that which is just now ringing in our ears. We have known some commanded to be humble, who have bowed down till they have become timorous and desponding. We have known others exhorted to be confident, who have gone far beyond a modest courage, and grown so presumptuous that they have presently fallen into gross transgressions. Is fidelity to the truth your cardinal virtue? Take heed of being uncharitable. Is love to God and man your highest aspiration? Beware lest you become the dupe of false apostles and foul hypocrites. Have you clad yourself with zeal as with a garment? Have a care now, lest by one act of indiscretion your garment should be rolled in blood. Oh, how easy it is to exaggerate a virtue until it becomes a vice. A man may look to himself, examine himself, and scrutinize all his actions and motives till he becomes deplorably selfish; or on the other hand, a man may look to others, counseling them and cautioning them, preaching to them and praying for them, till he grows oblivious of his own estate, degenerates into hypocrisy, and discovers to his surprise that his own heart is not right with God. There is a "way" about the precepts: there is a chime about them in which every bell gives out its note and makes up a tune. There is a mixture, as of old, of the anointing oil—so much of this and that and the other; and, if any ingredient were left out, the oil would have lost its perfect aroma. So is there an anointing of the holy life in which there is precept upon precept skillfully mingled, delicately infused, gratefully blended, and grace given to keep each of these precepts, and so the life becomes sweet like an ointment most precious unto the Lord. God grant us each, if we are to teach others—and I hope we shall all try to do that—to understand the way of his precepts.

As a prayer, too, this must certainly mean, Make me understand the way to keep thy precepts. It is not in human strength, for he that keeps the precepts of God must be kept by the God of the precepts. To keep the precepts we must keep him in the heart who gave the precepts, and whose life is the best exemplification of them. O Lord, teach us the way to observe and to do your commands. Give us such humble, dependent hearts, so receptive of the sweet influences of your Spirit, that we may understand the way in which those precepts are to be kept. Does it not signify—"Lord, make me to understand the Christian life, for that is the way of your precepts"? Dear friends, if you are teachers of others, you must be experimentally acquainted with the Christian life: you must know the great doctrines which support it and furnish motives for it—the great doctrines which are the pavement of the road along which the Christian travels. You must know the practical precepts themselves—what they are and how the Lord has worded them for each circumstance and each age of the Christian life. You must know the doctrinal and the practical; but you must know the experimental, and he is no preacher of any value who cannot tell the way of God's precepts by having experienced that way—having felt the joy of running in it—having taken the precepts and been guided by them, so as to have proved that "in keeping of them there is great reward." Yes, and he will be none the worse teacher if he has a lively memory of the bitterness that comes of having wandered from those commandments, for he can tell the sinner, with the tear starting to his own eyes, that he who wanders from the way of obedience will miss the paths of peace, for the way of God's commandments is exceedingly pleasant, but they that break the hedge and follow their own will shall find that their willfulness entails upon them grievous sorrow and sore pain. This is what we want—to understand the way of God's precepts. Let the prayer go up to heaven, especially from every young brother who is hoping to preach the Word before long, "Make me to understand the way of thy precepts."

Very obviously here a confession is implied. "Make me to understand the way of thy precepts." It means just this: "Lord, I do not understand it of myself. I am ignorant and foolish, and if I follow my own judgment—if I take to my own thinkings—I shall be sure to go wrong. Lord, make me to understand." It is a confession of a good man who did understand a great deal, but felt that he did not understand all. In this learning, he who understands most is the man who thinks he understands least. He who has the clearest knowledge of divine things is the very one to feel that there is a boundless ocean far beyond his observation, and he cries, "Make me to understand the way of thy precepts." It is a confession which should be made because it is intensely felt—the consciousness of folly and ignorance forcing the confession to the lip.

Our student's prayer asks a great boon when he says, "Make me to understand." This is something more than "Make me to know." He had said just before, "Teach me thy statutes." Every Christian needs this teaching for his own sake, but he that is to be an instructor of others must especially inquire for a thorough understanding. You Sunday school teachers who take the oversight of the children, and you elders of the church who look after inquirers and help them to the Savior, you must not be satisfied with knowing; you must understand. A superficial acquaintance with the Scriptures will not suffice for your important office. Your mind must penetrate into the deeper meaning, the hidden treasures of wisdom. "Make me to understand." A catechism may supply right answers; but we want the living teacher to give us true perceptions. Intelligence is not a faculty of babes: in understanding be men. Young pupils soon lose confidence in their preceptor if he does not seem up to the mark. I heard two schoolboys talking of their usher the other day. Says one, "I don't think he knows much more than we do." "Well, he always has to look at the book before he can tell us anything; has not he?" said the other little chap. Just now as I came along I watched two babies trying to carry another baby a little smaller than themselves, and they all three rolled down together. It is pretty to see little children anxious to help their little brother; but when the father comes up he lifts all three and carries them with ease. We have not many fathers, but every Christian man should aspire to that honorable and valuable estate in the church. The wisdom that comes of experience leads up to it. "Make me to understand." O Lord, the children are pleased with the flowers; help me to spy out the roots: take me into the secrets, let me know the deep things of God. Help me to discriminate: enable me to judge and weigh and ponder, and so to understand. Such reasons as you give enable me to comprehend. Where you give no reason, teach my reason to feel that there must be the best of reasons for no reasons having been given. So make me to understand what can be understood, and to understand that what I cannot understand is just as reliable as what I do understand. In understanding I can never find you out, O God, to perfection. In your sight I must still be a babe, though toward my fellow Christians I may be a man. "Make me to understand."

I love to meet with those of the Lord's people who have had their senses exercised in divine things, and their intelligence matured. For the most part we find disciples like babes, unskillful in the Word of Righteousness, using milk because unable to digest strong meat. Thank God for the babes; pray God they may soon grow and develop into men. He who knows that he is a sinner and that Christ Jesus is his Savior, knows enough to save him. But we have no wish to perpetuate childishness. The spelling book is essential as a primer, but not the spelling book for ever! A B C must not be sung for ever in wearisome monotone; nor must "Only believe" become the everlasting song! Are there not other truths deeper and higher? There is the grand analogy of the faith: there is the doctrine of the covenant, there is the doctrine of election, there is the doctrine of the union of the saints with Jesus Christ. These are the deep things of God, and I think we should pray, "Make me, Lord, to understand them." Yet the best understanding is that which aims at personal holiness. "Make me to understand the way of thy precepts." Lord, if I cannot grapple with doctrine, do let me know which is the right way for me to take in my daily life. If sometimes your truth staggers me, and I cannot see where this truth squares with that, yet Lord, grant that integrity and uprightness may preserve me. So make me to know and understand the way of your statutes that, if I be tempted, and the Tempter come as an angel of light, I may so understand the difference between a true angel of light and the mock angel of light that I may not be taken in the snare. "Make me to understand the way of thy precepts." May my eye be keen to know the right in all its tangles. May I follow the silken clue of uprightness where it seems to wind and twist. Give your servant such a clear understanding of what Israel ought to do, and of what he himself ought to do as a part of Israel, that he may never miss his way. This is the best kind of understanding in all the world.

The psalmist appeals to the fountain of all wisdom, the source from whence all knowledge springs. Who can put wisdom in the inward parts but the Lord? Or who can give understanding to the heart but God Most High? Our parents and our Sunday school teachers taught us the rudiments while we were supple and pliant with tender age. We thank them much, and we esteem them highly. Yet they could only teach the law and imprint, if possible, the letter of it on our memory, although even that we oft repeated and as oft forgot. It is the Lord that teaches us to profit by the divine Spirit. How very wonderfully the Lord does teach us. Some lessons have to be whipped into us. Well, he does not spare the rod for our crying. Other lessons can only be burnt into us as with a hot iron. Some of us can bless the Lord that we bear in our body the prints of the Lord Jesus, that he branded his truth into our very flesh and bones, so that we cannot now miss it, but must understand it. Into what strange places God will put his children! You have heard of colleges called by odd names—Brasennose, and the like; but the most singular college I ever heard of was the whale's belly. Jonah would never have bowed his self-will to sovereign grace had he not been cast into the deep, compassed about with floods, and overwhelmed with billows and waves. But the soundness of his doctrine was very palpable in the voice of his thanksgiving, for as soon as ever he came out of the whale's belly, he said, "Salvation is of the LORD." A singular college for a prophet; but we may be content to leave the college to God, and if we be like Joseph sold into Egypt, or like the Hebrew children carried captive into Babylon, or wherever it may be—so long as he makes us to understand the way of his precepts, we may be well content. Christ taught only three of his twelve apostles upon Tabor, but eleven of them in Gethsemane. Some, though favored much with high joys, learn more by deep sorrows. He takes but three of them into the chamber where he raises the dead girl, for all his wonders are not to be seen by all his followers; but they may all behold him on the cross, and learn the sweet wonders of his dying love. I would not be satisfied, dear brethren and sisters, without trying to understand all that can be understood of the love of Jesus Christ, and of all those precious truths that make up the way of God's precepts. He is a poor scholar who does not wish to learn more than lies within the bare compass of his task: a good pupil will try to get as much as ever he can out of his teacher. Be it your resolve and mine always to be learning! Let us never be content lightly to skim the wave or gently sip the river's brim. Rather let us delight ourselves with diving into the clear stream of knowledge. Revelation invites research, and it unfolds its choice stores only to those who search for them as for hidden treasures. O my God! I long to glean, to gather, to gain knowledge. I would fain yield up every hour I have to sit at your feet. To you I would surrender every faculty I have that I may be learning. By the ear, by the eye, by the taste would I imbibe instruction; yes, and in every season of recreation I would inhale the fragrance of your wondrous works; and when I seek repose I would lean my head upon your bosom, that I may learn your love by the touch as well as by every other sense. May each gate of Mansoul be filled with the traffic of the precious merchandise of heavenly knowledge. And, Lord, I would open the inmost depth of my soul that your light may shine into the most secret parts of my nature. Oh, hear my cry! Make me to understand the way of your precepts!

II. Now, dear friends, let us pass on to notice, in the next place, *the occupation of the instructed man.*

When the Lord has taught a man the way of his precepts, it behooves him rightly to use his sacred privileges: "So shall I talk of thy wondrous works." As a faithful teacher let him testify of God's works—his wondrous works. It is a sorry sermon that is all about man's works, especially if the preacher makes out our good works to be something very remarkable. We are to preach, not man's works, but God's works—not our own works, but the works of our great Substitute. There are two works, especially, that you Christian people must talk about to others—the work of Christ for us and the work of the Holy Ghost in us. These are themes that will never be exhausted. The work of God the Son for us in his life and death, resurrection, and ascension, his intercession at the right hand of God, and his second advent—what a theme is before you here! How great are the works of Christ on our behalf! Preach his substitution emphatically. Let there be no mistake about that. Let it be told that Christ stood in the place and stead of his people, and lived and died for them. Moreover, there is the work of the Holy Spirit in us—the vital interest and importance of which it would not be possible to exaggerate. I should not like any man to try and talk about this divine ministry unless he has been brought under its power, and been led by experience to understand it—the work of conviction, the work of regeneration, the work of emptying, humbling, and bringing down, the work of leading to repentance and to faith, the work of sanctification, the work of daily sustenance of the divine life, the work of perfecting the soul for heaven. There is plenty of room for blundering here if God does not make you to understand the way of his precepts! But if you have a good, clear knowledge of what Christian life is, then, my dear brothers and sisters, always be dwelling on these two things—what the Lord has done for us, and what the Lord is doing in us when he brings us out of darkness unto his marvelous light.

The wonderful character of these works of God opens up a study on which the devout mind can descant with ever-wakening emotions of awe and delight. There are a few things in the world that men may wonder at. They used to speak of the seven wonders of the world. I believe that there is not one of those seven wonders which some have not ceased to wonder at. If you see them a sufficient number of times, you get accustomed to them, and the wonder evaporates. But the works of the Lord, and these two works especially, you may think on them, meditate upon them, inspect them, enjoy them, every day of a long life; and the result will be, not a diminution, but an increase of your wonder. "Thy wondrous works!" God incarnate in the Son of Mary! Wondrous work, this! God in the carpenter's shop! The Son of God driving nails and handling a hammer! Wondrous work, this! Jesus at the loom, weaving a righteousness for his people, casting his soul into every throw of the shuttle, and producing such a matchless fabric for the wedding dress of his own chosen bride, that all the angels in heaven stand still and gaze at it, and marvel how such a fabric was wrought! Behold him—God himself in human flesh—dying, bearing human sin with a condescension that is wonderful beyond all wonder! Behold him casting all that sin into the depth of the sea, with wondrous might of merit, which drowned it in the bottomless abyss for ever! Wondrous work, that! Then see him going forth again, discharged from all his suretyship engagements, having paid the debt; and behold him nailing the handwriting of the ordinances that were against us to his cross. Oh, wondrous work! One might talk thereof by night and day, and never weary. View him rising as our representative, guaranteeing life to us; see him climbing the skies and casting a largesse of mercies among rebellious men. Consider the influence of his mediatorial authority, the power committed to him by his Father, for he has power given him over all flesh, that he may give eternal life to as many as the Father gave him. Listen, listen to his pleading as the Priest upon the throne. What wondrous work is that! Still through the apocalyptic vista gaze; gaze on all the glories of the future, when he shall come to reign upon the earth! There you have new fields of light breaking on your ravished view—fresh incentives to wonder, admire, and worship.

And what shall I say of these wondrous works which seem so near and so familiar to our observation, and yet baffle our investigation, till the more we scrutinize them the more amazement we feel? The church in the world is kept alive from generation to generation by One whose presence was promised, was bestowed, and is now felt and proved by the saints, the blessed Paraclete, the Comforter whom Jesus sent from the Father. By his agency long seasons of drought and despondency have been ever and anon succeeded by times of refreshing from the presence of the Lord, by revivals and renewals of signs and wonders such as began but did not end in the day of Pentecost. I never know which to wonder at most—God in human flesh, the incarnate Son, or the Holy Spirit dwelling in man. The indwelling is as wonderful as the incarnation. Let every gospel teacher yield up his own soul to the wonder and gratitude which these works of God are fitted to inspire. I like to see the preacher, when he is talking about these things, look like a man wonder struck, gazing forth on a vast expanse, lost in immensity, as if he were far out at sea, trembling with adoration, as if the chords of his nature vibrated to the mystery and awe that encircle him. There are lovely traces of God's transcendent skill in things minute when peered at through a microscope; but these wondrous works of God are of another order. They display his grander power. Tell not the old, old story as if it had grown trite and trifling in your ears, and tripped from off your tongue. Listen to the slow, deep, mellow voice of the mighty ocean of grace until your soul faints within you. Then speak in tones of strong emotion like those of Paul—"O the depth of the riches both of the wisdom and knowledge of God! how unsearchable are his judgments, and his ways past finding out!"

Yet it becomes you to speak very plainly. See how it is put. "So shall I talk of thy wondrous works." Talk is the simplest mode of speech. You cannot all preach, but you can all talk; and, if some preachers would refrain from rhetoric and tell their plain unvarnished tale, they would succeed better than they do now. Do you think that God meant his ministers to kill themselves in order come out on Sundays with one or two splendid displays of "intellect" and eloquence? Surely this is not God's way of doing things. I do not believe that Paul ever preached a fine sermon, or that Peter ever dreamed of any display of intellect. I asked the other day of one who had heard a sermon if it was likely that sinners would be converted by it. He said, "Oh no; by no means;

but it was an intellectual treat." Is there anywhere in the Bible a word about intellectual treats, or anything approximating to such an idea? Is there not a country on the other side of the sea, where they are attempting fine, flashy oratory—sermons that remind you of the way in which they finish up the fireworks; discourses made up of blue lights and blazes? They call it a "peroration," I believe. But the way for the Christian—the real Christian—is to talk of God's wondrous works. Tell me the old, old story. Tell it not stately, but do tell it simply, as to a little child. More glory will come to God from that, more comfort to your soul in reflection, and more benefit to the souls of those you teach, than from all the flights of poetry or the flourishes of rounded periods. They that would win souls must take David's words here, and say, "Make me to understand the way of thy precepts," so shall I give up all the "spread eagle," and "so shall I talk of thy wondrous works." "Blessed be God," said a farmer at a prayer meeting, "that we were fed last Sunday out of a low crib, for we have mostly had the fodder so high that we poor things could not reach it." When I read that farmer's thanksgiving, I thought it very wise.

When a man is instructed in the faith he will often speak about these things. Such conversation may be frequent without being irksome: he says, "I will talk." Preaching is an exercise to be undertaken now and then, but talking, I believe, is capable of being carried on by some people very nearly every minute of the day. Certainly few persons account it a hardship to talk every day; and when God makes us to understand the way of his precepts, we shall have the gospel at our fingers' ends, so that whoever we meet with, we shall be able to talk to them in an earnest and simple style about God's salvation. I would, dear friends, that our talk were always seasoned with salt—that our commonest conversation were bedewed with heavenly unction, ministering grace unto the hearers.

But though very plain and very frequent, the good psalmist's talk was very much to the point, and it did not lack propriety; for he says, "So shall I talk of thy wondrous works." How does he mean? Why, according to understanding. "Make me to understand, and then I shall talk like an intelligent man." May you, dear brethren and sisters, who do talk about Jesus Christ be enabled to talk about him in a wise way. Very serious mischief has often come from harping upon some one string. Some men are far more interested in stating their own notions than in unfolding God's counsels. If we understand the way of God's precepts, acquire the language of it, get into the groove of it, then we shall talk with understanding; and there will be a harmony and a wisdom about our utterances which will be blessed to the edification of the hearers.

III. We will close by noticing *the intimate relation between the prayer of the student and the pursuit that he subsequently followed.* "Make me to understand the way of thy precepts: so shall I talk of thy wondrous works."

The connection lies partly in the enchantment of this knowledge and the passion to communicate it. A man who understands Christ and his mediatorial work, and the Spirit and his sanctifying work, cannot be silent. The fire once kindled, the flames will spread. He will be so transported with wonder, admiration, and adoring gratitude at the great mercy and love of God, that it will cause a fermentation within his breast. He will be like a full vessel wanting vent, and he must have it. As with a fire in his bones, he will exclaim, "Woe is me if I preach not the gospel." I would to God there were a deeper understanding of the ways of God, for then many silent tongues must speak. The theme itself without any remarkable gifts on the part of the man would suffice to secure the attention it strongly claims. As the heart swells with thankfulness, the lips burst forth spontaneously into song. Doubtless Hannah would tell you that it was easier for a barren wife to restrain her tears than for a joyful mother to stifle her hymn of praise. Did Jesus love you when you were all forlorn? Did he find you when a stranger, and prove himself your friend? Did he shelter you when a sinner, and shield you from all harm? Did he die that you might live? Do you know that Jesus is your near kinsman, and that he takes great delight in redeeming you for himself? Let the truth of this but dawn on your heart, and though your tongue were dumb before, it must now begin to talk.

> Now will I tell to sinners round,
> What a dear Savior I have found,
> I'll point to thy redeeming blood
> And say, "Behold the way to God."

May this stir up some of you who love the Lord, and yet never talk about him; may it lead you to a holy searching of heart. Surely you have not such an understanding of him as you ought to have, or else sometimes your silence would be thawed, and your words would betray your strong emotions.

If I understand the way of God's precepts, then I shall be fully furnished with matter to talk of his wondrous works. What a dreadful thing it must be for a man to set up to be a teacher of others if he does not know the things of God experimentally himself. It can be done, you know, and done very cheaply. You can buy sermons ready lithographed and guaranteed not to have been preached within so many miles: price ninepence each. You can be furnished with them for ten shillings and sixpence a quarter. But there will be a heavy account at the last for the man who does that sort of thing. It is easy for you to teach in your class by reading the Sunday School Union notes, getting up the lesson, and having it all in the head. Ah, but, my dear friend, how will you answer for having taught children in the Sunday school when you have never been God's child and never have been taught of God yourself? "Unto the wicked God saith, What hast thou to do to declare my statutes, or . . . take my covenant in thy mouth?" Do not try to teach others what you do not understand yourself. Go down on your knees and cry, "Make me to understand the way of thy precepts, so shall I talk of thy wondrous works." Dear brethren, especially you who are to be ministers of the gospel and have begun to preach, seek a deeper understanding of divine things, or else your ministry will be lean and poverty-stricken. Unless you are taken into the confidence of God and initiated into his counsels, you cannot possibly discharge the solemn duties which lie upon the ambassador for Christ. Cry mightily to be well filled with an understanding of the gospel: so shall you overflow to others and talk of God's wondrous works.

Such sound education will clothe you with authority. A man who, in his own heart, knows what he is talking about, and preaches what he has tasted and handled of the good word of grace, will put weight into every utterance. It matters but little what language he uses; the power lies not in the garnishing, but in the truth itself which he proclaims. It is not the polish of his speech, but the fervor of his soul which gives force to his persuasions. Oh, how often my heart has been refreshed by a humble testimony from a poor man who has talked only about what the Lord has done for him. What a power there is about experimental talk. Dry doctrine and pious platitudes borrowed from books, fall flat on the ear and pall on the taste, but he who talks of the things which he has made touching the King, has a tongue like the pen of a ready writer. I know aged Christians who seem, every time they speak, to drop diamonds and emeralds from their lips; one could wish to treasure up every syllable they utter, not because there is anything very ingenious or original in any sentence, but because there is a sound of abundance of rain in every word; a divine depth, a sacred sweetness, a leaping of life, even in each broken utterance which is born on their lips. You say, "That man knows more than he tells. He does not expose all his wares in the window. He has been in the secret place of communion. His face shines though his voice falters." Such teachers may you and I prove in our riper years, having light in ourselves and illuminating all who are within the range of our influence. What God has led us to understand, may we be the means of communicating by our ordinary conversation, by speech easy, simple, unostentatious, yet earnest, faithful, and heavenly minded.

Brethren, be up and doing, teaching others what you know. Do not try to teach them what you do not know. As far as you know Christ, speak about him to your kinsfolk and acquaintances, your friends and neighbors. Our dear brother and elder, the late Mr. Verdon, on such a night as this would have been anxiously looking after any person who seemed to have heard with thankfulness, and he would not have suffered them to leave the place without accosting them in his own gentle manner, and beginning to talk to them about Christ. I want some more like him. He has gone home. I pray the Lord that some may be baptized for the dead, to stand in his place and fill up the gap which his removal has made in our ranks. We want a host of wise and prudent Christian talkers. I do not know that we have at present any more urgent need: people who can talk in the train, can talk by the roadside, can talk in the kitchen, can talk in the workshop, can talk across a counter, can, in fact, make opportunities to talk of Jesus. I want you, dear friends, to ask the Lord to qualify you for this service and lead you into it. Some of you appear to be marching backward, for you are even more reticent than you used to be. I would have you like Archimedes when he found out his secret and could not keep it for very joy, but ran down the street crying out, "I have found it! I have found it!" Come, break your guilty silence and cry aloud, "I have found him of whom Moses in the Law and the Prophets did write, and I cannot help talking about him."

As for others of you who are not believers, I pray the Lord that you may give a listening ear to the message which I ask others to tell out. Here it is: "Jesus Christ came into the world to save sinners. Whosoever believes in him has everlasting life." "He that believeth and is baptized shall be saved." The Lord bring you to accept these tidings, to believe in Jesus, and to find eternal life. Amen,

Jesus Interceding for Transgressors

～⁑～

Delivered on Lord's Day morning, November 18, 1877, at the Metropolitan Tabernacle, Newington. No. 1385.

And made intercession for the transgressors. — ISAIAH 53:12

Our blessed Lord made intercession for transgressors in so many words while he was being crucified, for he was heard to say, "Father, forgive them; for they know not what they do." It is generally thought that he uttered this prayer at the moment when the nails were piercing his hands and feet, and the Roman soldiers were roughly performing their duty as executioners. At the very commencement of his passion, he begins to bless his enemies with his prayers. As soon as the rock of our salvation was smitten, there flowed forth from it a blessed stream of intercession.

Our Lord fixed his eye upon that point in the character of his persecutors which was most favorable to them, namely, that they knew not what they did. He could not plead their innocence, and, therefore, he pleaded their ignorance. Ignorance could not excuse their deed, but it did lighten their guilt, and, therefore, our Lord was quick to mention it as in some measure an extenuating circumstance. The Roman soldiers, of course, knew nothing of his higher mission; they were the mere tools of those who were in power, and though they "mocked him, coming to him, and offering him vinegar," they did so because they misunderstood his claims and regarded him as a foolish rival of Caesar, worthy only to be ridiculed. No doubt the Savior included these rough gentiles in his supplication, and perhaps their centurion who "glorified God, saying, Certainly this was a righteous man," was converted in answer to our Lord's prayer. As for the Jews, though they had some measure of light, yet they also acted in the dark. Peter, who would not have flattered any man, yet said, "And now, brethren, I [know] that through ignorance ye did it, as did also your rulers." It is doubtless true that, had they known, they would not have crucified the Lord of glory, though it is equally clear that they ought to have known him, for his credentials were clear as noonday. Our Redeemer, in that dying prayer of his, shows how quick he is to see anything which is in any degree favorable to the poor clients whose cause he has undertaken. He spied out in a moment the only fact upon which compassion could find foothold, and he secretly breathed out his loving heart in the cry, "Father, forgive them; for they know not what they do." Our great Advocate will be sure to plead wisely and efficiently on our behalf; he will urge every argument which can be discovered, for his eye, quickened by love, will suffer nothing to pass which may tell in our favor.

The prophet, however, does not, I suppose, intend to confine our thoughts to the one incident which is recorded by the evangelists, for the intercession of Christ was an essential part of his entire life's work. The mountain's side often heard him, beneath the chilly night, pouring out his heart in supplications. He might as fitly be called the man of prayers as "the man of sorrows." He was always praying, even when his lips moved not. While he was teaching and working miracles by day, he was silently communing with God, and making supplication for men; and his nights, instead of being spent in seeking restoration from his exhausting labors, were frequently occupied with intercession. Indeed, our Lord's whole life is a prayer. His career on earth was intercession wrought out in actions. Since "He prayeth best who loveth best," he was a mass of prayer, for he is altogether love. He is not only the channel and the example of prayer, but he is the life and force of prayer. The greatest plea with God is Christ himself. The argument which always prevails with God is Christ incarnate, Christ fulfilling the law, and Christ bearing the penalty. Jesus himself is the reasoning and logic of prayer, and he himself is an ever-living prayer unto the Most High.

It was part of our Lord's official work to make intercession for the transgressors. He is a Priest, and as such he brings his offering and presents prayer on the behalf of the people. Our Lord is the Great High Priest of our profession, and in fulfilling this office we read that he offered up prayers and supplications with strong crying and tears; and we know that he is now offering up prayers for the souls of men. This, indeed, is the great work which he is carrying on today. We rejoice in his finished work, and rest in it, but that relates to his atoning sacrifice; his intercession springs out of his atonement, and it will never cease while the blood of his sacrifice retains its power. The blood of sprinkling continues to speak better things than that of Abel. Jesus is pleading now, and will be pleading till the heavens shall be no more. For all that come to God by him he still presents his merits to the Father, and pleads the causes of their souls. He urges the grand argument derived from his life and death, and so obtains innumerable blessings for the rebellious sons of men.

I. I have to direct your attention this morning to our ever-living Lord making intercession for the transgressors; and as I do so I shall pray God, in the first place, that all of us may be roused to admiration for his grace. Come, brethren, gather up your scattered thoughts and meditate upon him who alone was found fit to stand in the gap and turn away wrath by his pleading. If you will consider his intercession for transgressors, I think you will be struck with the love, and tenderness, and graciousness of his heart, when you recollect that he offered intercession verbally while he was standing in the midst of their sin. Sin heard of and sin seen are two very different things. We read of crimes in the newspapers, but we are not at all so horrified as if we had seen them for ourselves. Our Lord actually saw human sin, saw it unfettered and unrestrained, saw it at its worst. Transgressors surrounded his person, and by their sins darted ten thousand arrows into his sacred heart, and yet while they pierced him, he prayed for them. The mob compassed him around about, yelling, "Crucify him, crucify him," and his answer was "Father, forgive them": he knew their cruelty and ingratitude, and felt them most keenly, but answered them only with a prayer. The great ones of the earth were there, too, sneering and jesting—Pharisee and Sadducee and Herodian—he saw their selfishness, conceit, falsehood, and bloodthirstiness, and yet he prayed. Strong bulls of Bashan had beset him around, and dogs had compassed him, yet he interceded for men. Man's sin had stirred up all its strength to slay God's love, and, therefore, sin had arrived at its worst point, and yet mercy kept pace with malice, and outran it, for he sought forgiveness for his tormentors. After killing prophets and other messengers, the wicked murderers were now saying, "This is the heir; come, let us kill him, that the inheritance may be ours." And yet that heir of all things, who might have called fire from heaven upon them, died crying, "Father, forgive them." He knew that what they did was sin, or he would not have prayed "forgive them," but yet he set their deed in the least unfavorable light, and said, "they know not what they do." He set his own sonship to work on their behalf, and appealed to his Father's love to pardon them for his sake. Never was virtue set in so fair a frame before, never goodness came so adorned with abundant love as in the person of the Lord Jesus, and yet they hated him all the more for his loveliness, and gathered around him with the deeper spite because of his infinite goodness. He saw it all, and felt the sin as you and I cannot feel it, for his heart was purer, and, therefore, tenderer than ours: he saw that the tendency of sin was to put him to death, and all like him, yes and to slay God himself if it could achieve its purpose, for man had become a deicide and must needs crucify his God—and yet, though his holy soul saw and loathed all this tendency and atrocity of transgression, he still made intercession for the transgressors. I do not know whether I convey my own idea, but to me it seems beyond measure wonderful that he should know sin so thoroughly, understand its heinousness, and see the drift of it, and feel it so wantonly assailing himself when he was doing nothing but deeds of kindness; and yet with all that vivid sense of the vileness of sin upon him, even there and then he made intercession for the transgressors, saying, "Father, forgive them; for they know not what they do."

Another point of his graciousness was also clear on that occasion, namely, that he should thus intercede while in agony. It is marvelous that he should be able to call his mind away from his own pains to consider their transgressions. You and I, if we are subject to great pains of body, do not find it easy to command our minds, and especially to collect our thoughts and restrain them, so as to forgive the person inflicting the pain, and even to invoke blessings on his head. Remember that your Lord was suffering while he made intercession, beginning to suffer the pangs of death, suffering in soul as well as in body, for he had freshly come from the garden, where his soul was exceeding sorrowful, even unto death. Yet in the midst of that depression of spirit, which might well have made him forgetful of the wretched beings who were putting him to death, he forgets himself, and he thinks only of them, and pleads for them. I am sure that we should have been taken up with our pains even if we had not been moved to some measure of resentment against our tormentors; but we hear no complaints from our Lord, no accusations lodged with God, no angry replies to them such as Paul once gave—"God shall smite thee, thou whited wall"; not even a word of mourning or of complaining concerning the indignities which he endured, but his dear heart all ascended to heaven in that one blessed petition for his enemies, which there and then he presented to his Father.

But I will not confine your thoughts to that incident, because, as I have already said, the prophet's words had a wider range. To me it is marvelous that he, being pure, should plead for transgressors at all: for you and for me among them—let the wonder begin there. Sinners by nature, sinners by practice, willful sinners, sinners who cling to sin with a terrible tenacity, sinners who come back to sin after we have smarted for it; and yet the Just One has espoused our cause, and has become a suitor for our pardon. We are sinners who omit duties when they are pleasures, and who follow after sins which are known to involve sorrow: sinners, therefore, of the most foolish kind, wanton, willful sinners, and yet he who hates all sin has deigned to take our part, and plead the causes of our souls. Our Lord's hatred of sin is as great as his love to sinners; his indignation against everything impure is as great as that of the thrice-holy God who revenges and is furious when he comes into contact with evil; and yet this divine Prince, of whom we sing, "Thou lovest righteousness and hatest wickedness," espouses the cause of transgressors, and pleads for them. Oh, matchless grace! Surely angels wonder at this stretch of condescending love. Brethren, words fail me to speak of it. I ask you to adore!

Further, it is to me a very wonderful fact that in his glory he should still be pleading for sinners. There are some men who when they have reached to high positions forget their former associates. They knew the poor and needy friend once, for, as the proverb has it, poverty brings us strange bedfellows, but when they have risen out of such conditions they are ashamed of the people whom once they knew. Our Lord is not thus forgetful of the degraded clients whose cause he espoused in the days of his humiliation. Yet though I know his constancy I marvel and admire. The Son of Man on earth pleading for sinners is very gracious, but I am overwhelmed when I think of his interceding for sinners now that he reigns yonder, where harps unnumbered tune his praise and cherubim and seraphim count it their glory to be less than nothing at his feet, where all the glory of his Father is resplendent in himself, and he sits at the right hand of God in divine favor and majesty unspeakable. How can we hear without amazement that the King of kings and Lord of lords occupies himself with caring for transgressors—caring indeed for you and me. It is condescension that he should commune with the bloodwashed before his throne, and allow the perfect spirits to be his companions, but that his heart should steal away from all heaven's felicities to remember such poor creatures as we are and make incessant prayer on our behalf, this is like his own loving self—it is Christlike, Godlike. I think I see at this moment our great High Priest pleading before the throne, wearing his jeweled breastplate and his garments of glory and beauty, wearing our names upon his breast and his shoulders in the most holy place. What a vision of incomparable love! It is a fact, and no mere dream. He is within the Holy of Holies, presenting the one sacrifice. His prayers are always heard, and heard for us, but the marvel is that the Son of God should condescend to exercise such an office and make intercession for transgressors. This matchless grace well near seals my lips, but it opens the floodgates of my soul, and I would fain pause to worship him whom my words fail to set forth.

Again, it is gloriously gracious that our Lord should continue to do this; for lo, these eighteen hundred years and more he has gone into his glory, yet has he never ceased to make intercession for transgressors. Never on heaven's most joyous holiday when all his armies are marshaled, and in their glittering squadrons pass in review before the King of kings, has he forgotten his redeemed ones. The splendors of heaven have not made him indifferent to the sorrows of earth. Never, though, for all we know, he may have created myriads of worlds, and though assuredly he has been ruling the courses of the entire universe, never once, I say, has he suspended his incessant pleading for the transgressors. Nor will he, for the holy Scriptures lead us to believe that as long as he lives as Mediator he will intercede: "He is able also to save them to the uttermost that come unto God by him, seeing he ever liveth to make intercession for them." He lived and lives to intercede, as if this were the express object of his living. Beloved, as long as the great Redeemer lives and there is a sinner still to come to him, he will still continue to intercede. O my Master, how shall I praise you! Had you undertaken such an office now and then, and had you gone into the royal presence once in a while to intercede for some special cases, it would have been divinely gracious on your part, but that you should always be a suppliant, and ever cease to intercede, surpasses all our praise. Wonderful are his words as written in prophecy by Isaiah—"For Zion's sake will I not hold my peace, and for Jerusalem's sake I will not rest, until the righteousness thereof go forth as brightness, and the salvation thereof as a lamp that burneth." As the lamp in the temple went not out, so neither has our Advocate ceased to plead day nor night. Unwearied in his labor of love, without a pause, he has urged our suit before the Father's face. Beloved, I will not enlarge, I cannot, for adoration of such love quite masters me; but let your hearts be enlarged with abounding love to such an intercessor as this, who made, who does make, and who always will make intercession for the transgressors.

I have said, "will make," and indeed this is no bare assertion of mine, for my text may be read in the future, as well as in the past: indeed, as you will perceive upon a little thought, it must have been meant to be understood in the future, since the prophecy was written some 700 years before our Lord had breathed his intercessory prayer at the cross: although the prophet, in order to make his language pictorial and vivid, puts it in the past tense, it was actually in the future to him, and, therefore, we cannot err in reading it in the future, as I have done—"he shall make intercession for the transgressors." Constant love puts up a ceaseless plan. Endless compassion breathes its endless prayer. Till the last of the redeemed has been gathered home, that interceding breath shall never stay, nor cease to prevail.

II. Thus have I called you to feel admiration for his grace; and now, secondly, I do earnestly pray that we may be led of the Holy Ghost so to view his intercession for transgressors as to put our confidence in himself. There is ground for a sinner's confidence in Christ, and there is abundant argument for the believer's complete reliance in him, from the fact of his perpetual intercession.

Let me show you this first, because, beloved, his intercession succeeds. God hears him, of that we do not doubt; but what is the basis of this intercession? For whatever that is, seeing it makes the intercession to be successful, we may safely rest on it. Read carefully the verse: "Because he hath poured out his soul unto death: and he was numbered with the transgressors; and he [bore] the sin of many." See, then, the success of his plea arises out of his substitution. He pleads and prevails because he has borne the sin of those for whom he intercedes. The main stay and strength of his prevalence in his intercession lies in the completeness of the sacrifice which he offered when he bore the sin of many. Come, then, my soul, if Christ's prayer prevails because of this, so will your faith. Resting on the same foundation, your faith will be equally secure of acceptance. Come, my heart, rest on that truth—"He [bore] the sin of many." Throw yourself with all your sin upon his substitution and feel that this is a safe resting place for your believing, because it is a solid basis for your Lord's intercession. The perfect sacrifice will bear all the strain which can possibly come upon it; test it by the strongest faith and see for yourself; plead it with the boldest requests and learn its boundless prevalence. You may urge the plea of the precious blood with the Father, seeing the Lord Jesus has urged it, and has never failed.

Now, again, there is reason for transgressors to come and trust in Jesus Christ, seeing he pleads for them. You never need be afraid that Christ will cast you out when you can hear him pleading for you. If a son had been disobedient and had left his father's house, and were to come back again, if he had any fear about his father's receiving him, it would all disappear if he stood listening at the door and heard his father praying for him. "Oh," says he, "my coming back is an answer to my father's prayer; he will gladly enough receive me." Whenever a soul comes to Christ it need have no hesitancy, seeing Christ has already prayed for it that it might be saved. I tell you transgressors, Christ prays for you when you do not pray for yourselves. Did he not say of his believing people, "Neither pray I for these alone, but for them also which shall believe on me through their word"? Before his elect become believers they have a place in his supplications. Before you know yourselves to be transgressors and have any desire for pardon, while as yet you are lying dead in sin, his intercession has gone up even for such as you are. "Father, forgive them" was a prayer for those who had never sought forgiveness for themselves. And when you dare not pray for yourselves, he is still praying for you: when under a sense of sin you dare not lift so much as your eyes toward heaven, when you think, "Surely it would be in vain for me to seek my heavenly Father's face," he is pleading for you. Yes, and when you cannot plead, when through deep distress of mind you feel choked in the very attempt to pray, when the language of supplication seems to blister your lip because you feel yourself to be so unworthy, when you cannot force even a holy groan from your despairing heart, he still pleads for you. Oh, what encouragement this ought to give you. If you cannot pray, he can, and if you feel as if your prayers must be shut out, yet his intercession cannot be denied. Come and trust him! Come and trust him! He who pleads for you will not reject you: do not entertain so unkind a thought, but come and cast yourself upon him. Has he not said, "Him that cometh to me I will in no wise cast out"? Venture upon the assured truth of that word, and you will be received into the abode of his love.

I am sure, too, that if Jesus Christ pleads for transgressors as transgressors, while as yet they have not begun to pray for themselves, he will be sure to hear them when they are at last led to pray. When the transgressor becomes a penitent, when he weeps because he has gone astray, let us be quite sure that the Lord of mercy who went after him in his sin will come to meet him now that he returns. There can be no doubt about that. I have known what it is to catch at this text when I have been heavy in heart. I have seen my sinfulness, and I have been filled with distress, but I have blessed the Lord Jesus Christ that he makes intercession for the transgressors, for then I may venture to believe that he intercedes for me, since I am a transgressor beyond all doubt. Then again, when my spirit has revived, and I have said, "But yet I am a child of God, and I know I am born from above," then I have drawn a further inference—if he makes intercession for transgressors, then depend upon it he is even more intent upon pleading for his own people. If he is heard for those who are out of the way, assuredly he will be heard for those who have returned unto the shepherd and bishop of their souls. For them above all others he will be sure to plead, for he lives to intercede for all who come unto God by him.

In order that our confidence may be increased, consider the effect of our Lord's intercession for transgressors. Remember, first, that many of the worst of transgressors have been preserved in life in answer to Christ's prayer. Had it not been for his pleading they would have been dead long ago. You know the parable of the fig tree that cumbered the ground, bearing no fruit, and impoverishing the soil? The master of the vineyard said, "Cut it down," but the vinedresser said, "Let it alone this year also, till I shall dig about it, and dung it: and if it bear fruit, well." Need I say who he is that stays the ax which else had long ago been laid at the root of the barren tree? I tell you ungodly men and women that you owe your very lives to my Lord's interference on your behalf. You did not hear the intercession, but the great owner of the vineyard heard it, and in answer to the gracious entreaties of his Son, he has let you live a little longer. Still are you where the gospel can come at you, and where the Holy Spirit can renew you? Is there no ground for faith in this gracious fact? Can you not trust in him through whose instrumentality you are yet alive? Say to your heavenly Father,

Lord, and am I yet alive,
Not in torments, not in hell!
Still doth thy good Spirit strive—
With the chief of sinners dwell?

And then believe in him to whose pleading you owe the fact that you are within reach of mercy. Well does it become you to confide in him who has already been your preserver from death and hell. May the divine Spirit teach you the reasonableness of my argument and lead you at once into humble faith in Jesus.

Remember, next, that the gift of the Holy Spirit which is needful for the quickening of transgressors was the result of Christ's intercession. Our poet was right when he said.

'Tis by thine interceding breath
The Spirit dwells with men.

I do not doubt but that between the prayer of Christ for his murderers and the outpouring of the Holy Ghost at Pentecost there was an intimate connection. As the prayer of Stephen brought Saul into the church and made him an apostle, so the prayer of Christ brought in three thousand at Pentecost to become his disciples. The Spirit of God was given "to the rebellious also" in answer to the pleadings of our Lord. Now, it is a great blessing thus to have the Spirit of God given to the sons of men, and if this comes through Jesus' prayers, let us trust in him, for what will not come if we rely upon his power? Upon sinners he will still display his power; they will be pricked in their hearts, and will believe in him whom they have pierced.

It is through Christ's intercession that our poor prayers are accepted with God. John, in Revelation, saw another angel standing at the altar, having a golden censer, to whom there was given much incense, that he should offer it with the prayers of all saints upon the golden altar which was before the throne. Whence comes the much incense? What is it but Jesus' merits? Our prayers are only accepted because of his prayers. If, then, the intercession of Christ for transgressors has made the prayers of transgressors to be accepted, let us without wavering put our trust in him, and let us show it by offering our supplications with a full assurance of faith, and an unstaggering confidence in the promise of our covenant God. Are not all the promises yes and amen in Christ Jesus? Let us remember him, and ask in faith, nothing wavering.

It is through the prayers of Christ, too, that we are kept in the hour of temptation. Remember what he said to Peter, "I have prayed for thee, that thy faith fail not," when Satan desired to have him and sift him as wheat. "Father, . . . keep them from the evil" is a part of our Lord's supplication, and his Father hears him always. Well, if we are kept in the midst of temptation from being destroyed because Christ pleads for us, let us never fear to trust ourselves in his kind, careful hands. He can keep us, for he has kept us. If his prayers have delivered us out of the hand of Satan, his eternal power can bring us safely home, though death lies in the way.

Indeed, it is because he pleads that we are saved at all. He is "able also to save them to the uttermost that come unto God by him, seeing he ever liveth to make intercession for them." This, also, is one grand reason why we are able to challenge all the accusations of the world and of the devil, for "Who is he that condemneth? It is Christ that died, yea, rather, that is risen again, who is even at the right hand of God, who also maketh intercession for us." Satan's charges are all answered by our Advocate. He defends us at the judgment seat when we stand there like Joshua in filthy garments, accused of the devil; and therefore the verdict is always given in our favor—"Take away the filthy garments from him." O you that would bring slanderous accusations against the saints of God, they will not damage us in the court of the great King, for "if any man sin, we have an Advocate with the Father, Jesus Christ the righteous." Think, my dear brethren and sisters, of what the intercession of Jesus has done, and you will clearly perceive great inducements to place your sole reliance in your Lord. You who have never trusted him, will you not this very morning begin to do so? Come, weary heart, take the Lord Jesus to be your confidence—what more do you want? Can you desire a better friend than he is, a more prevalent advocate before the throne? Come, leave all other trusts, and yield yourselves to him this morning. I pray you accept this advice of love. And you, you saints, if you are foolish enough to have doubts and fears, come, see how Jesus pleads for you. Give him your burden to bear, leave with him your anxieties at this moment that he may care for you. He will carry on your suit before the eternal throne, and carry it through to success. He who engages a solicitor to manage his legal business among men leaves his affairs in his hands, and he who has such a pleader before God as Christ Jesus, the Wonderful, Counselor, has no need to torment himself with anxieties. Rather let him rest in Jesus, and wait the result with patience.

Give him, my soul, thy cause to plead,
Nor doubt the Father's grace.

So much, then, for the duty of exercising confidence in him. May the Holy Ghost fill you with faith and peace.

III. And now, in the third place, I pray that our text may inspire us with the spirit of obedience to his example. I say obedience to his example, for I take the example of Christ to be an embodied precept as much binding upon us as his written commands. The life of Christ is a precept to those who profess to be his disciples. Now, brethren in Christ, may I put a few practical matters before you, and will you endeavor by the help of God's Spirit to carry them out?

First, then, your Lord makes intercession for the transgressors, therefore imitate him by forgiving all transgressions against yourself. Have any offended you? Let the very recollection of the offense as far as possible pass from your minds, for none have ever injured you as men injured him; let me say, as you yourself have injured him. They have not nailed you to a cross, nor pierced your hands, and feet, and side; yet if he said, "Father, forgive them," well may you say the same. Ten thousand talents did you owe? Yet he forgave you all that debt, not without a grievous outlay to himself: your brother owes you but a hundred pence, will you take him by the throat? Will you not rather freely forgive him even to seventy times seven? Can you not forgive him? If you find it to be impossible, I will not speak to you any longer as a Christian, because I must doubt if you are a believer at all. The Lord cannot accept you while you are unforgiving, since he himself says, "Therefore if thou bring thy gift to the altar, and there rememberest that thy brother hath ought against thee; leave there thy gift before the altar, and go thy way; first be reconciled to thy brother, and then come and offer thy gift." If peace be not made, you will not be accepted. God hears not those in whose hearts malice and enmity find a lodging. Yet I would speak to you in tones of love rather than with words of threatening: as a follower of the gentle Christ I beseech you imitate him in this, and you shall find rest and comfort to your own soul. From the day in which Christ forgives you, rise to that nobility of character which finds a pleasure in forgiving all offenses fully and frankly for Christ's sake. Surely, the atonement which he offered, if it satisfied God, may well satisfy you, and make amends for the sin of your brother against you as well as against the Lord. Jesus took upon himself the transgressions of the second table of the law, as well as of the first, and will you bring a suit against your brother for the sin which Jesus bore? Brethren, you must forgive, for the blood has blotted the record! Let these words of Scripture drop upon your hearts like gentle dew from heaven—"Be ye kind one to another, tenderhearted, forgiving one another, even as God for Christ's sake hath forgiven you."

Next, imitate Christ, dear friends, in pleading for yourselves. Since you are transgressors, and you see that Jesus intercedes for transgressors, make bold to say, "If he pleads for such as I am, I will put in my humble petition and hope to be heard through him. Since I hear him cry, 'Father, forgive them,' I will humbly weep at his feet, and try to mingle my faint and trembling plea with his all-prevalent supplication." When Jesus says, "Father, forgive them," it will be your wisdom to cry, "Father, forgive me." Dear hearer, that is the way to be saved. Let your prayers hang, like the golden bells, upon the skirts of the great High Priest; he will carry them within the veil, and make them ring out sweetly there. As music borne on the breeze is heard afar, so shall your prayers have a listener in heaven because Jesus wafts them there. Since your prayers are feeble, yoke them to the omnipotence of his intercession: let his merits be as wings on which they may soar, and his power as hands with which they may grasp the priceless boons. What shall I say to those who refuse to pray when they have such an encouragement as the aid of Jesus? Tones of tenderness are suitable when addressing the ungodly, when we would persuade them to pray; but if they refuse the intercession of Jesus Christ himself, then must we add our solemn warnings. If you perish, your blood be on your own heads: we must say Amen to your condemnation, and bear witness that you deserve to be doubly punished. Rejecters of great mercy must expect great wrath. The intercession of your Savior, when refused, will be visited upon you most terribly in the day when he becomes your judge.

Let us imitate your Lord in a third point, dear friends: namely, if we have been forgiven our transgressions, let us now intercede for transgressors, since Jesus does so. He is the great example of all his disciples, and, if he makes it his constant business to supplicate for sinners, should not his people unite with him? Therefore would I stir up your pure minds by way of remembrance, to come together in your hundreds, and in your thousands, to pray. Never let our prayer meetings decline. Let us, as a church, make intercession for transgressors, and never rest from seeking the conversion of all around us. I trust that every day, so often as you bow the knee for yourselves, you will make intercession for the transgressors. Poor things, many of them are sinning against their own souls, but they know not what they do. They think to find pleasure in sin: in this also they know not what they do. They break the Sabbath, they despise the sanctuary, they reject Christ, they go downward to hell with mirth, singing merry glees as if they were going to a wedding feast: they know not what they do. But you do know what they are doing. By your humanity—scarcely shall I need to urge a stronger motive—I say, by mere humanity, I beseech you, do all you can for these poor souls, and especially pray for them. It is not much you are asked to do; you are not pointed to the cross and bidden to bleed there for sinners; you are but asked to make intercession. Intercession is an honorable service; it is an ennobling thing that a sinner like yourself should be allowed to entreat the King for others. If you could have permission to frequent the Queen's courts, you would not think it a hardship to be asked to present a petition for another; it would be to you a delight to be enjoyed, a privilege to be snatched at eagerly, that you should be permitted to present requests for others. Oh, stand where Abraham stood and plead for sinners: Sodom could scarce be worse than many portions of the world at this hour. Plead, then, with all your hearts. Plead again and again and again with the Lord, though you be but dust and ashes, and cease not till the Lord say, "I have heard the petition, I will bless the city, I will save the millions, and my Son shall be glorified."

I have not quite done, for I have a further duty to speak of, and it is this: let us take care, dear friends, that if we do plead for others we mix with it the doing of good to them, because it is not recorded that he made intercession for transgressors until it is first written, "He [bore] the sin of many." For us to pray for sinners without instructing them, without exerting ourselves to arouse them, or making any sacrifice for their conversion, without using any likely means for their impression and conviction, would be a piece of mere formality on our part. According to our ability we must prove the sincerity of our petitions by our actions. Prayer without effort is falsehood, and that cannot be pleasing to God. Yield up yourselves to seek the good of others, and then may you intercede with honest hearts.

Lastly, if Christ appears in heaven for us, let us be glad to appear on earth for him. He owns us before God and the holy angels; let us not be ashamed to confess him before men and devils. If Christ pleads with God for men, let us not be backward to plead with men for God. If he by his intercession saves us to the uttermost, let us haste to serve him to the uttermost. If he spends eternity in intercession for us, let us spend our time in intercession for his cause. If he thinks of us, we ought also to think of his people, and especially supplicate for his afflicted. If he watches our cases, and adapts his prayers to our necessities, let us observe the needs of his people, and plead for them with understanding. Alas, how soon do men weary of pleading for our Lord. If a whole day is set apart for prayer and the meeting is not carefully managed, it readily becomes a weariness of the flesh. Prayer meetings very easily lose their flame and burn low. Shame on these laggard spirits and this heavy flesh of ours, which needs to be pampered with liveliness and brevity, or we go to sleep at our devotions. For ever is not too long for him to plead, and yet an hour tries us here. On and on and on through all the ages, still his intercession rises to the throne, and yet we flag and our prayers are half dead in a short season. See, Moses lets his hands hang down, and Amalek is defeating Joshua in the plain! Can we endure to be thus losing victories and causing the enemy to triumph? If your ministers are unsuccessful, if your laborers for Christ in foreign lands make little headway, if the work of Christ drags, is it not because in the secret place of intercession we have but little strength? The restraining of prayer is the weakening of the church. If we aroused ourselves to lay hold upon the covenant angel and resolutely cried, "I will not let thee go, except thou bless me," we should enrich ourselves and our age. If we used more of the strong reasons which make up the weapon of all prayer, our victories would not be so few and far between. Our interceding Lord is hindered for lack of an interceding church; the kingdom comes not because so little use is made of the throne of grace. Get to your knees, my brethren, for on your knees you conquer. Go to the mercy seat and remain there. What better argument can I use with you than this—Jesus is there, and if you desire his company, you must oftentimes resort thither? If you want to taste his dearest, sweetest love, do what he is doing: union of work will create a new communion of heart. Let us never be absent when praying men meet together. Let us make a point of frequenting assemblies gathered for prayer, even if we give up other occupations. While we live, let us be above all things men of prayer, and when we die, if nothing else can be said of us, may men give us this epitaph, which is also our Lord's memorial—"He . . . made intercession for the transgressors." Amen.

Daniel, A Pattern for Pleaders

Published on Thursday, November 4, 1915; delivered on Lord's Day evening, September 25, 1870, at the Metropolitan Tabernacle, Newington. No. 3484.

"O LORD, hear; O LORD, forgive; O LORD, hearken and do; defer not, for thine own sake, O my God: for thy city and thy people are called by thy name."
—DANIEL 9:19

Daniel was a man in very high position in life. It is true he was not living in his own native land, but, in the providence of God, he had been raised to great eminence under the dominion of the country in which he dwelt. He might, therefore, naturally have forgotten his poor kinsmen; many have done so. Alas! we have known some that have even forgotten their poor fellow Christians when they have grown in grace, and have thought themselves too good to worship with the poorer sort when they themselves have grown rich in this world's goods. But it was not so with Daniel. Though he had been made a president of the empire, yet he was still a Jew: he felt himself still one with the seed of Israel. In all the afflictions of his people he was afflicted, and he felt it his honor to be numbered with them, and his duty and his privilege to share with them all the bitterness of their lot. If he could not become despised and as poor as they, if God's providence had made him to be distinguished, yet his heart would make no distinction: he would remember them and pray for them, and would plead that their desolation might yet be removed.

Daniel was also a man very high in spiritual things. Is he not one of God's three mighties in the Old Testament? He is mentioned with two others in a celebrated verse as being one of three whose intercessions God would have heard if he had heard any intercessions. But though thus full of grace himself (and for that very reason), he stooped to those who were in a low state. Rejoicing as he did before God as to his own lot, he sorrowed and cried by reason of those from whom joy was banished. It is a sad fault with those Christians who think themselves full of grace, when they begin to despise their fellows. They may rest assured they are greatly mistaken in the estimate they have formed of themselves. But it is a good sign when your own heart is fruitful and healthy before God, when you do condescend to those that backslide, and search after such as are weak, and bring again such as were driven away. When you have, like your Master, a tender sympathy for others, then are you rich in divine things. Daniel showed his intimate sympathy with his poorer and less gracious brethren in the way of prayer. He would have shown that sympathy in other ways had occasions occurred, and no doubt he did; but this time the most fitting way of proving his oneness with them was in becoming an intercessor for them.

My object here and now will be to stir up the people of God, and especially the members of this church, to abound exceedingly in prayer; more and more to plead with God for the prosperity of his Church, and the extension of the Redeemer's kingdom.

First, our text gives us a model of prayer; and secondly, it and its surroundings give us encouragement for prayer. First, then, our text gives us,

I. *A model of prayer.*

I think I may notice this first as to the antecedents of the prayer. This prayer of Daniel was not offered without consideration. He did not come to pray as some people do, as though it were a thing that required no forethought whatever. We are constantly told we ought to prepare our sermons, and I surely think that if a man does not prepare his sermons he is very blameworthy. But are we never to prepare when we speak to God, and only when we speak to man? Is there to be no preparation of the heart of man for God when we open our mouths before the Lord? Do not you think we often do, both in private and public, begin to pray without any kind of consideration, and the words come, and then we try to quicken the words rather than the desires coming, and the words coming like garments to clothe them withal?

But Daniel's considerations lay in this first, he studied the books. He had with him an old manuscript of the prophet Jeremiah. He read that through. Perceiving such and such things spoken of, he prayed for them. Perceiving such and such a time given, and knowing that that time was almost come, he prayed the more earnestly. Oh! that you studied your Bibles more! Oh! that we all did! How we could plead the promises! How often we should prevail with God when we could hold him to his word, and say, "Fulfill this word to your servant, whereon you have caused me to hope." Oh! it is grand praying when our mouth is full of God's Word, for there is no word that can prevail with him like his own. You tell a man, when you ask him for such and such a thing, "You yourself said you would do so and so." You have him then. And so when you can lay hold on the covenant angel with this consecrated grip, "You have said! you have said!" then have you every opportunity of prevailing with him. May our prayers then spring out of our scriptural studies; may our acquaintance with the Word be such that we shall be qualified to pray a Daniel prayer.

He had, moreover, it is clear if you read the prayer again, studied the history of his people. He gives a little outline of it from the day in which they came out of Egypt. Christian people should be acquainted with the history of the Church—if not with the Church of the past, certainly with the Church of today. We make ourselves acquainted with the position of the Prussian army, and we will buy new maps about once a week to see all the places and the towns. Should not Christians make themselves acquainted with the position of Christ's army, and revise their maps to see how the kingdom of God is progressing in England, in the United States, on the Continent, or in the mission stations throughout the world? All our prayers would be much better if we knew more about the Church, and especially about our own church. I am afraid I must say it—I am afraid there are some members of the Church that do not know what is doing—hardly know what is meant by some of our enterprises. Brethren, know well the Church's needs as far as you can ascertain them; and then, like Daniel, your prayer will be a prayer founded upon information; and with the promises of God and the fact of the Church's wants, you will pray prayers of the spirit, and of the understanding. Let that stand for earnest consideration.

But next, Daniel's prayer was mingled with much humiliation. According to the Oriental custom which expresses the inward thought and feeling by the outward act, he put on a coarse garment made of hair, black, called sackcloth, and then taking handfuls of ashes, he cast them on his head and over the cloth that covered him, and then he knelt down in the very dust in secret, and these outward symbols were made to express the humiliation which he felt before God. We always pray best when we pray out of the depths; when the soul gets low enough she gets a leverage; she can then plead with God. I do not say we ought to ask to see all the evil of our own hearts. One good man prayed that prayer very often. He is mentioned in some of the Puritan writers—a minister of the gospel. It pleased God to hear his prayer, and he never rejoiced afterward. It was with great difficulty that he was even kept from suicide, so deep and dreadful was the agony he experienced when he did begin to see his sin as he wanted to see it. It is best to see as much of that as God would have us see of it. You cannot see too much of Christ, but you might see even too much of your sin. Yet, brethren, this is rarely the case. We need to see much our deep needs, our great sins, for ah! that prayer shall go highest that comes from the lowest. To stoop well is a grand art in prayer. To pour out the last drop of anything like self-righteousness; to be able to say from the very heart, "Not for our righteousness' sake do we plead with you, O God, for we have sinned, and our fathers too." Put the negative, the weightiest negative, upon any idea of pleading human merit. When you can do this, then are you in the right way to pray a prayer that will move the arm of God, and bring you down a blessing. Oh! some of you ungodly ones have tried to pray, but you have not bowed yourselves. Proud prayers may knock their heads on mercy's lintel, but they can never pass through the portal. You cannot expect anything of God unless you put yourself in the right place, that is, as a beggar at his footstool; then will he hear you, and not until then.

Daniel's prayer instructs us in the next point. It was excited by zeal for God's glory. We may sometimes pray with wrong motives. If I seek the conversion of souls in my ministry, is not that a good motive? Yes, it is; but suppose I desire the conversion of souls in order that people may say, "What a useful minister he is," that is a bad motive, which spoils it all. If I am a member of a Christian church, and I pray for its prosperity, is not that right? Certainly; but if I desire its prosperity merely that I and others may be able to say, "See our zeal for the Lord! See how God blesses us rather than others!" that is a wrong motive. The motive is this, "Oh! that God could be glorified, that Jesus might see the reward of his sufferings! Oh! that sinners might be saved, so that God might have new tongues to praise him, new hearts to love him! Oh! that sin were put an end to, that the holiness, righteousness, mercy, and power of God might be magnified!" This is the way to pray; when your prayers seek God's glory, it is God's glory to answer your prayers. When you are sure that God is in the case, you are on a good footing. If you are praying for that which will greatly glorify him, you may rest assured your prayer will speed. But if it do not speed, and it be not for his glory, why, then you may be better content to be without it than with it. So pray, but keep your bowstring right; it will be unfit to shoot the arrow of prayer unless this be your bowstring, "God's glory, God's glory"—this above all; first, last, and midst; the one object of my prayer.

Then coming closer to the prayer, I would have you notice how intense Daniel's prayer was. "O LORD, hear; O LORD, forgive; O LORD, hearken and do; defer not, for thine own sake." The very repetitions here express vehemence. It is a great fault of some people in public prayer when they repeat the name, "O Lord, O Lord, O Lord," so often—it often amounts to taking God's name in vain, and is, indeed, a vain repetition. But when the reiteration of that sacred name comes out of the soul, then it is no vain repetition; then it cannot be repeated too often, and is not open to anything like the criticism which

I used just now. So you will notice how the prophet here seems to pour out his soul with "O Lord, O Lord, O Lord," as if, if the first knock at mercy's door does not open it, he will knock again, and make the gate to shake, and then the third time come with another thundering stroke if, perhaps, he may succeed. Cold prayers ask God to deny them: only importunate prayers will be replied to. When the church of God cannot take no for an answer, she shall not have no for an answer. When a pleading soul must have it, when the Spirit of God works mightily in him so that he cannot let the angel go without a blessing, the angel shall not go till he has given the blessing to such a pleading one. Brethren, if there be only one among us that can pray as Daniel did, with intensity, the blessing will come. Let this encourage any earnest man or woman here that fears that others are not excited to prayer as they should be. Dear brother, do you undertake it? Dear sister, in God's name, do you undertake it? and God will send a blessing to many through the prayer of one. But how much better would it be if many a score of men here, yes, the entire church of God, were stirred up to this, that we give him no rest until he establish and make Jerusalem a praise in the earth! Oh! that our prayers could get beyond praying, till they got to agonizing. As soon as Zion travailed—you know that word—as soon as she travailed she brought forth children. Not till it comes to travail—not till then—may we expect to see much done. God send such travailing to each one of us, and then the promise is near to fulfilling.

But coming still to the text, and a little more closely, I want to observe that this remarkable prayer was a prayer of understanding as well as earnestness; for some people in their earnestness talk nonsense, and I think I have heard prayers which God might understand, but I am sure I did not. Now here is a prayer which we can understand as well as God. It begins thus, "O LORD, hear." He asks an audience. This is how the petitioner does if he comes before an earthly majesty: he asks to be heard. He begins with that, O Lord, hear. "I am not worthy to be heard: if you shut me and my case out of hearing, it will be just." He asks an audience: he gets it, and now he goes at once to his point without delay, "O LORD, forgive." He knows what he wants. Sin was the mischief, the cause of all the suffering: he puts his hand on it. Oh! it is grand when one knows what one is praying for. Many prayers maunder and wander—the praying person evidently thinks he is doing a good thing in saying certain good phrases, but the prayer that hits the target in the center is the prayer it is good to pray. God teach us to pray so. "O Lord, forgive."

Then observe how he presses the point home. "O LORD, hearken and do." If you have forgiven—he does not stop a minute, but here comes another prayer quick on the heels of it. Do, good Lord, interpose for the rebuilding of

Jerusalem—do interpose for the redemption of your captive people; do interpose for the reestablishment of sacred worship. It is well when our prayers can fly fast, one after another, as we feel we are gaining ground. You know in wrestling (and that is a model of prayer) much depends on the foothold, but oftentimes there is much depending upon swiftness and celerity of action. So in prayer. "Hear me, my Lord! You have heard me; forgive me. Have I come so far, then work for me—work the blessings I want." Follow up your advantage; build another prayer on the answer that you have. If you have received a great blessing, say, "Because he has inclined his ear unto me, therefore will I call upon him; because he has heard me once, therefore will I call again." Such a prayer proves the thoughtfulness of him who prays. It is a prayer offered in the spirit, and with understanding also.

And now one other thing. The prayer of Daniel was a prayer of holy nearness. You catch that thought in the expression, "O my God." Ah! we pray at a distance oftentimes: we pray to God as if we were slaves lying at his throne-foot; as if we might, perhaps, be heard, but we did not know. But when God helps us to pray as we should, we come right to him, even to his feet, and we say, "Hear me, O my God." He is God; therefore, we must be reverent. He is my God; therefore, we may be familiar; we may come close to him. I believe some of the expressions that Martin Luther used in prayer, if I were to use them, would be little short of blasphemy, but as Martin Luther used them, I believe they were deeply devout and acceptable with God, because he knew how to come close to God. You know how your little child climbs your knee: he gives you a kiss, and he will say to you many little things that if a person in the market were to say, you could not bear; they must not be said. No other being may be so familiar with you as your child. But oh! a child of God—when his heart is right—how near he gets to his God; he pours out his child-like complaint in childlike language before the Most High. Brethren, this is to be noted well, that though he is thus pleading and in the position of humility, yet still he is not in the position of slavery. It is still "O my God"—he grasps the covenant; faith perceives the relationship to be unbroken between the soul and God, and pleads that relation: "O my God."

Now the last thing I shall call your attention to in this model prayer is this, that the prophet uses argument. Praying ought always to be made up of arguing. "Bring forth your strong reasons" is a good canon for a prevalent prayer. We should urge matters with God, and bring reasons before him—not because he wants reasons, but he desires us to know why we desire the blessing. In this text we have a reason given: first, "Defer not, for thine own sake," as much as if he had said, "If you suffer this people of yours to perish, all the world will revile your name; your honor will be stained. This is your own people; and because they are your property, suffer not your own estate to be endangered, but save Jerusalem for your own sake."

Then next, he puts it on the same footing in another shape, "For thy city and thy people"; he urges that this people were not like other people. They had sinned truly, but still there was a relationship between them and God that existed between God and no other people. He pleads the covenant, in fact, between Abraham and Abraham's seed and the God of the whole earth. Good pleading that! And then he puts in next, "[For they] are called by thy name." They were said to be Jehovah's people; they were named by the name of the God of Israel. "O God! let not a thing that bears your name be trundled about like a common thing. Suffer it not to be trailed in the dust; come to the rescue of it. Your stamp, your seal is upon Israel. Israel belongs to you; therefore, come and interpose." Now from this I gather that if we would prevail, we should plead arguments with God, and these are very many; and discreet minds, when they are fervent, will readily know how far to go in pleading, and where to stop. I remember one morning a dear brother, now present, praying in a way that seemed to me to be very prevalent when he spoke thus, "O Lord, you have been pleased to call your church your bride; now we, being evil, have such love toward our spouse that if there were anything in the world that would be for her good, we would not spare to give it to her; and will you not, O husband of the church, do the like with your spouse, and let your church receive a blessing now that she pleads for it?" It seemed good arguing, after Christ's own sort, "If ye then, being evil, know how to give good gifts unto your children: how much more shall your heavenly Father give the Holy Spirit to them that ask him?" Get a promise, and spread it before the Lord, and say, "O Lord, you have said it; do it." God loves to be believed in. He loves you to think he means what he says. He is a practical God himself. His word has power in it, and he does not like us to treat his promises as some of us do, as if they were wastepaper, as if they were things to be read for the encouragement of our enthusiasm, but not to be used as matters of real practical truth. Oh! plead them with God: fill your mouths with reasonings, and come before him. Make this your determination, that as a church, seeing we need his Spirit, and need renewed prosperity, we will not spare nor leave a single argument unused by which we may prevail with the God of mercy to send us what we want. Thus much, then, upon this as a model prayer. Now I shall want a little longer time to speak upon,

II. *The encouragement which the text and its surroundings give to us in prayer.*

Brethren, it is always an encouragement to do a thing when you see the best of men doing it. Many a person has taken a medicine only because he has known wiser men than himself take it. The best and wisest of persons in all ages have adopted the custom of prayer in times of distress, and, indeed, in all times. That ought to encourage us to do the same. I heard a dear Welsh brother speak last Thursday evening, who interested and amused me, too, but I cannot profess to repeat the way in which he told us a biblical story. It was something in this way. He told it as a Welshman, and not quite as I think I might. He said that after the Lord Jesus Christ had gone up to heaven, having told his disciples to wait at Jerusalem till the Spirit of God was given, Peter might have said, "Well, now we must not go out preaching till this blessing comes, so I shall be off fishing." And John might have said, "Well, there is the old boat over at the lake of Gennesaret; I think I shall go and see how that is getting on; it is a long time since I saw after it." And each one might have said, "Well, I shall go about my business, for it is not many days hence when it is coming, and we may as well be at our earthly calling." "No," says he, "they did not say that at all, but Peter said, 'Where shall we hold a prayer meeting?' and Mary said she had got a nice large room that would do for a prayer meeting. True it was in a back street, and the house was not very respectable, and, 'Besides,' says she, 'it is up at the very top of the house, but it is a big room.' 'Never mind,' says Peter, 'it will be nearer to heaven.' So they went into the upper room, and there began to pray, and did not cease the prayer meeting till the blessing came."

Then the brother told us the next story of a prayer meeting in the Bible. Peter was in prison, and Herod was so afraid that he would get out again that he had sixteen policemen to look after him, and the brethren knew they could not get Peter out in any other way than one; so they said, "We will hold a prayer meeting." Always the way with the church at that time, when anything was amiss, to say, "Where shall we have a prayer meeting?" So Mistress Mary said she had got a good room which would do very well for a prayer meeting. It was in a back street, so nobody would know of it, and they would be quiet. So they held that prayer meeting, and began to pray. I do not suppose they prayed the Lord to knock the prison walls down, nor to kill the policemen, nor anything of that kind, but they prayed only that Peter might get out, and they left how he was to get out to God. While they were praying there came a knock at the door. "Ah!" said they, "that is a policeman come after another of us. But Rhoda went to the door to look, and when she looked she started back in affright. What could she see? She looked again, however, and she was persuaded that it was no other than Peter. She went back to her mistress, and said, "There is Peter at the gate." Good souls! they had been praying that Peter might come out, but they could not believe it, and they said, "Why, it is his spirit—his angel." "No," said the girl, "I know Peter well enough; he has been here dozens of times, and I know it is Peter"; and in came Peter, and they all wondered at their unbelief. They had asked God to set Peter free, and free Peter was. It was the prayer meeting that did it. And rest assured we should, everyone, find it our best resource in every hour of need to draw near to God.

Prayer makes the darkest cloud withdraw,
Prayer mounts the ladder Jacob saw,
Gives exercise to faith and love,
Brings every blessing from above.

Restraining prayer, we cease to fight;
Prayer makes the Christian armor bright;
And Satan trembles when he sees
The weakest saint upon his knees.

It is prayer that does it, and this fact should encourage us to pray.

The success of Daniel's prayer is the next encouragement. He had not got to the end of his prayer before a soft hand touched him, and he looked up, and there stood Gabriel in the form of a man. That was quick work surely. So Daniel thought, but it was much quicker than Daniel expected, for as soon as ever he began to pray, the word went forth for the angel to descend. The answer to prayer is the most rapid thing in the world. "Before they call, I will answer; and while they are yet speaking, I will hear." I believe electricity travels at the rate of two hundred thousand miles in a second—so it is estimated; but prayer travels faster than that, for it is, "Before they call, I will answer." There is no time occupied at all. When God wills to answer, the answer may come as soon as the desire is given. And if it delay, it is only that it may come at a better time—like some ships that come home more slowly because they bring the heavier cargo. Delayed prayers are prayers that are put out to interest a while, to come home, not only with the capital, but with the compound interest too. Oh! prayer cannot fail—prayer cannot fail. Heaven may as soon fall as prayer fail. God may sooner change the ordinances of day and night, than he can cease to reply to the faithful, believing, spirit-wrought prayer of his own quickened, earnest, importunate people. Therefore, because he sends success, brethren, pray much.

It ought to encourage us, too, in the next place, to recollect that Daniel prayed for a very hard case. Jerusalem was in ruins; the Jews were scattered; their sins were excessive; but, nevertheless, he prayed, and God heard him. We are not in so bad a case as that with the church; we have not to mourn that God has departed from us; our prayer is that he may not, even in any measure, withdraw his hand. I do pray God that I may long be buried before he shall suffer this church to lose his presence. There is nothing that I know of in connection with our church life that is worth a single farthing, if the Spirit of God be gone. He must be there. Brethren, if you are not prayerful, if you are not holy, if you are not earnest, God does not keep priests, deacons, elders, and church members living near to him. The sorrow of heart which one will feel if one be kept right himself cannot be expressed. May the Lord prevent our declining. If you are declining, may he bring you back. Some of you, I am afraid, are so—getting cold. Now and then I hear of a person who finds it too far to come to the Tabernacle. It used to be very short one time, though it was four or five miles. But when the heart gets cold, the road gets long. Ah! there are some who want this little attention and the other. Time was when they stood in the aisle, in the coldest and draftiest place—if the word was blessed to them, they would not have minded it. May God grant that you may be a living people always, for years and years to come, until Christ himself comes. But oh! you that are living near to God, make this your daily, hourly, nightly prayer, that he would not withdraw from us for our sins, but continue to stretch out his hand in lovingkindness, even until he gathers us to our Father.

It ought, further, to encourage us in prayer to remember that Daniel was only one man, and yet he won his suit. But if two of you agree as touching any one thing, it shall be done—but a threefold cord, a fifty-fold cord—oh! if, out of our four thousand members, every one prayed instantly, day and night, for the blessing, oh! what prevalence there must be! Would God it were so!

Brethren, how about your private prayers: are they what they should be? Those morning prayers, those evening prayers, and that midday prayer, for surely your soul must go up to heaven, even if your knees are not bent—are those prayers as they should be? It will bring leanness upon you; there cannot be a fat soul and neglected prayer. There must be much praying if there be much rejoicing in the Lord.

And then your family prayers: do you keep them up? I was in a railway carriage the other day, and a gentleman said to me, who was sitting beside me, "My son is going to be married tomorrow—going to be married to one of your members." "I am glad to hear it," I said. "I hope he is a believer." "Oh! yes, sir; he has been a member of your church for some years. I wish you would write me something to give them tomorrow." Well, you know how the carriage will shake, but I managed to jot down something on a little bit of paper with a pencil. The words, I think, that I put were something like this, "I wish you every joy. May your joys be doubled; may your sorrow be divided and lightened." But then I put, "Build the altar before you build the tent. Take care that daily prayer begins your matrimonial life." I am sure we cannot expect our children to grow up a godly seed if there is no family prayer. Are your family prayers, then, what they ought to be?

Then next, let me say to each one, how about your prayers as members of the church? Perhaps I am the last person that might complain about a prayer meeting. It really is a grand sight to see so many of you, but I must confess I don't feel quite content, for there are some members whom I used to see, but don't see now. I know I see some fresh ones, and we are never short of praying men, but I want to see the others as well. I know those who are constantly at prayer meetings can say it is good to be there. It is the best evening in the week often to us, when we come together to entreat for the blessing. Do not, I pray you, get into the habit of neglecting the assembling of yourselves together for prayer. How often have I said, "All our strength lies in prayer"! When we were very few, God multiplied us in answer to prayer. What prayers we put up night and day when we launched out to preach the gospel in a larger building! And what an answer God sent us. Since then, in times of need and trouble we have cried to God, and he has heard us. Daily he sends us help for our college, for our orphanage, and for our other works, in answer to prayer. Oh! you that come here as members of the church, if you do not pray, the very beams out of these walls and the stones will cry out against you. This house was built in answer to prayer. If anybody had said that we, who were but few and poor, could have erected such a structure, I think it would have sounded impossible. But it was done—you know how readily it was done, how God raised us up friends, how he has helped us to this day. Oh! don't stop your prayers. You seem to me, good people, to be very like that king who, when he went to the dying prophet, was told, "Take the arrows . . . Smite upon the ground. And he smote thrice and stayed." And the prophet was angry and said, You should have shot many times, and then you would have utterly destroyed your enemies. And so we pray, as it were, but little. We ask but little, and God gives it. Oh! that we could ask much, and pray for much, and shoot many arrows, and plead very earnestly.

Look at this city of ours. I would not say a word in derogation of my country, but I am afraid there is not much to choose between the sin of London and the sin of Paris. And see what has come on Paris! One could hardly live in that city and know all the sin that was going on there without fearing that nation's sin would bring a national chastisement. And oh! this wicked city of London, with its dens of vice and filthiness! You are the salt of the earth; you that love Christ, let not your salt lose its savor. God forbid that you should sin against the Lord by ceasing to pray for this wicked people. Everywhere, sea and land, is compassed by the adversaries of the truth, to make proselytes. I beseech you compass the mercy seat, that their machinations may be defeated. At this time there ought to be special prayer. When God in providence seems to be shaking the papacy to its base, now should we cry aloud and spare not. Out of these convulsions God may bring lasting blessings. Let us not neglect to work when God works. Let the hand of the man be lifted up in prayer when the wing of the angel is moved in providence. We may expect great things if we can pray greatly, and wrestle earnestly. I call you, in God's name, to the mercy seat. Draw near there, with intense importunity; and such a blessing shall come as you have not yet imagined. Pray for some here present that are unconverted. There are a good many of them. They will not pray for themselves; let us pray them into prayer; let us pray God for them, until they at last pray God for themselves. Prayer can mercy's door unlock, for others as well as for our own persons; let us, therefore, abound in prayer, and God send us the blessing, for Jesus' sake. Amen.

"Lead Us Not into Temptation"

~~~

Delivered in 1878 at the Metropolitan Tabernacle, Newington. No. 1402.

"Lead us not into temptation."—MATTHEW 6:13

Looking over a book of addresses to young people the other day, I met with the outline of a discourse which struck me as being a perfect gem. I will give it to you. The text is the Lord's Prayer, and the exposition is divided into most instructive heads. "Our Father which art in heaven": a child away from home. "Hallowed be thy name": a worshiper. "Thy kingdom come": a subject. "Thy will be done in earth, as it is in heaven": a servant. "Give us this day our daily bread": a beggar. "And forgive us our debts, as we forgive our debtors": a sinner. "And lead us not into temptation, but deliver us from evil": a sinner in danger of being a greater sinner still. The titles are in every case most appropriate, and truthfully condense the petition.

Now if you will remember the outline you will notice that the prayer is like a ladder. The petitions begin at the top and go downward. "Our Father which art in heaven": a child, a child of the heavenly Father. Now to be a child of God is the highest possible position of man. "Behold, what manner of love the Father hath bestowed upon us, that we should be called the sons of God." This is what Christ is—the Son of God, and "Our Father" is but a plural form of the very term which he uses in addressing God, for Jesus says, "Father." It is a very high, gracious, exalted position, which by faith we dare to occupy when we intelligently say, "Our Father which art in heaven."

It is a step down to the next—"Hallowed be thy name." Here we have a worshiper adoring with lowly reverence the thrice-holy God. A worshiper's place is a high one, but it attains not to the excellence of the child's position. Angels come as high as being worshipers; their incessant song hallows the name of God; but they cannot say, "Our Father," "For unto which of the angels said he at any time, Thou art my son?" They must be content to be within one step of the highest, but they cannot reach the summit, for neither by adoption, regeneration, nor by union to Christ, are they the children of God. "Abba, Father," is for men, not for angels, and, therefore, the worshiping sentence of the prayer is one step lower than the opening, "Our Father."

The next petition is for us as subjects, "Thy kingdom come." The subject comes lower than the worshiper, for worship is an elevated engagement wherein man exercises a priesthood and is seen in lowly but honorable estate. The child worships and then confesses the Great Father's royalty.

Descending still, the next position is that of a servant, "Thy will be done in earth, as it is in heaven." That is another step lower than a subject, for her majesty the Queen has many subjects who are not her servants. They are not bound to wait upon her in the palace with personal service though they own her as their honored sovereign. Dukes and such like are her subjects, but not her servants. The servant is a grade below the subject.

Everyone will own that the next petition is lower by far, for it is that of a beggar, "Give us this day our daily bread"—a beggar for bread—an everyday beggar—one who has continually to appeal to charity, even for his livelihood. This is a fit place for us to occupy who owe our all to the charity of heaven.

But there is a step lower than the beggar's, and that is the sinner's place. "Forgive" is lowlier than "give." "Forgive us our debts, as we forgive our debtors." Here, too, we may each one take up his position, for no word better befits our unworthy lips than the prayer "Forgive." As long as we live and sin we ought to weep and cry, "Have mercy on us, O Lord."

And now, at the very bottom of the ladder, stands a sinner, afraid of yet greater sin, in extreme danger and in conscious weakness, sensible of past sin and fearful of it for the future: hear him as with trembling lip he cries in the words of our text, "Lead us not into temptation, but deliver us from evil."

And yet, dear friends, though I have thus described the prayer as a going downward, downward is in matters of grace much the same as upward, as we could readily show if time permitted. At any rate, the down-going process of the prayer might equally well illustrate the advance of the divine life in the soul. The last clause of the prayer contains in it a deeper inward experience than the earlier part of it. Every believer is a child of God, a worshiper, a subject, a servant, a beggar, and a sinner; but it is not every man who perceives the allurements which beset him, or his own tendency to yield to them. It is not every child of God, even when advanced in years, who knows to the full the meaning of being led into temptation; for some follow an easy path and are seldom buffeted; and others are such tender babes that they hardly know their own corruptions. Fully to understand our text, a man should have had sharp brushes in the wars and have done battle against the enemy within his soul for many a day. He who has escaped as by the skin of his teeth, offers this prayer with an emphasis of meaning. The man who has felt the fowler's net about him—the man who has been seized by the adversary and almost destroyed—he prays with awful eagerness, "Lead us not into temptation."

I purpose at this time, in trying to commend this prayer to you, to notice, first of all, the spirit which suggests such a petition; secondly, the trials which such a prayer deprecates; and then, thirdly, the lessons which it teaches.

I. *What suggests such a prayer as this?*—"Lead us not into temptation."

First, from the position of the clause, I gather, by a slight reasoning process, that it is suggested by watchfulness. This petition follows after the sentence, "Forgive us our debts." I will suppose the petition to have been answered, and the man's sin is forgiven. What then? If you will look back upon your own lives, you will soon perceive what generally happens to a pardoned man, for "As in water face answereth to face, so the heart of man to man." One believing man's inner experience is like another's, and your own feelings were the same as mine. Very speedily after the penitent has received forgiveness and has the sense of it in his soul, he is tempted of the devil, for Satan cannot bear to lose his subjects, and when he sees them cross the borderline and escape out of his hand, he gathers up all his forces and exercises all his cunning if, perchance, he may slay them at once. To meet this special assault, the Lord makes the heart watchful. Perceiving the ferocity and subtlety of Satan's temptations, the newborn believer, rejoicing in the perfect pardon he has received, cries to God, "Lead us not into temptation." It is the fear of losing the joy of pardoned sin which thus cries out to the good Lord—"Our Father, do not suffer us to lose the salvation we have so lately obtained. Do not even subject it to jeopardy. Do not permit Satan to break our newfound peace. We have but newly escaped; do not plunge us in the deeps again. Swimming to shore, some on boards and some on broken pieces of the ship, we have come safe to land; constrain us not to tempt the boisterous main again. Cast us not upon the rough billows any more. O God, we see the enemy advancing: he is ready if he can to sift us as wheat. Do not suffer us to be put into his sieve, but deliver us, we pray you." It is a prayer of watchfulness; and mark you, though we have spoken of watchfulness as necessary at the commencement of the Christian life, it is equally needful even to the close. There is no hour in which a believer can afford to slumber. Watch, I pray you, when you are alone, for temptation, like a creeping assassin, has its dagger for solitary hearts. You must bolt and bar the door well if you would keep out the devil.

Watch yourself in public, for temptations in troops cause their arrows to fly by day. The choicest companions you can select will not be without some evil influence upon you unless you be on your guard. Remember our blessed Master's words, "What I say unto you I say unto all, Watch," and as you watch, this prayer will often rise from your inmost heart:

From dark temptation's power,

From Satan's wiles defend;

Deliver in the evil hour,

And guide me to the end.

It is the prayer of watchfulness.

Next, it seems to me to be the natural prayer of holy horror at the very thought of falling again into sin. I remember the story of a pitman who, having been a gross blasphemer, a man of licentious life and everything that was bad, when converted by divine grace, was terribly afraid lest his old companions should lead him back again. He knew himself to be a man of strong passions, and very apt to be led astray by others, and, therefore, in his dread of being drawn into his old sins, he prayed most vehemently that sooner than ever he should go back to his old ways, he might die. He did die there and then. Perhaps it was the best answer to the best prayer that the poor man could have offered. I am sure any man who has once lived an evil life, if the wondrous grace of God has snatched him from it, will agree that the pitman's prayer was not one whit too enthusiastic. It were better for us to die at once than to live on and return to our first estate and bring dishonor upon the name of Jesus Christ our Lord. The prayer before us springs from the shrinking of the soul at the first approach of the tempter. The footfall of the fiend falls on the startled ear of the timid penitent; he quivers like an aspen leaf, and cries out, What, is he coming again? And is it possible that I may fall again? And may I once more defile these garments with that loathsome, murderous sin which slew my Lord? "O my God," the prayer seems to say, "keep me from so dire an evil. Lead me, I pray you, where you will—yes, even through death's dark valley, but do not lead me into temptation, lest I fall and dishonor you." The burnt child dreads the fire. He who has once been caught in the steel trap carries the scars in his flesh and is horribly afraid of being again held by its cruel teeth.

The third feeling, also, is very apparent; namely, diffidence of personal strength. The man who feels himself strong enough for anything is daring, and even invites the battle which will prove his power. "Oh," says he, "I care not; they may gather about me who will; I am quite able to take care of myself and hold my own against any number." He is ready to be led into conflict; he courts the fray. Not so the man who has been taught of God and has learned his own weakness; he does not want to be tried, but seeks quiet places where he may be out of harm's way. Put him into the battle and he will play the man; let him be tempted and you will see how steadfast he will be; but he does not ask for conflict, as, I think, few soldiers will who know what fighting means. Surely it is only those who have never smelled gunpowder, or seen the corpses heaped in bloody masses on each other, that are so eager for the shot and shell, but your veteran would rather enjoy the piping times of peace. No experienced believer ever desires spiritual conflict, though perchance some raw recruits may challenge it. In the Christian, a recollection of his previous weakness—his resolutions broken, his promises unkept—makes him pray that he may not in future be severely tested. He does not dare to trust himself again. He wants no fight with Satan, or with the world; but he asks that if possible he may be kept from those severe encounters, and his prayer is, "Lead us not into temptation." The wise believer shows a sacred diffidence—no, I think I may say an utter despair of himself: and even though he knows that the power of God is strong enough for anything, yet is the sense of his weakness so heavy upon him that he begs to be spared too much trial. Hence the cry, "Lead us not into temptation."

Nor have I quite exhausted, I think, the phases of the spirit which suggests this prayer, for it seems to me to arise somewhat out of charity. "Charity?" say you. "How so?" Well, the connection is always to be observed, and by reading the preceding sentence in connection with it we get the words, "as we forgive our debtors. And lead us not into temptation." We should not be too severe with those persons who have done wrong, and have offended us, but pray, "Lord, lead us not into temptation." Your maidservant, poor girl, did purloin a trifle from your property. I make no excuse for her theft, but I beseech you pause a while before you quite ruin her character for life. Ask yourself, "Might not I have done the same had I been in her position? Lord, lead me not into temptation." It is true it was very wrong in that young man to deal so dishonestly with your goods. Still, you know, he was under great pressure from a strong hand, and yielded only from compulsion. Do not be too severe. Do not say, "I will push the matter through; I will have the law of him." No, but wait a while; let pity speak, let mercy's silver voice plead with you. Remember yourself, lest you also be tempted, and pray, "Lead us not into temptation." I am afraid that badly as some behave under temptation, others of us might have done worse if we had been there. I like, if I can, to form a kind judgment of the erring; and it helps me to do so when I imagine myself to have been subject to their trials, and to have looked at things from their point of view, and to have been in their circumstances, and to have nothing of the grace of

God to help me: should I not have fallen as badly as they have done, or even gone beyond them in evil?

May not the day come to you who show no mercy in which you may have to ask mercy for yourselves? Did I say—may it not come to you? No, it must come to you. When leaving all below, you will have to take a retrospective view of your life, and see much to mourn over; to what can you appeal then but to the mercy of God? And what if he should answer you, "An appeal was made to your mercy, and you had none. As you rendered unto others, so will I render unto you." What answer would you have if God were so to treat you? Would not such an answer be just and right? Should not every man be paid in his own coin when he stands at the judgment seat? So I think that this prayer, "Lead us not into temptation," should often spring up from the heart through a charitable feeling toward others who have erred, who are of the same flesh and blood as ourselves. Now, whenever you see the drunkard reel through the streets, do not glory over him, but say, "Lead us not into temptation." When you take down the papers and read that men of position have betrayed their trust for gold, condemn their conduct if you will, but do not exult in your own steadfastness, rather cry in all humility, "Lead us not into temptation." When the poor girl seduced from the paths of virtue comes across your way, look not on her with the scorn that would give her up to destruction, but say, "Lead us not into temptation." It would teach us milder and gentler ways with sinful men and women if this prayer were as often in our hearts as it is upon our lips.

Once more, do you not think that this prayer breathes the spirit of confidence—confidence in God? "Why," says one, "I do not see that." To me—I know not whether I shall be able to convey my thought—to me there is a degree of very tender familiarity and sacred boldness in this expression. Of course, God will lead me now that I am his child. Moreover, now that he has forgiven me, I know that he will not lead me where I can come to any harm. This my faith ought to know and believe, and yet for several reasons there rises to my mind a fear lest his providence should conduct me where I shall be tempted. Is that fear right or wrong? It burdens my mind; may I go with it to my God? May I express in prayer this misgiving of soul? May I pour out this anxiety before the great, wise, loving God? Will it not be impertinent? No, it will not, for Jesus puts the words into my mouth, and says, "After this manner therefore pray ye." You are afraid that he may lead you into temptation; but he will not do so; or should he see fit to try you, he will also afford you strength to hold out to the end. He will be pleased in his infinite mercy to preserve you. Where he leads, it will be perfectly safe for you to follow, for his presence will make the deadliest air to become healthful. But since instinctively you have a dread lest you should be conducted where the fight will be too stern and the way too rough, tell it to your heavenly Father without reserve.

You know at home if a child has any little complaint against his father it is always better for him to tell it. If he thinks that his father overlooked him the other day, or half thinks that the task his father has given him is too severe, or fancies that his father is expecting too much of him—if he does not say anything at all about it, he may sulk and lose much of the loving tenderness which a child's heart should always feel. But when the child frankly says, "Father, I do not want you to think that I do not love you or that I cannot trust you, but I have a troubling thought in my mind, and I will tell it right straight out"; that is the wisest course to follow, and shows a filial trust. That is the way to keep up love and confidence. So if you have a suspicion in your soul that perhaps your Father might put you into temptation too strong for you, tell it to him. Tell it to him, though it seems taking a great liberty. Though the fear may be the fruit of unbelief, yet make it known to your Lord, and do not harbor it sullenly. Remember the Lord's Prayer was not made for him, but for you, and, therefore, it reads matters from your standpoint and not from his. Our Lord's Prayer is not for our Lord; it is for us, his children; and children say to their fathers ever so many things which it is quite proper for them to say, but which are not wise and accurate after the measure of their parents' knowledge. Their father knows what their hearts mean, and yet there may be a good deal in what they say which is foolish or mistaken. So I look upon this prayer as exhibiting that blessed childlike confidence which tells out to its father a fear which grieves it, whether that fear be altogether correct or not. Beloved, we need not here debate the question whether God does lead into temptation or not, or whether we can fall from grace or not; it is enough that we have a fear, and are permitted to tell it to our Father in heaven. Whenever you have a fear of any kind, hurry off with it to him who loves his little ones, and like a father pities them and soothes even their needless alarms.

Thus have I shown that the spirit which suggests this prayer is that of watchfulness, of holy horror at the very thought of sin, of diffidence of our own strength, of charity toward others, and of confidence in God.

II. Secondly, let us ask, *What are these temptations which the prayer deprecates*? Or say rather, what are these trials which are so much feared?

I do not think the prayer is intended at all to ask God to spare us from being afflicted for our good, or to save us from being made to suffer as a chastisement. Of course we should be glad to escape those things; but the prayer aims at another form of trial, and may be paraphrased thus—"Save me, O Lord, from such trials and sufferings as may lead me into sin. Spare me from too great trials, lest I fall by their overcoming my patience, my faith, or my steadfastness."

Now, as briefly as I can, I will show you how men may be led into temptation by the hand of God.

And the first is by the withdrawal of divine grace. Suppose for a moment—it is only a supposition—suppose the Lord were to leave us altogether, then should we perish speedily; but suppose—and this is not a barren supposition—that he were in some measure to take away his strength from us, should we not be in an evil case? Suppose he did not support our faith; what unbelief we should exhibit? Suppose he refused to support us in the time of trial so that we no longer maintained our integrity, what would become of us? Ah, the most upright man would not be upright long, nor the most holy, holy any more. Suppose, dear friend—you who walk in the light of God's countenance and bear life's yoke so easily because he sustains you—suppose his presence were withdrawn from you, what must be your portion?

We are all so like to Samson in this matter that I must bring him in as the illustration, though he has often been used for that purpose by others. So long as the locks of our head are unshorn, we can do anything and everything: we can rend lions, carry gates of Gaza, and smite the armies of the alien. It is by the divine consecrating mark that we are strong in the power of his might; but if the Lord be once withdrawn and we attempt the work alone, then are we weak as the tiniest insect. When the Lord has departed from you, O Samson, what are you more than another man? Then the cry, "The Philistines be upon thee, Samson," is the knell of all your glory. You do vainly shake those lusty limbs of yours. Now you will have your eyes put out, and the Philistines will make sport of you. In view of a like catastrophe we may well be in an agony of supplication. Pray then, "Lord, leave me not; and lead me not into temptation by taking your Spirit from me."

Keep us, Lord, oh keep us ever,
Vain our hope if left by thee;
We are thine, oh leave us never,
Till thy face in heaven we see;
There to praise thee
Through a bright eternity.

All our strength at once would fail us,
If deserted, Lord, by thee;
Nothing then could aught avail us,
Certain our defeat would be.
Those who hate us
Thenceforth their desire would see.

Another set of temptations will be found in providential conditions. The words of Agur, the son of Jakeh, shall be my illustration here. "Remove far from me vanity and lies: give me neither poverty nor riches; feed me with food convenient for me: lest I be full, and deny thee, and say, Who is the LORD? or lest I be poor, and steal, and take the name of my God in vain." Some of us have never known what actual want means, but have from our youth up lived in social comfort. Ah, dear friends, when we see what extreme poverty has made some men do, how do we know that we should not have behaved even worse if we had been as sorely pressed as they? We may well shudder and say, "Lord, when I see poor families crowded together in one little room where there is scarcely space to observe common decency; when I see hardly bread enough to keep the children from crying for hunger; when I see the man's garments wearing out upon his back, and by far too thin to keep out the cold; I pray you subject me not to such trial, lest if I were in such a case I might put forth my hand and steal. Lead me not into the temptation of pining want."

And, on the other hand, look at the temptations of money when men have more to spend than they can possibly need, and there is around them a society which tempts them into racing, and gambling, and whoredom, and all manner of iniquities. The young man who has a fortune ready to hand before he reaches years of discretion, and is surrounded by flatterers and tempters all eager to plunder him; do you wonder that he is led into vice, and becomes a ruined man morally? Like a rich galleon waylaid by pirates, he is never out of danger; is it a marvel that he never reaches the port of safety? Women tempt him, men flatter him, vile messengers of the devil fawn upon him, and the young simpleton goes after them like an ox to the slaughter, or as a bird hastens to the snare and knows not that it is for his life. You may very well thank heaven you never knew the temptation, for if it were put in your way, you would also be in sore peril. If riches and honor allure you, follow not eagerly after them, but pray, "Lead us not into temptation."

Providential positions often try men. There is a man very much pushed for ready money in business; how shall he meet that heavy bill? If he does not meet it, there will be desolation in his family; the mercantile concern from which he now draws his living will be broken up; everybody will be ashamed of him, his children will be outcasts, and he will be ruined. He has only to use a sum of trust money: he has no right to risk a penny of it, for it is not his, but still by its temporary use he may perchance tide over the difficulty. The devil tells him he can put it back in a week. If he does touch that money, it will be a roguish action, but then he says, "Nobody will be hurt by it, and it will be a wonderful accommodation," and so on. If he yields to the suggestion, and the thing goes right, there are some who would say, "Well, after all, there was not much harm in it, and it was a prudent step, for it saved him from ruin." But if it goes wrong, and he is found out, then everybody says, "It was a shameful robbery. The man ought to be transported." But, brethren, the action was wrong in itself, and the consequences neither make it better nor worse. Do not bitterly condemn, but pray again and again, "Lead us not into temptation. Lead us not into temptation." You see, God does put men into such positions in providence at times that they are severely tried. It is for their good that they are tried, and when they can stand the trial, they magnify his grace, and they themselves become stronger men: the test has beneficial uses when it can be borne, and God therefore does not always screen his children from it. Our heavenly Father has never meant to cuddle us up and keep us out of temptation, for that is no part of the system which he has wisely arranged for our education. He does not mean us to be babies in go-carts all our lives. He made Adam and Eve in the garden, and he did not put an iron palisade around the Tree of Knowledge, and say, "You cannot get at it." No, he warned them not to touch the fruit, but they could reach the tree if they would. He meant that they should have the possibility of attaining the dignity of voluntary fidelity if they remained steadfast, but they lost it by their sin; and God means in his new creation not to shield his people from every kind of test and trial, for that were to breed hypocrites and to keep even the faithful weak and dwarfish. The Lord does sometimes put the chosen where they are tried, and we do right to pray, "Lead us not into temptation."

And there are temptations arising out of physical conditions. There are some men who are very moral in character because they are in health; and there are other men who are very bad, who, I do not doubt, if we knew all about them, should have some little leniency shown them, because of the unhappy conformation of their constitution. Why, there are many people to whom to be cheerful and to be generous is no effort whatsoever, while there are others who need to labor hard to keep themselves from despair and misanthropy. Diseased livers, palpitating hearts, and injured brains are hard things to struggle against. Does that poor old lady complain? She has had the rheumatism only thirty years, and yet she now and then murmurs! How would you be if you felt her pains for thirty minutes? I have heard of a man who complained to everybody. When he came to die, the doctors opened his skull, and they found a close-fitting brainbox, and that the man suffered from an irritable brain. Did not that account for a great many of his hard speeches? I do not mention these matters to excuse sin, but to make you and me treat such people as gently as we can, and pray, "Lord, do not give me such a brainbox, and do not let me have such rheumatisms or such pains, because upon such a rack I may be much worse than they are. Lead us not into temptation."

So, again, mental conditions often furnish great temptations. When a man becomes depressed, he becomes tempted. Those among us who rejoice much often sink about as much as we rise, and when everything looks dark around us, Satan is sure to seize the occasion to suggest despondency. God forbid that we should excuse ourselves, but, dear brother, pray that you be not led into this temptation. Perhaps if you were as much a subject of nervousness and sinking of spirit as the friend you blame for his melancholy, you might be more blameworthy than he, therefore pity rather than condemn.

And, on the other hand, when the spirits are exhilarated and the heart is ready to dance for joy, it is very easy for levity to step in and for words to be spoken amiss. Pray the Lord not to let you rise so high nor sink so low as to be led into evil. "Lead us not into temptation" must be our hourly prayer.

Further than this, there are temptations arising out of personal associations, which are formed for us in the order of providence. We are bound to shun evil company, but there are cases in which, without fault on their part, persons are made to associate with bad characters. I may instance the pious child whose father is a swearer, and the godly woman lately converted, whose husband remains a swearer and blasphemes the name of Christ. It is the same with workmen who have to labor in workshops, where lewd fellows at every half a dozen words let fall an oath, and pour forth that filthy language which shocks us every day more and more. I think that in London our working people talk more filthily than ever they did; at least, I hear more of it as I pass along or pause in the street. Well, if persons are obliged to work in such shops, or to live in such families, there may come times when under the lash of jest and sneer and sarcasm the heart may be a little dismayed and the tongue may refuse to speak for Christ. Such a silence and cowardice are not to be excused, yet do not censure your brother, but say, "Lord, lead me not into temptation." How know you that you would be more bold? Peter quailed before a talkative maid, and you may be cowed by a woman's tongue. The worst temptation for a young Christian that I know of is to live with a hypocrite—a man so sanctified and demure that the young heart, deceived by appearances, fully trusts him while the wretch is false at heart and rotten in life. And such wretches there are who, with the pretense and affectation of sanctimoniousness, will do deeds at which we might weep tears of blood: young people are frightfully staggered, and many of them become deformed for life in their spiritual characteristics through associating with such beings as these. When you see faults caused by such common but horrible causes, say to yourself, "Lord, lead me not into temptation. I thank you for godly parents and for Christian associations and for godly examples; but what might I have been if I had been subjected to the very reverse? If evil influences had touched me when like a vessel I was upon the wheel, I might have exhibited even grosser failings than those which I now see in others."

Thus I might continue to urge you to pray, dear friends, against various temptations; but let me say, the Lord has for some men very special tests, such as may be seen in the case of Abraham. He gives him a son in his old age, and then says to him, "Take now thy son, thine only son Isaac, whom thou lovest, . . . and offer him . . . for a burnt offering." You will do right to pray, "Lord, lead me not into such a temptation as that. I am not worthy to be so tried. Oh, do not so test me." I have known some Christians sit down and calculate whether they could have acted as the patriarch did. It is very foolish, dear brother. When you are called upon to do it, you will be enabled to make the same sacrifice by the grace of God; but if you are not called upon to do it, why should the power be given? Shall God's grace be left unused? Your strength shall be equal to your day, but it shall not exceed it. I would have you ask to be spared the sterner tests.

Another instance is to be seen in Job. God gave Job over to Satan with a limit, and you know how Satan tormented him and tried to overwhelm him. If any man were to pray, "Lord, try me like Job," it would be a very unwise prayer. "Oh, but I could be as patient as he," say you. You are the very man who would yield to bitterness, and curse your God. The man who could best exhibit the patience of Job will be the first, according to his Lord's bidding, fervently to pray, "Lead us not into temptation." Dear friends, we are to be prepared for trial if God wills it, but we are not to court it; we are rather to pray against it, even as our Lord Jesus, though ready to drink the bitter cup, yet in an agony exclaimed, "If it be possible, let this cup pass from me." Trials sought after are not such as the Lord has promised to bless. No true child asks for the rod.

To put my meaning in a way in which it will be clearly seen, let me tell an old story. I have read in history that two men were condemned to die as martyrs in the burning days of Queen Mary. One of them boasted very loudly to his companion of his confidence that he should play the man at the stake. He did not mind the suffering; he was so grounded in the gospel that he knew he should never deny it. He said that he longed for the fatal morning even as a bride for the wedding. His companion in prison in the same chamber was a poor trembling soul, who could not and would not deny his Master; but he told his companion that he was very much afraid of the fire. He said he had always been very sensitive of suffering, and he was in great dread that when he began to burn, the pain might cause him to deny the truth. He besought his friend to pray for him, and he spent his time very much in weeping over his weakness and crying to God for strength. The other continually rebuked him, and chided him for being so unbelieving and weak. When they both came to the stake, he who had been so bold recanted at the sight of the fire and went back ignominiously to an apostate's life, while the poor trembling man whose prayer had been, "Lead me not into temptation," stood firm as a rock, praising and magnifying God as he was burned to a cinder. Weakness is our strength; and our strength is weakness. Cry unto God that he try you not beyond your strength; and in the shrinking tenderness of your conscious weakness breathe out the prayer, "Lead us not into temptation." Then if he does lead you into the conflict, his Holy Spirit will strengthen you, and you will be brave as a lion before the adversary. Though trembling and shrinking within yourself before the throne of God, you would confront the very devil and all the hosts of hell without one touch of fear. It may seem strange, but so the case is.

III. And now I conclude with the last head—*the lessons which this prayer teaches*. I have not time to enlarge. I will just throw them out in the rough.

The first lesson from the prayer, "Lead us not into temptation," is this: Never boast your own strength. Never say, "Oh, I shall never fall into such follies and sins. They may try me, but they will find more than a match in me." Let not him that puts on his harness boast as though he were putting it off. Never indulge one thought of congratulation as to self-strength. You have no power of your own; you are as weak as water. The devil has only to touch you in the right place, and you will run according to his will. Only let a loose stone or two be moved and you will soon see that the feeble building of your own natural virtue will come down at a run. Never court temptation by boasting your own capacity.

The next thing is, never desire trial. Does anybody ever do that? Yes; I heard one say the other day that God had so prospered him for years that he was afraid he was not a child of God, for he found that God's children were chastised, and, therefore, he almost wished to be afflicted. Dear brother, do not wish for that: you will meet with trouble soon enough. If I were a little boy at home, I do not think I should say to my brother, because he had been whipped, "I am afraid I am not my father's child, and fear that he does not love me because I am not smarting under the rod. I wish he would whip me just to let me know his love." No; no child would ever be so stupid. We must not for any reason desire to be afflicted or tried, but must pray, "Lead us not into temptation."

The next thought is, never go into temptation. The man who prays, "Lead us not into temptation," and then goes into it is a liar before God. What a hypocrite a man must be who utters this prayer, and then goes off to the theater! How false is he who offers this prayer and then stands at the bar and drinks and talks with depraved men and bedizened women! "Lead us not into temptation" is shameful profanity when it comes from the lips of men who resort to places of amusement whose moral tone is bad. "Oh," say you, "you should not tell us of such things." Why not? Some of you do them, and I make bold to rebuke evil wherever it is found, and shall do so while this tongue can move. There is a world of cant about. People go to church and say, "Lead us not into temptation," and then they know where temptation is to be found, and they go straight into it. You need not ask the Lord not to lead you there; he has nothing to do with you. The devil and you, between you, will go far enough without mocking God with your hypocritical prayers. The man who goes into sin willfully, with his eyes open, and then bends his knee and says half a dozen times over in his church on a Sunday morning, "Lead us not into temptation," is a hypocrite without a mask upon him. Let him take that home to himself, and believe that I mean to be personal to him, and to such bare-faced hypocrites as he.

The last word is, if you pray God not to lead you into temptation, do not lead others there. Some seem to be singularly forgetful of the effect of their example, for they will do evil things in the presence of their children and those who look up to them. Now I pray you consider that by ill example you destroy others as well as yourself. Do nothing, my dear brother, of which you have need to be ashamed, or which you would not wish others to copy. Do the right at all times, and do not let Satan make a cat's-paw of you to destroy the souls of others: do pray, "Lead us not into temptation"; then do not lead your children there. They are invited during the festive season to such and such a family party, where there will be everything but what will conduce to their spiritual growth or even to their good morals: do not allow them to go. Put your foot down. Be steadfast about it. Having once prayed, "Lead us not into tempta-tion," act not the hypocrite by allowing your children to go into it.

God bless these words to us. May they sink into our souls, and if any feel that they have sinned, oh, that they may now ask forgiveness through the pre-cious blood of Christ, and find it by faith in him. When they have obtained mercy, let their next desire be that they may be kept in future from sinning as they did before, and, therefore, let them pray, "Lead us not into temptation." God bless you.

Peter's Shortest Prayer

Published on Thursday, February 24, 1910; delivered on Thursday evening, October 2, 1873, at the Metropolitan Tabernacle, Newington. No. 3186.

"Lord, save me."—MATTHEW 14:30

I am going to talk about the characteristics of this prayer in the hope that there may be many who have never yet prayed aright who may make this their own prayer tonight, so that from many a person here present this cry may silently go up, "Lord, save me."

Where did Peter pray this prayer? It was not in a place set apart for public worship, or in his usual place for private prayer; but he prayed this prayer just as he was sinking in the water. He was in great peril, so he cried out, "Lord, save me." It is well to assemble with God's people for prayer if you can; but if you cannot go up to his house, it matters little, for prayer can ascend to him from anywhere all over the world. It is well to have a special spot where you pray at home; probably most of us have a certain chair by which we kneel to pray, and we feel that we can talk to God most freely there. At the same time, we must never allow ourselves to become the slaves even of such a good habit as that, and must always remember that, if we really want to find the Lord by prayer,

Where'er we seek him, he is found,
And every place is hallowed ground.

We may pray to God when engaged in any occupation if it is a lawful one; and if it is not, we have no business to be in it. If there is anything we do over which we cannot pray, we ought never to dare to do it again; and if there is any occupation concerning which we have to say, "We could not pray while engaged in it," it is clear that the occupation is a wrong one.

The habit of daily prayer must be maintained. It is well to have regular hours of devotion, and to resort to the same place for prayer, as far as possible; still, the spirit of prayer is better even than the habit of prayer. It is better to be able to pray at all times than to make it a rule to pray at certain times and seasons. A Christian is more fully grown in grace when he prays about everything than he would be if he prayed only under certain conditions and circumstances. I always feel that there is something wrong if I go without prayer for even half an hour in the day. I cannot understand how a Christian man can go from morning to evening without prayer. I cannot comprehend how he lives, and how he fights the battle of life without asking the guardian care of God while the arrows of temptation are flying so thickly around him. I cannot imagine how he can decide what to do in times of perplexity, how he can see his own imperfections or the faults of others without feeling constrained to say, all day long, "O Lord, guide me; O Lord, forgive me; O Lord, bless my friend!" I cannot think how he can be continually receiving mercies from the Lord without saying, "God be thanked for this new token of his grace! Blessed be the name of the Lord for what he is doing for me in his abounding mercy! O Lord, still remember me with the favor that you show to your people!" Do not be content, dear brethren and sisters in Christ, unless you can pray everywhere and at all times, and so obey the apostolic injunction, "Pray without ceasing."

I have already reminded you, dear friends, that Peter prayed his prayer when he was in circumstances of imminent danger. "Beginning to sink, he cried, saying, Lord, save me." But, asks someone, ought he not to have prayed before? Of course he ought; but if he had not done so, it was not too late. Do not say, concerning any trouble, "Now I am so deeply in it, I cannot go to God about it." Why not? "Is anything too hard for the Lord?" It would have been well if the disciples had prayed before the first rough breath of the tempest began to toss their little bark [sailing ship], yet it was not too late to pray when the vessel seemed as if it must go down. As long as you have a heart to pray, God has an ear to hear. Look at Peter; he is "beginning to sink." The water is up to his knees, it is up to his waist, it is up to his neck, but it is not yet too late for him to cry, "Lord, save me." And he has no sooner said it, than the hand of Jesus is stretched out to catch him, and to guide him to the ship. So, Christian, cry to God though the devil tells you it is no use to cry; cry to God even if you are beneath the tempter's foot. Say to Satan, "Rejoice not against me, O mine enemy: when I fall, I shall arise"; but do not forget to cry unto the Lord. Cry to God for your children even when they are most ungodly, when their ungodliness almost breaks your heart. Cry to God on behalf of those whom you are teaching in the Sunday school; even when you seem to think that their characters are developing in the worst possible form, still pray for them. Never mind though the thing you ask for them should appear to be an impossibility, for God "is able to do exceeding abundantly above all that we ask or think."

I would also say to any unconverted person who is here, under conviction of sin—dear friend, if you are beginning to sink, yet still pray. If your sins stare you in the face, and threaten to drive you to despair, yet still draw near to God in prayer. Though it seems as if hell had opened its mouth to swallow you up, yet still cry unto God. While there's life, there's hope.

While the lamp holds out to burn,

The vilest sinner may return;

and the vilest sinner who returns shall find that God is both able and willing to save him. Never believe that lie of Satan that prayer will not prevail with God. Only go as the publican did, smiting upon your breast, and crying, "God be merciful to me a sinner," and rest assured that God is waiting to be gracious to you.

I cannot help feeling that Peter's short, simple prayer was uttered in a most natural tone of voice: "Lord, save me." Let us always pray in just such a way as the Spirit of God dictates to us, and as the deep sorrow and humiliation of our heart naturally suggest to us. Many men who pray in public get into the habit of using certain tones in prayer that are anything but natural, and I am afraid that some even in private fail to pray naturally. Any language that is not natural is bad; the best tone is that which a man uses when he is speaking earnestly, and means what he says, and that is the right way to pray. Speak as if you meant it; do not whine it, or cant it, or intone it, but pour it out of your soul in the most simple, natural fashion that you can. Peter was in too great peril to put any fine language into his prayer; he was too conscious of his danger to consider how he might put his words together; but he just expressed the strong desire of his soul in the simplest manner possible: "Lord, save me." And that prayer was heard, and Peter was saved from drowning, just as a sinner will be saved from hell if he can pray after the selfsame fashion.

I. Now, coming to Peter's prayer itself, and suggesting that it is a suitable prayer for all who are able to pray at all, my first observation upon it is that *it was a very brief prayer.*

There were only three words in it: "Lord, save me." I believe that the excellence of prayer often consists in its brevity. You must have noticed the extreme brevity of most of the prayers that are preserved in Scripture. One of the longest is the prayer of our Savior recorded by John, which would, I suppose, have occupied about five minutes; and there is the prayer of Solomon at the dedication of the temple, which may have taken six minutes. Almost all the other prayers in the Bible are very short ones; and, probably, in our public services, we pray far longer than all of them put together. This may, perhaps, be excused when there are many petitions to be presented by one person on behalf of a large congregation; but at our prayer meetings, where there are many to speak, I am certain that, the longer the prayer is, the worse it is. Of course, there are exceptions to this rule. The Spirit of God sometimes inspires a man in such a way that, if he would keep on praying all night, we should be glad to join with him in that holy exercise; but, as a general rule, the Spirit of God does no such thing. There are some who pray longest, when they have least to say, and only go on repeating certain pious phrases which become almost meaningless by monotonous reiteration. Remember, dear friends, when you are praying, whether in public or in private, that you have not to teach the Lord a system of theology; he knows far more about that than you do. You have no need to explain to the Lord all the experience that a Christian ought to have, for he knows that far better than you do. And there is not necessity for you always to go around all the various agencies, and institutions, and mission stations. Tell the Lord what is in your heart in as few words as possible, and so leave time and opportunity for others to do the same.

I wonder if anyone here ever says, "I have no time for prayer." Dear friend, dare you leave your house in the morning without bowing the knee before God? Can you venture to close your eyes at night, and wear the image of death, without first commending yourself to the keeping of God during the hours of unconsciousness in sleep? I do not understand how you can live such a careless life as that. But, surely, you did not really mean that you had not time to offer such a prayer as Peter's "Lord, save me." How much time does that take, or this? "God be merciful to me a sinner." If you realized your true condition in God's sight, you would find time for prayer somehow or other, for you would feel that you must pray. It never occurred to Peter, as he was beginning to sink, that he had no time for prayer. He felt that he must pray; his sense of danger forced him to cry to Christ, "Lord, save me." And if you feel as you should feel, your sense of need will drive you to prayer, and never again will you say, "I have no time for prayer." It is not a matter of time so much as a matter of heart; if you have the heart to pray, you will find the time.

I would urge you to cultivate the habit of praying briefly all the day. I have told you before of the Puritan who, in a debate, was observed to be making notes; and when they were afterward examined, it was found that there was nothing on the paper except these words, "More light, Lord! More light, Lord! More light, Lord!" He wanted light upon the subject under discussion, and, therefore, he asked the Lord for it, and that is the way to pray. During the day, you can pray, "Give me more grace, God. Subdue my temper, Lord. Tell me, O my God, what to do in this case! Lord, direct me. Lord, save me." Pray thus, and you will be imitating the good example of brevity in prayer which our text sets before you.

II. Notice next that, brief as Peter's prayer was, *it was wonderfully comprehensive, and adapted for use on many different occasions*: "Lord, save me."

It covered all the needs of Peter at that time, and he might have continued to use it as long as he lived. When his Master told him that Satan desired to have him that he might sift him as wheat, he might well have prayed, "Lord, save me." When he had denied his Master, and had gone out, and wept bitterly, it would have been well for him to pray, "Lord, save me." When he was afterward journeying to and from preaching the gospel, he could still pray, "Lord, save me"; and when, at last, he was led out to be crucified for Christ's sake, he could hardly find a better prayer than this with which to close his life, "Lord, save me."

Now, as Peter found this prayer so suitable for him, I commend it to each one of you. Have you been growing rich lately? Then, you will be tempted to become proud and worldly; so pray, "Lord, save me from the evils that so often go with riches; you are giving me this wealth; help me to be a good steward of it, and not to make an idol of it." Or are you getting poor? Is your business proving a failure? Are your little savings almost gone? Well, there are perils connected with poverty; so pray, "Lord, save me from becoming envious or discontented; let me be willing to be poor rather than do anything wrong in order to get money." Do you, dear friend, feel that you are not living as near to God as you once did? Is the chilling influence of the world telling upon you? Then pray, "Lord, save me." Have you fallen into some sin which you fear may bring disgrace upon your profession? Well then, before that sin grows greater, cry, "Lord, save me." Have you come to a place where your feet have well near slipped? The precipice is just before you, and you feel that, if some mightier power than your own does not interpose, you will fall to your serious hurt, if not to your destruction. Then, at once breathe the prayer, "Lord, save me." I can commend this prayer to you when you are upon the stormy sea, but it will be equally suitable to you upon the dry land: "Lord, save me." I can commend it as suitable to you when you are near the gates of death, but it is just as much adapted to you when you are in vigorous health: "Lord, save me." And if you can add to the prayer, "and, Lord, save my children, and my kinsfolk, and my neighbors," it will be even better. Still, for yourself personally, it is an admirable prayer to carry about with you wherever you go: "Lord, save me."

III. Peter's prayer had a third excellence: *it was very direct.*

It would not have done for Peter just then to have used the many titles which rightly belong to Christ, or to have been asking for a thousand things; but he went straight to the point of his immediate need, and cried, "Lord, save me." When one of our dear friends, who has lately gone to heaven, was very ill, one of his sons prayed with him. He began in a very proper way, "Almighty Father, Maker of heaven and earth, our Creator"—but the sick man stopped him, and said, "My dear boy, I am a poor sinner, and I want God's mercy; say, 'Lord, save him.'" He wanted his son to get to the point, and I can sympathize with him; for often, when some of our dear brethren have been praying here, and have been beating about the bush, I have wished that they would come to the point, and ask for what they really needed. They have kept on walking around the house instead of knocking at the door and seeking to enter. Peter's prayer shows us how to go direct to the very heart of the matter: "Lord, save me."

Many persons fail to receive answers to their prayers because they will not go straight to God, and confess the sins that they have committed. There was a member of a Christian church who had, on one occasion, fallen very shamefully through drink. He was very penitent, and he asked his pastor to pray for him, but he would not say what his sin had been. The pastor prayed, and then told the brother himself to pray. The poor man said, "Lord, you know that I have erred, and done wrong," and so on, making a sort of general confession, but that brought him no peace of mind. He felt that he could not go away like that, so he knelt down again, and said, "Lord, you know that I was drunk; it was a shameful sin that I committed, but I am truly grieved for it; O Lord, forgive me, for Jesus' sake!" And before his prayer was finished, he had found peace because he had plainly confessed his sin to God, and had not sought to hide it any longer. You remember that David could get no peace until he came to the point, and prayed, "Deliver me from bloodguiltiness, O God, thou God of my salvation." Before that, he had tried to smother his great sin; but there was no rest for his conscience until he had made a full confession of his guilt, and after that he could say, "The sacrifices of God are a broken spirit: a broken and a contrite heart, O God, thou wilt not despise." Let our prayers, whether for ourselves or others, and especially our confessions of sin, go straight to the point, and not go beating about the bush. If any of you have been using forms of prayer, which have not obtained for you any answers to your supplications, put them all on one side, and just go and tell the Lord plainly what you want. Your prayer will then probably be something like this, "O God, I am a lost sinner! I have been careless about divine things; I have listened to the gospel, but I have not obeyed it. Lord, forgive me, save me, make me your child, and let me and my household, too, be yours for ever." That is the way to pray so that God will hear and answer you.

IV. Another characteristic of Peter's prayer was that *it was a very sound-doctrine prayer*: "Lord, save me."

Peter does not appear to have had any idea of saving himself from drowning; he does not seem to have thought that there was sufficient natural buoyancy about him to keep him afloat or that he could swim to the ship; but, "beginning to sink, he cried, saying, Lord, save me." One of the hardest tasks in the world is to get a man to give up all confidence in himself, and from his heart to pray, "Lord, save me." Instead of doing that, he says, "O Lord, I do not feel as I ought; I want to feel my need more, I want to feel more joy, I want to feel more holiness." You see, he is putting feelings in place of faith; he is, as it were, laying down a track along which he wants God to walk instead of walking in the way which God has marked out for all who desire to be saved. Another man is seeking to reform himself, and so to make himself fit for heaven; and he prays in harmony with that idea, and of course gets no answer. I like to hear such a prayer as this, "O Lord, I cannot save myself, and I do not ask you to save me in any way that I prescribe; Lord, save me anyhow, only do save me! I am satisfied to be saved by the precious blood of Jesus. I am satisfied to be saved by the regenerating work of the Holy Spirit. I know I must be born again if I am ever to enter heaven; quicken me; O you everblessed Spirit! I know I must give up my sins. Lord, I do not want to keep them; save me from them by your grace, I humbly entreat you. I know that only you can do this work; I cannot lift even a finger to help you in it; so save me, Lord, for your great mercy's sake!" This is sound doctrinal truth—salvation all of grace, not of man, nor by men; "not of blood, nor of the will of the flesh, nor of the will of man, but of God"; salvation according to the eternal purpose of God, by the effectual working of the Holy Spirit, through the substitutionary sacrifice of Jesus Christ. When a sinner is willing to accept salvation on God's terms, then the prayer shall ascend acceptably to the Most High, "Lord, save me."

V. Notice also that *Peter's prayer was a very personal one*: "Lord, save me."

Peter did not think of anybody else just then; and when a soul is under concern about its eternal interests, it had better at first confine its thoughts to itself, and pray, "Lord, save me." Yes, and in the Christian's afterlife, there will come times when he had better, for a while, forget all others, and simply pray, "Lord, save me." Here we are, a great congregation gathered together from very various motives; and perhaps some here, who are not yet personally interested in Christ, are vaguely hoping that God will bless somebody in this assembly; but if the Holy Spirit shall begin to work upon some individual heart and conscience, the convicted one will begin to pray, "Lord, save me. I hear of many others being brought to Jesus; but, Lord, save me. My dear sister has been converted, and has made a profession of her faith; but, Lord, save me. I had a godly mother, who has gone home to glory; and my dear father is walking in your fear; let not their son be a castaway; Lord, save me."

I entreat everyone here to pray this personal prayer, and I beg you who do love the Lord to join me in pleading with him that it may be so. I see some little girls over there; will not each one of you, my dear children, pray this prayer? I pray the Holy Spirit to move you to cry, "Lord, save little Annie," or "Lord, save little Mary"; and may you boys be equally moved to pray, "Lord, save Tom," or "Lord, save Harry." Pray for yourself in just that simple way, and who knows what blessing may come to you? Then you mothers will surely not let your children pray for themselves while you remain prayerless; will not each one of you pray, "Lord, save me"? And you working men, whom I am so glad to see at a weeknight service, do not go away without presenting your own personal petitions. The apostle Peter had to pray for himself, the most eminent servants of God had to pray for themselves, and you must pray for yourselves. If all the saints of God were to pray for you, with one united voice, as long as you live, you would not be saved unless you also cried to God for yourself. Religion is a personal matter; there is no such thing as religion by proxy. You must repent for yourselves and pray for yourselves and believe for yourselves if you would be saved. May God grant that you may do so!

VI. I want you to notice next, that *Peter's prayer was a very urgent one*: "Lord, save me."

He did not say, "Lord, come tomorrow," or "Lord, save me in an hour's time." He was "beginning to sink"; the hungry waves had opened their mouths to swallow him, and he would soon be gone. He had only time to cry, "Lord, save me," but he no doubt meant, "Lord, save me now, for I am in danger of being drowned. Lord, save me now, for, if you should delay, I shall sink to the bottom of the sea." "And immediately Jesus stretched forth his hand, and caught him," and so saved him. There are many people who would like Jesus to save them, but when? Ah! that is the point which they have not settled yet. A young man says, "I should like Christ to save me when I grow older, when I have seen a little more of life." You mean when you have seen a great deal more of death, for that is all you will see in the world; there is no real life except that which is in Christ Jesus. Many a man in middle life has said, "I mean to be a Christian before I die, but not just yet." He has been too busy to seek the Lord, but death has come to him without any warning; busy or not, he has had to die quite unprepared.

There is hope for a sinner when he prays, "Lord, my case is urgent, save me now. Sin, like a viper, has fastened itself upon me; Lord, save me now from its deadly venom. I am guilty now, and condemned already, because I have not believed in Jesus; Lord, save me now, save me from condemnation, save me from the damning sin of unbelief. Lord, for all I know, I am now upon the brink of death, and I am in danger of hell as well as of death as long as I am unforgiven. Therefore, be pleased to let the wheels of your chariot of mercy hasten, and save me even now, O Lord!" I have known some who have been so deeply under the influence of the Holy Spirit, that they have knelt down by their bedsides, and said, "We will never give sleep to our eyes, or slumber to our eyelids, till we have found the Savior," and before long they have found him. They have said, "We will wrestle in prayer until our burden of sin is gone," and when they have reached that determination, it has not been long before they have obtained the blessing they desire. When nothing else succeeds, importunity will surely prevail. When you will not take a denial from God, he will not give you a denial; but as long as you are content to be unsaved, you will he unsaved. When you cry with all the urgency of which you are capable, "I must have Jesus, or die; I am hungering, thirsting, pining, panting after him, as the hart pants after the waterbrooks," it shall not be long before you clasp that priceless treasure to your heart, and say, "Jesus is my Savior; I have believed in him."

VII. Now, lastly, I must remind you that *Peter's prayer was an effectual one*: "Lord, save me." And Jesus did save him.

There may be comfort to some here present in the thought that, although this was the prayer of a man in trouble, and a man in whom there was a mixture of unbelief and faith, yet it succeeded. Imperfections and infirmities shall not prevent prayer from speeding if it be but sincere and earnest. Jesus said to Peter, "O thou of little faith, wherefore didst thou doubt?" which shows that he did doubt although there was also some faith in him, for he believed that Christ could save him from a watery grave. Many of us also are strange mixtures, even as Peter was. Repentance and hardness of heart can each occupy a part of our being, and faith may be in our hearts together with a measure of unbelief, even as it was with the man who said to Jesus, "Lord, I believe; help thou mine unbelief."

Do any of you feel that you want to pray, and yet cannot pray? You would believe in Jesus, but there is another law in your members which keeps you back. You would pray an effectual prayer, like that of Elijah, never staggering at the promise through unbelief; but, somehow or other, you cannot tell why, you cannot attain to that prayer. Yet you will not give up praying; you feel that you cannot do that. You linger still at the mercy seat even when you cannot prevail with God in prayer. Ah, dear soul! it is a mercy that God does not judge your prayer by what it is in itself; he judges it from another point of view altogether. Jesus takes it, mends it, adds to it the merit of his own precious blood, and then, when he presents it to his Father, it is so changed that you would scarcely recognize it as your petition. You would say, "I can hardly believe that is my prayer, Christ has so greatly altered and improved it." It has happened to you as it sometimes happens to poor people who are in trouble, as it did happen to one whom I knew some time ago. A good woman wanted me to send in a petition to a certain government office, concerning her husband, who was dead, and for whose sake she wanted to get some help. She drew up the petition and brought it to me. About one word in ten was spelled correctly, and the whole composition was unfit to send. She wanted me to add my name to it, and post it for her. I did so, but I first rewrote the whole petition, keeping the subject matter as she put it, but altering the form and wording of it. That is what our good Lord and Master does for us only in an infinitely higher sense; he rewrites our petition, sets his own sign-manual [King's signature] to it, and when his Father sees that, he grants the request at once. One drop of Christ's blood upon a prayer must make it prosper.

Go home, therefore, you who are troubled with doubts and fears, you who are vexed by Satan, you who are saddened by the recollection of your own past sins; notwithstanding all this, go to God, and say, "Father, I have sinned against heaven, and before you," and ask for his forgiveness, and his forgiveness you shall receive. Keep on praying in such a fashion as this, "Lord, save me, for Jesus' sake. Jesus, you are the Savior of sinners; save me, I beseech you. You are mighty to save; Lord, save me. You are in heaven pleading for transgressors; Lord, plead for me." Do not wait till you get home, but pray just where you are sitting, "Lord, save me." May God give grace to everyone here to pray that prayer from the heart, for Jesus Christ's sake! Amen.

The Preparatory Prayers of Christ

Published on Thursday, December 30, 1909; delivered on Thursday evening, August 7, 1873, at the Metropolitan Tabernacle, Newington. No. 3178.

Now when all the people were baptized, it came to pass, that Jesus also being baptized, and praying, the heaven was opened, and the Holy Ghost descended in a bodily shape like a dove upon him, and a voice came from heaven, which said, "Thou art my beloved Son; in thee I am well pleased."—Luke 3:21–22

And it came to pass in those days, that he went out into a mountain to pray, and continued all night in prayer to God. And when it was day, he called unto him his disciples: and of them he chose twelve, whom also he named apostles. —Luke 6:12–13

And it came to pass about an eight days after these sayings, he took Peter and John and James, and went up into a mountain to pray. And as he prayed, the fashion of his countenance was altered, and his raiment was white and glistering.—Luke 9:28–29

And when he had sent the multitudes away, he went up into a mountain apart to pray: and when the evening was come, he was there alone. But the ship was now in the midst of the sea, tossed with waves: for the wind was contrary. And in the fourth watch of the night Jesus went unto them, walking on the sea.—Matthew 14:23–25

Then they took away the stone from the place where the dead was laid. And Jesus lifted up his eyes, and said, "Father, I thank thee that thou hast heard me. And I knew that thou hearest me always: but because of the people which stand by I said it, that they may believe that thou hast sent me." —John 11:41–42

And the Lord said, "Simon, Simon, behold, Satan hath desired to have you, that he may sift you as wheat: but I have prayed for thee, that thy faith fail not: and when thou art converted, strengthen thy brethren."—LUKE 22:31–32

And when Jesus had cried with a loud voice, he said, "Father, into thy hands I commend my spirit": and having said thus, he gave up the ghost.—LUKE 23:46

There is one peculiarity about the life of our Lord Jesus Christ which everybody must have noticed who has carefully read the four Gospels, namely, that he was a man of much prayer. He was mighty as a preacher; for even the officers who were sent to arrest him said, "Never man spake like this man." But he appears to have been even mightier in prayer, if such a thing could be possible. We do not read that his disciples ever asked him to teach them to preach, but we are told that, "as he was praying in a certain place, when he ceased, one of his disciples said unto him, Lord, teach us to pray." He had no doubt been praying with such wonderful fervor that his disciples realized that he was a master of the holy art of prayer, and they therefore desired to learn the secret for themselves. The whole life of our Lord Jesus Christ was one of prayer. Though we are often told about his praying, we feel that we scarcely need to be informed of it, for we know that he must have been a man of prayer. His acts are the acts of a prayerful man; his words speak to us like the words of one whose heart was constantly lifted up in prayer to his Father. You could not imagine that he would have breathed out such blessings upon men if he had not first breathed in the atmosphere of heaven. He must have been much in prayer or he could not have been so abundant in service and so gracious in sympathy.

Prayer seems to be like a silver thread running through the whole of our Savior's life, yet we have the record of his prayers on many special occasions; and it struck me that it would be both interesting and instructive for us to notice some of the seasons which Jesus spent in prayer. I have selected a few which occurred either before some great work or some great suffering, so our subject will really be the preparatory prayers of Christ, the prayers of Christ as he was approaching something which would put a peculiar stress and strain upon his manhood, either for service or for suffering; and if the consideration of this subject shall lead all of us to learn the practical lesson of praying at all times, and yet to have special seasons for prayer just before any peculiar trial or unusual service, we shall not have met in vain.

I. The first prayer we are to consider is *our Lord's prayer in preparation for his baptism.*

It is in Luke 3:21–22: "Now when all the people were baptized, it came to pass, that Jesus also being baptized, and praying," (it seems to have been a continuous act in which he had been previously occupied) "the heaven was opened, and the Holy Ghost descended in a bodily shape like a dove upon him, and a voice came from heaven, which said, Thou art my beloved Son; in thee I am well pleased."

The baptism of our Lord was the commencement of his manifestation to the sons of men. He was now about to take upon himself in full all the works of his messiahship; consequently, we find him very specially engaged in prayer, and, beloved, it seems to me to be peculiarly appropriate that, when any of us have been converted and are about to make a scriptural profession of our faith—about to take up the soldier life under the great Captain of our salvation—about to start out as pilgrims to Zion's city bound—I say that it seems to me to be peculiarly appropriate for us to spend much time in very special prayer. I should be very sorry to think that anyone would venture to come to be baptized, or to be united with a Christian church, without having made that action a matter of much solemn consideration and earnest prayer; but when the decisive step is about to be taken, our whole being should be very specially concentrated upon our supplication at the throne of grace. Of course, we do not believe in any sacramental efficacy attaching to the observance of the ordinance, but we receive a special blessing in the act itself because we are moved to pray even more than usual before it takes place and at the time. At all events, I know that it was so in my own case. It was many years ago, but the remembrance of it is very vivid at this moment, and it seems to me as though it happened only yesterday. It was in the month of May, and I rose very early in the morning, so that I might have a long time in private prayer. Then I had to walk about eight miles, from Newmarket to Isleham, where I was to be baptized in the river, and I think that the blessing I received that day resulted largely from that season of solitary supplication, and my meditation, as I walked along the country roads and lanes, upon my indebtedness to my Savior, and my desire to live to his praise and glory. Dear young people, take care that you start right in your Christian life by being much in prayer. A profession of faith that does not begin with prayer will end in disgrace. If you come to join the church, but do not pray to God to uphold you in consistency of life, and to make your profession sincere, the probability is that you are already a hypocrite; or if that is too uncharitable a suggestion, the probability is that, if you are converted, the work has been of a very superficial character, and not of that deep and earnest kind of which prayer would be the certain index. So again I say to you that, if any of you are thinking of making a profession of your faith in Christ, be sure then, in preparation for it, you devote a special season to drawing near to God in prayer.

As I read the first text, no doubt you noticed that it was while Christ was praying that "the heaven was opened, and the Holy Ghost descended in a bodily shape like a dove upon him, and a voice came from heaven, which said, Thou art my beloved Son; in thee I am well pleased." There are three occasions of which we read in Scripture when God bore audible testimony to Christ, and on each of these three occasions he was either in the act of prayer or he had been praying but a very short time before. Christ's prayer is specially mentioned in each instance side by side with the witness of his Father; and if you, beloved friends, want to have the witness of God either at your baptism or on any subsequent act of your life, you must obtain it by prayer. The Holy Ghost never sets his seal to a prayerless religion. It has not in it that of which he can approve. It must be truly said of a man, "Behold, he prays," before the Lord bears such testimony concerning him as he bore concerning Saul of Tarsus, "He is a chosen vessel unto me, to bear my name before the Gentiles."

So we find that it was while Christ was praying at his baptism that the Holy Ghost came upon him, "in a bodily shape like a dove," to qualify him for his public service; and it is through prayer that we also receive that spiritual enrichment that equips us as coworkers together with God. Without prayer, you will remain in a region that is desolate as a desert; but bend your knees in supplication to the Most High, and you have reached the land of promise, the country of benediction. "Draw nigh to God, and he will draw nigh to you," not merely as to his gracious presence, but as to the powerful and efficacious working of the Holy Spirit. More prayer, more power; the more pleading with God that there is, the more power will there be in pleading with men, for the Holy Ghost will come upon us while we are pleading, and so we shall be fitted and qualified to do the work to which we are called of God.

Let us learn, then, from this first instance of our Savior's preparatory prayer, at his baptism, the necessity of special supplication on our part in similar circumstances. If we are making our first public profession of faith in him, or if we are renewing that profession; if we are removing to another sphere of service, if we are taking office in the church as deacons or elders, if we are commencing the work of the pastorate, if we are in any way coming out more distinctly before the world as the servants of Christ, let us set apart special seasons for prayer, and so seek a double portion of the Holy Spirit's blessing to rest upon us.

II. The second instance of the preparatory prayers of Christ which we are to consider is *our Lord's prayer preparatory to choosing his twelve apostles*.

It is recorded in Luke 6:12–13: "And it came to pass in those days, that he went out into a mountain to pray, and continued all night in prayer to God. And when it was day, he called unto him his disciples: and of them he chose twelve, whom also he named apostles."

Our Lord was about to extend his ministry; his one tongue, his one voice, might have delivered his personal message throughout Palestine, but he was desirous of having far more done than he could individually accomplish in the brief period of his public ministry upon the earth. He would therefore have twelve apostles, and afterward seventy disciples, who would go forth in his name, and tell out the glad tidings of salvation. He was infinitely wiser than the wisest of mere men, so why did he not at once select his twelve apostles? The men had been with him from the beginning and he knew their characters, and their fitness for the work he was about to entrust to them; so he might have said to himself, "I will have James, and John, and Peter, and the rest of the twelve, and send them forth to preach that the kingdom of heaven is at hand, and to exercise the miraculous powers with which I will endow them." He might have done this if he had not been the Christ of God; but being the anointed of the Father, he would not take such an important step as that without long-continued prayer, so he went alone to his Father, told him all that he desired to do, and pleaded with him, not in the brief fashion that we call prayer, which usually lasts only a few minutes, but his pleading lasted through an entire night.

What our Lord asked for, or how he prayed, we cannot tell, for it is not revealed to us; but I think we shall not be guilty of vain or unwarranted curiosity if we use our imagination for a minute or two. In doing so, with the utmost reverence, I think I hear Christ crying to his Father that the right men might be selected as the leaders of the church of God upon the earth. I think I also hear him pleading that upon these chosen men a divine influence might rest, that they might be kept in character, honest in heart, and holy in life, and that they might also be preserved sound in doctrine and not turn aside to error and falsehood. Then I think I hear him praying that success might attend their preaching, that they might be guided where to go, where the blessing of God would go with them, that they might find many hearts willing to receive their testimony, and that when their personal ministry should end, they might pass on their commission to others, so that, as long as there should be a harvest to be reaped for the Lord, there should be laborers to reap it; as long as there should be lost sinners in the world, there should also be earnest, consecrated men and women seeking to pluck the brands from them. I will not attempt to describe the mighty wrestlings of that night of prayer when, in strong crying and tears, Christ poured out his very soul into his Father's ear and heart. But it is clear that he would not dispatch a solitary messenger with the glad tidings of the gospel unless he was assured that his Father's authority and the Spirit's power would accompany the servants whom he was about to send forth.

What a lesson there is in all this to us! What infallible guidance there is here as to how a missionary society should be conducted! Where there is one committee meeting for business, there ought to be fifty for prayer; and whenever we get a missionary society whose main business it is to pray, we shall have a society whose distinguishing characteristic will be that it is the means of saving a multitude of souls. And to you, my dear young brethren in the college, I feel moved to say that I believe we shall have a far larger blessing than we have already had when the spirit of prayer in the college is greater than it now is, though I rejoice to know that it is very deep and fervent even now. You, brethren, have never been lacking in prayerfulness; I thank God that I have never had occasion to complain or to grieve on that account; but, still, who knows what blessing might follow a night of prayer at the beginning or at any part of the session, or an all-night wrestling in prayer in the privacy of your own bedrooms? Then, when you go out to preach the gospel on the Sabbath day, you will find that the best preparation for preaching is much praying. I have always found that the meaning of a text can be better learned by prayer than in any other way. Of course, we must consult lexicons and commentaries to see the literal meaning of the words, and their relation to one another; but when we have done all that, we shall still find that our greatest help will come from prayer. Oh, that every Christian enterprise were commenced with prayer, continued with prayer, and crowned with prayer! Then might we also expect to see it crowned with God's blessing. So once again I remind you that our Savior's example teaches us that for seasons of special service we need not only prayers of a brief character, excellent as they are for ordinary occasions, but special protracted wrestling with God like that of Jacob at the brook Jabbok, so that each one of us can say to the Lord, with holy determination,

With thee all night I mean to stay,
And wrestle till the break of day.

When such sacred persistence in prayer as this becomes common throughout the whole church of Christ, Satan's long usurpation will be coming to an end, and we shall be able to say to our Lord, as the seventy disciples did when they returned to him with joy, "Even the devils are subject unto us through thy name."

III. Now, thirdly, let us consider *our Lord's prayer preparatory to his transfiguration*.

You will find it in Luke 9:28–29: "And it came to pass about an eight days after these sayings, he took Peter and John and James, and went up into a mountain to pray. And as he prayed, the fashion of his countenance was altered, and his raiment was white and glistering." You see that it was as he prayed that he was transfigured.

Now, beloved, do you really desire to reach the highest possible attainments of the Christian life? Do you, in your inmost soul, pine and pant after the choicest joys that can be known by human beings this side of heaven? Do you aspire to rise to full fellowship with the Lord Jesus Christ, and to be transformed into his image from glory to glory? If so, the way is open to you; it is the way of prayer, and only there will you find these priceless boons. If you fail in prayer, you will assuredly never come to Tabor's top. There is no hope, dear friends, of our ever attaining to anything like a transfiguration, and being covered with the light of God, so that whether in the body or out of the body we cannot tell, unless we are much in prayer.

I believe that we make more real advance in the divine life in an hour of prayer than we do in a month of sermon-hearing. I do not mean that we are to neglect the assembling of ourselves together, as the manner of some is; but I am sure that, without the praying, the hearing is of little worth. We must pray, we must plead with God if we are really to grow spiritually. In prayer, very much of our spiritual digestion is done. When we are hearing the Word, we are very much like the cattle when they are cropping the grass; but when we follow our hearing with meditation and prayer, we do, as it were, lie down in the green pastures, and get the rich nutriment for our souls out of the truth. My dear brother or sister in Christ, would you shake off the earthliness that still clings to you? Would you get rid of your doubting and your fearing? Would you overcome your worldliness? Would you master all your besetting sins? Would you glow and glisten in the brightness and glory of the holiness of God? Then, be much in prayer, as Jesus was. I am sure that it must be so, and that, apart from prayer, you will make no advance in the divine life; but that, in waiting upon God, you shall renew your spiritual strength, you shall mount up with wings as eagles, you shall run and not be weary, you shall walk and not faint.

IV. I must hasten on, lest time should fail us before I have finished; and I must put together two of *our Lord's prayers preparatory to great miracles*.

The first, which preceded his stilling of the tempest on the Lake of Gennesaret, is recorded in Matthew 14:23–25: "And when he had sent the multitudes away, he went up into a mountain apart to pray: and when the evening was come, he was there alone. But the ship was now in the midst of the sea, tossed with waves: for the wind was contrary. And in the fourth watch of the night Jesus went unto them, walking on the sea." He had been pleading with his Father for his disciples; and then, when their ship was tossed by the waves and driven back by the contrary winds, he came down to them from the lofty place where he had been praying for them, making a pathway for himself across the turbulent waters that he was about to calm. Before he walked upon those tossing billows, he had prayed to his Father; before he stilled the storm, he had prevailed with God in prayer.

Am I to do any great work for God? Then I must first be mighty upon my knees. Is there a man here who is to be the means of covering the sky with clouds and bringing the rain of God's blessing upon the dry and barren church which so sorely needs reviving and refreshing? Then he must be prepared for that great work as Elijah was when, on the top of Carmel, "he cast himself down upon the earth, and put his face between his knees," and prayed as only he could pray. We shall never see a little cloud, like a man's hand, which shall afterward cover all the sky with blackness, unless first of all we know how to cry mightily unto the Most High; but when we have done that, then shall we see what we desire. Moses would never have been able to control the children of Israel as he did if he had not first been in communion with his God in the desert, and afterward in the mount. So, if we are to be men of power, we also must be men of prayer.

The other instance to which I want to refer, showing how our Lord prayed before working a mighty miracle, is when he stood by the grave of Lazarus. You will find the account of it in John 11:41–42: "Then they took away the stone from the place where the dead was laid. And Jesus lifted up his eyes, and said, Father, I thank thee that thou hast heard me. And I knew that thou hearest me always: but because of the people which stand by I said it, that they may believe that thou hast sent me." He did not cry, "Lazarus, come forth," so that the people heard it, and Lazarus heard it, until first he had prayed, My Father, grant that Lazarus may rise from the dead, and had received the assurance that he would do so as soon as he was called by Christ to come forth from the grave.

But, brethren, do you not see that if Christ, who was so strong, needed to pray thus, what need there is for us, who are so weak, also to pray? If he, who was God as well as man, prayed to his Father before he wrought a miracle, how needful it is for us, who are merely men, to go to the throne of grace, and plead there with importunate fervency if we are ever to do anything for God! I fear that many of us have been feeble out here in public because we have been feeble out there on the lone mountainside where we ought to have been in fellowship with God. The way to be fitted to work what men will call wonders is to go to the God of wonders and implore him to gird us with his all-sufficient strength so that we may do exploits to his praise and glory.

V. The next prayer we are to consider is *our Lord's prayer preparatory to Peter's fall.*

We have the record of that in Luke 22:31–32: "And the Lord said, Simon, Simon, behold, Satan hath desired to have you, that he may sift you as wheat: but I have prayed for thee, that thy faith fail not: and when thou art converted, strengthen thy brethren."

There is much that is admirable and instructive in this utterance of our Lord. Satan had not then tempted Peter, yet Christ had already pleaded for the apostle whose peril he clearly foresaw. Some of us would have thought that we were very prompt if we had prayed for a brother who had been tempted, and who had yielded to the temptation; but our Lord prayed for Peter before he was tempted. As soon as Satan had desired to have him in his sieve, that he might sift him as wheat, our Savior knew the thought that was formed in the diabolic mind, and he at once pleaded for his imperiled servant, who did not even know the danger that was threatening him. Christ is ever beforehand with us. Before the storm comes, he has provided the harbor of refuge; before the disease attacks us, he has the remedy ready to cure it; his mercy outruns our misery.

What a lesson we ought to learn from this action of Christ! Whenever we see any friend in peril through temptation, let us not begin to talk about him, but let us at once pray for him. Some persons are very fond of hinting and insinuating about what is going to happen to certain people with whom they are acquainted. I pray you, beloved friends, not to do so. Do not hint that So-and-so is likely to fall, but pray that he may not fall. Do not insinuate anything about him to others, but tell the Lord what your anxiety is concerning him.

"But So-and-so has made a lot of money, and he is getting very purse proud." Well, even if it is so, do not talk about him to others, but pray God to grant that he may not be allowed to become purse proud. Do not say that he will be, but pray constantly that he may not be, and do not let anyone but the Lord know that you are praying for him.

"Then there is So-and-so; he is so elated with the success he has had that one can scarcely get to speak to him." Well, then, brother, pray that he may not be elated. Do not say that you are afraid he is growing proud, for that would imply what you would yourself be if you were in his place. Your fear reveals a secret concerning your own nature, for what you judge that he would be is exactly what you would be in similar circumstances. We always measure other people's corn with our own bushel; we do not borrow their bushel; and we can judge ourselves by our judgment of others. Let us cease these censures and judgments, and let us pray for our brethren. If you fear that a minister is somewhat turning aside from the faith, or if you think that his ministry is not so profitable as it used to be, or if you see any other imperfection in him, do not go and talk about it to people in the street, for they cannot set him right; but go and tell his Master about him, pray for him, and ask the Lord to make right whatever is wrong. There is a sermon by old Matthew Wilks about our being epistles of Christ, written not with ink, and not in tables of stone, but in fleshy tables of the heart; and he said that ministers are the pens with which God writes on their hearts' hearts, and that pens need nibbing every now and then, and even when they are well nibbed they cannot write without ink—so he said that the best service that the people could render to the preachers was to pray the Lord to give them new nibs, and dip them in the ink afresh, that they might write better than before. Do so, dear friends; do not blot the page with your censures and unkind remarks, but help the preacher by pleading for him even as Christ prayed for Peter.

VI. Now I must close with *our Lord's preparatory prayer just before his death.*

You will find it in Luke 23:46: "And when Jesus had cried with a loud voice, he said, 'Father, into thy hands I commend my spirit': and having said thus, he gave up the ghost."

Our Lord Jesus was very specially occupied in prayer as the end of his earthly life drew near. He was about to die as his people's Surety and Substitute; the wrath of God, which was due to them, fell upon him. Knowing all that was to befall him, "he stedfastly set his face to go to Jerusalem"; and in due time, he "endured the cross, despising the shame"; but he did not go to Gethsemane and Golgotha without prayer. Son of God as he was, he would not undergo that terrible ordeal without much supplication. You know how much there is about his praying in the later chapters of John's gospel. There is especially that great prayer of his for his church, in which he pleaded with wonderful fervor for those whom his Father had given him. Then there was his agonized pleading in Gethsemane, when "his sweat was as it were great drops of blood falling down to the ground." We will not say much about that, but we can well imagine that the bloody sweat was the outward and visible expression of the intense agony of his soul, which was "exceeding sorrowful, even unto death."

All that Christ did and suffered was full of prayer, so it was but fitting that his last utterance on earth should be the prayerful surrender of his spirit into the hands of his Father. He had already pleaded for his murderers, "Father, forgive them; for they know not what they do." He had promised to grant the request of the penitent thief, "Lord, remember me when thou comest into thy kingdom." Now nothing remained for him to do but to say, "'Father, into thy hands I commend my spirit': and having said thus, he gave up the ghost." His life, which had been a life of prayer, was thus closed with prayer—an example well worthy of his people's imitation.

Perhaps I am addressing someone who is conscious that a serious illness is threatening. Well, then, dear friend, prepare for it by prayer. Are you dreading a painful operation? Nothing will help you to bear it so well as pleading with God concerning it. Prayer will help you mentally as well as physically; you will face the ordeal with far less fear if you have laid your case before the Lord, and committed yourself, body, soul, and spirit, into his hands. If you are expecting, before long, to reach the end of your mortal life, either because of your advanced age or your weak constitution or the inroads of the deadly consumption, pray much. You need not fear to be baptized in Jordan's swelling flood if you are constantly being baptized in prayer. Think of your Savior in the garden and on the cross, and pray even as he did, "Not my will, but thine, be done . . . Father, into thy hands I commend my spirit."

While I have been speaking thus to believers in our Lord Jesus Christ, there may have been some here, who are still unconverted, who have imagined that prayer is the way to heaven; yet it is not. Prayer is a great and precious help on the road, but Christ alone is the way, and the very first step heavenward is to trust ourselves wholly to him. Faith in Christ is the all-important matter, and if you truly believe in him, you are saved. But the very first thing that a saved man does is to pray, and the very last thing that he does before he gets to heaven is to pray. Well did Montgomery write,

> *Prayer is the contrite sinner's voice,*
> *Returning from his ways;*
> *While angels in their songs rejoice,*
> *And cry, "Behold, he prays!"*
> *Prayer is the Christian's vital breath,*
> *The Christian's native air;*
> *His watchword at the gates of death:*
> *He enters heaven with prayer.*

The Redeemer's Prayer

~∼⁂∼~

Delivered on Sabbath morning, April 18, 1858, at the Music Hall, Royal Surrey Gardens. No. 188.

"Father, I will that they also, whom thou hast given me, be with me where I am; that they may behold my glory, which thou hast given me: for thou lovedst me before the foundation of the world."—JOHN 17:24

When the high priest of old entered into the most holy place, he kindled the incense in his censer, and waving it before him, he perfumed the air with its sweet fragrance and veiled the mercy seat with the denseness of its smoke. Thus was it written concerning him, "He shall take a censer full of burning coals of fire from off the altar before the LORD, and his hands full of sweet incense beaten small, and bring it within the veil: and he shall put the incense upon the fire before the LORD, that the cloud of the incense may cover the mercy seat that is upon the testimony, that he die not." Even so our Lord Jesus Christ, when he would once for all enter within the veil with his own blood to make an atonement for sin, did first offer strong crying and prayers. In this seventeenth chapter of John, we have, as it were, the smoking of the Savior's pontifical center. He prayed for the people for whom he was about to die, and before he sprinkled them with his blood, he did sanctify them with his supplications. This prayer therefore stands preeminent in Holy Writ as the Lord's Prayer—the special and peculiar prayer of our Lord Jesus Christ; and "if," as an old divine has it, "it be lawful to prefer one Scripture above another, we may say, though all be gold, yet this is a pearl in the gold; though all be like the heavens, this is as the sun and stars." Or if one part of Scripture be more dear to the believer than any other, it must be this which contains his Master's last prayer before he entered through the rent veil of his own crucified body. How sweet it is to see that not himself, but his people, constituted the staple of his prayer! He did pray for himself—he said, "Father, glorify thou me"; but while he had one prayer for himself, he had many for his people. Continually did he pray for them—"Father, sanctify them!" "Father, keep them!" "Father, make them one!" And then he concluded his supplication with, "Father, I will that they also, whom thou hast given me, be with me where I am." Melancthon well said there was never a more excellent, more holy, more fruitful, and more affectionate voice ever heard in heaven or in earth than this prayer.

We shall first notice *the style of the prayer*; secondly, *the persons interested in it*; and thirdly, *the great petitions offered*—the last head constituting the main part of our discourse.

I. First, notice *the style of the prayer*—it is singular: it is, "Father, I will."

Now, I cannot but conceive that there is something more in the expression "I will" than a mere wish. It seems to one, that when Jesus said, "I will," although perhaps it might not be proper to say that he made a demand, yet we may say that he pleaded with authority, asking for that which he knew to be his own, and uttering an "I will" as potent as any fiat that ever sprang from the lips of the Almighty. "Father, I will." It is an unusual thing to find Jesus Christ saying to God, "I will." You know that before the mountains were brought forth, it was said of Christ, "in the volume of the book it is written of me, I delight to do thy will, O my God"; and we find while he was on earth, that he never mentioned his own will, that he expressly declared, "I came down from heaven, not to do mine own will, but the will of him that sent me." It is true you do hear him when addressing men, saying "I will," for he says, "I will; be thou clean"; but in his prayers to his Father, he prayed with all humility;

With sighs and groans he offered up,
His humble suit below.

"I will," therefore, seems to be an exception to the rule; but we must remember that Christ was now in an exceptional condition. He had never been before where he was now. He was now come to the end of his work; he could say, "I have finished the work which thou gavest me to do," and therefore, looking forward to the time when the sacrifice would be complete and he should ascend on high, he sees that his work is done and takes his own will back again and says, "Father, I will."

Now, mark, that such a prayer as this would be totally unbecoming in our lips. We are never to say, "Father, *I will.*" Our prayer is to be, "Not my will, but thine, be done." We are to mention our *wishes*, but our *wills* are to subside into the will of God. We are to feel that while it is ours to desire, it is God's to will. But how pleasant, I repeat, it is to find the Savior pleading with such authority as this, for this puts the stamp of certainty upon his prayer. Whatsoever he has asked for in that chapter he shall have beyond a doubt. At other times, when he pleaded as a mediator, in his humility he was eminently successful in his intercessions; how much more shall his prayer prevail now that he takes to himself his great power, and with authority cries, "Father, I will." I love that opening to the prayer; it is a blessed guarantee of its fulfillment, rendering it so sure that we may now look upon Christ's prayer as a promise which shall be assuredly fulfilled.

II. Thus much concerning the style of the prayer; and now we *notice the persons for whom he prayed,*

"Father, I will that *they also, whom thou hast given me,* be with me where I am." This was not a universal prayer. It was a prayer including within it a certain class and portion of mankind who are designated as those whom the Father had given him. Now, we are taught to believe that God the Father did, from before the foundation of the world, give unto his Son Jesus Christ a number whom no man can number, who were to be the reward of his death, the purchase of the travail of his soul; who were to be infallibly brought unto everlasting glory by the merits of his passion and the power of his resurrection. These are the people here referred to. Sometimes in Scripture they are called the elect, because when the Father gave them to Christ he chose them out from among men. At other times they are called the beloved, because God's love was set upon them of old. They are called Israel; for like Israel of old, they are a chosen people, a royal generation. They are called God's inheritance, for they are especially dear to God's heart; and as a man cares for his inheritance and his portion, so the Lord cares especially for them.

Let me not be misunderstood. The people whom Christ here prays for are those whom God the Father out of his own free love and sovereign good pleasure ordained unto eternal life, and who, in order that his design might be accomplished, were given into the hands of Christ the Mediator, by him to be redeemed, sanctified, and perfected, and by him to be glorified everlastingly. These people, and none others, are the object of our Savior's prayer. It is not for me to defend the doctrine; it is scriptural, that is my only defense. It is not for me to vindicate God from any profane charge of partiality or injustice. If there be any wicked enough to impute this to him, let them settle the matter with their Maker. Let the thing formed, if it have arrogance enough, say to him that formed it, "Why have you made me thus?" I am not God's apologist; he needs no defender. "O man, who art thou that repliest against God?" Has he not, like the potter, power over the clay, to make one vessel to honor, and another to dishonor? Instead of disputing, let us inquire who are these people? Do we belong to them? Oh! let each heart now put the solemn query, "Am I included in that happy throng whom God the Father gave to Christ?" Beloved, I cannot tell you by the mere hearing of your names; but if I know your character, I can tell you decisively—or rather, you will need no telling, for the Holy Spirit will bear witness in your hearts that you are among the number. Answer this question—Have you given yourselves to Christ? Have you been brought by the constraining power of his own free love to make a voluntary surrender of yourself to him? Have you said, "O Lord, other lords have had dominion over me; but now I reject them, and I give myself up to you.

Other refuge have I none;

Hangs my helpless soul on thee;

and as I have no other refuge, so I have no other Lord. Little am I worth, but such as I am, I give all I have and all I am to you. It is true, I was never worth your purchasing, but since you have bought me, you shall have me. Lord, I make a full surrender of myself to you"? Well, soul, if you have done this, if you have given yourself to Christ, it is but the result of that ancient grant made by Jehovah to his son long before the worlds were made. And, once again, can you feel today that you are Christ's? If you cannot remember the time when he sought you and brought you to himself, yet can you say with the spouse, "I am my beloved's"? Can you now from your inmost soul say, Whom have I in heaven but you, and there is none upon earth that I desire besides you! If so, trouble not your minds about election, there is nothing troublesome in election to you. He that believes is elected; he who is given to Christ now was given to Christ from before the foundation of the world. You need not dispute divine decrees, but sit down and draw honey out of this rock and wine out of this flinty rock. Oh, it is a hard, hard doctrine to a man who has no interest in it; but when a man has once a title to it, then it is like the rock in the wilderness; it streams with refreshing water whereat myriads may drink and never thirst again. Well does the Church of England say of that doctrine, it "is full of sweet, pleasant, and unspeakable comfort to godly persons." And though it be like the Tarpeian rock, whence many a malefactor has been dashed to pieces in presumption, yet it is like Pisgah, from whose lofty summit the spires of heaven may be seen in the distance. Again, I say, be not cast down, neither let your hearts be disconsolate. If you be given to Christ now, you are among the happy number for whom he intercedes above, and you shall be gathered among the glorious throng, to be with him where he is and to behold his glory.

III. I very briefly pass over these two points, because I desire to dwell upon the third, which is, *the petitions which the Savior offers*.

Christ prayed, if I understand his prayer, for three things—things which constitute heaven's greatest joy, heaven's sweetest employment, and heaven's highest privilege.

The first great thing he prayed for is that which is *heaven's greatest joy*—"Father, I will that they also, whom thou hast given me, be with me where I am." If you notice, every word in the sentence is necessary to its fullness. He does not say—"I pray that those, whom thou hast given me, may be where I am"; but, *"with me* where I am." And he does not pray only that they might be *with him*, but that they might be with him in the same place *where he is*. And mark! he did not say he wished his people to be in heaven, but with him in heaven, because that makes heaven, heaven. It is the very pith and marrow of heaven to be with Christ. Heaven without Christ would be but an empty place; it would lose its happiness, it would be a harp without strings; and where would be the music?—a sea without water, a very pool of Tantalus. Christ prayed then that we might be with Christ—that is our companionship; with him where he is—that is our position. It seems as if he would tell us, that heaven is both a condition and a state—in the company of Christ and in the place where Christ is.

I might, if I chose, enlarge very much on these points, but I just throw out the raw material of a few thoughts that will furnish you with topics of meditation in the afternoon. Let us now pause and think how sweet this prayer is by contrasting it with our attainments on earth. "Father, I will that they also, whom thou hast given me, be with me where I am." Ah! brothers and sisters, we know a little of what it is to be with Christ. There are some happy moments, sweet pauses; between the din of the continued battles of this wearied life there are some soft times, like couches of rest, wherein we do repose. There are hours when our Master comes to us and makes us, or ever we are aware, like the chariots of Amminadib. It is true, we have not been caught up to the third heaven like Paul, to hear words which it is unlawful for us to utter; but we have sometimes thought that the third heavens have come down to us. Sometimes I have said within myself, "Well, if this be not heaven, it is next door to it," and we have thought that we were dwelling in the suburbs of the celestial city. You were in that land, which Bunyan calls the land Beulah. You were so near to heaven that the angels did flit across the stream and bring you sweet bunches of myrrh and bundles of frankincense, which grow in the beds of spices on the hills, and you pressed these to your heart and said with the spouse, "A bundle of myrrh is my well-beloved unto me; he shall lie all night betwixt my breasts," for I am ravished with his love and filled with his delights. He has made himself near to me, he has unveiled his countenance and manifested all his love.

But, beloved, while this gives us a foretaste of heaven, we may nevertheless use our state on earth as a complete contrast to the state of the glorified above. For here, when we see our Master, it is but at a distance. We are sometimes, we think, in his company, but still we cannot help feeling that there is a great gulf fixed between us, even when we come the nearest to him. We talk, you know, about laying our head upon his bosom, and sitting at his feet; but alas! we find it after all to be very metaphorical compared with the reality which we shall enjoy above. We have seen his face, we trust we have sometimes looked into his heart, and tasted that he is gracious, but still long nights of darkness lay between us. We have cried again and again with the bride, "O that thou wert as my brother, that sucked the breasts of my mother! when I should find thee without, I would kiss thee; yea, I should not be despised. I would lead thee, and bring thee into my mother's house, who would instruct me: I would cause thee to drink of spiced wine of the juice of my pomegranate." We were with him, but still he was in an upper room of the house, and we below; we were with him, but still we felt that we were absent from him, even when we were the nearest to him.

Again, even the sweetest visits from Christ, how short they are! Christ comes and goes very much like an angel; his visits are few and far between with the most of us, and oh! so short—alas, too short for bliss. One moment our eyes see him, and we rejoice with joy unspeakable and full of glory, but again a little time and we do not see him; our beloved withdraws himself from us; like a roe or a young hart he leaps over the mountain of division; he is gone back to the land of spices and feeds no more among the lilies.

If today he deigns to bless us
With a sense of pardoned sin,
He tomorrow may distress us,
Make us feel the plague within.

Oh, how sweet the prospect of the time when we shall not see him at a distance, but face to face. There is a sermon in those words, "face to face." And then we shall not see him for a little time, but,

Millions of years our wondering eyes,
Shall o'er our Savior's beauties rove;

And myriad ages we'll adore,
The wonders of his love.

Oh, if it is sweet to see him now and then, how sweet to gaze on that blessed face for ever, and never have a cloud rolling between, and never have to turn one's eyes away to look on a world of weariness and woe! Blessed days! when shall you come, when our companionship with Christ shall be close and uninterrupted?

And let us remark, again, that when we get a glimpse of Christ, many step in to interfere. We have our hours of contemplation when we do draw near to Jesus, but alas! how the world steps in and interrupts even our most quiet moments—the shop, the field, the child, the wife, the head, perhaps the very heart, all these are interlopers between ourselves and Jesus. Christ loves quiet; he will not talk to our souls in the busy market place, but he says, Come, my love, into the vineyard; get away into the villages; there will I show you my love. But when we go to the villages, behold the Philistine is there, the Canaanite has invaded the land. When we would be free from all thought except thought of Jesus, the wandering band of Bedouin thoughts come upon us, and they take away our treasures and spoil our tents. We are like Abraham with his sacrifice; we lay out the pieces ready for the burning, but foul birds come to feast on the sacrifice which we desire to keep for our God and for him alone. We have to do as Abraham did: when the birds came down upon the sacrifice, Abraham drove them away. But in heaven there shall be no interruption; no weeping eyes shall make us for a moment pause in our vision; no earthly joys, no sensual delights shall create a discord in our melody; there shall we have no fields to till, no garment to spin, no wearied limb, no dark distress, no burning thirst, no pangs of hunger, no weepings of bereavement; we shall have nothing to do or think upon but for ever to gaze upon that Sun of righteousness with eyes that cannot be blinded and with hearts that can never be weary. To lie in those arms for ever, throughout a whole eternity to be pressed to his bosom, to feel the beatings of his ever-faithful heart; to drink his love, to be satisfied for ever with his favor, and to be full with the goodness of the Lord—oh! if we have only to die to get to such delights as these—death is gain; it is swallowed up in victory.

Nor must we turn away from the sweet thought that we are to be with Christ where he is, until we have remembered that though we often draw near to Jesus on earth, yet the most we ever have of him is but a sip of the well. We sometimes come to the wells of Elim and the seventy palm trees, but when sitting beneath the palm trees, we feel that it is just like an oasis; tomorrow we shall have to be treading the burning sands with the scorching sky above us. One day we sit down and we drink from the sweet soft spring; tomorrow we know that we have to be standing with parched lips over Marah's fount, and crying, "Alas, alas! it is bitter; I cannot drink thereof." But oh, in heaven, we shall do what holy Rutherford says, we shall put the wellhead to our lips and drink right on from that well that never can be drained, we shall drink to our souls' utmost full. Yes, as much of Jesus as the finite can hold of infinity shall the believer receive. We shall not then see him for the twinkling of an eye and then lose him, but we shall see him ever. We shall not eat of manna that shall be like a small round thing, a coriander seed, but the manna whereof we feed shall be mountains, the broad hills of food; there we shall have rivers of delight and oceans of ecstatic joy. Oh, it is very hard for us to tell, with all that we can guess of heaven, how large, how deep, how high, how broad it is. When Israel ate of that one fair branch which came from Eshcol, they guessed what the clusters of Canaan must be; and when they tasted the honey, they guessed the sweetness. But I warrant no man in all that host had any idea of how full that land was of fertility and sweetness; how the very brooks ran with honey, and the very rocks did teem with fatness. Nor can any of us who have lived the nearest to our Master form more than the faintest guess of what it is to be with Jesus where he is.

Now all that is wanted to help my feeble description of being with Jesus is this—if you have faith in Christ, just think over this fact, that in a few more months you will know more about it than the wisest mortal before can tell. A few more rolling suns, and you and I shall be in heaven. Go on, O time! with your swiftest pinions fly! A few more years, and I shall see his face. Oh, can you say, my hearer, "I shall see his face"? Come, you gray-headed one nearing the goal of life, can you with confidence say, "I know that my Redeemer liveth"? If you can say that, it will fill your soul with joy. I can never think of it without being moved to tears. To think that this head shall wear a crown; that these poor fingers shall strike the harp strings of everlasting song; that this poor lip, which now faintly tells the wonders of redeeming grace, shall join with cherubim and seraphim and rival them in melody. Is it not too good to be true? Does it not seem sometimes as if the very greatness of the thought overwhelmed our faith? But true it is, and though too great for us to receive it, it is not too great for God to give. We *shall* be with him where he is. Yes, John; you laid your head upon your Savior's bosom once, and I have oftentimes envied you, but I shall have your place by and by. Yes, Mary; it was your sweet delight to sit at your Master's feet while Martha was cumbered with her much serving. I, too, am too much cumbered with this world, but I shall leave my Martha's cares in the tomb and sit to hear your Master's voice. Yes, O spouse, you did ask to be kissed with the kisses of his lips, and what you asked for, poor humanity shall yet see. And the poorest, meanest, and most illiterate of you who have trusted in Jesus shall yet put your lip to the lip of your Savior, not as Judas did, but with a true "Hail, Master!" you shall kiss him. And then, wrapped in the beams of his love, as a dim star is eclipsed in the sunlight, so shall you sink into the sweet forgetfulness of ecstasy, which is the best description we can give of the joys of the redeemed. "Father, I will that they also, whom thou hast given me, be with me where I am." That is heaven's sweetest joy—to be with Christ.

And now, the next prayer is, "that they may behold my glory, which thou hast given me." This is *heaven's sweetest employment*. I doubt not there are many joys in heaven which will amplify the grand joy which have just started; I feel confident that the meeting of departed friends, the society of apostles, prophets, priests, and martyrs, will amplify the joy of the redeemed. But still the sun that will give them the greatest light to their joy will be the fact that they are with Jesus Christ and behold his face. And now there may be other employments in heaven, but that mentioned in the text is the chief one, "That they may behold my glory." Oh, for the tongue of angel! Oh, for the lip of cherubim! for one moment to depict the mighty scenes which the Christian shall behold when he sees the glory of his Master, Jesus Christ! Let us pass as in a panorama before your eyes the great scenes of glory which you shall behold after death. The moment the soul departs from this body it will behold the glory of Christ. The glory of his person will be the first thing that will arrest our attention. There will he sit in the midst of the throne, and our eyes will first be caught with the glory of his appearance. Perhaps we shall be struck with astonishment. Is this the visage that was more marred than that of any man? Are these the hands that once rude iron tore? Is that the head that once was crowned with thorns? Oh, how shall our admiration rise and rise and rise to the very highest pitch, when we shall see him who was,

The weary man, and full of woes,
The humble man before his foes,

now King of kings, and Lord of lords. What! are those fire-darting eyes the very eyes that once wept over Jerusalem? Are those feet shod with sandals of light the feet that once were torn by the flinty acres of the Holy Land? Is that the man, who scarred and bruised, was carried to his tomb? Yes, it is he. And that shall absorb our thoughts—the Godhead and the manhood of Christ; the wondrous feet that he is God over all blessed for ever—and yet man, bone of our bone, flesh of our flesh. And when for an instant we have noted this, I doubt not the next glory we shall see will be the glory of his *enthronement*. Oh, how will the Christian stop at the foot of his Master's throne and look upward, and if there could be tears in heaven, tears of rich delight will roll down his cheeks when he looks and sees the man enthroned. "Oh," says he, "I often used to sing on earth, "Crown him! crown him! crown him King of kings and Lord of lords!" And now I see him; up those hills of glorious light my soul does not dare to climb. There, there he sits! Dark with unsufferable light his skirts appear. Millions of angels bow themselves around him. The redeemed before his throne prostrate themselves with rapture. Ah! we shall not deliberate many moments, but taking our crowns in our hands we shall help to swell that solemn pomp, and casting our crowns at his feet, we shall join the everlasting song, "Unto him that loved us, and washed us from our sins in his blood, . . . to him be glory . . . for ever and ever." Can you imagine the magnificence of the Savior? Can you conceive how thrones and princes, principalities and powers, all wait at his beck and command? You cannot tell how well the tiara of the universe does fit his brow, or how the regal purple of all worlds does gird his shoulders; but certain it is, from the highest heaven to the deepest hell, he is Lord of lords—from the furthest east to the remotest west, he is master of all. The songs of all creatures find a focus in him. He is the grand reservoir of praise. All the rivers run into the sea, and all the hallelujahs come to him, for he is Lord of all. Oh, this is heaven—it is all the heaven I wish, to see my Master exalted; for this has often braced my loins when I have been weary and often steeled my courage when I have been faint. "God also hath highly exalted him, and given him a name which is above every name: that at the name of Jesus every knee should bow, of things in heaven, and things in earth, and things under the earth."

And then the believer will have to wait a little while, and then he shall see more glorious things yet. After a few years, he will see the glories of the latter day. We are told in prophecy that this world is to become the dominion of Christ. At present, idolatry and bloodshed and cruelty and lusts do reign. But the hour is coming when this Augean stable shall be cleansed once and for ever; when these huge shambles of Aceldama shall yet become the temple of the living God. We believe that in these times, Christ with solemn pomp will descend from heaven to reign upon this earth. We cannot read our Bibles and believe them literally without believing that there are bright days coming when Christ shall sit upon the throne of his father David, when he shall hold his court on earth and reign among his ancients gloriously. But oh, if it be so, you and I shall see it, if we belong to the happy number who have put their trust in Christ. These eyes shall see that pompous appearance, when he shall stand in the latter day upon the earth. "Mine eyes behold, and not another." I could almost weep to think that I have lost the opportunity of seeing Christ on earth as crucified. I do think the twelve apostles were very highly favored, but when we shall see our Savior here, and shall be like our head, we shall think that all deficiencies are made up in the eternal weight of glory. When from the center to the poles the harmony of this world shall all be given to his praise, these ears shall hear it; and when all nations shall join the shout, this tongue shall join the shout also. Happy men and happy women who have such a hope, so to behold the Savior's glory.

And then, after that a little pause. A thousand years shall run their golden cycle, and then shall come the judgment. Christ, with sound of trumpet, in pomp terrific, shall descend from heaven—angels shall form his bodyguard, surrounding him on either hand. The chariots of the Lord are twenty thousand, even thousands of angels. The whole sky shall be clad with wonders. Prophecies and miracles shall be as rife and as plentiful as the leaves upon the trees. The earth shall totter at the tramp of the Omnipotent; the pillars of the heavens shall stagger like drunken men beneath the weight of the eternal splendor—heaven shall display itself in the sky while on earth all men shall be assembled. The sea shall give up its dead; the graves shall yield their tenants; from the cemetery and the graveyard and the battlefield, men shall start in their thousands; and every eye shall see him, and they who have crucified him. And while the unbelieving world shall weep and wail because of him, seeking to hide themselves from the face of him that sits upon the throne, believers shall come forward and, with songs and choral symphonies, shall meet their Lord. Then shall they be caught up together with the Lord in the air, and after he has said, "Come, ye blessed," they shall sit upon his throne, judging the twelve tribes of Israel; they shall take their seats as assessors upon that awful judgment bench; and when at the last he shall say, "Depart, ye cursed," and his left hand shall open the door of thunder and let loose the flames of fire, they shall cry, Amen; and when the earth shall vanish and men shall sink into their appointed doom, they, gladly seeing the triumph of their Master, shall shout again, again, again the shout of victory—"Alleluia: for the Lord God hath triumphed over all."

And to complete the scene, when the Savior shall ascend on high for the last time, his victories all completed and death himself being slain, he, like a mighty conqueror about to ride through heaven's bright streets, shall drag at his chariot wheel hell and death. You and I, attendants at his side, shall shout the victor to his throne; and while the angels clap their bright wings and cry, "the Mediator's work is done," you and I,

Louder than them all shall sing
While heaven's resounding mansions ring,
With shouts of sov'reign grace.

We shall behold his glory. Picture whatever splendor and magnificence you please, if you do but conceive it rightly, you shall behold it.

You see people in this world running through the streets to see a king or a queen ride through them. How they do climb to their housetops to see some warrior return from battle. Ah! what a trifle! What is it to see a piece of flesh and blood, though it be crowned with gold? But oh! what is it to see the Son of God with heaven's highest honors to attend him, entering within the pearly gates while the vast universe resounds with "Alleluia: for the Lord God omnipotent reigneth"?

I must close by noticing the last point, which is this. In our Savior's prayer *heaven's greatest privilege* is also included. Mark, we are not only to be with Christ and to behold his glory, but we are to be like Christ and to be glorified with him. Is he bright? So shall you be. Is he enthroned? So shall you be. Does he wear a crown? So shall you. Is he a priest? So shall you be a priest and a king to offer acceptable sacrifices for ever. Mark, that in all Christ has, a believer has a share. This seems to me to be the sum total and the crowning of it all—to reign with Christ, to ride in his triumphal chariot and have a portion of his joy; to be honored with him, to be accepted in him, to be glorified with him. This is heaven, this is heaven indeed.

And now, how many of you are there here who have any hope that this shall be your lot? Well said Chrysostom, "The pains of hell are not the greatest part of hell; the loss of heaven is the weightiest woe of hell"; to lose the sight of Christ, the company of Christ, to lose the beholding of his glories, this must be the greatest part of the damnation of the lost.

Oh, you that have not this bright hope, how is it that you can live? You are going through a dark world, to a darker eternity. I beseech you stop and pause. Consider for a moment whether it is worthwhile to lose heaven for this poor earth. What! pawn eternal glories for the pitiful pence of a few moments of the world's enjoyments? No, stop, I beseech you; weigh the bargain before you accept it. What shall it profit you to gain the whole world and lose your soul, and lose such a heaven as this?

But as for you who have a hope, I beseech you hold it fast, live on it, rejoice in it.

A hope so much divine,
May trials well endure,

May purge your soul from sense and sin,
As Christ the Lord is pure.

Live near your Master now, so shall your evidences be bright; and when you come to cross the flood, you shall see him face to face, and what that is only they can tell who enjoy it every hour.

John's First Doxology

—•••—

Delivered on Lord's Day morning, September 2, 1883, at Exeter Hall. No. 1737.

> *Unto him that loved us, and washed us from our sins in his own blood, and hath made us kings and priests unto God and his Father; to him be glory and dominion for ever and ever. Amen.*—REVELATION 1:5–6

John had hardly begun to deliver his message to the seven churches, he had hardly given in his name and stated from whom the message came, when he felt that he must lift up his heart in a joyful doxology. The very mention of the name of the Lord Jesus, "the faithful witness, and the first begotten of the dead, and the prince of the kings of the earth," fired his heart. He could not sit down coolly to write even what the Spirit of God dictated: he must rise; he must fall upon his knees; he must bless and magnify and adore the Lord Jesus. This text is just the upward burst of a great geyser of devotion. John's spirit has been quiet for a while, but on a sudden the stream of his love to Jesus leaps forth like a fountain, rising so high that it would seem to bedew heaven itself with its sparkling column of crystal love. Look at the ascending flood as you read the words, "Unto him that loved us, and washed us from our sins in his own blood, and hath made us kings and priests unto God and his Father; to him be glory and dominion for ever and ever. Amen."

Now, in the matter of this bursting out of devotion at unexpected times, John is one among the rest of the apostles. Their love to their divine Master was so intense that they had only to hear his footfall and their pulse began to quicken, and if they heard his voice, then were they carried clean away: whether in the body or out of the body, they could not tell, but they were under constraint to magnify the Savior's name; whatever they were doing they felt compelled to pause at once, to render direct and distinct homage unto the Lord Jesus by adoration and doxology. Observe how Paul breaks forth into doxologies: "Now unto him that is able to do exceeding abundantly above all that we ask or think, according to the power that worketh in us, unto him be glory in the church by Christ Jesus throughout all ages, world without end. Amen." Again: "Now unto the King eternal, immortal, invisible, the only wise

God, be honor and glory for ever and ever. Amen." The like is true of Jude, who cries, "Now unto him that is able to keep you from falling, and to present you faultless before the presence of his glory with exceeding joy, to the only wise God our Savior, be glory and majesty, dominion and power, both now and ever. Amen." The apostles overflowed with praise.

This explains to me, I think, those texts which bid us "rejoice evermore," "bless the LORD at all times," and "pray without ceasing": these do not mean that we are always to be engaged in devotional exercises, for that would cause a neglect of other duties. The very apostle who bids us "pray without ceasing" did a great many other things besides praying; and we should certainly be very faulty if we shut ourselves up in our private chambers and there continued perpetually upon our knees. Life has other duties, and necessary ones; and in attending to these we may render to our God the truest worship: to cease to work in our callings in order to spend all our time in prayer would be to offer to God one duty stained with the blond of many others. Yet we may "pray without ceasing" if our hearts are always in such a state that at every opportunity we are ready for prayer and praise; better still, if we are prepared to make opportunities, if we are instant in season and out of season and ready in a moment to adore and supplicate. If not always soaring, we may be as birds ready for instant flight: always with wings, if not always on the wing. Our hearts should be like beacons made ready to be fired. When invasion was expected in the days of Queen Elizabeth, piles of wood and combustible material were laid ready on the tops of certain hills, and watchmen stood prepared to kindle the piles should there be notice given that the ships of the enemy were in the offing. Everything was in waiting. The heap was not made of damp wood, neither had they to go and seek kindling; but the fuel waited for the match. The watch fire was not always blazing, but it was always ready to shoot forth its flame. Have you never read, "Praise waiteth for thee, O God, in Sion"? So let our hearts be prepared to be fired with adoring praise by one glimpse of the Redeemer's eyes; to be all on a blaze with delightful worship with one touch from that dear, pierced hand. Anywhere, wherever we may be, may we be clad in the robes of reverence and be ready at once to enter upon the angelic work of magnifying the Lord our Savior. We cannot be always singing, but we may be always full of gratitude, and this is the fabric of which true psalms are made.

This spontaneous outburst of John's love is what I am going to preach upon this morning. First of all I shall ask you to consider the condition of heart out of which such outbursts come, and then we will look more closely at the outburst itself; for my great desire is that you and I may often be thus transported into praise, carried off into ecstatic worship. I long that our hearts may be like harps through which each wind as it sweeps on its way makes charming music. As roses are ready to shed their perfume, so may we be eager to praise God, so much delighting in the blessed exercise of adoration that we shall plunge into it when colder hearts do not expect us to do so. I have read of Mr. Welch, a minister in Suffolk, that he was often seen to be weeping, and when asked why, he replied that he wept because he did not love Christ more. May not many of us weep that we do not praise him more? Oh, that our meditation may be used of the Holy Spirit to help us in that direction!

I. First, let us look at *the condition of heart out of which outbursts of adoration arise.*

Who was this man who when he was beginning to address the churches must needs lay down his pen to praise the Savior? We will learn the character of the man from his own devout language. We shall see his inmost self here, for he is carried off his feet and speaks out his very heart in the most unguarded manner. We shall now see him as he is and learn what manner of persons we must be if, like him, we would overflow with praise. It would be easy to talk at great length about John from what we know of his history from other parts of Scripture, but at this time I tie myself down to the words of the text, and I notice, first, that this man of doxologies, from whom praise flashes forth like light from the rising sun, is first of all a man who has realized the person of his Lord. The first word is, "Unto him"; and then he must a second time before he has finished say, "To him be glory and dominion." His Lord's person is evidently before his eye. He sees the actual Christ upon the throne. The great fault of many professors is that Christ is to them a character upon paper, certainly more than a myth, but yet a person of the dim past, a historical personage who lived many years ago and did most admirable deeds by the which we are saved, but who is far from being a living, present, bright reality. Many think of Jesus as gone away, they know not whither, and he is little more actual and present to them than Julius Caesar or any other remarkable personage of antiquity. We have a way, somehow, a very wicked way it is, of turning the facts of Scripture into romances, exchanging solidities for airy notions, regarding the august sublimities of faith as dreamy, misty fancies rather than substantial matters of fact. It is a grand thing personally to know the Christ of

God as a living existence, to speak into his ear, to look into his face, and to understand that we abide in him and that he is ever with us, even to the end of the world. Jesus was no abstraction to John; he loved him too much for that. Love has a great vivifying power: it makes our impressions of those who are far away from us very lifelike and brings them very near. John's great, tender heart could not think of Christ as a cloudy conception; but he remembered him as that blessed One with whom he had spoken and on whose breast he had leaned. You see that is so, for his song rises at once to the Lord's own self, beginning with, "Unto him."

He makes us see Jesus in every act of which he speaks in his doxology. It runs thus: "Unto him that loved us." It is not "Unto the love of God," an attribute or an influence or an emotion; but it is "Unto him that loved us." I am very grateful for love, but more grateful to him who gives the love. Somehow, you may speak of love and eulogize it; but if you know it only in the abstract, what is it? It neither warms the heart nor inspires the spirit. When love comes to us from a known person, then we value it. David had not cared for the love of some unknown warrior, but how greatly he prized that of Jonathan, of which he sang, "Thy love to me was wonderful, passing the love of women"! Sweet is it to sing of love, but sanctified hearts delight still more to sing, "Unto him that loved us."

So, too, with the washing from sin. It is enough to make us sing of pardoning mercy for ever and ever if we have been cleansed from sin, but the center of the joy is to adore him "that washed us from our sins in his own blood." Observe that he cleansed us, not by some process outside of himself, but by the shedding of his own blood of reconciliation. It brings the blood-washing into the highest estimation with the heart when we look into the wounds from whence the atonement flowed, when we gaze upon that dear visage so sadly marred, that brow so grievously scarred, and even peer into the heart which was pierced by the spear for us to furnish a double cleansing for our sin. "Unto him that . . . washed us." The disciples were bound to love the hands that took the basin and poured water on their feet and the loins which were girt with the towel for their washing; and we, brethren, must do the same. But as for the washing with his own blood, how shall we ever praise him enough? Well may we sing the new song, saying, "Thou art worthy . . . , for thou wast slain, and hast redeemed us to God by thy blood." This puts body and weight into our praise when we have realized him and understood how distinctly these precious deeds of love as well as the love itself come from him whose sacred heart is all our own.

So, too, if we are "kings and priests," it is Jesus who has made us so.

Round the altar priests confess:
If their robes are white as snow.
'Twas the Savior's righteousness
And his blood that made them so.

Our royal dignity and our priestly sanctity are both derived from him. Let us not only behold the streams but also consider the source. Bow before the blessed and only Potentate who does encrown and enthrone us, and extol the faithful high priest who does enrobe and anoint us. See the divine actor in the grand scene and remember that he ever lives, and, therefore, to him should we render perpetual glory. John worships the Lord himself. His mind is not set upon his garments, his crowns, his offices, or his works, but upon himself, his very self. "*I saw him,*" says the beloved apostle, and that vision almost blotted out the rest. His heart was all for Jesus. The censer must smoke unto him, the song must rise unto him—unto him, unto his very self.

I pray that every professor here may have a real Christ, for otherwise he will never be a real Christian. I want you to recognize in this realization of Christ by John this teaching—that we are to regard our holy faith as based on facts and realities. We have not followed cunningly devised fables. Do you believe in the divine life of Christ? Do you also believe that he who is "very God of very God" actually became incarnate and was born at Bethlehem? Do you put down the union of the godhead with our humanity as a historical fact which has the most potent bearing upon all the history of mankind? Do you believe that Jesus lived on earth and trod the blessed acres of Judea, toiling for our sakes, and that he did actually and really die on the behalf of sinners? Do you believe that he was buried and on the third day rose again from the dead? Are these stories in a book or facts in the life of a familiar friend? To me it is the grandest fact in all history, that the Son of God died and rose again from the dead and ever lives as my representative. Many statements in history are well attested, but no fact in human records is one-half as well attested as the certain resurrection of Jesus Christ from the dead. This is no invention, no fable, no parable, but a literal fact, and on it all the confidence of the believer leans. If Christ is not risen, then your faith is vain; but as he surely rose again, and is now at the right hand of God, even the Father, and will shortly come to be our judge, your faith is justified and shall in due season have its reward. Get a religion of facts and you will have a religion which will produce facts by operating upon your life and character; but a religion of fancies is but a fancied religion, and nothing practical will come of it.

To have a real, personal Christ is to get good anchor-hold for love and faith and hope. Somehow men cannot love that which is not tangible. That which they cannot apprehend they do not love When I was about to commence the orphanage at Stockwell, a gentleman who had had very large experience in an excellent orphanage said to me, "Begin by never expecting to receive the slightest gratitude from the parents of the children, and you will not be disappointed"; for, said he, "I have been connected with a certain orphanage," which he mentioned, "for a great many years, and except in the rarest case, I have never seen any tokens of gratitude in any of the mothers whose children have been received." Now, my experience is very different. I have had a great many grips of the hand which meant warm thanks, and I have seen the tear start from the mother's eyes full often, and many a grateful letter have I received because of help given to the orphan children. How do I explain the difference? Not that our orphanage has done more than the other, but the other orphanage is conducted by committee with no well-known head, and hence it is somewhat of an abstraction; the poor women do not know who is to be thanked and consequently thank nobody. In our own case the poor people say to themselves, "Here is Mr. Spurgeon, and he took our children into the orphanage." They recognize in me the outward and visible representative of the many generous hearts that help me. They know me, for they can see me, and they say, "God bless you," because they have someone to say it to. There is nothing particular about me, certainly, and there are others who deserve far more gratitude than that which comes to me; but it does come to me because the poor people know the name and the man and have not to look at a mere abstraction. Pardon the illustration: it suits my purpose well. If you have a Christ whom you cannot realize, you will not love him with that fervent affection which is so much to be desired. If you cannot reach the Lord in your mind, you will not embrace him in your heart; but if you have realized the blessed Master, if he has become a true existence to you, one who has really loved you and washed you from your sins, and made you a king and a priest, then your love must flow out toward him. You cannot resist the impulse to love one who has so truly loved you and is so well known to you.

This also gives foothold to faith. If you know the Lord Jesus, you feel that you can trust him. "They that know thy name will put their trust in thee." Those to whom Christ has become a well-known friend do not find it difficult to trust him in the time of their distress. An unknown Christ is untrusted; but when the Holy Spirit reveals Jesus, he also breeds faith. By the same means, your hope also becomes vivid, for you say, "Oh, yes; I know Jesus, and I am sure that he will keep his word. He has said, 'I will come again and receive you unto myself,' and I am sure that he will come, for it is not like him to deceive his own chosen." Hope's eyes are brightened as she thinks of Jesus and realizes him as loving to the end; in him believing, she rejoices with joy unspeakable and full of glory. To love, to trust, to hope are all easy in the presence of a real living Christ; but if, like the disciples at midnight on the Galilean lake, we think him to be a mere specter or apparition, we shall be afraid and cry out for fear. Nothing will suffice a real Christian but a real Christ.

Next, the apostle John, in whom we note this outburst of devotion, was a man firmly assured of his possession of the blessings for which he praised the Lord. Doubt has no outbursts; its chill breath freezes all things. Nowadays we hear Christian people talk in this way, "Unto him that we hope has loved us, and that we humbly trust has washed us, and that we sometimes believe has made us kings, unto him be glory." Alas! the doxology is so feeble that it seems to imply as little glory as you like. The fact is, if you do not know that you have a blessing, you do not know whether you ought to be grateful for it or not; but when a man knows he has covenant mercies, that divine assurance which the Holy Ghost gives to Christians works in him a sacred enthusiasm of devotion to Jesus. He knows what he enjoys, and he blesses him from whom the enjoyment comes. I would have you, beloved, know beyond all doubt that Jesus is yours, so that you can say without hesitation, "He loved me and gave himself for me." You will never say, "Thou knowest all things; thou knowest that I love thee," unless you are first established upon the point that Jesus loves you; for "we love him, because he first loved us." John was certain that he was loved, and he was furthermore most clear that he was washed, and, therefore, he poured forth his soul in praise. Oh, to know that you are washed from your sins in the blood of Jesus! Some professors seem half afraid to say that they are cleansed; but O my hearer, if you are a believer in Jesus, the case is clear, for "there is therefore now no condemnation to them which are in Christ Jesus"! He that believes in him has everlasting life. He that believes in him is justified from all things from which he could not be justified by the law of Moses. "Ye are clean," says Christ. "He that is washed needeth not save to wash his feet, but is clean every whit: and ye are clean."

O how sweet to view the flowing
Of the Savior's precious blood!
With divine assurance, knowing
He has made my peace with God.

This well-grounded assurance will throw you into ecstasy, and it will not be long before the deep of your heart will well up with fresh springs of adoring love. Then shall you also praise the Lord with some such words as these: "Unto him that loved us, and washed us from our sins in his own blood, . . . to him be glory and dominion for ever and ever. Amen."

Once more. I think we have brought out two points which are clear enough. John had realized his Master and firmly grasped the blessings which his Master brought him, but he had also felt, and was feeling very strongly, his communion with all the saints. Notice the use of the plural pronoun. We should not have wondered if he had said, "Unto him that loved me, and washed me from my sins in his own blood." Somehow there would have been a loss of sweetness had the doxology been so worded, and it would have hardly sounded like John. John is the very mirror of love, and he cannot live alone or rejoice in sacred benefits alone. John must have all the brotherhood around about him, and he must speak in their name, or he will be as one benefit of half himself. Beloved, it is well for you and me to use this "us" very often. There are times when it is better to say "me," but in general let us get away to the "us"; for has not our Lord taught us when we pray to say, Our Father which art in heaven. Give us this day our daily bread; forgive us our trespasses, and so on? Jesus does not bid us say, "My Father." We do say it, and it is well to say it, but yet our usual prayers must run in the "Our Father" style, and our usual praises must be "Unto him that loved us, and washed us from our sins." Let me ask you, beloved brethren, do you not love the Lord Jesus all the better and praise him all the more heartily because his grace and love are not given to you alone? Why, that blessed love has embraced your children, your neighbors, your fellow church members, myriads who have gone before you, multitudes that are around about you, and an innumerable company who are coming after; and for this we ought to praise the gracious Lord with unbounded delight. It seems so much the more lovely—this salvation, when we think of it, not as a cup of water of which one or two of us may drink, but as a well of water opened in the desert, ever flowing, ever giving life and deliverance and restoration to all who pass that way. "Unto him that loved us." O my Lord, I bless you for having loved me, but sometimes I think I could adore you for loving my wife, for loving my children and all these dear friends around me, even if I had no personal share in your salvation. Sometimes this seems the greater part of it, not that I should share in your compassion, but that all these poor sheep should be gathered into your fold and kept safe by you. The instinct of a Christian minister especially leads him to love Christ for loving the many, and I think the thought of every true worker for the Lord runs much in the same line. No man will burst out into such joyful adoration as we have now before us unless he has a great heart within him, full of love to all the brotherhood; and then, as he looks upon the multitude of the redeemed around about him, he will be prompted to cry with enthusiastic joy,

To him that lov'd the souls of men,
And wash'd us in his blood,
To royal honors raised our head,
And made us priests to God;

To him let every tongue be praise,
And every heart be love!
All grateful honors paid on earth,
And nobler songs above!

Thus much upon the condition of heart which suggests these doxologies.

II. Secondly, let us look at *the outburst itself.*

It is a doxology, and as such does not stand alone: it is one of many. In the book of the Revelation doxologies are frequent, and in the first few chapters they distinctly grow as the book advances. If you have your Bibles with you, as you ought to have, you will notice that in this first outburst only two things are ascribed to our Lord. "To him be glory and dominion for ever and ever." Now turn to the fourth chapter at the ninth verse, and read, "Those [living creatures] give glory and honor and thanks to him that sat on the throne." Here we have three words of honor. Run on to verse eleven, and read the same. "Thou art worthy, O Lord, to receive glory and honor and power." The doxology has grown from two to three in each of these verses. Now turn to chapter 5:13, "And every creature which is in heaven, and on the earth, and under the earth, and such as are in the sea, and all that are in them, heard I saying, Blessing, and honor, and glory, and power, be unto him that sitteth upon the throne, and unto the Lamb for ever and ever." Here we have four praise notes. Steadily but surely there is an advance. By the time we get to chapter 7:12, we have reached the number of perfection and may not look for more. "Blessing, and glory, and wisdom, and thanksgiving, and honor, and power, and might, be unto our God for ever and ever. Amen." If you begin praising God, you are bound to go on. The work engrosses the heart. It deepens and broadens like a rolling river. Praise is somewhat like an avalanche, which may begin with a snowflake on the mountain moved by the wing of a bird; but that flake binds others to itself and becomes a rolling ball. This rolling ball gathers more snow about it till it is huge, immense; it crashes through a forest; it thunders down into the valley; it buries a village under its stupendous mass. Thus praise may begin with the tear of gratitude; anon the bosom swells with love; thankfulness rises to a song; it breaks forth into a shout; it mounts up to join the everlasting hallelujahs which surround the throne of the Eternal. What a mercy it is that God by his Spirit will give us greater capacities by and by than we have here! For if we continue to learn more and more of the love of Christ which passes knowledge, we shall be driven to sore straits if confined within the narrow and drowsy framework of this mortal body. This poor apparatus of tongue and mouth is already inadequate for our zeal.

Words are but air and tongues but clay,
But his compassions are divine.

We want to get out of these fetters and rise into something better adapted to the emotions of our spirit. I cannot emulate the songsters of Immanuel's land though I would gladly do so; but as Berridge says,

Strip me of this house of clay,
And I will sing as loud as they.

These doxologies occur again and again throughout this book as if to remind us to be frequent in praise, and they grow as they proceed, to hint to us that we also should increase in thankfulness.

Now, this outburst carried within itself its own justification. Look at it closely and you perceive the reasons why, in this enthusiastic manner, John adores his Savior. The first is, "Unto him that loved us." Time would fail me to speak long on this charming theme, so I will notice only briefly a few things. This love is in the present tense, for the passage may be read, "Unto him that loveth us." Our Lord in his glory still loves us as truly and as fervently as he did in the days of his flesh. He loved us before the world was, he loves us now with all his heart, and he will love us when sun and moon and stars have all expired like sparks that die when the fire is quenched upon the hearth and men go to their beds. "He loves us." He is himself the same yesterday, today, and for ever, and his love is like himself. Dwell on the present character of it and be at this moment moved to holy praise.

He loved us first before he washed us: "Unto him that loved us, and washed us." Not "Unto him that washed us and loved us." This is one of the glories of Christ's love, that it comes to us while we are defiled with sin—yes, dead in sin. Christ's love does not go out to us only as washed, purified, and cleansed, but it went out toward us while we were yet foul and vile, and without anything in us that could be worthy of his love at all. He loved us and then washed us; love is the fountainhead, the first source of blessing.

Think of this as being a recognizable description of our Lord—"Unto him that loved us." John wanted to point out the Lord Jesus Christ, and all he said was, "Unto him that loved us." He was sure nobody would make any mistake as to who was intended, for no one can be said to love us in comparison with Jesus. It is interesting to note that, as John is spoken of as "that disciple whom Jesus loved," so now the servant describes the Master in something like the same terms, "Unto him that loved us." No one fails to recognize John or the Lord Jesus under their several love names. When the apostle mentioned "him that loved us," there was no fear of men saying, "That is the man's friend or father or brother." No, there is no love like that of Jesus Christ: he bears the palm for love; yes, in the presence of his love all other love is eclipsed, even as the sun conceals the stars by his unrivaled brightness.

Again, the word "him that loved us" seems as if it described all that Christ did for us, or, at least, it mentions first the grandest thing he ever did, in which all the rest is wrapped up. It is not, "Unto him that took our nature; unto him that set us a glorious example; unto him that intercedes for us"; but, "Unto him that loved us," as if that one thing comprehended all, as indeed it does.

He loves us; this is matter for admiration and amazement. O my brethren, this is an abyss of wonder to me! I can understand that Jesus pities us; I can very well understand that he has compassion on us; but that the Lord of glory loves us is a deep, great, heavenly thought, which my finite mind can hardly hold. Come, brother, and drink of this wine on the lees, well refined. Jesus loves you. Grasp that. You know what the word means in some little degree according to human measurements, but the infinite Son of God loved you of old, and he loves you now! His heart is knit with your heart, and he cannot be happy unless you are happy.

Remember, he loves you with his own love according to his own nature. Therefore he has for you an infinite love altogether immeasurable. It is also like himself, immutable, and can never know a change. The emperor Augustus was noted for his faithfulness to his friends, whom he was slow in choosing. He used to say, "Late ere I love, long ere I leave." Our blessed Lord loved us early, but he never leaves us. Has he not said, "I will never leave thee, nor forsake thee"? The love of Jesus is a pure, perfect, and divine love, a love whose heights and depths none can measure. His nature is eternal and undying, and such is his love. He could not love you more; he will never love you less. With all his heart and soul and mind and strength he loves you. Come; is not that a grand excuse, if excuse is wanted, for often lifting up our hearts and voices in hearty song unto the Lord? Why should we not seven times a day exult before him, saying, "Unto him that loved us, and washed us from our sins in his own blood, and hath made us kings and priests unto God and his Father, to him be glory and dominion for ever and ever. Amen"? Oh, for new crowns for his blessed brow! Oh, for new songs for his love-gifts ever new! Praise him! Praise him, all earth and heaven!

Then the apostle passes on to the second reason why he should thus magnify the Lord Jesus by saying, "And washed us from our sins in his own blood." "Washed us." Then we were foul; and he loved us though we were unclean. He washed us who had been more defiled than any. How could he condescend so far as to wash us? Would he have anything to do with such filthiness as ours? Would that sublime holiness of his come into contact with the abominable guilt of our nature and our practice? Yes, he loved us so much that he washed us from our sins, black as they were. He did it effectually too: he did not try to wash us, but he actually and completely washed us from our sins. The stains were deep and damnable; they seemed indelible, but he has "washed us from our sins." No spot remains, though we were black as midnight. "Wash me, and I shall be whiter than snow" has been realized by every believer here. But think of how he washed us—"with his own blood." Men are chary of their own blood, for it is their life; yet will brave ones pour it out for their country or for some worthy object; but Jesus shed his blood for such unworthy ones as we are, that he might by his atonement for ever put away the iniquity of his people. At what a cost was this cleansing provided! Too great a cost I had almost said. Have you never felt at times as if, had you been there and seen the Lord of glory about to bleed to death for you, you would have said, "No, my Lord, the price is too great to pay for such a one as I am"? But he has done it; brethren, his sin-atoning work is finished for ever: Jesus has bled, and he has washed us, and we are clean beyond fear of future defilement. Shall he not have glory for this? Will we not wish him dominion for this?

Worthy is he that once was slain,
The Prince of Peace that groan'd and died;
Worthy to rise, and live, and reign
At his Almighty Father's side.

Does not this doxology carry its justification in its own bowels? Who can refuse to praise at the remembrance of such grace as this?

Nor is this all. The Lord that loved us would do nothing by halves, and, therefore when he washed us in his own blood, he "made us kings." What is that? Are we kings this morning? We do not feel our crowns as yet, nor perhaps grasp our scepters as we might, but the Lord has made us a royal priesthood.

We reign over our own selves, and that is a dominion which is hard to gain, indeed, impossible without grace. We walk like kings among the sons of men, honored before the Lord and his holy angels—the peerage of eternity. Our thoughts, our aims, our hopes, and our longings are all of a nobler kind than those of the mere carnal man. Ours is a nature of a higher order than theirs, since we have been born again of the Spirit. Men know us not because they know not our Lord; but we have a heritage they have not, and we have prepared for us a crown of life which fades not away. The Lord has made us kings and endowed us with power before his presence; yes, he has made us rich since all things are ours. We read of the peculiar treasures of kings, and we have a choice wealth of grace. He has made us even now among the sons of men to possess the earth and to delight ourselves in the abundance of peace.

Furthermore our Lord has made us priests. Certain men impiously set up to be priests above the rest of the Lord's people. As Korah, Dathan, and Abiram are they, and they had need fear lest they and their evil system should go down into the pit. Whoever they may be, all the people of God are priests. Every man that believes in Jesus Christ is from that moment a priest, though he be neither shaven nor shorn nor bedecked in peculiar array. To the true believer his common garments are vestments, every meal is a sacrament, every act is a sacrifice. If we live as we should live, our houses are temples, our hearts are altars, our lives are an oblation. The bells upon our horses are holiness unto the Lord, and our common pots are as the bowls before the altar. It is the sanctification of the Holy Spirit which gives men a special character so that they are the priesthood of the universe. The world is dumb, and we must speak for it; the whole universe is as a great organ, but it is silent; we place our fingers on the keys, and the music rises toward heaven. We are to be priests for all mankind. Wherever we go we are to teach men and to intercede with God for them. In prayer and praise we are to offer up acceptable oblations, and we are ourselves to be living sacrifices, acceptable unto God by Jesus Christ our Lord. Oh, what dignity is this! How you and I are bound to serve God! Peter Martyr told Queen Elizabeth, "Kings and queens are more bound to obey God than any other persons; first as God's creatures, and secondly as his servants in office." This applies to us also. If common men are bound to serve God, how much more those whom he has made kings and priests unto his name!

What does the doxology say? "To him be glory and dominion." First, "To him be glory." Oh, give him glory, my beloved, this morning! Do I address any that have never yet accepted Christ's salvation? Accept it now, and thus give your Savior glory. Have you never trusted Jesus to save you? The best, the only thing you can do to give him glory is to trust him now, sinner as you are, that he may remove your transgressions. Are you saved? Then, dear brother, give him glory by speaking well of his name, and by perpetual adoration. Glorify him in your songs, glorify him in your lives. Behave yourselves as his disciples should do, and may his Spirit help you.

But the doxology also ascribes to him dominion. My heart longs for Jesus to have dominion. I wish he might get dominion over some poor heart this morning which has hitherto been in rebellion against him! Yield, rebel! Yield to your Sovereign and Savior! "Kiss the Son, lest he be angry, and ye perish from the way, when his wrath is kindled but a little." To him be dominion over hearts that have never submitted to him and assuredly to him be fullest dominion over hearts that love him. Reign, my Lord, reign in my bosom more and more; cast out every enemy and every rival; reign supreme, and reign eternally. Set up your throne also more and more conspicuously in the hearts and lives of all who call themselves Christians. O my brethren, ought it not to be so? Is it not clear to you that since he has loved and washed us, he should have dominion over us? Ah! let him have dominion over the wide, wide world, till they that dwell in the wilderness shall bow before him, and his enemies shall lick the dust. Reign for ever, King of kings and Lord of lords.

Then it is added, let him have glory and dominion "for ever and ever." I suppose we shall have some gentlemen coming up to prove that "for ever and ever" means only for a time. They tell us that everlasting punishment means only for a time, and, of course, everlasting life must mean just the same, and this praise must also have a limit. I mean not so, nor do you, beloved. I pray that our Lord may have endless glory, eternal dominion. I pray that Christ's power and dominion may be over this generation and the next and the next until he comes, and then that it may be said, "The Lord shall reign for ever and ever." Hallelujah! As long as there is wing of angel or song of man, as long as God himself shall live, may the Lord Jesus Christ that loved us and washed us have glory and dominion.

Now we have come to the last word of the text. It finishes up with "Amen." "For ever and ever. Amen." Can you heartily say "Amen" to this? Do you wish Christ to have glory and dominion for ever and ever? If you know he loved you, I am sure you do; if you know he washed you, I am sure you do. Now let our beating hearts in solemn silence say, "Amen"; and when we have done that, do you think you could join with one voice with me and say it out aloud, like thunder? Now, "Unto him that loved us, and washed us from our sins in his own blood, and hath made us kings and priests unto God and his Father, to him be glory and dominion for ever and ever. Amen"; and "Amen" yet again. (Here the great congregation joined aloud with the preacher.) The prayers of David the son of Jesse were ended when he came to that, and so may ours be, and so may this morning's service be. God bless you through his adorable Son. Amen and Amen.

The Prayers

of Christ

Christ's Prayer and Plea

⦅⦆

Published on Thursday, December 14, 1911; delivered on Thursday evening, January 18, 1866, at the Metropolitan Tabernacle, Newington. No. 3280.

Preserve me, O God: for in thee do I put my trust.—PSALM 16:1

I believe that we have in this verse a prayer of the Lord Jesus Christ. Some portions of this psalm cannot apply to anyone but the Savior; and we have the examples of Peter and Paul to warrant us in saying that in this psalm David spoke of Jesus Christ. There is no apparent division in the psalm, so that, as one part of it refers most distinctly to Christ, we are justified in concluding that the whole of it refers to him, and belongs to him. But we know that whatever belongs to Christ belongs also to all his people because of their vital union with him, so we shall treat the text, first, as our Savior's own prayer; and then, secondly, we shall regard it also as the prayer of the followers of the Lamb.

I. So, first, we will take these words as *our Savior's own prayer*:

"Preserve me, O God: for in thee do I put my trust"; and we will divide the text at once into two parts—the prayer itself: "Preserve me, O God:" and the argument or plea: "for in thee do I put my trust."

In considering these words as Christ's prayer, does it not immediately strike you as a very singular thing that Christ should pray at all? It is most certain that he was "very God of very God," that "Word" who was in the beginning with God, and who was himself God, the great Creator "without whom was not anything made that was made." But, without in any degree taking away his glory and dignity as God, we must never forget that he was just as truly man, one of the great family of mankind, and "as the children are partakers of flesh and blood, he also himself likewise took part of the same." Though he remained sinless, he "was in all points tempted like as we are." Being, therefore, man, and intending to make himself not only the atoning sacrifice for his people but also a perfect example that they might imitate, it became needful that he should pray. What would a Christian be without prayer, and how could a Christ who never prayed be an example to a Christian? Yet, notwithstanding the fact that it was necessary, it was marvelously condescending on our Savior's part. The Son of God, with strong crying and tears making known his requests unto his Father, is one of the greatest marvels in all the ages. What a wondrous stoop it was that Jesus—the unsinning Son of God, the thrice-holy One, the Anointed, the Christ—for whom prayer is to be made continually, should himself have prayed to his Father!

Yet, while there is much condescension in this fact, there is also much comfort in it. When I kneel in prayer, it is a great consolation to me to know that where I bow before the Lord, there is the print of my Savior's knees. When my cry goes up to heaven, it goes along the road which Christ's cry once traveled. He cleared away all impediments so that now my prayer may follow in the track of his. Be comforted, Christian, if you have to pray in dark and stormy nights, with the thought that your Master did the same.

Cold mountains and the midnight air
Witness'd the fervor of his prayer;
The desert his temptation knew,
His conflict and his victory too.

If you have to pray in sore agony of spirit fearing that God has forsaken you, remember that Christ has gone further even than that into the depths of anguish in prayer, for he cried in Gethsemane, "My God, my God, why hast thou forsaken me?"

In addition to being condescending and comforting, this fact of our Savior's praying shows the intimate communion there is between Christ and all the members of his mystical body. It is not only we who have to pray, but he who is our head bowed in august majesty before the throne of grace. Throughout the narratives of the four evangelists, one is struck with the many times that mention is made of Christ's prayers. At his baptism, it was while he was praying that "the heaven was opened, and the Holy Ghost descended in a bodily shape like a dove upon him, and a voice come from heaven, which said, Thou art my beloved Son; in thee I am well pleased." On another occasion, we read that "as he was praying in a certain place, when he ceased, one of his disciples said unto him, Lord, teach us to pray, as John also taught his disciples." On the Mount of Transfiguration, "as he prayed, the fashion of his countenance was altered, and his raiment was white and glistering." Jesus was emphatically "a man of prayer." After a long day of teaching the people and healing the sick, instead of seeking repose, he would spend the whole night in prayer to God; or, at another time, rising up a great while before day, he would depart into a solitary place and there pray for the needed strength for the new day's duties.

Having thus noticed the fact of Christ's praying, I want now to call your attention to the particular prayer in our text, and I ask you first to observe that it is addressed to God in a peculiar aspect. You do not see this in our translation, but in the Hebrew it is, " Preserve me, O El." That is one of the names of God, and the same name that the Savior used when he cried, "Eli, Eli, lama sabachthani?" "My God, my God, why hast thou forsaken me?" Many Christians seem to have only one name for God, but the Hebrew saints had many titles for the one living and true God. Worldlings generally talk of "the Almighty" as though his only characteristic was the omnipotent might which is displayed in great storms on the sea or terrible calamities on the land. But our Savior, whose knowledge of God was perfect, here selects a name of God peculiarly suitable to the condition in which he was when he offered this prayer; for, according to most commentators, the word "El" means "the strong One." So it is weakness crying to the strong for strength: "Preserve me, O you who are so strong, so mighty, that you uphold all things by the word of your power!" Others say that "El" means "the ever-present One." This is a delightful name for God, and one that is most appropriate for a believer to use when he is in peril on land or sea, in the den of lions or in the burning fiery furnace: " O you ever-present One, preserve me!" Jehovah is indeed "a very present help in trouble."

I wish we could acquire a more intimate knowledge of the divine character so that, in calling upon him in prayer, we could seek the aid of that special attribute which we need to have exercised on our behalf. What a blessed title is that of Shaddai which Bunyan uses in his *Holy War*—El Shaddai, God-all sufficient; or, as some render it, "the many-breasted God," the God with a great abundance of heart, full of mercy and grace, and supplying the needs of all his children out of his own fullness! Then take the other names or titles of God—Jehovah-Nissi, Jehovah-Shammah, Jehovah-Shalom, Jehovah-Tsidkenu, and any others that you can find—and think how much better we could pray if, instead of always saying, "O Lord!" or "O God!" we appealed to him under some title which indicated the attribute which we desired to be exerted on our behalf.

Next notice that this is a prayer produced by an evident sense of weakness. The suppliant feels that he cannot preserve himself. We believe that the human nature of Christ was altogether free from any tendency to sin, and that it never did sin in any sense whatsoever; yet, still, the Savior here appears not to rely upon the natural purity of his nature, but he turns away from that which might seem to us to be a good subject for reliance in order to show that he would have nothing to do with self-righteousness, just as he wishes us to have nothing to do with it. The perfect Savior prays, "Preserve me, O

God"; so, beloved, let us also pray this prayer for ourselves. Jesus Christ, the Son of God, who was without any tendency to sin, put himself under the shadow of the almighty wings; then shall I wickedly and presumptuously dare to go into danger trusting to my own integrity and relying upon my own strength of will? God forbid that you or I should ever act thus. Jesus was only weak because he had assumed our nature, yet in his weakness there was no tendency to sin; but our weakness is linked with a continual liability to evil; so, if Jesus prayed, "Preserve me, O God," with what earnestness should each one of us cry unto the Lord, " Hold me up, and I shall be safe."

I remark, next, that this prayer on the lips of Christ appeals for a promised blessing. "What!" says someone, "is there anywhere in God's Word a promise that Christ shall be preserved?" Oh, yes! Turn to the prophecy of Isaiah, the forty-ninth chapter, and the seventh and following verses, and there read, "Thus saith the LORD, the Redeemer of Israel, and his Holy One, to him whom man despiseth, to him whom the nation abhorreth, to a servant of rulers, Kings shall see and arise, princes also shall worship, because of the LORD that is faithful, and the Holy One of Israel, and he shall choose thee. Thus saith the LORD, In an acceptable time have I heard thee, and in a day of salvation have I helped thee: and *I will preserve thee*, and give thee for a covenant of the people, to establish the earth, to cause to inherit the desolate heritages." When the Savior prayed this prayer, he could remind his Father of the promise given through Isaiah, and say to him, "Thou hast said, 'I will preserve thee'; do as thou hast said, O my Father!"

Beloved brethren and sisters in Christ, let us learn from our Savior's example to plead the promises of God when we go to him in prayer. Praying without a promise is like going to war without a weapon. God is so gracious that he may yield to our entreaties even when he has not given a definite promise concerning what we are asking at his hands; but going to him with one of his own promises is like going to a bank with a check: he must honor his own promise. We speak reverently, yet very confidently, upon this point. To be consistent with his own character, he must fulfill his own word which he has spoken; so, when you approach the throne of grace, search out the promise that applies to your case, and plead it with your heavenly Father, and then expect that he will do as he has said.

Observe, next, that this prayer of Christ obtained an abundant answer. You recollect the many preservations which he experienced—how he was preserved while yet a child from the envy and malice of Herod, and how again and again he was delivered from those who sought his life. He was also preserved many times from falling into the snares set for him by scribes and

Pharisees and others who sought to entrap him in his talk. How wisely he answered the lawyer who came to him tempting him, and those who sought to catch him over the matter of paying tribute to Caesar! He was never taken as a bird ensnared by the fowler; he was always preserved in every emergency. He was like a physician in a hospital full of lepers, yet he was always preserved from the contagion.

Then, to close this part of the subject, notice that this prayer most deeply concerns the whole company of believers in Christ, for it strikes me that when our Savior prayed to his Father, "Preserve me," he was thinking of the whole of his mystical body, and pleading for all who were vitally united to him. You remember how in his great intercessory supplication he pleaded for his disciples, "Holy Father, keep through thine own name those whom thou hast given me, that they may be one, as we are." This is the same prayer as "Preserve me" if we understand the "me" to include all who are one with Christ. We also are included in that supplication, for he further said, "Neither pray I for these alone, but for them also which shall believe on me through their word; that they all may be one; as thou, Father, art in me, and I in thee, that they also may be one in us: that the world may believe that thou hast sent me." Yes, dear friend, though you may seem to yourself to be the meanest of the Lord's people, even though you are in your own apprehension but as his feet that glow in the furnace of affliction, even you are among those whom Christ entreated his Father to keep, and you may rest assured that he will certainly do so. Christ will never lose one of the members of his mystical body. If he could do so, his body would be imperfect and incomplete, but that it never can be. Paul tells us that Christ's church "is his body, the fullness of him that filleth all in all"; so that, if he were left without his fullness, he would have suffered an irreparable loss. That can never be the case, so this prayer will be answered concerning the whole body of believers in Jesus, who shall be presented "faultless before the presence of his glory with exceeding joy," blessed be his holy name!

Let us now turn *to the plea which Christ urged in support of his prayer*: "Preserve me, O God: for in thee do I put my trust." Did Christ put his trust in his Father? We surely need to ask the question, and we know at once what the answer must be. In the matter of faith, as in everything else, he is a perfect example to his people, and we cannot imagine a Christian without faith. Faith is the very life of a true believer in Jesus; indeed, without faith he is not a believer, so Christ was his model in this respect as well as in every other.

The words "in thee do I put my trust" may be translated "in you do I shelter." There is in them an allusion to running under something for shelter; in fact, the best figure I can use to give you the meaning of this sentence is that of the chicks running under the wings of the hen for shelter. Just so do we hide ourselves under the overshadowing wings of the Eternal. As a man, Christ used this plea with God, that he was sheltering from all evil under the divine wings of power and wisdom and goodness and truth. This is an accurate interpretation of the passage, and there are many instances recorded in Scripture in which Christ really did this. Take, for instance, that remarkable declaration in Psalm 22:9: "Thou didst make me hope when I was upon my mother's breasts," as though very early in life, probably far earlier than any of us were brought to know the Lord, Jesus Christ was exercising hope in the Most High. Then again, in the fiftieth chapter of the prophecy of Isaiah, we have these words which must refer to the Lord Jesus Christ, "I gave my back to the smiters, and my cheeks to them that plucked off the hair: I hid not my face from shame and spitting." That verse is immediately followed by this one: "For the Lord GOD will help me; therefore shall I not be confounded: therefore have I set my face like a flint, and I know that I shall not be ashamed." These words were peculiarly appropriate from the lips of Christ, yet each one of his followers may also say, "The Lord God will help me."

Even in his last agonies Christ uttered words which plainly prove that he had put his trust in God, "Father, into thy hands I commend my spirit." There is more faith in that final commendation of his soul to his Father than some of you might imagine, for it takes great faith to be able to speak thus in the circumstance in which Christ was then placed. Not only was he suffering the terrible pangs that were inseparable from death by crucifixion, but he had to bear the still greater grief that was his portion when his Father's face was withdrawn from him because he was in the place of sinners and, therefore, had to endure the separation from God which was their due. Job said, "Though he slay me, yet will I trust in him"; and this was what Jesus actually did. What wondrous faith it was that trusted in God even when he said, "Awake, O sword, against my shepherd, and against the man that is my fellow, saith the LORD of hosts!" Yet even then Jesus turned to his Father and said, "'Father, into thy hands I commend my spirit'; I commit myself into the hand that wields the sword of infallible justice, into the hand that has crushed me and broken me in pieces."

Talk of faith, did you ever hear of such sublime confidence as that having been displayed by anyone else? When a martyr has to lay down his life for the truth, his faith is sustained by the comforting presence of God; he believes in the God who is smiling upon him even while he is in the midst of the fire. But Christ on the cross trusted in the God who had forsaken him. O beloved, imitate this faith so far as it is possible in your case! What a glorious height of confidence Jesus reached; oh, that we may have grace to follow where he has so blessedly led the way!

I want you carefully to notice the argument that is contained in Christ's plea: "Preserve me, O God: for in thee do I put my trust." Christ, as God, had felt the power of that plea, so he knew that his Father would also feel the power of it. You remember that Jesus said to the woman of Canaan, " O woman, great is thy faith: be it unto thee even as thou wilt." Her faith prevailed with him, and he felt that his faith would prevail with his Father; so that, when he said, "In thee do I put my trust," he knew that he would obtain the preservation for which he pleaded. Jesus never forgot that the rule of the kingdom is, "According to your faith be it done unto you." He knew that we must "ask in faith, nothing wavering. For he that wavereth is like a wave of the sea driven with the wind and tossed. For let not that man think that he shall receive any thing of the Lord." So Jesus came to his Father with this plea, "I do trust in you. I have absolute confidence in you, therefore I pray you to preserve me."

My dear brother or sister in Christ, can you say the same? Can you look up to God and say, "In thee do I put my trust"? If so, you may use it as Christ used it in pleading with his Father. Perhaps you have gazed upon a weapon that has been wielded by some great warrior. If you had that weapon in your hand and were going forth to fight, you would feel, "I must not be a coward while I am grasping a brave man's sword, but I must play the man with it as he did." Well, you have in your grasp the very weapon which Christ used when he gained the victory. You can go before God with the very same argument that Christ used with his Father, and he will hear your plea even as he heard Christ's: "Preserve me, O God: for in thee do I put my trust."

II. I had intended, in the second place, to speak of my text as *the prayer of Christ's followers*; but, instead of preaching upon it as I would have done had time permitted, I will merely give you a few notes upon it, and then you can preach the second sermon yourselves by practicing it as you go your several ways to your homes.

First, *what does this prayer mean to a believer?* It means that you put yourself and all belonging to you under divine protection. Before you close your eyes, pray this prayer: " 'Preserve me, O God!' Preserve my body, my family, my house, from fire, from famine, from hurt or harm of every kind." Specially present the prayer in a spiritual sense. "Preserve me from the world; let me not be carried away with its excitements; suffer me not to be before its blandishments nor to fear its frowns. Preserve me from the devil; let him not tempt me above what I am able to bear. Preserve me from myself; keep me from growing envious, selfish, high-minded, proud, slothful. Preserve me from those evils into which I see others run, and preserve me from those evils into which I am myself most apt to run; keep me from evils known and from evils unknown. 'Cleanse thou me from secret faults. Keep back thy servant also from presumptuous sins; let them not have dominion over me.'"

This is a prayer which is more comprehensive in the original than it is in our version. It may be translated, " Save me," and this is a prayer that is suitable for many here. Those of you who have never prayed before can begin with this prayer, "Save me, O strong One! It will indeed need a strong One to save me, for I am so far gone that nothing but omnipotence can save me." It may also be rendered, "Keep me," or "Guard me." It is the word which we should use in speaking of the bodyguard of a king or of shepherds protecting their flocks. It is a prayer which you may keep on using from the time you begin to know the Lord until you get to heaven, and then you will need to alter Jude's Doxology only very slightly and to say, "Unto him who has kept us from falling, and presents us faultless before the presence of his glory with exceeding joy, to the only wise God our Savior, be glory and majesty, dominion and power, both now and ever. Amen."

Next, *when is this prayer suitable?* Well, it is suitable at this moment; you do not know what dangers you will meet with before you go to your bed tonight. Take special care when you come to what you consider the safe parts of the road, for you will probably be most in danger when you think you are in no danger at all. It is often a greater peril not to be tempted than to be tempted. This prayer is suitable to some of you who are going into new situations where you will have new responsibilities, new duties, and probably new trials and difficulties. In the old days of superstition, people were foolish enough to wear charms of various kinds to guard them from evil; but such a prayer as this is better than all their charms. If your pathway should lie through the enchanted fields or even through the valley of death-shade, you need not be afraid but may march boldly on with this prayer on your lips, " Preserve me, O God: for in thee do I put my trust."

Then, *in what spirit ought this prayer to be offered?* It should be offered in a spirit of deep humility. Do not pray, "Preserve me, O God," as though you felt that you were a very precious person; it is true that God regards you as one of his jewels if you are a believer in Jesus, but you are not to regard yourself as a jewel. Think of yourself as a brand plucked from the burning, and then you will pray with due humility. Pray as a poor feeble creature who must be destroyed unless God shall preserve you. Pray as if you were a sheep that had been shorn and that needed to have the wind tempered to it. Pray as a drowning man might pray, "Preserve me, O God." Pray as sinking Peter prayed, "Lord, save me," for so you shall be preserved even as he was.

With what motive ought you to pray this prayer? Pray it specially out of hatred to sin. Whenever you think of sin, the best thing you can do is to pray, "Preserve me, O God." Whenever you hear or read of others doing wrong, do not begin to plume yourself upon your own excellence, but cry at once, "Preserve me, O God, or it may be that I shall sin even as those others have done." If this night you are a Christian, the praise for this is not to be given to yourself, but to the Lord who has made you to differ from others. You are only what his grace has made you, so show how highly you value that grace by asking for more and more of it.

This must suffice concerning the prayer of the text, for I must, in closing, remind you of the plea and ask if each one here is able to use it: "Preserve me, O God: *for in thee do I put my trust.*" Can you, my friend, urge this plea with God tonight? Perhaps you say that you could do so years ago, then why not put your trust in the Lord now? It is present faith that you need in your present perils, and you cannot pray acceptably without faith, "for he that cometh to God must believe that he is, and that he is a rewarder of them that diligently seek him." You know what it is to trust a friend, and perhaps to be deceived, but do you know what it is to trust in God and not be deceived? Are you trusting for salvation only to Christ? Do you sing,

Thou, O Christ, art all I want,
More than all in thee I find?

Is this your plea continually; are you always trusting in God, in the dark as well as in the light? Many a man thinks he is strong until he begins to put forth his strength, and then he finds that it is utter weakness. There are many who fancy they are full of faith until they try to exercise it, and then they realize how little they have. They are fine soldiers when there is no fighting, and splendid sailors as long as they are on dry land; but such faith as that is of little service when some great emergency arises. The faith we need is that firm confidence which sings,

His love in time past forbids me to think
He'll leave me at last in trouble to sink;
Each sweet Ebenezer I have in review
Confirms his good pleasure to help me quite through.

If that is the kind of faith you have, you need not fear to pray, "Preserve me, O God," for he will be as a wall of fire around about you to guard you from all evil; and though you are now in the midst of those who would drag you down to their level if they could, or turn you aside from the paths of righteousness, the Lord in whom you have put your trust will never leave you nor forsake you, but will bring you in his own good time to that blessed place of which he has told you in his Word, and there,

Far from a world of grief and sin,
With God eternally shut in,

you shall be preserved from all evil for ever, and faith shall be blessedly exchanged for sight. God grant that every one of us may be able to pray the prayer of our text and to use the plea, "Preserve me, O God: for in thee have I put my trust," for Jesus' sake! Amen.

Our Lord's Solemn Inquiry

Published on Thursday, April 13, 1916; delivered on Lord's Day evening, April 7, 1872, at the Metropolitan Tabernacle, Newington. No. 3507.

> *"Eli, Eli, lama sabachthani?" that is to say, "My God, my God, why hast thou forsaken me?"*—MATTHEW 27:46

If any one of us, lovers of the Lord Jesus Christ, had been anywhere near the cross when he uttered those words, I am sure our hearts would have burst with anguish, and one thing is certain—we should have heard the tones of that dying cry as long as ever we lived. There is no doubt that at certain times they would come to us again, ringing shrill and clear through the thick darkness. We should remember just how they were uttered, and the emphasis where it was placed, and I have no doubt we should turn that text over and over and over in our minds. But there is one thing, I think, we should never have done if we had heard it—therefore, I am not going to do it—we should never preach from it. It would have been too painful a recollection for us ever to have used it as a text. No; we should have said, "It is enough to hear it." Fully understand it, who can? And to expound it, since some measure of understanding might be necessary to the exposition—that surely were a futile attempt. We should have laid that by; we should have put those words away as too sacred, too solemn, except for silent reflection and quiet, reverent adoration. I felt when I read these words again, as I have often read them, that they seemed to say to me, "You cannot preach from us," and, on the other hand, felt as Moses did when he put off his shoes from his feet in the presence of the burning bush, because the place whereon he stood was holy ground.

Beloved, there is another reason why we should not venture to preach from this text, namely, that it is probably an expression out of the lowest depths of our Savior's sufferings. With him into the seas of grief we can descend some part of the way; but when he comes where all God's waves and billows go over him, we cannot go there. We may, indeed, drink of his cup and be baptized with his baptism, but never to the full extent; and, therefore, where our fellowship with Christ cannot conduct us to the full, though it may in a measure—we shall not venture; not beyond where our fellowship with him would lead us aright, lest we blunder by speculation and "darken counsel by words without knowledge." Moreover, it comes forcibly upon my mind that though every word here is emphatic, we should be pretty sure to put the emphasis somewhere or other too little. I do not suppose we should be likely to put it anywhere too much. It has been well said that every word in this memorable cry deserves to have an emphasis laid upon it. If you read it, "'My God, my God, why have you forsaken me?' I marvel not that my disciples should, but why have you gone, my Father, God? Why could you leave me?" there is a wondrous meaning there. Then take it thus, "'My God, my God, why have you forsaken me?' I know why you have smitten me; I can understand why you do chasten me; but why have you forsaken me? Will you allow me no ray of love from the brightness of your eyes—no sense of your presence whatsoever?" This was the wormwood and the gall of all the Savior's bitter cup. Then God forsook him in his direst need. Or if you take it thus, "My God, my God, why have you forsaken me?" there comes another meaning. "Me, your well-beloved, your eternal well-beloved, your innocent, your harmless, your afflicted Son—why have you forsaken me?" Then, indeed, it is a marvel of marvels not that God should forsake his saints, or appear to do so, or that he should forsake sinners utterly, but that he should forsake his only Son. Then, again, we might with great propriety throw the whole force of the verse upon the particle of interrogation, "why." "My God, my God, why, ah! why have you forsaken me? What is your reason? What is your motive? What compels you to this, you Lord of love? The sun is eclipsed, but why is the Son of your love eclipsed? You have taken away the lives of men for sin, but why take you away your love, which is my life, from me who has no sin? Why and wherefore act you thus?"

Now, as I have said, every word requires more emphasis than I can throw into it, and some part of the text would be quite sure to be left and not dealt with as it should be; therefore, we will not think of preaching upon it, but instead thereof we will sit down and commune with it.

You must know that the words of our text are not only the language of Christ, but they are the language of David. You who are acquainted with the Psalms know that Psalm 22 begins with just these words, so that David said what Jesus said; and I gather from this that many a child of God has had to say precisely what the Lord Jesus, the first-born of the family, uttered upon the cross. Now as God's children are brought into the same circumstances as Christ, and Christ is considered the exemplar, my object tonight will be simply this—not to expound the words, but to say to believers who come into a similar plight, Do as Jesus did. If you come into his condition, lift up your hearts to God that you may act as he did in that condition. So we shall make the Savior now not a study for our learning, but an example for reproduction. The first out of these points in which, I think, we should imitate him is this,

I. *Under desertion of soul, the Lord Jesus still turns to God.*

At that time when he uttered these words, God had left him to his enemies. No angel appeared to interpose and destroy the power of Roman or Jew. He seemed utterly given up. The people might mock at him and they might put him to what pain they pleased; at the same time a sense of God's love to him as man was taken from him. The comfortable presence of God which had all his life long sustained him began to withdraw from him in the garden, and appeared to be quite gone when he was just in the article of death upon the cross; and meanwhile the waves of God's wrath on account of sin began to break over his spirit, and he was in the condition of a soul deserted by God. Now sometimes believers come into the same condition, not to the same extent, but in a measure. Yesterday they were full of joy, for the love of God was shed abroad in their hearts, but today that sense of love is gone; they droop; they feel heavy. Now the temptation will be at such times for them to sit down and look into their own hearts; and if they do, they will grow more wretched every moment until they will come well near to despair; for there is no comfort to be found within when there is no light from above. Our signs and tokens within are like sundials. We can tell what time it is by the sundial when the sun shines, but if it does not, what is the use of the sundial? And so marks of evidence may help us when God's love is shed abroad in the soul, but when that is gone, marks of evidence stand us in very little stead.

Now observe our Lord. He is deserted of God, but instead of looking in and saying, "My soul, why are you this? Why are you that? Why are you cast down? Why do you mourn?" he looks straightaway from that dried-up well that is within to those eternal waters that never can be stayed and which are always full of refreshment. He cries, "My God." He knows which way to look, and I say to every Christian here, it is a temptation of the devil when you are desponding and when you are not enjoying your religion as you did, to begin peering and searching about in the dunghill of your own corruptions, and stirring over all that you are feeling, and all you ought to feel, and all you do not feel, and all that. Instead of that, look from within, look above, look to your God again, for the light will come there.

And you will notice that our Lord did not at this time look to any of his friends. In the beginning of his sufferings he appeared to seek consolation from his disciples, but he found them sleeping for sorrow; therefore, on this occasion he did not look to them in any measure. He had lost the light of God's countenance, but he does not look down in the darkness and say, "John, dear faithful John, are you there? Have you not a word for him whose bosom was a pillow for your head? Mother Mary, are you there? Can you not say one soft word to your dying son to let him know there is still a heart that does not forget him?" No, beloved; our Lord did not look to the creature. Man as he was, and we must regard him as such in uttering this cry, yet he does not look to friend or brother, helper or human arm. But though God be angry, as it were, yet he cries, "My God." Oh! it is the only cry that befits a believer's lips. Even if God seems to forsake you, keep on crying to him. Do not begin to look in a pet and a jealous humor to creatures, but still look to your God. Depend upon it, he will come to you sooner or later. He cannot fail you. He must help you. Like a child if its mother strike it, still if it be in pain it cries for its mother; it knows her love; it knows its deep need of her, and that she alone can supply its need.

O beloved, do the same. Is there one in this house who has lately lost his comforts and Satan has said, "Don't pray"? Beloved, pray more than ever you did. If the devil says, "Why, God is angry; what is the use of praying to him?" he might have said the same to Christ—"Why do you pray to one who forsakes you?" But Christ did pray, "My God" still, though he says, "Why do you forsake me?" Perhaps Satan tells you not to read the Bible again. It has not comforted you of late; the promises have not come to your soul. Dear brother, read and read more; read double as much as ever you did. Do not think that because there is no light coming to you, the wisest way is to get away from the light. No; stay where the light is. And perhaps he even says to you, "Don't attend the house of God again; don't go to the communion table. Why, surely you won't wish to commune with God when he hides his face from you." I say the words of wisdom, for I speak according to the example of Christ; come still to your God in private and in public worship, and come still, dear brother, to the table of fellowship with Jesus, saying, "Though he slay me, yet will I trust in him," for I have nowhere else to trust; and though he hide his face from me, yet will I cry after him, and my cry shall not be "My friends," but "My God"; and my eye shall not look to my soul, my friends, or my feelings, but I will look to my God. and even to him alone. That is the first lesson, not an easy one to learn, mark you—easier to hear than you will find it to practice, but "the Spirit also helpeth our infirmities." The second lesson is this—observe that,

II. *Though under a sense of desertion, our Master does not relax his hold of his God.*

Observe it, "My God"—it is one hand he grips him with; "My God"—it is the other hand he grasps him with. Both united in the cry, "My God." He believes that God is still his God. He uses the possessive particle twice, "My God, my God."

Now it is easy to believe that God is ours when he smiles upon us, and when we have the sweet fellowship of his love in our hearts; but the point for faith to attend to, is to hold to God when he gives the hard words, when his providence frowns upon you, and when even his Spirit seems to be withdrawn from you. Oh! let go every thing, but let not go your God. If the ship be tossed and ready to sink and the tempest rages exceedingly, cast out the ingots, let the gold go, throw out the wheat, as Paul's companions did. Let even necessaries go, but oh! still hold to your God; give not up your God; say still, notwithstanding all, "In the teeth of all my feelings, doubts, and suspicions, I hold him yet; he is my God; I will not let him go."

You know that in the text our Lord calls God in the original his "strong One"—"Eli, Eli"—"my strong One, my mighty One." So let the Christian, when God turns away the brightness of his presence, still believe that all his strength lies in God and that, moreover, God's power is on his side. Though it seemed to crush him, yet faith says, "It is a power that will not crush me. If he smite me, what will I do? I will lay hold upon his arm, and he will put strength in me. I will deal with God as Jacob did with the angel. If he wrestle with me, I will borrow strength from him, and I will wrestle still with him until I get the blessing from him." Beloved, we must neither let go of God, nor let go our sense of his power to save us. We must hold to our possession of him, and hold to the belief that he is worth possessing, that he is God all-sufficient, and that he is our God still.

Now I would like to put this personally to any tried child of God here. Are you going to let go of your God because you have lost his smile? Then I ask you, Did you base your faith upon his smile? for if you did, you mistook the true ground of faith. The ground of a believer's confidence is not God's smile, but God's promise. It is not his temporary sunshine of his love, but his deep eternal love itself, as it reveals itself in the covenant and in the promises. Now, the present smile of God may go, but God's promise does not go; and if you believe upon God's promise, that is just as true when God frowns as when he smiles. If you are resting upon the covenant, that covenant is as true in the dark as in the light. It stands as good when your soul is without a single gleam of consolation as when your heart is flooded with sacred bliss. Oh! come then to this. The promise is as good as ever. Christ is the same as ever; his blood is as great a plea as ever; and the oath of God is as immutable as ever. We must get away from all building upon our apprehensions of God's love. It is the love itself we must build on—not on our enjoyment of his presence, but on his faithfulness and on his truth. Therefore, be not cast down but still call him, "My God."

Moreover, I may put it to you, if because God frowns you give him up, what else do you mean to do? Why, is not it better to trust in an angry God than not to trust in God at all? Suppose you leave off the walk of faith, what will you do? The carnal man never knew what faith was and, therefore, gets on pretty fairly in his own blind, dead way; but you have been quickened and made alive, enlightened, and if you give up your faith, what is to become of you? Oh! hold to him then.

> For if thine eye of faith be dim,
> Still hold on Jesus, sink or swim;
> Still at his footstool bow the knee,
> And Israel's God thy strength shall be.

Don't give him up.

Moreover, if faith give up her God because he frowns, what sort of a faith was it? Can you not believe in a frowning God? What, have you a friend who did the other day but give you a rough word, and you said, "At one time I could die for that man," and because he gives you one rough word, are you going to give him up? Is this your kindness to your friends? Is this your confidence in your God? But how Job played the man! Did he turn against his God when he took away his comforts from him? No; he said, "The LORD gave, and the LORD hath taken away; blessed be the name of the LORD." And do you not know how he put it best of all when he said, "Though he slay me, yet will I trust in him"? Yes, if your faith be only a fair-weather faith, if you can walk with God only when he sandals you in silver and smooths the path beneath your feet, what faith is this? Where did you get it from? But the faith that can foot it with the Lord through Nebuchadnezzar's furnace of fire and that can go walking with him through the valley of the shadow of death— this is the faith to be had and sought after, and God grant it to us, for that was the faith that was in the heart of Christ when forsaken of God. He yet says, "My God."

We have learned two lessons. Now we have learned them—(we have gone over them, but have we learned them?)—may we practice them, and turn to God in ill times and not relinquish our hold. The third lesson is this,

III. *Although our Lord uttered this deep and bitter cry of pain, yet learn from his silence.*

He never uttered a single syllable of murmuring or brought any accusation against his God. "My God, my God, why hast thou forsaken me?" There! look at those words. Can you see any blots in them? I cannot. They are crystallized sorrow, but there is no defilement of sin. It was just (I was about to say) what an angel could have said if he could have suffered; it is what the Son of God did say, who was purer than angels, when he was suffering. Listen to Job, and we must not condemn Job, for we should not have been half so good as he, I daresay; but he does let his spirit utter itself sometimes in bitterness. He curses the day of his birth and so on; but the Lord Jesus does not do that. There is not a syllable about "cursed be the day in which I was born in Bethlehem, and in which I came among such a rebellious race as this"—no, not a word, not a word. And even the best of men when in sorrow have at least wished that things were not just so. David, when he had lost Absalom, wished that he had died instead of Absalom. But Christ does not appear to want things altered. He does not say, "Lord, this is a mistake. Would God I had died by the hands of Herod when he sought my life, or had perished when they tried to throw me down the hill of Capernaum." No; nothing of the kind. There is grief, but there is no complaining; there is sorrow, but there is no rebellion.

Now this is the point, beloved, I want to bring to you. If you should suffer extremely, and it should ever come to that terrible pinch that even God's love and the enjoyment of it appears to be gone, put your finger to your lip and keep it there. "I was dumb [with silence], I opened not my mouth; because thou didst it." Believe that he is a good God still. Know that assuredly he is working for your good, even now, and let not a syllable escape you by way of murmuring, or if it does, repent of it and recall it. You have a right to speak to God, but not to murmur against him, and if you would be like your Lord, you would say just this, "Why hast thou forsaken me?" But you will say no more, and there will you leave him, and if there come no answer to your question you will be content to be without an answer.

Now again, I say, this is a lesson I can teach, but I do not know if I can practice it, and I do not know that you can. Only, again, "the Spirit helpeth also our infirmities," and he will enable us when we come to *"lama sabachthani"* to come so far, but not to go farther—to stop there with our Lord. The fourth lesson which, I think, we should learn is this,

IV. *Our Lord, when he does cry, cries with the inquiring voice of a loving child.*

"My God, why, ah! why hast thou forsaken me?" He asks a question not in curiosity, but in love. Loving, sorrowful complaints he brings. "Why, my God? Why? Why?" Now this is a lesson to us, because we ought to endeavor to find out why it is that God hides himself from us. No Christian ought to be content to live without full assurance of faith. No believer ought to be satisfied to live a moment without knowing to a certainty that Christ is his, and if he does not know it and assurance is gone, what ought he to do? Why, he should never be content until he has gone to God with the question, "Why have I not this assurance? Why have I not your presence? Why is it that I cannot live as once I did in the light of your countenance?" And, beloved, the answer to this question in our case will sometimes be, "I have forsaken you, my child, because you have forsaken me. You have grown cold of heart by slow degrees; gray hairs have come upon you, and you did not know; and I have made you know it to make you see your backsliding and sorrowfully repent of it."

Sometimes the answer will be, "My child, I have forsaken you because you have set up an idol in your heart. You love your child too much, your gold too much, your trade too much; and I cannot come into your soul unless I am your Lord, your love, your bridegroom, and your all." Oh! we shall be glad to know these answers because the moment we know them our heart will say,

The dearest idol I have known,
Whate'er that idol be,
Help me to tear it from its throne,
And worship only thee.

Sometimes the Lord's answer will be, "My child, I have gone from you for a little to try you, to see if you love me." A true lover will love on under frowns. It is only the superficial professor that wants sweetmeats every day, and loves his God only for what he gets out of him; but the genuine believer loves him when he smites him, when he bruises him with the bruises of a cruel one. Why, then we will say, "O God, if this is why you do forsake us, we will love you still, and prove to you that your grace has made our souls to hunger and thirst for you." Depend upon it, the best way to get away from trouble, or to get great help under it, is to run close in to God. In one of Quarles's poems he has the picture of a man striking another with a great nail. Now, the further off the other is, the heavier it strikes him. So the man whom

God is smiting runs close in, and he cannot be hurt at all. O my God, my God, when away from you affliction stuns me, but I will walk close with you, and then even my affliction I will take to be a cause of glory, and glory in tribulations also, so that your blast shall not sorely wound my spirit.

Well, I leave this point with the very same remark I made before. To cry to God with the inquiry of a child is the fourth lesson of the text. Oh! learn it well. Do practice it when you are in much trouble. If you are in such a condition at this time, practice it now, and in the pew say, "Show me wherefore you contend with me. Search me and try me, and see if there be any wicked way in me, and lead me in the way everlasting." Now the fifth observation is one to be treasured up,

V. *That our Lord, though he was forsaken of God, still pursued his father's work.*

Christ pursued the work he came to do. "My God, my God, why hast thou forsaken me?" But, mark you, he does not leave the cross; he does not unloose the nails as he might have done with a will; he did not leap down amid the assembled mockers and scorn them in return and chase them far away, but he kept on bleeding, suffering, even until he could say, "It is finished," and he did not give up the ghost till it was finished. Now, beloved, I find it, and I daresay you do, a very easy and pleasant thing to go on serving God when I have got a full sense of his love, and Christ shining in my face, when every text brings joy to my heart, and when I see souls converted, and know that God is going with the Word to bless it. That is very easy, but to keep on serving God when you get nothing for it but blows—when there is no success, and when your own heart is in deep darkness of spirit—I know the temptation. Perhaps you are under it. Because you have not the joy you once had, you say, "I must give up preaching; I must give up that Sunday school. If I have not the light of God's countenance, how can I do it? I must give it up." Beloved, you must do no such thing.

Suppose there were a loyal subject in a nation, and he had done something or other which grieved the king, and the king on a certain day turned his face from him—do you think that loyal subject would go away and neglect his duty because the king frowned? No; I think he would say to himself, "I do not know why the king seemed to deal hardly with me. He is a good king, and I know he is good; if he does not see any good in me, I will work for him more than ever. I will prove to him that my loyalty does not depend upon his smiles. I am his loyal subject and will stand to him still." What would you say to your child if you had to chasten him for doing wrong, if he were to go away and say, "I shall not attend to the errand that father has sent me upon, and I shall do no more in the house that father has commanded me to do because father has beaten me this morning"? Ah! what a disobedient child! If the scourging had its fit effect upon him, he would say, "I will wrong you no more, father, lest you smite me again." So let it be with us.

Besides, should not our gratitude compel us to go on working for God? Has not he saved us from hell? Then we may say with the old heathen, "Strike, so long as you forgive." Yes, if God forgives, he may strike if he will. Suppose a judge should forgive a malefactor condemned to die, but he should say to him, "Though you are not to be executed as you deserve, yet, for all that, you must be put in prison for some years," he would say, "Ah! my Lord, I will take this lesser chastisement, so long as my life is saved." And oh! if our God has saved us from going down to the pit by putting his own Son to death on our behalf, we will love him for that, if we never have anything more. If, between here and heaven, we should have to say, like the elder brother, "Thou never gavest me a kid that I might make merry with my friends," we will love him still; and if he never does anything to us between here and glory but lay us on a sick bed and torture us there, yet still we will praise and bless him, for he has saved us from going down to the pit; therefore, we will love him as long as we live. Oh! if you think of God as you ought to do, you will not be at ups and downs with him, but you will serve him with all your heart and soul and might whether you are enjoying the light of his countenance or not.

Now to close. Our Lord is an example for us in one other matter. He is to us our type of what shall happen to us, for whereas he said, "Why hast thou forsaken me?" yet,

VI. *He has received a glorious answer.*

And so shall every man that in the same spirit in the hour of darkness asks the same question. Our Lord died. No answer had he got to the question, but the question went on ringing through earth and heaven and hell. Three days he slept in the grave, and after a while he went into heaven, and my imagination, I think, may be allowed if I say that as he entered there the echo of his words, "Why hast thou forsaken me?" just died away, and then the Father gave him the practical answer to the question; for there, all along the golden streets, stood white-robed bands, all of them singing their Redeemer's praise, all of them chanting the name of Jehovah and the Lamb; and this was a part of the answer to his question. God had forsaken Christ that these chosen spirits might live through him; they were the reward for the travail of his soul; they were the answer to his question; and ever since then, between heaven and earth, there has been constant commerce.

If your eyes were opened that you could see, you would perceive in the sky not falling stars shooting downward, but stars rising upward from England, many every hour from America, from all countries where the gospel is believed, and from heathen lands where the truth is preached and God is owned, for you would see every now and then down on earth a dying bed, but upward through the skies, mounting among the stars, another spirit shot upward to complete the constellations of the glorified. And as these bright ones, all redeemed by his sufferings, enter heaven, they bring to Christ fresh answers to that question, "Why hast thou forsaken me?" And if stooping from his throne in glory the Prince of life takes view of the sons of men who are lingering here, even in this present assembly, he will see tonight a vast number of us met together around this table—I hope the most, if not all of us—redeemed by his blood and rejoicing in his salvation; and the Father points down tonight to this Tabernacle, and to thousands of similar scenes where believers cluster around the table of fellowship with their Lord, and he seems to say to the Savior, "There is my answer to your question, 'Why hast thou forsaken me?'"

Now, beloved, we shall have an answer to our question something like that. When we get to heaven, perhaps not until then, God will tell us why he forsook us. When I tossed upon my bed three months ago in weary pain that robbed me of my night's rest, and my day's rest too, I asked why it was I was there; but I have realized since the reason, for God helped me afterward so to preach that many souls were ingathered. Often you will find that God deserts you that he may be with you after a nobler sort—hides the light, that afterward the light of seven suns at once may break in upon your spirit, and there you shall learn that it was for his glory that he left you, for his glory that he tried your faith. Only mind you stand to that. Still cry to him, and still call him God, and never complain, but ask him why and pursue his work still under all difficulties; so being like Christ on earth, you shall be like Christ above, as to the answer.

I cannot sit down without saying just this word. God will never forsake his people for ever. But as many of you as are not his people, if you have not believed in him, he will forsake you for ever and for ever and for ever; and if you ask, "Why hast thou forsaken me?" you will get your answer in the echo of your words, "Thou hast forsaken me." "How shall we escape, if we neglect so great salvation?" "Believe on the Lord Jesus Christ, and thou shalt be saved."

But if your ears refuse
The language of his grace,
And hearts grow hard like stubborn Jews,
That unbelieving race;
The Lord in vengeance drest
Shall lift his hand and swear,
"You that despised my promised rest
Shall have no portion there."
God grant it may never be so with you, for Christ's sake. Amen

Special Protracted Prayer

Delivered on Lord's Day morning, March 1, 1868, at the Metropolitan Tabernacle, Newington. No. 798.

And it came to pass in those days, that he went out into a mountain to pray, and continued all night in prayer to God.—LUKE 6:12

If any man of woman born might have lived without prayer it was surely the Lord Jesus Christ. To us poor, weak, erring mortals, prayer is an absolute necessity; but it does not at first sight seem to be so to him who was "holy, harmless, undefiled, separate from sinners." In some parts of prayer our Lord Jesus Christ could take no share. As for instance, in that most important department, namely, personal confession of sin, he could take no portion. There were no slips in his outward life, there were no declensions in his inward heart. "Forgive us our debts as we forgive our debtors" is a very suitable prayer for him to teach us, but he could not use it himself. Nor had he any need to pray against inward corruptions, seeing he was born without them. We wrestle hard each day with original sin, but Jesus knew no such adversaries. It is as much as we can do, with all the weapons of our holy war, to keep down the foes of our own household, but our Lord had no sinful nature to subdue. The inner life is a daily struggle with some of us, so that Paul's exclamation, "O wretched man that I am!" is exceedingly familiar to our lips; but our Lord said truly of himself, "The prince of this world cometh, and hath nothing in me."

Moreover, our Lord had not to seek some of the things which are exceedingly needful to his disciples. One desire which I trust is ever present with us is for growth in grace, for advancement in the divine life; but our Lord was always perfect in holiness and love. I see not how there could have been any advancement in purity in him; he was always the spotless lily of innocence, incomparable, faultless, without spot or wrinkle, or any such thing. Our Lord had not need to make self-examination each night. When he retired for prayer, there would be no need to scan the actions of the day, to detect shortcomings and flaws; there would be no necessity to investigate secret motives to see whether he might not have been actuated by sinister principles. The deep wellsprings of his being were not of earth, but altogether divine. When he bowed

his knee in the morning, he had no need to pray to be protected from sin during the day. He went forth to his daily labor without the infirmities which we
bear within us and was free from the tendencies to evil which we bear about
us. Tempted he was in all points like as we are, but the arrows which wound
us glanced harmlessly from him.

Yet mark you carefully, although our glorious Master did not require to
pray in some of those respects in which it is most needful to us, yet never was
there a man who was more abundant in prayer and in supplication, nor one in
whom prayer was exercised with so much vehemence and importunity. He
was the greatest of preachers, but his prayers made even a deeper impression
on his disciples than his sermons, for they did not say, "Lord, teach us to
preach," but they did exclaim, "Lord, teach us to pray." They felt that he was
Master of that heavenly art, and at his feet they desired to sit that they might
learn how to move heaven and earth with sacred wrestlings.

Brethren, since our sinless Lord was this mighty in prayer, does not his
example say to us, with a voice irresistibly persuasive, "Watch and pray, that
ye enter not into temptation"? You are to be conformed to the image of
Christ—be conformed in this respect, that you be men of prayer. You desire
to know the secret of his power with men—seek to obtain his power with
God. You wish to obtain the blessings which were so copiously bestowed upon
him—seek them where he sought them, find them where he found them. If
you would adorn his doctrine and increase his kingdom, use the weapon of
all-prayer which ensures victory to all who use it as the Captain did.

Although our Lord Jesus Christ was most constant in his perpetual devotions, yet devout men have been wont to set apart times for extraordinary supplication. A man who does not pray usually is but a hypocrite when he
pretends to pray specially. Who would care to live in a miser's house who
starved you all the year around, except that now and then on a feast day he fed
you daintily? We must not be miserly in prayer, neglecting it regularly, and
abounding in it only on particular occasions when ostentation rather than sincerity may influence us. But even he who keeps a bounteous table sometimes
spreads a more luxurious feast than at other times; and even so must we, if we
habitually live near to God, select our extraordinary seasons in which the soul
shall have her fill of fellowship. Our Lord Jesus Christ in the text before us has
set us an example of extraordinary devotion, supplying us with all the details
and minutiae of the exercise.

Notice the place which he selected for it. He sought the solitude of a
mountain. He was so popular that he could not hope in any city or village to
be free from innumerable followers; he was so great a benefactor that he

could never be without sick folk entreating healing at his hands. He knew no leisure, no, not so much as to eat bread, and, therefore, to obtain a little respite, he sought the hollow of some lofty hill where foot of man could not profane his loneliness. If you would draw near to God in an extraordinary manner, you must take care to be entirely undisturbed. I know not how it is, but if ever one desires to approach very near to God, there is sure to be a knock at the door or some matter of urgent business or some untoward circumstance to tempt us from our knees. Is it so, that Satan knows how soul-fattening retirement and devotion are, and, therefore, if he can by any method stir up friend or foe to call us out of our closets, he will surely do so? Here our Lord was beyond call; the mountain was better than a closet with bolted doors. Far off was the din of the city and the noise of those who clamored with their merchandise: neither the shout of triumph nor the wail of sorrow could reach him there. Beloved friends, carefully seek if you can a perfect solitude, but if not, reach as near to it as you can, and as much as possible keep out the sound and thought of the outer world.

Did not our Lord resort to the mountain in order that he might be able to pray aloud? I cannot speak for others, but I often find it very helpful to myself to be able to speak aloud in private prayer. I do not doubt but that very spiritual minds can pray for a great length of time without the motion of the lips, but I think the most of us would often find it a spur and assistance if we could give utterance to our cries and sighs, no one being present to hear. We know that our Lord was accustomed to use strong cryings and tears, and these it would not have been desirable for a human ear to listen to; in fact, his natural modesty would have put him under a restraint. He therefore sought mountains far away that he might, in his Father's presence and in the presence of no one else, pour out his entire soul—groaning, struggling, wrestling, or rejoicing—as his spirit might be moved at the time.

Did he not also seek the mountain to avoid ostentation? If we pray to be seen of men, we shall have our reward, and a pitiful reward it will be; we shall have the admiration of shallow fools and nothing more. If our object in prayer be to obtain blessings from God, we must present our prayers unspoiled by human observation. Get alone with your God if you would move his arm. If you fast, appear not to men to fast. If you plead personally with God, tell none of it. Take care that this be a secret between God and your own soul, then shall your Father reward you openly; but if you gad about like a Pharisee to sound your trumpet in the corner of the streets, you shall go where the Pharisee has gone, where hypocrites feel for ever the wrath of God.

Jesus, therefore, to prevent interruption, to give himself the opportunity of pouring out his whole soul, and to avoid ostentation, sought the mountain. What a grand oratory for the Son of God! What walls would have been so suitable? What room would have worthily housed so mighty an intercessor? The Son of God most fittingly entered God's own glorious temple of nature when he would commune with heaven. Those giant hills and the long shadows cast by the moonlight were alone worthy to be his companions. No pomp of gorgeous ceremony can possibly have equaled the glory of nature's midnight on the wild mountain's side, where the stars, like the eyes of God, looked down upon the worshiper, and the winds seemed as though they would bear the burden of his sighs and tears upon their willing wings. Samson, in the temple of the Philistines moving the giant pillars, is a mere dwarf compared with Jesus of Nazareth moving heaven and earth as he bows himself alone in the great temple of Jehovah.

For purposes of extraordinary devotion, the time selected by our Master is also a lesson to us. He chose the silent hours of night. Now, it may so happen, that if we literally imitated him, we might altogether miss our way, for, no doubt, he chose the night because it was most convenient, congenial, and in every way appropriate. To some of us, the night might be most inappropriate and unsuitable; if so, we must by no means select it but must follow our Lord in the spirit rather than in the letter. We should give to heavenly things that part of the day in which we can be most quiet, those hours which we can most fairly allot to it, without despoiling our other duties of their proper proportion of time.

By day, our Savior was preaching; he could not cease from preaching even to spend the day in prayer. By day, the multitude needed healing; our Lord would not suspend his benevolent work for his private communions. We are to take care never to present one duty to God stained with the blood of another, but to balance and proportion our different forms of service so that our life's work may be perfect and entire, wanting nothing. Usually, however, night will be the favored season for wrestling Jacobs. When every man had gone to his own home to rest, the Man of Nazareth had a right to seek his solace where best he could, and if sleep refreshed others, and prayer more fully refreshed him, then by all means let him pray. Against this not a dog shall move his tongue. Set apart from remarkably protracted intercessions seasons which answer to this description, when the time is your own, not your master's, your own, not your family's, not pilfered from family devotion, not abstracted from the public assembly or the Sunday school, the time of quiet when all around you is in repose, the time congenial to solemnity, and the awe of a spirit hushed into reverent subjection, yet uplifted to rapt devotion. Such time, with many, may be the night, with others, it may be the day; let sanctified common sense be your direction.

Again, our Lord sets us a good example in the matter of extraordinary seasons of devotion in the protracted character of his prayer. He continued all night in prayer. I do not think that we are bound to pray long as a general rule. I am afraid, however, there is no great need to make the remark, for the most of Christians are short enough, if not far too short in private worship. By the aid of the Holy Spirit, it is possible to throw by holy energy and sacred zeal as much prayer into a few minutes as into many hours, for prevalent prayer is not measured by God by the yard or by the hour. Force is its standard rather than length. When the whole soul groans itself out in half-a-dozen sentences there may be more real devotion in them than in hours of mere wiredrawing and wordspinning. True prayer is the soul's mounting up to God, and if it can ride upon a cherub or the wings of the wind so much the better, yet in extraordinary seasons, when the soul is thoroughly wrought up to an eminent intensity of devotion, it is well to continue it for a protracted season.

We know not that our Lord was vocally praying all the time; he may have paused to contemplate; he may have surveyed the whole compass of the field over which his prayer should extend, meditating upon the character of his God, recapitulating the precious promises, remembering the wants of his people, and thus arming himself with arguments with which to return to wrestle and prevail. How very few of us have ever spent a whole night in prayer, and yet what boons we might have had for such asking! We little know what a night of prayer would do for us, its effect we can scarcely calculate. One night alone in prayer might make us new men, changed from poverty of soul to spiritual wealth, from trembling to triumphing. We have an example of it in the life of Jacob. Aforetime the crafty shuffler, always bargaining and calculating, unlovely in almost every respect, yet one night in prayer turned the supplanter into a prevailing prince and robed him with celestial grandeur. From that night he lives on the sacred page as one of the nobility of heaven.

Could not we, at least now and then, in these weary earthbound years, hedge about a single night for such enriching traffic with the skies? What, have we no sacred ambition? Are we deaf to the yearnings of divine love? Yet, my brethren, for wealth and for science men will cheerfully quit their warm couches; and cannot we do it now and then for the love of God and the good of souls? Where is our zeal, our gratitude, our sincerity? I am ashamed while

I thus upbraid both myself and you. May we often tarry at Jabbok, and cry with Jacob, as he grasped the angel,

With thee all night I mean to stay,
And wrestle till the break of day.

Surely, brethren, if we have given whole days to folly, we can afford a space for heavenly wisdom. Time was when we gave whole nights to chambering and wantonness, to dancing and the world's revelry; we did not tire then; we were chiding the sun that he rose so soon, and wishing the hours would lag a while that we might delight in wilder merriment, and perhaps deeper sin. Oh, wherefore, should we weary in our heavenly employment? Why grow we weary when asked to watch with our Lord? Up, sluggish heart, Jesus calls you! Rise and go forth to meet the heavenly friend in the place where he manifests himself.

Jesus has further instructed us in the art of special devotion by the manner of his prayer. Notice, he continued all night in prayer to God—to God. How much of our prayer is not prayer to God at all! It is nominally so, but it is really a muttering to the winds, a talking to the air, for the presence of God is not realized by the mind. "He that cometh to God must believe that he is, and that he is a rewarder of them that diligently seek him." Do you know what it is mentally to lay hold upon the great unseen One and to talk with him as really as you talk to a friend whose hand you grip? How heavenly to speak right down into God's ear, to pour your heart directly into God's heart, feeling that you live in him as the fish live in the sea, and that your every thought and word are discerned by him. It is true pleading when the Lord is present to you, and you realize his presence, and speak under the power and influence of his divine overshadowing.

That is to pray indeed, but to continue all night in such a frame of mind is wonderful to me, for I must confess, and I suppose it is your confession too, that if for a while I get near to God in prayer, yet distracting thoughts will intrude, the ravenous birds will come down upon the sacrifice, the noise of archers will disturb the songs at the place of drawing of water. How soon do we forget that we are speaking to God and go on mechanically pumping up our desires, perhaps honestly uttering them, but forgetting to whom they are addressed! Oh, were he not a gracious God, the imperfection of our prayers would prevent so much as one of them even reaching his ears; but he knows our frailty and takes our prayers, not as what they are, but as what we mean them to be, and, beholding them in Jesus Christ, he accepts both us and them in the Beloved. Do let us learn from our Master to make our prayers distinctly and directly appeals to God. That gunner will do no service to the army who takes no aim, but is content so long as he does but fire; that vessel makes an unremunerative voyage which is not steered for a port, but is satisfied to sail hither and thither. We must direct our prayers to God and maintain soul-fellowship with him, or our devotion will become a nullity, a name for a thing which is not.

The Ethiopic translation reads "in prayer with God." Truly this is the highest order of prayer, and though the translation may be indefensible, the meaning is correct enough, for Jesus was eminently with God all night. To pray with God, do you know what that is? To be the echo of Jehovah's voice! To desire the Lord's desires and long with his longings! This is a gracious condition to be in, when the heart is a tablet for the Lord to write upon, a coal blazing with celestial fire, a leaf driven with the heavenly wind. Oh, to be absorbed in the divine will, having one's whole mind swallowed up in the mind of God! This for a whole night would be blessed; this for ever bliss itself.

Note too, that some have translated the passage "in the prayer of God." This is probably an incorrect translation, though Dr. Gill appears to endorse it, but it brings out a precious meaning. The most eminent things were in the Hebrew language ascribed to God, so that by it would be meant the noblest prayer, the most intense prayer, the most vehement prayer, a prayer in which the whole man gathers up his full strength and spends it in an agony before the eternal throne. Oh, to pray like that! The great, deep, vehement prayer of God! Brethren, I am afraid that as a rule in our prayer meetings, we are much too decorous, and even in our private prayers feel too much the power of formality. Oh! how I delight to listen to a brother who talks to God simply and from his heart; and I must confess I have no small liking to those rare old-fashioned Methodist prayers which are now quite out of date. Our Methodist friends, for the most part, are getting too fine and respectable nowadays, too genteel to allow of prayers such as once made the walls to ring again. Oh, for a revival of those glorious violent prayers which flew like hot shot against the battlements of heaven! Oh, for more moving of the posts of the doors in vehemence; more thundering at the gates of mercy! I would sooner attend a prayer meeting where there were groans and cries all over the place, and cries and shouts of "Hallelujah!" than be in your polite assemblies where everything is dull as death and decorous as the whitewashed sepulcher. Oh, for more of the prayer of God, the whole body, soul, and spirit working together, the whole man being aroused and stirred up to the highest pitch of intensity to wrestle with the Most High! Such, I have no doubt, the prayer of Jesus was on the cold mountain's side.

Once more, we may learn from Jesus our Lord the occasion for special devotion. At the time when our Master continued all night in prayer he had been upbraided by the Pharisees. He fulfilled the resolve of the man after God's own heart. "Let the proud be ashamed; for they dealt perversely with me without a cause: but I will meditate in thy precepts." So David did, and so did David's Lord. The best answer to the slanderers of the ungodly is to be more constant in communion with God. Now, has it been so with any of you? Have you been persecuted or despised? Have you passed through any unusual form of trial? Then celebrate an unusual season of prayer. This is the alarm bell which God rings. Haste to him for refuge. See to it that in this your time of trouble you betake yourself to the mercy seat with greater diligence.

Another reason is also noticed in the context. Christ had said to his disciples, "Pray ye therefore the Lord of the harvest, that he will send forth laborers into his harvest." What he told them to do he would be sure to do himself. He was just about to choose twelve apostles, and before that solemn act of ordination was performed, he sought power for them from the Most High. Who can tell what blessings were vouchsafed to the twelve in answer to that midnight intercession? If Satan fell like lightning from heaven, Jesus' prayer did it rather than the apostles' preaching. So, Christian man, if you enter upon a new enterprise, or engage in something that is weightier and more extensive than what you have done before, select a night or a day, and set it apart for special communion with the Most High. If you are to pray, you must work, but if you are to work, you must also pray. If your prayer without your work will be hypocrisy, your work without your prayer will be presumption; so see to it that you are specially in supplication when specially in service. Balance your praying and working, and when you have reached the full tale of the one, do not diminish any of the other.

To any man here who asks me, "When should I give myself especially to a protracted season of prayer?" I would answer, these occasions will frequently occur. You should certainly do this when about to join the church. The day of your profession of your faith publicly should be altogether a consecrated day. I recollect rising before the sun to seek my Master's presence on the day when I was buried with him in baptism. It seemed to me a solemn ordinance not to be lightly undertaken or flippantly carried out; a duty which, if done at all, should be performed in the most solemn and earnest manner. What is baptism without fellowship with Christ? To be buried in baptism, but not with him, what is it? I would say to you young people who are joining the church now, mind you do not do it thoughtlessly, but in coming forward to enlist in the army of Christ, set apart a special season for self-examination and prayer. When you arrive at any great change of life do the same. Do not enter upon marriage, or upon emigration, or upon starting in business without having sought a benediction from your Father who is in heaven. Any of these things may involve years of pain or years of happiness to you; seek, therefore, to have the smile of God upon what you are about to do.

Should you not also make your times of peculiar trial to be also times of special prayer? Wait upon God now that the child is dying. Wrestle with him as David did about the child of Bathsheba. Draw near to God with fasting and prayer for a life that is specially dear to you if perhaps it may be preserved; and when the ax of death falls and the tree beneath which you found shelter is cut down, then again before the grave is closed, and the visitation is forgotten, draw near to God with sevenfold earnestness. And if you have been studying the Word of God, and cannot master a passage of Scripture, if some truth of revelation staggers you, now again is a time to set yourself like Daniel by prayer and supplication to find out what is the meaning of the Lord in the book of his prophecy.

Indeed, such occasions will often occur to you who are spiritual, and I charge you by the living God, if you would be rich in grace, if you would make great advances in the divine life, if you would be eminent in the service of your Master, attend to these occasions, get an hour alone, an hour, yes, two hours a day if you can, and go not away from the Master's presence till your face is made to shine as once the face of Moses did when he had been long upon the mount alone with God. And now having thus brought out the example of Christ as well as I can, I want to make an application of the subject to this church, which at this juncture has set apart a long season for special devotion. My words shall be few, but I earnestly desire that God may make them weighty to each member of this church.

A church, in order to have a blessing upon its special times of prayer, must abound in constant prayer at other times. I do not believe in spasmodic efforts for revival. There should be special occasions, but these should be the outgrowths of ordinary, active, healthy vigor. To neglect prayer all the year around, and then to celebrate a special week, is it much better than hypocrisy? To forsake the regular prayer meetings, but to come in crowds to a special one, what is this? Does it not betray superficiality or the effervescence of mere excitement? The church ought always to pray. Prayer is to her what salt and bread are to our tables. No matter what the meal, we must have salt and bread there, and no matter what the church's engagements, she must have her regular constancy of prayer. I think that in London our churches err in not having morning and evening prayer daily in every case where the church is large enough to maintain it. I am glad that our zealous brethren have here for some years maintained that constant prayer. I am thankful that in this church I cannot find much fault with you for non-attendance at the prayer meetings. There are some of you who never come, and I suppose you are such poor things that you are not of much good whether you come or stay away; but on the whole, the most of the people who fear God in this place are abundant in their attendance at the means of grace, not to be blamed in any measure whatever for forsaking the assembling of themselves together, for they do draw near to God most regularly; and such prayer meetings have we every Monday, as I fear are not to be found anywhere else. But we must see to it that we keep this up, and moreover, those who are lax and lagging behind, must ask forgiveness of their heavenly Father, and endeavor henceforth to be more instant in supplication.

If, brethren, men ought always to pray and not to faint, much more Christian men. Jesus has sent his church into the world on the same errand upon which he himself came, and that includes intercession. What if I say that the church is the world's priest? Creation is dumb, but the church is to find a mouth for it. Ungodly men are dumb of heart and will, but we who have the will and the power to intercede dare not be silent. It is the church's privilege to pray. The door of grace is always open for her petitions, and they never return empty-handed. The veil was rent for her, the blood was sprinkled upon the altar for her, God constantly invites her. Will she refuse the privilege which angels might envy her? Is not the church the bride of Christ? May she not go in unto her King at any time, at every time? Shall she allow the precious privilege to be unused? The church ever has need for prayer. There are always some in her midst who are declining, and frequently those who are falling into open sin. There are the lambs to be prayed for that they may be carried in Christ's bosom; there are the strong to be prayed for lest they grow presumptuous, and the weak lest they become despairing. In such a church as this is, if we kept up prayer meetings twenty-four hours in the day, three hundred sixty-five days in the year, we might never be without a special subject for supplication. Are we ever without the sick and the poor? Are we ever without the afflicted and the wavering? Are we ever without those who are seeking the conversion of their relatives, the reclaiming of backsliders, or the salvation of the depraved? No, with such congregations constantly gathering, with such a densely peopled neighborhood; with three millions of sinners around us, the most part of them lying dead in trespasses and sins; with such a country beginning to be benighted in superstition, over whom the darkness of Romanism is certainly gathering; in a world full of idols, full of cruelties, full of devilries; if the church does not pray, how shall she excuse her base neglect of the command of her loving Lord and covenant head? Let this church then be constant in supplication. There should be frequent prayer meetings; these prayer meetings should be constantly attended by all. Every man should make it a point of duty to come as often as possible to the place where prayer is wont to be made. I wish that all throughout this country the prayers of God's churches were more earnest and constant. It might make a man weep tears of blood to think that in our dissenting churches in so many cases the prayer meetings are so shamefully attended. I could indicate places that I know of, situated not many miles from where we now stand, where there are sometimes so few in attendance that there are scarcely praying men enough to keep up variety in the prayer meeting. I know towns where the prayer meeting is put off during the summer months as if the devil would be put off during the summer! I know of agricultural districts where they are always put off during the harvest, and I make some kind of excuse for them because the fruits of the earth must be gathered in, but I cannot understand large congregations, where the prayer meeting and lecture are amalgamated because there will not be enough persons coming out to make two decent services in the week. And then they say that God does not bless the Word. How can he bless the Word?

They say "Our conversions are not so numerous as they were," and they wonder how it is that we at the Tabernacle have so large an increase month by month. Do you wonder, brethren, that they have not a blessing when they do not seek it? Do you wonder that we have it when we do seek it? That is but a natural law of God's own government, that if men will not pray, neither shall they have; and if men will pray, and pray vehemently, God will deny them nothing. He opens wide his hand and says, "Ask what ye will, and it shall be given to you." I wish our denomination of Baptists and other denominations of Christians were greater believers in prayer, for this mischief of Ritualism and Rationalism which is coming upon us, this curse which is withering our nation, this blight and mildew which is devouring the vineyard of the Lord, has all come upon us because public prayer has almost ceased in the land as to its constancy, vehemence, and importunity. The Lord recover us from this sin!

But let the church be as diligent in prayer as she may on regular occasions, she ought still to have her special seasons. A thing which is regular and constant is sure to tire, and a little novelty is lawful; a little specialty may often tend to revive those who, otherwise, would be given to slumber. The church should have her special praying times because she has her special needs. There are times when spiritual epidemics fall upon churches and congregations. Sometimes it is the disease of pride, luxury, worldliness; at other times there are many falling into overt sin. Sometimes a black form of vice will break out in the very midst of the church of God; at other times it is a heresy or a doctrine carried to excess, or ill-will, or a want of brotherly love, or a general lethargy. At such special times of trial a church should have her extraordinary prayer meetings; as also when she is engaging in new enterprises and is about to break up new ground, she needs fresh strength, and she should seek it. Let her call her members together, and with heart and soul let them commend the work to God.

There should be special seasons of prayer because the Holy Spirit prompts us to it. "I believe in the Holy Ghost," is a sentence of the creed, but how few do really believe it! We seem to fancy that we have no motions of the Holy Spirit now among godly men as aforetime. But I protest before the living God that such is not the case. The Holy Spirit at this day moves in those who are conversant with him, and who are content to regard his gracious monitions, and he prompts us to especial fellowship. We speak what we do know, we declare what we have tasted and handled. The Holy Ghost, at certain times, prompts us to come together with peculiar earnestness and special desires. And then, if this suffice not, God has been pleased to set his seal to special seasons of prayer, therefore they ought to be held.

There have been more ingatherings, I was about to say, under special efforts of a month than under ordinary efforts of eleven months. I am sure that last year we saw very clearly God's blessing upon us during the month of February. All the year around—my dear brethren, the deacons and elders, can bear me out in it—there were always cases coming forward who said, "We were decided for Christ during the February meetings." God has always blessed the ministry here. I say it, not to boast, but to the glory to God. I do not know of any sermon preached here without conversions; but yet those times of special meeting, those solemn assemblies, have always been a hundredfold blessed of God, so that we have good reason to say we will continue them with renewed zeal because the Lord is with them.

Now, brethren, I must have just a word with you upon another matter, namely, that it should be our endeavor to bring power into these special meetings. They are lawful, they are necessary, let us make them profitable. The way to do so is to draw near to God as Christ did. When he prayed, it was a Son talking to his Father, the Son of God talking with the Father God, and unbosoming his heart in close communion. Come up tomorrow, my brethren, as sons of God to your Father; speak to him as to one who is very near akin to you. There will be no lack of power if such be the case. Jesus drew near to God in his prayer as a priest, the High Priest making intercession for the people. You are all priests and kings unto God, if you believe in Christ. Come with your breastplates on tomorrow; come that you may intercede before the throne, pleading the merit of the precious blood. There will be no flagging if every man put on his priestly miter. Jesus came before God with a burning zeal for his Father's glory. He could say, "The zeal of thine house hath eaten me up." Burn and blaze, my brethren, with love to God. Wait upon him this afternoon, let that be a special private season of prayer, and ask him to teach you how to love him, show you how to reverence him, and fire you with an intense ambition to spread abroad the savor of his name. Jesus Christ drew near to God in prayer with a wondrous love to the souls of men. Those tears of his were not for himself but for others; those sighs and cries were not for his own pangs, but for the sorrows and the sins of men. Try to feel as Christ did; get a tender heart, an awakened conscience, quickened sympathies, and then if you come up to the house of God, the prayer meetings cannot be dull.

Seek to be bathed in the blood of Christ. Go, my brethren, to the wounds of Christ and get life blood for your prayers. Sit down at Golgotha and gaze upon your dying Lord, and hear him say, "I have loved you, and given myself for you." Then rise up with this resolve in your soul,

Now for the love I bear his name,

What was my gain I count my loss,

and go forward determined in his strength that nothing shall be wanting on your part to win for him a kingdom, to gain for him the hearts of the sons of men. If such shall be your state of mind, I am quite sure there will be power with God in prayer.

In closing, I shall say to you, we, above all the churches of this country, have a special need and a special encouragement to make our prayers things of power. For, in the first place, my brethren, what a multitude we now are! I often wish, though I beg to be pardoned of the Lord for it, that I had never occupied the position that I now fill because of its solemn responsibilities. I tell you, when I feel them they crush me to the ground, and I can manage to sustain my spirits only by endeavoring to cast them upon the Lord. Why, three thousand seven hundred of you in church fellowship, or thereabouts, what can I do? Somebody complains that this sick one is not visited or that that sinning one is not rebuked. How can I do it? How can one man, how can twenty men, how can a hundred men do the work? God knows I would, if I could, cut myself in pieces, that every piece might be active in his service. But how can we rule and minister fully in such a church as this? God has supplied my lack of service very wonderfully, still there are things that make my heart ache day and night, as well as other matters that make my soul to leap for joy. Oh, pray for this great church! Where our power utterly fails us, let us implore the divine power to come in that all may be kept right. We have need to pray, for some have fallen. We have to confess it with a blush that crimsons our cheek, some have fallen shamefully. Oh, pray that others may not fall, and that the good men among us may be upheld by the power of God through faith unto salvation.

Think, my brethren, of the agencies which we are employing. If we do not pray for these they will be so much wasted effort. Every week the sermons preached here are scattered by tens of thousands all over the globe, not in this language only, but in all the languages of Christendom are they read. Pray that God's blessing may rest upon the Word which he has blessed aforetime. Our sons, our young ministers whom this church has trained at her feet, now are to be counted by hundreds, scattered all over this country and elsewhere. Intercede for them. Forget not your own sons, turn not your hearts away from your own children whom God has sent forth to be heralds of the cross. In your Sunday schools, in your tract distributions, in your city missions, in your street preachings, in your colportage, in your orphanage, everywhere you are seeking to glorify Christ. Do not, I beseech you, forget the one thing needful in all this. Do not be foolish builders, who will buy marble and precious stones at great cost, and then forget to lay the cornerstone securely. If it is worthwhile to serve God, it is worthwhile to pray that the service may be blessed. Why all this labor and cost? It is but offering to the Lord that which he cannot accept, except by prayer you sanctify the whole. I think I see you as a church standing by the side of your altar with the victims slain and the wood placed in order, but there is as yet still wanting the fire from on high. Oh, intercede, you Elijahs, men of like passions with us, but yet earnest men, upon whose hearts God has written prayer—intercede mightily! till at last the fire shall come down from heaven to consume the sacrifice and to make all go up like a pillar of smoke unto the Most High.

I cannot speak unto you as I would. The earnestness of my heart prevents my lips uttering what I feel, but if there be any bonds of love between us, above all, if there be any bonds of love between us and Christ, by his precious blood, by his death-sweat, by his holy life, and by his agonizing death, I do beseech you to strive together with us in your prayers that the Spirit of God may rest upon us, and to God shall be the glory. Amen and Amen.

The Joy of Jesus

Delivered on Sunday morning, December 5, 1880, at the Metropolitan Tabernacle, Newington. No. 1571.

In that hour Jesus rejoiced in spirit, and said, "I thank thee, O Father, Lord of heaven and earth, that thou hast hid these things from the wise and prudent, and hast revealed them unto babes: even so, Father; for so it seemed good in thy sight. All things are delivered to me of my Father: and no man knoweth who the Son is, but the Father; and who the Father is, but the Son, and he to whom the Son will reveal him."—LUKE 10:21–22

Last Lord's Day morning we considered the lamentations of Jesus; we will now turn our thoughts to the joys of Jesus. It is remarkable that this is the only instance on record in the gospels in which our Lord is said to have rejoiced. It stands alone, and is, therefore, the more to be prized: "In that hour Jesus rejoiced in spirit." He was the "man of sorrows and acquainted with grief" for our sakes, and, therefore, we are not astonished to find few indications of joy in the story of his life. Yet I do not think it would be fair to infer from the fact of a solitary mention of his rejoicing that he did not rejoice at other times; on the contrary, our Lord must, despite his sorrow, have possessed a peaceful, happy spirit. He was infinitely benevolent and went about doing good; and benevolence always finds a quiet delight in blessing others. The joy of the lame when they leaped and of the blind when they saw must have gladdened the soul of Jesus. To cause happiness to others must bring home to a sympathetic bosom some degree of pleasure. Sir Philip Sydney was wont to say, "Doing good is the only certainly happy action of a man's life"; and assuredly it is hard to see how the love of Jesus could refrain from rejoicing in blessing those around him.

Moreover, our Lord was so pure that he had a well of joy within which could not fail him. If it be indeed true that virtue is true happiness, then Jesus of Nazareth was happy. The poet said,

What nothing earthly gives, or can destroy,
The soul's calm sunshine and the heartfelt joy,
Is virtue's prize.

Such calm and joy must have been the Savior's, though for our sake he bowed beneath the heavy load of sorrow. The perfectly holy God is the perfectly happy God; and the perfectly holy Christ, had it not been that he had taken upon himself our griefs and sicknesses, would have been perfectly happy; but even with our griefs and sicknesses there must have been a deep peace of soul within him which sustained him in his deepest woe. Did not the Father himself say of his beloved Son, "Thou lovest righteousness, and hatest wickedness: therefore God, thy God, hath anointed thee with the oil of gladness above thy fellows"?

Nor is this all, for our blessed Lord lived in unbroken fellowship with the Father, and fellowship with God will not permit a soul to abide in darkness: for, walking with God, he walks in the light as God is in the light. Such a mind may, for certain purposes, come under clouds and glooms; but light is sown for the righteous, and it will speedily break forth as the dawn of day. Those nights of prayer and days of perfect service must have brought their own calm to the tried heart of the Son of God.

Besides, Christ Jesus was a man of faith—faith's highest exposition and example. He is "the author and the finisher of our faith," in whom we see its life, walk, and triumph. Our Lord was the incarnation of perfect confidence in the Father: in his life all the histories of great believers are summed up. Read Hebrews 11 and see the great cloud of witnesses, and then mark how in chapter 12 Paul bids us look to Jesus as though in his person the whole multitude of the witnesses could be seen. He it was, who "for the joy that was set before him endured the cross, despising the shame." His faith must, therefore, have anticipated the reward of his passion, and have brought the joy thereof home to him even while he sorrowed here. His joy was a light from the lamps of the future which were to be kindled by his death and victory. He had meat to eat that his disciples knew not of; for his long-sighted eye saw further than they, and while they mourned his departure, he saw the expediency of it, and told them that if they loved him they would rejoice because he was going to the Father. Be sure of this, that our Lord felt beneath the great water floods of outward affliction an undercurrent of joy, for he said, "These things have I spoken unto you, that my joy might remain in you, and that your joy might be full." What meant he by this if he had no joy in his people? Could he have spoken so many happy words, and so often have said to his disciples, "Be of good cheer," if he had been always downcast himself?

But still it is remarkable that our text should be the sole recorded instance of his joy, so far as the evangelists are concerned. It is clear that joy was not a distinguishing feature in our Lord's life, so as to strike the beholder. Peace may have sat serenely on his brow, but nothing of the exuberant spirits which are seen in some men, for his countenance was marred with lines of care and grief. We do not hear that he laughed, though it is thrice recorded that he wept; and here for once, as quite unique, we find the inspired assurance that he rejoiced. Because of its singularity the record deserves to be looked into with care that we may see the cause of delight so unusual.

The words here used are very emphatic. "He rejoiced." The Greek word is much stronger than the English rendering; it signifies "to leap for joy." It is the word of the blessed Virgin's song, "My spirit hath rejoiced in God my Savior." Strong emotions of delight were visible upon our Lord's face, and were expressed by the tones of his voice, as well as by his words. It is clear that he was greatly glad. The text also says he "rejoiced in spirit": that is, deep down in the very center of his nature, in that largest and most capacious part of his human being, the Redeemer rejoiced. Man is body, soul, and spirit; but the spirit is the nobler and most vital part, and it was with a spiritual, inward, and most living joy that the Lord Jesus Christ rejoiced. It was joy of the truest and fullest sort which made the Savior's heart to dance. Come we, then, near to this rejoicing Savior, who wraps the garments of praise about him, per-fumed with delight; and let us see if we cannot learn somewhat from his joys, since, I trust, we gathered something from his griefs.

I. First, let us look at our Lord and note that his joy was *joy in the Father's revelation of the gospel.*

"I thank thee, O Father, . . . that thou hast hid these things from the wise and prudent, and hast revealed them unto babes." He rejoices in his Father's revelation of the gospel. It was not joy in the fame which had gathered about his name insomuch that John heard of it in prison. It was not joy in the mani-fest tokens of power that went forth with his commissioners, though they rejoiced that devils were subject unto them; but it was joy in God's revealing the gospel to the sons of men.

I call your attention to the fact that he ascribed all that was done to the Father, and joyed that the Father was working with him. His disciples came back to him and said, "Even the devils are subject unto us through thy name"; and they spoke not amiss, for the name of Jesus was their strength and deserved honor; but the Lord, with that sacred self-abnegation which was so natural to him, replies, "I thank thee, O Father, . . . that thou . . . hast revealed [these things]." He takes no honor unto himself, but ascribes the glory unto the Father, who wrought with him. Imitate him, O you who call him Lord! Let the work of the Father be your joy. If God gives us any success in the preaching of the gospel, let our joy be that the Father's power is going forth with the Word. We are not so much to joy in our instrumentality as in the hand which uses the instrument and works by it. Oh, misery! misery! to be attempting gospel ministry without God! But oh, bliss, bliss unspeakable, to feel that when we lift our hand God's hand is lifted too, and when we speak the Word the voice of God is ringing through our feeble speech and reaching the hearts of men! It is to true believers a great joy that the Father is bringing home his wandering children and receiving penitents into his bosom.

The Savior's joy was that through the Father's grace men were being enlightened. The seventy disciples had been from city to city working miracles and preaching the gospel, and their Master was glad when they returned with tidings of success: "In that hour Jesus rejoiced in spirit." It pleases Jesus when the gospel has free course, and God is glorified thereby. Then, in measure, he sees of the travail of his Son and is filled with satisfaction. Shall we not find our joy where he finds his? Shall we not enter into the joy of our Lord? Whenever we hear good news of a village evangelized, of a township moved by the glad tidings, of a country long shut up from the gospel at length opened to the Word, let us feel our highest and deepest joy. Rather let us rejoice in this than in business prosperity or personal advantage. What if we can find no joy in our own circumstances, what if even spiritual affairs within our soul are full of difficulty; let us joy and rejoice that God the Father is revealing the light of his gospel among the sons of men. Be this our highest wish, "Thy kingdom come," and in that coming kingdom let us find our utmost happiness. Be sure that the joy which warmed the heart of Christ can do us no hurt: it must be a pure, sacred, and ennobling joy, and, therefore, let us indulge in it very largely. Christ's joy lay in the Father's sending forth his light and his truth, making men to see things which prophets and kings had desired to behold, but had not been favored to see. Jesus rejoiced in this, that the blessings of grace were being revealed by the Father.

Further, our Savior's joy lay very much in this, that this revelation to men was being made through such humble instruments. We read that "he lifted up his eyes on his disciples, and said, Blessed be ye poor: for yours is the kingdom of God." There was not among the twelve or the seventy, one person of any social status. They were the common people of the field and the sea. In after years Paul was raised up, a man richly endowed in learning, whose great abilities were used by the Lord; but the first ministers of Christ were a band of fishermen and countrymen, altogether unknown in the schools of learning and regarded as "unlearned and ignorant men." The grandest era in the world's history was ushered in by nobodies: by persons who, like their leader, were despised and rejected of men. To any one of them it might have been said, "For ye see your calling, brethren, how that not many wise men after the flesh, not many mighty, not many noble, are called: but God hath chosen the foolish things of the world to confound the wise; and God hath chosen the weak things of the world to confound the things which are mighty; and base things of the world, and things which are despised, hath God chosen, yea, and things which are not, to bring to nought things that are: that no flesh should glory in his presence."

Observe carefully that the persons whom our Lord had been employing were not only obscure in origin, but they were of a low degree of spiritual understanding, were in fact babes in grace as well as worldly wisdom. Their joy, when they came back to tell what had been done, was evidently childish as well as gracious. They joyed in their success as children do in their little achievements; but their Lord was thankful because he saw the openheartedness and the simplicity of their characters in the gladsome way in which they cried, "Lord, even the devils are subject unto us through thy name," and he thanked God that by such babes as these, such children, such true-hearted children, and yet such mere children, he was pleased to make known his Word among the sons of men. Rest sure that our Lord even at this day finds a delight in the weakness of the instruments he uses.

He takes the fool and makes him know
The mysteries of his grace;
To bring aspiring wisdom low,
And all its pride abase.

Not you, you scribes, who have counted every letter of the Old Testament, does he elect to be filled with the Spirit. Not you, you Pharisees, who so abound in outward religion, does he choose to spread the inward life and light. Not you, you Sadducees, who are versed in skeptical philosophy and boast your cleverness, does he call to preach his gospel to the poor. He has taken to be the heralds of his glory men from the Sea of Galilee whom you despise: men, simple-hearted, ready to learn, and then as ready to tell out again the message of salvation. Our Lord was by no means displeased with the absence of culture and learning in his followers, for the culture and learning of the period were utter vanity; but he was glad to see that they did not pretend to wisdom or astuteness, but came to him in all simplicity to accept his teaching because they believed him to be the Son of God. Jesus rejoiced in spirit about this.

And yet, further, his great joy was that the converts were of such a character as they were. "Thou hast hid these things from the wise and prudent, and hast revealed them unto babes." It is true that certain persons sneeringly asked, "Have any of the rulers or the Pharisees believed in him?" There were some who thought lightly of Jesus because those whom they imagined to be learned men had not signified their adhesion to his cause; our Lord himself had no concern in that direction, but called the Pharisees blind and the scribes hypocrites, as they assuredly were. Other voices may have inquired, "Who are these that follow Jesus? Of what class are his converts?" The answer would have been, "They are rustics, fishermen, and common people, with here and there a woman of substance and a man of means. The bulk of them are the poor to whom for the first time the gospel is preached. Such have gathered to Christ and received his Word." Some even said that a parcel of boys and girls were in the streets crying, "Hosanna," and this showed how commonplace the Preacher was. At this day I have heard the Lord's people spoken of as a poor set—people of no position, a lot of persons whose names will never be known, a mere assembly of Jack, Tom, Harry, Mary, Susan, and the rest. This was the very thing to which Jesus refers with thankfulness. He was glad that he was surrounded by unsophisticated, childlike natures, rather than by Pharisees and scribes, who, even if they be converted, are sure to bring some of their old manners with them.

He was glad that the Father had revealed his light and his salvation to those who were lowly and humble, who, though poor in this world, were "strong in faith, giving glory to God." Thus you see that the very fact which certain very superior people fling in our teeth as a disgrace was to our Savior a subject of joy. I have heard foolish ones sneer at certain churches which are earnest for the truth by affectedly asking, "Who are they? A mob of common people, tradesmen or working men, and the like. Are there any of the aristocracy among them? Do you find any of the highly intellectual in their ranks?" What if we do not, we shall not therefore sorrow, but join with Jesus in saying, "We thank thee, O Father, that thou hast hid these things from the wise and prudent, and hast revealed them unto babes." Christ found himself at home among those openhearted folks that gathered around him, for he was himself a child-man who wore his heart upon his sleeve, boasting of no wisdom though he was wisdom's self. Our Lord never sought himself as the wise and prudent of his age did; but he was meek and lowly in heart, and, therefore, found himself at home among a people who were willing to receive his teaching and eager to tell it out again to their countrymen; and so he blessed and praised God that such were chosen. O friends, it is not that Christ would not have the greatest come to him, it is not that Christ would not have the learned come to him; but so it is, that his greatest joy is that those come who, whatever the greatness or the littleness of their learning, are childlike in spirit, and like babes are willing to learn and prepared to receive what he shall teach to them. He was glad to receive persons with lowly notions of their own intelligence, and a supreme belief in the veracity of their great Teacher.

If those who are reckoned to be learned profess to come to Christ, they are generally a trial to the church. All the merely human learning that has ever come unto the church has, as a rule, been mischievous to it: and it always needs great grace to keep it in its right place. At first came the Gnostics with their philosophy, and into what perils they dragged the church of God I cannot stay to tell you: then arose others out of whose wisdom grew Arianism, and the church was well-nigh withered to her very heart by that deadly form of heresy. The schoolmen did for her much the same, and to this day whenever any of the would-be-thought-wise men meddle with religion, they tell us that the plain Word of God, as we read it, must be interpreted by modern thought, and that it bears another meaning which only the cultured can possibly comprehend. When philosophy invades the domain of revelation it ends in perverting the gospel, and in bringing in "another gospel which is not another." It is with human wisdom as it is with human riches, how hardly shall they that have it enter into the kingdom of God! True wisdom is another thing; that is a gift which comes from above and causes no puffing up of the heart, for it adores the God from whom it came. The wisdom which is true and real the Lord is prepared to give to those who confess their unwisdom, to those who will be babes in his sight. It is not ignorance which God loves, but conceit that he hates. Knowledge is good, but the affectation of it is evil. Oh, for more true wisdom! May God give us much of it, and may those who are babes as yet come to be men of full stature in Christ Jesus. Yet forget not your Lord's joy in the character of his converts, but remember the lines in which the poet of the sanctuary paraphrases our text:

Jesus, the man of constant grief,
A mourner all his days;
His Spirit once rejoiced aloud,
And turned his joy to praise.

"Father, I thank thy wondrous love,
That hath revealed thy Son
To men unlearned, and to babes
Hath made thy gospel known.

The mysteries of redeeming grace
Are hidden from the wise,
While pride and carnal reasoning join
To swell and blind their eyes.

Our Lord's joy sprang from one other source, namely, his view of the manner in which God was pleased to save his people. It was by revealing these things to them. There is, then, to every man who is saved a revelation, not of anything over and above what is given us in the Word of God; but of that same truth to himself personally and with power. In the Word is the light; but what is needed is that each man's eye should be opened by the finger of God to see it. Truth in the Scriptures will never save till it becomes truth in the heart: it must be "revealed" unto the most unprejudiced and true-hearted. Even men of childlike spirits and receptive natures will not see the truth unless it be specially revealed to them. There must be a work of the Father through the Holy Ghost upon each intellect and mind before it can perceive the truth as it is in Jesus. Hence, when unregenerate men tell us that they cannot see the beauty of the gospel, we are not at all astonished—we never thought they could: and when boastful men of "culture" declare that the old-fashioned gospel is unworthy of the nineteenth century with all its enlightenment, we are not surprised; for we knew that they would think so. Blind men are little pleased with color, and deaf men care little for music.

Human wisdom cannot make a man without eyes see the light. What do you know about the gospel, O you blinded wise men? What judges can you be of the light of revelation who seal up your eyes with the mud of your own cleverness, and then say you cannot see! Christ never intended that you should. He will reveal himself only as he pleases, and he has pleased to do this to another kind of person from what you are. you that are wise in your own conceit, the gate of true wisdom is barred against you! You cannot by searching find out God, and when he graciously reveals himself you refuse to see him, and, therefore, it is just that you should perish in the dark. Well do you deserve this judgment. Let justice be done. That God had been pleased to reveal himself to many through the preaching of the seventy was a great joy to Jesus; and let us also rejoice whenever God reveals himself to men. Let us be glad when one who is simple in heart is made a child by divine grace through being born again. Let us furthermore rejoice whenever conversion is wrought by instruments that cannot possibly claim the glory of it. Let us praise and bless God that salvation is his own work from first to last. Come, all you who love the Father, and say with the great Firstborn, "I thank thee, O Father, Lord of heaven and earth, that thou hast hid these things from the wise and prudent, and hast revealed them unto babes: even so, Father; for so it seemed good in thy sight."

II. I have thus tried, as far as I am able, to explain the cause of the Savior's joy; I would now call your attention to *his mode of expressing that joy.*

I have noticed some kind of joy in conversions which has not been wise in its expression, but has savored of glorying in the flesh. "Oh, we have had a wonderful time, we have had a blessed season! We have been visited by those dear men, and we have exerted ourselves in downright earnest to get up a revival. We have done wonders." Such talk will not do. Hear how the Savior speaks; his joy finds tongue in thanksgiving—"I thank thee, O Father." He ascribes the work to the Father, and then renders all the praise to him. This is the eloquence of joy—"I thank thee, O Father." Brethren, whenever you are happy, sing hymns of thanksgiving. "Is any merry? let him sing psalms." The fittest language for joy, whether it be on earth or in heaven, is adoration and thanksgiving to God. Blessed be the name of the Lord that we are gladdened in the harvest field of Christian work; for it is he that gives seed to the sower and causes the Word to spring up and bring forth fruit a hundredfold.

Our Lord found expression for his joy in declaring the Father's sovereignty. "I thank thee, O Father, Lord of heaven and earth." Some shrink back from the idea of God as Lord of all things above and below. To them the free will of man seems the greatest of all facts; and lest there should be the slightest intrusion upon man's domain, they would have God limited as to his absolute power. To magnify man they would minimize God. You will hear them talking against those of us who magnify divine sovereignty, and imputing to us the notion of a certain arbitrariness in God, although such a thought has never entered our minds. Jehovah, who gives no account of his matters, but orders all things according to the good pleasure of his will, is never arbitrary, unjust, or tyrannical: and yet he is absolute and uncontrolled, a sovereign who reigns by his own self-existent power, himself the source and origin of all law. He can be trusted with absolute sovereignty because he is infinite love and infinite goodness. I will go the utmost length as to the absolute supremacy of God, and his right to do as he wills, and especially to do as he wills with his own, which gospel grace most certainly is. He will have mercy on whom he will have mercy, and he will have compassion on whom he will have compassion. None can stay his hand or say unto him, What do you? When Christ was gladdest he expressed that gladness by ascribing unto God an infinite sovereignty, and shall that truth be gloomy to us? No, rather we will each one view the work of the Father's grace and cry, "I thank you, O Father, and I thank you all the more because I know that you are Lord of heaven and earth."

If I am addressing any who quarrel with the doctrine of the sovereignty of God, I would advise them to cease their rebellion, for "the LORD reigneth." Let them at least go as far as the Psalm, "Let the people tremble"; even if they cannot go a little further and sing, "The LORD reigneth; let the earth rejoice; let the multitude of isles be glad thereof." Power and rule are best in the hands of the great Jehovah who ever links together in his own single character both fatherhood and sovereignty. "I thank thee, O Father, Lord of heaven and earth." Dismiss from your minds all caricatures of the doctrine and receive it in its purest form—"the LORD is king for ever and ever." Hallelujah. Your joy, if it be deeply spiritual and very great, will never find room enough for the sweep of its Atlantic waves till you delight yourself in the absolute supremacy of God. The deep ground swell of delight within the Redeemer's soul could find no grander space over which it could expand its force than the unlimited power and dominion of the Lord of heaven and earth whose key it is which opens or shuts the kingdom of heaven, whose word it is which hides or reveals the things of eternity.

Our Lord delighted in the special act of sovereignty which was before him, that the Lord had "hid these things from the wise and prudent, and had revealed them unto babes." He communed with God in it, he took pleasure in it and said, "Even so, Father; for so it seemed good in thy sight." His voice, as it were, went with the Father's voice; he agreed with the Father's choice, he rejoiced in it, he triumphed in it. The will of the Father was the will of Christ, and he had fellowship with the Father in every act of his sovereign choice; yes, he magnified God for it in his inmost spirit. He says, "Even so, Father; for so it seemed good in thy sight"; for he knew that what seems good to God must be good. Some things seem good to us which are evil; but that which seems good to God is good. Jesus praises God about it for no other reason than it is God's good pleasure that it should be so. Oh, what a state of heart it will be for you and me to get into when we can express our highest joy by a perfect acquiescence in the will of God, whatever that will may be. See here, brethren, the road to contentment, to peace, to happiness, yes, heavenly life this side the grave. If you ever come to feel that what pleases God pleases you, you will be glad even in affliction and tribulation. If your heart is ever schooled down to accept as your will that which is God's will, and to believe anything to be good because God thinks it good, then you may go through the rest of your days singing and waiting till your Lord takes you to his own bosom. Soon will you rise to the place where all the singers meet and sing for ever unto God and the Lamb, all self and rebellion being for ever banished. Herein, then, Christ found a channel for his joy—in thanksgiving, in magnifying the divine sovereignty, in having communion with it, and in delighting in it.

III. Thirdly, and briefly, I want you to see *our Lord's explanation of the Father's act.*

The Father had been pleased to hide these things from the wise and prudent and to reveal them unto babes, and Jesus Christ is perfectly satisfied with that order of things, quite content with the kind of converts he has and the kind of preachers that God has given him.

For, first, the Lord Jesus does not need prestige. Read verse 22—"All things are delivered to me of my Father." A mere pretender, when he begins to prophesy and set himself up for a religious leader, how pleased he is when some learned doctor endorses his claims! If some man of wealth and station comes to his side how he plumes himself. The Savior of our souls sought no such aids. The verdict of the world's literati could not make his Word more truthful than it is, nor more convincing, for its power lies in the Spirit which reveals it. If great men say "Yes," they will not make his doctrine more sure; nor will they make it less truthful if they all say "No." Prestige for Christ! It is blasphemy to think of such a thing. "All things," says he, "are delivered to me of my Father." High priests and leaders of religion denounce him, but all things are delivered to him of his Father. The Sanhedrin determine to put him down, but all things are delivered to him of his Father. The learned deride his claims to be the Messiah! What matters it to Christ? The Father has committed all things into his hand. He stands alone and asks for no allies; his own power, unborrowed and unaided, is quite sufficient for his purposes. Do you think, brethren, that we are going to stay our preaching of the gospel until we shall have the so-called culture and intellect of the age upon our side to say, "It is even so"? Not we, but rather do we believe God in the teeth of the wiseacres, and say, "Let God be true, but every man a liar." Jesus needs no imprimatur from scholars, no patronage from princes, no apologies from orators. The pomp and power and wisdom and cunning of the world were not with him, and he thanks God that he is not encumbered with such doubtful gain, but that this truth has been revealed to those who are not wise in their own eyes, nor intelligent in their own esteem, but, like children, willing to learn from God, and glad to believe all that he reveals.

See how the Lord explains it yet further, by showing that human wisdom cannot find out God. "No man knoweth who the Son is, but the Father, and who the Father is, but the Son." No man; though he be a master in Israel. Men of science may puzzle their brains, and with great ingenuity they may try to thread the intricacies of the unknown, but they must err from the truth if they refuse revelation. Such a thing as natural religion, spontaneously born of man's intellect, does not exist. "Oh," say you, "surely there is much of it." I say that whatever is truly religious in it was borrowed from revelation and has been handed down by tradition. Talk of comparative religions—there is but one, and the other pretenders have stolen certain of its clothes. Men see, no doubt, much of God in nature, but they would not have done so had there been no revelation. First came the light through revelation, and then afterward, when men saw it reflected from various objects, they dreamed that the light came out of the reflectors.

Men hear something of revealed truth, and when their thoughts run in that line, that which they have heard is awakened in their minds, and they think themselves inventors. God is not known except as he reveals himself, nor can he be discovered by human ingenuity. Carnal wit and thought tend not that way, but tend from God unto blackest darkness. God is to be known only through Christ, so the text says: "No man knoweth who the Father is, but the Son, and he to whom the Son will reveal him." As the light, after God had created it was lodged in the sun, so is all knowledge of God treasured up in Christ as the Sun of righteousness. He it is that in himself has light, the light that lightens every man that comes into the world, if he be lightened at all. We must receive Christ or abide in darkness; yes, and the light which is in Christ is not perceptible by any man except by revelation. What says the text, "No man knoweth who the Son is, but the Father; and who the Father is, but the Son, and he to whom the Son will reveal him"? There must be a special and distinct revelation of Christ, and of the Father by Christ, to each man, or else he will remain in blindness to the day of his death.

The power, then, which lies in merely human wisdom is a force which often hinders men from coming under the influence of revelation. Only by revelation can they know and by a revelation personally receive. But the man is so wise that he does not want to be taught, he can find it out for himself. Yield himself to an infallible book or an infallible spirit? Not he! Well, then, because of his very wisdom he becomes incapable of learning. Truth to tell, what is human wisdom? The supposed wisdom of man is folly, that is the short for it all. They write a history sometime of religious thought, and of the various phases through which Christianity has gone, and on this they ground remarks; but I should like somebody to write a truthful history of philosophy. The history of philosophy is a record of the insanities of mankind: a catalog of lunacies. You shall see one generation of philosophers busily engaged in refuting those that went before them, and doing it very well indeed. But what will the next generation do? Why, refute this! The philosophies that were current one hundred years ago are all exploded now, and all the teachings of today, except such as are clear matters of fact, will be exploded before I go down to my grave, if I live to be gray-headed. There is not a philosopher now living that can be sure but what there is some other fact to be discovered yet which will upset every hypothesis that he has sent forth into the world. Philosophers who conceitedly glory over believers in revelation are fools, for they know nothing with certainty, and absolute certainty appertains only to divine revelation.

In those who pretend to wisdom apart from God folly abounds. There is no light in them, nor in any man except that which comes from the Spirit of God. That wisdom which sets itself up apart from God is atheism, because God knows, and he says to man, "I will teach you. I will reveal myself to you by my Son." But wisdom says, "We do not want to be taught. We know of ourselves." Then you are a rival to God! You pretend to be superior to God, since you are not willing to learn of him, but will rather trust yourself. This folly and this atheism are the reasons why God hides his mind from the wise and the clever; they reject him, and, therefore, he gives them over to a judicial blindness, and Christ thanks him that he does, for it is but justice that he should do so. When the Lord is pleased to give to any man a childlike spirit then is he on the road to knowledge.

This is true even in science itself. The secrets of nature will never be revealed to the man who believes that he already knows them. Nature herself does not teach the man who comes to her with prejudice. A man who thinks he knows beforehand sits down to study nature, and what does he generally discover? Well, he learnedly dreams of a universal solvent, or that the baser metals can be transmuted into gold, or that there is a perpetual motion. Those, you say, are things philosophers believed years ago. Yes, but their theories of today are just as stupid, and the science of today will be the jest of the next century. The greatest absurdities have been the pets of philosophy for hundreds of years, and why was it that men did not know better? Because they did not go to nature and ask her to teach them what was fact; they made a hypothesis, and then they went to nature to force her to prove it, as they do now; they start with a prejudgment of what they would like to be, and then take facts and twist them around into their system, and so they blind themselves by their own wisdom.

Well, if it be so in nature, and I am sure it is, it is certainly more so in grace, for when a man comes to the Word of God and says, "Now I know theology beforehand; I do not come here to find my creed in the Bible and learn it like a child, but I come to turn texts about and make them fit into my system." Well, he will blind himself and will be a fool, and it is right he should be blinded, for has he not done that willfully which must of necessity lead to such an end?

Brethren, simple teachableness is the first essential for the reception of a revelation from God, and if you have it today, if you are seeking after truth, if you are crying after her, and if you are willing that God should reveal her to you, if you are anxious that he should reveal truth to you in Christ, you are the sort of person upon whom God in sovereignty looks with divine favor, and unto such as you are will he reveal himself. What is wanted is faith, a childlike, receptive faith; not faith in a pope, not faith in a man, not faith in an old established creed, but faith in God. O my hearer, be willing to learn of him, and you shall not be left uninstructed.

Now a lesson or two, and I have done. The first lesson to be learned is this. If great men, if eminent men, if so-called learned men are not converted, do not be cast down about it—it is not likely they will be. In the next place, if many converts are obscure persons, persons without note or name, do not be at all disgusted with that fact. Who are you that you should be? Who are you that you should despise any upon whom God has looked in favor? Rather rejoice exceedingly with your Lord that God has chosen the despised, and you with them.

Next, learn that the sovereignty of God is always exercised in such a way that the pure in heart may always rejoice in it. God never did a sovereign act yet that the loving Christ himself could not rejoice in. Be content, therefore, to leave everything in the hand of God that you do not understand, and when his way is in the sea, be quite as glad as when his way is in the sanctuary; when his footsteps are not known, feel that they are quite as righteous and quite as holy as when you can perceive the path in which he moves.

The ultimate honor of the gospel is secured unto God alone; let that be our last lesson. When the wind up of all things shall come, there shall be no honor to any of us, nor would we desire it; but out of it all, out of the choice of each one, and out of the revelation made to each one will come up, multiplied into a thousand thunders, the voice as of Christ in his whole mystical body, "I thank thee, O Father." This shall be the song of heaven concerning the whole matter, as well concerning the lost as the saved. "I thank thee, O Father, Lord of heaven and earth." There shall be no cavils among the pure in heart, nor questions among the perfected spirits, but the whole family reviewing the whole of the Father's government, the hiding as well as the revealing, shall at the last say, Christ leading the utterance—" I thank thee, O Father, Lord of heaven and earth, that thou hast hid these things from the wise and prudent, and hast revealed them unto babes."

Brothers and sisters, let us learn our need of a personal revelation, let us seek it if we have not yet received it; with a childlike spirit, let us seek it in Christ, for he only can reveal the Father to us; and when we have it let it be our joy that we see him revealing it to others, and let this be our prayer, that the God of Jacob would yet bring others unto Christ, who shall rejoice in the light that has made glad our eyes. The Lord be with you. Amen.

Christ's Prayer for Peter

Intended for reading on Lord's Day, April 30, 1899; delivered on Lord's
Day evening, January 22, 1882, at the Metropolitan Tabernacle, Newington.
No. 2620.

"But I have prayed for thee, that thy faith fail not."—LUKE 22:32

Satan has a deadly hatred toward all good men; and they may rest assured that, somewhere or other, he will meet them on their way to the Celestial City. John Bunyan, in his immortal allegory, placed him in one particular spot and described him as Apollyon straddling across the road and swearing by his infernal den that the pilgrim should go no further, but that there and then he would spill poor Christian's soul. But the encounter with Apollyon does not happen in the same place to all pilgrims. I have known some of them assailed by him most fiercely at the outset of their march to Zion. Their first days as Christians have been truly terrible to them by reason of the satanic attacks they have had to endure; but, afterward, when the devil has left them, angels have ministered to them, and they have had years of peace and joy. You remember that, in the case of our Savior, no sooner was he baptized than he was led of the Spirit into the wilderness to be tempted of the devil. In like manner, there are those whose fiercest trials from the adversary come at the beginning of their public ministry.

Others meet with their greatest conflicts in middle life when, perhaps, they are too apt to think themselves secure against the assaults of Satan, and to fancy that their experience and their knowledge will suffice to preserve them against his wiles. I know some, like Martin Luther, in whose voyage of life the middle passage has been full of storm and tempest, and they have scarcely known what it was to have a moment's rest during all that period. Then there have been others, the first part of whose career has been singularly calm: their life has been like a sea of glass, scarcely a ripple has been upon the waters; and yet, toward the end, the enemy has made up for it, and he has attacked them most ferociously right up to the last. I have known many instances of eminent saints who have had to die sword in hand, and enter heaven—I was about to say, with the marks of their stern conflict fresh upon them. At any rate, they have been crowned on the battlefield and have fallen asleep at the close of a tremendous fight.

With the most of us who are really going to heaven—I will not say that it is a rule without any exception—but with the most of us, at some time or another, we shall know the extreme value of this prayer, "Lead us not into temptation [of any kind], but deliver us from [the] evil [one, who, beyond all others, is especially to be dreaded]." There is little to be got out of him, even if we conquer him. He usually leaves some mark of his prowess upon us, which we may carry to our graves. It were better to leap over hedge and ditch, and to go a thousand miles further on our pilgrim road than ever to have a conflict with him, except for those great purposes of which I shall presently speak a moment. The fight with Apollyon is a terrible ordeal—an ordeal, however, which a brave Christian will never think of shirking. No, rather will he rejoice that he has an enemy worthy of his steel, that true Damascus blade with which he is armed; and, in the name of God, he will determine, though he wrestles not with flesh and blood, that he will contend against principalities and powers, and with the very leader of them all, that there may be all the more glory to the great King who makes the weakest of his followers to be so strong that they put the old dragon himself to flight.

So, dear friends, rest assured that Satan hates every good man, and that, some time or other, he is pretty sure to show that hatred in a very cruel and deadly attack upon him.

Further, because of his hatred, Satan earnestly desires to put believers into his sieve that he may sift them as wheat—not that he wants to get the chaff away from them but simply that he may agitate them. You see the corn in the sieve, how it goes up and down, to and fro. There is not a single grain of it that is allowed to have a moment's rest; it is all in commotion and confusion, and the man who is sifting it takes care to sift first one way, and next another way, and then all sorts of ways. Now, that is just what Satan does with those whom he hates when he gets the opportunity. He sifts them in all manner of ways, and puts their whole being into agitation and turmoil. When he gets a hold of us, it is a shaking and sifting indeed; he takes care that anything like rest or breathing space shall be denied to us.

Satan desires thus to sift the saints in his sieve; and, at times, God grants his desire. If you look at the Revised Version, in the margin you learn the true idea of Satan having asked, or rather obtained by asking, the power to sift Peter as wheat. God sometimes gives Satan the permission to sift as wheat those who are undoubtedly his people, and then he tosses them to and fro indeed. That record in the book of Job of Satan appearing before God is just repeated in this story of Peter; for the devil had obtained from God liberty to try and test poor, boasting Peter. If Christ had not obtained of God in answer to his intercession the promise of the preservation of Peter, then had it gone ill indeed with the self-confident apostle. God grants to Satan permission to try his people in this way because he knows how he will overrule it to his own glory and their good.

There are certain graces which are never produced in Christians, to a high degree, except by severe temptation. "I noticed," said one, "in what a chastened spirit a certain minister preached when he had been the subject of most painful temptation." There is a peculiar tenderness, without which one is not qualified to shepherdize Christ's sheep, and to feed his lambs—a tenderness, without which one cannot strengthen his brethren, as Peter was afterward to do, a tenderness which does not usually come—at any rate, to such a man as Peter, except by his being put into the sieve, and tossed up and down by satanic temptation.

Let that stand as the preface of my sermon, for I shall not have so much to say upon that as upon another point.

First, observe, in our text, the grand point of Satan's attack. We can see that from the place where Jesus puts the strongest line of defense: "I have prayed for thee, that thy faith fail not." The point of Satan's chief attack on a believer, then, is his faith. Observe, secondly, the peculiar danger of faith: "That thy faith fail not." That is the danger—not merely lest it should be slackened and weakened, but lest it should fail. And then observe, thirdly, *the believer's grand defense:* "I have prayed for thee, that thy faith fail not."

I. Notice carefully, in the first place, *the grand point of Satan's attack.*

When he assails a child of God, his main assault is upon his faith; and I suppose that the reason is, first, *because faith is the vital point in the Christian.* We are engrafted into Christ by faith, and faith is the point of contact between the believing soul and the living Christ. If, therefore, Satan could manage to cut through the graft just there, then he would defeat the Savior's work most completely. Faith is the very heart of true godliness, for "the just shall live by faith." Take faith away, and you have torn the heart out of the gracious man. Hence, Satan, as far as he can, aims his fiery darts at a believer's faith. If he can only destroy faith, then he has destroyed the very life of the Christian. "Without faith it is impossible to please [God]." Therefore, if the devil could but get our faith away from us, we should cease to be pleasing to God and should cease to be "accepted in the Beloved." Therefore, brethren, look well to your faith. It is the very head and heart of your being as before God. The Lord grant that it may never fail you!

I suppose that Satan also attacks faith *because it is the chief of all our graces.* Love, under some aspects, is the choicest; but to lead the van in conflict, faith must come first. And there are some things which are ascribed solely and entirely to faith and are never ascribed to love. If any man were to speak of our being justified by love, it would grate upon the ears of the godly. If any were to talk of our being justified by repentance, those of us who know our Bible would be up in arms against such a perversion of the truth; but they may speak as long as they like of our "being justified by faith," for that is a quotation from the Scriptures. In the matter of justification, faith stands alone. It lays hold on Christ's sacrifice and his righteousness, and thereby the soul is justified. Faith, if I may so say, is the leader of the graces in the day of battle, and hence Satan says to his demoniacal archers, "Fight neither with small nor great, save only with the king of Israel; shoot at faith, kill it if possible." If faith is slain, where is love, where is hope, where is repentance, where is patience? If faith be conquered, then it is as when a standard-bearer faints. The victory is virtually won by the archenemy if he is able to conquer faith, for faith is the noble chieftain among the graces of a saint.

I suppose, again, that Satan makes a dead set upon the faith of the Christian became it is the nourishing grace. All the other graces within us derive strength from our faith. If faith be at a low ebb, love is sure to burn very feebly. If faith should begin to fail, then would hope grow dim. Where is courage? It is a poor, puny thing when faith is weak. Take any grace you please, and you shall see that its flourishing depends upon the healthy condition of faith in our Lord Jesus Christ. To take faith away, therefore, would be to take the fountain away from the stream; it would be to withdraw the sun from his rays of light. If you destroy the source, of course that which comes out of it thereupon ceases. Therefore, beloved, take the utmost possible care of your faith, for I may truly say of it that out of it are the issues of life to all your graces. Faith is that virtuous woman who clothes the whole household in scarlet, and feeds them all with luscious and strengthening food; but if faith be gone, the household soon becomes naked and poor and blind and miserable. Everything in a Christian fails when faith ceases to nourish it.

Next to this, Satan attacks faith *because it is the great preserving grace.* The apostle says, "Above all,"—that is, "over all," "covering all,"—"taking the shield of faith, wherewith ye shall be able to quench all the fiery darts of the wicked." Sometimes, the Eastern soldiers had shields so large that they were like doors, and they covered the man from head to foot. Others of them, who used smaller shields, nevertheless handled them so deftly and moved them so rapidly, that it was tantamount to the shield covering the entire person. An arrow is aimed at the forehead, up goes the shield, and the sharp point rings on the metal. A javelin is hurled at the heart, but the shield turns it aside. The fierce foe aims a poisonous dart at the leg, but the shield intercepts it. Virtually, the shield is all-surrounding; so it is with your faith. As one has well said, "It is armor upon armor, for the helmet protects the head, but the shield protects both helmet and head. The breastplate guards the breast, but the bucker or shield defends the breastplate as well as the breast." Faith is a grace to protect the other graces; there is nothing like it, and, therefore, I do not wonder that Satan attacks faith when he sees its prominent position and its important influence in the entire town of Mansoul.

I cannot help saying, also, that I wonder not that Satan attacks faith *because it is the effective or efficient grace.* You know what a wonderful chapter that Hebrews 11 is; it is a triumphal arch erected in honor of what? Of faith. According to that chapter, faith did everything; it quenched the fire, stopped the mouths of lions, turned to flight the armies of the aliens, received the dead who were raised, and so on. Faith is the soul's right hand. Faith works by love; but, still, it is faith that works, and you can do nothing acceptably before God unless you do it by that right hand of faith. Hence, Satan cannot endure faith; he hates that most of all. Pharaoh tried to have all the male children thrown into the river because they were the fighting force of Israel. He did not mind having the women to grow up to bear burdens, it was the men whom he feared. And, in like manner, the devil says, "I must stamp out faith, for that is the secret of strength." He will not trouble himself so much about your other graces, he will probably attack them when he can; but, first of all he says, "Down with faith! That is the man-child that must be destroyed"; and he aims his sharpest and deadliest darts at it.

I believe, also, that faith is attacked by Satan, most of all, *because it is most obnoxious to him.* He cannot endure faith. How do I know that? Why, because God loves it; and if God loves faith, and if Christ crowns faith, I am sure that Satan hates it. What are we told concerning the work of Jesus being hindered by unbelief? "He did not many mighty works there because of their unbelief." Now, I will turn that text around and say of Satan that he cannot do many mighty works against some men because of their faith. Oh, how he sneaks off when he discovers a right royal faith in a man! He knows when he has met his master, and he says, "Why should I waste my arrows upon a shield carried by such a man as that? He believes in God, he believes in Christ, he believes in the Holy Spirit; he is more than a match for me." To those that are under his leadership he cries, "To your tents!" He bids them flee away and escape, for he knows that there can be no victory for them when they come into collision with true God-given faith. He cannot bear to look at it. It blinds him; the lustrous splendor of that great shield of faith, which shines as though a man did hang the sun upon his arm, and bear it before him into the fray, blinds even the mighty prince of darkness. Satan does but glance at it, and straightaway he takes to flight, for he cannot endure it. He knows it is the thing which most of all helps to overthrow his kingdom and destroy his power; therefore, believer, cling to your faith! Be like the young Spartan warrior, who would either bring his shield home with him or be brought home dead upon his shield. "Cast not away your confidence, which hath great recompence of reward." Whatever else you have not, "have faith in God"; believe in the Christ of God; rest your soul's entire confidence upon the faithful promise and the faithful Promiser; and, if you do so, Satan's attacks upon you will all be in vain. That is my first point—observe the grand point of satanic attack.

II. Now, secondly, observe *the peculiar danger of faith*: "That thy faith fail not."

Did Peter's faith fail? Yes and no; it failed in a measure, but it did not altogether fail. It failed in a measure, for he was human; but it did not altogether fail, for, at the back of it, there was the superhuman power which comes through the pleading of Christ. Poor Peter! He denied his Master, yet his faith did not utterly fail; and I will show you why it did not. If you and I, beloved, are ever permitted to dishonor God and to deny our Lord as Peter did, yet may God in mercy keep us from the utter and entire failure of our faith as he kept Peter!

Notice, first, there was still some faith in Peter, even when he had denied his Master, for when the Lord turned and looked upon him, *he went out and wept bitterly.* If there had not been the true faith in Peter still, the Master might have looked upon him long before a tear would have coursed down his cheeks. The Lord not only looked on Judas, but he gave him a sop with him out of the dish; and he even let the traitor put his lips to him and kiss him; but all that had no weight with Judas. The reason why Christ's look had such an effect on Peter was because there was some faith in Peter still. You may blow as long as ever you like at the cold coals, and you will get no fire; but I have sometimes seen a servant kneel down when there has been just a little flame left in the coal in a corner of the grate, and she has blown it tenderly and gently so as to revive it. "It is not quite out," she says; and, at last, there has been a good fire once again. May God grant that we may never come to that sad condition; but, if we do, may he of his grace grant that there may still be that blessed little faith left, that weak and feeble faith which, through the breathing upon it of the Spirit of God, shall yet be fanned into a flame!

We are sure that there was this faith still in Peter, *or else, what would he have done?* What did Judas do? Judas did two things; first, he went to a priest, or to priests, and confessed to them, and then he went out and hanged himself; the two things were strangely connected. Peter did neither; yet, if he had not had faith, he might have done both. To publicly deny his Master three times, and to support his denial with oaths and curses even when that Master was close by, and in his greatest exigency, must have put Peter into most imminent peril; and if there had not been within his heart faith that his Master could yet pardon and restore him, he might, in his despair have done precisely what the traitor Judas did. Or, if he had not gone to that extremity of guilt, he would have hidden himself away from the rest of the apostles. But, instead of doing so, we soon find him again with John—I do not wonder that he was with John. They were old companions; but, in addition to that, the beloved John had so often leaned his head on the Master's bosom that he had caught the sweet infection of his Savior's tenderness; and, therefore, he was just the one with whom Peter would wish to associate. I think that if I had ever denied my Lord as Peter did, in that public way, I should have run away and hidden myself from all my former companions; but he did not, you see. He seemed to say to himself, "The Master, with his dear, tender heart, can still forgive me and receive me"; so he clings to the disciples, and especially to John. Yes, and notice that on the day of our Lord's resurrection Peter was the first discile to enter the sepulcher; for, though "the other disciple did outrun Peter" and reach the grave first, "yet went he not in" until Peter led the way. "The Lord is risen indeed, and hath appeared to Simon," is a remarkable passage. Paul, writing concerning Christ's resurrection, says that "he was seen of Cephas," that is, Peter. There was some special manifestation of our blessed Master to Simon Peter, who was waiting for it and privileged to witness it; and this showed that his faith was kept from failing through the Savior's prayers.

Now, beloved, I say no more about Peter, but I speak to you about your own faith. Are you greatly troubled? Then, I pray that your faith may not fail. It is shaken; it is severely tried; but God grant that it may not fail! Something whispers within your heart, "Give up all religion, it is not true." To that lie, answer, "'Get thee behind me, Satan'; for the religion of Jesus Christ is eternally, assuredly, infallibly true." Cling to it, for it is your life. Or, perhaps, the fiend whispers, "It is true enough to others; but it is not meant for you. You are not one of the Lord's people." Well, if you cannot come to Christ as a saint, come to him as a sinner; if you dare not come as a child to sit at his table, come as a dog to eat the crumbs that fall under it. Only do come, and never give up your faith.

If the arch-fiend whispers again, "You have been a deceiver; your profession is all a mistake or a lie," say to him, "Well, if it be so, there is still forgiveness in Christ for all who come unto God by him." Perhaps you are coming to the Savior for the first time; you mean to cast yourself upon the blood and merit of Jesus, even if you have never done so before. I pray for you, dear coming one. O gracious Savior, do not let Satan crush out the faith of even the weakest of your people! Blessed Intercessor, plead for that poor trembler in whom faith is almost dying out! Great High Priest, intercede for him that his faith may not utterly fail him, and that he may still cling to you!

What is to become of us if we have not faith in Jesus? I know that there are some who seem to get on well without it. So may the dogs; so may the wild beasts; they get on well enough without the children's garments or the children's bread; but you and I cannot. The moment I am unbelieving, I am unhappy. It is not a vain thing for me to believe in Christ; it is my life, it is my strength, it is my joy. I am a lost man, and it were better for me that I had never been born unless I have the privilege of believing. Give up faith? Remember what Satan said concerning Job, "Skin for skin, yea, all that a man hath will he give for his life"; and our life is wrapped up in our faith in Christ. We cannot give it up, and we will not give it up. Come on, fiends of hell or mockers of earth, we will not give it up; we will hold it fast, for it is part of the very warp and woof of our being. We believe in God and in his Son, our Lord and Savior Jesus Christ; and it is our great concern that our faith should be well guarded and protected, for we know the peculiar danger to which it is exposed when it is assailed by Satan.

III. Now I will close my discourse by speaking, for only a very few minutes, upon *the believer's great preservative and defense.*

What is the great protection of our faith? Our Savior's intercession. Prayer is always good, it is ever a blessed thing; but notice that great letter-word in the text, "I have prayed for thee." It is the intercession of Christ that preserves our faith, and there are three things about it which make it precious beyond all price; it is prevalent, prevenient, and pertinent. First, it is *prevalent;*

for if Jesus pleads, he must prevail. It is prevenient; for before the temptation comes to Peter, Jesus says, "I have prayed for you. Satan has but obtained, by his asking, the permission to tempt you; but I have already prayed for you."

And, then, it was pertinent; that is, to the point. Christ had prayed the best prayer possible: "that thy faith fail not." Peter would not have known that this was to be the chief point of attack by Satan; he might have thought that Satan would attack his love. The Lord seems to hint at his thought about that by saying to him afterward, "Simon, son of Jonas, lovest thou me?" But the Savior knew that the hottest part of the battle would rage around Fort Faith, and, therefore, he prayed that the fortress might be well garrisoned and never be captured by the enemy; and it was not.

Whenever I begin to talk to you about the intercession of Christ, I feel inclined to sit down and let you think and look up and listen till you hear that voice, matchless in its music, pleading, pleading, pleading with the Father. It were much better for you to realize it than for me to describe it. It was a blessed thing to hear one's mother pray—by accident, as we say, to pass the door that was ajar and to hear mother pleading for her boy or her girl. It is a very touching thing to hear your child praying for her father, or your wife breathing out her warm desires for her beloved. I do not know anything more charming than to hear, now and then, a stray prayer that was never meant to be heard on earth, but only in heaven; I like such eavesdroppings. Oh, but listen! It is Jesus who is praying; he shows his wounds and pleads the merit of his great sacrifice; and, wonder of wonders, he pleads for me and for you! Happy man, happy woman, to have our faith preserved by such a mighty preservative as this—the intercession of Christ!

I want you specially to notice that *this intercession is the pleading of One who*, in the text, *seems directly to oppose himself to the great adversary:* "Satan hath obtained thee by asking, that he may sift thee as wheat; but I have obtained thee by asking," (so I will venture to paraphrase it) "that thy faith fail not." There stands Satan. You cannot see him, and you need not want to; but that grim monster who has made kings and princes tremble, who has plucked angels from their spheres of light, and who has hurled bright spirits down from heaven to hell stands there to assail you. You may well be afraid, for God himself permits him to sift you. Ah! but there also stands the ever-blessed One before whom an angel, fallen or unfallen, is but a tiny spark compared with the sun; there he stands girt about the paps with the golden girdle of his faithfulness, robed in the fair white linen of his matchless righteousness, upon his head a crown of glory that far outshines all constellations of stars and suns;

and he opposes his divine pleading to the demoniacal asking of the fallen one. Are you afraid now? It does seem to me unspeakably blessed to see it written here, "Satan hath desired to have thee that he may sift thee as wheat," and then to see over the top of it this word, "but I have prayed for thee." Oh, blessed "but"! How it seems to cast the fallen angel back again into the bottomless pit, and to bind him with chains and set a seal upon his prison: "But I have prayed for thee." Tempt on, then, O devil; tempt at your worst, for there is no fear now when this glorious shield of gold, the intercession of the Savior, covers the entire person of the poor attacked one! "I have prayed for thee, that thy faith fail not."

And then my last word is this: *it is an intercession which is absolutely certain of success.* In fact, he who offers it anticipates its success and discounts it by giving this precept to his servant: "and when thou art converted"—sure pledge, then, that he will be converted, that he will be turned back, however far he wanders—when you are restored, "strengthen thy brethren." Then, for certain, he will be restored, or else the Savior would not have given him a precept which could be available only if a certain, unlikely contingency should occur. O you who are a true child of God, you may be drenched, but you shall never be drowned! O warrior of the cross, your shield may be covered with fiery darts, thickly as the saplings of a young forest grow; but no dart shall ever reach your heart! You may be wounded in head and hand and foot; you may be a mass of scars; but your life is given you. To Christ are you given as a prey, and you shall come out even from between the jaws of death, and you shall overcome Satan by Christ's power. Only trust Christ; only trust him. Cling to your faith, beloved; cling to your faith! I would like to get a hold of that young man who has lately been listening to skeptical teachers and to whisper in his ear, "Cling to your faith, young man; for, in losing that, you will lose all."

And to you who, alas! have fallen into sin after having made a profession of religion, let me say that however far you have gone astray, still believe that Jesus is able to forgive you; and come back to him, and seek his pardon now. And you, my hoary-headed brother whose hair is whitening for heaven, are you sorely beset by all sorts of temptations? Well, give me your hand, for I, too, know what this warfare means. Let us believe in God, my brother; let us both believe in God. Though he should break us down worse than ever, though he should set us up as a target and let the devil shoot at us all the arrows from his quiver, let us still believe in God; and come you to this pass, to which my soul has come full often and to which Job came of old, " 'Though he slay me, yet will I trust in him.' Whatever he does to me—if he shall never smile upon me again—I will still believe him. I can do no other." I dare not doubt him; I must confide in him. Where is there any ground for confidence if it be not in the God that cannot lie and in the Christ of the everlasting covenant whom he has set forth to be the propitiation for human sin, and in the Holy Ghost whose work it is to take of the things of Christ and reveal them unto us?

May the blessed Trinity save and keep us all, for our Lord Jesus Christ's sake! Amen.

Christ's Plea for Ignorant Sinners

❧❦❧

Intended for reading on Lord's Day, July 3, 1892; delivered on Lord's Day evening, October 5, 1890, at the Metropolitan Tabernacle, Newington. No. 2263.

Then said Jesus, "Father, forgive them; for they know not what they do."
—LUKE 23:34

What tenderness we have here; what self-forgetfulness; what almighty love! Jesus did not say to those who crucified him, "Begone!" One such word, and they must have all fled. When they came to take him in the garden, they went backward and fell to the ground when he spoke but a short sentence; and now that he is on the cross, a single syllable would have made the whole company fall to the ground or flee away in fright.

Jesus says not a word in his own defense. When he prayed to his Father, he might justly have said, "Father, note what they do to your beloved Son. Judge them for the wrong they do to him who loves them, and who has done all he can for them." But there is no prayer against them in the words that Jesus utters. It was written of old by the prophet Isaiah, "He made intercession for the transgressors"; and here it is fulfilled. He pleads for his murderers, "Father, forgive them."

He does not utter a single word of upbraiding. He does not say, "Why do you this? Why pierce the hands that fed you? Why nail the feet that followed after you in mercy? Why mock the Man who loved to bless you?" No, not a word even of gentle upbraiding, much less anything like a curse. "Father, forgive them." You notice, Jesus does not say, "I forgive them," but you may read that between the lines. He says that all the more because he does not say it in words. But he had laid aside his majesty and is fastened to the cross; and, therefore, he takes the humble position of a suppliant, rather than the more lofty place of one who had power to forgive. How often when men say, "I forgive you," is there a kind of selfishness about it! At any rate, self is asserted in the very act of forgiving. Jesus takes the place of a pleader, a pleader for those who were committing murder upon himself. Blessed be his name!

This word of the cross we shall use tonight, and we shall see if we cannot gather something from it for our instruction; for though we were not there and did not actually put Jesus to death, yet we really caused his death, and we, too, crucified the Lord of glory; and his prayer for us was, "Father, forgive them; for they know not what they do."

I am not going to handle this text so much by way of exposition as by way of experience. I believe there are many here to whom these words will be very appropriate. This will be our line of thought. First, *we were in measure ignorant*; secondly, *we confess that this ignorance is no excuse*; thirdly, *we bless our Lord for pleading for us*; and fourthly, *we now rejoice in the pardon we have obtained*. May the Holy Spirit graciously help us in our meditation!

I. Looking back upon our past experience, let me say, first, that *we were in measure ignorant*.

We who have been forgiven, we who have been washed in the blood of the Lamb, we once sinned in a great measure through ignorance. Jesus says, "They know not what they do." Now, I shall appeal to you, brothers and sisters, when you lived under the dominion of Satan, and served yourselves and sin, was there not a measure of ignorance in it? You can truly say, as we said in the hymn we sang just now,

Alas! I knew not what I did.

It is true, first, that we were ignorant of *the awful meaning of sin*. We began to sin as children; we knew that it was wrong, but we did not know all that sin meant. We went on to sin as young men; peradventure we plunged into much wickedness. We knew it was wrong, but we did not see the end from the beginning. It did not appear to us as rebellion against God. We did not think that we were presumptuously defying God, setting at nothing his wisdom, defying his power, deriding his love, spurning his holiness; yet we were doing that. There is an abysmal depth in sin. You cannot see the bottom of it. When we rolled sin under our tongue as a sweet morsel, we did not know all the terrible ingredients compounded in that deadly bittersweet. We were in a measure ignorant of the tremendous crime we committed when we dared to live in rebellion against God. So far, I think, you go with me.

We did not know, at that time, *God's great love to us*. I did not know that he had chosen me from before the foundation of the world; I never dreamed of that. I did not know that Christ stood for me as my Substitute to redeem me from among men. I did not know the love of Christ, did not understand it then. You did not know that you were sinning against eternal love, against infinite compassion, against a distinguishing love such as God had fixed on you from eternity. So far, we knew not what we did.

I think, too, that we did not know all that we were doing in *our rejection of Christ and putting him to grief.* He came to us in our youth; and impressed by a sermon we began to tremble and to seek his face; but we were decoyed back to the world, and we refused Christ. Our mother's tears, our father's prayers, our teacher's admonitions often moved us; but we were very stubborn, and we rejected Christ. We did not know that in that rejection we were virtually putting him away and crucifying him. We were denying his Godhead, or else we should have worshiped him. We were denying his love, or else we should have yielded to him. We were practically, in every act of sin, taking the hammer and the nails, and fastening Christ to the cross, but we did not know it. Perhaps, if we had known it, we should not have crucified the Lord of glory. We did know we were doing wrong, but we did not know all the wrong that we were doing.

Nor did we know fully *the meaning of our delays.* We hesitated; we were on the verge of conversion; we went back and turned again to our old follies. We were hardened, Christless, prayerless still; and each of us said, "Oh, I am only waiting a little while till I have fulfilled my present engagements, till I am a little older, till I have seen a little more of the world!" The fact is, we were refusing Christ and choosing the pleasures of sin instead of him; and every hour of delay was an hour of crucifying Christ, grieving his Spirit, and choosing this harlot world in the place of the lovely and ever-blessed Christ. We did not know that.

I think we may add one thing more. *We did not know the meaning of our self-righteousness.* We used to think, some of us, that we had a righteousness of our own. We had been to church regularly, or we had been to the meeting-house whenever it was open. We were christened; we were confirmed; or, peradventure, we rejoiced that we never had either of those things done to us. Thus, we put our confidence in ceremonies, or the absence of ceremonies. We said our prayers; we read a chapter in the Bible night and morning; we did— oh, I do not know what we did not do! But there we rested; we were righteous in our own esteem. We had not any particular sin to confess, nor any reason to lie in the dust before the throne of God's majesty. We were about as good as we could be; and we did not know that we were even then perpetrating the highest insult upon Christ; for, if we were not sinners, why did Christ die; and, if we had a righteousness of our own which was good enough, why did Christ come here to work out a righteousness for us? We made out Christ to be a superfluity by considering that we were good enough without resting in his atoning sacrifice. Ah, we did not think we were doing that! We thought we were pleasing God by our religiousness, by our outward performances, by our ecclesiastical correctness; but all the while we were setting up Antichrist in the place of Christ. We were making out that Christ was not wanted; we were robbing him of his office and glory! Alas! Christ could say of us, with regard to all these things, "They know not what they do." I want you to look quietly at the time past wherein you served sin, and just see whether there was not a darkness upon your mind, a blindness in your spirit, so that you did not know what you did.

II. Well now, secondly, *we confess that this ignorance is no excuse.*

Our Lord might urge it as a plea; but we never could. We did not know what we did, and so we were not guilty to the fullest possible extent; but we were guilty enough, therefore let us own it.

For first, remember, *the law never allows this as a plea.* In our own English law, a man is supposed to know what the law is. If he breaks it, it is no excuse to plead that he did not know it. It may be regarded by a judge as some extenuation; but the law allows nothing of the kind. God gives us the law, and we are bound to keep it. If I erred through not knowing the law, still it was a sin. Under the Mosaic law there were sins of ignorance, and for these there were special offerings. The ignorance did not blot out the sin. That is clear in my text; for, if ignorance rendered an action no longer sinful, they why should Christ say, "Father, forgive them"? But he does; he asks for mercy for what is sin, even though the ignorance in some measure be supposed to mitigate the criminality of it.

But, dear friends, *we might have known.* If we did not know, it was because we would not know. There was the preaching of the Word; but we did not care to hear it. There was this blessed Book; but we did not care to read it. If you and I had sat down and looked at our conduct by the light of the holy Scripture, we might have known much more of the evil of sin, and much more of the love of Christ, and much more of the ingratitude which is possible in refusing Christ and not coming to him.

In addition to that, *we did not think.* "Oh, but," you say, "young people never do think!" But young people should think. If there is anybody who need not think, it is the old man whose day is nearly over. If he does think, he has but a very short time in which to improve; but the young have all their lives before them. If I were a carpenter and had to make a box, I should not think about it after I had made the box; I should think, before I began to cut my timber, what sort of box it was to be. In every action, a man thinks before he begins or else he is a fool. A young man ought to think more than anybody else, for now he is, as it were, making his box. He is beginning his life's plan; he should be the most thoughtful of all men. Many of us who are now Christ's people would have known much more about our Lord if we had given him more careful consideration in our earlier days. A man will consider about taking a wife, he will consider about making a business, he will consider about buying a horse or a cow; but he will not consider about the claims of Christ and the claims of the Most High God; and this renders his ignorance willful and inexcusable.

Besides that, dear friends, although we have confessed to ignorance, *in many sins we did know a great deal.* Come, let me quicken your memories. There were times when you knew that such an action was wrong, when you started back from it. You looked at the gain it would bring you, and you sold your soul for that price and deliberately did what you were well aware was wrong. Are there not some here saved by Christ who must confess that, at times, they did violence to their conscience? They did despite to the Spirit of God, quenched the light of heaven, drove the Spirit away from them distinctly knowing what they were doing. Let us bow before God in the silence of our hearts and own to all of this. We hear the Master say, "Father, forgive them; for they know not what they do." Let us add our own tears as we say, "And forgive us, also, because in some things we did know; in all things we might have known; but we were ignorant for want of thought, which thought was a solemn duty which we ought to have rendered to God."

One more thing I will say on this head. When a man is ignorant and does not know what he ought to do, what should he do? Well, he should do nothing till he does know. But here is the mischief of it, that *when we did not know, yet we chose to do the wrong thing.* If we did not know, why did we not choose the right thing? But, being in the dark, we never turned to the right; but always blundered to the left from sin to sin. Does not this show us how depraved our hearts are? Though we are seeking to be right, when we are let alone, we go wrong of ourselves. Leave a child alone; leave a man alone; leave a tribe alone without teaching and instruction; what comes of it? Why, the same as when you leave a field alone. It never, by any chance, produces wheat or barley. Leave it alone, and there are rank weeds and thorns and briers showing that the natural set of the soil is toward producing that which is worthless. O friends, confess the innate evil of your hearts as well as the evil of your lives, in that, when you did not know, yet, having a perverse instinct, you chose the evil and refused the good; and, when you did not know enough of Christ and did not think enough of him to know whether you ought to have him or not, you would not come unto him that you might have life. You needed light; but you shut your eyes to the sun. You were thirsty; but you would not drink of the living spring; and so your ignorance, though it was there, was a criminal ignorance which you must confess before the Lord. Oh, come to the cross, you who have been there before and have lost your burden there! Come and confess your guilt over again and clasp that cross afresh, and look to him who bled upon it and praise his dear name that he once prayed for you, "Father forgive them; for they know not what they do."

Now, I am going a step further. We were in a measure ignorant, but we confess that that measurable ignorance was no excuse.

III. Now, thirdly, *we bless our Lord for pleading for us.*

Do you notice when it was that Jesus pleaded? It was *while they were crucifying him.* They had not just driven in the nails, they had lifted up the cross and dashed it down into its socket, and dislocated all his bones, so that he could say, "I am poured out like water, and all my bones are out of joint." Ah, dear friends, it was then that instead of a cry or groan, this dear Son of God said, "Father, forgive them; for they know not what they do." They did not ask for forgiveness for themselves; Jesus asked for forgiveness for them. Their hands were imbrued in his blood; and it was then, even then, that he prayed for them. Let us think of the great love wherewith he loved us, even while we were yet sinners, when we rioted in sin, when we drank it down as the ox drinks down water. Even then he prayed for us. "When we were yet without strength, in due time Christ died for the ungodly." Bless his name tonight. He prayed for you when you did not pray for yourself. He prayed for you when you were crucifying him.

Then think of his plea; *he pleads his Sonship.* He says, "Father, forgive them." He was the Son of God, and he put his divine Sonship into the scale on our behalf. He seems to say, "Father, as I am your Son, grant me this request and pardon these rebels. Father, forgive them." The filial rights of Christ were very great. He was the Son of God, not as we are by adoption, but by nature. By eternal filiation he was the Son of the Highest, "Light of light, very God of very God," the second Person in the Divine Trinity; and he puts that Sonship here before God and says, "Father, forgive them." Oh, the power of that word from the Son's lips when he is wounded, when he is in agony, when he is dying! He says, "Father, Father, grant my one request; O 'Father, forgive them; for they know not what they do'"; and the great Father bows his awful head in token that the petition is granted.

Then notice that Jesus here silently, but really, *pleads his sufferings.* The attitude of Christ when he prayed this prayer is very noteworthy. His hands were stretched upon the transverse beam; his feet were fastened to the upright tree; and there he pleaded. Silently his hands and feet were pleading, and his agonized body from every sinew and muscle pleaded with God. His sacrifice was presented there before the Father's face; not yet complete, but in his will complete; and so it is his cross that takes up the plea, "Father, forgive them." O blessed Christ! It is thus that we have been forgiven, for his Sonship and his cross have pleaded with God and have prevailed on our behalf.

I love this prayer, also, because of the *indistinctness* of it. It is, "Father, forgive them." He does not say, "Father, forgive the soldiers who have nailed me here." He includes them. Neither does he say, "Father, forgive sinners in ages to come who will sin against me." But he means them. Jesus does not mention them by any accusing name: "Father, forgive my enemies. Father, forgive my murderers." No, there is no word of accusation upon those dear lips. "Father, forgive them." Now into that pronoun "them" I feel that I can crawl. Can you get in there? Oh, by a humble faith, appropriate the cross of Christ by trusting in it, and get into that big, little word "them"! It seems like a chariot of mercy that has come down to earth into which a man may step, and it shall bear him up to heaven. "Father, forgive them."

Notice, also, what it was that Jesus asked for; to omit that would be to leave out the very essence of his prayer. *He asked for full absolution for his enemies*: "Father, forgive them. Do not punish them; forgive them. Do not remember their sin; forgive it, blot it out; throw it into the depths of the sea. Remember it not, my Father. Mention it not against them any more for ever. Father, forgive them." Oh, blessed prayer, for the forgiveness of God is broad and deep! When man forgives, he leaves the remembrance of the wrong behind; but when God pardons, he says, "I will forgive their iniquity, and I will remember their sin no more." It is this that Christ asked for you and me long before we had any repentance or any faith; and in answer to that prayer, we were brought to feel our sin, brought to confess it, and to believe in him; and now, glory be to his name, we can bless him for having pleaded for us and obtained the forgiveness of all our sins.

IV. I come now to my last remark, which is this: *we now rejoice in the pardon we have obtained.*

Have you obtained pardon? Is this your song?
Now, oh joy! My sins are pardon'd,
Now I can, and do believe.

I have a letter in my pocket from a man of education and standing who has been an agnostic; he says that he was a sarcastic agnostic, and he writes praising God and invoking every blessing upon my head for bringing him to the Savior's feet. He says, "I was without happiness for this life, and without hope for the next." I believe that that is a truthful description of many an unbeliever. What hope is there for the world to come apart from the cross of Christ? The best hope such a man has is that he may die the death of a dog, and there may be an end of him. What is the hope of the Romanist when he comes to die? I feel so sorry for many of the devout and earnest friends, for I do not know what their hope is. They do not hope to go to heaven yet, at any rate; some purgatorial pains must be endured first. Ah, this is a poor, poor faith to die on to have such a hope as that to trouble your last thoughts. I do not know of any religion but that of Christ Jesus which tells us of sin pardoned, absolutely pardoned. Now, listen. Our teaching is not that when you come to die you may, perhaps, find out that it is all right, but, "Beloved, now are we the sons of God." "He that believeth on the Son hath everlasting life." He has it now, and he knows it, and he rejoices in it. So I come back to the last head of my discourse, we rejoice in the pardon Christ has obtained for us. We are pardoned. I hope that the larger portion of this audience can say, "By the grace of God, we know that the larger portion of this audience can say, 'By the grace of God, we know that we are washed in the blood of the Lamb.'"

Pardon has come to us through Christ's plea. Our hope lies in the plea of Christ, and specially in his death. If Jesus paid my debt, and he did it if I am a believer in him, then I am out of debt. If Jesus bore the penalty of my sin, and he did it if I am a believer, then there is no penalty for me to pay, for we can say to him,

> *Complete atonement thou hast made,*
> *And to the utmost farthing paid*
> *Whate'er thy people owed:*
> *Nor can his wrath on me take place,*
> *If shelter'd in thy righteousness,*
> *And sprinkled with thy blood.*
>
> *If thou hast my discharge procured,*
> *And freely in my room endured*
> *The whole of wrath divine:*
> *Payment God cannot twice demand,*
> *First at my bleeding Surety's hand,*
> *And then again at mine.*

If Christ has borne my punishment, I shall never bear it. Oh, what joy there is in this blessed assurance! Your hope that you are pardoned lies in this, that Jesus died. Those dear wounds of his bled for you.

We praise him for our pardon because *we do know now what we did*. O brethren, I know not how much we ought to love Christ because we sinned against him so grievously! Now we know that sin is "exceeding sinful." Now we know that sin crucified Christ. Now we know that we stabbed our heavenly Lover to his heart. We slew, with ignominious death, our best and dearest Friend and Benefactor. We know that now; and we could almost weep tears of blood to think that we ever treated him as we did. But it is all forgiven, all gone. Oh, let us bless that dear Son of God who has put away even such sins as ours! We feel them more now than ever before. We know they are forgiven, and our grief is because of the pain that the purchase of our forgiveness cost our Savior. We never knew what our sins really were till we saw him in a bloody sweat. We never knew the crimson hue of our sins till we read our pardon written in crimson lines with his precious blood. Now we see our sin, and yet we do not see it; for God has pardoned it, blotted it out, cast it behind his back for ever.

Henceforth *ignorance*, such as we have described, *shall be hateful to us*. Ignorance of Christ and eternal things shall be hateful to us. If, through ignorance, we have sinned, we will have done with that ignorance. We will be students of his Word. We will study that masterpiece of all the sciences, the knowledge of Christ crucified. We will ask the Holy Ghost to drive far from us the ignorance that engenders sin. God grant that we may not fall into sins of ignorance any more; but may we be able to say, "I know whom I have believed. Henceforth I will seek more knowledge till I comprehend, with all saints, what are the heights and depths and lengths and breadths of the love of Christ, and know the love of God which passes knowledge"!

I put in a practical word here. If you rejoice that you are pardoned, *show your gratitude by your imitation of Christ*. There was never before such a plea as this, "Father, forgive them; for they know not what they do." Plead like that for others. Has anybody been injuring you? Are there persons who slander you? Pray tonight, "Father, forgive them; for they know not what they do." Let us always render good for evil, blessing for cursing; and when we are called to suffer through the wrongdoing of others, let us believe that they would not act as they do if it were not because of their ignorance. Let us pray for them and make their very ignorance the plea for their forgiveness: "Father, forgive them; for they know not what they do."

I want you also to think of the millions of London just now. See those miles of streets pouring out their children this evening or look at those public houses with the crowds streaming in and out. Go down our streets by moonlight. See what I almost blush to tell. Follow men and women, too, to their homes, and be this your prayer: "Father, forgive them; for they know not what they do." That silver bell—keep it always ringing. What did I say? That silver bell? No, it is the *golden* bell upon the priest's garments. Wear it on your garments, you priests of God, and let it always ring out its golden note, "Father, forgive them; for they know not what they do." If I can set all God's saints imitating Christ with such a prayer as this, I shall not have spoken in vain.

Brethren, I see *reason for hope in the very ignorance that surrounds us*. I see hope for this poor city of ours, hope for this poor country, hope for Africa, China, and India. "They know not what they do." Here is a strong argument in their favor, for they are more ignorant than we were. They know less of the evil of sin and less of the hope of eternal life than we do. Send up this petition, you people of God! Heap your prayers together with cumulative power; send up this fiery shaft of prayer straight to the heart of God while Jesus from his throne shall add his prevalent intercession, "Father, forgive them; for they know not what they do."

If there be any unconverted people here, and I know that there are some, we will mention them in our private devotion as well as in the public assembly; and we will pray for them in words like these, "Father, forgive them; for they know not what they do." May God bless you all, for Jesus Christ's sake! Amen.

Christ's Pastoral Prayer for His People

⟨⟩

Intended for reading on Lord's Day, October 22, 1893; delivered on Lord's Day evening, September 1, 1889 at the Metropolitan Tabernacle, Newington. No. 2331.

> *"I pray for them: I pray not for the world, but for them which thou hast given me; for they are thine. And all mine are thine, and thine are mine; and I am glorified in them."*—JOHN 17:9–10

To begin with, I remark that our Lord Jesus pleads for his own people. When he puts on his priestly breastplate, it is for the tribes whose names are there. When he presents the atoning sacrifice, it is for Israel whom God has chosen; and he utters this great truth, which some regard as narrow, but which we adore, "I pray for them: I pray not for the world." The point to which I want to call attention is this, the reason why Christ prays not for the world, but for his people. He puts it, "For they are thine," as if they were all the dearer to him because they were the Father's: "I pray for them: I pray not for the world, but for them which thou hast given me, for they are thine." We might have half thought that Jesus would have said, "They are mine, and, therefore, I pray for them." It would have been true, but there would not have been the beauty of truth about it which we have here. He loves us all the better, and he prays for us all the more fervently, because we are the Father's. Such is his love to his Father that our being the Father's sheds upon us an extra halo of beauty. Because we belong to the Father, therefore does the Savior plead for us with all the greater earnestness at the throne of the heavenly grace.

But this leads us on to remember that our Lord had undertaken suretyship engagements on account of his people; he undertook to preserve the Father's gift: "Those that thou gavest me I have kept, and none of them is lost." He looked upon the sheep of his pasture as belonging to his Father, and the Father had put them into his charge, saying to him, "Of thine hand will I require them." As Jacob kept his uncle's flocks, by day the heat devoured him, and at night the frost, but he was more careful over them because they were

Laban's than if they had been his own; he was to give an account of all the sheep committed to him, and he did so, and he lost none of Laban's sheep; but his care over them was partly accounted for by the fact that they did not belong to him, but belonged to his uncle Laban.

Understand this twofold reason, then, for Christ's pastoral prayer for his people. He first prays for them because they belong to the Father, and, therefore, have a peculiar value in his eye; and next, because they belong to the Father, he is under suretyship engagements to deliver them all to the Father in that last great day when the sheep shall pass under the rod of him that tells them. Now you see where I am bringing you tonight. I am not going to preach at this time to the world any more than Christ upon this occasion prayed for the world; but I am going to preach to his own people as he in this intercessory prayer pleaded for them. I trust that they will all follow me, step by step, through this great theme; and I pray the Lord that in these deep central truths of the gospel we may find real refreshment for our souls tonight.

I. In calling your attention to my text, I want you to notice, first, *the intensity of the sense of property which Christ has in his people.*

Here are six words setting forth Christ's property in those who are saved— "Them which thou hast given me"—(that is one); "for they are thine. And all mine are thine, and thine are mine; and I am glorified in them." There are certain persons so precious to Christ that they are marked all over with special tokens that they belong to him; as I have known a man to write his name in a book which he has greatly valued, and then he has turned over some pages, and he has written his name again; and as we have sometimes known persons, when they have highly valued a thing, to put their mark, their seal, their stamp, here, there, and almost everywhere upon it. So, notice in my text how the Lord seems to have the seal in his hand, and he stamps it all over his peculiar possession: "They are thine. And all mine are thine, and thine are mine." It is all possessive pronouns to show that God looks upon his people as his portion, his possession, his property. "They shall be mine, saith the LORD of hosts, in that day when I make up my jewels." Every man has something or other which he values above the rest of his estate; and here the Lord, by so often reiterating the words which signify possession, proves that he values his people above everything. Let us show that we appreciate this privilege of being set apart unto God; and let us each one say to him,

Take my poor heart, and let it be
For ever closed to all but thee!

Seal thou my breast, and let me wear
That pledge of love for ever there.

I call your attention, next, to the fact that while there are these six expressions here, they are all applied to the Lord's own people. "Mine" (that is, the saints) "are thine" (that is, the saints); "and thine" (that is, the saints) "are mine" (that is, the saints). These broad arrows of the King of kings are all stamped upon his people. While the marks of possession are numerous, they are all set upon one object. What, does not God care for anything else? I answer, No; as compared with his own people, he cares for nothing else. "The LORD's portion is his people; Jacob is the lot of his inheritance." Has not God other things? Ah, what is there that he has not? The silver and the gold are his, and the cattle on a thousand hills. All things are of God; of him and by him and through him and to him are all things; yet he reckons them not in comparison with his people. You know how you, dearly beloved, value your children much more than you do anything else. If there were a fire in your house tonight, and you could carry only one thing out of it, mother, would you hesitate a moment as to what that one thing should be? You would carry your babe, and let everything else be consumed in the flames; and it is so with God. He cares for his people beyond everything else. He is the Lord God of Israel, and in Israel he has set his name, and there he takes his delight. There does he rest in his love, and over her does he rejoice with singing.

I want you to notice these different points, not because I can fully explain them all to you; but if I can give you only some of these great truths to think about and to help you to communion with Christ tonight, I shall have done well. I want you to remark yet further concerning these notes of possession that they occur in the private relationship between the Father and the Son. It is in our Lord's prayer when he is in the inner sanctuary speaking with the Father that we have these words, "All mine are thine, and thine are mine." It is not to you and to me that he is talking now; the Son of God is speaking with the Father when they are in very near communion one with the other. Now, what does this say to me but that the Father and the Son greatly value believers? What people talk about when they are alone, not what they say in the market, not what they talk of in the midst of the confused mob, but what they say when they are in private, that lays bare their heart. Here is the Son speaking to the Father, not about thrones and royalties, nor cherubim and seraphim, but about poor men and women, in those days mostly fishermen and peasant folk, who believed on him. They are talking about these people, and the Son is taking his own solace with the Father in their secret privacy by talking about these precious jewels, these dear ones that are their peculiar treasure.

You have not any notion how much God loves you. Dear brother, dear sister, you have never yet had half an idea, or the tithe of an idea, of how precious you are to Christ. You think because you are so imperfect and you fall so much below your own ideal that, therefore, he does not love you much; you think that he cannot do so. Have you ever measured the depth of Christ's agony in Gethsemane and of his death on Calvary? If you have tried to do so, you will be quite sure that apart from anything in you or about you, he loves you with a love that passes knowledge. Believe it. "But I do not love him as I should," I think I hear you say. No, and you never will unless you first know his love to you. Believe it; believe it to the highest degree, that he so loves you that when there is no one who can commune with him but the Father, even then their converse is about their mutual estimate of you, how much they love you: "All mine are thine, and thine are mine."

Only one other thought under this head, and I do but put it before you and leave it with you, for I cannot expound it tonight. All that Jesus says is about all his people, for he says, "All mine are thine, and thine are mine." These high, secret talks are not about some few saints who have reached a "higher life," but about all of us who belong to him. Jesus bears all of us on his heart, and he speaks of us all to the Father: "All mine are thine." "That poor woman who could never serve her Lord except by patient endurance, she is mine," says Jesus. "She is thine, great Father." "That poor girl, newly converted, whose only spiritual life was spent upon a sickbed, and then she exhaled to heaven like a dewdrop of the morning, she is mine, and she is thine. That poor child of mine who often stumbles, who never brought much credit to the sacred name, he is mine, and he is thine. All mine are thine." I seem as if I heard a silver bell ringing out; the very tones of the words are like the music from the harps of angels: "Mine—thine; thine—mine." May such sweet risings and fallings of heavenly melodies charm all our ears!

I think that I have said enough to show you the intensity of the sense of property which Christ has in his people: "All mine are thine, and thine are mine."

II. The next head of my discourse is *the intensity of united interest between the Father and the Son concerning believers.*

First, let me say that Jesus loves us because we belong to the Father. Turn that truth over. "My Father has chosen them, my Father loves them; therefore," says Jesus, "I love them, and I lay down my life for them, and I will take my life again for them, and live throughout eternity for them. They are dear to me because they are dear to my Father." Have you not often loved another person for the sake of a third one upon whom all your heart was set? There is an old proverb, and I cannot help quoting it just now; it is, "Love me, love my dog." It is as if the Lord Jesus so loved the Father that even such poor dogs as we are get loved by him for his Father's sake. To the eyes of Jesus we are radiant with beauty because God has loved us.

Now turn that thought around the other way: the Father loves us because we belong to Christ. At first, the Father's love in election was sovereign and self-contained; but now, today, since he has given us over to Christ, he takes a still greater delight in us. "They are my Son's sheep," says he; "he bought them with his blood." Better still, "That is my Son's spouse," says he, "that is my Son's bride. I love her for his sake." There was that first love which came fresh from the Father's heart, but now, through this one channel of love to Jesus, the Father pours a double flood of love on us for his dear Son's sake. He sees the blood of Jesus sprinkled on us; he remembers the token, and for the sake of his beloved Son he prizes us beyond all price. Jesus loves us because we belong to the Father, and the Father loves us because we belong to Jesus.

Now come closer still to the central thought of the text, "All mine are thine." All who are the Son's are the Father's. Do we belong to Jesus? Then we belong to the Father. Have I been washed in the precious blood? Can I sing tonight,

> The dying thief rejoiced to see
> That fountain in his day;
> And there have I, though vile as he,
> Washed all my sins away?

Then, by redemption I belong to Christ; but at the same time I may be sure that I belong to the Father: "All mine are thine." Are you trusting in Christ? Then you are one of God's elect. That high and deep mystery of predestination need trouble no man's heart if he be a believer in Christ. If you believe in Christ, Christ has redeemed you, and the Father chose you from before the foundation of the world. Rest happy in that firm belief, "All mine are thine." How often have I met with people puzzling themselves about election! They want to know if they are elect. No man can come to the Father but by Christ; no man can come to election except through redemption. If you have come to Christ and are his redeemed, it is certain beyond all doubt that you were chosen of God and are the Father's elect. "All mine are thine." So, if I am bought by Christ's precious blood, I am not to sit down and say how grateful I am to Christ as though he were apart from the Father, and more loving and more tender than the Father. No, no; I belong to the Father if I belong to Christ; and I have for the Father the same gratitude, the same love, and I would render the same service as to Jesus; for Jesus puts it, "All mine are thine."

If, tonight, also, I am a servant of Christ, if, because he bought me I try to serve him, then I am a servant of the Father if I am a servant of the Son. "All mine, whatever position they occupy, belong to you, great Father," and they have all the privileges which come to those who belong to the Father. I hope that I do not weary you; I cannot make these things entertaining to the careless. I do not try to do so; but you who love my Lord and his truth ought to rejoice tonight to think that, in being the property of Christ, you are assured that you are the property of the Father. "All mine are thine."

With Christ our Lord we share our part
In the affections of his heart;
Nor shall our souls be thence removed
Till he forgets his first-beloved.

But now you have to look at the other part of it: "and thine are mine." All who are the Father's are the Son's. If you belong to the Father, you belong to the Son. If you are elect, and so the Father's, you are redeemed, and so the Son's. If you are adopted, and so the Father's, you are justified in Christ, and so you are the Son's. If you are regenerated, and so are begotten of the Father, yet still your life is dependent upon the Son. Remember that while one biblical figure sets us forth as children who have each one a life within himself, another equally valid figure represents us as branches of the Vine which die unless they continue united to the stem. "And thine are mine." If you are the Father's, you must be Christ's. If your life is given you of the Father, it still depends entirely upon the Son.

What a wonderful mixture all this is! The Father and the Son are one, and we are one with the Father and with the Son. A mystic union is established between us and the Father by reason of our union with the Son and the Son's union with the Father. See to what a glorious height our humanity has risen through Christ. By the grace of God, you who were like stones in the brook are made sons of God. Lifted out of your dead materialism, you are elevated into a spiritual life, and you are united unto God. You have not any idea tonight of what God has already done for you, and truly it does not yet appear what you shall be. A Christian man is the noblest work of God. God has here reached the fullness of his power and his grace in making us to be one with his own dear Son, and so bringing us into union and communion with himself. Oh, if the words that I speak could convey to you the fullness of their own meaning, you might spring to your feet electrified with holy joy to think of this, that we should be Christ's, and the Father's, and that we should be thought worthy to be the object of intricate transactions and intercommunions of the dearest kind between the Father and the Son! We, even we, who are but dust and ashes at our very best, are favored as angels never were; therefore let all praise be ascribed to sovereign grace!

III. And now, I shall detain you only a few minutes longer while I speak upon the third part of our subject, that is, *the glory of Christ.*

"And I am glorified in them." I must confess that while the former part of my subject was very deep, this third part seems to me to be deeper still: "I am glorified in them."

If Christ had said, "I will glorify them," I could have understood it. If he had said, "I am pleased with them," I might have set it down to his great kindness to them; but when he says, "I am glorified in them," it is very wonderful. The sun can be reflected, but you need proper objects to act as reflectors; and the brighter they are, the better will they reflect. You and I do not seem to have the power of reflecting Christ's glory; we break up the glorious rays that shine upon us; we spoil, we ruin so much of the good that falls upon us. Yet Christ says that he is glorified in us. Take these words home, dear friend, to yourself, and think that the Lord Jesus met you tonight, and as you went out of the Tabernacle, said to you, "You are mine, you are my Father's; and I am glorified in you." I dare not say that it would be a proud moment for you; but I dare to say that there would be more in it to make you feel exalted for him to say, "I am glorified in you," than if you could have all the honors that all the kings can put upon all men in the world. I think that I could say, "Lord, now lettest thou thy servant depart in peace, according to thy word," if he would but say to me, "I am glorified in your ministry." I hope that he is; I believe that he is; but, oh, for an assuring word, if not spoken to us personally, yet spoken to his Father about us as in our text, "I am glorified in them"!

How can this be? Well, it is a very wide subject. Christ is glorified in his people in many ways. He is glorified by saving such sinners, taking these people, so sinful, so lost, so unworthy. When the Lord lays hold upon a drunkard, a thief, an adulterer; when he arrests one who has been guilty of blasphemy, whose very heart is reeking with evil thoughts; when he picks up the far-off one, the abandoned, the dissolute, the fallen, as he often does; and when he says, "These shall be mine; I will wash these in my blood, I will use these to speak my word," oh, then he is glorified in them! Read the lives of many great sinners who have afterward become great saints, and you will see how they have tried to glorify him, not only she who washed his feet with her tears, but many another like her. Oh, how they have loved to praise him! Eyes have wept tears, lips have spoken words, but hearts have felt what neither eyes nor lips could speak of adoring gratitude to him. "I am glorified in them." Great sinners, Christ is glorified in you. Some of you Pharisees, if you were to be converted, would not bring Christ such glory as he gets through saving publicans and harlots. Even if you struggled into heaven, it would be with very little music for him on the road, certainly no tears and no ointment for his feet, and no wiping them with the hairs of your head. You are too respectable ever to do that; but when he saves great sinners, he can truly say, "I am glorified in them," and each of them can sing,

> It passeth praises, that dear love of thine,
> My Jesus, Savior: yet this heart of mine
> Would sing that love, so full, so rich, so free,
> Which brings a rebel sinner, such as me,
> Nigh unto God.

And Christ is glorified by the perseverance which he shows in the matter of their salvation. See how he begins to save and the man resists. He follows up his kind endeavor, and the man rebels. He hunts him, pursues him, dogs his footsteps. He will have the man, and the man will not have him. But the Lord, without violating the free will of man, which he never does, yet at length brings the one who was most unwilling to lie at his feet, and he that hated most begins to love, and he that was most stouthearted bows the knee in lowliest humility. It is wonderful how persevering the Lord is in the salvation of a sinner; yes, and in the salvation of his own, for you would have broken loose long ago if your great Shepherd had not penned you up within the fold. Many of you would have started aside and have lost yourselves if it had not been for constraints of sovereign grace which have kept you to this day and will not let you go. Christ is glorified in you. Oh, when you once get to heaven, when the angels know all that you were and all that you tried to be, when the whole story of almighty, infinite grace is told, as it will be told, then will Christ be glorified in you!

Beloved, we actively glorify Christ when we display Christian graces. You who are loving, forgiving, tenderhearted, gentle, meek, self-sacrificing, you glorify him; he is glorified in you. You who are upright and who will not be moved from your integrity, you who can despise the sinner's gold and will not sell your conscience for it, you who are bold and brave for Christ, you who can bear and suffer for his name's sake, all your graces come from him. As all the flowers are bred and begotten of the sun, so all that is in you that is good comes from Christ, the Sun of righteousness; and, therefore, he is glorified in you.

But, beloved, God's people have glorified Christ in many other ways. When they make him the object of all their trust, they glorify him; when they say, "Though I am the chief of sinners, yet, I trust him; though my mind is dark, and though my temptations abound, I believe that he can save to the uttermost; I do trust him." Christ is more glorified by a sinner's humble faith than by a seraph's loudest song. If you believe, you do glorify him. Child of God, are you tonight very dark and dull and heavy? Do you feel half dead, spiritually? Come to your Lord's feet and kiss them, and believe that he can save, no, that he has saved you, even you; and thus you will glorify his holy name. "Oh!" said a believer the other day, "I know whom I have believed; Christ is mine." "Ah!" said another, "that is presumption." Beloved, it is nothing of the kind; it is not presumption for a child to own his own father; it might be pride for him to be ashamed of his father; it is certainly great alienation from his father if he is ashamed to own him. "I know whom I have believed." Happy state of heart, to be absolutely sure that you are resting upon Christ, that he is your Savior, that you believe in him, for Jesus said, "He that believeth on me hath everlasting life." I believe on him, and I have everlasting life. "He that believeth on him is not condemned." I believe on him, and I am not condemned. Make sure work of this, not only by signs and evidences, but do even better; make the one sign and the one evidence to be this, "Jesus Christ came into the world to save sinners; I, a sinner, accept his great sacrifice, and I am saved."

Especially, I think that God's people glorify Christ by a cheerful conversation. If you go about moaning and mourning, pining and complaining, you bring no honor to his name; but if, when you fast, you appear not unto men to fast, if you can wear a cheerful countenance, even when your heart is heavy, and if, above all, you can rally your spirit out of its depths and begin to bless God when the cupboard is empty and friends are few, then you will indeed glorify Christ.

Many are the ways in which this good work may be done; let us try to do it. "I am glorified in them," says Christ; that is, by their bold confession of Christ. Do I address myself to any here who love Christ, but who have never owned it? Do come out, and come out very soon. He deserves to have all the glory that you can give him. If he has healed you, be not like the nine who forgot that Christ had healed their leprosy. Come and praise the name of the great Healer, and let others know what Christ can do. I am afraid that there are a great many here tonight who hope that they are Christians, but they have never said so. What are you ashamed of? Ashamed of your Lord? I am afraid that you do not, after all, love him. Now, at this time, at this particular crisis of the history of the church and the world, if we do not publicly take sides with Christ, we shall really be against him. The time is come now when we cannot afford to have go-betweens. You must be for him or for his enemies; and tonight he asks you, if you are really his, to say it. Come forward, unite yourself with his people, and let it be seen by your life and conversation that you do belong to Christ. If not, how can it be true, "I am glorified in them"? Is Christ glorified in a non-confessing people, a people that hope to go slinking into heaven by the byroads or across the fields, but dare not come into the King's highway and travel with the King's subjects, and own that they belong to him?

Lastly, I think that Christ is glorified in his people by their efforts to extend his kingdom. What efforts are you making? There is a great deal of force in a church like this; but I am afraid that there is a great deal of waste steam, waste power here. The tendency is, so often, to leave everything to be done by the minister, or else by one or two leading people; but I do pray you, beloved, if you be Christ's, and if you belong to the Father, if, unworthy though you be, you are claimed with a double ownership by the Father and the Son, do try to be of use to them. Let it be seen by your winning others to Christ that he is glorified in you. I believe that by diligent attendance to even the smallest Sunday school class, Christ is glorified in you. By that private conversation in your own room, by that letter which you dropped into the post with many a prayer, by anything that you have done with a pure motive, trusting in God in order to glorify Christ, he is glorified in you.

Do not mistake my meaning with regard to serving the Lord. I think it exceedingly wrong when I hear exhortations made to young people, "Quit your service as domestics, and come out into spiritual work. Businessmen, leave your shops. Workmen, give up your trades. You cannot serve Christ in that calling; come away from it altogether." I beg to say that nothing will be more pestilent than such advice as that. There are men called by the grace of God to separate themselves from every earthly occupation, and they have special gifts for the work of the ministry; but ever to imagine that the bulk of Christian people cannot serve God in their daily calling is to think altogether contrary to the mind of the Spirit of God. If you are a servant, remain a servant. If you are a waiter, go on with your waiting. If you are a tradesman, go on with your trade. Let every man abide in the calling wherein he is called, unless there be to him some special call from God to devote himself to the ministry. Go on with your employment, dear Christian people, and do not imagine that you are to turn hermits or monks or nuns. You would not glorify God if you did so act. Soldiers of Christ are to fight the battle out where they are. To quit the field and shut yourselves up alone would be to render it impossible that you should get the victory. The work of God is as holy and acceptable in domestic service, or in trade, as any service that can be rendered in the pulpit, or even by the foreign missionary.

We thank God for the men specially called and set apart for his own work; but we know that they would do nothing unless the salt of our holy faith should permeate the daily life of other Christians. You godly mothers, you are the glory of the church of Christ. You hard-working men and women who endure patiently "as seeing him who is invisible" are the crown and glory of the church of God. You who do not shirk your daily labor, but stand manfully to it, obeying Christ in it, are proving what the Christian religion was meant to do.

We can, if we are truly priests unto God, make our everyday garments into vestments, our meals into sacraments, and our houses into temples for God's worship. Our very beds will be within the veil, and our inmost thoughts will be as a sweet incense perpetually smoking up to the Most High. Dream not that there is anything about any honest calling that degrades a man or hinders him in glorifying God; but sanctify it all, till the bells upon the horses shall ring out, "Holiness to the LORD," and the pots in your houses shall be as holy as the vessels of the sanctuary.

Now, I want that we should so come to the communion table tonight that even here Christ may be glorified in us. Ah, you may sit at the Lord's table wearing a fine dress or a diamond ring, and you may think that you are somebody of importance, but you are not! Ah, you may come to the Lord's table and say, "Here is an experienced Christian man who knows a thing or two." You are not glorifying Christ that way; you are only a nobody. But if you come tonight saying, "Lord, I am hungry, you can feed me," that is glorifying him. If you come saying, "Lord, I have no merit and no worthiness, I come because you have died for me, and I trust you," you are glorifying him. He glorifies Christ most who takes most from him, and who then gives most back to him. Come, empty pitcher, come and be filled; and when you are filled, pour all out at the dear feet of him who filled you. Come, trembler, come and let him touch you with his strengthening hand, and then go out and work, and use the strength which he has given you. I fear that I have not led you where I wanted to bring you, close to my Lord and to the Father, yet I have done my best. May the Lord forgive my feebleness and wandering, and yet bless you for his dear name's sake! Amen.

Christ's Negative and Positive Prayer

Intended for reading on Lord's Day, April 8, 1894; delivered on Lord's Day evening, February 5, 1888, at the Metropolitan Tabernacle, Newington. No. 2355.

"I pray not that thou shouldest take them out of the world, but that thou shouldest keep them from the evil."—JOHN 17:15

Notice in the prayer of our Divine Lord what honor he always puts upon God the Father. He ascribes to God everything—the taking the disciples out of the world or the keeping them from the evil in the world. Let us never neglect to look for God's hand in all that happens to the saints; and let us not fall into the error of those who deny the Great First Cause and are always dealing with appearances, forgetting the Mighty God who shapes our ends and rules our destinies. If we die, it is not by chance, but because God takes us out of the world. Believers fall asleep in Jesus, neither before nor after the predestined time. No disease or accident can cut short their lives; and it would not be possible to prolong their existence beyond the time appointed by the Lord. I like to believe—whatever it may be to some of you, to me it is very sweet to believe that

All must come, and last, and end,
As shall please my heavenly Friend.

Plagues and deaths around me fly,
Till he bids I cannot die:
Not a single shaft can hit
Till the God of love thinks fit.

Our lives are entirely in the keeping of our loving Father. You can see that truth in the text. Jesus speaks of God as taking the beloved ones out of the world; and it is even so. This fact should make us cease to be anxious about when or how we shall die; and it should, at the same time, reconcile us to the time and the manner of the homegoing of any whom we love most dearly. They were not snatched away by the robber Death; they were taken out of the world by our dear Father's gracious hand. Let us say concerning them what Job said of his loved ones, "The LORD gave, and the LORD hath taken away; blessed be the name of the LORD."

See, also, how our Lord Jesus honors the Father by ascribing to him the keeping of the saints from evil, for he says, "I pray not that thou shouldest take them out of the world, but that thou shouldest keep them from the evil." Beloved, our escape from evil, at the first, was by the Father's grace. Our persevering in righteousness until now has been wrought in us by the Father's hand through the Divine Spirit; and this day, if we have not apostatized, if we have not denied the faith and proved traitors to Christ, we must ascribe it entirely to the grace of God. As the psalmist says, "It is he that hath made us, and not we ourselves," and it is he who keeps us, and not we ourselves; for, again quoting the hundredth Psalm, "We are his people, and the sheep of his pasture."

I want you, as far as you possibly can, to be constantly recognizing God's overruling hand; God, in our death, taking us out of the world, and God, in our life, keeping us from evil and upholding us in our integrity. When you get thus near to God and realize that God is ever present with you, you are in the right frame of mind for prayer. You are also in the state and condition of heart which will give you courage in time of danger; you are, indeed, ready for anything and for everything, whatever may come to you, when God is thus consciously overshadowing your spirit. This much, I think, the prayer of our Lord plainly suggests.

Observe, again, that God has us absolutely at his disposal. Let us ever remember that great truth. The prayer of Jesus recognizes his Father's sovereignty; but we ourselves must also recognize that we are entirely in God's hand. He can take us out of the world; or he can keep us in the world and preserve us from evil. We are glad to be at the disposal of our God; as his people, we would have no voice or choice in fixing our own position, but with the psalmist we would say, "He shall choose our inheritance for us." Whether we stay or whether we go depends entirely upon the Lord's will; and Christ in his prayer recognizes that it is so. He would not pray for a matter which was not in the hand of him to whom he prayed. He felt that his people were absolutely at his Father's disposal, and, therefore, he presented the prayer which is to be the subject of our meditation tonight.

Now, in this petition, there are two things. There is, first, *the negative prayer:* "I pray not that thou shouldest take them out of the world"; and then, secondly, there is *the positive prayer:* "But that thou shouldest keep them from the evil."

I. There is here, first, *the negative prayer:*

"I pray not that thou shouldest take them out of the world." At first sight that seems almost unkind on our Savior's part. What could happen better than for those whom the world hated to be taken out of the world? Jesus himself was going out of the world; what could he do that should have greater love in it than to pray that they might go with him? I have often felt as Thomas did when he said, "Let us also go, that we may die with him." Has Jesus gone? Why should we tarry here? Has Jesus entered the glory? Let us be with him where he is that we may behold his glory. There is nothing left to detain us below since he has ascended to his Father's right hand; but there is everything to attract us upward since he is there who is our heart's Lord, our all in all. Have you not often felt inclined to pray for yourself that the Lord would take you out of the world? I mean, not merely in times of depression, when, like Elijah, who never died, you are ready to pray, "Now, O LORD, take away my life"; but in times of exultation when you have been near to the gates of heaven in ecstatic joy and holy gladness, have you not wished to slip in? "Lord, it is good for us to be here: if thou wilt, let us make here three tabernacles." Have you not said so in your heart, if not with your voice? No, have you not wished, not to stay on the Mount of Transfiguration, but from that point to take your heavenward flight and land yourself in the New Jerusalem, to go no more out for ever? I know that, sometimes, on a Sunday when we have been singing to the tune Prospect,

On Jordan's stormy banks I stand,
And cast a wishful eye
To Canaan's fair and happy land,
Where my possessions lie.

I have felt that I could from my heart sing the last verse of the hymn,

Fill'd with delight, my raptured soul
Can here no longer stay:
Though Jordan's waves around me roll,
Fearless I'd launch away,

Yet the Savior says, "I pray not that thou shouldest take them out of the world." I am sure, therefore, that it is a better thing for us to stop here till our appointed time than it is for us to be taken out of the world. It may not be better in all respects; but there are some points in which it is an advantage for believers to remain here. Our Savior loves us so much that he would be certain to ask the very best thing for us. Therefore, for us to be taken out of the world at once would not be, all things considered, the best disposition of us that the Lord could make.

How is that? Well, first, if we, who are Christ's people, were taken out of the world, then *the world itself could perish*. Do we contemplate, with any pleasure, such a catastrophe as that? "Ye are the light of the world." Take all the lights away and the murky atmosphere, which is dark enough even now, would become dense as Egyptian midnight, and life would be intolerable. "Ye are the salt of the earth." Should the salt be taken away, putrefaction would revel without limit, corruption would then have nothing to contend with it, and the world would reek in the nostrils of God himself till he would be obliged to destroy it.

I look along the ages, and I see mankind given up to debauchery and eaten up with worldliness, yet the sinners are permitted to live on year after year; but I also see a strange-looking ship that has been built on dry land, and I watch the only family in the earth that fears God going up into that queerly-shaped vessel, and the door is shut by God himself. I hear it as it closes, and the moment that door is shut, what happens? The world is doomed; God pulls up the sluices of the great deep that lies under, and he throws open the floodgates of heaven; the fountains gush up from below, and the rains pour down from above, till the whole world is drowned. This awful judgment did not begin till Noah, the one righteous man, was taken away from the rest of mankind and shut in the ark: *"The same day* were all the fountains of the great deep broken up, and the windows of heaven were opened. And the rain was upon the earth forty days and forty nights. *In the selfsame day* entered Noah, and Shem, and Ham, and Japheth, the sons of Noah, and Noah's wife, and the three wives of his sons with them, into the ark."

I look again and away yonder, I behold, in the vale of Siddim, the cities of Sodom and Gomorrah. If I go within their gates, I hear and see that which disgusts my soul; things that it were a shame even to speak of are done in those cities. There is one good man who lives there, and only one; and I see him, early one morning, flying with his wife and daughters out of the city. The moment he has passed beyond the bounds of the condemned cities and escaped to little Zoar, what happens? Destruction is poured out of heaven upon the guilty people: "The sun was risen upon the earth when Lot entered into Zoar. *Then* the LORD rained upon Sodom and upon Gomorrah brimstone and fire from the LORD out of heaven; and he overthrew those cities, and all the plain, and all the inhabitants of the cities, and that which grew upon the ground."

Because we do not wish such awful destruction as that, either by water or by fire, to fall upon this guilty world, we ask God to permit the salt to remain in the earth, the light still to burn in it, the Noah still to linger, the Lot still to dwell here yet a little while. When the Lord shall begin rapidly to gather his saints home, as he may do by and by, and when the wail is heard, "The faithful fail from among the children of men," then shall come dark days indeed, and the earth shall know the terrible vengeance of Almighty God.

This, then, is one reason why Christ does not pray that we should be taken out of the world, because it would be the ruin of guilty men if the saints were removed from the earth which is preserved only for their sake.

Does not the Lord also wish the righteous to stay in the world a while that *they may be the means of the salvation of others?* How came Jesus here himself? He came to seek and to save that which was lost; and when he went away he did not take his disciples out of the world because their ministry was to be blessed to many of their fellow creatures. In this very prayer to his Father, he said, "As thou hast sent me into the world, even so have I also sent them into the world." They who might be safely housed in heaven stay here that they may be the means of saving others. Mother is still here, though her son has well near broken her heart; she is left on the earth that she may yet win that boy for Christ. And our old, gray-headed friend, whose infirmities are multiplying, is still among us, though he would be far happier among the harps of angels; but he is detained here that his grandson, or his still-unconverted daughter, may hear from his lips once more a loving, living testimony for the Lord Jesus and may thereby be turned to God.

I do think that there are many of you who do not yourselves love the Lord, who, nevertheless, ought to be very grateful to him for saying, "I pray not that thou shouldest take them out of the world." Oh, dear man, you do not want to lose that loving wife of yours! She has brought you here tonight after a good deal of coaxing and tender persuasion; you do not think of her God or care about the Lord Jesus; but your wife is still living to seek the salvation of your soul. I believe she will win you yet, by God's grace. There are many who might, long ago, have received their reward and would have been thrice happy to do so, but they have yet to preach the everlasting gospel, and yet to win more souls to Christ. It is more needful for sinners that Paul should abide in the flesh a little longer, though he himself has a desire to depart and to be with Christ, which is far better.

Beloved Christian brothers and sisters, if the Lord is keeping any of us here with the object of using us in the salvation of others, let us take care that we answer the purpose of our continued existence on the earth; let us be up and doing, let us be earnestly seeking the souls of our relatives, let us be zealously endeavoring to bring others to Christ. I am sometimes saddened when

I hear of households conducted by professedly Christian people, places where one would think that God's name would be upon every tongue, and yet servants may live for years in such families, and their masters and mistresses never speak to them about their souls. And many men, employing hundreds of workpeople, will give them their wages as if they had no souls to care about; for they take no interest in the eternal welfare of those who work for them in temporal things. Do not let it be so with you, dear friends. Masters and mistresses, there are occasions in which you can go to your servants, and those employed by you, and without being at all intrusive, can seek to interest them in the things of God. You can call at their homes, perhaps; and the offering of a prayer and speaking to them about the gospel of Christ may reach them and bring them to the Savior, where our sermons have failed to do so. I charge you, by him who bought you by his blood, either go to heaven and glorify Christ there, or else, if you remain in the world, glorify him here; but whether you live or whether you die, do see to this matter, that you answer the divine purpose which is that, being saved yourself, you may become the means of saving others.

There is a second reason, then, for our Lord's wishing his disciples to stop here, that they may be the means of the salvation of others.

Next, I think the Lord lets his people stay in the world *that they may serve him in the place where they sinned against him.* If I had been converted just now, and the Lord were to open the gates of heaven and say, "Come in," I think that I should step back and say, "Dear Master, may I stop here just a little while to undo some of the mischief that I did in my ungodly state?" I can fancy that someone here would pray, "Lord, there is my friend who used to go to the theater and the music hall with me, and I taught him much that was mischievous; will it please you to let me tarry here and tell him about your great salvation?" I think that another would say, "Lord, I spent so many years in the service of the devil; now, before I go home to see your face, let me have a few years in your service! I would like to undo at least a portion of the evil that I have done before I stand in your presence amid the eternal splendors of heaven." It seems to me that it is most gracious of the Lord to let us remain here to serve him where we sinned against him, and not to take us home as soon as we are converted. I think that we shall congratulate ourselves even in heaven that we had some opportunity of contending for the faith, or of bearing reproach for Christ's sake, or of seeking to win souls for him before we entered upon our everlasting rest.

Is not that a good reason why the Savior did not pray that his disciples might be taken out of the world?

And is not this another good reason why saints are left in the world? *The Lord keeps his people here that he may exhibit in them the power of divine grace.* Just as he permitted Job to be tempted of the devil that all the world might see how God can enable a man by patience to triumph, so he keeps us here to let the devil and all men know what his grace can do for his people, and also to let angels and principalities and powers in the heavenly places behold what saints God can make out of guilty sinners. He takes those who had gone far away in sin and brings them near by the blood of Jesus. He fashions the rough, knotty timber that did not seem as if it ever could be shaped and uses it in the building of his temple. He makes wonders of grace out of sinful men and women, such marvels of mercy that the angels will stand and gaze at them throughout eternity as they say, "How could God make such perfect beings as these out of such sinful material?" All this will be "to the praise of the glory of his grace, wherein he hath made us accepted in the beloved." You see, we cannot exhibit patience in heaven; so far as we now know anything about heaven, it does not seem possible that there will be any need of patience there. We cannot manifest strength of faith in heaven, for faith will be lost in sight. We can take our love into glory; there are some flowers that will sweetly open in the land where they have no need of the sun, for Christ is better than the sun. There are certain flowers of less sweet perfume, and those can be developed only in the earth; and the Lord, therefore, bids us tarry here a while that he may show what grace can do in sustaining us in suffering, upholding us under trial, and protecting us against temptation. O soldiers of the cross, do you want crowns without having contended for them?

Must you be carried to the skies
On flowery beds of ease;
While others fought to win the prize,
And sailed through bloody seas?

Ask no such thing; be satisfied to take your share in the conflict, or else I do not see how you can so sweetly relish the triumph which God will give to his people in due time.

Thus, the Lord exhibits the power of his grace in us; and that is another reason why we have to tarry here a while.

Next, I shall have to say many things very briefly where I could have wished to have had time for enlargement. Do you not think that we are kept here *to prepare us for heaven?* Are we not as yet like children who need education for that truer, higher life? When a boy first goes to school, you do not put into his hand the higher classics. He must plod through his grammar, he must learn many elementary lessons; and then he must work hard on dry and dreary roots, and afterward you will give him some classic poet that he may read intelligently. So must you and I, here below, go plodding through our primers; we must work hard at our grammars, we must have a slate and pencil still; and when we have become proficient in all we have to learn here, we shall the better enjoy the holy rest and perfect service which make up the heaven of the blessed.

Let me give you an illustration of what I mean. A boy is sent to school, and his parents pinch themselves to pay for him to have a good education. It is not every boy who will say this to himself; but if he does, he is a first-rate lad: "My poor father and mother are doing all they can to give me a first-class education here. They want to make something of me; and I am going to learn with all my heart, so that I may be worthy of all that my parents design for me, and not waste one single shilling of the money they are spending upon me." Such a boy is diligent at his books; he labors where others loiter, and treasures up in his mind everything that he learns while others forget it. Now the Lord Jesus Christ is thus putting some of us to school, training us for high employment hereafter. He means to make something of us by and by; and our desire now is to be prepared as far as possible for what Christ intends for us that we may be the more to his praise and glory, and our own completeness for ever and ever.

I have often been puzzled by those words of the Lord Jesus, "I go to prepare a place for you." What there was about heaven that was not ready, I do not know; except it was that Jesus himself was not there; but I can easily understand this truth, that we are not ready for heaven yet, for heaven consists more in character than in place. We have to be more completely sanctified, more truly developed in all good things than we are at present. We are not yet fit for the glory land, so Jesus does not pray that we should be taken out of the world; but we are to wait here a little longer till his grace has more fully fitted us for glory.

Does not the Lord also, by keeping us here, mean us *to see more of the wisdom, the power, the grace, and the truth of God?* Within this last month—a month of remarkable pain and travail to me—I have had certain experiences which I shall never forget, and I would pass through seas ten times as deep and boisterous merely for the sake of having those experiences repeated. There are some of them which I could not tell here. There are facts connected with them that would be discreditable to some who had to do with them, though greatly honorable to others; but as to my God, they have shown me his faithfulness, his power, his tenderness, his wisdom; and I believe that, had I been in heaven, I should not have seen as much of some of the attributes of

God as I have seen here below. If you had been an angel, for ever praising God in glory, could you tell how faithful he is to a tried saint? Could you say, if you had not experienced it here on earth, how surely he comforts his people in their deepest sorrows? There are some pearls in these troubled waters that the sea of glass itself can never contain. There are some bright eternal lessons that we should never have known, if it had not been for our earthly trials, even if we might have had an archangel for a schoolmaster. Therefore, we must stop here a while and suffer affliction, temptation, depression of spirit, and slander and abuse that we may learn thereby the deeper truths of God's revelation.

I shall have to abandon the second part of my subject, I see, for my time has nearly gone already. I must, however, make just one more remark upon our first head.

I think that our Lord Jesus does not pray that we may be called out of the world because *he knows that we shall be taken to heaven in due time.* He scarcely thinks of that as a matter of prayer; it is so entirely in the Father's hands that he leaves it there. I would not encourage anybody here to pray that he might die; and on the other hand, I do not know that I would incite anybody here to pray very earnestly that he might live. Hezekiah prayed that his life might be lengthened, and his prayer was granted. Manasseh would not have been born if Hezekiah had not lived those extra fifteen years; and it would have been a good thing if Manasseh had never been born. Those sins and iniquities with which he made Judah to sin with his idols, though they were forgiven, yet filled up the cup of the nation's perversion from God and fixed the doom of that apostate people. I do not know, if the lifting of our finger could make us live for another twenty years, whether we had not better hesitate to lift that finger.

At any rate, I feel quite clear about the other side of the question—we have no business to pray that we may die. As I have already reminded you, the man who did pray that he might die never died at all. How foolish he was to pray that he might die when God had intended that he should go to heaven by a whirlwind with a chariot and horses of fire! We shall die all in good time, unless the Lord shall come in the splendor of his Second Advent. If you and I had the choice of the time of our death, there would be just a tinge of the element of suicide about it, and that is the very worst form of murder. This is clearly our duty, to leave ourselves wholly and unreservedly in the hand of him to whom belong the issues of life; it is certainly our best course.

This, then, is our Lord's negative prayer: "I pray not that thou shouldest take them out of the world."

II. Secondly, if time had permitted, I was also to have spoken to you about *the positive prayer*. I will only hint at this.

What did Jesus pray for his disciples? That God would keep them from evil. This is the right prayer for you to offer for yourself. Do not pray to get out of the battle; ask of God that you may never be a coward, but that you may bravely play the man in the day of danger. Do not seek to be screened from affliction; but plead that you may never be driven to sin by your affliction. You need not even pray that you may not have prosperity; but you may entreat the Lord that prosperity may not make you proud or worldly. Let your condition be as God wills it; but let your great anxiety be that you may be kept from all sin in every condition.

"I pray not that thou shouldest take them out of the world, but that thou shouldest keep them from the evil." We need to be kept from the evil of *apostasy*, the evil of *worldliness*, from the evil of *unholiness*, from the evil of getting to be as men of the world are; that is the main point. I do not think that it matters much what the condition of a man is so long as his heart is above his condition. I remember that Saint Bernard, as he is usually called— Bernard of Clairvaux—one of the holiest and humblest of men, was one day riding on a mule to a certain monastery; and one who saw him said, "I think Bernard is getting proud, because he is riding on a mule, and sitting upon a cloth which has a fringe of gold lace to it." Now Bernard was a man who cared nothing for that sort of thing; and when the other charged him with pride, he said, "Perhaps it may be so, but I never noticed that I had any cloth at all." Someone else had put that fine cloth upon the mule without his knowing anything about it, and he really thought that he was riding on the animal's bare back, for his mind was taken up with something far more important.

If you are rich and you have a cloth with a gold fringe to it, do not be conscious of its existence; let your soul rise above it. If you are poor and you have no saddle at all, do not notice your lack; but let your soul soar above such matters. Pray not that you may be taken out of this or that, be it poverty or be it wealth, be it sickness or be it health; but pray that you may be kept from the evil of it, for there is an evil in every case. If you are making money, we ought to have a special prayer meeting for you to pray that you may be kept from evil. I said to a brother who was going to a banquet the other day, "Well, we will pray for you, dear friend, for you are going into a place of peril." I do not think there was any great risk to such a man in going; perhaps some of those who stopped at home and complained of him were in more danger. The great point is, not where you are, not what you are as to circumstances, but that you

may be kept by almighty power from evil which might come out of any circumstances unless you were divinely preserved from evil. Oh, that the Lord
Jesus may say this concerning us tonight: "I pray not that thou shouldest take
them out of the world, but that thou shouldest keep them from the evil"! If
so, we can leave everything else in his dear hands.

But, brothers, do not let us be anxious to get to heaven just yet. Let us
seek to fight our way there in valiant fashion. Do not let us be so earnest about
the end as about the way, laying hold on Christ and uplifting his dear cross as
our banner. Oh, that all of you would do this and follow the Lamb whither-
soever he goes! We will just bend our thoughts to this one point and not think
so much of going to heaven as of avoiding sin. Lord, keep me out of evil!
Then let me live or let me die, hold me up or press me down, let me dance
with joy of heart, or let me lie and pine in an agony of pain, with anguish rack-
ing every bone in my body, it shall be all the same to me; so long as nothing
of the evil of surrounding circumstances enters into me, do with me as you
will, O my God!

God bless you, dear friends, for Jesus' sake! Amen.

The Character of Christ's People

⟨∘⟩

Delivered on Sabbath morning, November 22, 1855, at New Park Street Chapel, Southwark. No. 78.

"They are not of the world, even as I am not of the world."—JOHN 17:16

Christ's prayer was for a special people. He declared that he did not offer a universal intercession. "I pray for *them*," said he. "I pray not for the world, but for them which thou hast given me; for they are thine." In reading this beautiful prayer through, only one question arises to our minds: Who are the people that are described as "them," or as "they"? Who are these favored individuals, who share a Savior's prayers, are recognized by a Savior's love, have their names written on the stones of his precious breastplate, and have their characters and their circumstances mentioned by the lips of the High Priest before the throne on high? The answer to that question is supplied by the words of our text. The people for whom Christ prays are an unearthly people. They are a people somewhat above the world, distinguished altogether from it. "They are not of the world, even as I am not of the world."

I shall treat my text, first of all, *doctrinally*; secondly, *experimentally*; and thirdly, *practically*.

I. First, we shall take our text and look at it *doctrinally*.

The doctrine of it is that God's people are a people who are not of the world, even as Christ was not of the world. It is not so much that they are not of the world as that they are "not of the world, *even as [Christ was] not of the world.*" This is an important distinction, for there are to be found certain people who are not of the world, and yet they are not Christians. Among them I would mention sentimentalists—people who are always crying and groaning in affected sentimental ways. Their spirits are so refined, their characters are so delicate, that they could not attend to ordinary business. They would think it rather degrading to their spiritual nature to attend to anything connected with the world. They live much in the air of romances and novels; they love to read things that fetch tears from their eyes; they would like continually to live in a cottage near a wood or to inhabit some quiet cave where they could read *Zimmerman on Solitude* for ever; for they feel that they are "not of the world." The fact is, there is something too flimsy about them to stand the wear and tear of this wicked world. They are so preeminently good that they cannot bear to do as we poor human creatures do. I have heard of one young lady, who thought herself so spiritually-minded that she could not work. A very wise minister said to her, "That is quite correct! You are so spiritually-minded that you cannot work; very well, you are so spiritually-minded that you shall not eat unless you do." That brought her back from her great spiritual-mindedness.

There is a stupid sentimentalism that certain persons nurse themselves into. They read a parcel of books that intoxicate their brains, and then fancy that they have a lofty destiny. These people are "not of the world," truly; but the world does not want them, and the world would not miss them much if they were clean gone for ever. There is such a thing as being "not of the world" from high order of sentimentalism, and yet not being a Christian after all. For it is not so much being "not of the world," as being "not of the world, even as [Christ was] not of the world." There are others, too, like your monks and those other individuals of the Catholic church who are not of the world. They are so awfully good that they could not live with us sinful creatures at all. They must be distinguished from us altogether. They must not wear, of course, a boot that would at all approach to a worldly shoe, but they must have a sole of leather strapped on with two or three thongs like the far-famed Father Ignatius. They could not be expected to wear worldly coats and waistcoats; but they must have peculiar garbs, cut in certain fashions, like the Passionists. They must wear particular dresses, particular garments, particular habits. And we know that some men are "not of the world" by the peculiar mouthing they give to all their words—the sort of sweet, savory, buttery flavor they give to the English language because they think themselves so eminently sanctified that they fancy it would be wrong to indulge in anything in which ordinary mortals indulge. Such persons are, however, reminded, that their being "not of the world" has nothing to do with it. It is not being "not of the world" so much as being "not of the world, even as [Christ was] not of the world."

This is the distinguishing mark—being different from the world in those respects in which Christ was different. Not making ourselves singular in unimportant points as those poor creatures do, but being different from the world in those respects in which the Son of God and the Son of man, Jesus Christ, our glorious Exemplar, was distinguished from the rest of mankind. And I think this will burst out in great clearness and beauty to us if we consider that Christ was not of the world in nature; that he was not of the world again in office; and above all, that he was not of the world in his character.

First, *Christ was not of the world in nature*. What was there about Christ that was worldly? In one point of view his nature was divine; and as divine, it was perfect, pure, unsullied, spotless; he could not descend to things of earthliness and sin. In another sense he was human; and his human nature, which was born of the Virgin Mary, was begotten of the Holy Ghost, and, therefore was so pure that in it rested nothing that was worldly. He was not like ordinary men. We are all born with worldliness in our hearts. Solomon well says, "Foolishness is bound up in the heart of a child." It is not only there, but it is bound up in it, it is tied up in his heart and is difficult to remove. And so with each of us: when we were children, earthliness and carnality were bound up in our nature. But Christ was not so. His nature was not a worldly one; it was essentially different from that of everyone else, although he sat down and talked with them. Mark the difference! He stood side by side with a Pharisee; but everyone could see he was not of the Pharisee's world. He sat by a Samaritan woman; and though he conversed with her very freely, who is it that fails to see that he was not of that Samaritan woman's world—not a sinner like her? He mingled with the publicans, no, he sat down at the publican's feast, and ate with publicans and sinners; but you could see by the holy actions and the peculiar gestures he there carried with him that he was not of the publicans' world, though he mixed with them. There was something so different in his nature that you could not have found an individual in all the world whom you could have set beside him and said, "There! he is of that man's world." No, not even John, though he leaned on his bosom and partook very much of his Lord's spirit, was exactly of that world to which Jesus belonged; for even he once in his Boanergean spirit said words to this effect, "Let us call down fire from heaven on the heads of those who oppose you"—a thing that Christ could not endure for a moment, and thereby proved that he was something even beyond John's world.

Well, beloved, in some sense, the Christian man is not of the world even in his nature. I do not mean in his corrupt and fallen nature, but in his new nature. There is something in a Christian that is utterly and entirely distinct from that of anybody else. Many persons think that the difference between a Christian and a worldling consists in this: one goes to chapel twice on a Sunday, another does not go but once or perhaps not at all; one of them takes the sacrament, the other does not; one pays attention to holy things, the other pays very little attention to them. But, ah, beloved, that does not make a Christian.

The distinction between a Christian and a worldling is not merely external, but internal. The difference is one of nature, and not of act.

A Christian is as essentially different from a worldling as a dove is from a raven, or a lamb from a lion. He is not of the world even in his nature. You could not make him a worldling. You might do what you liked; you might cause him to fall into some temporary sin; but you could not make him a worldling. You might cause him to backslide; but you could not make him a sinner as he used to be. He is not of the world by his nature. He is a twice-born man; in his veins runs the blood of the royal family of the universe. He is a nobleman; he is a heaven-born child. His freedom is not merely a bought one, but he has his liberty by his newborn nature. He is begotten again unto a lively hope. He is not of the world by his nature; he is essentially and entirely different from the world. There are persons in this chapel now who are more totally distinct from one another than you can even conceive. I have some here who are intelligent and some who are ignorant; some who are rich and some who are poor; but I do not allude to those distinctions: they all melt away into nothing in that great distinction—dead or alive, spiritual or carnal, Christian or worldling. And, oh, if you are God's people, then you are not of the world in your nature; for you are "not of the world, even as [Christ was] not of the world."

Again, *you are not of the world in your office.* Christ's office had nothing to do with worldly things. "Are you a king, then?" Yes; I am a king; but my kingdom is not of this world. "Are you a priest?" Yes; I am a priest; but my priesthood is not the priesthood which I shall soon lay aside or which shall be discontinued as that of others has been. "Are you a teacher?" Yes; but my doctrines are not the doctrines of morality, doctrines that concern earthly dealings between man and man simply; my doctrine comes down from heaven. So Jesus Christ, we say, is "not of the world." He had no office that could be termed a worldly one, and he had no aim which was in the least worldly. He did not seek his own applause, his own fame, his own honor; his very office was not of the world.

And, O believer! what is your office? Have you none at all? Why, yes, man! You are a priest unto the Lord your God; your office is to offer a sacrifice of prayer and praise each day. Ask a Christian what he is. Say to him, "What is your official standing? What are you by office?" Well, if he answers you properly, he will not say, "I am a draper or druggist," or anything of that sort. No; he will say, "I am a priest unto my God. The office unto which I am called is to be the salt of the earth. I am a city set on a hill, a light that cannot be hid. That is my office. My office is not a worldly one." Whether yours be the office of the minister or the deacon or the church member, you are not of this world in your office, even as Christ was not of the world; your occupation is not a worldly one.

Again, you *are not of the world in your character,* for that is the chief point in which Christ was not of the world. And now, brethren, I shall have to turn some what from doctrine to practice before I get rightly to this part of the subject; for I must reprove many of the Lord's people that they do not sufficiently manifest that they are not of the world in character, even as Christ was not of the world. Oh! how many of you there are who will assemble around the table at the supper of your Lord who do not live like your Savior. How many of you there are who join our church and walk with us, and yet are not worthy of your high calling and profession. Mark you the churches all around, and let your eyes run with tears when you remember that of many of their members it cannot be said, "ye *are not* of the world," for they *are* of the world. O, my hearers, I fear many of you are worldly, carnal, and covetous; and yet you join the churches and stand well with God's people by a hypocritical profession. O you whitewashed sepulchers! you would deceive even the very elect! You make clean the outside of the cup and platter, but your inward part is very wickedness. Oh, that a thundering voice might speak this to your ears!— "Those whom Christ loves are not of the world," but you are of the world; therefore you cannot be his even though you profess so to be; for those that love him are not such as you.

Look at Jesus' character, how different from every other man's—pure, perfect, spotless; even such should be the life of the believer. I plead not for the possibility of sinless conduct in Christians, but I must hold that grace makes men to differ, and that God's people will be very different from other kinds of people. A servant of God will be God's everywhere. As a chemist, he could not indulge in any tricks that such men might play with their drugs; as a grocer—if indeed it be not a phantom that such things are done—he could not mix sloe leaves with tea or red lead in the pepper; if he practiced any other kind of business, he could not for a moment condescend to the little, petty shifts called "methods of business." To him it is nothing what is called "business"; it is what is called God's law. He feels that he is not of the world; consequently, he goes against its fashions and its maxims. A singular story is told of a certain Quaker. One day he was bathing in the Thames, and a waterman called out to him, "Ha! there goes the Quaker." "How do you know I'm a Quaker?" "Because you swim against the stream; it is the way the Quakers always do." That is the way Christians always ought to do—to swim against the stream. The Lord's people should not go along with the rest in their worldliness. Their characters should be visibly different. You should be such men that your fellows can recognize you without any difficulty and say, "Such a man is a Christian." Ah! beloved, it would puzzle the angel Gabriel himself to tell whether some of you are Christians or not if he were sent down to the world to pick out the righteous from the wicked. None but God could do it, for in these days of worldly religion they are so much alike. It was an ill day for the world when the sons of God and the daughters of men were mingled together, and it is an ill day now when Christians and worldlings are so mixed that you cannot tell the difference between them. God save us from a day of fire that may devour us in consequence! But O beloved! the Christian will be always different from the world. This is a great doctrine, and it will be found as true in ages to come as in the centuries which are past. Looking back into history we read this lesson: "They are not of the world, even as I am not of the world." We see them driven to the catacombs of Rome; we see them hunted about like partridges; and wherever in history you find God's servants, you can recognize them by their distinct, unvarying character—they were not of the world, but were a people scarred and peeled, a people entirely distinct from the nations. And if in this age there are no different people, if there are none to be found who differ from other people, there are no Christians; for Christians will be always different from the world. They are not of the world, even as Christ is not of the world. This is the doctrine.

II. But now for treating this text *experimentally*.

Do we, dearly beloved, feel this truth? Has it ever been laid to our souls so that we can feel it is ours? "They are not of the world, even as I am not of the world." Have we ever felt that we are not of the world? Perhaps there is a believer sitting in a pew tonight who says, "Well, sir, I can't say that I feel as if I was not of the world, for I have just come from my shop, and worldliness is still hanging about me." Another says, "I have been in trouble and my mind is very much harassed—I can't feel that I am different from the world; I am afraid that I am of the world." But, beloved, we must not judge ourselves rashly because just at this moment we discern not the spot of God's children. Let me tell you, there are always certain testing moments when you can tell of what kind of stuff a man is made. Two men are walking. Part of the way their road lies side by side. How do you tell which man is going to the right and which to the left? Why, when they come to the turning point. Now, tonight is not a turning point, for you are sitting with worldly people here, but at other times we may distinguish.

Let me tell you one or two turning points when every Christian will feel that he is not of the world. One is, when he gets into very *deep trouble*. I do believe and protest that we never feel so unearthly as when we get plunged down into trouble. Ah! when some creature comfort has been swept away, when some precious blessing has withered in our sight like the fair lily snapped at the stalk, when some mercy has been withered like Jonah's gourd in the night—then it is that the Christian feels, "I am not of the world." His cloak is torn from him, and the cold wind whistles almost through him; and then he says, "I am a stranger in the world, as all my fathers were. Lord, you have been my dwelling place in all generations." You have had at times deep sorrows. Thank God for them! They are testing moments. When the furnace is hot, it is then that the gold is tried best. Have you felt at such a time that you were not of the world? Or have you rather sat down and said, "Oh! I do not deserve this trouble"? Did you break under it? Did you bow down before it and let it crush you while you cursed your Maker? Or did your spirit, even under its load, still lift itself unto him like a man all dislocated on the battlefield, whose limbs are cut away but who still lifts himself up as best he can and looks over the field to see if there be a friend approaching. Did you do so? Or did you lie down in desperation and despair? If you did that, I think you are no Christian; but if there was a rising up, it was a testing moment, and it proved that you were "not of the world" because you could master affliction; because you could tread it under foot and say,

When all created streams are dry,
His goodness is the same;
With this I well am satisfied
And glory in his name.

But another testing moment is *prosperity*. Oh! there have been some of God's people who have been more tried by prosperity than by adversity. Of the two trials, the trial of adversity is less severe to the spiritual man than that of prosperity. "As the fining pot for silver, so is a man to his praise." It is a terrible thing to be prosperous. You had need to pray to God, not only to help you in your troubles, but to help you in your blessings. Mr. Whitfield once had a petition to put up for a young man who had—stop, you will think it was for a young man who had lost his father or his property. No! "The prayers of the congregation are desired for a young man who has become heir to an immense fortune, and who feels he has need of much grace to keep him humble in the midst of riches." That is the kind of prayer that ought to be put up, for prosperity is a hard thing to bear. Now, perhaps you have become almost intoxicated with worldly delights, even as a Christian. Everything goes well with you; you have loved, and you are loved. Your affairs are prosperous; your heart rejoices, your eyes sparkle; you tread the earth with a happy soul and a joyous countenance; you are a happy man, for you have found that even in worldly things "godliness with contentment is great gain." Did you ever feel,

These can never satisfy;

Give me Christ, or else I die?

Did you feel that these comforts were nothing but the leaves of the tree and not the fruit, and that you could not live upon mere leaves? Did you feel they were after all nothing but husks? Or did you not sit down and say, "Now, soul, take your ease; 'Thou hast much goods laid up for many years; eat, drink, and be merry'"? If you did imitate the rich fool, then you were of the world; but if your spirit went up above your prosperity so that you still lived near to God, then you proved that you were a child of God, for you were not of the world. These are testing points: both prosperity and adversity.

Again, you may test yourselves in this way *in solitude and in company*. In solitude you may tell whether you are not of the world. I sit me down, throw the window up, look out on the stars, and think of them as the eyes of God looking down upon me! And oh! does it not seem glorious at times to consider the heavens when we can say, "Ah! beyond those stars is my house not made with hands; those stars are milestones on the road to glory, and I shall soon tread the glittering way, or be carried by seraphs far beyond them and be there"! Have you felt in solitude that you are not of the world? And so again in company? Ah! beloved, believe me, company is one of the best tests for a Christian. You are invited to an evening party. Sundry amusements are provided which are not considered exactly sinful, but which certainly cannot come under the name of pious amusements. You sit there with the rest; there is a deal of idle chat going on; you would be thought puritanical to protest against it. Have you not come away—and notwithstanding all has been very pleasant, and friends have been very agreeable—have you not been inclined to say, "Ah! that does not do for me. I would rather be in a prayer meeting; I would rather be in an old, broken-down cow lodge with six old women, so long as I could be with the people of God, than in fine rooms with all the dainties and delicacies that could be provided without the company of Jesus. By God's grace I will seek to shun all these places as much as possible." That is a good test. You will prove in this way that you are not of the world. And you may do so in a great many other ways which I have no time to mention. Have you felt this experimentally, so that you can say, "I know that I am not of the world; I see it; I experience it." Don't talk of doctrine. Give me doctrine ground into experience. Doctrine is good; but experience is better. Experimental doctrine is the true doctrine which comforts and which edifies.

IV. And now, lastly, we must briefly apply this in *practice*.

"They are not of the world, even as I am not of the world." And, first, allow me, man or woman, to apply this to you. You *who are of the world*, whose maxims, whose habits, whose behavior, whose feelings, whose everything is worldly and carnal, listen to this. Perhaps you make some profession of religion. Hear me, then. Your boasting of religion is empty as a phantom and shall pass away when the sun rises, as the ghosts sleep in their grave at the crowing of the cock. You have some pleasure in that professed religion of yours wherewith you are arrayed, and which you carry about you as a cloak and use as a stalking horse to your business, and a net to catch the honor in the world, and yet you are worldly, like other men. Then I tell you if there be no distinction between yourself and the worldly, the doom of the worldly shall be your doom. If you were marked and watched, your next-door tradesman would act as you do, and you act as he does; there is no distinction between you and the world. Hear me, then; it is God's solemn truth. You are none of his. If you are like the rest of the world, you are of the world. You are a goat and with goats you shall be cursed; for the sheep can always be distinguished from the goats by their appearance. O you worldly men of the world! you carnal professors, you who crowd our churches and fill our places of worship, this is God's truth! Let me say it solemnly. If I should say it as I ought, it would be weeping tears of blood. You are, with all your profession, "in the gall of bitterness"; with all your boastings, you are "in the bond of iniquity"; for you act as others, and you shall come where others come; and it shall be done with you as with more notorious heirs of hell.

There is an old story which was once told of a dissenting minister. The old custom was that a minister might stop at an inn and not pay anything for his bed or his board; and when he went to preach from place to place, he was charged nothing for the conveyance in which he rode. But on one occasion, a certain minister stopped at an inn and went to bed. The landlord listened and heard no prayer; so when he came down in the morning, he presented his bill. "Oh! I am not going to pay that, for I am a minister." "Ah!" said the landlord, "you went to bed last night like a sinner, and you shall pay this morning like a sinner; I will not let you go." Now, it strikes me that this will be the case with some of you when you come to God's bar. Though you pretended to be a Christian, you acted like a sinner, and you shall fare like a sinner too. Your actions were unrighteous; they were far from God; and you shall have a portion with those whose character was the same as yours. "Be not deceived"; it is easy to be so. "God is not mocked," though we often are, both minister and people. "God is not mocked: for whatsoever a man soweth, that shall he also reap."

And now we want to apply this to many *true children of God* who are here by way of caution. I say, my brother Christian, you are not of the world. I am not going to speak hardly to you because you are my brother, and in speaking to you I speak to myself also, for I am as guilty as you are. Brother, have we not often been too much like the world? Do we not sometimes in our conversation talk too much like the world? Come, let me ask myself, are there not too many idle words that I say? Yes, that there are. And do I not sometimes give occasion to the enemy to blaspheme because I am not so different from the world as I ought to be? Come, brother; let us confess our sins together. Have we not been too worldly? Ah! we have. Oh! let this solemn thought cross our minds: suppose that after all we should not be his! for it is written, "Ye are not of the world." O God! if we are not right, make us so; where we are a little right, make us still more right; and where we are wrong, amend us!

Allow me to tell a story to you. I told it when I was preaching last Tuesday morning, but it is worth telling again. There is a great evil in many of us being too light and frothy in our conversation. A very strange thing once happened. A minister had been preaching in a country village, very earnestly and fervently. In the midst of his congregation there was a young man who was deeply impressed with a sense of sin under the sermon; he therefore sought the minister as he went out in hopes of walking home with him. They walked till they came to a friend's house. On the road the minister had talked about anything except the subject on which he had preached, though he preached very earnestly, and even with tears in his eyes. The young man thought within himself, "Oh! I wish I could unburden my heart and speak to him, but I cannot. He does not say anything now about what he spoke of in the pulpit." When they were at supper that evening, the conversation was very far from what it should be, and the minister indulged in all kinds of jokes and light sayings. The young man had gone into the house with eyes filled with tears, feeling like a sinner should feel; but as soon as he got outside after the conversation, he stamped his foot and said, "It is a lie from beginning to end. That man has preached like an angel and now he has talked like a devil." Some years after the young man was taken ill and sent for this same minister. The minister did not know him. "Do you remember preaching at such-and-such a village?" asked the young man. "I do." "Your text was very deeply laid to my heart." "Thank God for that," said the minister. "Do not be so quick about thanking God," said the young man. "Do you know what you talked of that evening afterward, when I went to supper with you? *Sir, I shall be damned!* And I will charge *you* before God's throne with being the author of my damnation. On that night I did feel my sin, but you were the means of scattering all my impressions." That is a solemn thought, brother, and teaches us how we should curb our tongues, especially those who are so lighthearted after solemn services and earnest preachings that we should not betray levity. Oh! let us take heed that we are not of the world, even as Christ was not of the world.

And Christian, lastly, by way of practice, let me comfort you with this. You are not of the world for your home is in heaven. Be content to be here a little for you are not of the world, and you shall go up to your own bright inheritance by and by. A man in traveling goes into an inn; it is rather uncomfortable. "Well," says he, "I shall not have to stay here many nights; I have only to sleep here tonight. I shall be at home in the morning, so that I don't care much about one night's lodging being a little uncomfortable." So, Christian, this world is never a very comfortable one; but recollect, you are not of the world. This world is like an inn; you are lodging here only a little while. Put up with a little inconvenience because you are not of the world, even as Christ is not of the world; and by and by, up yonder, you shall be gathered into your father's house, and there you will find that there is a new heaven and a new earth provided for those who are "not of the world."

Believers Sent by Christ, as Christ Is Sent by the Father

Delivered on Lord's Day morning, May 11, 1890, at the Metropolitan Tabernacle, Newington. No. 2144.

"As thou hast sent me into the world, even so have I also sent them into the world."—JOHN 17:18

Here is a great fact mentioned, namely, that the Father sent the Son into the world. In this our Lord's disciples had believed. Jesus says himself, "They have believed that thou didst send me." It is one of the first essentials of saving faith to believe in Christ as the sent one of God. They had proved, in their own experience, that Jesus was sent of God; for they had found him to be sent to them. Especially they knew this because they had found in him eternal life. To them it had been life eternal "to know the only true God, and Jesus Christ, whom he had sent." They had entered into the possession of a new and heavenly life, and they rejoiced therein; so that to them the fact that God had sent his Son into the world was indisputable. It was a fact upon which they based their salvation. It was their hope, their joy, their theme of thought, and subject of converse. They declared it with the accent of assurance.

Our Lord based upon that fact another. He says to his Father, "As thou hast sent me into the world, even so have I also sent them into the world." As surely as Christ was sent into the world by the Father, so surely are the saints sent into the world by Christ. Note well, that I say "the saints." I mean not the apostles only, but all the saints. I dare not limit the reference to what are called ordained ministers or apostles, for I believe it includes all the chosen of God. Was the prayer, contained in this seventeenth chapter of John, for the apostles only? I think not. Surely our Lord prayed for all whom the Father had given to him and not for ministers only. Beyond question, our great Intercessor pleaded for all those whom the Father gave to him; and hence it is of all these that he speaks in the words of our text. He mentions not only the officers, but the rank and file of the chosen host who have been called by grace to know him as the Sent of God. He says to them all, without exception, "As my Father hath sent me, even so send I you." I do not for a moment dispute the need of a special call to the office of pastor or elder in the church of God, nor do I question that there are officers in the church of God upon whom peculiar responsibility rests; but no class of men may be exalted into a caste of Brahmins, who are alone sent into the world by the great Head of the church. We who spend our lives in teaching are your servants for Christ's sake; but we rejoice that you also have a high calling of God in Christ Jesus. If we have fuller knowledge of Scripture or larger gift of utterance, accept us as your fellow servants whose talents are cheerfully employed for your sakes; but if you have not these same talents, yet you have others, and you are equally given to Christ to be by him sent into the world.

This is no trifle, but a very solemn business. To our Lord it was a special matter of prayer. It is here in that prayer which always seemed to me to be the core of the whole Bible. Our Lord pleads not only about our being saved, but about our being sent. There is something here which deserves our deepest thought.

There are two petitions in our Lord's prayer which bear upon this. First comes the petition—"Holy Father, keep them." You cannot serve God unless he preserves you. You will never keep the Lord's flock unless he first shepherds you. The Lord of the vineyard must keep the keepers, or their vineyards will not be kept. The other prayer immediately precedes the text: "Sanctify them." You cannot go out into the world as the sent ones of Christ unless you are sanctified. God will use no unholy messenger; you must be consecrated and cleansed, devoted and dedicated to God alone, or else you will not have the first qualification for the divine mission. Christ's prayer is, "Sanctify them through thy truth." The more truth you believe, the more sanctified you will be. The operation of truth upon the mind is to separate a man from the world unto the service of God. Just in proportion as truth is given up, worldliness and frivolity are sure to prevail. A church which grows so enlightened as to neglect the doctrines of grace also falls in love with the vain amusements of the world. It has been so in all past ages, and it is sadly so today. But a church which, in a living way, holds fast the truth once for all delivered to the saints will also separate itself from the ways of the world: in fact, the world and the worldly church will shun it and push it into the place of separation. The more separated we are after our Master's fashion, the more fit shall we be to do his bidding.

Our Lord was evidently most careful as to our commission which he bases upon his own commission, and declares to be as certain and real as his own sending by the Father. He so values this that he prays, "[Father], keep them," and "[Father], sanctify them." May those two prayers be heard for us, and then we shall stand with our loins girt, our shoes on our feet, our lamps trimmed, and our lights burning, ready to go forth at the command of the Most High to the very ends of the earth. Our mission by Jesus grows out of his mission by the Father, and we may learn much about it by considering how the Father sent the Son to be the Savior of the world.

I. I would open up this subject by asking you, first, to *what our Lord's being sent involved to himself.*

To a large extent, there will be a parallel between his being sent and ours. The parallel is drawn by way of quality, not of equality. Christ's commission is on a higher scale than ours; for he was sent to be a propitiation and covenant-head, and so came into positions which it would be presumption for us to dream of occupying. Still, there is a likeness, though it be only that of a drop to the sea.

Our Lord's mission involved *complete subjection to the Father's will.* He said, "My Father is greater than I." This did not relate to his essential nature and dignity as God, but to the position which he took up in reference to the Father when he was sent to be our Savior. He that sends is greater than he that is sent. The Savior took up that subordinate position that he might do the Father's will. From that time forth, so long as he remained under his commission, he did not speak his own words nor do his own deeds; but he listened to the Father's will, and what the Father said to him he both spoke and did. That is exactly where you and I have to place ourselves now, deliberately and unreservedly. Our Lord sends us, and we are to be, in very deed, subordinate to his command in all things. We are no longer masters; we have become servants. Our will is lost in the will of our glorious superior. If we are ambitious and our ambition is guided by wisdom, it will take us down to that basin and the towel, and we shall be willing to wash the disciples' feet to show that we are sent by our condescending Lord. We shall henceforth have no respect unto our own dignity or interest but shall lay ourselves out to serve him to whom we belong. Whatsoever he says unto us we shall aim to do. Although we are sons of God, yet now we are also servants; and we would not do our own will but the will of him that sent us. Oh, to be sound on this point so as to yield our members in perfect obedience, and even bring every thought into subjection to Christ! Oh, to die to self and live in Christ! Can you drink of this cup, and be baptized with this baptism? I trust you can; and if so, you shall fulfill the errand upon which he sends you.

This meant for our Lord *the quitting of his rest.* He reigned in heaven, all angels paid him homage; but when the Father sent him, he left his high abode.

He was laid in the manger, for there was no room for him in the inn. Where the horned oxen fed, there must the holy child be cradled. The royalties of heaven are left behind; the rest which he enjoyed in the bosom of the Father must be renounced for toil and hunger and thirst and weariness and the death of the cross. Dear friends, you may serve the Lord, and yet be as happy as your Lord was; but if Jesus has sent you into the world you are not to seek ease or comfort; you are not even to make your own spiritual comfort the first object of your thought. How nice that evening at home would be! But you are sent, and, therefore, must turn out to win souls. How delightful it would be to read that book through, and to leave the class alone! But you must not, for you are sent to instruct and save. Henceforth you are to consider nothing but how you can answer the design of him who has sent you. Your aim must be to do the utmost possible for your Lord. The Christian who does much is still an idler if he could do more. We have never reached the point of diligence till we are doing all that lies in us and are even then wishing to do far more. Bought with his precious blood, the vows of the Lord are upon us, and we renounce our natural love of ease that we may please him who has sent us.

When sent of God, the Savior also had *to forgo even heaven itself*. He was here on earth the God-man, the Mediator, and he did not return to the splendor of his Father's court till he could say, "I have finished the work which you gave me to do. And now, O Father, glorify me." We must not sigh for heaven while so much is to be done on earth. The rest of glory will come soon, but just now we have to do with the work of grace. Let us stick to our work here below and do it thoroughly well, for our Lord has gone above and is preparing a place for us. Is it not wonderful how God even now denies himself for the salvation of men? Why does not our Lord come at once in his glory? Why do we not see the millennial reign begin? It is because of the long-suffering of God: he waits and puts off the closing scene because he is "not willing that any should perish, but that all should come to repentance." He keeps back even the glorious advent to give men space for salvation. That for which Jesus longs and the Spirit longs and the spouse longs is kept back in mercy to the guilty. The Bridegroom postpones his marriage day that men may be brought to him by the divine long-suffering. If Jesus can do this, surely we may well wait out of compassion to our fellowmen. Even our hope of being for ever with the Lord may wait a while. So long as there is another sinner for us to rescue, we will remain in this land of our exile. That is what our Lord means: the Father has sent me from heaven and kept me out of heaven for the sake of men; and even so shall I detain you among the tents of Kedar for a while that you may bring in my redeemed through the gospel.

The words of our text are, "As thou hast sent me *into the world*"; and this implies *affinity with men*. Our Lord was not sent to the edge of the world to look over the fence and converse hopefully from a distance, but he was sent right into the world. He took on him human nature and became bone of our bone. We read, "Then drew near unto him all the publicans and sinners for to hear him." He was a man among men. In this way Jesus has sent you, my brethren, into families, into offices, into establishments, into places where you labor for daily bread among a company of ungodly men. Do not cry out because you have thus to mingle with them. Your Lord was sent into the world, not, I say, to the outskirts of it nor to some elevated mountain high above it from which he might look down. He was sent into the world in an emphatic sense; and so are you sent, wisely sent, to tarry even among unconverted, infidel, and impure men that you may do for Christ his great work and make known his salvation.

He was sent into the world, and this involved *abiding in humiliation*. "The world knew him not," therefore the world knows us not because it knew him not. You are not sent into the world to be honored and pampered; nor even to receive your righteous due. If God aimed at your immediate glorification, he would take you to heaven; but he aims at your humiliation that you may be like his Firstborn. You are to have fellowship with the Only-begotten in many ways; and among the rest, you are to be partakers of his suffering. Expect to be misunderstood, misrepresented, belied, ridiculed, and so forth; for so was the Sent of the Father. You are to look for evil treatment; for as the Father sent his Son into a world which was sure to treat him ill, so has he sent you into the same world which will treat you in the same manner if you are like your Lord. Be not surprised at persecution, but look for it and take it as part of the covenant entail; for as Ishmael mocked Isaac, so will the seed after the flesh persecute that which is born according to promise.

In a word, your being sent of Christ involves *unreserved dedication to his work*. When Christ came into the world he did nothing but what his Father sent him to do. He had no secondary object of any sort. From the reservoir of his being, no little stream trickled away in waste, but the whole of it went to turn the great mill wheel of his life. The whole current and force of his nature went in one way, working out one design. Now, as the Father sent Jesus, so has Jesus sent you to be henceforth by occupation a Christian. You are to be consecrated wholly and alone to the one object for which Christ has set you apart. There may be other lawful objects, but these you render subsidiary to the one object of your life. You have but one eye, and that eye looks to your Lord. Henceforth you belong to Christ, body, soul, and spirit—from the morning light to the evening shade and through the night watches. There is not a hair of your head but what Jesus values, for he has put it down in the inventory— "the very hairs of your head are all numbered." Give him, then, every single power, however feeble; every part of your nature, however insignificant. Let your whole being be the Lord's, for "ye are not your own. For ye are bought with a price." "This is a high standard," says one. My brethren, it is none too high; and it is sad that any should think it so. God help you to know that you are sent and clearly to perceive what your mission involves. We, too, are missioned from above; we, too, are to have a hand in the saving of the world.

II. Secondly, having thus shown you the parallel so far, I now ask you to *consider why our Lord was sent into the world.*

Our Lord came here with one design. Christ was not sent to teach a correct system of philosophy. He was not Plato, but Jesus; not a sage, but a Savior. He could have solved the problems of the universe, but he did not even allude to them. He was not an Aristotle ruling the world of human thought, although he could have done so easily had he chosen. Blessed be his name, he came to save from sin; and this no Plato or Aristotle could have done. All the sages and philosophers put together are not worth so much as the little finger of a Christ. Christ entered into no rivalry with the academy; he came on a very different errand. Neither was our Lord sent to be an inventor or a discoverer. All the discoveries that have been made in modern times could have been at once revealed by him; but that was not his object, and he kept scrupulously to his one design. He could have told us the secret of the Dark Continent, but he was not sent for that end. He could have anticipated all that we have slowly learned and saved the world the long processes of experiment and observation, but this was not the object of his mission.

He did not come to be a conqueror. God gave us in him neither Alexander nor Caesar: of such slaughterers the world has always had enough and to spare. He conquers evil, but not by the sword. Our Lord did not come even to be a politician, a reformer of governments, a rectifier of social economics. There came one to him who said, "Master, speak to my brother, that he divide the inheritance with me." You might have supposed that the Lord would have arbitrated in that case; but he did not do so, for he said, "Who made me a judge or a divider over you?" He kept to his one business, and we shall be wise to do the same. Point me to a single instance in which he interfered with the government of Pilate or of Herod. Had he anything to say about the tyranny of Caesar? When he takes Caesar's penny in his hand, he simply says, "Render therefore unto Caesar the things which are Caesar's, and unto God the things that are God's." He was none of Caesar's, for he belonged to God and to God alone.

Should not Christian people take heed that they follow Christ in this unity of aim and purpose? This I know, I am not sent to preach to you any new philosophical system, nor to advocate any political party, nor to meddle with any of those social matters which can be better managed by others. It is mine to preach the gospel of the grace of God, and this one thing I do. If you can serve Christ and your fellowmen in any way, do it; but never get away from your one aim and purpose. If we are enabled to save men's souls by the Holy Ghost resting upon our teaching we may die content, even though we have left fifty other excellent things undone. There are enough of the dead to bury the dead. Burying the dead is a good work, but this will be a labor more congenial to the dead around us than to ourselves. Let us leave it to them. We cannot do everything. Let us do that which we are sent to do.

Oh, that every Christian would feel that, whatever else he would like to be, his first business is to be a servant of Christ. Your first concern is to serve Christ, and it ought to be your second thing to serve Christ. Then I would claim that it should be your third thing, and I shall get far on in numbers before I should allow any other character to take a leading position. May no possible object bear my comparison in your desires and endeavors in comparison with your resolve to glorify God your Savior!

Notice, further, that *our Lord was not sent to be ministered unto, but to minister.* I fear that many of his professed servants think they have been sent to be ministered unto. Their religion consists in coming to places of worship to be ministered unto. Through the week they would like to have very particular attention from the pastor and the church officers, and you hear them grumbling that they are not sufficiently looked after. Surely, they must have been sent, not to minister, but to be ministered unto. Brethren, let us give them as much as we can of our services, for they evidently need them; but Jesus was not sent to be visited and waited on and served. He came to minister to others; and he did so to the full and could truly say, "I am among you as he that serveth." Beloved friend, you know that it is more blessed to give than to receive; therefore feel it to be your joy to live as one who is sent by Jesus to be the servant of the church and the winner of souls.

Let us inquire what was Christ's work upon earth. It was, first, *to teach.* Wherever he went he was an instructor of the ignorant. He preached of the kingdom and of faith and of grace. We are to teach. "I do not know anything," says one. Then do not tell it, but first go to the Lord and ask him to teach you something; and as soon as ever you know the A B C of the gospel, go and teach somebody that A B C. You need not teach him D E F and G H I till you have advanced so far yourself, but teach all you are taught. Learn first; but when you have learned, then let others learn from you. This is what Jesus did. We need to be teaching the gospel everywhere.

Forget not that *he lived*, and his living was teaching. His actions were so many heads of his life's sermon. His every movement was instructive. He went about doing good. Make your life tally with your teaching, and make your life to be a part of your teaching; no, the best part of your discourse. The most solid and most emphatic teaching that comes from you should be what you do rather than what you say; and Christ has sent you into the world for that end.

Our Lord came also *to suffer for the cause of truth and righteousness*. If you follow him closely, you must expect to suffer also. Do not cry out about it as though some strange thing had happened unto you. Take joyfully the spoiling of your good name. If Christ has sent you forth like sheep in the midst of wolves, wonder not that the wolf gives you a bite or two: is it not his nature? Let the wolf howl, but do not trouble yourself about it; for what else should a wolf do? When pain and weakness and bodily infirmity seize on you, and you lie for days and weeks tossed with pain all through the sleepless nights, take it all patiently and say, "I am sent to show patience, that men may see what grace can do."

You are sent *to save men*. It is true that you have not to redeem them by blood, that the Lord has done most effectually. You have not to suffer as a substitute, for his one sacrifice has sufficed; but you are sent to seek and to save that which was lost by proclaiming salvation by Christ Jesus. Every man who is saved himself should feel that he is called at once to labor for the salvation of others. Your election is not only election to personal salvation, but to personal service. You are chosen that, through your being saved, others may be called into the like felicity. View this very clearly and get it fixed in your minds, and then carry it out in your daily lives.

"Ah!" say you, "our Lord might very well give himself up to his work; for if he had not done so, the whole world must have perished." Listen! *Your work also is indispensable*. How is the work of Christ to be made effectual among the sons of men for their salvation? Must they not hear it that they may believe it? How shall they hear without a preacher? I venture to say that as the salvation of man depended upon Christ, so, in another sense, the salvation of men at this hour depends upon the church of God. If believers do not go and preach Christ, who will? If you that love him do not commend him, who will? Do you think that the Houses of Parliament will ever meet together to consider the evangelization of the heathen? If the government did take such work in hand, it could do nothing, for it is not a fit agent, and it would hinder rather than help the good design. Do you think the worldlings, the skeptics, the critics will ever unite to spread the kingdom of Christ and save the souls of men? Do not dream it. If the church of God does not go forth on her holy errand, nothing will be done. "But it might be done by angels," says one. I know it might, but "unto the angels hath he not put in subjection the world to come, whereof we speak." He has committed unto us the word of reconciliation, even to us who are men; and we must attend to it or great guilt will be upon us.

I should like every Christian to feel that he has to be the instrument of salvation to certain persons. It is all allotted; the whole country is measured and divided, and we have each our portion, which we must conquer for our Lord. If I belong to the tribe of Judah, I have to help my brethren to drive out the Canaanites from our portion. If you belong to the tribe of Issachar or Benjamin, you must look to your own allotment and clear it of the enemy. Joshua is the leader, but every Israelite is in his army. Christ has power over all flesh as the head of the body, and he has given to each of his members a portion of his power, so that each member of his body has power over some portion of the "all flesh"; and that power must be used in the giving of eternal life to as many as the Father has given to Jesus. God grant that you may feel this and may go to your work as Christ went to his!

III. This leads me a little further, and I now invite you to *consider how our Lord came*; for this will show us how we ought to go forward when we are sent.

First, our Lord came *with alacrity*. The work of our Redeemer was no forced work. He was sent, but he willingly came.

Down from the shining seats above
With joyful haste he fled.

"Lo, I come to do thy will, O God," said he. He came cheerfully among the sons of men. You that are sent of Christ must always go gladly to your service; never look as if you were driven to the field like oxen which love not the plow. God does not delight in a slavish spirit. If we serve Christ because of the yoke of duty, we shall serve badly; but when our service is our pleasure, when we thank God that to us is this grace given that we should "preach among the Gentiles the unsearchable riches of Christ," then we shall labor wisely, zealously, and acceptably.

Next, our Lord came *with authority*. The Lord God had sent him. He had the Father at his back. Be sure that, when Jesus sends you, you are invested with authority, and they that despise you do it at their peril. Your blunders and mistakes are not authorized; but so far as you speak his Word with a desire for his glory, he that receives you receives Christ, even as our Lord said, "He that receiveth me receiveth him that sent me." God is with you, be not afraid; your Lord will not let your words fall to the ground.

Our Lord came *with ability* too. What did his ability consist in? Mainly in this—"The Spirit of the Lord is upon me, because he hath anointed me." This is also where your sufficiency must be found, and you can have as much as you please of it. You cannot get every faculty of the brain, but you can have every influence of the Spirit. It may be you cannot reach the highest form of education or of utterance, but these things are not vital. God can speak by your stammering tongue, even as in the case of Moses. You shall do the Lord's work, and do it well, if you are anointed of the Holy Ghost. He who does Christ's work in Christ's power works an abiding work which will eternally glorify God. He who sends us out into the world to carry the gospel to every creature will give us grace to obey his bidding.

Our Lord came *with absorption*. Jesus came, as I have said before, to do what he was sent to do and nothing else. He meddled with nothing beyond his vocation. Every thought of his manhood, every power of his Godhead, he devoted to fulfilling the errand on which he came. His zeal had eaten him up. He was covered with it as with a cloak. The man Christ was all on fire, and all on fire with one desire, that he might finish the work which his Father had given him to do. For this joy he endured the cross, despising the shame.

Our Lord came *with abiding resolve* to go through with his mission to the end. He never thought of going back. He steadfastly set his face to go to Jerusalem. He pressed through shame, through death to accomplish our redemption. In these days we shall not do much unless we have a desperate determination to persevere in the teeth of difficulties. Those who can go back will go back. Remember how Gideon proclaimed throughout the host that if any man was fainthearted he might go home; so do we proclaim today: go home if you are wavering. If you do not love Christ enough to be resolved to serve him to the last, what is the good of you? You will break down and lose us the victory at some important crisis. He that has been bought with the blood of Christ and knows it, feels that he must endure to the end, for only he that endures to the end shall be saved. We go because our Lord's sending constrains us. "Woe is unto me, if I preach not the gospel!" Woe is unto you if you do not teach the children or speak to individuals or write letters or in some way fulfill your mission!

IV. Bear with me a little, while I bid you *consider how our Lord behaved as the Sent One.* Oh, that we may learn from him how to fulfill our own mission!

Our Lord *began early.* While he was yet a youth, he said, "Wist Know ye not that I must be about my Father's business?" As soon as ever a man is converted, he should inquire, "Lord, what will you have me to do?" Young believer, do not let many weeks pass over your head before you have attempted somewhat for your Lord. I will correct that exhortation. I wish you would not let a single day pass away without your bearing testimony for your Master.

But, next, *our Lord waited very patiently.* He was thirty years old before he preached openly. We do not know all that he did in the workshop at Nazareth. Is it not possible that he supported his widowed mother by his hand-labor? We do not know; but of this we are sure, that it is the duty of many young men to look after their parents first. It is the duty of all to "show piety at home." Many Christian women will have done well if they have carried out home duties. She was a holy woman upon whose grave they placed this epitaph, "She made home happy." This is what Jesus did for the first thirty years of his life. He was doing the Father's will when he was a young man at home. Though he did not preach, yet while he was working and learning he was carrying out the purpose for which he was sent.

When the time came for him to commence his more public service, *he sought proper entrance* into it. He did not blunder into God's work by a rush and a leap, but he went to John to be baptized and to be publicly recognized as the Messiah. John was the porter, and he opened the gate to the Good Shepherd, who came in by the door and did not climb up some other way. He came to John, who represented the prophetic chair of the Jewish church, and so he entered into his work as minister in a lawful and proper way. I like our young friends, when they feel their time has come for public service, to begin in right style and due order, carrying out the Lord's mind in the Lord's way. Willfulness in beginning may throw a man out of gear as to his future work; and it argues a spirit ill prepared for acceptable service.

That being passed, *see how he labored at his work.* He was always doing the Father's will. He worked all the day, every day, everywhere, with everybody. Some Christian people can render only occasional service. They are very good at a convention. They save up their holiness for meetings. At a religious gathering they are in fine form, but they are not everyday saints. The kind of person the church needs most is the maid-of-all-work, the worker who can turn his hand to anything which providence allots him and is glad to do so, however humbling it may be. My venerated grandmother owned a set of choice china, which is, I believe part of it, in existence now. Why does it exist now? It has seen little service. It came out only on high-days and holidays— say once in six months when ministers and friends came to tea. It was a very nice set of old china—too good for children to break. Some Christians are like that fine old ware: it would not do to use them too often. They are too good for every day. They do not teach their servants and try to win the poor people in their own neighborhood to Christ; but they talk well at a conference. O you fine bits of egg-shell china, I know you! Don't fear. I am not going to break you. Yet I would somewhat trouble you by the remark that in the case of such ware as you are, more pieces get broken in the cupboard than on the table. You will last all the longer if you get to work for Christ in everyday work. Jesus was not sent out for particular occasions, and neither are you. We use our Lord for a thousand hallowed purposes, and even so will he use us from time to time, if we are but ready and willing.

Notice about our Lord's service that *his prayers always kept pace with his work*. This is where most of us fail. When our Lord had a long day's work, we find him taking a long night's prayer. "I have so much to do," says one, "that I could not be long in prayer." That is putting the case the wrong way upward. When you have most to do, you have most need to pray; and unless you keep up the proportion, your offering will fail in quality. The holy incense was sweet before God because in that sacred compound there was a proportion of each spice; and so in our lives there must be a due measure of Word and work and prayer and praise. I may say of prayer what one said of salt in the Scripture, "Salt without prescribing how much." Prayer can never be in excess. You can salt meat too much, but you cannot salt your service too much with prayer. If you are accustomed to pray in your walk and works, at all hours and seasons, you do not err. There never will be in any of us a superfluity of devotion. God help you to be like his Son who, though he was sent and had the Father with him, yet could not live without prayer. May you not only feel your need of prayer, but fill up that need abundantly!

Once more, in all that Jesus did *he remained in constant fellowship with the Father*. He said, "He that sent me is with me." That is a beautiful sentence. Let me repeat it—"He that sent me is with me." The great Father had never to call to Jesus and say, "Come nearer. You are departing from me. You are too busy with Mary and Lazarus and Peter and John, and so you are forgetting me." No, no. He did always the things that pleased God, and he was always in communion with the great Father in everything that he did. "Ah!" says one, "it is hard to commune with God and be very busy." Yes, but it will prove harder still to have been very busy and not to have dwelt with God. It is easy to do much when you walk with God, and easier still to make a great fuss and do nothing because the Lord is away. To get near omnipotence will not make you omnipotent, but it will make you feel omnipotence working with you. Oh, that we might thus dwell with God as Jesus did; for he has sent us for this even as the Father sent him.

I would leave with you four words. We are sent; therefore, whenever we try to press Christ upon men *we are not guilty of intrusion*. We have sometimes known strangers asked in this place about their souls by certain of our friends, and they have grown angry at such a question. This is very silly of them, is it not? But I hope the friend who meets with an angry answer will not be at all hurt. You are not intrusive, though the angry person says you are. You are sent, and where Jesus sends you, you have a right to go. The postman frequently knocks at the door as late as ten o'clock. I suppose you want to be asleep. Do you cry out—"How dare you make that noise"? No, he is the postman, an officer of Her Majesty, and he is sent out with the last mail and must deliver the letters. You cannot blame him for doing that for which he is sent. Go you and knock at the doors of the careless and the sleepy. Give them a startling word. Do not let them perish for want of a warning or an invitation. Go on without fear; your commission is your warrant. If Jesus has sent you, you have a right to speak even to princes and kings.

Next, we are sent; therefore, *we dare not run away*. If Jesus bids us go forward, we must not retreat. If what we have preached and taught be of God, if we are ridiculed for it, let us take no notice, but steam ahead. Put more coals in the furnace, get the steam up, and go faster than ever in the same course. We defy the devil to stop us, for we are sent.

Next, we are sent; therefore, *we are sure to be helped*. Our King never sends a servant on an errand at his own charges. *Our* own power fails us, but he never allows *his* power to fail us when engaged in his service. Those who are sent shall be sustained.

But, if we are sent, remember lastly, *we have to give in an account*. Our Lord does not call for the time sheet every night, but a time sheet is kept all the same; and there will be a day for passing in the checks, and we shall have to answer for what we have done. I speak not now to you ungodly ones, whose account will be terrible at that last great day. God save you! May you believe on him whom God has sent! But now I speak to Christian people: you will have to render in your account, and may God grant you may not have to make a lamentable return in this fashion—"On such a day so much wood, and on such a day so much hay, and on such a day so much stubble." Let there be down in your book nothing but gold, silver, and precious stones, for it must all be tried with fire; and if you yourself are saved and your work is burned up, you will suffer loss. What pain to find your life's work to be a lot of wood, hay, and stubble which will blaze furiously and die out in ashes! You know what I mean: so much time spent in planning frivolous amusements for the people, so much talent expended in teaching what is not the gospel, so much zeal consumed upon matters which do not concern eternal things, all this will burn. Beloved, do your Master's work, win souls, preach Christ, expound your Bibles, pray men to be reconciled to God, plead with men to come to Christ. This kind of work will stand the fire; and when the last great day shall dawn, this will remain to glory and honor. God bless you, brethren, for Christ's sake!

"I Will"; yet, "Not as I Will"

Intended for reading on Lord's Day, September 2, 1894; delivered on Lord's Day evening, July 1, 1883, at the Metropolitan Tabernacle, Newington. No. 2376.

"Father, I will."—JOHN 17:24

"Not as I will."—MATTHEW 26:39

We have here two prayers uttered by the same Person; yet there is the greatest possible contrast between them. How different men are at different times! Yet Jesus was always essentially the same: "the same yesterday, and today, and for ever." Still, his mood and state of mind varied from time to time. He seemed calmly happy when he prayed with his disciples and said, "Father, I will that they also, whom thou hast given me, be with me where I am; that they may behold my glory, which thou hast given me"; but he was in agony when in Gethsemane, having withdrawn from his disciples and fallen on his face, he prayed, saying, "O my Father, if it be possible, let this cup pass from me: nevertheless not as I will, but as thou wilt." It is the same man, and an unchangeable Man, too, as to his essence, who uttered both prayers; yet see how different were his frames of mind, and how different the prayers he offered.

Brother, you may be the same man, and quite as good a man, when you are groaning before God as when you are singing before him. There may be more grace even in the submissive "Not as I will" than in the triumphant "Father, I will." Do not judge yourselves to have changed in your standing before God because you have undergone an alteration as to your feelings. If your Master prayed so differently at different times, you, who have not the fullness of grace that he had, must not wonder if you have a great variety of inward experiences.

Notice, also, that it was not only the same Person, but that he used these two expressions almost at the same time. I do not know how many minutes— I had better say minutes rather than hours—intervened between the last supper, and the wonderful high-priestly prayer, and the agonizing cries of Gethsemane. I suppose that it was only a short walk from Jerusalem to the olive garden, and that it would not occupy long to traverse the distance. At one end of the walk, Jesus prays, "Father, I will"; and at the other end of it, he says, "Not as I will." In like manner, we may undergo great changes and have to alter the tone of our prayers in a few minutes. You prayed just now with holy confidence; you took firm hold of the covenant angel and with wrestling Jacob you said, "I will not let thee go, except thou bless me"; and yet it may be equally becoming on your part within an hour to lie in the very dust and in an agony to cry unto the Lord, "Pardon my prayers, forgive me that I was too bold, and hear me now as I cry to you and say, 'Not as I will, but as thou wilt.'"

If but my fainting heart be blest
With thy sweet Spirit for its guest,
My God, to thee I leave the rest;
Thy will be done!

Never be ashamed because you have to mend your prayers; be careful not to make a mistake if you can help it; but, if you make one, do not be ashamed to confess it and to correct it as far as you can. One of our frequent mistakes is that we wonder that we make mistakes. Whenever a man says, "I should never have thought that I could have done such a foolish thing as that," it shows that he did not really know himself; for had he known himself, he would rather have wondered that he did not do worse, and he would have marveled that he acted as wisely as he did. Only the grace of God can teach us how to run our prayers down the scale from the high note of "Father, hear me, for you have said, 'Ask what thou wilt,'" right down to the deep, deep bass of "Father . . . not as I will, but as thou wilt."

I must further remark that these two prayers were equally characteristic of Christ. I think that I should know my Lord by his voice in either of them. Who but the eternal Son of God may dare to say, "Father, I will"? There speaks Incarnate Deity; that is the sublime utterance of the well-beloved Son. And yet who could say as he said it, "If it be possible, let this cup pass from me: nevertheless not as I will, but as thou wilt"? Perhaps you have uttered those words, dear friend; but in your case they were not concerning such a cup of woe as Christ emptied. There were but a few drops of gall in your cup. His was all bitterness from the froth to the dregs; all bitterness, and such bitterness as, thank God, you and I can never taste! That cup he has drained to the dregs, and we shall not have to drink one drop from it; but it was of that cup that he said—and I detect the voice of the Son of God, the Son of man, in that brief utterance—"Not as I will, but as thou wilt."

My two texts make up a strange piece of music. Blessed are the lips that know how to express the confidence that rises to the height as far as we can go with Christ, and descends even to the deeps as far as we can go with him in full submission to the will of God. Does anybody say that he cannot understand the contrast between these two prayers? Dear friend, it is to be explained thus. There was a difference of position in the Suppliant on these two occasions. The first prayer, "Father, I will," is the prayer of our great High Priest with all his heavenly garments on—the blue and purple and fine twined linen, and the pomegranates and the golden bells and the breastplate with the twelve precious stones bearing the names of his chosen people. It is our great High Priest, in the glory of his majestic office and power, who says to God, "Father, I will." The second Suppliant is not so much the Priest as the Victim. Our Lord is there seen bound to the altar, about to feel the sacrificial knife, about to be consumed with the sacrificial fire; and you hear him as though it were a lamb bleating, and the utterance is, "Not as I will, but as thou wilt." The first petition is the language of Christ in power pleading for us; the second is the utterance of Christ made sin for us that we might be made the righteousness of God in him. That is the difference of position that explains the contrast in the prayers.

Let me tell you also that there is a difference in the subject of his supplication, which is full of instruction. In the first prayer where our Lord says so majestically, "Father, I will," he is pleading for his people, he is praying for what he knows to be the Father's will, he is officiating there before God as the very mouthpiece of God, and speaking of something about which he is perfectly clear and certain. When you are praying for God's people, you may pray very boldly. When you are pleading for God's cause, you may speak very positively. When you know you are asking what is definitely promised in the Scriptures as part of the covenant ordered in all things and sure, you may ask without hesitation as our Lord did. But, in the second case, Jesus was praying for himself: "If it be possible, let this cup pass from me." He was praying about a matter concerning which he did not, as man, know the Father's will, for he says, "If it be possible." There is an "if" in it: "If it be possible, let this cup pass from me." Whenever you go upstairs in an agony of distress and begin to pray about yourself and about a possible escape from suffering, always say under such circumstances, "Nevertheless not as I will, but as thou wilt." It may be given you sometimes to pray very boldly even in such a case as that; but, if it is not given you, take care that you do not presume. I may pray for healing for my body, but not with such confidence as I pray for the prosperity of Zion and the glory of God. That which has to do with myself I may ask as a child of God asks of his Father; but I must ask submissively, leaving the decision wholly in his hands, feeling that, because it is for myself rather than for him,

I must say, "Nevertheless not as I will, but as thou wilt." I think that there is a plain lesson here for Christians to take heed that, while they are very confident on one subject for which they pray, they are equally submissive on another, for there is a heavenly blending in the Christian character, as there was in Christ's character, a firm confidence and yet an absolute yielding to the will of God, let that will be what it may.

> *Lord, my times are in thy hand;*
> *All my sanguine hopes have plann'd,*
> *To thy wisdom I resign,*
> *And would make thy purpose mine.*

Now all this while you may say that I have only been going around the text. Very well; but, sometimes, there is a good deal of instruction to be picked up around a text. The manna fell around about the camp of Israel; peradventure there is some manna around about this text. May the Lord help every one of us to gather his portion!

I want you now, for a few minutes, to view this great Suppliant in the two moods in which he prayed, "Father, I will," and "Not as I will," and then to combine the two. We will, first, view *Jesus in the power of his intercession;* next, we will talk of *Jesus in the power of his submission;* and in the third place, we will try to *combine the two prayers,* "I will"; yet, "Not as I will."

I. First, let us view Jesus *in the power of his intercession,* saying, "Father, I will."

Whence did he derive that power? Who enabled him thus to speak with God and say, "Father, I will"? First, *Jesus prayed in the power of his Sonship.* Sons may say to a father what strangers may not dare to say; and such a Son as Jesus was—so near to his Father's heart, one who could say, "The Father hath not left me alone; for I do always those things that please him"; one of whom the Father had said, "This is my beloved Son, in whom I am well pleased"—well might he have power with God so as to be able to say, "Father, I will."

Next, he derived this power from *the Father's eternal love to him.* Did you notice how, in the very verse from which our text is taken, Jesus says to his Father, "Thou lovedst me before the foundation of the world"? We cannot conceive what the love of the Father is to Christ Jesus his Son. Remember, they are one in essence. God is one—Father, Son, and Holy Spirit; and as the Incarnate God, Christ is unspeakably dear to the Father's heart. There is nothing about him of which the Father disapproves; there is nothing lacking in him which the Father would desire to see there. He is God's ideal of himself: "In him dwelleth all the fullness of the godhead bodily." Well may one who is the subject of his Father's eternal love be able to say, "Father, I will."

But *our Lord Jesus also based this prayer upon his finished work.* I grant you that he had not yet actually died, but in the certain prospect of his doing so he had said to his Father, "I have glorified thee on the earth: I have finished the work which thou gavest me to do." Now he has actually finished it; he has been able in the fullest sense to say, "It is finished," and he has gone up to take his place in glory at his Father's side. You remember the argument with which Paul begins his Epistle to the Hebrews: "God, who at sundry times and in divers manners spake in time past unto the fathers by the prophets, hath in these last days spoken unto us by his Son, whom he hath appointed heir of all things, by whom also he made the worlds; who being the brightness of his glory, and the express image of his person, and upholding all things by the word of his power, when he had by himself purged our sins, sat down on the right hand of the Majesty on high; being made so much better than the angels, as he hath by inheritance obtained a more excellent name than they. For unto which of the angels said he at any time, Thou art my Son, this day have I begotten thee? And again, I will be to him a Father, and he shall be to me a Son?" When the Father looks at Christ, he sees in him atonement accomplished, satisfaction presented, sin annihilated, the elect redeemed, the covenant ratified, the everlasting purpose settled on eternal foundations. O beloved, since Christ has magnified God's law and made it honorable, and since he has poured out his soul unto death, he may well possess the power to say, "Father, I will."

Remember, too, that *Jesus still possesses this power,* and possesses it for you and for me. O my dear hearers, you may well go to Christ and accept him as your Mediator and Intercessor since all this power to say "Father, I will" is laid up in him on purpose for poor believing sinners who come and take him to be their Savior! You say that you cannot pray. Well, he can; ask him to plead for you. I thank God that, sometimes, when we do not ask him to plead for us, he does it all the same as he did for Peter when Satan had desired to have him, but Christ had prayed for him. Peter did not know his danger, but the Savior did, and he pleaded for him at once. What a blessing it is to think of Christ, clothed with divine authority and power, using it all for us! Well does Toplady sing,

With cries and tears he offer'd up
His humble suit below;
But with authority he asks,
Enthroned in glory now.

For all that come to God by him,
Salvation he demands;
Points to their names upon his breast,
And spreads his wounded hands.
His covenant and sacrifice
Give sanction to his claim;
Father, I will that all my saints
Be with me where I am.

Further, that power of Christ will land every believer in heaven. Notice how Christ turns all his pleading with God that way; he says, "Father, I will, that they also, whom thou hast given me, be with me where I am; that they may behold my glory." The devil says that we shall never get to heaven; but we remember that declaration of Moses, "Thine enemies shall be found liars unto thee," and the archenemy will be found to be the arch-liar, for the Lord's Prayer will be heard. As he pleads that those whom the Father gave him should be brought up to be with him where he is, you may depend upon it that they will all arrive safely in heaven; and you, if you are among those who are given to Christ—and you may know that by your faith in him—shall be among that blessed company.

I shall have finished with this first point when I have said this, *that power which Christ had may, in a measure, be gained by all his people.* I dare not say, and I would not say, that any one of us will ever be able to utter our Savior's words, "Father, I will"; but I do say this: if you abide in Christ, and his words abide in you, you may attain to such power in prayer that you shall ask what you will, and it shall be done unto you. This is not a promise to all of you; no, not even to all of you who are God's people; but only to those of you who live wholly unto God and serve him with all your heart. You can, by an established relationship with God, attain to such power with the Most High that men shall say of you what they used to say of Luther, "There goes a man who can ask what he likes of God and have it." You may attain to that glorious altitude. Oh, I would that every one of us would seek to reach this height of power and blessing! It is not the feeble Christian, it is not the worldly Christian who has just enough grace to make him miserable, the man who has only about enough grace to keep him from being absolutely immoral; that is not the man who will prevail with God. You paddlers in Christianity who scarcely wet your toes, you who never go in beyond your ankles or your knees, God will never give you this privilege unless you go in for it. Get where the waters are deep enough to swim in and plunge in. Be perfectly consecrated to God;

yield your whole lives to his glory without reserve; then may you obtain something of your Master's power in prayer when he said, "Father, I will."

II. Now I ask you kindly to accompany me, in the second place, to notice *Jesus in the power of his submission.*

Our second text is all submission: "Not as I will." This utterance, "Not as I will," proved that *the shrinkings of Christ's nature from that dreadful cup were all overcome.* I do not believe that Christ was afraid to die; do you believe that? Oh no; many of his servants have laughed at death. I am sure that he was not afraid to die; what was it, then, that made that cup so awfully terrible? Jesus was to be made sin for us, he was to come under the curse for us, he was to feel the Father's wrath on account of human guilt; and his whole nature, not alone his flesh, but his whole being shrank from that fearful ordeal. It was not actual defilement that was to come upon him, but it looked like it; and as man, he could not tell what that cup of wrath must contain.

> *Immanuel, sunk with dreadful woe,*
> *Unfelt, unknown to all below—*
> *Except the Son of God*
> *In agonizing pangs of soul,*
> *Drinks deep of wormwood's bitterest bowl,*
> *And sweats great drops of blood.*

After dwelling in the love of God from all eternity, he was in a few hours to bear the punishment of man's sin; yet he must bear it, and, therefore, he said, "Not as I will, but as thou wilt." Do you wonder that he prayed, "If it be possible, let this cup pass from me"? Is Christ to be blamed for these shrinkings of nature? My dear friends, if it had been a pleasure to him and he had had no shrinkings, where would have been his holy courage? If it had not been a horrible and dreadful thing to him, where would have been his submission, where would have been the virtue that made atonement of it? If it had been a thing that he could not, or must not, shrink from, where would have been the pain, the wormwood, and the gall of it? The cup must be, in the nature of things, something from which he that bears it must shrink, or else it could not have been sufficient for the redemption of his people and the vindication of the broken law of God. It was necessary, then, that Christ should, by such a prayer as this, prove that he had overcome all the shrinkings of his nature.

"Not as I will" is also an evidence of *Christ's complete submission to the will of his Father.* "He is brought as a lamb to the slaughter, and as a sheep before her shearers is dumb, so he openeth not his mouth." There is no resistance, no struggling, he gives himself up completely. "There," he seems to say to the Lord, "do what you will with me; I yield myself absolutely to your will." There was on Christ's part no reserve, no wish even to make any reserve. I go further and say that Jesus willed as God willed, and even prayed that the will of God, from which his human nature at first shrank, might be fulfilled. "Nevertheless not as I will, but as thou wilt."

O brothers and sisters—for you both need this grace—pray God to help you to learn how to *copy your Lord in total submission!* Have you submitted to the Lord's will? Are you submitting now? Are not some of you like bullocks unaccustomed to the yoke? There is a text, you know, in the one hundred and thirty-first Psalm, "My soul is even as a weaned child." I have sometimes thought that, for some of the Lord's children, the passage would have to be read, "My soul is even as a weaning child," and there are many of God's people who are very long in the weaning. You cannot get satisfaction and quiet and contentment, can you? Can you give yourself up entirely to God that he may do whatever he likes with you? Have you some fear of a tumor or a cancer? Is there before you the prospect of a painful and dangerous operation? Is business going badly with you so that you will probably lose everything? Is a dear child sickening? Is the mother likely to be taken away? Will you have to lose your position and reputation if you are faithful to the Lord? Will you be exposed to cruel slanders? Will you probably be cast out of your situation if you do what is right? Come now, whatever you dread or expect, can you give yourself up wholly to God and say, "It is the LORD, let him do what seemeth him good"? Your Lord and Master did so; he said, "Not as I will." Oh, that he might teach you this divine art of absolute resignation to the purpose and ordinance of God till you also should be able to say, "Not as I will"! Thus you will sing,

I bow me to thy will, O God,
And all thy ways adore;
And every day I live I'll seek
To please thee more and more.

III. I'll have finished my discourse when I have just twisted these two sayings together a little; so, thirdly, let us *combine the two prayers*: "I will"; yet, "Not as I will."

First, let me say, *Number One will help you very much to Number Two.* If you learn to pray with Christ, with the holy boldness that almost says, "Father, I will," you are the man who will know how to say, "Not as I will." Is it not strange that it should be so? It looks like a contradiction; but I am sure that it is not so. The man who can have his will with God is the very man who does not want his own way with God. He who may have what he likes is the man who wishes to have what God likes. You remember the good old woman who lay near to death, and one said to her, "Do you not expect soon to die?" She answered, "I do not know whether I shall live or die; and what is more, I have no concern which way it is." Then the friend asked, "But if you had your choice whether you should live or die, which would you choose?" She replied, "I would rather that the Lord's will should be done." "But suppose the Lord's will were to leave it entirely to you to choose whichever you liked?" "Then," she said, "I would kneel down and pray the Lord to choose for me." And I do think that is the best way to live; not to have any choice at all, but to ask the Lord to choose for you. You can always have your way, you know, when your way is God's way. The sure way to carry out self-will is when self-will is nothing else but God's will. Oh, that the Lord would teach us this mighty power with him in prayer! It will not be given without much close fellowship with him. Then, when we know that we can have what we will of him, we shall be in the right state to say, "Not as I will."

The next remark that I would make is, that *Number Two is needful for Number One;* that is to say, until you can say, "Not as I will," you never will be able to say, "Father, I will." I believe that one reason why people cannot prevail in prayer is because they will not yield to God; and they cannot expect God to yield to them. God does this and that with you, and you quarrel with him; and then you go upstairs and begin to pray. Go down on your knees and make your peace with him first; for if you must not come to the altar till you have become reconciled unto your brother, how can you come to the throne of grace till you have given up your quarrel with God? But some people are never at peace with God. I have heard of a good friend who lost a child, and he was wearing mourning several years afterward. He was always fretting about the dear child, till a Quakeress said to him, "What! have you not forgiven God yet?" and there are some people who have not yet forgiven God for taking their loved ones. They ought always to have blessed him, for he never takes away any but those whom he lent to us, and we should bless his name as much for taking them again as for lending them to us. Dear friends, you must submit to the will of God or else you cannot have power with him in prayer. "Well," say you, "you will not let me have my own way at all." Certainly, I will not let you have your own way; but when you just say, "There, Lord, I have no quarrel with you now; do what you will with me," then he will say, "Rise, my child, ask what you will, and I will give it you; open your mouth wide, and I will fill it."

Notice, also, dear friends, that *Jesus will help us to have Number One and Number Two.* He gives himself over to us to teach us the power of prevailing prayer, but he also gives himself over to teach us the art of blessed submission in prayer; and it is his will that these two should not be separated. "Father, I will" is Christ's word on our behalf; and "Not as I will" is equally Christ's word on our behalf. When you cannot pray either of these prayers as you would, fall back upon Christ's prayer and claim it as your own.

Lastly, I think that *true sonship will embody both Number One and Number Two.* It is the true child of God who knows that he is his Father's child, who says, "Father, I will." He is often very bold where another would be presumptuous. Oh, I have heard full often of somebody's prayers—I will not say who the somebody is—he seemed so familiar with God in his prayer. Oh yes; I know! You love those very stately prayers in which the bounds are set about the mount and no man may dare to come near. You make the throne of grace to be like Sinai was of old, of which the Lord said, "Whosoever toucheth the mount shall be surely put to death: there shall not an hand touch it, but he shall surely be stoned, or shot through; whether it be beast or man, it shall not live." "Oh, but," you say, "so-and-so is so familiar at the mercy seat!" Yes, I know; and you think that is a pity, do you not? Perhaps you are acquainted with a judge; look at him on the bench wearing his wig and robe of office; but you will not dare to speak to him there unless you address him as "My lord," and behave very respectfully to him. By and by he goes home, and he has a little boy there, Master Johnny. Why, the child has seized hold of his father's whiskers, there he is up on his father's back! "Why, Johnny, you are disrespectful!" "Oh, but he is my father!" says the boy; and his father says, "Yes, Johnny, that I am; and I do not want you to say, 'My lord,' and talk to me as they do in the court." So, there are certain liberties which God's children may take with him which he counts no liberties at all; but he loves so to be treated by them. He will let each one of them say, "Father, I will," because they are his children.

Then, mark you, you are not God's child unless you can also say, "Father, not as I will." The true child bends before his father's will. "Yes," says he, "I would like so and so." His father forbids it. "Then I do not want it, and I will not touch it"; or he says, "I do not like to take that medicine, but my father says I am to take it," and he takes the cup, and he drinks the whole of its contents. The true child says, "Not as I will," although, after his measure, he also says, "Father, I will."

I have been talking only to you who are the Lord's people. I hope you have learned something from this subject; I know you have if the Lord has taught you to pray after the fashion of these two prayers, as you humbly yet believingly may, copying your Lord.

But oh, what shall I say to those of you who are not the Lord's people? If you do not know how to pray at all, may the Lord teach you! If you do not yet know your needs, may the Lord instruct you! But let me tell you that if ever there shall come a time when you feel your need of a Savior, the Lord Jesus will be willing to receive you. If ever you should yearn after him, be sure that he is also yearning after you. Even now,

Kindled his relentings are,

and if you will but breathe the penitent's prayer, "God be merciful to me a sinner," and turn your eye Christ-ward, and cross-ward, there is salvation for you even now. God grant that you may have it, for Jesus' sake! Amen.

"Love and I"—A Mystery

Delivered on Lord's Day morning, July 2, 1882, at the Metropolitan Tabernacle, Newington. No. 1667.

"I have declared unto them thy name, and will declare it: that the love where-with thou hast loved me may be in them, and I in them."—JOHN 17:26

For several Sabbath mornings my mind has been directed into subjects which I might fitly call the deep things of God. 1 think I have never felt my own incompetence more fully than in trying to handle such subjects. It is a soil into which one may dig and dig as deep as ever you will, and still never exhaust the golden nuggets which lie within it. I am, however, comforted by this fact, that these subjects are so fruitful that even we who can only scratch the surface of them shall yet get a harvest from them. I read once of the plains of India, that they were so fertile that you had only to tickle them with a hoe and they laughed with plenty, and surely such a text as this may be described as equally fruitful, even under our feeble husbandry. Pearls lie on the surface here as well as in the depth. We have only to search its surface and stir the soil a little, and we shall be astonished at the plenitude of spiritual wealth which lies before us. Oh, that the Spirit of God may help us to enjoy the blessed truths which are herein set forth! Here is the priceless treasure, but it lies hid till he reveals it to us.

You see, this text is taken out of our Lord's last prayer with his disciples. He did as good as say, "I am about to leave you; I am about to die for you. For a while you will not see me; but now, before we separate, let us pray." It is one of those impulses that you have felt yourselves. When you have been about to part from those you love, to leave them perhaps in danger and difficulty, you have felt you could do no less than say, "Let us draw near hither unto God." Your heart found no way of expressing itself at all so fitting, so congenial, so satisfactory as to draw near unto the great Father and spread the case before him. Now, a prayer from such a one as Jesus, our Lord and Master; a prayer in such a company, with the eleven whom he had chosen and who had consorted with him from the beginning; a prayer under such circumstances, when he was just on the brink of the brook of Cedron, and was about to cross that gloomy stream and go up to Calvary, and there lay down his life—such a prayer as this, so living, earnest, loving, and divine, deserves the most studious meditations of all believers. I invite you to bring hither your best thoughts and skill for the navigation of this sea. It is not a creek or bay, but the main ocean itself. We cannot hope to fathom its depths. This is true of any sentence of this matchless prayer; but for me the work of exposition becomes unusually heavy because my text is the close and climax of this marvelous supplication. It is the central mystery of all. In the lowest depth there is still a lower depth, and this verse is one of those deeps which still exceed the rest. Oh, how much we want the Spirit of God. Pray for his bedewing: pray that his balmy influences may descend upon us richly now.

You will observe that the last word of our Lord's prayer is concerning love. This is the last petition which he offers, "That the love wherewith thou hast loved me may be in them, and I in them." He reaches no greater height than this, namely, that his people be filled with the Father's love. How could he rise higher? For this is to be filled with all the fullness of God, since God is love, and he that loves dwells in God and God in him. What importance ought you and I to attach to the grace of love! How highly we should esteem that which Jesus makes the crown jewel of all. If we have faith, let us not be satisfied unless our faith works by love and purifies the soul. Let us not be content indeed until the love of Christ is shed abroad in our hearts by the Holy Ghost which is given to us. Well did the poet say,

Only love to us be given,
Lord, we ask no other heaven.

For indeed there is no other heaven below, and scarcely is there any other heaven above than to reach to the fullness of perfect love, for this is where the prayer of the Son of David ends, in praying "that the love wherewith thou hast loved me may be in them." What a subject! The highest that even our Lord Jesus reached in his noblest prayer. Again with groanings my heart cries, "Holy Spirit, help."

I shall this morning try to speak first upon the food of love, or what love lives upon; secondly, upon the love itself, what kind of love it is; and then, thirdly, upon the companion of love. "That the love wherewith thou hast loved me may be in them, and I in them."

I. First is *the food of love* to God.

What is it? It is knowledge. "I have declared unto them thy name, and will declare it." We cannot love a God whom we do not know; a measure of knowledge is needful to affection. However lovely God may be, a man blind of soul cannot perceive him and, therefore, is not touched by his loveliness. Only when the eyes are opened to behold the loveliness of God will the heart go out toward God who is so desirable an object for the affections. Brethren, we must know in order to believe; we must know in order to hope; and we must especially know in order to love. Hence the great desirableness that you should know the Lord and his great love which passes knowledge. You cannot reciprocate love which you have never known, even as a man cannot derive strength from food which he has not eaten. Till first of all the love of God has come into your heart, and you have been made a partaker of it, you cannot rejoice in it or return it. Therefore our Lord took care to feed his disciples' hearts upon the Father's name; he labored to make the Father known to them. This is one of his great efforts with them, and he is grieved when he sees their ignorance and has to say to one of them, "Have I been so long time with you, and yet hast thou not known me, Philip? He that hath seen me hath seen the Father; and how sayest thou then, Show us the Father?" Study much, then, the Word of God: be diligent in turning the pages of Scripture and in hearing God's true ministers that the flame of love within your hearts may be revived by the fuel of holy knowledge which you place upon it. Pile on the logs of sandalwood, and let the perfumed fires burn before the Lord. Heap on the handfuls of frankincense and sweet odors of sacred knowledge that on the altar of your heart there may always be burning the sacred flame of love to God in Christ Jesus.

The knowledge here spoken of is a knowledge which Jesus gave them. "I have known thee, and these have known that thou hast sent me. And I have declared unto them thy name, and will declare it." O beloved, it is not knowledge that you and I pick up as a matter of book learning that will ever bring out our love to the Father. It is knowledge given us by Christ through his Spirit. It is not knowledge communicated by the preacher alone which will bless you; for however much he may be taught of God himself, he cannot preach to the heart unless the blessed Spirit of God comes and takes of the things that are spoken and reveals them and makes them manifest to each individual heart, so that in consequence it knows the Lord. Jesus said, "O righteous Father, the world hath not known thee," and you and I would have been in the same condition—strangers to God, without God and without hope in the world—if the Spirit of God had not taken of divine things and applied them to our souls so that we are made to know them. Every living word of knowledge is the work of the living God. If you know only what you have found out for yourself or picked up by your own industry apart from Jesus, you know nothing aright. It must be by the direct and distinct teaching of God the Holy Ghost that you must learn to profit. Jesus Christ alone can reveal the Father. He himself said, "No man cometh unto the Father but by me." He that knows not Christ knows not the Father; but when Jesus Christ reveals him, ah! then we do know him after a special, personal, peculiar, inward knowledge. This knowledge brings with it a life and a love with which the soul is not puffed up, but built up. By such knowledge we grow up into him in all things who is our head, being taught of the Son of God.

This knowledge, dear friends, comes to us gradually. The text indicates this. "I have declared unto them thy name, and will declare it." As if, though they knew the Father, there was far more to know and the Lord Jesus was resolved to teach them more. Are you growing in knowledge, my brothers and sisters? My labor is lost if you are not growing in grace and in the knowledge of our Lord and Savior Jesus Christ. I hope you know much more of God than you did twenty years ago when first you came to him. That little knowledge which you received by grace when you found "life in a look at the Crucified One" has saved you; but in these after years you have added to your faith knowledge, and to your knowledge experience; you have gone on to know more deeply what you knew before, and to know the details of what you seemed to know in the gross and the lump at first. You have come to look into things as well as upon things—a look at Christ saves; but oh, it is the look into Christ that wins the heart's love and holds it fast and binds us to him as with fetters of gold. We ought every day to be adding something to this inestimably precious store that as we are known of God so we may know God and become thereby transformed from glory unto glory through his Spirit.

Are you not thankful for this blessed word of the Lord Jesus: "I will declare it"; "I will make it known"? He did do so at his resurrection when he taught his people things they knew not before; but he did so much more after he had ascended up on high when the Spirit of God was given. "He shall teach you all things, and bring all things to your remembrance, whatsoever I have said unto you." And now today in the hearts of his people he is daily teaching us something that we do not know. All our experience tends that way. When the Spirit of God blesses an affliction to us, it is one of the Savior's illuminated books out of which we learn something more of the Father's name, and consequently come to love him better. That is the thing Christ aims at. He would so make known the Father that the love wherewith the Father has loved him may be in us, and that he himself may be in us.

This knowledge distinguishes us from the world. It is the mark by which the elect are made manifest. In the sixth verse of this chapter our Lord says, "I have manifested thy name unto the men which thou gavest me out of the world: thine they were, and thou gavest them me; and they have kept thy word." The world does not know the Father and cannot know him, for it abides in the darkness and death of sin. Judge yourselves therefore by this sure test, and let the love which grows out of gracious knowledge be a token for good unto you.

Now let me try to show you what the Savior meant when he said, "I have declared unto them thy name, and will declare it." This knowledge which breeds love is knowledge of the name of God. What does he mean by "thy name"? Now, I do not think I should preach an unprofitable sermon if I were to stop with the connection and say that the "name" here meant is specially the name used in the twenty-fifth verse: "O righteous Father, the world hath not known thee." This is the name which we most need to know—"righteous Father." Observe the singular combination here. Righteous, and yet a Father. "Righteous"—to us poor sinners that is a word of terror when first we hear it. "Father"—oh, how sweet. That is a word of good cheer even to us prodigals; but we are afraid to lay hold upon it for our sins arise and our consciences protest that God must be righteous and punish sin.

Our joy begins when we see the two united: "righteous Father"—a Father full of love, and nothing but love, to his people, and yet righteous as a Judge, as righteous as if he were no Father. Dealing out his righteousness with stern severity as the Judge of all the earth must do, and yet a Father at the same time. I do protest that I never did love God at all, nor could I embrace him in my affections, till I understood how he could be just and yet the justifier of him that believes in Jesus: how, in a word, he could be the "righteous Father." That satisfied my conscience and my heart at the same time, for my conscience said, It is well. God has not put away sin without a sacrifice and has not winked at sin nor waived his justice in order to indulge his mercy, but he remains just as he ever was—the same thrice-holy God who will by no means spare the guilty. He has laid the punishment of our sins upon Christ; he has made him to be sin for us who knew no sin that we might be made the righteousness of God in him. And all this he has done that he might act to us as a Father and save his own children from the result of their transgressions.

He has given his only begotten Son to die in our stead that many sons might be brought to glory through him. It is at the cross we understand this riddle. Here we see the righteous Father. But the world will not learn it, and a large part of the professing church, which is nothing better than the world wrongfully named with Christ's name, will not learn it. They do anything they can to get away from atonement: love without righteousness is their idol. Substitution is a word that is hard for the world to spell: they cannot abide it. That Christ should suffer in the stead of the guilty and bear that we might never bear the Father's righteous wrath—this they cannot away with. Many pretend to keep the atonement, and yet they tear the bowels out of it. They profess to believe in the gospel, but it is a gospel without the blood of the atonement; and a bloodless gospel is a lifeless gospel, a dead gospel, and a damning gospel. Let those take heed who cannot see God as a righteous Father, for they are numbered among the world who know him not. "These have known thee," says our Lord. These who have been taught by Christ, and these alone, come to find as much joy in the word "righteous" as in the word "Father."

Blending the two together they feel an intense love to the "righteous Father," and their hearts rejoice in a holy gospel, a message of mercy consistent with justice, a covenant salvation ordered in all things and sure, because it does no violence to law and does not bind the hands of justice. Beloved, if this revelation of the atoning blood does not make your heart love Jesus and love the Father, it is because you are not in him; but if you know this secret as to how righteousness and peace have kissed each other, you know the name that wins the affection of believers to God. My own heart is glad and rejoices every hour because I find rest in substitution, safety in the vindication of the law, and bliss in the glory of the divine character.

> Lo! in the grace that rescued man
> His brightest form of glory shines!
> Here, on the cross, 'tis fairest drawn
> In precious blood and crimson lines.
>
> Here I behold His inmost heart,
> Where grace and vengeance strangely join,
> Piercing his Son with sharpest smart,
> To make the purchased pleasure mine.
>
> Oh, the sweet wonders of that cross,
> Where God the Savior loved and died!
> Her noblest life my spirit draws
> From his dear wounds and bleeding sides.

Still, I would take the word "name" in a wider sense. "I have declared unto them thy name," which signifies "thy character." The word "name" is used as a sort of summary of all the attributes of God. All these attributes are well adapted to win the love of all regenerate spirits. Just think for a minute. God is holy. To a holy mind there is nothing in the world, there is nothing in heaven more beautiful than holiness. We read of the beauties of holiness; for to a soul that is purified, holiness is superlatively lovely. Now, beauty wins love. Consequently when Jesus Christ makes known his holy Father, and shows us in his life and in his death the holiness of the Ever-blessed, then our heart is won to the Father. "Oh," say you, "but holiness does not always win love." No, not the love of the defiled hearts that cannot appreciate it; but those who are pure in heart, and can see God, no sooner behold his holiness than they are enamored of it, and their souls at once delight in their Lord.

Moreover, we learn from our Lord Jesus that God is good. "There is none good but one, that is, God." How inexpressibly good he is! There is no goodness but what comes from God. His name, "God," is but short for "good," and all the good things that we receive in this life and for the life to come are but enlargements of his blessed name. "Every good gift and every perfect gift is from above, and cometh down from the Father of lights." Blessings enjoyed by us are streams that flow from the fountainhead of God's infinite goodness to the sons of men. A man cannot help loving God when once he knows him to be good, for all men love that which they apprehend to be good to them. A man says, "Gold is good; rest is good; fame is good"; and, therefore, he seeks after these things, and when he comes to know that God is good, oh, then his spirit follows hard after him. He cannot help but love that which he is persuaded is in the highest sense good. The soul that knows the name of the Lord rejoices at the very mention of him.

To sinners like ourselves perhaps the next word may have more sweetness. God is merciful; he is ever ready to forgive. Note how the prophet says, "Who is a God like unto thee, . . . and passeth by the transgression?" He does not say, "Who is a man like unto thee?" for none among our race can for a moment be compared with him; but even if the gods of the heathen were gods, none of them could be likened unto the Lord for mercy. Now, when a man knows that he has offended, and yet the person offended readily and freely forgives, why, it wins his love. If he is a right-hearted man he cries, "I cannot again offend one who so generously casts all my offenses behind his back." The mercy of God is such a love-winning attribute that, as I told you the other Sunday, twenty-six times in a single psalm the ancient church sang, "His mercy endureth for ever." Free grace and pardoning love sensibly known in the soul will win your hearts unto God for ever, so that you shall be his willing servants as long as you have any being.

But then there is a higher word still. God is love, and there is a something about love which always wins love. When love puts on her own golden armor and bares her sword bright with her own unselfishness, she goes on conquering and to conquer. Let a man once apprehend that God is love, that this is

God's very essence, and he must at once love God. I do not mean merely "apprehend" that God is love in the cold intellect; but when this heart begins to glow and burn with that divine revelation, then straightaway the spirit is joined unto the Lord, and rests with delight in the great Father of spirits. Love knits and binds. Oh, to feel more of its uniting power.

Thus have I shown you the manna which love feeds upon, the nectar which it drinks. Everything in God is lovely, and there is no trait in his character that is otherwise than lovely. All the lovelinesses that can be conceived are heaped up in God without the slightest admixture of adulteration. He is love altogether, wholly, and emphatically. Oh, surely our Lord and Master was wise when he fed his people's love upon such meat as this.

II. Brethren, we have as yet only been standing at the furnace mouth: let us now enter into the devouring flame while we speak, in the second place, upon *the love itself.*

Observe, first, what this love is not. "I have declared unto them thy name, and will declare it: that the love wherewith thou hast loved me may be in them." Do notice that the prayer is not that the Father's love may be set upon them or moved toward them. God does not love us because we know him, for he loved us before we knew him, even as Paul speaks of "his great love wherewith he loved us, even when we were dead in sins." Jesus has not come to set his Father's love upon the chosen. Oh no; he did not even die with that object, for the Father's love was upon the chosen from everlasting. "The Father himself loveth you" was always true. Christ did not die to make his Father loving, but because his Father is loving: the atoning blood is the outflow of the very heart of God toward us. So do not make any mistake. Our Lord speaks not of the divine love in itself, but in us. This is not the eternal love of God toward us of which we are now reading, but that love in us. We are inwardly to feel the love which proceeds from the Father, and so to have it in us. We are to have the love of God shed abroad in our hearts by the Holy Ghost which is given to us. It is to be recognized by us, felt in us, made the subject of inward joy; this it is that our Lord wishes to produce, that the love of God may be in us, dwelling in our hearts, a welcome guest, the sovereign of our souls.

And this love is of a very peculiar sort. Do let me read the verse again: "That the love wherewith thou hast loved me may be in them." It is God's own love in us. The love of the Father toward Jesus springs up like a crystal fountain, and then the sparkling drops fall and overflow, as you have seen the fountains do, and we are the cups into which this overflowing love of God toward Christ Jesus flows, and flows till we too are full. The inward love so much desired for us by our Lord is no emotion of nature, no attachment proceeding from the unregenerate will, but it is the Father's love transplanted into the soil of these poor hearts and becoming our love to Jesus, as we shall have to show in the next point. But is not this a wonderful thing—that God's own love to Jesus should dwell in our hearts? And yet it is so. The love wherewith we love Christ, mark you, is God's love to Christ: "That the love wherewith thou hast loved me may be in them." All true love, such as the Father delights in and accepts at our hands, is nothing but his own love which has come streaming down from his own heart into our renewed minds.

But what can this mean? I must ask you to observe that it includes within itself four precious things.

First, the text means that our Lord Jesus Christ desires us to have a distinct recognition of the Father's love to him. He wants the love wherewith the Father loves him to be felt in us, so that we may say, "Yes, I know the Father loved him, for I, who am such a poor, unworthy, and foolish creature, yet love him; and oh, how his Father must love him." I love him! Yes, by his grace, it were a blessed thing to die for him; but if I love him, oh, how must his Father love him who can see all his beauty, and can appreciate every distinct piece of loveliness that is in him! God never loved anything as he loves Christ, except his people, and they have had to be lifted up to that position by the love which the Father has to his Son. For, first and foremost, the Father and the Son are one: they are one in essence. The Savior has been with the Father from the beginning, and his delight has been with him, even as the Father testified, "This is my beloved Son, in whom I am well pleased." Oh, do try to feel, if you can, the love of the Father to his Son, or else you will not love the Father as you should for the amazing sacrifice which he made in giving Jesus to us. Think what it cost him to tear his well Beloved from his bosom and send him down below to be "despised and rejected." Think what it cost him to nail him up to yonder cross, and then forsake him and hide his face from him because he had laid all our sins upon him. Oh, the love he must have had to us thus to have made his best Beloved to become a curse for us, as it is written, "Cursed is every one that hangeth on a tree." I want you to get this right into your souls, dear friends. Do not hold it as a dry doctrine, but let it touch your heart. Let it flow into your heart like a boiling stream till your whole souls become like Icelandic geysers, which boil and bubble up and send their steam aloft into the clouds. Oh, to have the soul filled with the love of the Father toward him who is altogether lovely.

Now, go a step further and deeper. Our text bears a further reading. Remember that you are to have in your heart a sense of the Father's love to you, and to recollect that it is precisely the same love wherewith he loves his Son. "That the love wherewith thou hast loved me may be in them." Oh, wonder of wonders, I feel more inclined to sit down and meditate upon it than to stand up and talk about it! The love wherewith he loved his Son— such is his love to all his chosen ones. Can you believe it, that you should be the object of God's delight, even as Christ is, because you are in Christ; that you should be the object of the Father's love as truly as Christ is, because he sees you to be part and parcel of the mystical body of his well-beloved Son? Do not tell me that God the Father does not love you as well as he does Christ; the point can be settled by the grandest matter of fact that ever was. When there was a choice between Christ and his people which should die of the two, the Father freely delivered up his own Son that we might live through him. Oh, what a meeting there must have been of the seas of love that day, when God's great love to us came rolling in like a glorious springtide, and his love to his Son came rolling in at the same time. If they had met and come into collision, we cannot imagine the result; but when they both took to rolling together in one mighty torrent, what a stream of love was there! The Lord Jesus sank that we might swim; he sank that we might rise, and now we are borne onward for ever by the mighty sweep of infinite love into an everlasting blessedness which tongues and lips can never fully set forth. Oh, be ravished with this. Be carried away with it; be in ecstasy at love so amazing, so divine. The Father loves you even as he loves his Son; after the same manner and sort he loves all his redeemed.

But now this goes to a third meaning, and that is that we are to give back a reflection of this love and to love Jesus as the Father loves him. A dear old friend speaking to me the other day in a rapturous tone said, "I love Jesus as the Father loves him." This is true; not equally, but like. Is not this a blessed thought? I said, "O friend, that is a strong thing to say!" "Ah," said he, "but not stronger than Jesus would have it when he prays that 'the love wherewith thou hast loved me may be in them, and I in them.'" His people love Christ as the Father loves him—in the same way, though from want of capacity they cannot reach to the same immeasurable force of love. Oh, to throw back on Christ his Father's love. The Father is the sun and we are the moon, but the moonlight is the same light as the sunlight. We can see a difference because reflection robs the light of much of its heat and its brilliance, but it is the same light. The moon has not a ray of light but what came from the sun, and we have not a live coal of love to Christ but what came from the Father. We are as the moon, shining by reflected light, but Jesus loves the moonlight of our love and rejoices in it. Let us give him all of it; let us try to be as the full moon always, and let us not dwindle down to a mere ring of love or a crescent of affection; let us render no half-moon love; let us not be half dark and cold, but let us shine on Christ with all the light we can possibly reflect of his Father's love, saying in our very soul,

My Jesus, I love thee, I know thou art mine;
For thee all the follies of sin I resign.

And then, fourthly, this love of the Father in us is to go beaming forth from us to all around. When we get the love wherewith the Father loves the Son into our hearts, then it is to go out toward all the chosen seed. He that loves him that begat loves also them that are begotten of him. Yes, and your love is to go forth to all the sons of men, seeking their good for God's glory, that they may be brought in to know the same Savior in whom we rejoice. Oh, if the love of the Father to Christ once enters into a man's soul it will change him; it will sway him with the noblest passion; it will make him a zealot for Christ; it will cast out his selfishness; it will change him into the image of Christ and fit him to dwell in heaven where love is perfected.

So I conclude this second head by saying that this indwelling of the Father's love in us has the most blessed results. It has an expulsive result. As soon as ever it gets into the heart it says to all love of sin, "Get you hence, there remains no room for you here." When the light enters in, the darkness receives immediate notice of ejectment; the night is gone as soon as the dawn appears. It has also a repulsive power by which it repels the assaults of sin. As though a man did snatch the sun out of the heaven and make a round shield with it, and hold it in the very face of the prince of darkness, and blind him with the light, so does the love of God the Father repel the enemy. It girds the soul with the armor of light. It repels the devil, the love of the world, the love of sin, and all outward temptations.

And then what an impulsive power it has. Get the love of Christ into you, and it is as when an engine receives fire and steam, and so obtains the force which drives it. Then have you strengthening, then have you motive power, then are you urged on to this and that heroic deed which, apart from this sublime love, you never would have thought of. For Christ you can live, for Christ you can suffer, for Christ you can die, when once the Father's love to him has taken full possession of your spirit. And, oh, how elevating it is. How it lifts a man up above self and sin; how it makes him seek the things that are above! How purifying it is; and how happy it makes the subject of its influence.

If you are unhappy you want more of the love of God. "Oh," say you, "I want a larger income." Nonsense. A man is not made happy by money. You will do very well in poverty if you have enough of the love of God. Oh, but if your soul be filled with the love of God your spirit will be ready to dance at the very sound of his name. You murmur and repine at providence because the fire of your love is burning low. Come, get the ashes together; pray the Spirit of God to blow upon them. Beg him to bring fresh fuel of holy knowledge till your soul becomes like Nebuchadnezzar's furnace, heated seven times hotter. This is the kind of love we should have toward Christ. No blessing can excel it. Oh, Savior, let your prayer be fulfilled in me and in all your dear people this morning, and may the love wherewith the Father has loved you be in us.

III. Thirdly, here is *the companion of love.*

"I in them." Look at the text a minute and just catch those two words. Here is "love" and "I"—love and Christ come together. O blessed guests! "Love and I," says Christ; as if he felt he never had a companion that suited him better. "Love" and "I"—Jesus is ever at home where love is reigning. When love lives in his people's hearts, Jesus lives there too. Does Jesus, then, live in the hearts of his people? Yes; wherever there is the love of the Father shed abroad in them he must be there. We have his own word for it, and we are sure that Jesus knows where he is.

We are sure that he is where love is; for, first, where there is love there is life, and where there is life there is Christ, for he himself says, "I am the . . . life." There is no true life in the believer's soul that is divided from Christ. We are sure of that; so that where there is love there is life, and where there is life there is Christ. Again, where there is the love of God in the heart there is the Holy Spirit; but wherever the Holy Spirit is, there is Christ, for the Holy Spirit is Christ's representative; and it is in that sense that he tells us, "Lo, I am with you alway," namely, because the Spirit is come to be always with us. So where there is love there is the Spirit of God, and where there is the Spirit of God there is Christ. So it is always "love and I."

Furthermore, where there is love there is faith, for faith works by love, and there never was true love to Christ apart from faith; but where there is faith there is always Christ, for if there is faith in him he has been received into the soul. Jesus is ever near to that faith which has himself for its foundation and resting place. Where there is love there is faith, where there is faith there is Christ, and so it is "love and I."

Yes, but where there is the Father's love toward Christ in the heart God himself is there. I am sure of that, for God is love. So if there is love within us there must be God, and where God is there Christ is, for he says, "I and my Father are one." So you see where there is love there must be Jesus Christ, for these reasons and for many others besides.

"I in them." Yes, if I were commanded to preach for seven years from these three words only, I should never exhaust the text, I am quite certain. I might exhaust you by my dullness, and exhaust myself by labor to tell out the sacred secret, but I should never exhaust the text. "I in them." It is the most blessed word I know. You, beloved, need not go abroad to find the Lord Jesus Christ. Where does he live? He lives within you. "I in them." As soon as ever you pray you are sure he hears you because he is within you. He is not knocking at your door; he has entered into you, and there he dwells and will go no more out for ever.

What a blessed sense of power this gives to us. "I in them." Then it is no more "I" in weakness, but, since Jesus dwells in me, "I can do all things through Christ which strengtheneth me." "I in them." It is the glory of the believer that Christ dwells in him. "Unto you therefore which believe he is precious."

Hence we gather the security of the believer. Brother, if Christ be in me, and I am overcome, Christ is conquered too, for he is in me. "I in them." I cannot comprehend the doctrine of believers falling from grace. If Christ has once entered into them, will he not abide with them? Paul says, "I am persuaded, that neither death, nor life, nor angels, nor principalities, nor powers, nor things present, nor things to come, nor height, nor depth, nor any other creature, shall be able to separate us from the love of God which is in Christ Jesus our Lord." To that persuasion I set my hand and seal. Well, then, if Christ is in us, whatever happens to us will happen to him. We shall be losers if we do not get to heaven; but so will he be, for he is in us and so is a partaker of our condition. If it is an indissoluble union—and so he declares it is, "I in them,"— then his destiny and ours are linked together; and if he wins the victory, we conquer in him. If he sits at the right hand of God, we shall sit at the right hand of God with him, for he is in us.

I know not what more to say, not because I have nothing more, but because I do not know which to bring forward out of a thousand precious things; but I leave the subject with you. Go home and live in the power of this blessed text. Go home and be as happy as you can be to live, and if you get a little happier that will not hurt you, for then you will be in heaven. Keep up unbroken joy in the Lord. It is not "I in them" for Sundays and away on Mondays; nor "I in them" when they sit in the Tabernacle and out of them when they reach home. No; "I in them," and that for ever and for ever. Go and rejoice. Show this blind world that you have a happiness which as much outshines theirs as the sun outshines the sparks which fly from the chimney and expire. Go forth with joy and be led forth with peace; let the mountains and the hills break forth before you into singing.

All that remains for me
Is but to love and sing,
And wait until the angels come,
To bear me to the King.

"Oh, but I have my troubles." I know you have your troubles, but they are not worthy to be compared with the glory that shall be revealed in you, nor even with your present glory. I feel as if I could not think about troubles, nor sins, nor anything else when I once behold the love of God to me. When I feel my love to Christ, which is but God's love to Christ, burning within my soul, then I glory in tribulation, for the power of God shall be through these afflictions made manifest in me. "I in them." God bless you with the knowledge of this mystery, for Jesus' sake. Amen.

Christian Resignation

∼≈∼

Delivered on a Thursday evening, early in the year 1859, at New Park Street Chapel, Southwark. No. 2715.

"Not as I will, but as thou wilt."—MATTHEW 26:39

The apostle Paul, writing concerning our Lord Jesus Christ, says, "Though he were a Son, yet learned he obedience by the things which he suffered." He who, as God, knew all things had to learn obedience in the time of his humiliation. He, who is in himself Wisdom Incarnate, did himself condescend to enter the school of suffering, there to learn that important lesson of the Christian life, obedience to the will of God; and here, in Gethsemane's garden, you can see the Divine Scholar going forth to practice his lesson. He had been all his lifetime learning it, and now he has to learn it for the last time in his agony and bloody sweat, and in his terrible death upon the cross. Now is he to discover the utmost depths of suffering and to attain to the height of the knowledge of obedience. See how well he has learned his lesson; note how complete and ripe a scholar he is. He has attained to the very highest class in that school; and in the immediate prospect of death, can say to his Father, "Not as I will, but as thou wilt."

The object of this discourse is to commend to you the blessed example of our Lord Jesus Christ; and as God the Holy Spirit shall help me to urge you to be made like unto your glorious Head, and yourselves to learn, by all the daily providences with which God is pleased to surround you, this lesson of resignation to the will of God and of making an entire surrender to him.

I have been struck, lately, in reading works by some writers who belong to the Romish Church, with the marvelous love which they have toward the Lord Jesus Christ. I did think, at one time, that it could not be possible for any to be saved in that church; but, often, after I have risen from reading the books of those holy men and have felt myself to be quite a dwarf by their side, I have said, "Yes, despite their errors, these men must have been taught of the Holy Spirit. Notwithstanding all the evils of which they have drunk so deeply, I am quite certain that they must have had fellowship with Jesus, or else they could not have written as they did." Such writers are few and far between; but, still, there is a remnant according to the election of grace even in the midst of that apostate church. Looking at a book by one of them the other day, I met with this remarkable expression, "Shall that body, which has a thorn-crowned Head, have delicate, pain-fearing members? God forbid!" That remark went straight to my heart at once. I thought how often the children of God shun pain, reproach, and rebuke, and think it to be a strange thing when some fiery trial happens to them. If they would but recollect that their Head had to sweat as it were great drops of blood falling down to the ground, and that their Head was crowned with thorns, it would not seem strange to them that the members of his mystical body also have to suffer. If Christ had been some delicate person, if our glorious Head had been reposing upon the soft pillow of ease, then might we, who are the members of his church, have expected to go through this world with joy and comfort; but if he must be bathed in his own blood, if the thorns must pierce his temples, if his lips must be parched, and if his mouth must be dried up like a furnace, shall we escape suffering and agony? Is Christ to have a head of brass and hands of gold? Is his head to be as if it glowed in the furnace and are not we to glow in the furnace too? Must he pass through seas of suffering, and shall we

> Be carried to the skies,
>
> On flowery beds of ease?

Ah! no! we must be conformed unto our Lord in his humiliation if we would be made like him also in his glory. So, brethren and sisters, I have to discourse to you upon this lesson, which some of us have begun to learn, but of which as yet we know so little—this lesson of saying, "Not as I will, but as thou wilt." First, let me *explain the meaning of this prayer; then, urge you, by certain reasons, to make this your constant cry.* Next, let me *show what will be the happy effect of its being the paramount desire of your spirits.* We will conclude with a practical inquiry—*what can bring us to this blessed condition?*

I. First, then, *what is the meaning of this prayer,* "Not as I will, but as thou wilt"?

I shall not address myself to those Christians who are but as dwarfs, who know little about the things of the kingdom. I will speak rather to those who do business in the deep waters of communion, who know what it is to pillow their heads upon the bosom of Jesus, to walk with God as Enoch did, and to talk with him as Abraham did. My dear brethren, only such as you can understand this prayer in all its length and breadth. Your brother, who as yet scarcely knows the meaning of the word communion, may pray thus in some feeble measure. Yet it is not to be expected that he should discern all the spiritual teaching that there is in these words of our Lord; but to you who are Christ-taught, you who have become ripe scholars in the school of Christ, to you I may speak as unto wise men—judge what I say.

If you and I mean this prayer and do not use it as a mere form of words, but mean it in all its fullness, we must be prepared for this kind of experience. Sometimes, when we are in the midst of the most active service, when we are diligently serving God both with our hands and our heart, and when success is crowning all our labors, *the Lord will lay us aside*, take us right away from the vineyard, and thrust us into the furnace. Just at the very time when the church seems to need us most, when the world's necessities are most of all appealing to us, and when our hearts are full of love toward Christ and toward our fellow creatures, it will often happen that, just then, God will strike us down with sickness or remove us from our sphere of activity. But if we really mean this prayer, we must be prepared to say, "Not as I will, but as thou wilt."

This is not easy, for does not the Holy Spirit himself teach us to long after active service for our Savior? Does he not, when he gives us love toward our fellowmen, constrain us, as it were, to make their salvation our meat and our drink? When he is actively at work within our hearts, do we not feel as if we could not live without serving God? Do we not then feel that to labor for the Lord is our highest rest, and that toil for Jesus is our sweetest pleasure? Does it not then seem most trying to our ardent spirit to be compelled to drink the cup of sickness and to be incapable of doing anything actively for God? The preacher is seeing men converted and his ministry successful; but, on a sudden, he is compelled to cease from preaching. Or the Sunday school teacher has, by the grace of God, been the means of bringing his class into an interesting and hopeful condition; yet, just when the class needs his presence most, he is smitten down so that he cannot go on with his work. Ah! then it is that the spirit finds it hard to say, "Not as I will, but as thou wilt." But if we adopt this prayer, this is what it means: that we should be prepared to suffer instead of to serve, and should be as willing to lie in the trenches as to scale the walls, and as willing to be laid aside in the King's hospital as to be fighting in the midst of the rank and file of the King's army. This is hard to flesh and blood, but we must do it if we present this petition.

If we really mean this prayer, there will be a second trial for us. Sometimes, *God will demand of us that we labor in unpropitious fields*; he will set his children to plow the rock and to cast their bread upon the waters. He will send his Ezekiel to prophesy in a valley full of dry bones, and his Jonah to carry his message to Nineveh. He will give his servants strange work to do—work which seems as if it never could be successful, or bring honor either to God or to themselves. I doubt not that there are some ministers who toil and labor with all their might, yet who see but little fruit. Far away in the dark places of heathendom, there are men who have been toiling for years with scarcely a convert to cheer them; and here, too, in England, there are men who are preaching, in all sincerity and faithfulness, the Word of the Lord, yet they do not see souls converted. They know that they are unto God a sweet savor of Christ, both in them that perish and in them that are saved. Our hearts are, I trust, so full of the Spirit prompting us to cry, like Rachel, "Give me children, or else I die," that we cannot rest content without seeing the success of our labors. Yet the Master, in effect, says to us, "No, I tell you to continue to toil for me, though I give you no fruit for your labor; you are to keep on plowing this rock simply because I tell you to do it." Ah! then, brethren, it is hard to say, "Not my will, but thine be done." But we must say it; we must feel that we are ready to forgo even the joy of harvest and the glory of success if God wills it.

At other times, God will remove his people from positions of honorable service to other offices that are far inferior in the minds of men. I think that I should feel it hard if I had to be banished from my large congregation and from my thousands of hearers to a small village where I could preach the gospel to only a little company of people; yet I am sure that, if I entered fully into the spirit of our Lord's words—"Not as I will, but as thou wilt"—I should be quite as ready to be there as to be here. I have heard that among the Jesuits such is the extraordinary obedience which they are compelled to pay to their superiors that, on one occasion, there was a president of one of their colleges who had written some of the most learned books in any language—a man of the highest talents—and the superior of the order took a freak into his head, for some reason, to send him straightaway from the country where he was to Bath, to stand there in the street for a year and sweep the crossing. And the man did it. He was compelled to do it; his vow obliged him to do anything that he was told to do.

Now, in a spiritual sense, this is hard to perform; but, nevertheless, it is a Christian's duty. We remember the saying of a good man that the angels in heaven are so completely given up to obedience to God that, if there should be two works to do, ruling an empire and sweeping a crossing, neither of the two angels who might be selected to go on these two errands would have any choice in the matter, but would just leave it with their Lord to decide which part they were to fulfill. You may, perhaps, be called from the charge of the services in a place of worship to become one of the humblest members in another church; you may be taken from a place of much honor and put in the very lowest ranks of the army. Are you willing to submit to that kind of treatment? Your flesh and blood say, "Lord, if I may still serve in your army, let me be a captain; or, at least, let me be a sergeant or a corporal. If I may help to draw your chariot, let me be the leading horse, let me run first in the team, let me wear the showy ribbons." But God may say to you, "I have put you there in the thick of the battle, now I will place you behind; I have given you vigor and strength to fight with great success, now I will make you tarry by the stuff; I have done with you in the prominent position, now I will use you somewhere else." But if we can only pray this prayer, "Not as I will, but as thou wilt," we shall be ready to serve God anywhere and everywhere, so long as we know that we are doing his will.

But there is another trial which we shall all have to endure in our measure, which will prove whether we understand by this prayer what Christ meant by it. Sometimes, *in the service of Christ, we must be prepared to endure the loss of reputation, of honor, and even of character itself.* I remember when I first came to London to preach the Word, I thought that I could bear anything for Christ; but I found myself shamefully slandered, all manner of falsehoods were uttered concerning me, and in agony I fell on my face before God and cried unto him. I felt as though that was a thing I could not bear; my character was very dear to me, and I could not endure to have such false things said about me. Then this thought came to me, "You must give up all to Christ; you must surrender everything for him—character, reputation, and all that you have. If it is the Lord's will, you shall be reckoned the vilest of the vile; so long as you can still continue to serve him, and your character is really pure, you need not fear. If it is your Master's will that you shall be trampled and spit upon by all the wicked men in the world, you must simply bear it, and say, 'Not as I will, but as thou wilt.'" And I remember then how I rose from my knees and sang to myself that verse,

If on my face, for thy dear name,
Shame and reproaches be,
All hail reproach, and welcome shame,
If thou remember me.

"But how hard it was," you say, "for you to suffer the loss of character and to have evil things spoken against you falsely for Christ's name's sake!" And what was the reason why it was so hard? Why, it was just because I had not fully learned how to pray this prayer of our Lord Jesus Christ—and I am afraid that I have not completely learned it yet. It is a very delightful thing to have even our enemies speaking well of us, to go through this world with such holiness of character that men who pour scorn upon all religion cannot find fault with us. But it is an equally glorious thing for us to be set in the pillory of shame, to be pelted by every passerby, to be the song of the drunkard, to be the byword of the swearer, when we do not deserve it, and to endure all this for Christ's sake. This is true heroism; this is the meaning of the prayer of our text.

Again, some of you have at times thought, "Oh, if the Master will only be pleased to open a door for me where I may be the means of doing some good! How glad I should be if I could have either more wealth, or more influence, or more knowledge, or more talents with which I might serve him better!" You have prayed about the matter and thought about it, and you have said, "If I could only get into such and such a position, how excellently should I be able to serve God!" You have seen your Master give to some of his servants ten talents, but he has given you only one; you have gone on your knees and asked him to be good enough to trust you with two, and he has refused it. Or you have had two and you have asked him to let you have ten; and he has said, "No, I will give you two talents, and no more." But you say, "Is it not a laudable desire that I should seek to do more good?" Certainly; trade with your talents, multiply them if you can. But suppose you have no power of utterance, suppose you have no opportunities of serving God, or even suppose the sphere of your influence is limited, what then? Why, you are to say, "Lord, I hoped it was your will that I might have a wider sphere, but if it is not, although I long to serve you on a larger scale, I will be quite content to glorify you in my present narrower sphere. I feel that here is an opportunity for the trial of my faith and resignation, and again I say, 'Not as I will, but as thou wilt.'"

Christian men, are you prepared heartily to pray this prayer? I fear there is not a single individual among us who could pray it in all its fullness of meaning. Perhaps you may go as far as I have already gone; but if God should take you at your word and say, "My will is that your wife should be smitten with a fatal illness and, like a fading lily, droop and die before your eyes; that your children should be caught up to my loving bosom in heaven; that your house should be burned with fire; that you should be left penniless, a pauper dependent on the charity of others; it is my will that you should cross the sea; that you should go to distant lands and endure unheard-of hardships; it is my will that, at last, your bones should lie bleaching on the desert sand in some foreign clime." Are you willing to endure all this for Christ? Remember that you have not attained unto the full meaning of this prayer until you have said "Yes" to all that it means. Until you can go to the uttermost lengths to which God's providence may go, you have not gone to the full extent of the resignation in this cry of our Lord.

Many of the early Christians, I think, did know this prayer by heart; it is wonderful how willing they were to do anything and be anything for Christ. They had got this idea into their heads that they were not to live to themselves; and they had it also in their hearts. They believed that to be martyred was the highest honor they could possibly wish for. Consequently, if they were brought to the tribunals of the judges, they never ran away from their persecutors; they almost courted death, for they thought it was the highest privilege that they could possibly have if they might be torn in pieces by the lions in the arena or be decapitated with the sword. Now, if we also could but get that idea into our hearts, with what courage would it gird us. How fully might we then serve God, and how patiently might we endure persecution if we had but learned the meaning of this prayer, "Not as I will, but as thou wilt."

II. In the second place, *I am to try to give you some reasons why it will be best for us all to seek to have the Holy Spirit within us so that we may be brought into this frame of mind and heart.*

And the first reason is because it is simply *a matter of right.* God ought to have his way at all times, and I ought not to have mine whenever it is contrary to his. If ever my will is at cross-purposes to the will of the Supreme, it is but right that mine should yield to his. If I could have my own way—if such a poor, feeble creature as I am could thwart the Omnipotent Creator—it would be wrong for me to do it. What! has he made me, and shall he not do as he wills with me? Is he like the potter, and am I but as the clay, and shall the thing formed say to him that formed it, "Why have you made me thus"? No, my Lord, it is but right that you should do what you please with me, for I am yours—yours, for you have made me; yours, for you have bought me with your blood. If I am a jewel purchased with the precious blood of Jesus then he may cut me into what shape he pleases, he may polish me as he chooses. He may let me lie in the darkness of the casket, or let me glitter in his hand or in his diadem; in fact, he may do with me just as he wills, for I am his; and so long as I know that he does it, I must say, "Whatever he does is right; my will shall not be in opposition to his will."

But, again, this is not only a matter of right, *it is a matter of wisdom with us.* Depend upon it, dear brethren, if we could have our own will, it would often be the worst thing in the world for us. But to let God have his way with us, even if it were in our power to thwart him, would be an act of wisdom on our part. What do I desire when I wish to have my own will? I desire my own happiness; well, but I shall get it far more easily if I let God have his will, for the will of God is both for his own glory and my happiness. So, however much I may think that my own will would tend to my comfort and happiness, I may rest assured that God's will would be infinitely more profitable to me than my own; and that, although God's will may seem to make it dark and dreary for me at the time, yet from seeming evil he will bring forth good, such as never could have been produced from that supposed good after which my weak and feeble judgment is so apt to run.

But, again, suppose it were possible for us to have our own will, would it not be an infringement of that loving reliance which Christ may well ask at our hands that we should trust him? Are we not saved by trusting our Lord Jesus Christ? Has not faith in Christ been the means of saving me from sin and hell? Then, surely I must not run away from this rule when I come into positions of trial and difficulty. If faith has been superior to sin through the blood of Christ, it will certainly be superior to trial through the almighty arm of Christ. Did I not tell him when I first came to him that I would trust no one but him? Did I not declare that all my other confidences were burst and broken, and scattered to the winds? Did I not ask that he would permit me to put my trust in him alone? Shall I, after that, play the traitor? Shall I now set up some other object in which to place my trust? Oh no! my love to Jesus, my gratitude to him for his condescension in accepting my faith, binds me henceforth to trust to him, and to him alone.

We often lose the force of a truth by not making it palpable to our own mind; let us try to make this one so. Imagine the Lord Jesus to be visibly present in this pulpit. Suppose that he looks down upon one of you, and says, "My child, your will and mine do not, just now, agree; you desire such and such a thing, but I say, 'No, you must not have it.' Now, my child, which will is to prevail, mine or yours?" Suppose you were to reply, "Lord, I must have my will." Do you not think he would look at you with eyes of infinite sadness and pity, and say to you, "What! did I give up my will for you, and will you not give up your will for me? Did I surrender all I had, even my life, for your sake, and do you say, you self-willed child, 'I must have these things according to my will, and contrary to your wish and purpose, O my Savior?'" Surely you could not talk like that; rather, I think I see you instantly falling on your knees and saying, "Lord Jesus, forgive me for ever harboring such evil thoughts. No, my Lord, even if your will be hard, I will think it pleasant. If it be bitter, I will believe that the bitterest draft is sweet. Let me but see you dying on the cross for me. Let me know only that you love me. Wherever you shall put me, I will be in heaven as long as I can feel that it is your will that is being done with me. I will be perfectly content to be just wherever you choose me to be, and to suffer whatever you choose for me to endure." Yes, dear friends, it would show a sad want of that love which we owe to Christ, and of that gratitude which he deserves, if we were once to set our wills up in opposition to his. Therefore, again, beloved, for love's sake, for wisdom's sake, for right's sake, I beseech you ask the Holy Spirit to teach you this prayer of our Lord Jesus Christ and to impart to you its blessed meaning.

III. I notice, in the next place, *the effect of truly saying and feeling,* *"Not as I will, but as thou wilt."*

The first effect is *constant happiness*. If you would find out the cause of most of your sorrows, dig at the root of your self-will, for that is where it lies. When your heart is wholly sanctified unto God and your will is entirely subdued to him, the bitter becomes sweet, pain is changed to pleasure, and suffering is turned into joy. It is not possible for that man's mind to be disturbed whose will is wholly resigned to the will of God. "Well," says one, "that is a very startling statement." Another says," I have really sought to have my will resigned to God's will, yet I am disturbed." Yes, and that is simply because though you have sought, like all the rest of us, you have not yet attained to full resignation to the will of the Lord. But when once you have attained to it—I fear you never will in this life—then shall you be free from everything that shall cause you sorrow or discomposure of mind.

Another blessed effect of this prayer, if it is truly presented, is, that it will give a man holy courage and bravery. If my mind is wholly resigned to God's will, what have I to fear in all the world? It is with me then as it was with Polycarp; when the Roman emperor threatened that he would banish him, he said, "Thou canst not, for the whole world is my Father's house, and thou canst not banish me from it." "But I will slay thee," said the emperor. "Nay, thou canst not, for my life is hid with Christ in God." "I will take away all thy treasures." "Nay, thou canst not, for I have nothing that thou knowest of; my treasure is in heaven, and my heart is there also." "But I will drive thee away from men, and thou shalt have no friend left." "Nay, that thou canst not do, for I have a Friend in heaven from whom thou canst not separate me; I defy thee, for there is nothing that thou canst do unto me." And so can the Christian always say, if once his will agrees with God's will. He may defy all men, and defy hell itself, for he will be able to say, "Nothing can happen to me that is contrary to the will of God; and if it be his will, it is my will too; if it pleases God, it pleases me. God has been pleased to give me part of his will, so I am satisfied with whatever he sends."

Man is, after all, only the second cause of our sorrows. A persecutor says, perhaps, to a child of God, "I can afflict you." "No, you cannot, for you are dependent on the first Great Cause, and he and I are agreed." Ah! dear friends, there is nothing that makes men such cowards as having wills contrary to the will of God; but when we resign ourselves wholly into the hands of God, what have we to fear? The thing that made Jacob a coward was that he was not resigned to God's will when Esau came to meet him. God had foretold that the elder of the two sons of Isaac should serve the younger; Jacob's business was to believe that and to go boldly forward with his wives and children, and not to bow down before Esau, but to say, "The promise is, 'The elder shall serve the younger.' I am not going to bow down to you; it is your place to fall prostrate before me." But poor Jacob said, "Perhaps it is God's will that Esau should conquer me, and smite the mothers and their children; but my will is that it shall not be so." The contest is well pictured at the ford Jabbok; but if Jacob had not disbelieved God's promise, he would never have bowed himself to the earth seven times before his brother Esau. In the holy majesty of his faith he would have said, "Esau, my brother, you can do me no harm, for you can do nothing contrary to the will of God. You can do nothing contrary to his decree, and I will be pleased with whatsoever it is."

So, this resignation to God's will gives, first, joy in the heart, and then it gives fearless courage; and yet another thing follows from it. As soon as anyone truly says, "Not as I will, but as thou wilt," this resolve *tends to make every duty light, every trial easy, every tribulation sweet.* We should never feel it to be a hard thing to serve God. Yet there are many people, who, if they do a little thing for the Lord, think so much of it. If there is ever a great thing to be done, you have, first, to plead very hard to get them to do it; and when they do it, very often it is done so badly that you are half sorry you ever asked them to do it. A great many people make very much out of what is really very little. They take one good action which they have performed and hammer it out till it becomes as thin as gold leaf, and then they think they may cover a whole week with that one good deed. The seven days shall all be glorified by an action which takes only five minutes to perform; it shall be quite enough, they even think, for all time to come. But the Christian, whose will is conformed to God's will, says, "My Lord, is there anything else for me to do? Then, I will gladly do it. Does it involve want of rest? I will do it. Does it involve loss of time in my business? Does it involve me, sometimes, in toil and fatigue? Lord, it shall be done if it is your will, for your will and mine are in complete agreement. If it is possible, I will do it; and I will count all things but loss that I may win Christ and be found in him, rejoicing in his righteousness and not in mine own."

IV. There are many other sweet and blessed effects which this resignation would produce; but I must close by observing that *the only way in which this Spirit can be attained is by the unction of the Holy One*, the outpouring and the indwelling of the Holy Spirit in our hearts.

You may try to subdue your own self, but you will never do it alone. You may labor, by self-denial, to keep down your ambition; but you will find that it takes another shape and grows by that wherewith you thought to poison it. You may seek to concentrate all the love of your soul on Christ, and in the very act you will find self creeping in. I am sometimes astonished—and yet not astonished when I know the evil of my own heart—when I look within myself and find how impure my motive is at the very moment when I thought it was most pure; and I expect it is the same with you, dear friends. You perform a good action—some almsgiving to the poor, perhaps. You say, "I will do it very quietly." Someone speaks of it, and you say at once, "I wish you had not spoken of that. I do not like to hear anyone talk of what I have done; it hurts me." Perhaps it is only your pride that makes you say that it hurts you, for some folk make their modesty to be their pride; it is, in fact, their secret pride that they are doing good, and that people do not know it. They glory in that supposed secrecy, and by its coming out they feel that their modesty is spoiled. They are afraid that people will say, "Ah, you see that it is known what they do; they do not really do their good deeds in secret." So that even our modesty may be our pride; and what some people think their pride may happen to be the will of God, and may be real modesty. It is very hard work to give up our own will; but it is possible, and that is one of the lessons we should learn from this text, "Not as I will, but as thou wilt."

Again, if there is anybody of whom you are a little envious—perhaps a minister who takes a little of the gloss off you by preaching better than you do, or a Sunday school teacher who is more successful in his work—make that particular person the object of your most constant prayer, and endeavor as much as lies in you to increase that person's popularity and success. Someone asks, "But you cannot bring human nature up to that point, can you—to try and exalt one's own rival?" My dear friends, you will never know the full meaning of this prayer till you have tried to do this and actually sought to honor your rival more than yourself. That is the true spirit of the gospel, "in honor preferring one another." I have sometimes found it hard work, I must confess; but I have schooled myself down to it. Can this be done? Yes, John the Baptist did it; he said of Jesus, "He must increase, but I must decrease." If you had asked John whether he wished to increase, he would have said, "Well, I should like to have more disciples; still, if it is the Lord's will, I am quite content to go down and that Christ should go up."

How important, therefore, it is for us to learn how we may attain to this state of acquiescence with our heavenly Father's will! I have given you the reasons for it, but how can it be done? Only by the operation of the Spirit of God. As for flesh and blood, they will not help you in the least, they will go just the other way; and when you think that, surely, you have gotten flesh and blood under control, you will find that they have gotten the upper hand of you just when you thought you were conquering them. Pray the Holy Spirit to abide with you, to dwell in you, to baptize you, to immerse you in his sacred influence, to cover you, to bury you in his sublime power; and so, and only so, when you are completely immersed in the Spirit and steeped, as it were, in the crimson sea of the Savior's blood, shall you be made fully to realize the meaning of this great prayer, "Not as I will, but as thou wilt." "Lord, not self, but Christ; not my own glory, but your glory; not my aggrandizement, but yours. No, not even my success, but your success; not the prosperity of my own church or my own self, but the prosperity of your church, the increase of your glory—let all that be done as you will, not as I will."

How different this is from everything connected with the world! I have tried to take you up to a very high elevation; and if you have been able to get up there, or even to pant to get up there, how striking has the contrast been between this spirit and the spirit of the worldling! I shall not say anything to those of you who are unconverted, except this: Learn how contrary you are to what God would have you be, and what you must be, before you can enter the kingdom of heaven. You know that you could not say, "Let God have his will," and you know also that you could not humble yourself to become as a little child. This shows your deep depravity; so, may the Holy Spirit renew you, for you have need of renewing that you may be made a new creature in Christ Jesus! May he sanctify you wholly, spirit, soul, and body, and at last present you, faultless, before the throne of God, for his dear name's sake! Amen.

Indexes

Sermon Index by Key Scripture

Alphabetical Listing
of Sermon Titles

Chronological Listing of Sermon Titles

(by delivery date)

Spurgeon's Sermons on Prayer

The text of this book is set in Dante 11/14 and Delphin IA, with Poetica® Ornaments.

Typeset in QuarkXPress.

Preface by Patricia Klein.

Copyediting by Suzanne Tilton.

These sermons by Charles Spurgeon have been gently edited and updated for the modern reader.

Interior design and typesetting by Rose Yancik, of Y Designs. www.ydesigns.us